DAVID B. OLSEN

INTEGRATIVE
THEOLOGY

VOLUME ONE

INTEGRATIVE THEOLOGY

KNOWING ULTIMATE REALITY
THE LIVING GOD

Bruce Demarest

and

Gordon Lewis

Academie Books Grand Rapids, Michigan
Zondervan Publishing House

INTEGRATIVE THEOLOGY
Copyright © 1987 by the Zondervan Corporation
Grand Rapids, Michigan

ACADEMIE BOOKS are published by Zondervan
Publishing House, 1415 Lake Drive, SE,
Grand Rapids, Michigan 49506

Library of Congress Cataloging in Publication Data

Lewis, Gordon Russel, 1926–
    Integrative theology.

    Bibliography: v. 1, p.
    Includes indexes.
    Contents: v. 1, pt. 1. Knowing ultimate reality;
pt. 2. The living God.
    1. Theology, Doctrinal.   2. Theology—Methodology.
I. Demarest, Bruce A., 1935–   . II. Title.
BT75.2.D37   1987   230   86–24564

ISBN 0-310-39230-6   (v. 1)

All Scripture quotations, unless otherwise noted, are taken from the HOLY BIBLE: NEW INTERNATIONAL VERSION (North American Edition). Copyright © 1973, 1978, 1984 by The International Bible Society. Used by permission of Zondervan Bible Publishers.

Edited by Gerard Terpstra
Designed by Louise Bauer

Printed in the United States of America

87 88 89 90 91 92 / AF / 10 9 8 7 6 5 4 3 2 1

CONTENTS

CONTENTS

Preface

Coherent thinking and authentic living in the modern world require that a person view life holistically rather than in fragments. For some people a meaningful world view is provided by the data of lived experience, while for others empirical analysis of the external world supplies the "big picture." Christians, however, believe that a coherent understanding of reality begins with God's perspective mediated by general and special revelation. In order to develop a comprehensive view of the real, the true, and the valuable and so to arrive at viable convictions by which to live and serve, we propose that Christians consider the paradigm of integrative theology.

Bernard Ramm, in his book *After Fundamentalism*, argues that Evangelicals must devise a new paradigm for doing theology in the post-Enlightenment world. The traditional approach to doing theology, he argues, will not suffice for the future. Ramm believes that Evangelicals "have not developed a theological method that enables them to be consistently evangelical in their theology and to be people of modern learning. That is why a new paradigm is necessary."[1] Ramm chooses the method of Karl Barth as the preferred model for doing theology in the future. "Barth's paradigm has resulted in an authentic methodology," he claims.[2] In response to such felt needs for a new theological methodology, we propose the paradigm of integrative theology. This approach, we believe, follows a more reliable method than that of Barth and yields results that are more consistent with Scripture and the historic Christian faith.

The approach we call integrative theology involves six successive stages. The first involves identification of the problem under consideration. The investigator delineates the parameters of the theological problem and senses its significance for personal and societal existence.

Second, one identifies the various solutions to the problem that have been suggested in the history of Christian thought. Devout and gifted minds may have acquired insights that later Christians have not considered. But since equally competent scholars differ on many issues, we should view the alternative proposals as hypotheses to be tested by the primary biblical data.

Third, one goes behind the secondary testimony of history to the prime source of theological knowledge—inspired and inerrant Scripture. Following the method of biblical theology and employing a responsible hermeneutic, one finds the relevant teachings of the Old and New Testaments in their chronological development. This stage also involves relating one portion of Scripture to other portions that deal with the same subject in the progress of revelation.

Fourth, the investigator orders the relevant data of general and special revelation into a coherent doctrine and relates the same to the other doctrines similarly derived. The person commits himself to the thesis that satisfies the test for truth with the fewest number of difficulties. The commended test for truth is threefold: (1) logical consistency, (2) agreement with the data of revelation, and (3) existential viability.

Fifth, the Christian defends this doctrinal position in interaction with contrary positions in theology, philosophy, and new religions. At this stage the offensive component of an integrative theology becomes evident as the truth encounters and challenges alien ideologies. The goal of theology is to bring every dimension of thought and action under the lordship of the sovereign God.

Sixth, theology is applied to specific life situations in the world. This final stage assumes (1) that truth does not terminate in abstract contemplation and (2) that faithful living flows from truth as water flows from a fountain. It is imperative that Christians live by their convictions authentically before God, in relationship with others, and in service to the world. The ethical dimension of theology is apparent in this final stage.

The integrative approach to theology proposed in this volume thus may be summarized by six key phrases: The Problem; Historical Hypotheses; Biblical Teaching; Systematic Formulation; Apologetic Interaction; and Relevance for Life and Ministry. Due to space limitations each of these sections will be less than exhaustive and can only initiate thought in the given area.

Our contention is that integrative theology as implemented in this series offers more promise than alternative theological methods practiced in the past. It is superior to *confessional theology*, which presents the tenets that constitute a particular ecclesiastical tradition and invites adherence on that basis. The difficulty with confessional theology is that frequently few reasons are given why one tradition (Reformed, Lutheran, Anabaptist) is held to be superior to another. Such an approach seems to be closed rather than open to new insights from special or general revelation.

The integrative approach would also appear superior to *fideistic theology*, which enjoins belief on the authority of the speaker who claims to possess God's Word. It may not be clear to the hearer of such a presentation that the claimant does in fact possess the truth of God. The element of unsubstantiated dogmatism present in the fideistic approach likewise may hinder the reception of the message.

The approach of integrative theology may be superior to traditional *systematic theology* for several reasons. The latter (1) usually does not develop a comprehensive history of the doctrine with a view to identifying hypotheses to be tested; (2) often does not follow the method of biblical theology but relies on proof-texting without the developmental context; (3) may not employ a comprehensive test for truth and thus not attain a high degree of objective validity in deciding which proposal is true and which views are spurious; (4) may not defend each doctrine in interaction with opposing views; and (5) may not show the relevance of each doctrinal issue for Christian life in the church and in the world.

Integrating our thoughts is something that we must do for ourselves— others cannot do it for us. These volumes provide several sets of data that should be coherently related in our minds. They also indicate ways in which the authors express their attempts at a coherent formulation. In the final analysis, however, we cannot organize your thoughts for you. Readers are urged to digest the material and to begin integrating their own thinking. If that seems discouraging at first, do not be surprised. Integrating our thoughts and then living by the convictions based on this integration is a life-time challenge. If a good start is made in that direction, the purpose of these volumes will have been achieved.

The method of integrative theology herein set forth is biblically grounded, historically related, culturally sensitive, person-centered, and profoundly related to life. Its goal is to set forth a comprehensive picture of the cosmos, of persons, and of history that is logically consistent, factually adequate, and capable of maximizing personal meaning and fulfillment. We propose a method for doing theology that follows a coherent research method, that avoids callous indoctrination, and that encourages the learner to come to his or her own conclusions and create his or her own commitments face-to-face with the Word of God and under the gentle guidance of the Holy Spirit. Our hope is that this approach may enable theology to overcome the impasse in which it finds itself in the contemporary situation, and that it might enable theology once again to speak convincingly to a church in need of instruction and to a world in need of God's liberating truth and light.

After reviewing a few chapters of *Integrative Theology*, you may find yourself asking some of the following questions:

Question: Should the problem addressed in the first section of each chapter focus more directly on the urgent cultural problems of our times?

The immediate issues of a given culture provide valuable conversational starting points, but the study of each basic Christian doctrine begins with a problem of permanent, transcultural significance. A theological treatment of the multitudes of specific issues in each culture and subculture is important, but that can best be done by Christians who have specialized in the areas of the sciences, history, psychology, sociology, etc. Furthermore multitudes of contemporary issues may pass out of date almost as quickly as daily newspapers. The classical issues and doctrines have exhibited universal and permanent relevance because they are common to all men and women from the Near East, the Far East, and the West, in the two-thirds world and the one-third world, in rural areas and the large cities.

Question: Before looking at the "alternative proposals in the church" regarding a problem, should not theological research examine the biblical teaching? Would it not be wise to examine biblical truth inductively without theological biases?

Attempts to begin inductive research with the "objective" biblical evidence overlook the impossibility of obtaining complete objectivity in any comprehensive field. Nothing has become more evident recently than that all researchers and writers in any field have presuppositions. The ideal of objectivity is worthy and not in question here. The problem is to find a critical method by which to move toward greater objectivity. The most effective way we know for students of the Bible to identify their biases is to survey the alternative perspectives and so become aware of their own assumptions. By stating the alternative doctrines as mere hypotheses to be tested we not only become aware of the similarities and differences between our perspectives and those of others, but also of the need of verifying our own doctrine. This critical approach is necessary if we are to get out of our closed hermeneutical circles and in a spirit of openness do genuine research with any hope of making some progress. We make no claim to exhaustiveness but have attempted to state succinctly the most significant options from the beginning of the history of a given doctrine to the present time as a means of exposing assumptions so that they can be tested for their consistency and adequacy with the biblical evidence.

Question: Must a person adopt only one of the alternative views or can he be eclectic?

The section Systematic Formulation seeks to develop with clarity and some creativity a coherent interpretation of the primary biblical data in the space allotted—an interpretation that encompasses elements of truth from several of the different historical views and avoids their weaknesses. Beginning students may tend to take one of those views and reject everything in the others. Only where the others contradict a biblical position must they logically be dismissed. Often there is something to learn from views that have had major historical or contemporary influence. From their own historical and biblical studies professors and students may wish to formulate their conclusions with different emphases. So the formulation presented may serve as the springboard for further discussion.

Question: Could other views be considered in the sections under Apologetic Interaction?

The apologetic interaction sections are generally more concerned with the major non-Christian contemporary contradictory options than with fine tuning the evangelical position adopted as against other evangelical versions. It is our view that within the framework of an evangelical position there may be freedom to vary in specifics. Teachers and students in different traditions should feel free to focus in greater detail on the intramural refinements as they wish. Having tried to incorporate the values of the alternative options in the section Systematic Formulation, it is important not to undermine those elements of truth while opposing the nonbiblical elements or the system in general.

Question: Can other points of personal and social relevance be noted?

Readers are encouraged to supplement the section Relevance for Life and Ministry with their own applications of the doctrine. Teachers and students are free to consider other ways in which the revealed truth can make a difference in their own specific life situations and vocations. Keep in mind that the ministry here envisioned is not just that of ordained ministers, but more generally that of all Christians in their service to others, whether vocationally or avocationally.

Question: How can the review questions at the end of each chapter be used?

The review questions may help readers determine how well they can recall and express the major ideas of each section. The review questions may also stimulate discussions among students in larger or smaller groups. And they may be used as examination questions for essay tests.

Question: Can you briefly explain the relationship between the sections of each chapter? They are closely related as logically ordered steps in a verificational method of researching one basic issue. The verificational method of devising truth is not purely inductive, nor deductive. Rather, it is an abductive or retroductive method often called the hypothetical, critical, or scientific method of reasoning. The diagram on page 12 may clarify this.[3]

After a problem has been delimited, the verificational method does not begin with an allegedly blank mind (as in inductive methods), or with a confessional statement presupposed to be true (as in deductive methods), but with several historical and contemporary answers as hypotheses to be tested. These proposals are evaluated and confirmed or disconfirmed by the primary biblical evidence. Then the elements confirmed are formulated topically and logically in a consistent way that accounts for the biblical teaching. The section Apologetic Interaction indicates how the opposing hypotheses are inconsistent and inadequate in accounting for the evidence. Finally, the section Relevance for Life and Ministry indicates some of the viability of the conclusion for life and ministry.

Please note: because of the important connections of the sections of each chapter to each other in this verificational approach, no single section can be taken out of its context in the entire chapter to stand by itself as a

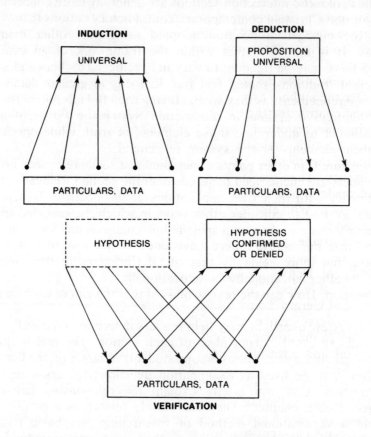

INDUCTION

UNIVERSAL

PARTICULARS, DATA

HYPOTHESIS

DEDUCTION

PROPOSITION
UNIVERSAL

PARTICULARS, DATA

HYPOTHESIS
CONFIRMED
OR DENIED

PARTICULARS, DATA

VERIFICATION

Three Methods of Justifying Beliefs

This diagram was taken from Gordon R. Lewis, "Schaeffer's Apologetic Method" in *Reflections on Francis Schaeffer*, ed. Ronald W. Ruegsegger (Grand Rapids: Zondervan, 1986), 71. Used by permission.

complete discussion of any topic or school of thought. If, for example, people want to study the neoorthodox view of special revelation, it will not be sufficient to look at the references to it in just one section of the chapter. That view is stated in Alternative Proposals (section two), is tested in Biblical Teaching, its strengths and weaknesses may be incorporated in Systematic Formulation, and its lack of consistency or adequacy reflected in Apologetic Interaction.

Each part of this integrative work, particularly, must be read in the broader context of its chapter with understanding of the contribution of each section to the overall method. Many analytical works on theological words have been written. The purpose of this integrative work is to construct a more synthetic, big picture. We ask the patience of the analytically inclined who try to pursue this synthetic work. Before judging a given specific discussion of a topic or view in any one section of a chapter, readers are urged to integrate it with the teaching of the entire chapter. To help with this the review questions at the end of each chapter are provided.

Question: How did the authors work together in writing this work?

After the authors agreed on the basic approach and the issues, Bruce Demarest contributed the first half of each chapter, defining the problem, surveying the historical views, and summing up the relevant biblical evidence. Gordon Lewis contributed the second half of each chapter, formulating the doctrine systematically, defending it, and applying it to life and ministry. Then we interacted with each other's materials and with several readers' and editors' suggestions, making revisions accordingly.

Question: Who else significantly contributed to the production of this publication?

Innumerable people have contributed to our lives and thinking through the years. We are particularly indebted to our stimulating colleagues at Denver Seminary and to the administration's thoughtful policy on sabbaticals. Special thanks go to Zondervan editors Stanley Gundry and Gerard Terpstra. We benefited also from the suggestions of several readers—above all, from those of Daniel B. Wallace of Probe Ministries. In the production of the manuscript we express our gratitude to the skillful and cheerful assistance of Doris Haslam, our secretary at Denver Seminary.

Question: Can you suggest other ways to help people become involved in doing theology?

Many have been helped to struggle with some of the issues, interpret some relevant passages for themselves, and formulate their own conclusions by doing studies in Gordon R. Lewis, *Decide for Yourself: A Theological Workbook* (Downers Grove: InterVarsity, 1970). This workbook has been widely used by lay people and by college, seminary, and extension-seminary students. For some classes the workbook may appropriately serve as a student manual, and *Integrative Theology* as a teacher's manual.

Abbreviations

AB	*The Anchor Bible*, ed. W. F. Albright and D. N. Freedman
BAGD	Walter Bauer, William F. Arndt, F. Wilbur Gingrich, and Frederick W. Danker, *A Greek-English Lexicon of the New Testament* (Chicago: University of Chicago Press, 1979)
CD	Karl Barth, *Church Dogmatics*, ed. G. W. Bromiley and T. F. Torrance, 13 vols. (Edinburgh: T. & T. Clark, 1936–69)
CGTC	*The Cambridge Greek Testament Commentary*, ed. C. F. D. Moule
EBC	*The Expositor's Bible Commentary*, ed. Frank E. Gaebelein (Grand Rapids: Zondervan, 1976–)
EDT	*Evangelical Dictionary of Theology*, ed. Walter A. Elwell (Grand Rapids: Baker, 1984)
EP	*Encyclopedia of Philosophy*, ed. Paul Williams, 8 vols. (New York: Macmillan, 1967)
HNTC	*Harper's New Testament Commentary*, ed. Henry Chadwick
ICC	*The International Critical Commentary*, ed. J. A. Emerton and C. E. B. Cranfield
ISBE	*The International Standard Bible Encyclopedia*, ed. G. W. Bromiley, 4 vols. (Grand Rapids: Eerdmans, 1979–)
LCC	*Library of Christian Classics*, 25 vols. (Philadelphia: Westminster, 1953–69)
LW	*Luther's Works*, ed. J. Pelikan and H. T. Lehman, 55 vols. (St. Louis: Concordia and Philadelphia: Fortress, 1955–76)
NBCRev	*The New Bible Commentary*, revised. (London: Inter-Varsity, 1970)
NBD	*New Bible Dictionary* (Wheaton, Ill.: Tyndale, 1982)
NCBC	*New Century Bible Commentary*, 6 vols. (Grand Rapids: Eerdmans, 1980–84)
NICNT	*The New International Commentary of the New Testament*, ed. F. F. Bruce. 17 vols. (Grand Rapids: Eerdmans, 1952–84)
NICOT	*The New International Commentary of the Old Testament*, ed. R. K. Harrison (Grand Rapids: Eerdmans, 1965–82)
NIDNTT	*The New International Dictionary of New Testament Theology*, ed. Colin Brown, 4 vols. (Grand Rapids: Zondervan, 1975–78)

NIGTC *New International Greek Testament Commentary*, 4 vols. (Grand Rapids: Eerdmans, 1978–82)

NLBC *The New Layman's Bible Commentary*, ed. G. C. D. Howley, F. F. Bruce, and H. L. Ellison (Grand Rapids: Zondervan, 1979)

OTL *The Old Testament Library*, ed. G. Ernest Wright, John Bright, James Barr, and Peter Ackroyd

SCG Thomas Aquinas, *Summa Contra Gentiles*, 4 vols. (Notre Dame: Notre Dame University Press, 1975)

ST Thomas Aquinas, *Summa Theologica*, 22 vols. (London: R. & T. Washbourne, 1912–25)

TDNT *Theological Dictionary of the New Testament*, ed. G. Kittel and G. Friedrich, 9 vols. (Grand Rapids: Eerdmans, 1965)

TDNTAbr *Theological Dictionary of the New Testament*, ed. G. Kittel and G. Friedrich and abridged in one volume by G. W. Bromiley (Grand Rapids: Eerdmans, 1985)

TDOT *Theological Dictionary of the Old Testament*, ed. G. Johannes Botterweck and H. Ringgren, 6 vols. (Grand Rapids: Eerdmans, 1977)

TI Karl Rahner, *Theological Investigations*, 14 vols. (New York: Seabury: 1974–76)

TNTC *Tyndale New Testament Commentaries*, ed. R. V. G. Tasker (Grand Rapids: Eerdmans, 1975–83)

TOTC *Tyndale Old Testament Commentaries*, ed. D. J. Wiseman, 17 vols. (Downers Grove, Ill.: InterVarsity, 1968–84)

TWOT *Theological Wordbook of the Old Testament*, ed. R. Laird Harris, Gleason L. Archer, Jr., and Bruce K. Waltke, 2 vols. (Chicago: Moody, 1980)

WA *D. Martin Luthers Werke: Kritische Gesamtausgabe* (Weimar, 1883–)

WBC *Word Biblical Commentary*, ed. David A. Hubbard and Glenn W. Barker (Waco: Word, n.d.)

ZPEB *Zondervan Pictorial Encyclopedia of the Bible*, ed. Merrill C. Tenney, 5 vols. (Grand Rapids: Zondervan, 1976)

PART ONE

KNOWING
ULTIMATE REALITY

CHAPTER 1

THEOLOGY'S CHALLENGING TASK

Theology's Challenging Task

INTRODUCTION

The Need for Integrative Thinking

We seldom find time to put all the bits and pieces of our learning together in a meaningful whole. The rapid growth of knowledge makes it difficult to keep up in one field, let alone develop a unified world view encompassing all fields of knowledge.

The diversity of experiences and cultures accessible to us adds to the difficulty of comprehensive knowledge. The radically different kinds of experiences of people in East and West, North and South complicate the challenge of relating areas of learning cohesively on a shrinking globe. And even within the same culture people's interests vary greatly.

Difficult as it may be for us, with a multiplicity of experiences and interests in an exploding information age, to "put it all together," we need to relate our thinking about our particular specialty to reliable thought about other areas. The importance of seeing life whole is illustrated in ecology. Before unnecessarily exhausting a limited source of energy for personal profit, a person ought to consider, as far as possible, the potential effect on the earth's whole ecological system.

A coherent world view and way of life provides a necessary context for our ethical decision making in general. Without the "big picture" it is difficult to determine wisely what values are worth living and dying for in a fast-moving, pluralistic world. Francis Schaeffer diagnosed the basic problem of Christians in America in this way: "They have seen things in bits and pieces instead of totals."[1] In the social issues of life it is important to be able to detect the underlying assumptions about reality (metaphysics) and about how we know reality (epistemology).

Not all those who reject skepticism and try to make sense out of life accept the existence of special revelation as their starting point. A variety of unifying principles are proposed. Many naturalists find the ultimate integrative factor in nature's energy-matter and its uniform laws. For secular humanists the highest reality that gives meaning to everything else is not impersonal, but personal: humanity. Pantheists think the supreme being is an impersonal god: the dynamic underlying energy of nature and our inner being.

Theists on the other hand see everything in the cosmos as the creation of a personal God who is distinct from the world but active in it. And Christian theists find that the existence, meaning, and purpose of energy, nature, and persons derive from the purposes of the transcendent Lord of all, disclosed in Jesus Christ and the Bible.

Developing a theology that relates biblically revealed truth to humanity and nature is not an elective for Christians who believe in the Lord of all, but a requirement. God knows, sustains, and gives purpose to all that is. God provides a focal point not only for our limited personal experiences or special interests but for all thought. The question for Christians is not whether they will relate all their fields of knowledge to God's purposes, but whether they, as stewards of God's truth, will do so poorly or well.

Entry Points for Serious Thinking About Revealed Truth

As new Christians begin to further their understanding of what changed their lives, language functions not only to communicate vague feelings but to define the experienced reality. Usually new believers express the same beliefs about God and his purposes as those held by the people who were most influential in their conversion to Christ.

Denominationally, their earliest influences may have come from Baptists, Pentecostalists, Nazarenes, Presbyterians, Methodists, Episcopalians, Roman Catholics, or independents. Transdenominationally, the earliest influences may have come from systems of theology primarily evangelical, liberal, neoorthodox, ecumenical, liberation, process, fundamentalist, or charismatic.

Whatever our original enthusiasm and psychological certitude, subsequent experiences may cause us to think more carefully about particular beliefs. In this shrinking, pluralistic world we discover other Christians with quite different and even contradictory views. Our relatives, co-workers, neighbors, or friends may have significantly different perspectives, and their loyalties challenge us to know why we should maintain beliefs that until now we accepted without question.

There are many points in life at which we are forced to think more deeply about what we believe and why. While each of us has his or her specific "entry points" for serious thinking about revealed truth, there are some broad areas of experience that provide the "entry points" for many. Involved in church *outreach* programs, we confront people involved in non-Christian philosophies, religions, and cults. Dialogue with non-Christians may raise difficult issues that motivate further study. Compassion for people genuinely struggling with issues of basic beliefs may also motivate the search for answers.

Christians who have dedicated their lives to *vocational service* must decide in which doctrinal tradition they can serve with intellectual integrity and fervent commitment. A preliminary form of that decision may be the choice of a college or seminary. In training, courses in church history present many alternative theological traditions. Other challenging issues may be raised by studies in psychology and counseling, sociology, philosophy of religions, and crosscultural missions. Even the study of the Old and New Testaments discloses conflicting beliefs among knowledgeable and dedicated interpreters of the biblical languages. And responsible courses in theology involve the student in comparing and contrasting live options in the field. In order to establish normative beliefs to guide life and ministry, people considering Christian vocations will evaluate the relevance of alleged biblical evidence and the cogency of the arguments drawn from it.

Members of committees and boards of various organizations are often called on to discern the implications of doctrine that may determine the future of organizations and their personnel. The vitality of churches may depend on the theological discernment of pulpit committees who must make a choice from among candidates with radically different doctrinal loyalties to recommend for their pastorate. For the integrity of their mission agencies and schools board members must determine what beliefs are nonnegotiable.

A well-founded, personally appropriated faith becomes crucial when one is experiencing serious *illness* and facing *death.* Do the anxieties of a seemingly meaningless life, real guilt, and death have an answer that stands examination? In times of crisis it may not be enough to hunt for a verse here and there. When pressures gang up on us we need well-formulated, well-founded convictions that will not let us down. Even under the more ordinary pressures of life we need well-established convictions by which to live in a faithful, loving relation to God and others.

Experiences at some of these "entry points" motivate Christians to investigate the work others have done in theology and to become involved in the discipline themselves. Throughout our lives we need the guidance of revealed truths. Our spiritual Master asked us to grow, not only in grace, but also in knowledge of him and his revealed purposes (Eph. 4:15; 2 Peter 3:18).

Developing *intellectual maturity* takes Christians through at least four stages. (1) As they become aware of other religions, philosophies, and theologies, they can think and speak of them fairly. (2) Then they grow in an ability to evaluate alternative doctrines objectively by reliable criteria of truth. (3) Mature people do not remain in an undecided state but decide in favor of the most coherent account of the relevant data with the fewest difficulties. (4) Having personally accepted a well-founded conviction, they grow in their ability to live by it authentically, state it clearly, defend it adequately, and communicate it effectively.

SYSTEMATIC FORMULATION

Systematic Theology

The root meaning of the word "theology" is the "organized study (*logos*) of God (*theos*)." However, in this work we do not claim to know anything about God apart from God's disclosure of himself in nature and in Scripture. As used here, therefore, *theology* is the topical and logical study of God's revealed nature and purposes.

Theology is more comprehensive than the study of separate doctrines. *Doctrinal studies* consider individual biblical topics without logically relating them to other biblical or nonbiblical tenets in a developing belief system. *Systematic theology* not only derives coherent doctrines from the entirety of written revelation but also systematically relates them to each other in developing a comprehensive world view and way of life.

Systematic theology differs from *biblical theology* in its aim and organizing principle. Both systematic and biblical theology derive their data from the same primary source, the Bible. But biblical theology, aiming to be a descriptive science, is organized around the chronological and cultural development of a given biblical writer's own terms, categories, and thought forms in his historical and cultural context. Systematic theology, on the other hand, aims to produce normative guidelines to spiritual reality for the present generation; it organizes the material of divine revelation topically and logically, developing a coherent and comprehensive world view and way of life.[2]

23

During centuries of attempts to develop systematics, the discipline has met with much opposition, as is true of any ethical or social attempt to state normative principles that people *ought* to accept and live by unhypocritically. But the opposition has targeted particularly systematic theology's *method of reasoning*. The discipline of systematics has sometimes been dominated by a given philosophical emphasis and paid insufficient attention to the history of doctrine and to biblical teaching in its literary, historical, and cultural contexts.

Not only biblical and historical scholars but also philosophers opposed (and oppose) premature systematizing. Some of the most influential recent philosophies (such as positivism, linguistic analysis, existentialism, and pragmatism) abandoned all hope of developing coherent and comprehensive world views. A similarly based anti-systematic temper is also evident in influential twentieth-century theologies such as liberalism, neoorthodoxy, and biblical theology.

Instead of systematic theology, graduate schools and publishers by and large emphasized psychology of religion, philosophy of religion, comparative religions, Old Testament studies, the faith of Israel (as evidenced in stories or case studies), New Testament studies, and the faith of the church. Even Karl Barth, who tried to call liberalism back to the transcendent God of the Bible, failed to regard the Bible itself as a coherent, divine revelation and wrote his extensive series of volumes on *church* dogmatics rather than systematic theology.

Charges Against Systematic Theology

These trends produced some very powerful charges against the discipline of systematic theology, and these charges led many to think it presumptuous and arrogant even to attempt coherence in all our thought about God, humanity, history, and nature. These charges, described below, cannot be overlooked by anyone approaching the field today.

1. Systematic theology organized a system of Christian thought around one central theme (such as sovereignty, freedom, covenant, dispensation, or kingdom) chosen a priori and imposed on the rest of revelation in a contrived interrelatedness.

2. Systematic theology failed to do justice to the multiplicity of relevant lines of biblical information seen in their cultural and historical contexts.

3. Systematic theology paid insufficient attention to the history of doctrine in the church.

4. Systematic theology tended to regard a system of theology as closed rather than open to new discoveries from God's Word or God's world.

5. Systematic theology passed its teachings on to the next generation by sheer indoctrination—an unworthy approach to education.

6. Finally, systematic theology failed to display the relevance of its content to the burning personal and social issues of its day.

Responses of Systematic Theologians

In spite of the measure of validity and power in criticisms like these, some evangelical theologians have made few methodological changes, while others have made major changes without explicitly formulating a new method of decision making.

Apparently unmoved by charges like those above are presuppositionalists (such as Cornelius Van Til and Rousas Rushdoony)[3] and the deductive rationalists (such as Gordon Clark and Carl Henry).[4] Valuable as the contributions of these writers have been in many ways, their presuppositional and axiomatic methodologies remain unchanged. Consequently, charges of a priori assumptions of the things to be proved, eisegesis, insufficient attention to the history of the doctrines, closed-mindedness, indoctrination, and insufficient relevance continue to limit the extent of their outreach and impact.

A change from such presuppositional approaches is evident in Millard Erickson's *Christian Theology*. Called "systematic theology" in chapter 1, this work displays a heightened consciousness of biblical contexts, the history of doctrine, an openness to investigation, avoidance of sheer indoctrination, and a meeting of contemporary needs. Some of these advantages are reflected in Erickson's definition of systematic theology as "that discipline which strives to give a coherent statement of the doctrines of the Christian faith, based primarily on the Scriptures, placed in the context of culture in general, worded in contemporary idiom, and related to issues of life."[5]

Although Erickson devotes valuable chapters to methodology, biblical criticism, and philosophy, his systematic theology is not explicitly developed on the basis of a distinctive method of decision making. (A similar weakness appears in the helpful work of John Jefferson Davis.)[6] Commendable as the elements discussed in Erickson's chapter on methodology and related chapters are, a procedure by which a reader might be expected to relate these elements to each other is not explicitly outlined. The telling criticisms leveled against systematic theology seem to require a more developed methodological proposal than either Erickson or Davis offers.

Contemporary theologians generally announce their intention to do justice to historical, biblical, contemporary, and practical aspects. However, the data may not always be made available to students who want to evaluate the evidence for themselves, and the relationship between the data and the decision-making process may not always be clear. Assuming a participatory philosophy of education in such a comprehensive field, a methodological paradigm becomes an essential tool for both research and teaching.

Integrative Theology

The Meaning of "Integrative Theology"

Integrative theology utilizes a distinctive verificational method of decision making as it defines a major topic, surveys influential alternative answers in the church, amasses relevant biblical data in their chronological development, formulates a comprehensive conclusion, defends it against competing alternatives, and exhibits its relevance for life and ministry.

Integrative theology is a *science*. On the basis of the entirety of special and general revelation, it develops a comprehensive, noncontradictory set of convictions on topics significant for Christian life and service. As a comprehensive science, integrative theology, like synthetic philosophy, tries to draw upon relevant lines of evidence from God's external world as responsibly interpreted by the empirical sciences, and from internal experience as responsibly interpreted by psychology, axiology, ethics, epistemology, and ontology.

Like other sciences, integrative theology works with *interrelated criteria* of truth (logical noncontradiction, empirical adequacy, and existential viability), accepting only those hypotheses that upon testing are discovered to be (1) noncontradictory, (2) supported by adequate evidence, and (3) affirmable without hypocrisy.

Integrative theology is not only a comprehensive science but also an *art* that requires student participation. It is one thing to learn a field by reading the research of others. It is quite another thing to do theological research for oneself. The art of research in integrative theology employs a consciously chosen methodology that answers the charge of starting with a priori presuppositions and imposing these on Scripture. The use of a research methodology assumes that Christians are illumined by the Holy Spirit, not only in preaching and teaching but also in their stewardship of Bible college and seminary assignments and in personal study. We seek to provide the data that will enable readers to follow these steps and integrate their own thinking for themselves. In the final analysis, no one can integrate other people's thinking for them.

The method used here seeks to involve the reader in six distinct steps: (1) defining and distinguishing one distinct topic or problem for inquiry; (2) learning alternative approaches to it from a survey of Spirit-led scholars in the history of the church; (3) discovering and formulating from both the Old and the New Testament a coherent summary of relevant biblical teaching by making use of sound principles of hermeneutics, worthy commentaries, and biblical theologies; (4) formulating on the basis of the relevant data a cohesive doctrine and relating it without contradiction to other biblically founded doctrines and other knowledge; (5) defending this formulation of revealed truth in interaction with contradictory options in theology, philosophy, science, religion, and cults; and (6) applying these convictions to Christian life and ministry in the present generation.[7] These six steps provide the outline for each of the following chapters: The Problem; Historical Hypotheses; Biblical Teaching; Systematic Formulation; Apologetic Interaction; and Relevance for Life and Ministry.

Integrative Theology and Systematic Theology

Consider how integrative theology preserves the values of systematics and avoids its weaknesses:

1. If systematic theology involves reading an a priori central organizing idea into the Bible, an integrated, verificational approach, by contrast, seeks coherence at the *end* of its investigation, not by eisegesis, but by exegesis. The methodology of integrative theology does not start with indefensible presuppositions or axioms. The logical starting point in verificational research discovers alternative hypotheses to be tested. It will accept only those proposals that cohere with adequate evidence from special revelation or general revelation. Several *checks and balances* in the method help a person avoid a contrived interrelatedness (historical surveys of alternatives, surveys of relevant biblical evidence, and interaction with conflicting views). The criteria are designed to permit only as much integration as the data of Scripture and experience permit.

Erickson's central motif is "the magnificence of God."[8] Although his emphasis on the greatness of God's natural and moral attributes is intended to center all of life and theology on God, this could be accomplished more explicitly if we formulate the central and all-important theme of divine revelation in a more comprehensive way. The overarching *great idea* of divine revelation focuses on the *Father's* eternal purposes revealed in *promises* to do gracious things for *his redeemed people* and *through them* individually and collectively for the *whole world*.[9]

This verificationally derived central theme of Scripture integrates such basic doctrines as trinitarianism, decrees, grace, revealed promises or covenants, Christ's atonement, the Holy Spirit's work, and the mission of people in the world, both as persons and as members of such social institutions as families, the Israelite nation, and churches.

2. If systematic theology fails to distinguish human interpretations of the divine revelation from the revelation as given, integrative theology's method requires this distinction. This integrative approach to theology assumes (from the argumentation of apologetics and evidence concerning revelation) that God can reveal information to people who are created in his image to think his thoughts after him. Nevertheless, the method emphasizes the difference between what is *given* in divine revelation and what is *taken from* it by human interpreters. We seek to avoid premature claims to finality of interpretations, or conclusiveness on every point beyond reasonable doubt. Interpretive conclusions have degrees of probability according to the extent and the present state of clarity of their supporting evidence. Thus *the attempt to state our partial understanding of revealed truth without logical contradiction involves no claim to our full comprehension of any complex reality such as God, humans, historical events, or the church.*

3. If systematic theology begins a study of each doctrine presupposing the conclusion, integrative theology begins by surveying the historical and contemporary options as hypotheses. Hypotheses may be confirmed or invalidated upon testing. This survey of options helps people to interact consciously with alternatives other than the one most influential in their lives up to this point. And it asks people to consider their own position as one among many hypotheses to be verified or invalidated.*

4. If systematic theology involves a closed system, integrative theology does not. Integrative theology can never be completely finished and its content as presently formulated can never become a final and closed system. It is always open to new discoveries about the significance of God's Word and God's world. The verificational method sees all truth as God's truth, wherever it is found. And all truth is ours (1 Cor. 3:21–23). On this approach one need not fear the reexamination of any doctrine. If what has been held is not true, it ought to be revised; if what has been held is true, it will stand reexamination.

5. If systematic theology is taught by indoctrination, integrative theology is not. Given its methodology, it cannot be communicated by sheer indoctrination, but only by challenging the coming generation to become sharers of the adventure of doing theology for themselves. The appropriate philosophy of education for communicating integrative theology calls for the participation of students in each step of the research methodology. To gain most from their study of theology, students will struggle with the issues, consider alternative answers, examine the relevant data, arrive at their own conclusions, and think through the import of these con-

---

*The importance of reexamining the biblical data may be seen in the following statement by a noted Presbyterian in another context, "In this [formulation of the doctrine of God], as in most other matters, the truly original contributions of the Reformation are not to be found in 'classic Protestantism' (Lutheranism, Calvinism, Anglicanism), but in the thinkers of 'radical or sectarian Protestantism' (Baptists, Congregationalists, Quakers, etc., and later Methodists) who sought to press behind theological formulations of the centuries and recover the 'pure' faith of primitive Christianity. However, only in the present period has their influence begun to become significant within the mainstream of Protestantism." Henry P. Van Dusen, in *A Handbook of Christian Theology,* ed. Marvin Halvorson (New York: Meridian, 1958), 148–49.

clusions for their own lives and ministries.

6. If systematic theology fails to exhibit its relevance, integrative theology has a built-in demand to do so. The approach endeavors to exhibit the practical significance for Christian life and service of the doctrines it establishes. It endeavors to display the contemporary relevance of the doctrines formulated without reducing theology to a trendy tract for the fleeting times.

Integrative Theology: Benefits and Limitations

Practicing the art of doing theology for oneself has many *benefits*. The discipline of doing his or her own theological research along with us will help the student to (1) relate the teaching of one portion of Scripture to others on the same subject; (2) integrate the distinct doctrines of Scripture into a coherent whole; (3) develop a biblical view of the real, the true, and the valuable; (4) compare and contrast a biblical world view and way of life with nonbiblical perspectives; (5) apply criteria of truth to distinguish authentic from counterfeit religious experiences; (6) develop personal and social convictions and values worth living and dying for; (7) build confidence to speak up in favor of his or her experience with the God who is there, acting and speaking; and (8) teach biblically based, historic Christian doctrine with its moral significance to children, young people, and adults. The art of integrative theology involves skill at each of these steps.

Integrative theology also has its evident *limitations*. It is no simple task to build a full-orbed world view and way of life based on God's universal revelation in nature, humanity, and history; on God's special revelation in the life and teachings of Christ; and on the thirty-nine Old Testament books and twenty-seven New Testament books, and the history of doctrine derived from

them. The best we can do is to work *toward* comprehensiveness and adequacy, *toward* an integrative theology. None can even come close to God's omniscient understanding, and most certainly this limited work does not. It seeks only to make a significant attempt in the direction of an integrative comprehensiveness of five fields: the historical, biblical, systematic, apologetic, and practical. Others are more qualified to add substantial sections on psychology and sociology and all the other lines of relevant data from the diverse fields of knowledge.

Given the vast and varied amount of material available to Christians, it is not surprising that Spirit-illumined people from all different backgrounds organize and apply it in quite different ways. Some consider certain facts of history and teachings of Scripture more important and determinative than others for organizing purposes (as the historical surveys show). The remarkable thing is that Christian theologians in very different cultures and using very different methodologies through the history of the church have reflected such agreement on basic Christian doctrines.

The Contribution of Other Fields to Integrative Theology

Apologetics: The Defense of Theological Presuppositions. In an increasingly complicated world, no discipline, and certainly not a comprehensive discipline, can put it all together by itself. In doing theology it is therefore necessary to assume what has been established particularly in apologetics.

Apologetics, having examined epistemological issues and alternatives with an openness to all sources of knowledge, establishes reliable criteria by which to evaluate truth claims in religion. Accepted as true are those hypotheses about reality that are logically noncontradictory, factually adequate, and existentially viable.

After examining numerous alternative world views, apologists argue that logical, empirical, and existential data are best accounted for by the Christian theistic world view.[10] The basic tenets of Christian theism affirm (1) the existence of the God of creation disclosed in (2) the Jesus of history and (3) the teaching of Scripture. Since that three-fold conclusion is defended in apologetics, we here presuppose that God has acted and spoken in creation, Christ, and Scripture. The challenging theological task is to explicate the enriching world view and way of life that follows from those presuppositions for people individually and collectively.

Biblical Studies: The Primary Source of Theological Information. A philosophy student who plans to devote his life to teaching the thought of Plato's classic Dialogues must learn what other experts from ancient to modern times have taught about Plato's philosophy. But a thorough student will not be satisfied with second-hand interpretations. From the Dialogues themselves, preferably in the original Greek and from the best manuscripts, he must find out for himself what Plato taught. Similarly, people who devote their lives to teaching and preaching a biblical message must know what the most influential scholars in the history of the church have said about it. But beyond these secondary sources, they must determine what the primary source, the Bible itself, teaches.

The student of Plato regards the varied interpretations as alternative hypotheses to be tested. He critically determines which writings are indeed Plato's and how well the text has been preserved through the centuries. To relate the thought of the Dialogues to each other, their dates must be determined as far as possible. And the more thorough the knowledge of Greek culture and history of Plato's time, the

better the milieu for understanding the famous philosopher's objectives and meaning. Similarly, in a lifelong study of Scripture, textual, linguistic, historical, critical, and cultural studies are valuable. Students who lack a background in the biblical languages, logic (critical thinking), history, and culture sooner or later may regret their lack of resources for determining what is genuinely biblical.

But critical studies are not an end in themselves. They are a means to identifying the divinely inspired writings in order that they may be studied, lived, taught, and preached. The content of the inspired writings, as other chapters and apologetics extensively support, is the primary source and only inerrant norm of Christian theology.

Christians confident of biblical revelation minister, like the apostle Paul, not only to the "foolish" but also to the "wise" (Rom. 1:14). They have a secure base from which to dialogue daily with skeptics, naturalists, pantheists, and other kinds of theists (Acts 17:1, 17; 18:4, 19). Christian ministers who hold "firmly to the trustworthy message" can not only "encourage others by sound doctrine" but also "refute those who oppose it" (Titus 1:9).

With all the stress on Christianity's relevance to alternative world views and ways of life, evangelical theology is grounded in the teaching of Scripture, God's written Word. Through all critical and philosophical interpretation, what the Bible teaches remains the primary source and final court of appeal. And in all decisions between biblical interpreters and theologians, reflective commitment is granted to the position coherently taught in the only writings that are inerrant.

Hermeneutics: Antidote to Theological Subjectivism. Supporting theological positions from Scripture is not as simple as it often appears to beginning students. All references to the Bible in support of a theological position involve interpretations, as the egregious use and open abuse of biblical quotations in cultic movements show. Listing a reference does not necessarily mean that one's interpretation of it is faithful to the biblical meaning.

After hearing a Bible study or sermon on a controversial theme, a listener may say, "But that is just your interpretation!" And after listening to the critic, the speaker may reply, "And that is just *your* interpretation!" Any resolution of such a conflict between those holding opposing views is hopeless if there is no escape from *eisegesis*, from reading their own ideas into the Bible. To engage in *exegesis*, the deriving of ideas *from* the Bible, both need to acknowledge that their views are hypotheses to be tested. Both need to be willing to submit their views to the test of standard logical criteria of truth and hermeneutical principles for interpreting literature in general and the literature of the Bible in particular. Without respect for hermeneutical guidelines, doctrinal differences among even those who believe the Bible may lack any hope of resolution. Some of those standards of responsible interpretation follow.

1. The meaning of a biblical statement is the ordinary, or normal, meaning of the statement (usually literal with some figures of speech) in terms of its context and the author's purpose. "Jesus died" is a cognitive assertion that is either true or false in fact. The assertion is not merely emotive, nor is it merely of spiritual significance (as Christian Science alleges). The fact of Christ's death (and the deaths of others) cannot be changed to fit the assumption that in reality there is no death. Assumptions must be changed to fit the given facts of Scripture about nature and history.

2. The meaning of a biblical statement fits the historical and cultural setting of the writer and the first readers. Their frame of reference cannot be ignored and replaced by one foreign to them. For example, a Hindu cyclical view of history cannot be introduced into the Jewish-Christian linear view of history. Given the present stress on the differences between cultures, one of the major theological issues today focuses on the question of what teaching applies only to the one culture addressed and what applies to all people of all times. In supporting a doctrine as authoritative today, one of the basic questions that must be answered is, "How does the normative teaching of this passage in its immediate context fit into the total pattern of God's progressive revelation relevant to this subject?"[11] But while we must take cultural differences seriously, we must remember that human beings in all times and places are human beings with more commonalities than differences. All peoples of all cultures are created in the image of God and fallen, inclined to all the works of the flesh, dependent upon God, obligated to God, alienated from God, in all justice guilty before God's moral norms, and in need of mercy and grace, etc.[12]

3. The meaning of a sentence is the one most coherent with the writer's own context. The author's usage of a word as traced throughout his writings is a stronger indication of its meaning than the derivation of the word. A word should not be interpreted apart from its sentence, the basic unit of the writer's thought. Then the sentence should be understood in its paragraph and the paragraph in its place in the progress of thought in the book. Each book of the Bible needs to be understood in relation to the other books in its Testament. And the two Testaments need to be related to each other.

4. The meaning of any single biblical statement is not contradictory to any teaching of other Scripture on the sub-

ject. God's Word, presumably, does not affirm and deny the same thing at the same time in the same respect. So a verse should be taken in accord with the broader theological context. This is involved in the Reformers "analogy of faith." Scripture interprets Scripture.

5. The intended meaning is the one, literal, historical, grammatical, contextual meaning, not a "deeper" or "secret" meaning. Although the applications of a passage are many, the meaning in context is one. Many groups today, such as Theosophy, Divine Science, and the New Age movements in general, assume plural meanings in biblical statements. They regard the normal, literal meaning as the simple meaning, to be superceded by the "deeper" meaning, which turns out to teach an unbiblical monism and support mystical, metaphysical, or occult practices. For examples of this, see Unity's *Metaphysical Bible Dictionary* or the "Glossary" in Mary Baker Eddy's *Science and Health with Key to the Scriptures*.[13]

6. Extensive passages on a subject take priority for theological purposes over brief allusions. We are more likely to misinterpret a single sentence than a whole series of statements on a topic in a paragraph. For example, on the subject of what is necessary for salvation it is unwise to base the eternal life of millions on a single allusion to baptism for the dead (1 Cor. 15:29).

7. Doctrinal passages have initially a greater importance than historical narratives that may report ideas and practices not normative for others. Hence the meaning of the baptism of the Spirit is more clearly defined in the teaching of 1 Corinthians 12:13 than in references to the practice in Acts (1:5; 2:4; 8:14–17; 10:44–48). The allusion to the Jerusalem believers having everything in common and selling their possessions (Acts 2:44–45) does not take priority over the general exhortation to work, to

have something (private ownership), and to share with those in need as generous stewards (Eph. 4:28).

8. What is central in scriptural teaching should be central in our theologies and ministries. The basic human problem throughout the world is sin against our Creator and against others. The universal prescription to resolve the problem is justification through faith on the basis of Christ's death for our sins. Christ's atonement was anticipated throughout the Old Testament, achieved in the Gospels, proclaimed in Acts, and explicated in the rest of the New Testament. To give preeminence to any other teaching, however good, is to distort the central message of special revelation to which the Holy Spirit witnesses.[14]

Logic: A Tool to Sharpen Theological Thinking. Students of theology often misunderstand each other's view and interpretation of the primary biblical source. The same words may be used with different meanings, or very different words may be used for the same belief. Merely verbal disputes are counterproductive. So it is important to avoid hasty labeling of one another and to define terms with increasing precision. Diligence is needed to develop proficiency in the discipline of logic. This discipline specializes, for one thing, in how to define terms. Introductory logic texts explain that good definitions are not circular, figurative, negative, or synonymous attempts at explaining meaning. Rather, a concept to be defined is placed under the next more general genus (kind) and then distinguished from other things of the same kind. So it becomes important to know the varieties of genus common in a biblical world view, and the varieties within each.[15]

If biologists and other scientists give careful thought to logical classifications and definitions, surely theologians can

31

and must do so. Knowing when humankind originated on earth, for example, depends on how theologians and scientists define humanness. We cannot limit ourselves to existential truth, truth about our own passionate existence, important as that is. We can know both existential truth and essential truth. Without knowledge of the essence of humanity, we have no way to know which creatures deserve respect as humans and have distinctively human rights and which are not made in the image of God.

Early theologians, seriously seeking to distinguish Christian truth from non-Christian opinions, carefully chose and defined their terms. At great cost, the early Christian thinkers explained the respect in which God is one and the respect in which God is threefold. Similarly they worked hard and long to explain the respect in which Jesus Christ was human and the respect in which he was divine. Contemporary carelessness in clarifying trinitarian distinctions and the ontological deity and humanity of Christ has contributed to many leaving churches with classical Christian teaching for those with unorthodox teaching and for other religions and cults. Much unnecessary ambiguity and debate can be avoided if people speaking and writing about Christian theology will discipline themselves to define their terms as they use them.

Logic also helps people who think about the God of the Bible to realize that the final authority includes not only what the Bible explicitly asserts but also what biblical assertions presuppose. Many important controversial issues today are not addressed explicitly in Scripture, but guidance concerning these issues may come from understanding the presuppositions of Christ and the biblical writers. The biblical record does not indicate that Jesus asserted explicitly that all people are sinners. But from his concern to seek and to save the lost, we may argue that Jesus presupposed that all are sinful.

Logical presuppositions may be not only of content but also of method, or principles of reasoning. Acquaintance with the methods of logical reasoning used in certain passages can also provide data to aid students in their theological reasoning. Paul, arguing that Israel's election was by grace, not works, says, "If it were [by works], grace would no longer be grace" (Rom. 11:6). Here Paul presupposes classical logic's three laws of thought: (1) the principle of *identity*: A is A, grace is (unmerited) grace; (2) the principle of the *excluded middle*: A is not non-A, (unmerited) grace is not nongrace (or works with merit); and (3) the principle of *noncontradiction*: a thing cannot be both A and non-A, God's choice cannot be according to both grace and nongrace (works).

Some modern logicians regard these three laws as mere tautologies, but their objective validity and general applicability is presupposed by Paul's inspired argument and reflected in their usefulness for over two thousand years in all fields of disciplined thought and meaningful communication. Opponents' arguments against these laws of thought cannot be understood or even given an appearance of validity unless these three laws of thought hold for their words and sentences. Not even one side of a paradox or dialectical antithesis can mean what it says if the three laws do not hold.[16]

Given the truth of biblical assertions, logic helps students of theology draw valid inferences from them. Logically one may draw an immediate inference from a universal affirmative proposition ("all people are sinners") to a particular affirmative proposition ("John Jones is a sinner"). The Bible does not list each sinner by name. All who try to help others see the need for Christ's salvation depend on the logical validity of this inference from the truth of the universal proposition in Scripture to its truth for each particular person.[17]

The basic need for logic in religion and Christian theology is often challenged. Mystics think it inhibits experience—but logic only asks that they make sense when they interpret their experience and speak about it to others. Some biblical theologians think it is alien to the Jewish mind. But it was not alien to Paul's mind or to the thinking of other biblical writers. Differences between the Hebrew and Greek cultures may be exaggerated. Both the Hebrew Old Testament and the Greek New Testament assert that God is not a man that he should lie. Basic principles of logic may have been discovered and formulated by Aristotle, but they were not invented by Aristotle.

Logical principles, like moral principles, are rooted ultimately in the mind and nature of the Creator. Common intellectual grids enable people from vastly different cultures to overcome initial difficulties and eventually communicate with each other. Logic is as indispensable to meaningful thought as grammar is to understandable language. In this God has made no exceptions, not even for born-again students of theology. Life can become very complicated and thought confused, but it will not help in those difficult periods to throw away such a valuable tool as logic. We may need to slow down, call for division of the question, and deal with one issue at a time.

The persistent may allege that "consistency is the mark of a small mind." But as one scholar aptly replied, "Better a small mind than none at all!" No theologian claims fully to comprehend human beings, atoms, or the Bible, let alone God. But Christians who believe that God revealed truth in the Bible's sentences have a basis for speaking about that truth in coherent sentences. We know in part, as Paul said. When speaking or writing about the part we do know, Christians studying theology seek to make sense. People cannot follow our preaching or teaching if we contradict ourselves.

Like any other instrument, logical reasoning can be used either for the ultimate glory of God or for the glorification of created beings. The misuse of reason by people who made logic or something in creation their God need not keep others from responsible use of the tool in support of God's revealed purposes in the church and throughout the world. Logic is not an invention of unbelieving philosophers, but a reflection of God's mind in minds made in his image. Our ability to reason, like every other capacity, has been affected by our fallen sensuality and pride, but it has not been destroyed. The Holy Spirit renews the minds of believers so that they grow not only in grace, but also in knowledge (Col. 3:10). We will never fully comprehend God or his purposes, but we can and ought to know God and his purposes in part.

Logical reasoning helps God's will get done on earth in at least three additional ways: (1) Logical thinking helps display the coherence of the world view and way of life based on revealed truth. (2) Logically developed sermons and Bible studies help people know unequivocally what is expected of them as they face appealing contradictory options. (3) Also living consistently by a coherent belief system helps avoid hypocrisy and exemplifies Christianity's relevance for contemporary ethical and social issues.[18]

Previous Theologies: Secondary Sources With Provisional Authority. The challenging task of integrative theology cannot be accomplished by one person alone. Each theologian depends on many others, for in divine providence many have been enabled to make significant contributions to the field for nearly two thousand years. Whether ancient or recent, their interpretations, insights, syntheses, and applications are ignored to our loss. Doctrinal studies, Old or New Testament theologies, biblical theologies, and systematic theologies of others may suggest hypotheses that we would otherwise not consider. These hypotheses may deserve to be tested by the primary biblical data and, if more coherent than contradictory alternatives, applied in life and ministry.

Fortunately, some of the finest work in the past has been summed up through painstaking efforts in confessions of faith and creeds recognized in the church as being in harmony with the biblical standard. These deserve special attention as representative of a wide scholarly consensus and serve as provisional authorities for Christians as yet unable to do theological research for themselves. In this Protestant approach, creeds are not rules that rule Scripture (*norma normans*), but they are ruled by Scripture (*norma normata*).[19]

Particularly when new in the faith, like young children under the authority of their parents, Christians wisely depend rather heavily on their received traditions. But valuable as well-founded traditions in classical Christianity are, at best they can serve only as provisional authorities. They function as authorities until we have been able to check out their faithfulness to Scripture for ourselves. To the extent that they provide the most coherent account of the biblical data, they will continue to serve as consciously chosen authorities. But, and here is the provision, to the extent that received traditions do not measure up to the primary scriptural materials, they will no longer serve as norms. The only nonnegotiable authority in theology is Scripture quoted in an appropriate context from a reliable text or translation. With the Protestant Re-

formers, we affirm that although there are many sources of theological knowledge, there is but one inerrant, final authority: *sola scriptura*. In seeking to integrate biblical truth with other knowledge, we constantly face, for example, the issue of whether the biblical or the scientific has the priority. The liberal tradition tended to accommodate the biblical to the psychological or philosophical in order to communicate to contemporary society. Natural theology corrected scriptural theology.[20] In the process, the essence of revealed truth was lost. We must adapt our communication of theology to our generation but be alert to the great danger of accommodating the message to its errors. As Fulton J. Sheen once said, "He who marries the spirit of the age will become a widower in the age to come."

We may hope that educated young people will mature to the place of doing research for themselves. And educated Christians who desire to minister to others will mature to the place of examining alternative doctrinal hypotheses, responsibly evaluating them, and arriving at their own reflective commitments. To decide for ourselves does not mean that our conclusions will be entirely new. It does mean that they should be entirely ours.

Research Methodology: Key to Responsible Theological Decision Making. Sound theology does not arise from wishful thinking, naïve gullibility, or arbitrary leaps into the dark. Nor does it come from a haphazard quoting of creeds, Scriptures, or favorite Bible-conference speakers. Too often people have sought to do theology without giving sufficient attention to research methodology. Some such surveys of historical and contemporary theologies have left many in an anchorless sea of relativism.

How can anyone determine religious

truth in our times? Even in biblical hermeneutics many have been influenced by the impact of relativism. No one can be objective, we are told, for all come to a subject with preunderstandings. Anthony Thiselton's *The Two Horizons* contrasts the presuppositional horizon of the biblical writers and the presuppositional horizon of biblical interpreters some two thousand years later.[21] Charles Kraft's *Christianity in Culture* complicates the issue further, and properly so, by adding a third horizon, that of the people to whom we present the biblical message.[22] In the midst of at least three different sets of cultural presuppositions (not to mention possible generation gaps or subcultural perspectives within each), how can anyone know any normative propositional truth, let alone presume to declare God's truth to others with very different horizons?[23]

Admittedly no one is free from preunderstandings in any field, including Old Testament, New Testament, and theology. In all knowing, the knower actively participates, a point sometimes overlooked by pure empiricists. There is an element of subjectivity in all human knowing. Karl Marx showed that as active knowers we bring with us to any field an ideological taint. Our economic status as "haves" or "have nots" influences our outlook on life, including our theological or philosophical world views. According to Sigmund Freud, our belief system is also influenced by psychological factors resulting from early childhood experiences. John Dewey underlined the impact of early educational experiences on a scholar in any discipline. Anthropologists and missionaries have pointed to the varying influences of cultures and subcultures on Christians seeking to take essentials of the gospel to the people of these cultures for the first time.

The cumulative impact of all of these

and other disciplines has led many toward a total relativism, pragmatism, and functionalism, even in theology. People are said to be not only culturally influenced but culturally determined to think and believe as they do. If God did give absolute truth in Scripture centuries ago to people with an entirely different set of preunderstandings than ours, we are hopelessly removed from that truth. And some think these considerations make it impossible even for God to have given changelessly true affirmations of truth to biblical writers in human propositions expressed in sentences in human languages.

Note on the Cultural Factor in Interpretation

People are the essentially human and fallen in all places and all times and in all cultures, but there are also real differences of art forms, music, diets, ceremonies, family customs, and governmental forms. Some imagine everything always the same; others, always totally different.

Careful interpreters of biblical literature must do justice to the similarities and the differences. They will acknowledge both the normative principles universally applicable to all people of all times and some principles normative only for a specific person or group in a specific situation. In certain situations an action may not be governed by principle but merely by wisdom or consideration of others. In delineating principles in biblical teaching, seek the biblical author's *reason* for the given principle.[24]

1. Is the reason for the principle rooted in the unchanging nature of God? (Love others because God first loved you [1 John 4:19]?) God's nature, transcending all cultural variables and racial prejudices, does not change.

2. Is the reason for the principle rooted in the uniform nature of creation, mankind, or moral law? Natural

35

laws, essential humanness, and creation mandates are not altered by cultural differences. However distorted or suppressed the universal requirements of the Ten Commandments—written by God on human hearts, given by Moses, and repeated in the New Testament—may be, they are universally binding (though the Sabbath need not be on the seventh day).

3. Is the principle rooted in the unchanging redemptive principles of God's plan of salvation (sheer grace, faith, the righteousness provided by the Messiah)? These do not change with the passing of a changing institution such as circumcision.

4. Is the principle rooted in character traits of Jesus Christ and produced by the Holy Spirit? Humility may be expressed in other cultures in a different way than by washing one another's feet in a society where people walked on dirt roads (John 13:12–16).

5. Are Old Testament principles reiterated in the New Testament? If so, they transcend the earlier cultures and express absolute norms (e.g., condemnation of occult practices of all sorts). But the Old Testament dietary requirements are not repeated in the New Testament and so would not be normative, though in some similar conditions (e.g., lack of refrigeration) they might be wise.

6. Even culturally specific principles may apply to others because a culture may be similar to other cultures in many respects. Eugene Nida observed that in choosing the Jewish people, God chose the greatest number of world cultures (*Message and Missions*). Also the Greek language and culture was inherited by great sectors of the human family.

To respond to the challenge of relativism we need more than a set of hermeneutical principles. Those principles themselves are in question. We need a reliable method for research derived from a reliable epistemology that has successfully interacted with relativism. Assuming a critical realism,* we hasten to point out that the

---

*Critical realism as here used is a theory of human knowing about what is (metaphysics). It maintains the reality of persons, things, and events independent of knowing them to the extent that hypotheses concerning them are confirmed by a critical (verificational) method of justifying beliefs. Critical realism is not naïve realism. For naïve realists, the oar halfway in the water is believed to be bent in reality as well as in appearance. And naïve realists believe that the railroad tracks not only appear to meet in the distance, but actually do meet. Reality is as they uncritically see it.

Neither is critical realism to be confused with common-sense (Scottish) realism. Not all the intuitions or "natural judgments" of "common sense" are true even though our minds have been made by God to know and govern reality. For finite and fallen minds to know which of our impressions conform to what is real requires a testing of hypotheses by reliable criteria of truth. A critical or verificational method is needed to distinguish actual persons, things, and events from illusions, dreams, fantasies, and hallucinations, however common (e.g., flat earth, rising sun).

Again, critical realism is not to be confused with idealism. Idealists think that since all our knowledge involves ideas, there is no reality independent of human or divine perceiving of them. However, the fire in the fireplace is not recreated when I come into the room after an hour's absence. Neither is it sustained only in the mind of the divine Perceiver during the absence of a human observer. But idealists are correct in holding that ideas (as distinct from things) are involved in all knowing. Critical realism concedes to idealism that whenever a thing is perceived, it is an object for the mind, but it does not conclude that things have no existence except in the mental perception.

The difference critical realists make between objects known and data derived from them in the mind explains several important aspects of experience. That difference makes memory

fact of multiple influences on human knowers presents an insufficient basis for concluding that we know *nothing but* our own subjective opinions. A political crisis may be reported from a variety of perspectives in *The World Press Review,* but it does not follow that its readers know nothing about the facts or events that stirred up such conflicting opinions. Furthermore, some of the reports may be better informed of the relevant data than others. While no journalist can claim total objectivity, all may agree on certain elements. Critically trained, morally responsible political observers and scientific historians may significantly overcome economic, psychological, cultural, and linguistic hurdles to write on a crisis with commendable objectivity and substantial truth.

Analogously, the fact that no theologian can claim complete objectivity does not mean that no theological statement conveys any truth. We must, however, develop our ability to identify how we have been influenced by our background and environment and consider our preunderstandings as tentative hypotheses that must be tested as severely as other people's preunderstandings in the light of objective criteria in order to arrive at responsible conclusions.

To contribute toward the ends of objective validity and maturity in doing theology, the following verificational method is proposed. Growing out of a critically realistic epistemology, it provides many checks and balances to avoid naïve, unsupported "horizons" or preunderstandings from overruling relevant principles and data. In our writing we seek to adhere to this demanding methodology in the development of each doctrine. We hope that the product will therefore be more than an exercise in bias or tradition and that it will have a higher degree of objective validity than theologies less conscious of these methodological checks and balances. But none can be more aware than we that we have not attained!

The verificational method includes five steps:

1. Genuine inquiry begins with defining a problem to be researched and becoming aware of its significance. It is impossible to work effectively on everything at once. So we must limit the scope of each doctrinal study. If too much is attempted initially, it may become necessary to divide the question into two or more studies. If the problem is to understand a scriptural passage relating to a subject, it is also helpful to try to feel what the writer felt in accord with his purpose for this writing. To research existentialist emphases on authenticity, students need to feel their disgust for hypocrisy and its effects throughout christendom. To engage in a genuine inquiry of neoorthodox emphases on God's distinctness from na-

---

possible and explains differences of appearances under different conditions, such as a distant light in a fog or an oar halfway submerged in water. This difference between a thing and mental data derived from it also accounts for different interpretations of the same events, and it accounts for error or illusions (for example, of a person on drugs).

In sum, critical realism retains the belief of common-sense realism in independent things but admits that these are not directly and homogeneously presented to very different knowers in very different or even similar perceptual situations. Hence a critical procedure becomes indispensable to verify or disconfirm any religious beliefs, whether derived from common sense, sensory observation, mystical intuition, rational intuition, or Holy Spirit–illumined *interpretation* of Scripture on any subject.

For further thoughts on this subject, see Elton Trueblood, *General Philosophy* (Grand Rapids: Baker, 1963), 29–45; Antony Flew, *A Dictionary of Philosophy* (New York: St. Martin's, 1979), 77; D. F. Kelly, "Scottish Realism," in *EDT, 990–91.*

ture and humanity, scholars need to feel Barth's disillusionment with liberalism's unrealistic view of human nature, its unfounded faith in the inevitability of progress, and its humanistic worship and service of the self. People need to feel poverty and powerlessness to appreciate Latin American liberation theology, seemingly endless chauvinism to begin to understand feminist theology, and discrimination and slavery to research black theology. The motivation for painstaking theological research often comes from enigmatic and even traumatic experiences in life. Sheltered students need to do their best to identify with the experiences and motivations of the leaders who shape the thinking of the theological world.

2. The theological method then discovers alternative answers to the problem by surveying relevant literature or interviewing theologians from many perspectives. No limits are placed on sources of possible hypotheses to be tested. Stimulation of thought may come from the whole spectrum of theologies, religions, philosophies, new consciousness groups, cults, and the occult. Creative contextualizations of the Christian faith may come from any cultural horizon in any country in the world. An objective survey of varied perspectives helps students become aware of their own presuppositions, much like travel overseas helps them become conscious of assumptions taken for granted as universal in their own culture. Elements of the different answers that do not contradict teachings of Scripture or each other may be combined in new syntheses.

3. All hypotheses, even those whose truth we have assumed for years, must be tested for their coherence and viability on standard criteria of truth. If they are true, we need not fear reexamination. True doctrines will not be found self-contradictory, or unrelated to reality in the external or internal worlds of human experience. Sound interpretations of a disputed passage of Scripture will without self-contradiction account for all the relevant lines of evidence: the author's purpose, grammar, and word usage; the immediate biblical context; and the broader theological context. Fitting the external givens, the hypotheses should also fit the internal givens. That is, one should be able to live by it without disillusionment or inauthenticity.

These criteria derive, not from one theological tradition, but from the Creator, his image in humanity, and common grace. On these bases we insist that however great the cultural, educational, economic, social, political, religious, and theological differences people may have, they are still human. All human beings have this in common that they all deserve respect, have inalienable rights, and ought to be treated fairly or justly as self-determined, responsible agents, not as mere victims of their environments. Furthermore, truth for all human beings is equally related to the data of reality, including logical principles of meaningful thought and communication. Among the most significant givens in human experience is the Bible. It cannot be erased from human experience, history, literature, philosophy, or theology. Every world view must give some account of its teachings. And for Christians, every theological hypothesis considered true must without contradiction account for all the relevant biblical lines of evidence.

4. After resolving preliminary or subordinate issues between alternatives that are live options, we seek to formulate the overall conclusion to the issue under inquiry. The most coherent and viable position is stated in a way faithful to the revealed truth and at the same time clear and significant for the present generation of Christians and the unreached people we serve.

5. The method applies the conclusion to the burning issues of life by determining worthy ends and values in life and service and, when possible, by suggesting more concrete ways in which to implement the conclusions as persons in families, churches, and nations.

Without a theological method of this kind, liberals and Evangelicals, Baptists and Roman Catholics will not break out of their hermeneutical circles and will fail to reduce the misunderstanding and carnal divisiveness that threaten our world.[25] Important as piety is in the doing of theology, spirituality will not by itself settle conflicting presuppositions and truth claims. Faith is indispensable to progress in any field, but fideism alone will not change the conflicting claims made by believers. Although the object of faith may be unseen, the evidence for a belief is seen and needs to be examined with sound methodology.

Without the witness of the Holy Spirit to the truth of the gospel and our appropriation of its benefits, Christian theology is about an alien universe. But the Spirit witnesses to truth discovered in evidence. Apart from evidence of truth about reality in general or special revelation, the Holy Spirit does not provide a method for resolving conflicting theological claims. The Spirit of truth guides people into truth through illumined, accountable uses of the mental capacities he gave the church.

Intuitive insights may come from God or other sources independently of historical and scriptural evidence. Any intuitive insights alleged to be from God must fit together into a consistent whole that squares with Scripture and reality as we face it daily. Carefully interpreted scriptural teaching must test intuitions, not the other way around (1 John 4:1–3).

Much spiritual-life teaching today seems to make intuition not only a source of truth but also the highest test of truth. Watchman Nee's trichotomy elevates the intuitive capacity to the highest "part" of a human being (the spirit) and demotes the reasoning capacity to a lower "part" (the soul).[26] On this analysis, direct intuitions ("word of knowledge," "prophecies," etc.) are often believed to constitute a higher, "spiritual knowledge" than knowledge that comes through a reasoned exegesis of Scripture: Reasoning from nature or the Scriptures is considered "soulish." However, depravity has seriously affected not only our reasoning capacities but also our intuitive capacities. Ideas derived intuitively can be as carnal as those derived by misuse of reasoning from the Scriptures. Either source of knowledge may be deceptive. If there is to be growth in grace and knowledge, the entire person, including the intuitive abilities, must be brought into harmony with the truth of the Creator-God revealed in the historic Christ and the inspired Scriptures. And the God of nature, Christ, and Scripture is maturely known through some method such as that outlined in the five steps above, not merely through direct intuitions without checks and balances.

All who would do more than report the theology of others, must determine whether in controversial issues the final court of appeal is immediate intuitive insight independent of scriptural study or thorough research of the issue in a verificational method. Faithful stewards of divine revelation have found no successful substitute for the disciplined use of a fruitful research method. The sooner gifted young people devote their best intellectual efforts to such a systematic study of the Word with faithful prayer, the sooner they will meet qualifications for ministry and lead thinking people and churches to greater piety, faith, Spirit-attested truth, and wholesome spirituality. The ultimate key to spirituality is not our own immediate experience, however sincere, life-transforming, and important that may be, but divinely revealed truth. Truth is not falsified by our lack of experience but the authenticity of our experience is tested by truth.

Summation

We can now succinctly state what integrative theology is ideally and what it is not. The significance of these points will become increasingly clear in the development of subsequent chapters.

Integrative theology seeks to be human, not humanistic; person-related, not merely relational; situation-related, not situation-bound; biblical, not biblicistic; subjective, not subjectivistic; historically related, not culture-bound or historicistic; verifiable, not positivistic; experience-related, not experience-bound; critically realistic, not naïvely realistic; rational, not rationalistic; classically relevant, not relativistic; normative, not merely descriptive; presuppositionally conscious, not uncritical; scientific, not scientistic; assertive, not arbitrary; systematic, not omniscient; coherent, not fully comprehended; substantially viable, not liveable to perfection in this life.

APOLOGETIC INTERACTION

Influenced by the analytic approaches of the twentieth century, both biblical scholars and philosophers tended to abandon integrative syntheses of thought such as systematic theologies and comprehensive philosophies. Can some of their antisystematic reasoning be answered from an integrative approach?

Is an Integrative Theology Possible Philosophically?

Among the philosophies arrayed against systematic and integrative theology are logical positivism, philosophical analysis, nontheistic existentialism, pragmatism, and Marxism-Leninism. In their opposition to developing a theological *Weltanschauung* (world view) they form a kind of secular humanist consensus. Opposition also arises from a humanist consensus of Eastern Hindu and Buddhist, occult, and the new-consciousness movements. It is impossible to respond here to each of these, but we can give a brief indication of directions answers might take.

The powerful impact of the positivists' verifiability criterion of meaning and truth led Clark Pinnock to say, "The question of questions for our time is the very possibility of any theology at all."[27] An invisible divine Spirit cannot be verified according to a strict interpretation of the verifiability criterion, and thus talk about God is meaningless. Theological definitions are either tautologies or merely the venting of feelings. Testimonies of religious experiences, said A. J. Ayer, provide interesting material for abnormal psychology.[28]

However, the positivists' own division of sentences into but two categories, meaningful and meaningless, turned out to be nonsense because it is unverifiable. Verifiability "died the death of a thousand qualifications." In these times of nuclear proliferation anyone who declares nonsensical sentences about justice (also invisible), cannot be taken seriously. In 1980 A. J. Ayer himself signed the Secular Humanist Declaration, which contains a number of invisible and unverifiable values. For example, the statement about the value of the scientific method ("We believe the scientific method, though imperfect, is still the most reliable way of understanding the world") cannot be verified by the five senses in a laboratory experiment. It is more a philosophical or epistemological judgment than a scientific statement. People who accept the case of logical positivism or scientism against theology must on the same grounds be prepared to give up *all* of the highest values in life.

The end result of mere empiricism is the loss of the empiricist's self. Limiting all knowledge to mere sensory impressions, David Hume received no impression of his soul or self receiving impressions. This led to the loss of inner dignity and responsibility. In an attempt to enhance human worth, secular humanism tends to destroy the self-determining, personal agent who was to have dominion over his environment rather than be determined by it. One total empiricist vainly trying to live by the philosophy greeted another one morning, saying, "You are fine; how am I?"

Existentialists sought to overcome the tragic oversight of the self in empiricism by giving priority to the individual, existing person. We must first become aware that the full responsibility of our existence rests on ourselves. No fixed human nature limits human freedom. No God, Jean-Paul Sartre insists, prescribes values or issues commands. We cannot abstract a universal essence of goodness from good acts, nor a universal essence of humanness from a number of persons. The slogan "Existence precedes essence" means, among other things, that no essences can be known.

It follows that, if there is no God and if there are no objectively valid ethical principles, there can be not only no normative theology but no objectively valid statements about anything. Why then should Sartre expect us to consider the assertion, "Existence precedes essence" as anything more than an expression of his own feeling? Has that statement any value beyond a description of his subjectivism? We have acknowledged an element of subjectivity in our knowledge of objectively valid truths. If Sartre wants an element of objectivity in his basic theses, then objective validity is possible. Other truths that are true for everyone may eventually be found and related to one

another coherently so that a synthesis of these truths might gradually develop. We may even find that such changeless truths rest ultimately in a changeless mind, the Logos of God!

Marx reacted against Hegel's talk of empty consciousness and spoke persuasively of practical activity in real life. If theology or philosophy is viewed as an independent branch of activity apart from the taintedness of economics and dialectical determinations, it has no value whatever.

Opposing abstraction as much as Marx did, William James, psychologist and pragmatist, even dismissed the notion of "truth" as an abstraction. The question "What is truth?" is not a real question because it is not relative to any conditions. The concept of truth, James said, is a mere abstraction from truths (in the plural). Mistakenly, James thought that if one system was right, every other must be wrong. He failed to allow for elements of truth in systems that need be logically wrong only where they contradicted the Christian faith. Needless to say, William James rejected those elements of other philosophies that contradicted the presuppositions of pragmatism, implying the objective validity of the law of noncontradiction.

If William James or John Dewey had adequately defined pragmatism, the definition would constitute an abstraction that all ought to accept. If all knowledge must operationally work for us, satisfy us, or promote our adaptation to our environment, we have some normative abstractions (depending on the definition of "work" and "satisfy" and whether the "environment" includes eternal surroundings) according to which a system develops. The writings of James and Dewey were basically consistent with their assumptions, except for their claim to avoid abstractions from particulars in universal and normative truths. An absolute relativism is self-contradictory. Some truths are known and advanced as valid for all. What we know we need to understand and communicate coherently. In doing that, like it or not, we are involved in culture-transcending systems of thought.

Another attack on integrative syntheses has come from a very different perspective, that of Eastern and occult monism. Hinduism in its countless forms has affirmed the ultimate reality of Brahman, but allegedly no true statements can be made about that transcendent being. Although alleged to be beyond all thought, Brahman can be experienced in an ineffable, temporary, passive, mystical union. In this union distinctions between the knower and the known, subject and object become meaningless. All is one. No duality can be maintained in reality, even between good and evil. Distinctions are made only in *maya* (appearance). Illusory propositional truth *seems* to be of value, but in reality it is not of value. Any theology claiming propositional revelation true for God and humanity is consigned to the illusions of maya. And any theology based on a distinction between good and evil that holds for God and dependent man becomes illusory.

The Buddhist doctrine of maya, Alan Watts found, has remarkable similarity to the Western doctrine of relativism. It alleges that things, events, and persons are delineated not by nature, but by human description, and the way in which we divide or describe them is relative to our varying illusory points of view. We can know no distinct thing or person in reality. A thing or person can be said to be nothing more than the sum total of these relationships, dependencies, influences, effects, and determinations. Things in themselves cannot be known. Only relationships can be known. Personal identity has slipped into the "reality" of the shining sea, never to be distinguished again.

Those who on the basis of Eastern relativistic assumptions oppose systematic doctrines about God as he is revealed to be in himself need to remember that the same assumptions rule out any knowledge of themselves, others, and things. No universals can be known, only changing relationships, whatever these may be or, rather, become. Not even ideals can survive. So Watts writes, "Be not concerned with right and wrong. The conflict between right and wrong is the sickness of the mind."[29] Instead, cultivate a bland indifference. Decide without having the faintest understanding of how you do it. Yet Alan Watts published 222 relatively coherent pages about unspeakable religious experience in *Beyond Theology: The Art of Godmanship,* in addition to numerous other books.[30]

The self-contradictions inherent in these challenges to systematic thought in general, and systematic thought in theology in particular, are evident. Their relativism and amorality does not adequately fit the facts of human valuational or moral experience. The perspectives underlying these challenges are impossible to live by without assuming our continuous identity and responsibility. But that responsibility would be meaningless if there were no moral Judge to whom we will give account.

We need not reject coherent thought in order to find existentially, pragmatically, and mystically significant experience. Rather, fulfilling Christian experience of the living God comes through a growing appreciation of the coherent truth and vital relevance of his revelation in the person of Christ and the teachings of Scripture.

Is an Integrative Theology Possible Biblically?

Much recent "biblical theology" opposes generalizations or abstractions from the Scripture's immediate historical and cultural contexts and considers systematic theology impossible and illegitimate. The Bible's message, many biblical theologians argue, is timebound and limited to the events to which it refers in their historical, cultural contexts. Of relative validity only, the writers' messages cannot be harmonized with each other or generalized with normative authority for all people of all times and places. The practical outcome for ministers is that they can present only a situational theology from case studies in "expository" messages and not normative doctrinal messages with legitimate authority for all situations.

John Bright, for example, in *The Authority of the Old Testament* claims that the normative authority does not rest in the Bible's timeless abstract teachings but in its events. Bright's Bible as such has no final authority and is not given by God.[31] It is not to be used as a compendium of doctrine, since a harmonious system of biblical teaching is considered impossible.[32] Not even Paul's letters justify systematics, for their propositions are not revelation, nor are the sentences conveying them verbally inspired.[33] Paul's letters simply summon people to new life in Christ.[34]

Bright's caricature of systematic theology bears little resemblance to the discipline here presented. Except for affirming that the Bible is fully inspired in all its parts, Bright's notion of theology deserves rejection. According to Bright, systematic theology quotes verses in a mechanical way to set forth what is intelligible to the individual theologian or his denomination. It introduces categories foreign to the Bible's historical nature and terminology that is not part of the faith of its writers in their own times and cultures.

The conventional rubrics—God, man, sin, and salvation—force the biblical materials into a Procrustean bed of nonbiblical, Greek philosophical origin.[35]

Bright's inductive approach to the historical events is as incapable of discovering changeless kerygmatic truth as scientism is of discovering moral absolutes. Behind the varieties of biblical expression, the biblical theologian finds one common center of unity, namely, that history is the theater of God's purposive activity. But beliefs are not to be identified with the biblical expressions.[36] These beliefs do not permit metaphysical or ontological knowledge of God, for Bright's horizon is limited to the phenomenal realm of history.

Bright's approach raises some of the most basic issues between biblical and systematic theology. Is it possible to abstract normative principles for all times from the detailed historical and cultural context of biblical narratives? In the diversity of biblical writings addressing a variety of situations, can we find unified teaching on basic topics or do we have many conflicting christologies and soteriologies? Is there a noncontradictory harmony of biblical doctrines contained in the biblical text? Is a biblically rooted theology totally discontinuous with philosophy or is there some common ground?

In response to these questions Bright has overlooked scriptural examples of condensed, transferable statements of duty and doctrine. The Bible itself on occasion abstracts generalizations applicable in every context in all times and places. Apparently the extensive legislation of the Pentateuch could be summed up in the Book of the Covenant (Exod. 20–24) and condensed further in the Ten Commandments (Exod. 20:1–17). Jesus even further condensed the ten into two (Matt. 22:36–40). The writer of Hebrews abstracted several elementary teachings from their historical contexts: repentance from acts of laying on of hands, the resurrection of the dead, and eternal judgment (Heb.

6:1-2). These doctrines may summarize emphases of the previous Jewish dispensation preparing the way for Christ's coming. Whether they reflect pre-Christian or early Christian teaching, or both, the point is the same: a condensed statement of doctrines abstracted from their initial settings in literary narrative is not contrary to biblical precedent.

The New Testament also recognizes certain coherent patterns of gospel teachings in faithful words. The supposition that early Christians had no fixed pattern of teachings that regulated thought and practice is entirely alien to the apostle's ethic.[37] Paul summed up the core of the gospel that was according to the Scriptures, not merely behind them in events (1 Cor. 15:3-4). And Paul judged people's lives by what was "contrary to the sound doctrine that conforms to the glorious gospel of the blessed God," which God had entrusted to him (1 Tim. 1:10-11). The gospel was expressed in faithful sayings passed on to Timothy (1 Tim. 1:15), and these sayings were worth defending (1 Tim. 1:18; 2 Tim. 1:13-14) and transmitting to other reliable men (2 Tim. 2:1-2).

Paul praised members of the church at Rome for wholeheartedly obeying the form (*typos,* pattern) of teaching received (Rom. 6:17). The Thessalonians' faith in "the Lord's message" was well known (1 Thess. 1:7), and Paul exhorted them to "hold to" and "live according to the teaching" received from the apostles" (2 Thess. 3:6).

Just as the tabernacle was built according to a pattern (*typos,* Heb. 8:5), so faith and life conformed to a pattern of sound doctrine. The same pattern applied not only in different geographical areas but to both Jews and Greeks (Acts 20:21), showing that the gospel message conveyed in human language transcended prejudicial cultural boundaries and did not fluctuate in different cultural settings. Of greater concern

than life itself to Paul was "testifying to the gospel of God's grace" (Acts 20:24). And in his parting plea to pastors Paul called on them to guard the gospel, the word of God's grace (Acts 20:28-32).

Granting that the Bible summarizes and abstracts both law and gospel from their original historical situations, do we depart from Scripture when we consider how law and gospel relate to each other? If it is proper to do so within the work or works of one writer, is it impossible to find a coherent teaching on law and gospel in all the different summations of them by all the writers in the same Testament? And then would there not be value in relating teaching on law and on the gospel in both Testaments? Might it then not also be helpful to consider the relation of law and gospel to the law written on all human hearts (Rom. 2:14-15)? Would it be departing from Scripture (or too "philosophical") to consider the relation of all that revelation teaches on law to all that it teaches on gospel?

For integrative theology to "put all Scripture on a subject together" is no less biblical than for biblical theologians who accept propositional revelation to do the same with a selected part of the biblical corpus. The Scriptures are the primary source of information for systematic theology as much as for biblical theology. The main difference between the two types of theology lies in their organizing principles, which are chronological and logical respectively. Biblical theology stresses the concepts of law and gospel in different writers at their particular stage in the progress of revelation. Systematic theology synthesizes the teaching of all the biblical writers on basic topics in a logical order.

Can either discipline accomplish its purpose while limiting itself to biblical words and categories of thought alone? With due respect for the Holy Spirit's inspiration of the original wording, must we stay with the original languages? To be obliged to stay with the words of Scripture alone would destroy all exposition and interpretation of Scripture, not systematic theology alone. What interpreters take from Scripture must be distinguished from what is given by Scripture, as the differences among commentators and biblical theologians indicate. If different wordings cannot be used, interpreters cannot make clear in what way they are taking the Bible's teaching. Furthermore, truth is not merely a matter of words but of propositional content, and the same assertion can be made in different words in different languages, or in the same language in direct or indirect quotations or active and passive moods.

To allege that we must use the same words as Scripture does would render useless all preaching and teaching of the Bible. A minister or teacher could do nothing but read Scripture. Authors could not write about Scripture. A Calvinist could not be distinguished from an Arminian or a Pelagian, nor a trinitarian from a nontrinitarian. Sometimes a given word is used with different meanings in different biblical contexts. Only by expressing the sense of the context can the meanings of even biblical terms be clear. The contextual sense can be determined only by the wording, but its expression is not limited to the wording of a sentence, paragraph, or book.

Biblical theologians suggest that systematic theologians often introduce categories alien to the Scriptures. Can we use different general ways of thinking in systematics? Existentialist and neo-orthodox theologians speak of authenticity as persons and of personal encounters. Relational theologians emphasize personal relationships. Process theologians limit themselves to process forms of thought. Functional theologians speak repeatedly of functions. Orthodox theologians have for centuries spoken also of substances or essences and attributes of things and of persons in relationships.

All students of theology must determine which ways of thinking are validly inferred from Scripture, and none can avoid the use of categories of thought in understanding and communicating its teaching. Often fundamentalists, Barthians, and biblical theologians who imagine themselves most free from philosophical categories are subconsciously influenced by them. Biblical theologians who attack systematic theologians as too influenced by philosophy exhibit the phenomenalistic and antiabstractionist tendencies of certain modern philosophies. Thinkers cannot avoid categories. But categories are not explicitly set forth in Scripture. So theologians, whether organizing their material chronologically or logically, use "philosophical" categories such as existence, being, person, relationship, or function. The only questions are whether they choose their categories consciously or unconsciously and whether the choice is based on valid scriptural inferences or not.

In summary, biblical theology interprets passages relevant to a given topic and abstracts the teaching of those passages for a given writer or period of Old Testament or New Testament history. Having summed up the teaching for different periods of biblical history, some may abstract further to the teaching of all the biblical materials in progressive revelation on a given topic in a logical manner.

Biblical theology brings out differences of emphasis in the concepts by different writers at different periods, and ideally it does so without doing injustice to their unity. Systematic theology shows the unity of the teaching throughout the Scriptures, and ideally it does so without doing injustice to the differences at different stages in the progress of revelation.

Systematic theology then relates the different doctrines to each other coherently. This it does by presenting a unified view of theology proper, humanity, moral law, sin, Christ, the atonement, the gospel, the Spirit and the experience of salvation, and the church and its mission.

If in their initial steps biblical theologians do not limit themselves to biblical language and categories, why should systematic theologians in the next stage of abstraction be considered unbiblical? If generalizations are possible in dealing with individual books, writers, and periods of biblical history, why not for all the periods together? If the abstractions of biblical theologians can be documented from Scripture without a charge of proof-texting, may not also those of systematic theologians?

The case against systematics from the side of biblical theology has provided a healthy warning to avoid biblically unjustified importations into integrative theology. But the case either proves too much and so also destroys biblical theology or it fails to justify a bias against all verificationally derived systematic thinking about scriptural revelation. The challenging task remains, then, for people in integrative theology to derive from the primary and secondary sources a coherent world view and way of life in harmony with the explicit and implicit teaching of Scripture.

RELEVANCE FOR LIFE AND MINISTRY

Integrative theology contributes to healthy spiritual experience and service to others in a number of ways.

Truth Essential to Spirituality

Truth is not spirituality, but without it authentic spiritual experience is impossible. Spirituality is not merely a feeling of dependence on God (as Schleiermacher taught). Neither is spirituality merely a life poured out in service to others (as Paul Van Buren declared in his view of secular theology). Genuine spirituality is not an ecstatic experience of union with a nonpersonal Ground of Being (as held by Paul Tillich and Eastern mysticism). Distinctively Christian spiritual experience is not merely encountering a person believed without evidence to be divine (as neoorthodoxy and relational theology maintain). Christian spirituality is experience directed away from idols and demons to the living God by revealed scriptural truths. By reliable biblical doctrine those who are wise test the spirits to see whether they are of God. Then they enjoy personal fellowship with the God of the Bible and, dependent on his grace, pour out their lives in service to others.

Truth Important to Fellowship Between Persons

Truth expressed in words is a means of fellowship between persons. Words are utterances of spirit. Although there may be nonverbal indications of fellowship, through words spirits hold the most meaningful fellowship with spirits. As Andrew Murray said long ago, "In a man's words he reveals himself to the one who receives his promise. In his commands he sets forth his will."[38] Analogously, Murray said of God:

When God speaks forth Himself in His words, He does indeed give Himself, His love, His life, His will and His power to those who receive these words, in a reality passing comprehension. In every promise He puts Himself in our power to share with Him His will, His Holiness, His perfection. In God's Word is nothing less than the Eternal Son, Jesus Christ. And so all Christ's words and God's words are full of a Divine quickening life and power.[39]

Truth a Vehicle of Life and Power

Jesus himself is not the only dynamic source of spiritual life. The truth of the Old Testament, Jesus maintained, will remain, though heaven and earth disappear (Matt. 5:17, 18). Jesus, endued with the Holy Spirit, quoted the Old Testament and withstood Satan's three great temptations (Matt. 4:1–11). Of his own words Jesus said, "The *words* I have spoken to you are spirit and they are life" (John 6:63). Jesus later said, "If you hold to my teaching, you are really my disciples. Then you will know the truth, and the truth will set you free" (John 8:31–32). The words of Scripture need not become an idol standing between a person and the living God. They are vehicles of enduring meaning that the Spirit illumines in order to convey to mankind life, truth, power, and freedom.

Truth an Ingredient in Personal Faithfulness

"Truth" can mean both instruction and faithfulness.[40] As instruction it conveys a witness concerning what is and ought to be. Thus, Jesus taught in words what was and what ought to be. He also exemplified the personal fidelity of one who knows ultimate reality and God's ethical demands. Jesus not only taught the truth, he is the truth. In the mind truth is reliable information; in the life truth is faithfulness to the realities of which it speaks.

Truth the Criterion of Authentic Spiritual Experiences

The key to authentic spiritual experiences is assent to God's revelation as reliably informative about what is in reality and what ought to be. Then life can be faithfully devoted to the truly real and the most significant.

Without reliable information one may expend his life for nothing; without faithfulness to the highest values, one may be a hypocrite. On the one hand a merely doctrinaire view of truth may lead to an empty idealism or an arrogant legalism. On the other hand, an undirected commitment may lead to a blind emotionalism, a frustrated activism, or a tragic discontinuity with what is or ought to be.[41]

So it is by doctrinal truth concerning Christ that we must test encountered spirits to see whether they are of God (1 John 4:1–3).

It has been in vogue to say that today the important thing is not Christianity's truth but its relevance. That is like saying to the sick that the important point is not the accuracy of the prescription, but taking the medicine. In determining which of the innumerable kinds of medicine to take, how much, and how often, nothing is more important than the accuracy of the doctor's prescription. In the taking of the proper medicine in the proper amounts at the proper times, nothing is more important than faithfulness. If we choose between accurate information and fidelity, we do so to our own harm. *Both* are crucial for their respective purposes. One is not a good substitute for the other. Accurate information from reliable Scriptures concerning authentic spirituality and faithfulness to it are both necessary to a healthy spiritual life.

Truth Indispensable to Distinctively Christian Service

Sound theological understanding underlies distinctively Christian ministry. Servants who understand their master's purposes have a clearer sense of mission. Theological perception of God's program in the world helps formulate long-range goals in life for those who would do his will on earth. Servants who know who they are can function more freely with a sense of identity as

47

not only metaphysical but also moral and spiritual children of God.

Theology determines whether the world needs to be evangelized, whether evangelism is urgent, and why. Theological considerations are important to formulating the message that is initially to be proclaimed to non-Christians. It helps Christian servants understand their roles in relation to the work of the Holy Spirit as they endeavor to lead people to faith in Christ. Theological reflection enables Christians to determine priorities in a maturing Christian life.

Theology contributes to determining whether a church is necessary and what is needed to make a church what it ought to be. From a theological base we determine what is essential to a Christian church, whether conditions of membership, reasons for discipline, ordinances, offices, and ministries and mission in the world today.

The theologically reflective grow in seeing all of life, individually and collectively, from the perspective of God's revealed truth. As they do so they respond with gratitude in devotional commitment to God. "Christian discipleship focuses on the authentic meaning of faith; Christian mission focuses on its consequences for life." Again, "If action lacks rootage in a characteristic Christian motivation, it will lose its identity as witness to the gospel and becomes simply our own good works. . . . There is only one remedy for this malaise: a conscious recovery of the life principle of the church, Christian devotion."[42]

ALTERNATIVE APPROACHES TO THEOLOGY IN THE CHURCH

The Patristic Period

Systematic theology first found expression in the East, particularly in Alexandria, where in 185 a Christian catechetical school was founded. In that cosmopolitan center Clement (c. 155–c. 200) used Greek philosophy to show on the one hand that Christianity is the one rational philosophy and to expose on the other hand the fallacies of Gnosticism. Ordering his theology around the doctrine of the Logos, Clement stressed the eternal preexistence, incarnation, and redemptive work of the Word. Against heretics who claimed an esoteric *gnosis,* Clement insisted that Christianity is the true *gnosis* and that followers of Christ are the true gnostics. Clement's theology is set forth in three works: *Address to the Greeks, The Tutor,* and *Miscellanies.*

Origen (c. 185–c. 254), who taught at catechetical schools in Alexandria and Caesarea, was described by Jerome as "a teacher second only to the great Apostle." A gifted philologist, exegete, dogmatician, and apologist, Origen is regarded as the leading theologian of the early church. His work *On First Principles* (218–230) was the first major systematic formulation of Christian doctrine. Origen's theology represents a synthesis of scriptural teaching (often allegorically derived) and contemporary Greek philosophy.

The school of Asia Minor is represented by Irenaeus (c. 130–c. 202), the anti-Gnostic theologian. In his classic work *Against Heresies* (181–189) Irenaeus refuted Gnostic doctrines and expounded the leading tenets of the Christian system. He asserted the unity of the Godhead against the Gnostic demiurges, the incarnation of God in flesh, redemption through the God-man, and the future resurrection of the body. Compared with the Logos theology of earlier fathers, Irenaeus's theology is a theology of the historic Christ.

During this golden age of exegesis and theology, the main doctrines of the Christian faith were refined through the process of refuting sundry errors. Athanasius (296–373), bishop of Alexandria, defended for fifty years the deity of the incarnate Word against the Arians. His classic essay *The Incarnation of the Word* (318) discusses the fall of the race and the dilemma this posed for God. In order to destroy sin and redeem the creature, God became man in Jesus of Nazareth. To be an effectual Savior, Jesus Christ had to be coequal, coeternal, and consubstantial with God the Father. Athanasius's exposition of the Trinity is one of the outstanding theological essays of all time.

The three Cappadocian theologians Basil of Caesarea (c. 329–379), Gregory of Nazianzus (330–389), and Gregory of Nyssa (c. 334–395) were largely responsible for the formula that settled the Arian controversy. Gregory of Nazianzus, acclaimed "The Theologian," preached five celebrated *Theological Orations* against the Arians, in which he argued for the equality of the Father and the Son and the consubstantiality of the Spirit with the Father and the Son. Gregory of Nyssa wrote an important *Catechetical Oration* (383)—a manual for new converts—that expounded the essential Christian doctrines: God, Creation, Fall, the Incarnation of Christ, the Atonement, the sacraments, and eschatology. John of Damascus (c. 675–c. 794), the last of the Greek fathers, wrote *The Orthodox Faith* in one hundred chapters. This work served as the classic statement of Greek patristic theology.

In the West, Hilary of Potiers (315–386) wrote *On the Trinity*, an important treatise against the Arians. Ambrose (340–397), the leading churchman of the fourth century, drafted several theological treatises dealing with the Incarnation, the Resurrection, and the Holy Spirit. Jerome, the great biblical scholar, wrote many exegetical commentaries and numerous letters, some of which were rich in theological content. The greatest Latin theologian and the towering figure of Christendom's first 750 years was Augustine (354–430), bishop of Hippo. Augustine wrote profound theological treatises against the Manichaeans, Donatists, Arians, and Pelagians. His monumental essay *On the Trinity* (399–419) summarized patristic teaching and advanced his own understanding of the Godhead. His *Enchiridion,* or *Handbook,* outlined, via an exposition of the Apostles' Creed, the main features of Augustine's theology. *The City of God* presents the first comprehensive philosophy of history within an explicitly theological framework. Augustine's views on church and sacraments reflected a growing trend toward Roman theology, whereas his emphases on universal inherited guilt, the bondage of the will, election, and the effectual grace of God in salvation was a catalyst for the thought of Luther and Calvin.

Medieval Theology

During the medieval era, patristic authorities were collected and arranged according to preestablished categories. In time, tradition was placed on a par with the Bible as the source of theology. Medieval theology also reflected a shift from the spirituality of the fathers to an external sacramentalism. The theology of the Eucharist, for example, developed into the dogma of transubstantiation and the Mass. Medieval Catholic theology also became increasingly Pelagian, thus provoking the protest of the sixteenth-century Reformers. The twelfth century saw the rise, the thirteenth the zenith, and the fourteenth and fifteenth centuries the decline of medieval scholasticism.

Because of the speculative and dialectical character of his theology, Anselm of Canterbury (c. 1033–1109) earned the title "the father of medieval scholasticism." Anselm's *Monologion* and *Proslogion* set forth, respectively, the bishop's cosmological and ontological arguments for God's existence. *Cur Deus Homo* (*Why God Became Man*), perhaps the greatest work on the Atonement ever written, propounds a biblical rationale for Christ's work on the cross. Another important scholastic theologian, Peter Abelard (1079–1142), emphasized the role of reason in theology: "A doctrine is believed not because God has said it, but because it has been proven to be so." His chief work, *Yes and No*, presents seemingly contradictory views from the fathers on a wide range of doctrines and practices. Abelard also wrote an *Introduction to Theology* in three books (1136). A third leading theologian of the period was Peter Lombard (c. 1100–60), bishop of Paris. His *Four Books of Sentences* (c. 1150) brought together sayings from the fathers ordered around the main theological headings, namely, the Trinity, Creation, Redemption, and the Sacraments and Last Things. The *Sentences*, Aristotelian in orientation, became a leading textbook for several hundred years.

Stimulated by the rise of the universities and the revival of Aristotelianism in the West via Latin translations of Arabic texts, the thirteenth century is known as "the golden age of scholasticism." In this period was Thomas Aquinas, the chief theologian of the second 750 years of the church. The "Angelic Doctor" affirmed a rational ontology that drew a sharp distinction between philosophy and theology, between nature and grace. Thomas's Aristotelian theology is set forth in *Summa Contra Gentiles* (1261–64) and in the seventeen large volumes of the unfinished *Summa Theologica* (1265–72). For centuries it has remained the classic treatment of medieval Roman Catholic theology.

The decline of medieval theology in the fourteenth and fifteenth centuries need not long detain us. William of Ockham (c. 1280–1349), the English commentator on Peter Lombard's *Sen-*

tences, attacked the scholastic procedure of wedding Aristotelian philosophy to Christian theology. God is known, not by rational inference, but by reception of divine revelation by faith. The nominalist theology of Ockham and of Gabriel Biel (1420–95) further asserted the power of human free will and weakened the operation of divine grace. The gradual demise of speculative theology prompted the renewed medieval quest for God through mystical experience. Thus Meister Eckhart (c. 1260–1327), John Tauler (c. 1300–61), and Henry Suso (c. 1300–66) promoted in sermons and tracts the merger of the human soul into the reality of God. Suso, for example, strove to become one with God "as a drop of water mingles with a cask of wine."

Era of the Reformation

During the medieval era Roman Catholic theology became corrupted with the doctrine of salvation by works, the veneration of relics, the idea of a treasury of merit, and the sale of indulgences. Abuses such as these led to the protest movement known as the Reformation. Guided by the themes *sola scriptura, sola gratia,* and *sola fide,* the Protestant Reformers forged a return to the teachings of the Bible as the primary authority.

Martin Luther (1483–1546), the Augustian monk and Wittenberg professor, turned from legalistic works and guilt to the Bible, where he discovered the theme of justification by grace through faith. Luther's theology followed the main outlines of Augustinianism. A churchman and biblical scholar, Luther wrote no systematic theology. His doctrinal distinctives are set forth in numerous treatises, particularly in two epoch-making commentaries, *Lectures on Romans* (1515) and *Lectures on Galatians* (1535). Philip Melanchthon

(1497–1560) was the leading theologian of the Lutheran wing of the Reformation. His work *Leading Conceptions in Theology (Loci communes,* 1521) was the first systematic theology of the Reformation, focusing on the authority of the Bible, law and Gospel, justification by faith, and the forgiveness of sins.

Ulrich Zwingli (1484–1531) was the first of the Reformed theologians. From his humanistic background Zwingli wrestled with the issues of original sin, predestination, the work of Christ, the nature of the church, and the two sacraments. A succinct statement of Zwingli's position is preserved in his *Sixty-Seven Theses* (1523) and in *An Exposition of the Faith* (1529). The leading theologian of the modern era is John Calvin (1509–64). Melanchthon designated St. Paul as "the apostle," St. Thomas as "the philosopher," and Calvin as "the theologian." As Luther stressed the doctrine of justification by faith, Calvin emphasized the sovereignty of God and his inscrutable will. Calvin's theological treatises, commentaries, and sermons (some eight hundred in all) occupy fifty-nine quarto volumes. Calvin's *Institutes of the Christian Religion* (1559) engaged the Reformer's energies for thirty years. Calvin's purpose in the *Institutes* was to expound the "Christian philosophy" that God gave in the Bible. It has been said that "no system exceeds it in comprehensiveness, precision, lucidity, and literary elegance."[43]

The Protestant Reformation forced Rome to reexamine and redefine its own doctrinal stance. At the Council of Trent (1545–63) the diverse strands of medieval theology were woven together into a tapestry of authoritative dogma. Trent established (1) Scripture (the Apocrypha included) and tradition as coequal authorities; (2) the Roman Catholic church as the authoritative determiner of the canon and interpreter of Scripture; (3) the doctrine of justification by faith and subsequent works; and (4) the validity of the seven sacraments through which saving grace is mediated. In addition, at Trent the dogma of transubstantiation and the practice of indulgences were commended to the faithful.

Modern Theology

Protestant orthodoxy in the seventeenth century produced numerous dogmatic theologies from both Lutheran and Reformed perspectives. Energetic theologians strove to consolidate the theological positions of the Reformers. There is some validity in the criticism that rational definition of doctrines tended to supplant the freshness and vigor of Reformational theology. Scholasticizing tendencies appear in the writings of both Lutheran and Reformed theologians of the period.[44]

The leading dogmatician of Lutheran orthodoxy, John Gerhard of Jena (1582–1637), prepared the massive *Theological Commonplaces* in twenty-three volumes (1610–22). Although it emphasized Aristotelian categories and terminology, the work became the classic of Lutheran theology. Abraham Calov (1612–86), the prodigious Wittenberg theologian, wrote the twelve-volume *System of Theological Themes* (1655–77). Calov's militant passion for orthodoxy is reflected in his prayer, "Fill me, O Lord, with hatred of heretics."[45] Dogmatic texts with a decided scholastic bent were prepared by J. A. Quenstedt (1617–88), J. W. Baier (1647–95), and David Hollaz (1707).

For Reformed theology the seventeenth century was an era of controversy. Jacob Arminius of Leyden (1560–1609) protested the extreme supralapsarianism of Theodore Beza (1519–1605). Arminius's followers published the *Five Articles of the Remonstrants* (1610) that limited the salvific decree to those whom God foresaw would trust Christ. The Synod of Dort (1618–19) settled the dispute in favor of the majority Reformed party. Not a few of the Remonstrants (free-spirited successors to the Arminians) lapsed into Socinianism or rationalism (e.g., Grotius, Limborch, Wettstein).

In the mainstream of Calvinist orthodoxy Johannes Wollebius (1586–1629) prepared *Compendium of Christian Theology* (1626), a classic work developed under the two headings, "The Knowledge of God" and "The Service of God." Gisbert Voetius of Holland (1589–1676) wrote the pious yet polemical five-volume dogmatics *Selected Theological Disputations* (1648–69), while Johannes Cocceius (1602–69) forged a new direction by ordering theology about the poles of the covenant of works and the covenant of grace. In Geneva Francis Turretin's (1623–87) four-volume *Institutio Theologiae Elencticae* (1688) exercised much influence on Reformed theology, especially on nineteenth-century American Presbyterianism. Meanwhile in France, Moïse Amyraut (1596–1664) of the Saumur Academy propounded in *Treatise on Predestination* (1634) the theory of hypothetical universalism that was opposed by both the *Formula Consensus Helvetica* (1675) and the Zurich theologian J. H. Heidegger (1633–98) in *Body of Christian Theology* (1700).

The Puritans in England and America were preacher-theologians who viewed theology practically as the act of living unto God. Thus, rather than being pure scholars, the Puritans practiced the craft of practical exegesis by applying Bible and theology to Christian faith and life. The Puritans upheld the full authority of the Bible, the mystery of sovereign election, the moral corruption of the sinner, and the finality of Christ and his saving work on the cross. The Puritans are known primarily for their excellent biblical commentaries and theological treatises on nearly every aspect of the faith. Leading Puritan theologians include Thomas Manton (1620–77), John Owen (1616–83), Stephen Charnock (1628–80), Jonathan Edwards (1703–58), and Samuel Hopkins (1721–1803).

The pietistic movement in eighteenth-century Europe arose as a lively reaction to the dry intellectualism of Protestant scholasticism. The Pietists replaced dogmatics with practical instruction in the spiritual life. They emphasized the necessity of conversion, devotional study of the Bible, the priesthood of believers, and foreign missions. The Pietists often gathered in homes in cell groups that later developed into movements that were known as "inner missions." Leading Pietist spokesmen include Philip J. Spener (1635–1705), the "Father of Pietism" who wrote *Pious Longings;* A. H. Francke (1663–1727), the Halle theologian; and J. A. Bengel (1687–1752), the Wittenberg exegete whose *Gnomon of the New Testament* (1742) remains one of the finest word-by-word expositions of the Greek Testament.

The Romantic movement in the eighteenth and nineteenth centuries arose in reaction to the sterility of theological rationalism, which viewed reason as the all-sufficient system builder. According to the Romantic theologians, the source of theology resided in the feelings and in the imagination of the human agent. F. D. E. Schleiermacher (1768–1834), acclaimed the greatest theologian between Calvin and Barth, may be viewed as the father of modern theology. His work *The Christian Faith* (1821) was the most influential theology of the nineteenth century. Schleiermacher played on the fringes of pantheism, for he viewed God as the creative Eros immanent in all things. Religion is not a collection of dogmas certified by some external authority; rather, it is a set of convictions that arise from a person's feelings of absolute dependence on God.

In the latter half of the nineteenth century a new impulse was generated by Albrecht Ritschl (1822–89), whose theology was heavily influenced by Kant's *Critique of Practical Reason.* In his three-volume doctrinal work *The Christian Doctrine of Justification and Reconciliation* (1870–74), Ritschl, the antimetaphysical theologian, rejected as "fact" the traditional doctrines of Christ's incarnation and resurrection, original sin, and forensic justification. His theory of "moral value" focused on the gradual realization of the kingdom of God via actualization of the ethic of Jesus. Ritschl had a profound influence on the social gospel in America. Disciples of Ritschl include J. W. Herrmann (1846–1922), who outlined his moralistic theology in *The Communion of the Christian With God* (1886) and a posthumous *Systematic Theology* (1925), and Adolf Harnack (1851–1930) who, in *What Is Christianity?* (1901), substituted the fatherhood of God and the infinite value of the human soul for the so-called culturally conditioned doctrines of Christianity. Walter Rauschenbusch (1861–1918), the author of *A Theology for the Social Gospel* (1917), was an influential Ritschlian theologian in America.

The Contemporary Period

Neoorthodoxy, also known as the "theology of crisis" or "dialectical theology," was a vehement protest against various immanentalistic theologies prominent around the turn of the present century. Neoorthodox theologians, while certain that the faith of the Reformers required reworking in the light of modern critical knowledge, sought to forge a return to the theology of the Reformation.

Karl Barth (1886–1968), driven back to the Scriptures and to Calvin by the practical inadequacies of liberal theology, launched neoorthodox theology with his monumental *Romans* commentary (1919). The Swiss scholar's main work is the unfinished thirteen-volume *Church Dogmatics* (1935–67), larger than Thomas's *Summa Theologica* and nine times the size of Calvin's *Institutes.* Barth's theology emphasizes the freedom and transcendence of God, the threefold form of the Word, and the radical sinfulness of the creature. Somewhat to the left of Barth was his Swiss colleague Emil Brunner (1889–1966), who wrote the three-volume *Dogmatics* (1946–60). Brunner differed from Barth in that he accepted a preliminary revelation of God in nature and history and the sinner's retention of the *imago Dei.* Unlike Barth, Brunner denied the virgin birth of Christ. Reinhold Niebuhr (1893–1971) moved in the direction of Barthianism from the early liberalism of his teachers. Niebuhr made insightful observations on the human condition and its social and political consequences. His most systematic work is *The Nature and Destiny of Man* (1941). H. Richard Niebuhr (1894–1962), the younger brother of Reinhold, articulated a relativistic view of the divine self-disclosure in *The Meaning of Revelation* (1941) and wrestled with the Christian's relation to the modern world in *Christ and Culture* (1951).

John Henry Newman (1801–90), the Anglican convert to Catholicism, anticipated recent developments in the church with his programmatic essay *Development of Christian Doctrine* (1845). The Cardinal challenged the notion of fixed and inviolable dogmas by asserting that through the course of history truth undergoes development. Moreover, since Scripture does not contain the whole of revelation the Bible must be supplemented by insights gleaned from experience. The rise of Catholic modernism around the turn of the century enlarged the distance between traditional theology and the new ideas. George Tyrrell (1861–1909), in *Christianity at the Cross-Roads* (1909), argued that Christians should retain Jesus' religious spirit but abandon many of the dogmas that have grown up around him. Alfred Loisy (1857–1940), the leader of Catholic modernism in France, insisted that traditional dogmas must be revised or rejected in the light of new knowledge. His book *The Gospel and the Church* (1902) boldly claims that the Roman church has departed from the way of Christ. The Catholic modernist movement was condemned by Pius X in the encyclical *Pascendi* (1907). The new impulses in Catholic theology came to the fore at the Second Vatican Council (1962–65), summoned by Pope John XXIII. Vatican II was traditional on such matters as papal infallibility, Mary, the Mass, and purgatory. But in other important areas liberal and radical perspectives prevailed. The notion of "dogmatic relativism" was endorsed by the Council, thus throwing open the door to many new ideas. Vatican II acknowledged that, since the reality of God naturally wells up within, all people possess "implicit faith." Moreover, the exclusivity of the Roman church as the only means of salvation was denied. Non-Christians and atheists were said to be recipients of saving grace. The missionary task thus was envisaged as announcing the news that God has accepted the world in Christ.

A leading spokesman for the new Catholicism is Karl Rahner (b. 1904), the German Jesuit author of the fourteen-volume *Theological Investigations* (1974–76), whom some rank on a par with Barth. Rahner propounds a system of "transcendental Thomism," which is a reinterpretation of Aquinas guided by insights from Kant, Heidegger, and Marechal, the Belgian Jesuit (d. 1944). Central to Rahner's theology is the "supernatural existential," the dynamic impulse that drives the person toward the immediate presence of God. Since all people subconsciously are oriented toward the Absolute, the entire world is an "anonymous Christianity."[46] The most outspoken critic of traditional Catholic polity and theology is Hans Küng (b. 1927), the Swiss-born theologian who in 1979 was disqualified as an official Catholic teacher by Pope John Paul II. In *The Church* (1967) Küng charges that both the papacy and its claim of infallibility are without biblical warrant. Küng describes his *On Being a Christian* (1976) as "a kind of small 'Summa' of the Christian faith."[47] Küng's theology begins with the human situation, redefines the God-idea, asserts the fallibility of the Bible and its doctrines, and claims that the non-Christians are part of God's plan for the salvation of the world. Rahner charges Küng with speaking like a "liberal Protestant." Edward Schillebeeckx (b. 1914), the Flemish Catholic theologian, synthesizes insights from Thomism, existentialism, and linguistic philosophy to forge new directions in Christology, the phenomena of human existence, and the church as agent of social change.

The religious existentialism of Heidegger and Kierkegaard had a substantial impact on twentieth-century Protestant theology. One of the most prominent existentialists was Paul Tillich (1886–1965), whose "existential-ontological theism" sought to forge a middle way between supernaturalism and naturalism. Tillich insisted that modern theology must affirm the "God beyond God"[48] or "the God above the God of theism."[49] Tillich's mystical system of Being-Itself, set forth in his *Systematic Theology* (1951–63) encouraged later secular theologians to pronounce God dead. Rudolf Bultmann (1884–1976) was an existentially oriented biblical theologian who shared common ground with dialectical theology. In his 1941 programmatic essay, "New Testament and Mythology," Bultmann, on the basis of form-critical analysis, distinguished between the pure kernel of revelation and the more extensive husk of Jewish and Gnostic myths that allegedly had encrusted the simple Christian message. In Bultmann's mind Christ's incarnation, miracles, sacrificial atonement, resurrection, and second coming are nonhistoric myths. The German scholar launched the program of demythologization, interpreting the alleged biblical myths via an existential hermeneutic. The main outlines of Bultmann's system are set forth in *New Testament Theology* (1949–53; ET: 1952–55). The leading systematic theology based on philosophical existentialism is *Principles of Christian Theology* (1977) by the English theologian John Macquarrie (b. 1919). Stimulated by Bonhoeffer, Tillich, and Bultmann, J. A. T. Robinson (b. 1919) radically redefined the Christian faith in *Honest to God* (1963) and *The Human Face of God* (1973).

Two turbulent but short-lived liberal impulses from the 1960s were the so-called secular theology and the death-of-God movement. The former was stimulated in part by Dietrich Bonhoeffer's enigmatic expressions "man come of age" and "religionless Christianity." Paul van Buren (b. 1924) left his early Barthian theology after concluding that the word "God" makes little sense to the modern mind. *The Secular Meaning of the Gospel* (1963) expounds a non-metaphysical view of the religion of the historical Jesus. Meanwhile Harvey Cox (b. 1929) in *The Secular City* (1965) argues that industrialization and urbanization offer a fruitful context in which modern man lives before God with a mature sense of this-worldiness. More radical yet, Thomas J. J. Altizer (b. 1927) in *The Gospel of Christian Atheism* (1967) and Altizer and William

Hamilton in *Radical Theology and the Death of God* (1966) claimed that at the Incarnation God died. Yet the Good News is that God, though dead, lives on in the man Jesus. In the death-of-God movement, religious skepticism came to its logical end. God is eliminated, but Jesus is retained as a figure who offers some measure of spiritual solace.

Process theology is an influential form of philosophical theology indebted to the thought of A. N. Whitehead (1861–1947) and Charles Hartshorne (b. 1897). Process thought postulates that reality consists not of bits of substance but of subatomic moments of experience called "actual occasions" or "occasions of experience." With great rapidity each actual occasion "prehends" (i.e., grasps or feels) prior actual occasions, incorporating these into its own universe, thus forming a creative and novel synthesis. In process theology, also known as neoclassical theism, God is a special kind of energy event continually being shaped by relations with other actual occasions. Moreover, each person apprehends God in every moment of human experience in a manner not unlike ESP or mental telepathy. John B. Cobb, Jr., outlines the main features of process theology in *A Christian Natural Theology* (1965), as does Norman Pittenger in *God in Process* (1967) and *The Divine Triunity* (1977).

Heightened social, political, and economic tensions in the modern world have prompted the rise of a broad movement known as political theology. An early form, the theology of hope, was developed by the German theologian Jürgen Moltmann in *Theology of Hope* (1964). Indebted to Hegel, Marx, and the Marxist Ernst Bloch, Moltmann maintains that humanity's hope lies in openness to a future that has been given meaning by the resurrection of Jesus. Moltmann stresses that the Christian hope must be worked out in radical political and social action. A similar emphasis is enunciated by Johannes Metz (b. 1928), the leading Catholic political theologian in Germany.

A second from of political theology, the theology of liberation, was developed in Latin America in the late 1960s. The systematic charter of the liberation movement is *A Theology of Liberation* (1971; ET: 1973) by the Peruvian Catholic theologian Gustavo Gutièrrez (b. 1928). Other titles from this perspective include *Revolutionary Theology Comes of Age* (1975), by Jose Miguiz Bonino and Juan Luis Segundo's *The Liberation of Theology* (1977). Theology, according to the liberationists, consists not in meditative reflection on supernaturally revealed truths but in *praxis,* namely, involvement in the plight of the poor and powerless of this world. Much of liberation theology is indebted to the Marxist critique of society and its program of violent revolution. Black theologians such as James Cone (*A Black Theology of Liberation* [1970] and *God of the Oppressed* [1975]) undertake a similar program from the Black American perspective. In a similar vein feminist theologies address the alleged oppression of women in Western culture (e.g., Georgia Harkness, *Women in Church and Society* [1971]; Mary Daley, *Beyond God the Father* [1973]; and Philis Trible, *God and the Rhetoric of Sexuality* [1978]).

The aim of this final section is to identify several more or less conservative theologies of the last hundred years or so. Charles Hodge (1797–1878), who taught at Princeton Seminary for fifty years, is the most prominent nineteenth-century American theologian. His three-volume *Systematic Theology* (1871–73) that defended the Calvinism of the old Princeton school is still referred to today. His son A. A. Hodge (1823–86) is the author of the useful *Outlines of Theology* (1878). The scholarly three-volume *Dogmatic Theology* of W. G. T. Shedd is rich in philosophical interaction. The Presbyterian B. B. Warfield (1851–1921), who succeeded A. A. Hodge at Princeton, wrote no systematic theology; yet his scores of books and essays on biblical theological subjects are widely read and highly valued.

On the Continent Abraham Kuyper (1837–1920), described by one authority as "the greatest Calvinist since Calvin,"[50] wrote the three-volume *Encyclopedia of Sacred Theology* (1894). The Dutch theologian successfully integrated the theological enterprise with human achievements in science, government, and the arts. An equally staunch defender of the Reformed faith was Herman Bavinck (1854–1921), who wrote the erudite four-volume *Reformed Dogmatics* in Dutch (1895–1901). A one-volume English synopsis bears the title *Our Reasonable Faith* (1956).

G. C. Berkhouwer (b. 1903), author of the thirteen-volume series *Studies in Dogmatics* (1949–67), professes a confessional method in theology but in recent times appears to have adopted a relational neoorthodox understanding of revelation and knowledge (see especially his *Holy Scripture* [1967; ET: 1975]). Hendrikus Berkhof's *Christian Faith* (1973; ET: 1979) interacts in depth with the world of critical theological scholarship. Louis Berkhof has written a succinct and widely read *Systematic Theology* (1941). J. O. Buswell's two-volume *Systematic Theology of the Christian Religion* (1962–65) contains extensive exegetical sections and represents a premillennial position. Thomas F. Torrance (b. 1913), the Edinburgh dogmatician, is an important modern thinker who seeks to unify the worlds of theology and science. *Theology in Reconstruction* (1965) represents his most unified theological work. Donald Bloesch (b. 1928), in the two-volume *Essentials of Evangelical Theology* (1978–79), attempts to articulate "a

Catholic Evangelicalism" that takes issue with both fundamentalism and liberalism. The readable work reflects a special sympathy for Barth and elements of Roman Catholic theology.

In the Lutheran tradition Francis Pieper (1852–1931) wrote the modern classic theology (three volumes plus index) under the title *Christian Dogmatics* (1917–24; ET: 1950–57). A one-volume condensation of Pieper bearing the same title (1934/55) was prepared by John Theodore Mueller. A noteworthy modern dogmatics is Helmut Thielicke's (b. 1908) three-volume *The Evangelical Faith* (1968–78; ET: 1974–82). Thielicke's broadly evangelical theology incorporates some features from the thought of Kant, Kierkegaard, and Barth. Thielicke is guided by the salutary premise that "the value of dogmatics depends upon whether it can be preached." Wolfhart Pannenberg (b. 1928), in *Revelation as History* (1961), argues that God reveals himself in universal history, the whole of which is summed up in the resurrection of Jesus. His *Jesus, God and Man* (1964; ET: 1968) develops a Christology from below from the data of Jesus' life, death, and resurrection.

Representing the Wesleyan-Arminian tradition, John Miley (1813–95) has left the church a thorough, albeit traditional, *Systematic Theology* (1892–94) in two volumes. H. Orton Wiley, writing from a Nazarene standpoint, prepared the equally scholarly *Christian Theology* (1940–43) in three volumes. *A Contemporary Wesleyan Theology* (1983), a two-volume work edited by Charles W. Carter, expounds the main features of Wesleyan doctrine and ministry.

The Baptist theologian A. H. Strong (1836–1921) wrote the often-reprinted *Systematic Theology* (1886) that upholds evolution as the mode of God's working in nature. The Southern Baptist theologian Edgar Y. Mullins, who wrote *The Christian Religion in Its Doctrinal Expression* (1917), shaped in nontechnical language a theology that mediates between Calvinism and Arminianism, while focusing on evangelical experience. More recently from the same tradition Dale Moody has written the scholarly work *The Word of Truth* (1981), which makes concessions to critical liberal scholarship in the areas of revelation, the person of Christ, and the justification of the sinner.

The Anglican tradition in modern times has made only minor contributions to systematic theology. A. C. Headlam, whose *Christian Theology* (1934) covers only revelation and theology proper, offers the following observation: "It is one of the characteristics of the English church that it has never produced a great work on systematic theology. English people do not love system, or order, or completeness."[51] The conservative Anglican W. H. G. Thomas has provided a theological exposition of the Thirty-Nine Articles of the Church of England in *The Principles of Theology* (1930).

Within the broad evangelical movement Louis Sperry Chafer (1871–1952) provided the classic exposition of the older dispensationalism (from a modified Calvinist perspective) in his eight-volume *Systematic Theology* (1947–48). Recent reformulations of the dispensationalist position have rendered Chafer's work increasingly obsolete. *Lectures in Systematic Theology* by Henry C. Thiessen (1949–79) is a nontechnical work written from a moderate dispensational point of view. The revised edition is more Calvinistic than the original.

Finally, but not least in importance, Carl F. H. Henry (b. 1913) has produced the six-volume opus *God, Revelation and Authority* (1976–83) that covers the limited areas of prolegomena, revelation, and the Godhead. The incisive analyses and penetrating criticisms that Henry offers represent mature evangelical scholarship. Millard J. Erickson in *Christian Theology* (1983–85) offers a fresh restatement of the Christian faith from a baptistic perspective.

REVIEW QUESTIONS

To Help Relate Each Section of This Chapter to Doing Theology

1. Explain why integrative thinking is needed in a diversified world.

2. What entry points for serious thinking about divinely revealed truth have you experienced in your own life?

3. List the charges that have been brought against the discipline of systematic theology recently and indicate how other theologians responded?

4. What is integrative theology?

5. How does integrative theology relate to systematic theology and how does it answer charges against systematics?

6. Explain the relationship of integrative theology to other fields such as the following:

apologetics
biblical studies
hermeneutics
logic
historical theology
research methodology

7. How is integrative theology possible philosophically?

8. How is integrative theology possible biblically?

9. How does integrative theology compare and contrast with alternative approaches to doing theology in the history of the church?

10. In what ways are well-founded, well-formulated theological truths relevant for your life and service to others?

CHAPTER 2

DIVINE REVELATION TO ALL PEOPLE OF ALL TIMES

Divine Revelation
to All People of All Times

THE PROBLEM: DOES EVERY RATIONAL PERSON COMPREHEND SOMETHING OF GOD?

Christianity differs from religion, commonly understood, in that it involves God's gracious quest for the person rather than the person's groping search for God. Central to the Christian way is the claim that God has taken the initiative and has, in intelligible ways, disclosed himself to people. It is of fundamental importance, however, to understand to whom God reveals himself, at what times, and in what ways. Has God given a revelation of himself and his will only to his covenant people Israel and the Christian church, or has the Creator somehow disclosed himself to all people who have ever lived? Did God first make a meaningful disclosure of himself in Jesus Christ, or has there been a valid revelation since the beginning of time? Moreover, is God revealed only through mighty signs and miracles, or has he made a disclosure in the ordinary operations of nature and in the course of history? Does only the reader of the Bible or the believer in Christ know God, or does every rational person comprehend something of the reality of God?

To clarify these issues, Christian theology has made a distinction between two kinds of revelation: general and special. *General revelation* refers to the disclosure of God in nature, in providential history, and in the moral law within the heart, whereby all persons at all times and places gain a rudimentary understanding of the Creator and his moral demands. *Special revelation* refers to God's self-disclosure through signs and miracles, the utterances of prophets and apostles, and the deeds and words of Jesus Christ, whereby specific people at particular times and places gain further understanding of God's character and a knowledge of his saving purposes in his Son.

On the one hand, a denial that knowledge of God is mediated through general revelation appears to undermine the basis for enduring moral values and the meaningfulness of human existence; for the Christian it would also mean the elimination of common ground in witness to the unsaved. On the other hand, an overestimation of the value of general revelation might imply that saving knowledge of God is available to all people quite apart from the gospel message about Jesus Christ.

The issues surrounding God's general disclosure thus involve the spiritual condition of people who make no profession of Christ, be they our friends and relatives or far-off pagans who have not heard the gospel. The issues raised also relate to the current debate over the value of the non-Christian religions as vehicles for mediating knowledge of God and salvation. Thus even the missionary enterprise has a profound stake in these basic theological considerations.

It is no exaggeration to say that the foundational issue in Christian theology deals with the nature and scope of divine revelation. A. C. Headlam has rightly maintained that "the primary question in theology must be, what is the source of our knowledge of God."[1] Hence it is appropriate and necessary that our study of Christian theology should begin with these chapters on revelation.

ALTERNATIVE PROPOSALS IN THE CHURCH

In the history of the Christian church, several influential answers have been given to the question as to whether all people know God and, if so, to what extent and with what consequences?

Aquinas and the Thomistic Tradition

Thomists maintain that rational induction from the data of nature leads to a demonstration of God's existence and the infinity of his perfections. Saving knowledge of God, however, comes only through Scripture and church teachings. Thomas Aquinas, rejecting the Platonic scheme of innate ideas, favored the Aristotelian method of rational induction from temporal effects. Aquinas created a metaphysical model consisting of two realms (nature and grace), two kinds of knowledge (natural and revealed), and two independent methods of knowing (reason and faith). The "Angelic Doctor" came to theology with three presuppositions, by virtue of which he judged the human mind competent to reason its way to knowledge of God: (1) human beings, made in the image of God, are endowed with the power of a rational mind; (2) the intellect was not seriously affected by the Fall; and (3) God's existence is analogous to human existence (analogy of being), hence the former is not totally other to the latter.

With regard to the realm of nature, Aquinas argued that the empirical data of the sensible world interpreted by the principle of cause and effect lead to proof of God's existence and the infinity of his perfections. Via rational induction from created effects, he sought to prove both that God exists (the famous Five Ways) and that God is infinite, eternal, incorporeal, immutable, intelligent, and so on. This general disclosure in the cosmos, quite apart from propositional revelation, leads to a substantial natural theology or philosophical science. He was quite clear, however, that this corpus of natural theology is inadequate to save a person. Only God's revelation in Christ and the Scriptures imparts the knowledge necessary for salvation—knowledge of God's being and purpose (e.g., Trinity, Incarnation, and Atonement). Concerning the way of rational ascent and the way of revelational descent, Aquinas concludes: "We have a more perfect knowledge of God by grace than by natural reason."[2]

Empirically Orientated Liberalism

Liberals of an empirical bent argue that knowledge of God is obtained by rational evaluation of the so-called assured results of the natural and social sciences. The insights afforded by modern learning are judged superior to those possessed by prescientific biblical writers. Henry Van Dusen argues that knowledge of God is gained through the study of the universe and of persons. The empirical sciences shed considerable light on nature, whereas philosophy, sociology, and the psychology of religion impart understanding of persons and human values. According to Van Dusen, modern learning is "an all-sufficient interpreter of reality and guide for life."[3] He argues that the disciplines of human knowledge correct the fallible teachings of the Bible concerning God, man, and the universe. Van Dusen and other liberals stress the continuity between general and special revelation, between natural and supernatural knowledge, and between reason and faith.

Similarly, L. H. DeWolf, who affirms "the powers of human thought to find and recognize the truth,"[4] postulates the universal availability of a substantial corpus of natural theology. The data of experience, interpreted by reason and tested by the principle of comprehensive coherence, affords a considerable knowledge of God and of human destiny. DeWolf insists that the traditional distinction between general and special revelation is difficult to sustain; human experience of the world and reflection are caused by God and are expressive of his thought. Thus "the line cannot be drawn between nature and the Bible on the ground of the more direct, unmediated character of the latter."[5] Indeed, DeWolf prefers to speak of the difference between usual and unusual, or spectacular, forms of revelation. The latter might include a rainbow, a particularly bright and starry sky, or a sudden flash of intuition. In the liberal scheme, then, knowledge of God and his will is secured by rational observation and is available to all persons of sound mind.

Existentially Orientated Liberalism

Liberals in the existential tradition, assuming the unity of being and knowing, postulate the knowability of all being—including Being-itself (God)—via an immediate, illuminatory preapprehension. Thus human beings, *qua* human beings, know God in a mystical, life-changing experience of grace. Schleiermacher, an important precursor of this emphasis, taught that through the noncognitive faculty of feeling or ineffable intuition the human soul is brought into immediate contact with the Soul of the universe. Thus God is not found in the external world through the modalities of natural revelation. Rather, through the "feeling of absolute dependence" or the intuition of immediate self-consciousness, in which the subject-object duality is overcome, the human soul is united with the Soul of the universe. Since the sense and taste for the Infinite is universal, it follows that all people everywhere "know God." Argued Schleiermacher: "This feeling of absolute dependence . . . is therefore not an accidental element, or a thing which varies from person to person, but a universal element of life."[6]

In the twentieth century, Paul Tillich replaced the categories of general and special revelation with "primary revelation" and "secondary revelation." In primary revelation the focus is not the objective cosmos or history but the reflection of Being-itself within the person's awareness of Primal Reality that transcends the subject-object duality. Tillich describes this experience as a moment of the gnostic insight in which human eyes are opened to "the abysmal element in the ground of Being."[7] Thus all people are said to know God via primary revelation, namely, through the experience of being grasped by "ultimate, unconditional, total, infinite concern."[8] Clearly, Tillich has propounded a natural theology of ecstatic religious experience centering on the mystical intuition of Being-itself within the depths of the person's own being. Secondary revelation, according to Tillich, involves the formal representation of this mystical experience in the symbols and myths of religion.

Karl Rahner, by means of a Heideggerian interpretation of Aquinas, reaches roughly the same conclusions as Tillich. Since, Rahner argues, an a priori transcendental relationship exists between the human person and God, in every moment of consciousness human beings find their life oriented toward the life of God; the dynamic impulse that drives every person toward the immediate presence of God is the "supernatural existential."[9] By virtue of this preconceptual encounter with Being-itself, all people possess an experienced, albeit unthematic, knowledge of God. According to Rahner, those who permit the supernatural existential to shape their existence are Christians, even though they may reject the name. Indeed, since all people respond positively to this transcendental experience, the entire world constitutes an "anonymous Christianity."[10] Rahner's vision of the person as transcendental consciousness continually shaped by holy Mystery eliminates the objective basis of revelation in favor of a mysticism of the emotions. Revelation imparts no new knowledge, only a new consciousness. Thus, according to the transcendental Thomism of Rahner and other contemporary Catholic thinkers, nature and grace have merged. The old Catholic scholastic theology is viewed as an antiquated anachronism.

The Neoorthodox Tradition

Karl Barth and many neoorthodox theologians deny the existence of any revelation outside of God's radical address through the Word. The wholly otherness of the Creator and the thoroughgoing sinfulness of the creature mandate that God can be known only through God. Thus, against liberalism's assertion of a natural theology derived either from science or from the religious affections and against medieval Catholicism's postulate of a natural theology established by reason, Karl Barth affirmed that God reveals himself solely through his threefold Word of address.

Barth's polemic against natural knowledge of God from below was rooted in three assumptions: (1) The infinite qualitative difference between God and persons; time and eternity are viewed as two mutually exclusive realms without any natural connecting links. (2) The annihilation of the *imago Dei* by the Fall; corrupted reason is incapable of apprehending the transcendent Majesty. (3) Rejection of an analogy of being (*analogia entis*) between the Creator and the creature; Barth boldly characterized the latter Thomistic tenet as an "invention of the Antichrist."[11]

Thus Barth intoned that no general revelation is given "in reason, in conscience, in the emotions, in history, in nature, and in culture and its achievements."[12] No knowledge is mediated by the modalities of so-called general revelation, for God is known only in his entirety, namely, in his Trinitarian nature. The meeting between God and persons must be actualized entirely from God's side—and particularly through his reconciling grace in Christ. Any alleged disclosure that does not involve the unveiling of grace to the sinner is not revelation. Thus we see that Barth upheld a rigorous Christomonism of revelation: "Revelation means the incarnation of the Word of God."[13]

To maintain consistency with his thesis, Barth radically reinterprets Romans 1:18–20. This text, according to Barth, affirms nothing about Gentiles gaining knowledge of God's invisible nature from created effects. When Paul states, "What may be known about God is plain to them, because God has made it plain to them" (Rom. 1:19), Barth appeals to the immediately preceding context (vv. 15–17), which discusses the apostolic proclamation of the gospel. Thus, according to Barth, the revelation discussed in verses 18–20 is not a general disclosure in nature; rather it is the message of God's supernatural revelation in Christ. Argues Barth, "We cannot isolate what Paul says about the heathen in Romans 1:19–20 from the context of the apostolic preaching, from the incarnation of the Word."[14] But how, on this showing, does Barth interpret Paul's repeated insistence that the Gentiles *know* God (vv. 19–21)? Barth's answer is that the pagan *theoretically* knows God on the basis of God's universal election of humankind in Christ, even though *in actual fact* the pagan is not conscious of such knowledge.[15] For Barth, the burden of Romans 1:18–20 is the paradox of election!

Dutch Reformed Theology

Most Dutch Reformed theologians postulate the reality of general revelation and a knowledge of God implanted within the sinner's moral and psychological constitution. But because sin has blinded the mind, natural human beings attain no knowledge of God by reflection on the *indicia* of the space-time universe. Abraham Kuyper argues that sin has bolted shut the door to general knowledge of God; only those who approach nature and history with regenerate eyes and minds find the cosmos to be a legible book.

G. C. Berkouwer maintains that Scripture touches on the subject of a general knowledge of God mediated by the cosmos only incidentally and infrequently. The clear thrust of biblical teaching on the subject is the sinner's thoroughgoing *ignorance* of God (Gal. 4:8; 1 Thess. 4:5; 2 Thess. 1:8). According to Berkouwer, Paul in Romans 1 teaches only that sinners *confront* or *make contact with* revelation in nature. Paul's saying that the Gentiles "knew God" (Rom. 1:21) must be viewed as hyperbole. General revelation is *there*, and natural man encounters it. But, due to epistemic inability, it fails to register in one's mind as knowledge. Insists Berkouwer, "The Christian church, in speaking of general revelation, never intended to assert that *true* knowledge of God is possible through the natural light of reason."[16] Following Kuyper, Berkouwer claims that knowledge of God as Creator is possible only on the basis of prior knowledge of God as Redeemer.

Cornelius Van Til arrives at a similar conclusion from an involved epistemological analysis. He argues that there are two schemes for viewing reality: the Christian and the non-Christian. The former postulates the triune God of the Bible as its universal, while the latter centers on rebellious, autonomous man. If a person wants to know anything about God, he or she must adopt the correct referent by presupposing the God revealed in authoritative Scripture. But sinful human beings, consistently dismissing God from their lives, are incapable of drawing right conclusions about God from nature or any other source. Thus general revelation affords the sinner no knowledge. Epistemologically, all the unsaved are atheists.[17] The God of the Bible is known only by those persons who renounce the reckless quest for autonomy and who presuppose the truth of the Bible and its interpretation of human life and experience.

Many Fathers, Reformers, and Evangelicals

A significant number of Fathers, Reformers, and evangelical theologians maintain that the rational mind intuits God as a first principle and thereafter draws further conclusions about God's character and moral requirements by contemplating the magnitude and precision of the universe. This nonsalvific knowledge of God establishes human responsibility and provides the basis for God's redemptive revelation in Christ and in the Scriptures.

Thus the Apologists, in defending the faith against pagan assaults, appealed to what any person concludes about God from the surrounding world. Theophilus argued that "God cannot be seen by human eyes, but is beheld and perceived through His providence and works."[18] Clement argued that "there always was a natural manifestation of the one Almighty God among all right-thinking men."[19] Tertullian, who polemicized against philosophical speculation, argued that knowledge of God is innate in the soul and subsequently enlarged by rational inspection of created things.[20] Many Fathers—e.g., Origen, Athanasius, Cyril of Jerusalem, and Gregory of Nyssa—insisted that although human beings cannot behold God's essence, they can observe the clear imprint of Deity from the design of the universe and from the works of providence.[21]

Augustine argued that God's universal self-disclosure affords all people a rudimentary knowledge of himself. The knowledge of God that all possess is first of all a priori. Enabled by a divine general illumination, the person effably intuits eternal changeless principles, including the reality of God. By virtue of this immediate act of "seeing" facilitated by the Logos (John 1:4, 9), none can justly claim to be atheists. This a priori meeting of the soul with God is subsequently enlarged by a knowledge content that is a posteriori. From the signs or data displayed in nature and in providential history, the rational mind, blessed by common grace, draws fur-

ther conclusions about the character and moral demands of the Creator God. By these two means, Augustine argued, "Noble philosophers looked and knew the Maker from His handiwork."[22] But instead of cultivating the preliminary knowledge of God ("wisdom") thus provided, the sinner moves to dismiss God and thus sinks into moral debauchery. Augustine clearly insisted that general revelation does not save. Rather, it serves only to establish the person's accountability to the Judge of the universe. Redemptive knowledge ("saving wisdom") is acquired by faith in (assent to) the incarnate Christ, whose atoning death and saving life are recorded in Holy Scripture.

Luther likewise propounded a twofold scheme of revelation and knowledge, under the rubric "general knowledge of God" (which he also called "legal" and "left-handed" knowledge) and "particular knowledge of God" (or "evangelical" and "right-handed" knowledge). On the basis of immediate intuition of the divine Being and reflection on the data of nature, "all men have the general knowledge, namely that God is, that He has created heaven and earth, that He is just, that He punishes the wicked, etc."[23] This universal general knowledge that establishes a person's accountability to God is incomplete, and so it cannot save.

Calvin's twofold understanding of revelation is set forth in the first two books of his *Institutes*, which bear the titles "The Knowledge of God the Creator" and "The Knowledge of God the Redeemer." God is known as Creator by general revelation and by the added light of special revelation. General revelation mediates knowledge of God as Creator by an immediate intuition (which Calvin calls the universal "sense of divinity" and "seed of religion"), by the moral law implanted in the heart, and by the imprint of Deity on nature, the human frame, and providential history. Of the revelation of God in nature Calvin asserts, "Even wicked men are forced, by the mere view of the earth and sky, to rise to the Creator."[24] Calvin, therefore, believed that all persons know God as Creator—both from within themselves and from the world without. General revelation, however, does not save; it only serves to condemn. Hence, God graciously grants to sinners his Word, whereby the elect know him as efficacious Redeemer.

The same Reformational stance on general revelation appears in Article II of the French Confession of Faith (1559), Article II of the Belgic Confession (1561/1619), and Article I.1 of the Westminster Confession of Faith (1647). Evangelical authorities who support the mediation of a limited knowledge of God by the modalities of general revelation include Charles Hodge,[25] Carl F. H. Henry,[26] Henry C. Thiessen,[27] Dale Moody,[28] and Millard J. Erickson.[29]

BIBLICAL TEACHING

We cannot subscribe to all the conflicting views on universal revelation, but we can examine them in terms of their conformity to the primary, biblical sources.

Pentateuch

"In the beginning God . . ." (Gen. 1:1). The very first statement of the Bible assumes the reality of the living, active, powerful God. Thirty-five times in the first chapter of Genesis, with no attempt to explain his reality, Moses identifies *Elohim* as the Creator and Sovereign of all that is. There is no definition of God, no explication of his character, no proof of his existence. *Elohim* simply is *there*—a universal given—the living God! Whether we treat the early chapters of Genesis as history or as "a proclamation of God's

decisive dealing with His creation,"[30] the idea of the Creator is assumed.[31] The forthright manner in which God is presented in the first chapter of the Bible leads us to believe that the fundamental concept of God was the common property of all people from the very beginning.

Poetry and Wisdom

Elihu's speech to Job (esp. Job 36:24–37:24) sheds further light on God's revelation to all persons at all times and places. The clouds and rain that faithfully water the earth (Job 36:27–28), the clap of thunder and flash of lightning that strike terror in the heart (36:29–37:5), the snow and ice of winter that remind humans that they are dependent creatures (37:6–10), the fury of a howling thunderstorm (37:11–15), and the sun that, following the storm, shines brilliantly through the windswept sky (37:21–22) amply attest the power, majesty, goodness, and severity of the God of creation. Elihu observes that God's revelation of himself in nature is not limited to those who possess a prior faith: "All mankind has seen it; men gaze on it from afar" (36:25).

God's retort to Job (Job 38:1–39:30) elaborates on the revelation of God in the created order. The vast expanse of earth and sea (38:4–11), the daily rising of the sun (38:12–15), snow and hail, wind and rain, frost and ice (38:22–30), the mighty constellations that grace the heavens (38:31–38), and the incredible complexity and harmonious interrelationships of the animal kingdom (38:39–39:30) clearly reflect the infinite Mind that created and orders all these phenomena. The burden of this section of Job is that both the inanimate and the animate worlds attest the existence and glory of God.[32] Through the medium of a magnificent cosmos the observer plainly perceives the reality of the God who made and who upholds all that is.

Several so-called "nature psalms" (e.g., Pss. 8, 19, 29, 65, 104, 148) uphold the reality of a general revelation of God in the created order. But since many of these psalms are songs to God from the perspective of faith, our attention turns to two psalms that speak to the issue of God's self-disclosure in a more didactic manner. According to Psalm 14:1 (cf. Ps. 53:1), "The fool says in his heart, 'There is no God.'" The fool (*nābāl*; cf. 1 Sam. 25:25; Rom. 1:22) is the person who deliberately and volitionally closes the mind to God and his instruction. The psalmist is persuaded that the person who utters the sentence "There is no God" is afflicted with a certain perversity, since the reality of God inexorably impresses itself on all right-minded people at all times. That is to say, the knowledge of God is divinely implanted in all and is strengthened by daily contemplation of the natural world. On the basis of a general, universal revelation of God, all mankind confronts God as supreme Creator and Judge. Hence, the one who affirms the contrary, namely, the nonexistence of God, is properly a "fool." The psalmist proceeds to underscore the fact that those who defiantly deny God's existence inevitably sink to a life of moral corruption (Ps. 14:1b–3).

Psalm 19 mainly teaches that the natural order displays the existence and glory of God. This psalm of David consists of two books: the book of nature (vv. 1–6)—which teaches that God reveals himself to all people as *Elohim*, the God of creation—and the book of the law (vv. 7–13)—which states that God reveals himself as *Yahweh* to the covenant community. The modalities of God's self-disclosure in nature are the starry heavens (vv. 1–4a) and, more particularly, the sun (vv. 4b–6). With respect to the former the psalmist makes two direct assertions that establish the validity of a general revelation of God in nature: "The heavens declare the glory of God" (v. 1a) and "the skies proclaim the work of his hands" (v. 1b). The verbs "declare" (*mᵉsapprîm*) and "proclaim" (*maggîd*) are participles that indicate that the revelatory activity is continuous. That which the heavens declare is the divine glory (*kābôd*), namely, the external manifestation of God's character. David affirms of the revelation of God's glory through the heavens that it is uninterrupted and perpetual (v. 2), that it is wordless, being cast, not in language, but in sensations perceptible to the senses (v. 3), and that it is universal, extending to the ends of the earth (v. 4).

The psalmist saw in the sun a second testimony to the existence and glory of God, even if his knowledge of earth's nearest star was limited. Surely the psalmist David would have echoed the conviction recorded by the prophet Isaiah, "The whole earth is full of his glory" (Isa. 6:3). The psalmist in particular and the Jewish people in general believed that God is displayed in nature and that—in rudimentary fashion, at least—he is known there. As expressed in Wisdom of Solomon 13:5, "The greatness and beauty of created things give us a corresponding idea of their Creator."

Primitive Christianity/Acts

In their remarks to the largely Gentile audience in the Roman colony of Lystra (Acts 14:15–17), Paul and Barnabas appealed to two factors from the realm of everyday experience with which their hearers were familiar: (1) God is Creator of all (v. 15) and (2) he is the providential Provider of basic human needs (v. 17). Even though they had distorted the knowledge of God and worshiped idols, the pagan people of Lystra were not strangers to "the living God, who made heaven and earth and sea and everything in them" (v. 15).

The works of the Creator God were displayed with sufficient clarity to be seen by all. Similarly, by the providential supply of the means for the maintenance of life, God did "not leave himself without testimony" (*amartyron*)— that is, unattested or unknown. God's witness to himself consisted in doing good (*agathourgon*) to all by sending rain, ordering the cycle of the seasons, providing full harvests, and filling the people's hearts with gladness (v. 17). Behind these providential provisions, people should have apprehended the living God who governs the nations. Their fall into idolatry and spiritual confusion was their own fault.

In his Areopagus address to sophisticated Athenian pagans (Acts 17:24–31), Paul, as was his custom, sought for a meaningful point of contact with his audience. Before proclaiming specific redemptive truths (v. 31), the apostle sought to establish areas of agreement between his hearers and himself. The common ground Paul chose here was the elementary knowledge of God that the Stoics possessed on the basis of common grace and general revelation. Although their knowledge was partial and distorted, the Athenians were aware of a number of things about God on the basis of his universal self-disclosure: (1) God is the invisible Creator and Sovereign of the universe (v. 24); (2) God is self-sufficient and dependent on the creature for nothing (v. 25a); (3) God is the source of life and everything humans value as good (v. 25b); (4) God is an intelligent Being, for he has established the times and bounds of man's habitation on the earth (v. 26); (5) God is immanent in the world (v. 27); and (6), amplifying the idea advanced in verse 25b, God is the very ground of human existence (v. 28). Gärtner, in his definitive study of the Acts 17 text, draws the following conclusion: "Creation and history provide a revelation of God apprehensible by man and imparting to him a certain knowledge of what God is."[33] The Athenians had sufficient knowledge of God to move to a relationship of dependence and obligation. But because they chose to extinguish the light God had given to them, Paul described their condition as one of "ignorance" (*agnoia*, v. 30) and moral culpability (v. 31).

A brief additional comment is warranted in connection with verse 28, where the apostle cites two pieces of Stoic wisdom; namely, "In him we live and move and have our being" and "We are his offspring." The Stoics believed that divine Reason, or the Logos, was immanent in man. Paul turned that belief around, insisting that the whole of man's life is grounded in God.[34] The continual existence of mankind's physical life and the exercise of intellectual and emotional faculties are so dependent on God that the apostle could say that all persons exist "in him." Moreover, Paul's second citation refutes the supposition of pantheism and conveys his conviction that human beings by creation bear the image and likeness of the Creator. Synthesizing these two lines of thought, we arrive at Paul's conviction that, made in the image of God and sustained in rationality by God's common grace, humans as humans cognitively apprehend the reality of God as an inviolable datum. Therefore, although they know God as Creator, they are motivated by a sinful heart and repress this elemental knowledge and give themselves to the worship of idols (v. 23).

The Pauline Literature

The classic text that treats the universal revelation of God in nature is Romans 1:18–21. Paul's thesis in this passage is that the human race is judicially guilty; for although all people know God from his works, all have willfully excluded him from their lives. The larger passage, Romans 1:18–32, makes four principal assertions concerning revelation and the knowability of God:

1. All people everywhere acquire a rudimentary knowledge of God as Creator (vv. 18–21). Paul's opening statement is clear: "What may be known [*to gnōston*] about God is plain to them [*en autois*], because God has made it plain to them" (v. 19). Moreover, "God's invisible qualities—his eternal power and divine nature—have been clearly seen" and "understood" (v. 20). What is perceived and grasped by the mind are God's "eternal power" and his "divine nature" (*theiotēs*). The latter term signifies the aggregate of God's invisible attributes or perfections. Yet again, lest he be misunderstood, the apostle states the conclusion: "They knew God" (*gnontes ton theon*, v. 21).

2. Knowledge of God as Creator is acquired by rational reflection on created effects (v. 20). Many biblical scholars (e.g., Godet, Hodge, Hughes, Litton) believe that the general statement of verse 19 ("What may be known about God is plain to them, because God has made it plain to them") includes both knowledge of God intuited as a first truth and knowledge gained by rational contemplation of the natural world. Yet in the next verse Paul plainly asserts that God's invisible qualities are discerned "from what has been made" (v. 20). Twice (vv. 19, 21) the apostle uses the verb *ginōskō* ("to know"), which involves the idea of perceiving with the senses and grasping with the mind. In verse 32 he uses the intensive form of the verb, *epiginōskō*, which means to "know exactly, completely, through and through"[35]; and in verse 28 we find the intensive noun form, *epignōsis*. If further evidence were needed, Paul adds in verse 20 that the divine perfections "have been clearly seen," the verb *kathoraō* denoting the process of observation and perception by the senses. In addition, the phrase "being understood" (*nooumena*) signifies the acquisition of knowledge by the workings of the rational mind. We concur with the conclusion of Murray, Kant notwithstanding, that "phenomena disclose the noumena of God's transcendent perfection and specific divinity."[36]

3. The sinful heart consistently suppresses the knowledge, derived from nature, of God as Creator (vv. 21–22, 28). Although the knowledge of God was impressed on human hearts and minds, Paul asserts that "they did not think it worthwhile to retain the knowledge of God" (v. 28). The verb *dokimazō* suggests the idea of testing or proving. People tasted the knowledge of God as Sovereign and Judge, found it not to their liking, and thus summarily dismissed it from their lives. Determined to seek meaning apart from God, they proceeded to fashion lifeless idols in the form of birds, animals, and reptiles (v. 23). The result of this rejection of the light of general revelation is that they "exchanged the truth of God for a lie, and worshiped and served created things rather than the Creator" (v. 25). Wherefore three times (vv. 24, 26, 28) Paul insists that "God gave them over" to the impulses of their lower nature. Rejection of the knowledge of God as Creator resulted in defilement of the human body (vv. 24–27), chiefly in the form of sexual perversions, and in defilement of the human spirit (vv. 28–32), namely, in the form of a host of crimes against the neighbor and the community.

4. Finally, humanity's deliberate repudiation of the light of the knowledge of God establishes human guiltworthiness before the bar of divine justice (v. 20). All people, having perceived God's eternal power and divine nature and having rejected it, are said to be "without excuse" (*anapologētos*), that

is, lacking any defense against an accusation. The divine revelation in nature thus is an instrument not of salvation but of judgment. Because the knowledge of God (both innate and acquired) is trampled underfoot, God justly sentences all to death (v. 32).

In Romans 2:14–15, the apostle Paul teaches that all people at all times and places possess an intuitive knowledge of God's moral law. Apart from any contact with the written law of God, humans *qua* humans instinctively know that God requires goodness and abhors evil. In the wider context of Romans 2:12–16, the apostle states that all people stand condemned before God, since all have violated his holy laws. The Jews are guilty because they have transgressed the law given through Moses; and the Gentiles, who have not the Mosaic Law, are likewise guilty because they have violated the unwritten law of God inscribed on their hearts. "The requirements of the law" (*to ergon tou nomou*, v. 15), said by Paul to be written on the Gentiles' hearts, should be understood not as the set of moral values that the sinner learns from a religious and social milieu (the so-called affects of the law).[37] Rather, the phrase signifies the statutory dimension of the law engraved on the heart by virtue of which all people know the difference between good and evil. The apostle in verses 14–15 draws a precise parallel between the written law of Moses accessible to the Jews and the unwritten law implanted on the hearts of the Gentiles. Paul concludes his discussion by affirming that conscience (*syneidēsis*, co-knowing), the universal faculty of moral judgment, testifies to each person's compliance or noncompliance with the moral law within. Although a person's conscience may be hardened or seared, the accusations of conscience nevertheless convey the realization that there is a supreme Lawgiver and Judge who rewards good and requites evil. In sum, the moral law implanted within and the testimony of conscience provide additional means by which all people gain a rudimentary knowledge of God and his moral requirements.

The Johannine Literature

John's contribution to the issue focuses on the illuminatory operation of the Logos. John affirms of the eternal Word, "In him was life, and that life was the light of men" (John 1:4). Moreover, the Word is "the true light that gives light to every man who comes into the world" (John 1:9).[38] John's use of the Logos represents the synthesis of the Old Testament Word of the Lord (*dᵉbār Yahweh*) and Hellenistic (Stoic) usage that finds many parallels in the Wisdom motif in late Judaism. The Stoics saw in the Logos the divine power that pervades all things and that undergirds rational and moral life. The Book of Proverbs semihypostatizes and portrays Wisdom (the parallel Jewish motif) as the first of all created entities. In the Wisdom of Solomon 7:22–9:18, wisdom, among other functions, leads people to the attainment of knowledge of God. Thus in late Jewish thought, Wisdom is analogous to the power of God—operative in the world, creating, enlightening, and renewing. An identical pattern is found in John's use of the Logos motif in the fourth Gospel. The eternal Word created the universe (John 1:3), illumines human intellectual and moral faculties (John 1:4, 9), and, having become incarnate, renews spiritually those who believe in him (John 3:3, 16). Thus it seems clear that in John 1:4, 9 the apostle teaches that through the universal operation of the Logos the mind of every person is divinely illumined so as to perceive God as the inescapable datum of human existence. All people, by virtue of the general illumination of the Logos, reflect—in the manner of Calvin's "sense of divinity" or "seed of religion"—awareness of the reality of God within their hearts or minds. Tasker, among other exegetes, agrees with this interpretation, claiming that "the source of man's intellectual and spiritual perception, his conscience as well as his consciousness, is the divine Word."[39] Plummer concurs, adding the perceptive observation, "The Light illumines every man, but not every man is better for it; that depends on himself."[40]

SYSTEMATIC FORMULATION

After gathering primary biblical data and secondary historical views of a subject, the next task of a student of theology is to organize those data coherently and to develop a comprehensive biblical doctrine.

Information Revealed to All
(General Revelation)

What God Has Universally Revealed

As we have seen, the reality of a universal revelation through creation is clear from such passages as Psalm 19 and Romans 1–2. Exactly what has God made known to all people in and through creation?

1. God is one. In spite of the diversity of peoples and cultures, the evident unity of mankind indicates one source (Acts 17:26), and the order of the cosmos similarly indicates one sustainer God (Ps. 19:1–5; Rom. 1:20).

2. The Creator, who has life in himself, is the source of all that has life (Acts 17:25).

3. God is eternal and independent of everything else (Ps. 93:2; Rom. 1:20; Acts 17:25).

4. God is invisible and powerful (Rom. 1:20).

5. God is personal and wise (Ps. 104:24).

6. Although distinct from the universe, God is active in it (Acts 17:24, 26–27).

7. The Creator of mankind is the continuous source of earth's life-support system (Acts 14:15–16; 17:24–28).

8. The living and relating God is moral and just in himself and in his judgment of people and nations (Acts 14:17; Rom. 1:32; 2:14–15).

9. God alone, as the ultimate source and support of values, is of supreme worth and deserving of ultimate concern and worship. Idolaters exchange this truth for a lie (Acts 14:15; 17:23; Rom. 1:25).[41]

It is important to see that there are no redemptive truths here! What *is* revealed through nature is the heart of a theistic world-and-life view. "Theism signifies belief in one God (*theos*) who is (1) personal, (2) worthy of adoration, and (3) separate from the world, but (4) continuously active in it."[42] The ultimate reality is not an impersonal Thatness or energy, but a personal, knowing, and active God. The world is not a part or a mode of God, as pantheists and panentheists think, but a temporal creation of an eternal God distinct from it. People are not divine and cannot hope to become like God. Although distinct from the world (transcendent), God is also continuously relating to it (immanent). God did not create the world and then leave it to run on its own, as deists think.

The truths revealed universally imply an irreducible twofold nature of reality that must not be overlooked in the quest for a unified world-and-life view. Reality is not all of one kind. Ever since Creation there has been a *metaphysical dualism:* the eternal Creator cannot be reduced to the level of any part of creation, and creatures ought never to confuse themselves with deity (Rom. 1:20–25). Furthermore, an *ethical dualism* is presupposed in the truths of universal revelation (Rom. 2:14–15):

Never call evil good or good evil. Similarly implied is an ineradicable *epistemological dualism* between truth and falsehood (Rom. 1:25): truth ought not be reduced to error, and error ought never be regarded as true.

This latter difference between truth and falsehood relates to the fact that revealed truth concerning God can be asserted in universally significant propositions expressed in sentences. "A proposition is an assertion which proposes or denies something, and is capable of being judged true or false."[43] A proposition is expressed in indicative sentences with a subject (S), some form of the verb "to be" (e.g., is), and a predicate nominative (P); a proposition thus has the general form "S is P." Although in ordinary conversation people may not emphasize such indicative sentences, when their deepest beliefs about what is real and important are challenged, propositions become crucial. The languages in which the assertion is expressed may be as diverse as English, Sanskrit, or Chinese, but the logical content affirmed can in essence be the same. The meaning of the nine propositions listed above is made known universally, whatever the language in which it is spoken or written, and can be understood even by the nonliterate.

It also follows that, since these propositions are true, their contradictories are false, or "lies" (as Paul calls them in Rom. 1:25), presupposing the validity of the logical law of noncontradiction (i.e., both the affirmation and the denial of the same thing cannot be true at the same time and in the same respect). The law of noncontradiction is important in evaluating the claim that it does not matter what one calls God so long as one worships God. Names for God convey meanings ascribed to the ultimate reality. Divine names are not mere signs without significance. Names for God in any language or religion are acceptable logically if they convey the meanings listed above or are not contradictory to them, other considerations being equal. But divine names designating concepts contradictory to the content of general revelation cannot be accepted on logical principle. If one's ultimate concern is the Creator, it cannot be temporal process, evolution, "mother nature," or one's own inner self viewed as divine. Our ultimate loyalties ought not be to gurus, witch doctors, teachers, rabbis, preachers, parents, political leaders, or any historical institutions or processes.

Not every difference of thought or wording is a logical contradiction, however. Only logical contradictions of revealed truths must necessarily be rejected on logical principles. Theists may profitably study comparative religions, anthropology, the psychology of religious experience, and philosophy of religion with an openness to learn from varieties of thought and expression that supplement or confirm but do not flatly contradict what God has disclosed to be true.

In view of this data supporting a universal cognitive revelation of the essence of theism, we conclude that existentialist and Barthian hypotheses insofar as they deny a universal revelation fail to fit the relevant facts.

Where God's Universal Revelation May Be Seen

Granting that God has made his existence, power, and moral demands known in creation, where, more specifically, may these truths be perceived? God's universal revelation is made known in (1) the universal human consciousness of dependence on a higher being, (2) the universal capacity to distinguish right from wrong, (3) the order, regularity and intelligibility of nature, and (4) the continuous judgments in history on persons and nations.

First, God has revealed his presence *in human consciousness of dependence on a higher being.* Millions of Hindus sense an inner awareness of the "thatness" beyond themselves and the observable world. Life touches on a reality beyond itself. People from varied cultures through the centuries have testified to a sense of dependence on something greater than they, even though this sense of dependence may not be perceived as a distinctly religious experience. Schleiermacher referred to a universal consciousness or feeling of "unqualified dependence,"[44] and many who try to suppress this awareness are haunted by the feeling that "there must be something more." Augustine's attempt to suppress this sense of dependence led to increasing anxiety and a feeling of emptiness. Out of years of unfulfilled experience he prayed, "Thou hast created us for thyself, and our hearts are restless until they find their rest in thee."

Second, God discloses his moral nature *in human conscience with its sense of obligation or "oughtness."*[45] People in cultures throughout the world acknowledge a difference between what is just and what is unjust, particularly if they are treated unjustly themselves. People *ought* not treat other people unfairly. Researchers *ought* not represent their findings dishonestly. People *ought* to respect honesty. The universality and necessity of such norms indicate that these norms are more than the results of public opinion polls and more than the probable conclusions of social scientists. No one ought ever to treat others unjustly or dishonestly, not teachers, students, judges, legislators, law-enforcement people, parents, children, spouses, or neighbors.

Normative moral distinctions, however different in application in different cultures, permeate every culture. Expectations of moral decency within nations and among nations and cultures presuppose the objective validity of moral distinctions. The biblical explanation that a transcendent God has "written" the requirements of moral law on our hearts (Rom. 2:14–15) accounts most adequately for the nonnegotiable principles of justice that ought to be maintained without respect of persons.

Third, God reveals his intelligence, power, and personal qualities *in nature's intelligibility and awesome power and in life, especially human life.* Indications of the divine existence are seen, not only in subjective human consciousness and conscience, but also in objective givens in the universe. The world we observe is not self-derived, self-explanatory, or self-sufficient. It points to a source beyond itself, the Source already known in humanity's moral experience. Both the world's raw materials and its form come from God. God is both creative will and Logos, both the source of vitality and the source of conceptual meaning.[46] Nature exists but is not eternal. Nature has a beginning in the finite past: God created it all out of nothing (*ex nihilo*). Nature displays order on the microscopic and macroscopic levels, as well as on the levels of ordinary human experience. Nature displays an exceptional amount of power; and nature presents us with life, not only plant and animal life, but also human, personal life. In view of these data, it is improbable that nature's source is nonintelligent and purposeless, nonliving and nonpersonal. Nature makes more explicit the revelation in human consciousness that God is both transcendent and immanent, wise and powerful. And since persons are the highest reality in nature, their most likely source is also intelligent, powerful, and personal.

Fourth, God reveals his moral uprightness *in history's judgment of people and nations.* Human history is not merely a record of humanity's quest for God or of increasingly adequate definitions of God. It is rather the record of the tendency of persons and nations to rebel against creatureliness and dependence on God. People seek to be as independent, as secure, and as autonomous as God. Having received the truths of general revelation, they sometimes do by nature the things required by God's law. But more often, their knowledge is better than their actions. Knowing the requirements of God's just principles, they fail to live by them, and then they experience the deserved consequences.

Given these lines of internal and external human experience, we concur with Aquinas, Schleiermacher, Tillich, and Rahner (against Barth) on theological significance in empirical, historical, moral, and spiritual experience.

Human Perception of Universal Revelation (Natural Theology)

The Scriptures teach both that God makes reliable information available to people and that people universally perceive it. *General revelation* is God's activity of making known to people his eternal existence, and *natural theology* as used here is the people's activity of perceiving this truth. In other contexts, "natural theology" often refers only to Thomas Aquinas's five arguments from the sensory observation of nature, but here it refers to knowledge of God from creation derived from any sort of inner as well as external experience and any valid form of interpretation or argument utilizing those data.

The reality of natural theology, though devalued or denied in some Barthian and Reformed thinking, is explicitly and repeatedly taught in Scripture. As we have seen in the previous section, several times in Romans 1 the ungodly are said to know God. They are not held guilty for rejecting the gospel they did not know but for

disbelieving and disobeying the Creator they *did* know. The ungodly must have been aware of the Creation truths in order to have "suppressed the truth" (Rom. 1:18). Indeed, the presence of these truths is the basis of their culpability in disobedience to God and his moral principles.

The texts often used by Barth and Reformed theologians to deny the actuality of a natural knowledge of God fail to take sufficiently into account the two kinds of knowledge of God required by the respective contexts: knowledge of a moral theism and knowledge of God's redemptive plan. Passages of Scripture that state that people do not know God deny, not a knowledge of theism, but a knowledge of *God's redemptive plan* in the incarnate, crucified, and risen Christ. Before Paul says that the Galatians formerly did not know God (Gal. 4:8), he spoke of their being sons of God through faith in Jesus Christ (Gal. 3:26), and he said that having the witness of the Holy Spirit in the heart one is a child of God spiritually (Gal. 4:1–7). Although no one is by nature a spiritually reborn child of God, everyone is by nature a child of the Creator, deriving life and breath from him (Acts 17:28). The lack of redemptive sonship does not deny the reality of a metaphysical creaturely sonship.

Does the teaching that some truth can be known through the creation contradict the teaching that depraved minds cannot understand the things of God apart from faith in Christ (1 Cor. 2:14)? Again, the context has to do with redemptive truth—the message of the Cross (1 Cor. 1:18), Jesus Christ and him crucified (1 Cor. 2:2). If by some effort we extend depravity to include the absence of any knowledge of God's existence, then it is important to recall the Augustinian emphasis on a universal as well as a special work of divine illumination.[47] God's Logos, through whom all things were made, gave people life, and "that life was the light of men" (John 1:4). And "the true light that gives light to every man was coming into the world" (John 1:9). Even more explicitly, Paul argues that the ungodly have a knowledge of theism "because God has made it plain to them" (Rom. 1:19). Thus, in addition to the divine activity of general revelation and the human activity of learning from this revelation, there is another divine activity that enables fallen, fleshly minds clearly to see and understand the theistic content that has been revealed.

It is true, of course, that the nature psalms and Romans 1 were written by people of faith. Can it be inferred from this that what is taught in these passages can apply only to believers? No. What is taught is the universal, continuous, and clear revelation to all, the perception of all, and the accountability of all. One might as well affirm that Paul's description of the basis of condemnation (Rom. 3:9–20) still holds for believers because the passage was written by a believer. If believers today can discuss the status of unbelievers before God, surely biblical writers could.

The teaching of Scripture that all human beings do know the truths of theism and inexcusably fail to live up to them does not automatically support any particular type of argument for God's existence and moral administration of the world. People asked to state the reasons for their belief in God give quite different arguments. But with different starting points, intermediate steps, degrees of probability, and psychological certitude, all conclude that God exists.

Prior to faith in Christ, some theists have only a vague feeling of a Creator, others a rational intuition. Many have followed the five arguments of Aquinas from observed data to an adequate cause. Some simply testify to their own mystical experiences of God. Others presuppose God's existence and show how that assumption lends meaning to everything else. People propose the hypothesis of God's existence and find it verified rather than disconfirmed by many converging lines of external and internal data.

The Bible does not support any one of these forms of argument explicitly. It simply asserts that, from the things made, people do know (by whatever type of reasoning) God's eternal power and personhood. Although one may find one argument for concluding that God exists more convincing than another, we may need to recognize the cumulative impact of all external and internal data and the valid elements in all lines of reasoning based on them. For the weighing of strengths and weaknesses of each type of reasoning, it is wise to examine textbooks on Christian apologetics.[48]

The Dutch Reformed and Barthian hypotheses denying natural knowledge of God do not account for this evidence as adequately as the Augustinian evangelical doctrine does.

Human Accountability for Universal Revelation

God's intention in the giving of universal revelation, as in the giving of the Mosaic Law, was that any who would live in accordance with it would be right with him. "God did this so that men would seek him and perhaps reach out for him and find him" (Acts 17:27). People who perfectly and continuously keep the requirements written on their own heart (Rom. 2:14–15) or in the Mosaic Law, or who worship and serve the Creator more than the creature (Rom. 1:25), need not fear divine condemnation.

The question is whether anyone ever meets these just requirements continuously and perfectly all of his or her life. The Scriptures clearly teach that no one does. Righteousness before God cannot be achieved by depraved sinners attempting to keep God's moral law. All non-Jews (Gentiles) are accountable before God's general revelation (Rom. 1:18–2:16). All Jews are accountable in addition before the written law of Moses (Rom. 2:17–3:8). On the basis of what they *know*, God finds all Gentiles and Jews without respect of persons to be "under sin" (Rom. 3:9–18). God's standard is "holy, just and good" (Rom. 7:12). The problem is not with the divine demands but with fallen human nature, with what the "flesh" cannot do (Rom. 8:3). Hence, it is descriptively a fact that all who have not by faith received the gift of Christ's perfect righteousness remain under condemnation (John 3:18, 36).

But, in view of the teaching of Romans 1–3, it is simply inaccurate to affirm that rejection of Christ is the only reason anyone will ever be found guilty by God. The present-tense verbs throughout Romans 1 indicate that the universal revelation is continuous and actually perceived. On that basis an omniscient and uncompromisingly moral Judge finds all people inexcusably idolatrous in relation to himself and unjust in relationships with other people, regardless of whether they have heard of Christ or not.

The universality of moral accountability, of failure to attain the moral ideal, and of divine condemnation often raises the objection that God is unjust. Dale Moody asks the hard question, which no one can sidestep: "But what kind of God is he who gives man enough knowledge to damn him but not enough to save him?"[49] Moody argues that the possibilities resulting from general revelation must be positive as well as negative, redemptive as well as condemnatory. Hypothetically, he is right. Anyone who could keep the moral law continuously and perfectly would not be justly found guilty of any injustice. Prior to the Fall, general revelation was

indeed both redemptive and condemnatory: Adam and Eve could have obeyed God, and had they done so, the result would have been positive and not negative. But reality for us is the fallen human condition: no one born of the flesh with a fleshly nature (John 3:6) loves God and neighbors perfectly. God wrote the requirements of morality on our hearts that we might find him, not that we might be condemned. We, of our own will, have rebelled against those requirements. Moody's inference that it is unjust of God to demand justice because we may be condemned by those standards reminds one of a college dean who argued that the students should have no rules so that they would not feel guilty for breaking them.

Granting the propensities toward evil in the fallen race and the pervasiveness of greed, hate, murder, lust, and rape—even in the presence of the restraints imposed by God's universal moral law—we can imagine how intolerable and impossible life would be without a universal sense of uncompromising justice and fair play. As a restraint on flagrant evils, the revelation of moral principles to all constitutes a manifestation of God's universal concern for the well-being of all. How could God remain just, we ask, and not call injustice wrong?

The God of the Bible does not arbitrarily condemn anyone but judges according to people's works, according to the truth they knew. These principles hold true without respect of persons, not only within certain subcultures (such as evangelicalism) or cultures (such as that of North America), but for all nations and peoples in the world. And we need not fear that the all-knowing Judge of all the earth will not do right. None will be punished more than they deserve.

Thus the fundamental significance of the revelation in creation is this: that through

77

it man as man is a *person*, a responsible being, a being related to God, "standing before" him; and also that by this revelation man is responsible for his sin, and is therefore inexcusable. This is why it is the presupposition of the saving revelation in Jesus Christ, although in itself it has no saving significance.[50]

One question that remains in debate is whether the Holy Spirit brings conviction of sin and repentance to people who never hear the message about Jesus Christ. Evangelicals know that no one lives up to the light he or she has received through general revelation or the law of Moses. No one is absolved of real guilt, changed in nature, and restored to fellowship with God by trying to be as good as possible or by being as good as or better than others.

However, some suggest that although no one is perfectly good, a person can repent of sin without having heard of Christ. They believe that those who realize their guilt and throw themselves on the mercy of the divine court with a sincerity that shows in their lives will find mercy because of the cross of Christ, even though they have never heard of it.[51] Others believe that probably no such people exist. The latter view appears to be more in harmony with the overall teaching of Scripture. Repentance, like every other good gift, is from above, the result of a preliminary work of the Holy Spirit in bringing people to Christ. Faith comes by hearing, through a human instrument (Rom. 10:9–14). All who receive the preliminary work of the Spirit leading to a repentant heart (rather than merely a temporary intention) in God's providence hear the gospel in some way, whether it be through a believer, literature, or the media. That is why the Savior left his disciples with the unforgettable words of the Great Commission as recorded by Luke: "Repentance and forgiveness of sins will be preached in his [Christ's] name to all nations,

beginning in Jerusalem. You are my witnesses of these things" (Luke 24:47–48).[52]

APOLOGETIC INTERACTION

Those who accept a universal revelation and knowledge of God's existence and moral demands will need to be prepared for rejection on the basis that the doctrine does not fit the facts of experience. Can we claim a universal knowledge of a personal God when atheists and pantheists explicitly deny his existence? Liberal and other universalist thinkers who regard natural knowledge of God sufficient for relating to God challenge the conclusion that universal knowledge of God's existence and moral demands does not put people morally and spiritually right with God. Then Barthian theologians flatly deny that either Scripture or experience justifies belief in any universal revelation and knowledge of the true God.

One caution before investigating the data of human experience to determine whether the biblical teachings fit the facts. The biblical hypothesis asserts not only a general revelation and natural theology but also the universal tendency in sinful people to suppress this truth.

We ought not expect, then, that Gallup polls will disclose that 100 percent of respondents affirm belief in the one true God or that those who do affirm it live up to his moral norms. Rather, if the scriptural position is in harmony with the experience of mankind, we should expect to find in each generation traces of a prior awareness of the truths revealed: (1) some consciousness of a higher power on which life depends, (2) a sense of a real difference between right and wrong, (3) a consciousness of moral purpose and accountability in history, and, at the same time, (4) indications of sinful rebellion against these truths in atheistic suppressions and religious distortions. These four points together coherently account for the elements of truth and of error in the world's philosophies and religions.

Atheistic Suppression

We do not claim that atheists are believers in disguise, but rather that, having cognitive knowledge of God, it is foolish for them to say in their hearts that God is nonexistent (Ps. 53:1). Knowing better, they are foolish not to yield themselves to God and to claim that assertions about God are meaningless (according to logical-positivist or existentialist categories). An atheist can neither live meaningfully as a human being nor understand himself without adhering to some ultimate loyalty and concern.

Nontheists, for example, will often pledge loyalty to many of the same values as theists: the dignity of man; human rights; the obligation to remove racial, social, and economic injustices; the promotion of understanding and peace among nations; and the alleviation of natural evils such as earthquakes and moral evils such as alcoholism. But if ultimate reality is nonmoral and reducible to a quantifiable scientific explanation, then there is no *nonnegotiable* basis for these values. Thus secular humanist presuppositions tend to suppress the truth that their inherent value derives from a higher source. Nontheists cannot account for the universality and necessity of principles of justice.

What amazes theists is not that nontheists have no ultimate concerns, but that they find it possible to worship and serve. Corliss Lamont, author of *The Philosophy of Humanism*, finds it unreasonable to worship a personal God distinct from the world, but he does find it reasonable to call the scientific method "an instrument of infinite power."[53] He accepts the impersonal, nonpurposive universe as "self-existing" and history as "a continuous process" (eternal).[54] Could this be worship and service of the creature rather than the Creator (Rom. 1:25)?

Pantheistic Distortions

Scholars studying world religions find differently worded but rather similar vestiges of original general revelation and natural theology in the world's religions. S. H. Kellogg lists four basic similarities among the world's theistic, pantheistic, nontheistic, and animistic religions. First, all religions "assume the existence of a Power (or powers) superior to man, on which he is dependent, and which is able to influence his destiny." Second, "because of man's relation to this Supreme Power, certain things are obligatory on him, and other things must be avoided at the peril of suffering." Third, "between man and the Supreme Power or powers, something is wrong." Fourth, "there is for man a state of being after death; and the consequence of wrongdoing or rightdoing in this present life will follow a man after death."[55] Kellogg's findings include both the theistic consciousness and its distortions in pantheistic worship of the creation.

Aldous Huxley's portrayal of "the perennial philosophy" in various forms in culture after culture over a period of twenty-five centuries slants these truths toward monistic pantheism.[56] At the core of the perennial philosophy Huxley finds four fundamental doctrines:

> First, the phenomenal world of matter and of individualized consciousness . . . is the manifestation of a Divine Ground . . . apart from which they would be nonexistent. Second: human beings are capable not merely of knowing about the Divine Ground by inference; they can also realize its existence by a direct intuition. . . . This immediate knowledge unites the knower with that which is

known. Third: men possess a double nature, a phenomenal ego and an eternal Self, which is the inner man, the spirit, the spark of divinity within the soul. Fourth: man's life on earth has only one end and purpose: to identify himself with his eternal Self and so to come to unitive knowledge of the Divine Ground.[57]

Huston Smith prefers to speak of "the primordial tradition" rather than the "perennial religion," because he thinks these beliefs express less an intellectual philosophy than a tradition. The author of *The Religions of Man* wrote *Forgotten Truth: The Primordial Tradition* to show that beyond the quantifiable limits of science people have found values, purposes, and meanings in life through the tradition, which includes the recognition of infinite being, infinite awareness, and infinite bliss.[58] Smith moves toward Vedanta Hinduism when he says that theism is "true," but not the final truth. God's personal mode is not the final reality, he thinks, because the final reality is spoken of literally only in negative terms, and in positive terms only analogically and paradoxically.[59]

Smith's typical allegation that conceptual knowledge limits God confuses assertions with their referents. Do we limit Niagara Falls by defining water? And Smith has failed to show the superiority of impersonal analogies of God to personal ones. Smith also misses the mark of truth when he supposes that the human mind was made for knowing facts and fictions but not ultimates.[60] The mind of man was and is renewed to know God in part (1 Cor. 13:12; Col. 3:10). In the first use of language reported in Scripture, God communicated with man (Gen. 1:28–30; 2:16). Univocal knowledge is denied whenever the realm of time, space, and human thought is consigned to the relative and changing and whenever God is said to be totally different. Indeed God is changeless, but God created mankind to

think his thoughts after him, using analogies with univocally valid points, as shown above in the propositional content of universal revelation.

C. S. Lewis observes that people generally prefer to distort the theistic belief in a concrete, choosing, commanding, prohibiting God with determinate character and purposes into a pantheistic being in general, about which nothing can be truly asserted, who does nothing and demands nothing, who is there if you wish for him, like a book on a shelf, but will not pursue you. But the point of general revelation is that God is "the fountain of facthood." God invents, acts, and creates. He creates concrete, individual, determinate things that do exist: things like flamingoes, lovers, pineapples, comets, and kangaroos. This concreteness is not accounted for by abstractions of logic or scientific law. "If God is the ultimate source of all concrete, individual things and events, then God Himself must be concrete and individual in the highest degree."[61]

The impulse of fallen humanity toward pantheism has been revitalized today in the rejuvenation of Eastern religions, the New Age movement, new-consciousness groups, and human potential movements. "Yet by a strange irony, each new relapse into this immemorial 'religion' is hailed as the last word in novelty and emancipation."[62] Pantheists—however perennial, traditional, or "new" their religion may seem to be—distort the original, theistic revelation and worship and serve created energy rather than the Creator (Rom. 1:25).

Liberal Theology's Inflation

Liberalism traditionally assumed a naturalistic, evolutionary view of the world, an optimistic view of man as inherently good, and a reductive view of Scripture as little more than a collection of minute segments written and compiled by children of their respective times. Mankind having no supernaturally inspired propositions from above, DeWolf's natural theology "corrects" the Bible.[63] No distinctive special revelation remains. Redemption is unnecessary. Revelation in nature is made the determinative revelation.

Here is a crucial issue with liberalism. Do the traditions of the world religions and philosophies represent the final truth by which to correct Scripture, or do the Scriptures (when validly interpreted) represent the final truth by which to correct the religious philosophies? Because the data of experience can be readily misinterpreted, the more specific biblical corrective is needed and was "breathed out" by God.

Misinterpretations of Scripture may be corrected by responsibly interpreted data from history and the sciences. And irresponsible historical and scientific interpretations can be corrected by responsibly interpreted Scripture.

Given the best efforts at adhering faithfully to sound scientific, historical, epistemological, and hermeneutical principles, we may nevertheless be confronted with contradictory assertions from nature and Scripture. When this happens, the view that is drawn from sound exegesis of Scripture and confirmed by people of varied cultural perspectives throughout the creedal history of the church is the least likely to be the one in error. Even apart from the supernatural inspiration of Scripture, linguistic statements permit greater precision in communication than nonverbal types of communication. We are less likely to misinterpret language on a subject than mere objects or events. Special revelation must not be demoted and understood as inferior to general revelation.

Neoorthodox Denials

Karl Barth represents one of the most vigorous recent writers in opposition to both universal revelation and natural theology. He speaks for a host of experience-oriented people from varied theological perspectives who consider divine revelation essentially noninformational. What God reveals is himself, we are told, and not information *about* himself.[64] This concept of revelation is based on extreme views of God's transcendence,[65] making God's mind totally different from the human mind, thus undercutting the fact that our minds are made in the image of God's (Col. 3:10).[66] Barth also fails to distinguish nonredemptive knowledge of God from redemptive knowledge, confusing revelation with redemption and imagining that there is no revelation if there is no positive human response (which contradicts Romans 1).[67] Barth and others also think that a direct Person-to-person encounter excludes information from the essence of revelation. However, the author of Psalm 19 appreciated both the way God's written Word "revives the soul" (vv. 7–10) and the way nature "declares God's glory" (vv. 1–6). And Paul, who so personally met Christ on the Damascus road (Acts 9:1–19), fully appreciated the knowledge of God's existence and moral norms mediated through nature (Rom. 1:18–25; 2:14–15).

Barth also denied general revelation and natural theology because he feared that any belief taken to be propositionally true in itself would become an idol (antichrist) and stand between a person and a personal relationship with Christ.[68] All who hold to objectively valid religious truths ought to share this concern. A system of theistic beliefs can become our ultimate concern rather than a means to lead us away from idols to a personal relationship with the One of whom the belief system speaks. But the belief system of theism is necessary to lead us away from the idols of materialism and pantheism to seek the Most High God. Such reliable assertions led people at Thessalonica away from idols to the living God (1 Thess. 1:9; 2:13). Conceptual truth is not an end in itself but a means to the end of avoiding worship and service of the unreal, the visible material creation, and the invisible demonic hosts.

On the basis of his presuppositions Barth considered the teaching of passages like Psalm 19 and Romans 1 incidental and contradictory to the major biblical teaching that unbelievers do not know God (1 Cor. 1:20–21). Commenting on the statement "The invisible things of God are clearly seen" (Rom. 1:20) Barth wrote, "And what does this mean but that we know nothing of God. . . ?"[69] However, it is hardly incidental to the teaching of Romans and other Scripture to affirm the essentials of a theistic world-and-life view in which all people are dependent on and accountable to God. Redemptive knowledge of God teaches the just basis on which God can forgive all who have failed to worship and serve him faithfully all of their lives. Moral knowledge helps people see their need for the gospel. Hence the moral law within and the knowledge of its source, the moral Creator, is not rendered unnecessary by the gospel. Natural theology and morality are the forerunners of the gospel.

An objectively valid revelation of God, then, is in fact true and important, not as an end in itself, but as a means of avoiding the worship and service of idols. It also provides a means of thankful acknowledgment of our dependence on God and of our obligation to the ultimate Source who created us in his image. The inexorable moral judgments within, like Moses' written law, become a strict teacher, enabling us to realize our need for a just amnesty and for the restoration of right relationships with God, ourselves, and our neighbors. General revelation must not be stripped of its significance by special revelation.

Of the historical and contemporary options available, an Augustinian-Reformed-Evangelical view provides the most coherent and viable account of the relevant biblical and experiential data with the fewest difficulties.

RELEVANCE TO LIFE AND MINISTRY

It would be advantageous if people working for a better world did so from a sound theological base and if well-grounded theologians were at the same time actively involved in promoting just relationships in the family, church, and society.

Assuming the validity of practicing what we know, preach, and teach, we here introduce some suggestions in application of the truth of a universal revelation. We make little attempt to delineate strategies and methods of influencing human life, leaving that to specialists in related fields (such as ethics, education, legislation, practical theology, and missions). But we try to highlight some practical ends and goals worth living, ministering, and dying for.

A universal revelation and a universal knowledge of God by common grace at this point is no longer a mere hypothesis. Its truth has been confirmed by Scripture and experience. What, then, are the values and purposes for life and ministry that follow from the truth about the reality of God's general revelation?

Pro-Life Universally

The above research has shown that the giving of rain, crops, food, and joy are "testimonies" to God's "kindness" (Acts 14:17). Can those who worship the *King* as Lord of all be unkind to their neighbors? Since our God "gives life and breath and everything else" (Acts 17:25) to all mankind, shall we unnecessarily pollute the air and waste planet earth's life support resources? Believing that God supports human life universally, we will be pro–human life in the broadest sense of the words. Regardless of economic, political, cultural, racial, educational, or religious differences, understanding theists, like their God, will be known for their kindness to all other persons as persons.

Among the values of people under God is the desire that all people should have the resources for a happy life. Theists whose resources have been met experience the joy of giving generously for the sake of those who lack the necessities of life. Persons, families, and communities who share God's objectives will contribute and work that all people may have adequate resources to pursue happiness.

Nontheists imagine that to believe in a personal God is to lose happiness. But among the values of believers in the great personal Giver of every good gift is the joy of giving.[70] By serving ends in harmony with those of the wise giver of the entire life-support system, theists discover the most lasting joy. Experience indicates that human happiness is seldom found when it is pursued as an end in itself.[71] Our highest and most lasting happiness is experienced when we do not make our happiness, but the well-being of others among our highest values.

Whatever else we may lose in this changing life, if we serve changeless God-given norms, our highest values cannot be taken away. Total relativists, materialists, and naturalists of all sorts face the loss of their highest loyalties, none of which is absolute or enduring. But God and the moral values of God's nature and law are incorruptible. Whatever losses occur in this fallen world,

those who serve the living God's values cannot lose the final source of inner joy. So in God's universal revelation theists discover a more enduring ground for supporting human values than humanists who are naturalists or atheists. However tragically some theists may have failed to realize this pro-life truth in history, theistic humanism better motivates and more permanently sustains human values than naturalistic or pantheistic humanisms.

Pro-Truth Universally

Although human knowers have their varied perspectives as relativists have so emphasized, a universal ability to *know* some objective truth about creation and the Creator is implied in a natural theology as a product of common grace. We know the difference between being in the presence of a person and being in the presence of a thing. We know that we ought to respect the rights of human beings. We know that we ought to treat people justly as we would be treated. We know that there is a real difference between right and wrong. Such knowledge is necessary to morally responsible behavior.

All the ordered, intelligible relationships or criteria in the world come from the creative mind of God. Beyond the multitudes of varying opinions in the world are unchanging principles of thought (logic), communication, education, aesthetics (rhyme, verse, proportion, scales, harmony), arithmetic, geometry, astronomy, physics, nuclear energy, anthropology, sociology, and psychology. By these principles we evaluate claims concerning these areas. Some theories in these fields are found to be better informed and closer to reality than others. Valid truths in a university's different departments and colleges are not ultimately irreconcilable.

Confidence in the theistic basis for unifying research in all fields motivated many of the early scientists and the founders of the great *uni*versities. Unfortunately the exaggerated individualism and total relativism of recent times has shattered confidence in a comprehensive world view and philosophy of life. Relativistic scientists have become so absorbed in the differences between revolutionary models and paradigms that they have forgotten the similarities. Many of the first scientists worked creatively because they were guided by the conviction that "the enduring rationality of the cosmos made sense only so long as the world, its laws and its constants were *given* in the deepest ontological sense."[72]

Pro-Justice Universally

A universal natural morality by common grace is part of a natural theology. "Conscience," whether clear or guilty, bears witness to the requirements of God's moral law inscribed on human hearts (Rom. 2:14–15). Humans universally discriminate between right and wrong. In their hearts, all human beings understandably demand justice and know that they ought to treat others fairly. The basic requirements of God's universal moral law were expressed by Moses. If we were to sum up the moral law of God, the Ten Commandments, in one word, God expects from all people justice. The prophets constantly called people back to basic morality under God. "And what does the LORD require of you? To act justly . . . and to walk humbly with your God" (Mic. 6:8).

What is just or unjust is not decided by the moral consensus. Fifty-one percent of a society may be wrong, as in the Nazi regime. What *is* does not decide what *ought* to be. A total relativism is inadequate to account for the universal sense of obligation to be a just person and act justly. Can theists who preach and teach a universal moral revelation, think that they will escape judgment for their injustice to their spouses? to their children? to neighbors? to students? to administrators? to faculty? to employees? to employers? Justice as an absolute is nonnegotiable. And the Administrator of Justice judges without respect of persons.

After examination of injustice in their own lives, contemporary theists, like the prophets of old, may be prepared to challenge the injustice and immorality in others whether in high or low places. Can theists place their highest values in the Lord of all and remain uninvolved with injustice to the poor, widows, orphans, prisoners, and refugees? However popular relativism may become, is there no objective and real difference between right and wrong? Is there no objective difference between helping a person and hurting a person? Even in the name of "law and order" it is wrong to oppress and exploit others! And even in the name of "liberation" it is wrong to seek personal vindictive vengeance. Freedom does not mean license to violate and destroy others.[73] Theists challenge immorality and injustice in high places when these threaten the well-being of creatures made in God's image.[74]

Pro–Human Accountability Universally

Talk about justice is cheap if no Administrator of Justice can be found. Unenforced moral norms in human hearts are of little use in a fallen world. But the doctrine of universal revelation shows that all people are not only dependent on God but also obligated to God the giver of every good. People are stewards of God's resources. He is their ultimate owner. Temporarily we are stewards accountable for sharing these resources for the benefit of all. Unfaithful stewardship fails to conserve the earth's finite life support resources, to develop them fully, and to distribute them generously.[75]

In a day of increasing disrespect for private property it seems relevant to note that half of the commandments are prohibitions against theft of what belongs to another. I must not covet anything that belongs to my neighbor or rob him of his life, wife, property, or reputation. I cannot deprive him of God's purpose through nature to provide my neighbor with freedom to grow crops, harvest them, and give to assist the less fortunate. Injustices resulting from private or state ownership come from attempts to be independent of the Creator who knows our thoughts and acts. Permanent improvements in economic and social situation will not come from communist programs that deceive people into thinking themselves to be autonomous and unaccountable to God. Correctives to selfish abuses of private ownership in accord with the moral law of God do not abolish private ownership, but they should abolish the irresponsibility and thanklessness of private owners who disregard the universal revelation (Rom. 1:21). Thankful theists, knowing that they are accountable to God, will exhibit generous, risk-taking stewardship of whatever they have from God's common grace.[76]

Accountability to God becomes essential for improved conditions in all realms. Whatever the form of government, no branch of government and no person in power may usurp ultimate authority or be given our ultimate loyalty. Whether in legislative, administrative, or executive branches, every leader has power under God. Every leader in any country ought to recognize his accountability to the highest Ruler of all. Given human experience, any form of political power can be corrupted. But absolute power is corrupted absolutely. No human being, as Plato's *Republic* vividly showed, is wise enough or good enough to be given

unaccountable power. Even where human accountability is built into political structures, the fullest alleviation of political injustice will not come without ultimate accountability to the all-knowing God.

The major objective of a pastor-teacher may not be to change political structures as such, if these structures have built-in checks and balances against the leader's absolute pretensions. But the major responsibility of Christian ministers is to call political leaders to accountable stewardship before the God on whom they depend for their life and breath. Under God human leaders are accountable in their governing to provide for their subjects a just ability to procure food and drink, the right to justice, and the freedom to pursue happiness. Like Paul at Athens, we must deliver the divine summons to repent to leaders who are inexcusable for not living up to the moral and spiritual truth they ought to see clearly.

Similarly theists will work for universal justice in education. More ultimate than school buildings and strategies and methods of teaching is the acknowledgment of dependence on the Creator and obligation to the moral Lawgiver and Administrator. All school teachers, administrators, and staff members are inexcusable for intellectual dishonesty. All educators will give account of prejudices that deprive qualified students of their right to learn. Public schools cannot justly serve only one segment of a pluralistic society. Does not the principle of justice indicate that since theists pay taxes equally, that theists' children should be able to hear a theistic interpretation of any field of learning in the curriculum as well as naturalistic and pantheistic interpretations? If so, justice works in the other direction also. Public schools cannot be made exclusively theistic if others besides theists pay for them. Academic freedom implies academic responsibility to the basic world views of the community served.

Although ministers and average church leaders as general practitioners may not be specialists in economics, politics, and education, they have an important contribution to make in each of these and other fields. If they know that all people in all fields are dependent on God, accountable to God, and guilty before God, they can call all people everywhere to repent.

In calling people to repent of injustice and to treat others justly as they would be treated, no church leaders need fear that they are thus imposing denominational, evangelical, or even distinctively Christian standards on non-Christians. This appeal to universal moral law is based on human nature and universal revelation, not on revelation to some persons and not on sectarian values. A Christian theist simply calls on people everywhere to uncover the nonnegotiable original requirements of God's law in their own hearts, however suppressed. Although evangelical theists may not be able to cooperate with nonevangelicals for evangelistic and missionary purposes, they may consistently cooperate with other theists (liberal Christian, Jewish, etc.) for concerted religious efforts for greater justice in school districts, neighborhoods, cities, states, and nations. And in the political arena theists may also, on the ground of the universal revelation and knowledge of justice, cooperate with nontheists who happen at the moment to be working for just causes.

Pro—Moral Education Universally

Another implication of a universal natural theology by common grace is the universal capacity in normal human beings for moral education to action on the basis of moral principles (derived from the nature and revelation of God). Before young people assume responsibilities in business, education, and government, they need to be morally mature and responsible. Increasing crime rates in high places have led to a concern for clarifying values and helping children to own them. The recent work of Lawrence Kohlberg has served as a catalyst for many studies on this subject.[77] Kohlberg found that children may justify or condemn their own actions in various ways: (1) They may choose to do something for a reward or to avoid punishment. (2) They may choose on mere pragmatic considerations. (3) They may be motivated by conventional approval or (4) by authoritative law and order considerations. (5) They may develop a respect for social contracts and legal concerns. Finally, (6) they may justify their moral actions by their harmony with universal ethical principles.

Where do children and adults get the capacity for deciding right and wrong on the basis, not of what is being done by their peers, but of universal moral principles? Nontheistic total relativism fails to provide an adequate answer. On the hypothesis of a universal implantation of the requirements of the moral law on human hearts, theists have an adequate explanation. Moral education brings students to a level at which they recall the moral principles God incorporated in their being.

Beyond accounting for absolute moral principles of justice, theists add an even higher motive—the ultimate motive—for deciding and acting on principle: not legalistic necessity, but thankful love. In church and family education theists will seek to develop in their children love for the Source and Support of moral values. And with love for God will come love for all people, to whom God universally gives life and breath.

The moral education of people on the basis of universal revelation takes logical precedence over their spiritual education on the basis of redemptive revelation to prophets and apostles. Before young children are asked to believe in Jesus' saving provision for them, they need to understand their ultimate dependence on the Creator, their obligation to his moral laws and their guilt before his just judgment. Children of all ages need to know that there is a real or objective difference between right and wrong, truth and falsehood. And they need to learn well that they will give account to God for what they choose to think, say, and do. Christian parents, child evangelists, and youth ministers need to remember this order. General revelation precedes special revelation.

Only after coming to an age of moral accountability for their actions can children be expected to understand what it is to be sinners guilty of injustice before God and in need of the Savior. After children are old enough to realize real guilt before divine justice, they are old enough to realize their need for the Savior. Then they can grasp to some degree that the sinless Jesus, who came from God, gave his life a just payment for the forgiveness of all their sins and their complete acceptance with God.

In a pluralistic world frantically seeking to suppress the truth of dependence on God and obligation to God, parents and teachers will start early to help children understand that important and loved as they are, they are not the center of the universe. God is. God-centered moral development also emphasizes that with our rights as persons come as many responsibilities before God and mankind.

Pro–Common Ground for Apologetic Purposes

A universal revelation and theology in a pluralistic world makes cross-philosophical communication possible. When people from other world views challenge the truth of Christianity, can Christians discover any points of contact on which both can agree? As Christians begin conversations with non-Christians, are there any common principles of sound thought or valid argument to which both can appeal? Are there any ground rules in common by which they can engage in a respectable debate?

Although nontheists may suppress and distort the truths of universal revelation and misuse the perceptual and reasoning capacities that make them possible, the doctrine of universal revelation implies common ground in several respects. Non-Christians as well as Christians are dependent on adequate provisions of air, food, and water to live. Both demand justice and can rediscover the moral law within them. Both are themselves moral-lawbreakers. Both are accountable to know the reality God created and to use the laws of sound reasoning that come from God. Both need to consciously affirm the truth that Someone cares about them, and both need love.

However different Christian and non-Christian prescriptions for restoring moral and spiritual fellowship may be, there is common ground in metaphysical dependence on God, moral accountability to God, and need for acceptance by God. While Dutch Reformed thinkers fear that acknowledgments of common ground make unsaved people independent of God, in fact no atheist exists apart from God's common grace. To deny that he is dependent makes him no less dependent. Again the fear that common ground makes humans autonomous is unfounded, for the admission of a common principle of justice does not make non-Christian philosophers independent of God's moral demands, but accountable to universal principles of morality.[78]

Christians speaking up for their faith may count on common ground as did Paul, the apostle to the pagans (nontheistic Gentiles) at Athens. Although in preaching to the Jews in the synagogues Paul reasoned out of the Scriptures (Acts 17:2), with pretheists and pre-Christians he reasoned out of God's revelation in nature, history, and the human heart. Addressing the atheistic Epicurean materialists, Stoic pantheists, and idolaters, Paul presented the truth about the God they worshiped as unknown (vv. 22–23). Although his points about God were in accord with Old Testament Scripture, Paul did not quote the Old Testament as of divine authority. Rather, he reminded the educated Athenians that their life and breath depended on the personal God (vv. 24–29) and that they were accountable to God, guilty before God, and in need of repentance (v. 30).

Paul at Athens established the truth about God as Creator and as giver of the moral law by recovering distorted common ground in the writings of one of the Stoic pantheists' own poets (v. 28). Paul's use of the common ground did not make the Athenians independent of God or autonomous. It made them more responsible for what they knew. Paul's approach began with theism and moved to the gospel of the crucified and risen Christ. Although some sneered and some put off deciding, Paul's approach was highly successful. Well-known leaders Dionysius and Damaris and several others came to believe in Christ (v. 34). And, according to church history, Dionysius became the first pastor of a Christian church in that influential ancient city. Paul, especially called and prepared for presenting the gospel to the pagans, first built on common ground to help naturalistic, pantheistic, and idolatrous people recover the truths of theism from general revelation. Paul's approach to the Athenians provides the most extensive New Testament example of reasoning with nontheistic unbelievers. The multiplying numbers of naturalists and

pantheists in post-Christian cultures need to believe that God is (Heb. 11:6) before they are asked to believe the gospel of the Lord Jesus Christ.

Pro–Common Ground Crossculturally in Missiology

A universal revelation and theology by common grace in a pluralistic world provides the basis for crosscultural communication. Christian missions, as observed by Lit-sen Chang in the Far East, reflected diminished effectiveness when missionaries failed to understand the importance of the distinctive content of universal revelation or confused it with the redemptive message of special, redemptive revelation.

On one extreme, liberal missionaries in the Far East tended to magnify the universal revelation into the entirety of revelation. Finding elements of theism and morality in non-Christian religions, liberals tended to regard theists as Christians. But if a moral theism were the whole essence of the Christian faith, then it would never have become distinct from Judaism's moral theism.[79] It would have been one more sect like those of the Pharisees and the Sadducees. The gospel message concerning the redemptive provisions of Christ's atonement differed not merely in degree but also in kind from the teaching of meritorious works in Eastern religions. It set forth, not what we must do to be just, but what Christ did for the best of people who come short of absolute justice.

Paul understood the theism that Judaism and Christianity held in common. But as one who had come to grasp the redemptive provision of Jesus as the Messiah, he considered his Jewish relatives and friends zealous, but unsaved (Rom. 10:1–2). The more they emphasized the justice of the law, the more they should have realized how short they themselves came from meeting it themselves. By trying to establish their own righteousness, they did not receive Christ's perfect righteousness as a gift by faith (vv. 3–4).

Similarly, liberal Christianity has missed the distinctive importance of Christ's once-for-all objective provision by which God remains just and justifies the ungodly who believe. Liberal missionaries found so much in common with non-Christians because they lost the heart of the good news about the incarnate, crucified, and risen Christ they came to present. So liberalism also lost the urgency to present the gospel of God's grace. The research above shows that missionary outreach is urgent. No fallen person has perfectly satisfied God's absolute justice by trying to live up to the moral law within. Given only general revelation, the best of us is not good enough.

Some Evangelicals seek to alleviate the awesome urgency to reach the unreached with the gospel by suggesting that people who never heard the gospel may be acceptable to God, not on the basis of works, but on the basis of their repentance for insufficient meritorious works. Even though they have never heard of Christ or his atonement and its provisions, this view suggests, they may be accepted through repentance without faith.[80] We ask, however, whether the Holy Spirit ever convicts of sin to bring about authentic repentance without also providentially directing missionaries so that the permanently repentant may hear and believe the gospel of Christ?

Of course God is free to bring the gospel to anyone at any time independently of human missionary agents, and we must not limit him. But we must respect what God has revealed about his freely chosen way of bringing a knowledge of Christ's provisions to the unreached. Although the end of Romans 10 alludes to the hearing of the universal revelation (vv. 18–20), the earlier verses make clear that people must call on Christ to be saved (v. 13) and so must believe in Christ and hear about Christ from a preacher in order to believe (v. 14).[81]

On the other extreme in the Far East were pietistic fundamentalists and neoorthodox missionaries who urgently proclaimed the person of Christ and the gospel but failed to have a point of contact with non-Christians. Fundamentalism has characteristically neglected to develop a doctrine of universal revelation. So fundamentalist missionaries were isolated from contact with the people they sought to reach. They failed to capitalize on their common knowledge and to learn of cultural points of contact. This led to one-directional communication and insensitivity to people's needs. As a result, the Christian message seemed meaningless and irrelevant. Reacting against ecumenical missions, some fundamentalists sought "to serve the Creator by ignoring his creation."[82]

Christian missionaries (and what Christian in this shrinking world does not communicate crossculturally?) need general revelation for points of contact with people in every culture on earth. But since general revelation is law, not gospel, every missionary urgently needs to preach the good news of grace in Christ, not the message of salvation by works.

What is the relationship between general and special revelation? It is not one of sheer contrast and opposition, as B. B. Warfield saw it, but "rather one of supplement and completion."[83] "All religion and all morality which has ever been in the world is of God. Whether natural or revealed, it is he who has given it; and it is he alone who has maintained it, yea, and will maintain it, enlarge and enriched to meet sinful man's clamant needs and renewed man's deeper desires. Both religion and morality are rooted in God, live in God, and in all the states of their development, and phases of their manifestation alike reflect man's essential relations to God—relations of dependence and obligation."[84]

As Lit-sen Chang more succinctly put it, "Although we thoroughly realize the absolute insufficiency of general revelation for salvation, nevertheless, we should also realize that general revelation has certain value for the Christian religions and that there is a close relationship between the two. Special revelation has incorporated, corrected, and interpreted general revelation."[85]

The specially revealed gospel is *not* suspended in air, so to speak; it presupposes the order of nature and speaks to life everywhere in the world at its ultimate level. Special revelation itself shows the connection between common and special grace, between the order of nature and the order of redemptive grace.

Not everything practiced in a non-Christian culture need be given up, then, as people receive Christ's perfect righteousness. All that evangelical missionaries need to ask people to give up is their sin. All the true and good elements of the former religion and culture by common grace can be incorporated in a Christian world view and way of life. The Christ who saves is the Christ who created and sustains all that is, whether visible or invisible, and by him all things "hold together" (Col. 1:16–17). So evangelical Christian missionaries need not limit themselves to the special revelation contained in Scripture or to Christian sources like Paul, Apollos or Cephas. "All things are yours, . . . the *world* or life or death or the present or the future—all are yours, and you are of Christ, and Christ is of God" (1 Cor. 3:21–23).

Evangelical Christian missionaries have a basis in general revelation for drawing as many nonredemptive analogies from a culture as possible for illustrating the truths of metaphysical dependence on God and moral accountability to God. And although illustrations of aspects of the gospel may be found in a culture, it may be misleading to call the analogies redemptive as has become popular since the exciting account of *Peace Child*. No analogies are in themselves redemptive, and to speak of "redemptive analogies" from nature and culture may be misleading in terms of the conclusions drawn above.

REVIEW QUESTIONS

To Help Relate and Apply
Each Section in This Chapter

1. *Briefly state the classical problem* this chapter addresses and indicate reasons why genuine inquiry into it is important for your world view and your existence personally and socially.

2. *Objectively summarize the influential answers* given to this problem in history as hypotheses to be tested. Be able to compare and contrast their real similarities and differences (not merely verbal similarities or differences).

3. *Highlight the primary biblical evidence* on which to decide among views—evidence found in the relevant teachings of the major divisions of Scripture—and decide for yourself which historical hypothesis (or synthesis of historical views) provides the most consistent and adequate account of the primary biblical data.

4. *Formulate in your own words your doctrinal conviction* in a logically consistent and adequate way, organizing your conclusions in ways you can explain clearly, support biblically, and communicate effectively to your spouse, children, friends, Bible class, or congregation.

5. *Defend your view* as you would to adherents of the alternative views, showing that the other views are logi-

cally less consistent and factually faced with more difficulties than your view in accounting for the givens, not only of special revelation but also of human experience in general.

6. *Explore the differences the viability of your conviction can make in your life.* Then test your understanding of the viability of your view by asking, "Can I live by it authentically (unhypocritically) in relation to God and to others in my family, church, vocation, neighborhood, city, nation, and world?"

MINISTRY PROJECTS

To Help Communicate This Doctrine in Christian Service

1. *Memorize one major verse or passage* that in its context teaches the heart of this doctrine and may serve as a text from which to preach, teach, or lead small group studies on the topic. The memorized passages from each chapter will build a body of content useful also for meditation and reference in informal discussions.

2. *Formulate the major idea of the doctrine in one sentence* based on the passage memorized. This idea should be useful as the major thesis of either a lesson for a class (junior high to adult) or a message for a church service.

3. *State the specific purpose or goal of your doctrinal lesson or message.* Your purpose should be more than informative. It should show why Christians need to accept this truth and live by it (unhypocritically). For teaching purposes, list indicators that would show to what extent class members have grasped the truth presented.

4. *Outline your message or lesson in complete sentences.* Indicate how you would support the truth of the doctrine's central ideas and its relevance to life and service. Incorporate elements from this chapter's historical, biblical, systematic, apologetic, and practical sections selected according to the value they have for your audience.

5. *List applications of the doctrine* for communicating the difference this conviction makes in life (for sermons, lessons, small-group Bible studies, or family devotional Bible studies). Applications should make clear what the doctrine is, why one needs to know it, and how it will make differences in thinking. Then show how the difference in thought will lead to differences in values, priorities, attitudes, speech, and personal action. Consider also the doctrine's possible significance for family, church, neighborhood, city, regional, and national actions.

6. *Start a file and begin collecting illustrations* of this doctrine's central idea, the points in your outline, and your applications.

7. *Write out your own doctrinal statement on this subject in one paragraph* (in half a page or less). To work toward a comprehensive doctrinal statement, collect your formulations based on a study of each chapter of *Integrative Theology*. As your own statement of Christian doctrine grows, you will find it personally strengthening and useful when you are called on for your beliefs in general and when you apply for service with churches, mission boards, and other Christian organizations. Any who seek ordination to Christian ministry will need a comprehensive doctrinal statement that covers the broad scope of theology.

CHAPTER 3

DIVINE REVELATION THROUGH CHRIST, PROPHETS, AND APOSTLES

Divine Revelation Through Christ, Prophets, and Apostles

THE PROBLEM: HOW DOES A MAN, WOMAN, OR CHILD, CREATED AND LOVED BY GOD, COME TO KNOW THE LORD OF THE UNIVERSE IN A PERSONAL, SAVING RELATION?

In the preceding chapter we showed that by means of general revelation God reveals himself to all people at all times and in all places so that his existence and something of his character and moral demands are known. No person, we have shown, is without a rudimentary knowledge of God and the moral law. But we have also seen that due to the debilitating effects of sin on the mind and will, God's revelation in nature, history, and the implanted moral law fails to accomplish the purpose for which it was given. Scripture plainly testifies that, motivated by a darkened heart, sinners repudiate the rudimentary knowledge of God mediated by general revelation and devote themselves to idols. Thus in the end, general revelation does not save; it serves only to condemn.

Consequently, if anyone is to be saved, the sovereign God must move to communicate further dimensions of his hidden person and redemptive plan. No amount of inductive inference from God's past activity can bring to light his inner purposes. No amount of deduction from permanent principles of operation can make known salvific grace. Since manifestly not all people are saved, a number of important questions follow. To whom does God disclose his redemptive grace? Furthermore, what is it that God reveals? Does he disclose himself alone? Or does he disclose his saving plan as well? The problem for the thoughtful Christian, then, is to determine by what means God has made known his saving purposes and how finite, alienated persons can identify and appropriate the several modes of special revelation.

A further issue of considerable importance today is whether God in the present continues to give added special revelation to his people. Did special revelation end with the exaltation of Christ and the close of the canon of Scripture, or does God continue to reveal heretofore undisclosed aspects of his redemptive purposes through specially appointed spokespersons?

The tendency in recent theology, both Protestant and Roman Catholic, has been to deny that objective knowledge or intellectual concepts are revealed by God and to insist that saving revelation takes the form of ineffable encounters. One authority, for example, states, "Nowhere in the Bible is revelation the disclosure of a transcendental mystery, or an element of information."[1] What is revealed, most non-evangelical scholars assert, is not information about God, but God himself in ecstatic experience. Thus a primary issue in regard to special revelation is whether God's self-disclosure is propositional or nonpropositional, or perhaps something of both.

Clearly special revelation is foundational to the entire Christian scheme of things. It constitutes the prerequisite for the formulation of a theology that is properly Christian. Moreover, it forms the basis whereby a person comes to know God savingly, to worship him, and to serve him meaningfully in life.

ALTERNATIVE PROPOSALS IN THE CHURCH

The sources of information about God's redemptive plan are so important to every person that it is not surprising that over the centuries strong differences about them have arisen in the church.

Roman Catholic Scholasticism

Traditional Roman Catholic theologians taught that natural knowledge of God is supplemented by a supernatural knowledge mediated by the teachings of the prophets, apostles, and Jesus Christ. God's redemptive revelation preserved in Scripture is enriched by oral tradition and interpreted by the teaching office of the church.

Thomas Aquinas postulated both an ascent to God by the light of reason and nature and a descent by God in the form of revelation to be received by faith. Revelation transcends but does not contradict truths about God secured by reason. Aquinas affirmed that God gave saving revelation in the events of sacred history, in the words of chosen prophets and apostles, and supremely in the enfleshment of God's eternal Son. The permanent record of saving revelation was inerrantly recorded on the pages of the Bible. Aquinas stressed the cognitive character of special revelation. What God supernaturally revealed for faith's acceptance is described as "truths that exceed reason," "knowledge," "doctrine," and "sacred science." Aquinas, however, held that the Bible and the teachings of the church constitute two sources (*principia*) of Christian belief. Later Roman Catholic authorities were more insistent that church tradition represents a second source of revelation.

The Council of Trent opposed the *sola scriptura* principle of the Protestant Reformers and insisted that divine revelations were preserved both in Scripture and in ecclesiastical tradition. Thus the Council stated that the gospel, which is "the source of all saving truth and rule of conduct," is contained "in the written and unwritten traditions that have come down to us, having been received from the apostles from the mouth of Christ Himself, or from the apostles by the dictation of the Holy Spirit, and have been transmitted as it were from hand to hand . . . and preserved in continuous succession in the Catholic church."[2]

Enlightenment Skepticism

Enlightenment theologians and their modern disciples deny the possibility and necessity of supernatural revelation. Human reason, experience, and the scientific method are judged sufficient to provide modern people with the knowledge needed to forge their future. Spinoza, a pantheist, attacked the Christian concept of propositional revelation. The Word of God, he argued, cannot be captured in a book, in paper and ink. Enlightenment skepticism regarding special revelation was greatly abetted by Hume's rejection of miracles and his radical empiricist claim that theological statements, being non-verifiable by the senses, lack meaning. Moreover, Kant's denial of theoretical or metaphysical knowledge of God in favor of practical knowledge struck at the very foundations of the classical model of special revelation.

The consistent deists denied the reality of special revelation. Following the lead of Lord Herbert of Cherbury, they maintained that divine revelation to specific people at certain times conflicts with God's all-sufficient revelation in the Creation. As put by Matthew Tindal, "Can revelation . . . add anything to a religion thus absolutely perfect, universal, and immutable?"[3] Special revelation was judged unnecessary, since the rational mind and the scientific method could uncover all truth.

The German rationalists, following the deductive reasoning of Leibnitz and Wolff, likewise undermined the validity of special revelation. G. E. Lessing, for example, claimed: "All revealed religion is nothing but a reconfirmation of the religion of reason. Either it has no mysteries, or, if it does, it is indifferent whether the Christian combines them with one another, or with none at all."[4] Lessing envisaged revelation as the natural process whereby God effects his educative program for the human race.

In his book, *Has Christianity a Revelation?* F. Gerald Downing protests the intellectualist position that argues for the attainment of clear knowledge of God. Downing insists that from the biblical perspective God cannot be said to have revealed himself. "If God intended to 'reveal himself' in Christ, in the events of his life and death and resurrection and in his teaching, he failed."[5] The word "revelation" is best reserved for the future consummation.

Kierkegaard and Neoorthodoxy

Neoorthodox authorities and proponents of the so-called "biblical theology" maintain that God's saving purposes are revealed through mighty acts in the history of Israel and the church, and supremely in the Christ-event. In the present, revelation consists in the event of God speaking to a person in Jesus Christ through the medium of the biblical witness.

Kierkegaard inaugurated this emphasis with his postulate of the "infinite qualitative difference" between God and man, which implied the incomprehensibility of God to finite minds. Since God is unfathomable to discursive reason and the emotions, Kierkegaard insisted that the abyss between eternity and time must be closed by God himself. Thus the focus of God's revelation was said to be the Incarnation of the God-man in the form of a servant. God is known, not by an analysis of nature or history, but by the radical inbreaking of God in Jesus Christ. But given the severe chasm between eternity and time, Jesus Christ appears to the mind as an offense and a scandal, indeed, as the absolute paradox. Thus God's revelation must be received by a radical and passionate leap of faith.

Barth, following Kierkegaard, insisted that the transcendent Word is the only revelation. God discloses himself, not through propositional information, but only as the Ineffable breaks into a person's existence in an experience of crisis, evoking the response of decision and trust. In Barth's own words:

> Real revelation puts man in God's presence. . . . It is the revelation which is attested to ourselves. . . . An objective revelation as such, a revelation which consists statically only in its sign-giving, in the objectivity of Scripture, preaching and sacrament, a revelation which does not penetrate to man: a revelation of this

kind is an idol like all the rest, and perhaps the worst of idols.[6]

Barth grants that God worked through mighty events in the history of Israel and the church. But he posits revelation, not in the bare historical events (*Historie*), but in the events interpreted according to the faith response of the believer (*Geschichte*). Thus for Barth revelation is a noncognitive inner confrontation with the Divine, rather than the rational communication of information. Moreover, revelation is an ongoing event in the believer's experience, rather than a "frozen" deposit from the past. Consequently the Bible is not itself revelation, but is only a fallible witness to revelatory events and encounters. Barth concludes that "when divine revelation meets us and we respond in faith and obedience the Bible becomes the Word of God."[7]

Brunner developed in greater detail the notion of revelation as an "I-Thou" personal encounter. "Divine revelation is not a book or a doctrine; the revelation is God Himself in His self-manifestation within history. Revelation is something that happens."[8] Through the fallible biblical witness to past revelations (i.e., theophanies, dreams, visions, words of prophets and apostles, and the life of Christ), God sovereignly brings the individual face to face with himself as Lord and as Love. In that moment of personal encounter the individual participates in the mysterious event of revelation. For Brunner, as for Barth, the human, errant Bible becomes the Word of God as the Sovereign graciously speaks to people through it.

H. Richard Niebuhr forged a path between neoorthodoxy and liberalism in *The Meaning of Revelation* (1941). Rejecting the classical view as formal and static, Niebuhr viewed revelation as relational, contextual, and relative. Revelation is relational in that its locus is the "I-Thou" encounter that invites the person's trust and devotion. Revelation is contextual in the sense that Jesus and the biblical writers were sufficiently bound by their culture to teach falsehoods. Finally, revelation is relative in that, because culturally skewed, it is not objectively true for all people of all times. "Such a theology of revelation is objectively relativistic, proceeding with confidence in the independent reality of what is seen, though recognizing that its assertions about that reality are meaningful only to those who look upon it from the same standpoint."[9]

Hans Küng maintains that God revealed himself to believers in Israel and the church as "I," thus becoming for them a "Thou"—i.e., a subject rather than a predicate. The biblical writers were "witnesses of faith" to their revelatory encounters with the "Wholly Other." The Scriptures therefore are not divine revelation; they are human testimonies ("unequivocally man's word") to past revelatory experiences. Nevertheless man's word in the Bible *becomes* God's Word for those who submit in faith to its testimony. "For someone who accepts the invitation . . . the Bible does not remain man's word, but—despite all the problems—becomes God's assisting, liberating, saving Word."[10]

Pannenberg's Revelation as History

Wolfhart Pannenberg proposes that God has provided revelation in the course of world history and chiefly in the resurrection of Christ, both of which are explicated by the historical method. Against the position of his mentor Barth that faith is suprahistorical, Pannenberg strives to ground faith in the verifiable basis of universal world history. Appealing to Hegel's vision of world history as an indirect revelation of God, Pannenberg insists that the only permissible revelation is the single revelation that is identical with the totality of history. *Heilsgeschichte*, he argues, created a false dichotomy between the narrow stream of special redemptive history and the broader stream of secular history. Pannenberg thus defines revelation as the temporal process of a history that is not yet completed, open to all, and open to a future that is anticipated in the history and teachings of Jesus. Pannenberg maintains that the end of history had its "advance-enactment" in the life and resurrection of Jesus Christ. Through Christ's resurrection the God of Israel has substantiated his Deity in an ultimate way and so is manifest as the God of all mankind.

Theistic Existentialism

Existentialist theologians such as Bultmann and Macquarrie view revelation as an ongoing process in which a person, when confronted with the mythical kerygma, realizes the meaning of Being and is thereby transformed to a condition of authentic existence. Following Heidegger, Bultmann rejects both "objective knowledge" that involves an "I-It" relation and "personal knowledge" that centers on the "I-Thou" relation in favor of "primordial knowledge" that corresponds to the demands of being (as understood by the existentialist tradition). Revelation consequently is not the transmission of information (orthodoxy) nor the soul's meeting with God (neoorthodoxy). Revelation is the encounter one has with the kerygma, whereby human eyes are opened to the possibility of true being. Argues Bultmann:

> What has been revealed? Nothing at all, so far as the question concerning revelation asks for doctrines—doctrines, say, that no man could have discovered for himself—or for mysteries that become known once for all as soon as they are communicated. On the other hand, however, *everything has been revealed insofar as man's eyes are opened concerning*

his own existence and he is once again able to understand himself.[11]

In the existentialist schema, revelation is entirely horizontal. It is an experience that occurs *within* the human subject as self-understanding and a new mode of being are grasped by faith. Moreover, revelation is never completed, for the encounter and resultant insight may be repeated again and again.

Most Church Fathers, Reformers, and Evangelicals

Many leading authorities within the church insist that God has revealed himself to particular persons at specific times through personal encounters and miraculous deeds that are explicated by inspired, truth-bearing propositions. The Bible, as the record of God's purposes in deeds and words among men, is an authoritative revelation of God's heart.

Like many other church fathers, Irenaeus posited revelation in the theophanies of the Old Testament, the law of Moses, the utterances of prophets and apostles, the person of Christ, and the Rule of Faith. The pinnacle of redemptive revelation was Christ incarnate, who mediated sure knowledge of God. Athanasius observed that since general revelation was insufficient to lead people to salvation, God made a higher disclosure. He noted that if the subjects of a king should go astray, "he warns them by letters, and often sends to them friends, or if need be, he comes in person to put them to rebuke in the last resort by his presence."[12] Likewise God has revealed himself to sinners by giving the law, by sending prophets and apostles to deliver heavenly instruction, and supremely, by his self-manifestation in Christ. Consequently, "they who would not know him from his providence and rule over all things, may even from the works done by his actual body know the Word of God which is in the body, and through him the Father."[13]

Augustine noted that God specially revealed himself to the patriarchs, to Moses in the burning bush and the giving of the law, and to the Old Testament prophets. In the fullness of time, however, God laid bare his person and his saving purposes through the observable life, death, and resurrection of Christ. Spirit-illumined prophets and apostles bore witness to Christ, and their testimony is inerrantly recorded in Holy Scripture. Said Augustine, "We were too weak by unaided reason to find out the truth, and for this cause needed the authority of holy writings."[14] For Augustine, reason (*ratio*) illumined by the Logos attains from the inscripturated data of special revelation a fund of knowledge (*sapientia*) about God's hidden character and redemptive purposes. This knowledge about God's saving provision in the incarnate Christ (*scientia*) provides the objective basis for faith's decision. Faith, according to Augustine, is not blind but rests on knowledge of the object to be believed and the reasons why one is to believe.

Calvin similarly held that God revealed himself to the Fathers by means of oracles and visions, through the law of Moses, by the preaching of prophets and apostles, and paramountly through the living Word, Jesus Christ. The sum of saving wisdom is recorded in Holy Scripture, which descended, as it were, from God in heaven. "We must come to the Word, where God is truly and vividly described to us from his works, while these very works are appraised not by our depraved judgment but by the rule of eternal truth."[15] Only through the written Word that testifies to Christ, the living Word, does the sinner gain knowledge of God as Redeemer.

Carl F. H. Henry describes revela-

tion as the "critical center" of the crisis in modern theology.[16] Revelation, defined as God's free and personal communication of himself that offers persons privileged communication with the Creator, flows entirely from God's free purpose and grace. The modalities of special revelation include unique saving acts in the history of Israel and the church, the communication of the meaning of such events to chosen prophets and apostles, and consummately the incarnation, crucifixion, and resurrection of Christ. Holy Scripture, which contains the inspired interpretation of all God's disclosures, is itself supernatural revelation. Henry underscores the rational intelligibility of the oral and written special revelation: "God's revelation is rational communication conveyed in intelligible ideas and meaningful words, that is, in conceptual-verbal form."[17]

Further discussion of special revelation from an Evangelical perspective can be found in the writings of B. B. Warfield,[18] and Millard J. Erickson.[19] Valuable monographs on the subject include Bernard Ramm's *Special Revelation and the Word of God*[20] and Ronald Nash's *The Word of God and the Mind of Man*.[21]

BIBLICAL TEACHING

Pentateuch

Divine revelation to specific persons at particular times and places began immediately following Adam and Eve's fall into sin. In Eden God announced the goal of all ensuing revelations, namely, the person and mission of Jesus Christ (Gen. 3:15). The *protoevangelium,* as this declaration is called, attests the fact that the religion of Israel and the church would be rooted in special revelation.

An important modality of special revelation in the Pentateuch is *divine speech*. When irreligion was rife, God spoke to Noah and divulged his plan to destroy the world by a mighty flood (Gen. 6:13). God supernaturally communicated the design of the ark and told Noah how to use it to preserve life during the forty-day deluge. Later God called Abram to Canaan and gave him promises that served as the core of subsequent Old Testament revelations (Gen. 12:1–4). At Horeb God spoke to Moses from the burning bush and communicated his intention to deliver the Israelites from Egyptian bondage (Exod. 3:1–4:17). At Sinai God not only communicated verbally the Ten Commandments (Exod. 20:3–17) but also gave Moses the extensive Law code (Exod. 20:22–23:33) and instructions for building and furnishing the tabernacle (Exod. 25–27).

In the Pentateuch God also disclosed himself through dreams, visions, and theophanies. The dream (*hªlôm*) was a common mode of revelation in the patriarchal era when written revelation did not exist. Thus Jacob had a dream at Bethel in which God confirmed the covenant made with Abraham (Gen. 28:10–17). Joseph dreamed a dream that depicted his prominence over his brothers (Gen. 37:5–9). Revelatory dreams were also given to non-Israelites, viz., Abimelech (Gen. 20:3–6), Laban (Gen. 31:24), and Pharaoh (Gen. 41:1–7). Far from being abstruse mystical experiences, these dreams, when rightly interpreted, conveyed objective knowledge of God's unfolding purposes.

Whereas the dream generally occurred during sleep, the revelatory vision (*hazôn*) commonly was given to one awake. Visions were given almost exclusively to holy men in the service of God. In visions God confirmed his covenant with Abraham (Gen. 15:1), directed Jacob to go down to Egypt, and promised him that he would bring Israel out as a nation (Gen. 46:2–4).

God gave Balaam a vision that conveyed divine guidance and instruction (Num. 22:31–35).

A higher modality of revelation was the theophany, or visible manifestation of God. The angel of the Lord told Hagar of the fortunes of her soon-to-be-born son Ishmael (Gen. 16:7–13). It is clear from verse 13 that the angel of the Lord was Yahweh in his self-manifestation. The three men who conversed with Abraham at the entrance to his tent (Gen. 18:1–5) were likewise a theophany. The men are plainly identified as "the LORD" (vv. 10, 13–14), yet two of the men are further designated as "angels" (Gen. 19:1) sent by God to execute his purposes (Gen. 19:13). The identity of the angel who encountered Moses in the flaming fire at Horeb is given as "the God of Abraham, the God of Isaac and the God of Jacob" (Exod. 3:6). The Lord who visibly manifested himself unfolded to his servant plans for Israel's deliverance from Egypt (vv. 7–22). The theophany was thus accompanied by intelligible words of command and encouragement. The pillar of cloud and the pillar of fire that guided Israel on their journey through Sinai (Exod. 13:21–22; cf. 24:16–17) likewise were visible symbols of God's presence with his people. When God said to Moses, "My Presence will go with you" (Exod. 33:14), Scripture identifies the "Presence" (*pānîm*) as the angel of the Lord (Isa. 63:9), that is, as God himself mediated to the human senses.

Special revelation in the Old Testament also came in the form of mighty acts wrought on the stage of Israel's history. All events, in a certain sense, are revealing. But God was operative in Israel's history in a way that he is not at work in the general history of the world.

God specially revealed himself and his saving purposes through the plagues meted out on Egypt (Exod. 7–10). Nine times God did "miraculous signs" (*môs^etîm*) and "wonders" (*'ôtôt*) that Pharaoh and his magicians were powerless to oppose (Exod. 7:3).[22] Israel's passage through the Sea of Reeds (Exod. 14:13–31) after their release from Egypt was another instance of revelation as miraculous event. Yahweh announced in advance that the purpose of the miracle was that "the Egyptians will know that I am the LORD" (Exod. 14:4, 18). As the sea retreated, allowing the Israelites safe passage, and as the same waters caved in on the pursuing Egyptians, God's power, holiness, and salvation were openly displayed.

The judgments God meted out on his disobedient people during their sojourn in the Sinai peninsula (Num. 11:1–3; 12:10–12) were revelatory of God's justice and hatred of sin. Likewise, the forty years of wandering in the wilderness was a revelatory event (Num. 14:33).

Historical Books

In the historical books, God gave commands, provided information, and communicated promises. His special revelations to Joshua are introduced by the formula "The LORD said to Joshua" (Josh. 1:1; 3:7; 4:1, et al.). The Lord also spoke to Samuel and instructed him to anoint Saul as Israel's first king. Later, when the disobedient Saul was rejected as king, God directed Samuel to identify David as Israel's next king (1 Sam. 16:1–12). When David sought to build the temple, the Lord told Nathan that David's son Solomon would construct it, but God promised David a dynasty that would endure forever. The account closes with the words "Nathan reported to David all the words of this entire revelation" (1 Chron. 17:15).

In the same period revelation also came in the form of theophany. Near

Jericho, Joshua saw standing before him with drawn sword "the commander of the LORD's army" (Josh. 5:13–15). This military figure, identified by the text as "the LORD" (*Yahweh*, Josh. 6:2), delivered instructions to Joshua concerning the march his forces were to make around Jericho. Gideon likewise was comforted by an angel of the Lord (Judg. 6:11–24), whom the Hebrew warrior designates as the "Sovereign LORD" (v. 22). The Lord, through the modality of the theophany, imparted a message to encourage Gideon in his battle with the Midianites.

The historical books also attest revelation in the form of space-time events with accompanying interpretation. The miracle that parted the flood waters of the Jordan (Josh. 3:14–4:18) took place so that people might fear the all-powerful God (Josh. 4:24). Israel's defeat by the Canaanites at Ai (Josh. 7:1–24), together with God's interpretation of the disaster, revealed the heinousness of sin. The contest on Carmel between Elijah and the prophets of Baal (1 Kings 18:16–39), in which the man of God called the fire of God down from heaven, prompted the confession of the onlookers, "The LORD—he is God! The LORD—he is God!" (1 Kings 18:39). Israel's exile at the hand of Assyria (2 Kings 17) and Judah's captivity at the hand of Babylon (2 Kings 24–25), as the commentary on the judgments attests, were revelatory events in which Yahweh's holiness and anger were openly displayed.

Wisdom and Poetry

The Book of Job makes clear that finite beings of themselves cannot penetrate the hidden reality of God. Thus Zophar poses the question, "Can you fathom the mysteries of God? Can you probe the limits of the Almighty? They are higher than the heavens—what can we do? They are deeper than the depths of the grave—what can you know?'' (Job 11:7–8). Since people cannot find God by themselves (Job 23:8–9), God must initiate contact through his special self-disclosure.

Commonplace in the Psalms is the theme of God's redemptive revelation to Israel through mighty acts of deliverance and judgment. Thus Psalms 77–78, 103, and 105–107 rehearse God's manifold saving acts, such as the giving of the Law at Sinai, the career of Joseph, the plagues on Egypt, the passage through the Sea of Reeds, the miraculous guidance in the wilderness, and the capture of Canaan. In describing these saving events the singers of Israel use such words as "wonders" (*môp^etîm*, Pss. 78:43; 105:27), "miracles" (*p^elā'îm*, Pss. 77:11; 78:12), "judgments" (*mišpātîm*, Pss. 97:8; 105:5, 7), "wonderful deeds" (*niplā'ôt*, twenty-seven times in the Psalms, e.g., Pss. 26:7; 75:1; 106:22), "miraculous signs" (*'ôtôt*, Pss. 78:43; 105:27), and "awesome deeds" (*nôrā'ôt*, Pss. 65:5; 106:22). Through these works God's character and will were powerfully impressed on the hearts of his people.

God revealed his purposes to Israel by the direct disclosure of laws, statutes, and commands (Ps. 78:5). God distinguished Israel from all the other nations by disclosing his word to them. "He has revealed his word to Jacob, his laws and decrees to Israel. He has done this for no other nation; they do not know his laws" (Ps. 147:19–20). God's specially revealed precepts and ordinances effect spiritual revitalization in the believer (Pss. 19:7; 119:93), impart spiritual understanding (Pss. 19:7; 119:104, 130), give peace to troubled consciences (Ps. 119:165), and implant the hope of final salvation (Ps. 119:81).

The Prophets

Of old God gave his word to chosen prophets. Thus the prophetic literature contains frequent introductory formulas, such as, "The LORD came to me" (Jer. 1:2, 4; Jonah 1:1; Zech. 1:1, 7). While worshiping in the temple Isaiah heard the exalted Lord say, "Whom shall I send? And who will go for us?" (Isa. 6:8). When Isaiah volunteered, the Lord spoke to the prophet the message he wanted delivered to the people. God spoke to Jeremiah, conveying his call, purposes, and message (Jer. 1:4–2:3; 11:1–23, et al.). Likewise, God spoke his word to other prophetic messengers (Ezek. 2:1–3, 8; Hos. 1:2–11; Hab. 1:5–11). God spoke in the Old Testament both audibly and inaudibly. The important point is that his revelation through speech involved the communication of objective knowledge. Biblical faith affirms, with Amos, "The Sovereign LORD has spoken" (Amos 3:8)!

Not only did God speak *to* the prophets, he also spoke *through* them. The utterances of the prophets constitute the final modality of special revelation in the Old Testament. The prophets predicted events that would come to pass in the future (Isa. 42:9; Amos 5:27; Obad. 19), but they also proclaimed the Word and the will of God (Deut. 18:18). Thus the prophetic ministry involved both foretelling and forthtelling. With respect to the latter aspect of the prophet's ministry, God put his words in Jeremiah's mouth (Jer. 1:9) so that they became to him as "a burning fire" (Jer. 20:9). Similarly God sent Ezekiel to the obstinate Israelites armed with his message (Ezek. 2:4). Ezekiel must eat the scroll on which were written the words of God (Ezek. 3:1–3). This symbolism teaches that the Word of God was so much a part of Ezekiel's being that the prophet's message and God's message were one and the same.

When Hosea opened his mouth he said, "Hear the word of the LORD, you Israelites" (Hos. 4:1). Joel's prophetic message is identified as "The word of the LORD that came to Joel" (Joel 1:1).

So also, Amos's message to the northern kingdom was punctuated by the oft-repeated phrase, "This is what the LORD says" (Amos 1:3, 6, 9, et al.). Similar epithets from Obadiah, Nahum, Micah, Haggai, and Zechariah prove that the proclamation of the prophets was identical with the Word of God. The prophecies of Nahum (1:1) and Habakkuk (1:1) are specifically designated an "oracle" (*dābār*), namely, an utterance from the mouth of God himself.

"Word of God" in the Old Testament thus evolved into a technical term for the prophetic proclamation of God's truth. This word was first spoken by the Spirit-anointed prophets and later set down in writing. Hence not only the prophetic utterances but also the prophets' writings are forms of special revelation. In the same era Nebuchadnezzar had dreams (Dan. 2:1; 4:5–18), the meaning of which was revealed to Daniel in a night vision (Dan. 2:19, 31–45). Later God gave Daniel a revelatory dream and vision (Dan. 7) in which four beasts came out of the sea, representing the four world empires that would precede the eternal kingdom of the Son of Man. Through visions God called persons to a prophetic vocation (Isa. 6:1–10), communicated the content of the prophets' message (Isa. 1:1; Jer. 1:11–17; Amos 7:1–9), pointed out the sinfulness of the nation (Ezek. 8:1–18), and comforted God's people (Zech. 1:8–17; 2:1–5). In both dreams and visions specific truths were imparted.

The prophets testify that God made himself known through mighty deeds in Israel's history. God's preservation of Daniel in the den of lions (Dan. 6:16–27) was a miraculous work that elicited a remarkable confession from Darius the Persian king (Dan. 6:26–27). Moreover, God's holy name would be vindicated when the sovereign Lord established his people back in the land.

Israel's return from exile thus was a revelatory event (Ezek. 36:24–38).

Although rich in content, special revelation in the Old Testament was preparatory and incomplete (1 Peter 1:10–12). The consummate revelation of God's saving purposes awaited the coming of Christ, the living Word of God.

Synoptic Gospels

The modalities of special revelation in the synoptic Gospels are diverse. First, there is the direct revelation of God through dreams, visions, and theophanies. An angel of the Lord (identified as Gabriel) appeared to Zechariah bearing the message that his wife Elizabeth would bear a son John and that this Spirit-anointed servant would pave the way for the coming of the Lord (Luke 1:11–20). The same angel appeared to Mary and told her that she would conceive through the power of the Spirit and give birth to the Son of God (Luke 1:26–38). An angel of the Lord appeared to Joseph in a dream (Matt. 1:20–24) and to shepherds near Bethlehem (Luke 2:9–15), communicating additional messages. When Jesus was baptized by John, the Spirit of God descended on him in the form of a dove and the Father spoke the audible words, "This is my Son, whom I love; with him I am well pleased" (Matt. 3:16–17).

Second, God revealed himself to specific persons at particular times and places through Jesus' miracles. In the prologue to his Gospel, Luke wrote, "Many have undertaken to draw up an account of the things [*ta pragmata*, i.e., events or deeds] that have been fulfilled among us" (Luke 1:1). In her song of praise Mary uttered the words "The Mighty One has done great things [*megala*] for me" (Luke 1:49). Peter later declared to the Jews that Jesus was "accredited by God to you by miracles [*dynameis*], wonders [*terata*] and signs [*sēmeia*]" (Acts 2:22). Jesus demonstrated his power over nature by the miracle of calming the storm on the Sea of Galilee (Mark 4:37–41), over the consequences of sin by healing people of numerous afflictions and diseases (Mark 5:22–29; 8:22–25), and over sin itself by exorcising demons and forgiving offenses against God (Matt. 9:2–8; Mark 5:2–13). The Gospels attest that the miracles done by Jesus affirmed his compassion for people, his mighty power, and his heavenly authority. Some who witnessed his mighty revelatory works confessed him to be the Son of God (Matt. 14:33). The supreme event that demonstrated Jesus to be the all-powerful Son of God (cf. Rom. 1:4) was his resurrection from death and the grave (Matt. 28:1–10 and parallels).

Third, special revelation in the Synoptics also took the form of a direct communication of truth from God. The Holy Spirit disclosed (*chrēmatizō*, to "impart a revelation")[23] to Simeon that he would live to see the Christ of God (Luke 2:26). After his pronouncement of judgment on the unrepentant cities Jesus praised the Father because he had "hidden these things from the wise and learned, and revealed [*apokalyptō*] them to little children" (Matt. 11:25). After Peter had confessed Jesus as the Christ and the Son of God, the Lord commended him with the words, "This was not revealed [*apokalyptō*] to you by man, but by my Father in heaven" (Matt. 16:17). The verb *apokalyptō*, which occurs twenty-six times in the New Testament, signifies the removal of a covering and hence the disclosure of what was previously hidden or unknown.

Fourth, the Synoptics represent Jesus and his teaching as an important modality of special revelation. Filled with the Holy Spirit, Simeon cradled the infant Jesus in his arms and described him as "a light for revelation [*apokalypsis*] to the Gentiles and for

glory to your people Israel" (Luke 2:32). The noun *apokalypsis* occurs eighteen times in the New Testament in the sense of a divine disclosure or revelation. In language reminiscent of John's Gospel, Matthew observes that by virtue of Jesus' filial relation to God he is eminently capable of revealing the Father to those he chooses (Matt. 11:27). When Jesus in the synagogue read from Isaiah 61:1–2 and applied to himself the words "The Spirit of the LORD is on me, because he has anointed me to preach good news to the poor," we conclude that both his teaching and his deeds were vehicles of special revelation (cf. Acts 3:22).

Primitive Christianity/Acts

An important modality of revelation in Acts is the vision, often accompanied by messages mediated by an angel of the Lord or the Holy Spirit. In Acts 10:3–8 Cornelius had a vision of an angel of God (described as "a man in shining clothes," v. 30) who instructed him to send for Peter. The next day Peter had a vision and heard the voice of God telling him not to despise what God had made clean (10:9–16; cf. v. 28). While Peter was reflecting on this vision, the Holy Spirit told him to receive the messengers who were sent to him (vv. 19–20; cf. 11:12). When Peter arrived at Caesarea, Cornelius urged him to relate "everything the Lord has commanded you to tell us" (v. 33). Whereupon Peter replied, "You know the message God sent to the people of Israel" (v. 36).

Elsewhere in Acts Stephen had a revelatory vision of the heavenly Jesus (Acts 7:55–56), and Saul had a vision of the glorified Christ who told him of his purpose to make him an apostle (9:3–6; 22:6–11). Thereafter God gave Ananias a vision and instructed him to lay hands on Saul so that the latter might receive the Holy Spirit (9:10–18). Later Paul had a vision of a man of Macedonia urging the apostle to preach the gospel in that region (16:9-10). When certain Jews opposed Paul's ministry in Corinth, the Lord spoke to the missionaries in a vision with words of spiritual encouragement (18:9-10).

In the ministry of the apostolic church an angel of the Lord gave instructions to the apostles who were freed from jail (Acts 5:19-20), spoke to Philip (8:26-29), and gave words of assurance to Paul aboard the storm-tossed ship (27:23-26). Similarly the Holy Spirit instructed the church at Antioch to set apart Barnabas and Saul for the work of the ministry (13:2, 4) and warned Paul of impending hardships (20:23). The Lord himself spoke to Paul in Jerusalem, informing the apostle of what lay in store for him in Rome (23:11).

A second modality of special revelation in Acts is found in the miracles God wrought through the apostles. Luke reports that "The apostles performed many miraculous signs [sēmeia] and wonders [terata] among the people" (Acts 5:12; cf. 4:30; 6:8). The outpouring of the Holy Spirit at Pentecost (2:1-4), accompanied by strong winds, tongues of fire, and spontaneous utterances in foreign languages, was a striking revelation of the power and holiness of God. When the Jews assembled in Jerusalem heard the Spirit-anointed Christians speak, they remarked, "we hear them declaring the wonders [ta megaleia] of God in our own tongues" (2:11). Peter stated that these things happened in fulfillment of the prophecy of Joel (2:28-32), namely, that in the latter days God "will show wonders [terata] in the heaven above and signs [sēmeia] on the earth below" (2:19). Thus Peter's healing of the crippled beggar (3:1-8), the judgment meted out on Ananias and Sapphira (5:1-11), and the resuscitation of Eutychus at Troas (20:7-10) were miraculous works that

certified Jesus as the Son of God and the apostles as his authoritative spokesmen.

Finally, the Spirit-given message of the apostles was itself revelatory. Luke relates that after being filled with the Holy Spirit the early Christians "spoke the Word of God boldly" (Acts 4:31). The preaching of Peter and John in Samaria (8:25), the teaching and preaching of Barnabas and Paul on Cyprus (13:7), in Pisidian Antioch (13:46), and at Syrian Antioch (15:35) are all designated as "the word of God." Luke describes the content of the apostles' preaching and teaching as "God's salvation" (28:28). The oral teaching of the apostles in due course was set down in writing and valued equally with the Old testament Scriptures.

The Pauline Corpus

Nothing is more certain than the fact that Paul's ministry was rooted in supernatural revelation. Divine revelation to Paul was first of all subjective in character. Reflecting on his Damascus road experience, Paul asked, "Have I not seen Jesus our Lord?" (1 Cor. 9:1; cf. 15:8). Some six or eight years after his conversion Paul was taken up by the Spirit into Paradise where he was given visions and revelations from the Lord and "heard inexpressible things, things that man is not permitted to tell" (2 Cor. 12:1-4). But Paul's teaching also focused on revelation that was objective in character. Defending his apostleship, Paul claimed that the gospel he preached was received by revelation from Christ (Gal. 1:12). A theme often enunciated in Paul is that God disclosed to him "the mystery hidden for long ages past" (Rom. 16:25). Specifically what God revealed to Paul was that believing Gentiles would be given equal status with believing Jews in the body of Christ in fulfillment of the promise (Eph. 3:6). But in the larger sense the mystery is synonymous with the gospel of God's grace in Jesus Christ. In this sense "the mystery is the total meaning of God's redemptive purpose, which he has accomplished in Christ."[24] Thus it is clear that God disclosed to Paul both himself as a person and his Word and will. Revelation encompasses not only the messenger but also the message.

It follows that the Spirit-guided teaching and preaching of the apostle was revelation. Paul testified that "the message [logos] of the cross," while appearing foolish to the unsaved, is in truth to the believer "the power [dynamis] of God" (1 Cor. 1:18). Moreover, Paul spoke "in words taught by the Spirit, expressing spiritual truths in spiritual words" (1 Cor. 2:13). Elsewhere Paul's preaching is identified as "the word of God" (2 Cor. 2:17; 4:2; 1 Thess. 2:13) since, as the apostle testifies, Christ was speaking through him (2 Cor. 13:3).

Paul believed that the historical Jesus Christ was the pinnacle of all God's revelations to mankind. The apostle described the eternal second person of the Trinity as "the image [eichōn] of the invisible God" (Col. 1:15). In Koine Greek, eichōn could refer to, among other things, a portrait. A soldier on duty in a remote outpost, for example, could write to his sweetheart, "I send you an eichōn of myself." Christ, then is the portrait of the ineffable God sent to finite, feeble-sighted people. Repeatedly the apostle affirms that at the Incarnation the invisible God took visible form in Jesus of Nazareth. As the fragment of a hymn of the early church put it, "He [God] appeared in a body" (1 Tim. 3:16; cf. Titus 2:11; the aorist tense in both texts points to the event of the Incarnation). Likewise, "in Christ all the fullness [plēroma] of the Deity [theotēs] lives in bodily form" (Col. 2:9; cf. 1:19). The verb "lives" (katoikei) is present continuous tense, signifying that the reflection of the divine essence through Jesus of Nazareth was a continuous mode of revelation as long as he lived on earth.

Not only the Incarnation but also the visible return of Christ to consummate the present age was viewed by Paul as a modality of special revelation. The apostle denotes the Second Advent as an unveiling (apokalypsis, 1 Cor. 1:7; 2 Thess. 1:7) and as a shining appearance (epiphaneia, 1 Tim. 6:14; 2 Tim. 4:1; Titus 2:13). This application of revelation language to Christ's first advent as well as his second advent prompts one authority to conclude: "To speak of revelation in the fullest biblical sense is to speak of Jesus Christ."[25] Just as Christ's first coming was a powerful revelation of God's grace, so his second coming will be a potent revelation of God's unsurpassing glory.

The Johannine Literature

Special revelation, according to John, was given in the first instance through various "miraculous signs" (sēmeia, John 6:30; 11:47; 12:37; 20:30) and "miracles" (ergo, John 7:3, 21; 10:25, 32) wrought by Jesus. Thus John describes Jesus' miracle of changing water to wine at Cana (John 2:1–11) as "the first of his miraculous signs," the healing of the royal official's son (John 4:46–54) as the "second miraculous sign," and so on. Rightly Jesus said to the unbelieving Jews, "I have shown you many great miracles [ergo] from the Father" (John 10:32). Appropriately the victorious saints in the Book of Revelation sing the song, "Great and marvelous are your deeds [erga], Lord God Almighty" (Rev. 15:3). Jesus' revelatory works were performed for several purposes: (1) to demonstrate that the Father sent him into the world (John 5:36), (2) to validate his extraordinary claims (10:25), (3) to affirm the unique relationship that exists between him and the Father (10:38), and (4) to engender the faith in himself that issues in eternal life (20:30–31). In sum, Jesus performed mighty revelatory works to manifest (*phaneroō*) his eternal glory (2:11).

Given the strong christological focus of John's Gospel and Epistles, it is natural that Jesus Christ is upheld as the supreme embodiment of special revelation. Throughout his writings John implies that God is known by the coming of a personal representative. Thus in the theologically pregnant prologue to the fourth Gospel John teaches that the Word (*logos*), coeternal and coequal with the Father, became a man and dwelt in our midst. Adds John, "We have seen his glory, the glory of the One and Only, who came from the Father, full of grace and truth" (John 1:14). The historical Jesus thus was the revelation of the *shekinah* glory of God.

John continues by saying that the fleshly eye has never seen God (v. 18). But by virtue of the unique relationship the Son sustains to the Father, Christ has made God known (*exēgeomai*). This verb is variously translated in the New Testament as "tell" (Acts 10:8; 15:12), "describe" (15:14), and "report in detail" (21:19). It is the verb from which comes the English word "exegete," which means to interpret or unfold the meaning of a thing. The eternal Son thus most fully "exegetes" for mortals the reality of the invisible God. It is he who tells us who God is and what God is like. Hence the culminating Word of all God's words is Jesus Christ who has become man in our space and time. The third chapter of John's Gospel adds that Jesus, who has come from the Father in heaven (John 3:13), testifies to what he has seen and heard there (v. 32). Commissioned by God and anointed by the Spirit he "speaks the words of God" (v. 34). Later in the Upper Room Peter asked

Jesus to show them the Father, perhaps hoping to be given a theophany. Jesus' answer was powerful in its simplicity: "Anyone who has seen me has seen the Father" (John 14:9). Our Lord's character, deeds, and words provided a perfect revelation of the Father to the world (John 17:6, 26). This role of our Lord as the revelation of God is confirmed by the titles John ascribes to him: "faithful witness" (Rev. 1:5; 3:14), the "divine glory" (John 1:14; 17:24), "light of the world" (8:12; 9:5); "teacher" (11:28; 13:13); and "prophet" (7:40; 9:17).[26]

Other New Testament Writings

A powerful text that identifies Christ as God's final, redemptive revelation is Hebrews 1:1–2. The writer affirms that under the old economy revelation had a long history ("at many times") and came in a multiplicity of modes ("in various ways"). This revelation, which was chiefly a "speaking," was a gradually unfolding reality. But at the juncture between the old and the new eras God "has spoken [*elalēsen*] to us by his Son" (Heb. 1:2). The aorist tense of the verb "to speak" (*laleō*) signifies that God's revelation through Christ is full and complete. Except for the apostolic explication of the gospel, God's final word of revelation was spoken through the total reality of the Son's incarnation, death, resurrection, and second coming (so the anarthrous *en huiō*). As the supreme modality of special revelation the Son is the visible outshining (*apaugasma*) of God's glory and the exact expression (*charaktēr*) of God's invisible reality (v. 3). The same verse asserts that God's final disclosure through the Son is a saving revelation, for it involves "purification for sins." Peter, moreover, identifies Christ's second coming as a specifically revelatory datum. To this immanent eschatological event he applies the verb *apokalyptō*

(1 Peter 1:5) and the noun *apokalypsis* (v. 7). The revelation of Christ at his second coming is likened to the rising of the morning star and the dawning of a new day (2 Peter 1:19).

SYSTEMATIC FORMULATION

A distinctively Christian doctrine of special revelation begins with a distinctively Christian view of God. Skeptics, deists, and liberals often find a cognitive communication from God in time unthinkable because their concept of eternity makes it impossible. And neoorthodox ministers consider God so totally other that any relation to people in history becomes paradoxical or dialectical. So people who would communicate information from God today need first to make clear both *who* the eternal God is and *how* this God has related to the spokesmen he especially appointed in time.

God's Word in Eternity

A Christian understanding of eternity begins with the triune God: Holy Father, Holy Word, and Holy Spirit. The ultimate Revealer expressed his very nature in his Word and in his Spirit. From eternity communication was normal and enhanced the relationships of the three divine persons.

Before the world was, "the Word was with God" (John 1:1). God was never *alogos*, without reason or speech like the animals (2 Peter 2:12; Jude 10). Within the divine Being, John's personal Logos was face to face ("with") the Father, in significant communication with him (cf. John 17:5, 24). The Holy Spirit, like Jesus, was a person "whom" he would send from the Father (John 15:26). Based on biblical data like this, the early confessions affirm trinitarianism against a mere divine singularity. The unbroken fellowship of the three persons before the

foundation of the world involved intercession (Rom. 8:26). Meaningful communication thus is not foreign to God. Communication is inherent in the triune God eternally. Transcending the limits of space and time in the Godhead are personal relationships involving contentful communication.[27]

In the eternal Word, furthermore, were the patterns or forms of everything that would be created. "Through him [the eternal Word] all things were made; without him nothing was made that has been made" (John 1:3). Since God made nothing without reason, the divine "Word" or "Son" gives the whole world figuratively "light" (John 1:3–5; cf. 8:12), or knowability. The creation is not chaotic, but an ordered cosmos with regular laws because everything received its intelligible nature from God. Eternal "wisdom" served as "the craftsman" at God's side during creation (Prov. 8:22–31). Hence we see that "wisdom" personified speaks what is worthy, right, true, just, and faultless (Prov. 8:6-9).

"If anyone denies the existence of this eternal wisdom [*sapienta*]," St. Augustine explained, "then logically— if a plan of Creation was not present to God—He must hold that without any plan God made what He made, or that, either when He made it or before He made it, He did not know what He made or would make."[28]

God's eternal Logos not only gave meaning to the things in the world but also gave purpose to the course of events in history. God planned to create men and women to share his fellowship and his rule of creation. And God made the world to be ruled by people. It follows that categories that exist in the mind of God, though not limited like those of finite, fallen people, are not totally removed from theirs or totally different in every respect. God is not impersonal energy. God is not nonrational. Rational meaning and purpose is not an afterthought but prior to creation. Existence is not prior to essence, as Jean-Paul Sartre alleged, but essences are prior in the mind of God (not abstract concepts as in Plato's world of ideas).[29] The archetypes of knowledge of principles of physics, music, morality, and thought (logic) are in the divine mind. Our ectypal knowledge is true when it corresponds with God's original and more complete knowledge.[30]

God disclosed himself to be "faithful and true" (Isa. 65:16; John 3:33; 16:13; 17:17; Rom. 3:5–7). He who is "faithful" (Heb. 10:23) "remains faithful forever" (Ps. 146:6). Hence we can depend on the fact that God is "faithful to all his promises" (Ps. 145:13). One's concept of revelation reflects one's concept of God. The God of the Bible speaks only in accord with truth. No discrepancy can be found between God's statements and his acts. It is impossible for God to err or "lie" (Heb. 6:17–18). In other words, because God in himself, in his eternal Son, is faithful, his word in eternity is true (inerrant) and reliable (infallible).[31]

God's Word in Time

Theological relativists may grant absolute truth in God but find impossible the communication of God's undistorted truth to errant sinners conditioned by a given culture in space and time. In an age of conceptual relativism those who would minister God's revealed truth must prepare to address the difficulties raised by different cultural, conceptual, and linguistic influences in time. On the basis of the extensive biblical data above, we here propose that in addition to a universal revelation God has communicated objectively valid truths to specific people in particular cultures at specific places and times.

Formally *defined*, "special revelation" refers to the eternal God's disclosure of his redemptive purposes in the Near East (1) supremely *through* Jesus Christ's character, life, and conceptual teachings (in human words) confirmed by miraculous acts, and also (2) in various ways *to* prophetic and apostolic spokesmen whose teachings from God in human words were confirmed by their consistency with one another and by signs, wonders, and mighty acts.

God's Word Incarnate

The eternal Logos or second person of the Trinity "became flesh and made his dwelling among us" (John 1:14). He came to make God known (1:18) to people in the Near East in the first century and through them to the whole world in every generation (Matt. 28:19; Heb. 1:3).

Jesus Christ entered history not as a mere symbol of divine love, but as an actual demonstration of transcendent love. He was truly human as well as truly divine. The account of Jesus' birth is not a myth analogous to the birth of Krishna and many other Hindu avatars. Jesus literally lived, atoned for sin, and rose from the dead. Because of his once-for-all signs, wonders, and mighty acts, he ranks above all mere religious leaders and indeed above the angels (Heb. 1:5–14). "In Christ all the fullness of the Deity lives in bodily form" (Col. 2:9).

For all people of all times and cultures Jesus of Nazareth vividly displayed the fact that the living God is personal, wise, caring, intelligent, and purposive. Jesus displayed a holiness from beyond fallen human history. Jesus' judgments, like the Father's, were "faithful and true" (Rev. 3:7; 16:5, 7; 19:2, 11). Jesus disclosed an objectively valid universal purpose of God to satisfy justice and deliver sinners from the slave markets of selfishness by giving his life a ransom in their place (Mark 2:9–10). Jesus demonstrated a transcendent *agapē* love as the friend of tax collectors and sinners (Luke 7:34). No greater love could have been displayed than the laying down of his life for others (John 15:13). And the power that raised Christ from the dead clearly came from above and hence normatively declares with power that the son of David was indeed the Son of God (Rom. 1:3–4). The first Christians confessed on the basis of many confirming signs, wonders, and mighty acts, not only that Jesus exemplified the eternal Christ in time, but that Jesus *was* the Christ (John 20:31).

What did Jesus Christ teach about his own teaching, either by direct statement or by implication?[32] Many who emphasize revelation only in the person of Christ seem to ignore this crucial question. Emphasizing nonconceptual "encounters" with Christ's person or his "mighty acts," people may neglect what he taught in human categories and words. It is hard to find a discussion of his teaching about his own doctrine. Let us return to one of the most important questions of contemporary theology: What did Jesus teach his first-century disciples about his own teaching? From Jesus' teaching what implications can be drawn about the possibility of stating the Father's eternal truth in history in human thought forms and languages?

1. Jesus' teaching *originated*, not with himself, but *with God the Father*. When the amazed Jews asked, "How did this man get such learning without having studied?" Jesus replied, "My teaching is not my own. It comes from him who sent me" (John 7:15–16). In his high priestly prayer, Jesus could say, "I have revealed you to those whom you gave me. . . . Now they know that everything you have given me comes from you" (John 17:6–8). May we not infer that the conceptual content of Jesus' teaching in history conformed to the Father's in eternity?

2. Jesus taught that divine revelation could be communicated *in human concepts and words.* "For I gave them the words you gave me" (John 17:8). Jesus did not speak a special heavenly language, but the Aramaic or Greek of the common people. May we not infer that the propositional content of Jesus' teaching could be expressed verbally in culturally influenced human languages?

3. Jesus also taught that human words reveal a person's inner heart. Just as a tree can be recognized by its fruit, so good or evil persons can be recognized by the "fruit" of their lips (Matt. 12:35; 7:15–20): "Out of the overflow of the heart the mouth speaks" (Matt. 12:34). Jesus spoke out of the overflow of his own heart and therefore not only his deeds but also his words disclose his inner divine nature. Concepts and words enhance personal, heartfelt relationships. May we not infer that Jesus' words revealed his personal, inner convictions, feelings, and purposes, enriching personal relationships with those who received them?

4. The information Jesus taught in human concepts and languages was conceptually true—consistent and factual. In humbling himself to become a human, Jesus adapted himself to the human level, but did not accommodate himself to human sin or error. In prayer to the Father he exclaimed, "I gave them the words you gave me. . . . Your word is truth" (John 17:8, 17).

Although Christ emphasized eternal life, he taught reliable assertions about a great variety of subjects: the Pharisees, God's moral law in the Sermon on the Mount, the demonic, illness, the kingdom of God, the new birth, faith, the cost of discipleship, paying taxes, offending children, riches, his coming betrayal and denial and death, signs of the end of the age, and the Great Commission. Jesus' teaching on all of these and other matters conformed to reality and the mind of God the Father. May we not infer that Jesus taught no error on any subject of which he spoke (his plenary inerrancy)?

5. The teaching of Jesus was not only conceptually true but also existentially viable and effectual. Far from a static hindrance to vitality, his teaching was rejuvenating. It served as a viable instrument of the Holy Spirit to give spiritual life. "The Spirit gives life; the flesh counts for nothing. The words I have spoken to you are spirit and they are life" (John 6:63). People also found Jesus' conceptual truth to be liberating. It served as an instrument of the Holy Spirit to free people from moral and spiritual slavery to sinful desires. Jesus said, "If you hold to my teaching, you are really my disciples. Then you will know the truth, and the truth will set you free" (John 8:31–32).

Further, Jesus' teaching was sanctifying. As an instrument of the Holy Spirit in the disciples' lives, it helped them become spiritually mature. Jesus prayed, "Sanctify them by the truth; your word is truth" (John 17:17). May we not infer that Jesus' teaching was infallible in accomplishing the ends for which it was given?

6. All that Jesus affirmed on any subject was not only true and viable, but also authoritative for his immediate and subsequent disciples, as follows from the evidence in statements 1 through 5. Furthermore, the Father granted him "authority over all people that he might give eternal life . . . " (John 17:2).

His hearers recognized his authority; the people in the town of Capernaum "were amazed at his teaching, because his message had authority" (Luke 4:31–32). At the conclusion of the Sermon on the Mount "the crowds were amazed at his teaching, because he taught as one who had authority, and not as their teachers of the law" (Matt. 7:28–29).

Before ascending to the Father Jesus said, "All authority in heaven and on earth has been given to me." On that basis he asked them to make disciples, "teaching them to obey *everything*" he had commanded them (Matt. 28:18–20). May we not infer that all of Jesus' teaching had normative authority in his own time?

7. Jesus' teaching was *not time-bound, but classically time-related.* "Heaven and earth will pass away," Jesus said, "but my words will never pass away" (Mark 13:31). Disciples today may need the best critical procedures to determine what indeed Jesus said, and what he meant by what he said, but any teaching known to be from the first-century incarnate Christ remains normative for authentic disciples until his return. Remember his words, "If anyone loves me, he will obey my teaching" (John 14:23). May we not infer that Jesus' teaching had normative authority for all times and cultures?

The biblical data thus support Jesus' revelation of himself, the Father, and the Holy Spirit in human concepts and languages. He communicated truth in two major senses:[33] (1) His teaching conveyed reliable information concerning what is and normative principles concerning what ought to be, and (2) his life reflected fidelity to the ultimate reality, God the Father, and his will on earth. He affirmed what is the case essentially, and he lived by it existentially. Those who find the supreme revelation of God in Jesus Christ need put no distance between propositional and relational truth. In Christ essential and existential truth are inseparable. Barth's and Bultmann's views are less adequate insofar as they separate the conceptual from the experiential.

God's Word Through Prophetic Spokesmen

Just as Jesus' teachings originated with God the Father, *true prophets' teachings originated with God* and *were given by the supernatural power of the Holy Spirit.* The problem is not how a totally other God could possibly speak with finite and fallen people in concepts and words. A conceptual communication is possible because the living God made mankind to think his thoughts after him. As Jesus' teaching has demonstrated, God's truth can be communicated in human, culturally influenced categories and languages.

Is it not one thing, however, for the incarnate Christ to convey truth in human languages and another for finite, fallen sinners to do so? Indeed! How could authentic prophets transcend the limits of their finiteness and the corruption of their sinfulness to convey objectively valid truth from God? God providentially prepared them for this task (Jer. 1:5) and then supernaturally enabled them to overcome their innate propensities to err in receiving and speaking God's truth through sentences in human language (Zech. 7:12). That the Spirit's work on their behalf should be supernatural is not strange. The Logos entered the fallen world as God's Son (the Holy One) by supernatural conception (Luke 1:35). So also the Logos entered the fallen world of the prophets as God's Word by supernatural mental conceptions.

The Spirit of God disclosed divine truth to prophets in different ways: (1) by means of an audible voice (Exod. 19:3–6), though God as spirit (John 4:24) has no physical body or larynx (John 5:37); (2) through internal suggestion or silent hearing of the Word by a prophet but not by others around him (1 Kings 13:18–22; Isa. 7:3–4); (3) by presenting a vision or imaginary picture (Ezek. 37; Micah 4:1–4); and (4) through an opening of the prophet's eyes to see realities otherwise invisible (Num. 22:31; 2 Kings 6:15–17).[34] However varied the modes, the *point* of the

figurative visions (et al.) could be stated in unfigurative language.

The basic problem was distinguishing between two kinds of prophets. *Presumptuous prophets* claimed to speak for God, but in fact did not (Deut. 18:20). They would wag their own tongues but say, "The Lord declares . . . " (Jer. 23:31), and they could "speak visions from their own minds, not from the mouth of the LORD" (Jer. 23:16) and so distort the words of the living God and raise false hopes. In that situation "every man's own word becomes his oracle" (Jer. 23:36).

True prophets received the content of their messages from God as Aaron did from Moses. Aaron served as "prophet" or spokesman for Moses, and Moses was to Aaron as "God" (Exod. 7:1; 4:16). True prophets did not just give fallible advice (cf. 2 Sam. 7:1–3), they also spoke on behalf of God (cf. vv. 4–17). They were not mere automata but real persons facing real situations to which they spoke for God. As finite, the prophets were limited in knowledge; as fallen, they could make mistakes or intentionally deceive. But when prophets received messages from God and conveyed them to the people, they functioned as God's spokesmen inerrantly. God, the all-knowing and all-wise, did not make untrustworthy promises. His Word did not err in what it affirmed of objective reality or subjective feelings. And God's Word through the prophets infallibly achieved its objectives.

The crucial issue for the people was not deciding what to accept and reject from among the prophets' teachings, but whether the alleged prophets communicated truth from God or spoke presumptuously. The people naturally cried out, "How can we know when a message has not been spoken by the LORD?" (Deut. 18:21). God's people were not condemned for asking that question, but were given *criteria* to use for detecting religious deceivers.

First, the alleged prophet's *signs must take place* as predicted (Deut. 18:22). God's predictions never fail to come true as foreseen. One who speaks for God does not misrepresent reality but presents assertions that fit the facts (sustained and known by God). God does not raise false hopes, but teaching from God conforms to reality. Special revelation involved more than words and concepts; it included also signs, wonders, and mighty acts supernaturally performed by God in support of his redemptive program.

Second, the alleged prophet's *teaching concerning God must be consistent* with what has been given by previous revelation, whether through Moses or other prophets. Whatever signs and wonders might occur, if a prophet asked the Israelites to follow other gods and worship idols, God's people ought not listen to the words of that prophet (Deut. 13:3–4). God does not deny himself nor contradict himself. Any self-contradictory religious teaching not only cannot be meaningfully communicated but neither can it originate with the living God, who is faithful.

Only after a prophet's credentials had been verified should his message be accepted as from God. God still wants his people to use their critical capacities for distinguishing true from false religious claims. In a day of many prophets, the people had to "inquire, probe and investigate [them] thoroughly" (Deut. 13:14).

Once the credentials of Moses, for example, were verified, his teaching was to be received as true on his authority and obeyed as God's teaching. The prophet's teaching was not merely a fallible witness to a noncognitive divine act, encounter, or relationship. What an accredited prophet taught was the *normative* Word of God. It ought to be received as true and

obeyed. The tendency today seems to encourage criticism of revealed content (in theology) to the neglect of critical examination of the credentials of the alleged divine representatives (in apologetics).

God made known his redemptive plans and purposes in various ways (Heb. 1:1), including (1) revealed assertions in sentences, (2) miraculous deeds, and (3) the prophet's personal experiences of God. Personal encounters (Isa. 6:1–5), mighty acts (Exod. 14:13, 31), and propositional assertions (1 Sam. 2:27; 3:21) were intertwined as the prophets called people to a life of fellowship with God and service for God. Their faith, hope, and love was not fraudulently evoked but motivated by truth concerning God's nature, purposes, and acts.

The basic element of revealed conceptual truth is not an isolated concept or single word but an assertion expressed in an indicative sentence. Of course, the sentence ordinarily occurs in a paragraph, and the paragraph in a series of such units of thought. Hence a word communicated by a prophet was understood in the context of its sentence, paragraph, and broader cultural and theological world view.

Like Christ's teaching, the prophetic teaching was not only coherent, but also *permanently viable and authoritative.* Jesus said, "Do not think that I have come to abolish the Law or the Prophets; I have not come to abolish them but to fulfill them. I tell you the truth, until heaven and earth disappear, not the smallest letter, not the least stroke of a pen, will by any means disappear from the Law until everything is accomplished" (Matt. 5:17–18). In the subsequent points of the Sermon on the Mount Jesus refuted not only the teaching of the Old Testament prophets but also the misunderstandings of them in Pharisaic legalism.

By way of summary and definition,

then, prophets were providentially prepared people of God whose claims to receive messages from God were accredited and who affirmed with divine authority and power reliable information about significant events in the past, present, and future and normative principles about how people ought to relate to God and one another.

God's Word Through Apostolic Spokesmen

Jesus as an "apostle" sent by the Father "was faithful to the one who appointed him" (Heb. 3:1–2). As Jesus preached with the Father's delegated authority, so Jesus appointed apostles to preach with his delegated *authority* (Mark 6:7) and Spirit-endued *power* (John 20:21; Acts 1:8; 2:4). Hence Peter asked people to remember not only the words spoken in the past by the holy prophets but also "the command given by our Lord and Savior through your apostles" (2 Peter 3:2).

What was the *source* of the prophetic and apostolic message? Peter insisted that "prophecy never had its origin in the will of man, but men spoke from God as they were carried along by the Holy Spirit" (2 Peter 1:21). Paul claimed to speak "not in words taught us by human wisdom but in words taught by the Spirit, expressing spiritual truths in spiritual words" (1 Cor. 2:13), even when giving his own judgment on subjects on which no quotation from Jesus was available (1 Cor. 7:25; 14:37). And Paul thanked God that the Thessalonians "received the word of God," which they heard from the apostles "not as the word of men, but as it actually is, the word of God" (1 Thess. 2:13).

By what *criteria* could people in the first century know whether an alleged apostle was speaking for God or speaking presumptuously? The tests of a true apostle were similar to those of a true prophet. The first-century Christians had every reason to expect that Saul should give evidence of being transformed into Paul, the apostle to the Gentiles. In defense of his apostolic ministry Paul stressed the consistency of his one gospel with that of the other apostles (Gal. 1:9–11; 2:7–9). Paul also had become an eyewitness of the risen Christ, a requirement for an apostle (Acts 1:22–23; 1 Cor. 15:7). And Paul's miracles came to pass. "The things that mark an apostle—signs, wonders and miracles—were done among you with great perseverance" (2 Cor. 12:12; Heb. 2:4).

God's people needed to be critical rather than gullible, for there were already many false apostles in the first century. Not all that was supernatural was of God. First-century Christians were not to believe every spirit but to "test the spirits to see whether they [were] from God" (1 John 4:1). This major test was doctrinal. "Every spirit that acknowledges that Jesus Christ has come in the flesh is from God, but every spirit that does not acknowledge Jesus is not from God" (1 John 4:2–3). Anyone who departs from the teaching of (about) Christ does not have God (2 John 9). Revelation allegedly from God that comes through people who deny the deity of Christ is clearly not from the Most High but from a lesser source.

What an accredited apostle taught, God taught. The *contents* of the apostles' messages were not subject to critical testing and possible acceptance or rejection, because the apostles' *credentials* had been verified. The early Christians did not think of rejecting the apostolic teaching. The teaching of the apostles was all normative for establishing doctrine, making value judgments in life, overseeing the church, and disciplining church members.

Like the messages of Christ, the apostle's messages originated with God the Father, came through human concepts and words, were supernaturally kept from error by the power of the Holy Spirit, taught only truth authoritatively and effectually, and were not time-bound, but classically time-related and relevant.

APOLOGETIC INTERACTION

Are There Additional Revelations Today?

Since prophets and apostles were instrumental to special revelation, the question may be restated. Do the offices of prophet and apostle continue in the church? If so, in what form? With respect to prophets, after about 400 B.C. no more prophets appeared in Israel. Three times the writer of 1 Maccabees mentions that there were no prophets in Israel (4:46; 9:27; cf. 14:41). And Josephus said that at about the time of Artaxerxes of Persia "the exact succession of the prophets" had ceased.[35] The Old Testament being completed, after four centuries of prophetic silence John the Baptist is the last of the prophets of the old covenant and the precursor of Jesus.

Since it was God's will to give another Testament presenting the accomplishment of redemption as predicted in the Old Testament, another period of prophecy would be expected. Jesus Christ is the greatest prophet (Deut. 18:15–19; Matt. 7:29). There were several prophets mentioned by name in the New Testament (Luke 1:67; Acts 11:28; 13:1; 15:32; 21:9–10). Before the New Testament had been completed many false prophets had appeared (Acts 13:6; 1 John 4:1; Rev. 2:20).

The new period of prophecy, like the earlier one, came to an end when this portion of God's Word was completed. The end of this period, when new divine revelations would no longer be given, was not immediately apparent. As in the case of the OT, they simply ceased. The entire Bible was written. Thereafter people in the Church were called prophets only in the extended sense of presenting God's people truths received, not by direct revelation, but from careful study of the completed and infallible Word of God.[36]

The work of noncanonical prophets emphasized application of the teaching of written revelation to specific situations, not adding books to the canon of either the Old Testament or the New. The authentic successor to the prophets is the Old Testament itself, since it continues their ministry to the world and the people of God. In a secondary sense those who instruct and challenge people or encourage and comfort people from the Old or New Testament Scriptures may be said to have a prophetic ministry and may be called prophets (1 Cor. 14:3).

Is there a succession of apostles from the first century until today? The Church of England and Episcopalian terminology of apostolic succession is not found in the New Testament, and there is little evidence for the idea. One passage used emphasizes the continuity of apostolic doctrine, not the office (2 Tim. 2:2). The idea of a succession of apostles is absent in the first two centuries. There could be no more apostles in the original (revelatory) sense of the word (Acts 1:21–22). "The real successor to the apostolate is the NT itself, since it continues their ministry within the church of God. Their office was incommunicable."[37]

Since the completion of the biblical books, there is no further divine *inspiration* for the writing of Scripture. Divine *illumination* produces no new revelation; illumination opens the mind and will to the reception of revelation (1 Cor. 2:14). Jesus Christ has done all that he can do in his redemptive purposes until his return to the earth. And in the available canon we have all the truths necessary to acceptance with

God and for an abundant life. All the noncontradictory teachings of alleged recent revelations together do not add anything significant to scriptural teachings on God, mankind, sin, salvation, the church, and things to come.

The commission of the apostles was unique and nonrepeatable. The apostles were eyewitnesses of the incarnate and risen Christ. Apostolic ministry was distinguished from all other ministries, was not local but universal, and was not derived from the church, but was foundational to it.[38] Just as the enduring product of the Incarnation was the teaching of the divine-human person of Christ, the enduring product of revelation through prophets and apostles was their divine-human teaching (doctrine). The question is this: Does revelation continue today through the church?

Note that the revelation came *to* the people of God through specially gifted prophets and apostles as well as through Jesus Christ. The revelation did not come *from* the church as a whole or its permanent officers. The evidence does not support the traditional Roman Catholic position stated by Thomas Aquinas: "Revelation is the truth that God communicates through the prophets, Christ, the Apostles, *and the Church.*"[39]

Church leaders (elders, pastors, bishops) serve as provisional authorities for teaching new converts and others until they can discover and relate revealed truth for themselves. Christians are all priests indwelt and illumined by the Holy Spirit in the study of special revelation. When leaders in the church stray from its teaching, the mature members can call them back to the supernaturally originated Word of God. However, they do not receive new revelation to add to the Bible.

The provisional authority of ecclesiastical leaders as *interpreters* of the Word, however, deserves respect, especially where reflected in thoroughly prepared doctrinal statements such as the creeds of the early church. Nevertheless, if contradiction appears between the explicit teaching of church authorities and responsibly interpreted revealed truth, people must obey the revelation that originated with God and was supernaturally given through the specially gifted prophets and apostles who were authenticated by supernatural signs, wonders, and mighty acts.

To preserve the unique authority of the foundational and only inerrant revelation (*sola scriptura*), Christians often challenge the pretensions of any church or cult that sees itself as an additional source of revelation for these latter days alongside the Lord, the prophets, and the apostles. Israel and the church were not *above* but *under* the authority of the Word. The tendency to speak of the church as a continuation of the incarnation must avoid the inference that it can add new revelation to the foundational truth of the prophets and apostles.

Is revelation continuous today? Facing many alleged revelations from both occult and established sources, people must develop discernment and overcome gullibility. False as well as true prophets may produce signs, wonders, and mighty acts (Matt. 24:24). Not all that is supernatural in our times is of God. Examine contemporary claims of revelation by the same criteria as in Old and New Testament times. Determine whether the advertised miracles in fact took place and whether the central teachings contradict teachings known to be from God in the Old and New Testaments.

All the alleged revelations of spiritists, Latter-Day Saints, Christian Scientists, and others put together do not add anything significant to the teaching of Scripture. Remember that Christ has completed all that can be done for the salvation of the world until he returns again to the earth. What people need now is not more revelation but more faithfulness to the Spirit-illumined applications of biblical principles to specific situations. To protect the uniqueness of biblical revelation we do not call applications "revelations," but "illuminations."

Just as the Word must always test the spirits, the Holy Spirit must always attest the Word. Although we may not anticipate additional objective truth mediated through propositions, the Holy Spirit continues to work with believers immediately, enabling them to *receive* the deep things of God's divine wisdom and to grow in understanding toward the mind of Christ (1 Cor. 2:10–16). The continuing immediate aspect of special revelation in the inner witness of the Holy Spirit is indispensable to spiritual growth. Commitment to the objective truth of redemptive revelation is no substitute for keeping in step with the Spirit or illumination (Gal. 5:25). And "abiding in the Spirit" cannot for long serve as a satisfactory substitute for adherence to objectively revealed truths.

The Particularity of Special Revelation

The occurrence of divine disclosures to specific persons at specific times and places seems unfair to those to whom no special revelation was given. However, special revelation does not preclude the reality of general revelation in the repeated laws of nature, events of history, and human consciousness universally (as established in the previous chapter). Through general revelation God justly approaches all people everywhere in the same manner.

Although special revelation underlines what all deserve equally, it focuses centrally on undeserved mercy and grace. Since justice has been served, does it follow that God could not mercifully grant certain benefits to some people and not to others? Has he not

freely given some gifts to certain leaders that are not given to others?

The gifts of grace are given not for people to spend for their own pleasures, but to use for the benefit of all. The purpose of the covenant with Abraham and the choice of Israel as a nation was not to encourage their pride, arrogance, or self-indulgence, but rather that Abraham's descendants might bring blessing to the whole world (Gen. 12:2–3). Jesus ministered to the specially chosen disciples in a way he did not to others. But our Lord's ministry to the Twelve was also for their becoming equipped to make disciples throughout the world and teach all that Jesus had disclosed to them. God chose Saul to become an apostle to the Gentiles, not to provide him with selfish ease and comfort, but to give him a mission to reach the world with the gospel of grace.

If revelation was to become something more than general revelation, it would necessarily have to be given to a person in history at a particular time and place. If Jesus was to become incarnate at all, (1) it would have to be in some century—so why not the first? (2) It would have to be in some place—so why not the Near East? (3) It would necessarily be in the context of some people—so why not the Jewish people?

"What advantage, then, is there in being a Jew? . . . First of all, they have been entrusted with the very words of God" (Rom. 3:1–2). The choice of the Jewish prophets and apostles in particular was not based on some special merit on their part. All have sinned; none is deserving of divinely bestowed benefits. Paul wrote to the Corinthians, as much concerning himself as anyone else, "God chose the foolish things of the world to shame the wise; God chose the weak things of the world to shame the strong . . . so that no one may boast before him" (1 Cor. 1:27–29). Clearly, to be chosen by God to receive and communicate revelation as a prophet or apostle was not grounds for feelings of superiority. Paul could ask anyone, "What do you have that you did not receive?" (1 Cor. 4:7).

Beyond all this, the particular instrument through which divine revelation comes faces great responsibility. The Pharisees who failed to understand grace relied on the law and bragged about their relationship to God, but Paul wrote, "You, then, who teach others, do you not teach yourself? . . . God's name is blasphemed among the Gentiles because of you" (Rom. 2: 21–24). Paul's indictment of humanity concludes, "Are we any better? Not at all! We have already made the charge that Jews and Gentiles alike are all under sin" (Rom. 3:9). In the Old Testament context, Israel would receive the same judgments as the nations driven out before her if she disobeyed the Lord in the way they had.

The particularism of special revelation is not that of an ethnic or geographical favoritism, but of a redeemed remnant called out from the masses to serve them. Belief in a God who cares enough for the lost to come into the world as their Savior and to communicate the redemptive message through his prophetic and apostolic spokespeople remains essential to Christian faith. If this gracious, spiritual particularism is rejected, Christianity is rejected. God's special redemptive program takes place not in a vacuum but in the context of God's universal providential program that includes every person and every culture throughout history.

By way of contrast, if the alleged incarnation of the Hindu Krishna is not particularistic, it is because according to the myths Krishna could not have a literal body in space and time without becoming evil. According to Christian teaching, matter is not evil; it is the creation of God. Humanness also, as created, is not inherently evil. So a literal incarnation is not morally impos-

sible. Because Christianity is actually incarnational, it is uniquely particularistic and essentially so.

Although the differences between various historical periods and cultures are often emphasized and should not be overlooked, there are also many similarities in human beings of all times and places. All are persons and have inalienable human rights, all demand justice and intellectual honesty, all need mercy and love, all have to relate to reality, and all ought to speak coherently in order to understand and be understood. All have failed to live up to the norms of general revelation. Hence all need salvation by grace through faith.

So, while there is an inescapable truth in Christianity's particularism, its particularism does not render it negotiable, nor is it irrelevant to people of other times and places. Like the particularism of a classical work of art or music, special revelation speaks relevantly and normatively to people around the world in generation after generation, whether yellow, black, brown, red, or white, male or female, Eastern or Western, poor or rich, educated or uneducated.

Because of the marked differences between human cultures and even within the same culture over a period of fifteen hundred years, special revelation was *progressive*. Not everything could be taught at once and the divine spokesman is responsible only for the new element introduced at a given time. As prophet after prophet spoke, their messages did not contradict earlier communications. At times paradoxes (apparent contradictions) stimulated thought. But further investigation showed that the divine spokesmen were not affirming and denying the same thing at the same time or in the same respect. Jesus' communiques did not "destroy" but "fulfilled" earlier revelations from the prophets (Matt. 5:17–18). And the apostles, including Paul, did not destroy but carried through to completion the teaching of their Lord.[40] The spokesmen for a God who cannot deny himself did not contradict themselves. Before attributing contradictory nonsense to God's spokesmen, interpreters do well to exhaust every possible way of understanding the harmony and continuity of authority that the authors sensed in the ultimate Author's plan.

Special Revelation:
Personal and Propositional

Contemporary existentialist, neoorthodox, and biblical theology has repeatedly alleged that what God reveals is himself, not information about himself. "God does not give us information by communication; He gives us Himself in communion."[41] Again, "there appears a remarkable breadth of agreement in recent discussions about revelation. It is that what is fundamentally revealed is God Himself, not propositions about God."[42]

The claim to have received propositional revelation is not to be confused with occult or magical claims to guidance from hidden spirit sources. In animistic and occult practice questions are asked requiring a yes or no answer through involuntary signs in a liver or on a Ouija board and the voluntary signs of "familiar spirits." By contrast, the propositional revelation given to prophets and apostles produced promises, covenants, unconditional predictions, conditional predictions, epistles, gospels, histories, psalms, proverbs, exhortations, doctrinal teaching, and laws. Furthermore, this has come from openly acknowledged, tested, and confirmed prophets and apostles. The happenings these people report were not done in a corner, a darkened room, or among believers only. They were observed by Egyptians, Baal worshipers, Roman guards, and other nonbelievers as well as many questioning believers and people who became believers.

A defense of propositional revelation may also be misunderstood as a claim that all revealed information came in the form of "S is P" (a subject, some form of the verb to be, and a predicate nominative). Although many revealed assertions are not in this form, propositions in logical form may be presupposed or inferred from the poetry, letters, biographical descriptions and narratives. Assumptions and inferences about God and humanity are implied in what has been stated in nonpropositional form.

Misunderstandings also occur when a "proposition" is taken to be so inflexible and static as to be inapplicable to meaningful personal existence and relationships.

In philosophy, but not in business or sexual activity, a proposition is whatever can be asserted, denied, contended, maintained, assumed, supposed, implied, or presupposed. In other words, it is that which is expressed by a typical indicative sentence.[43]

The content of a proposition needs to be distinguished from the sentence conveying it. The same assertion can appear very differently in different languages. "God knows you and cares about you" may be communicated in totally different wordings in Hebrew, Greek, Spanish, Sanskrit, Russian, Swahili, and Chinese. The same affirmation can be expressed in these and hundreds of other languages.

Truth is a quality of propositions; sentences either convey the proposition effectively or ineffectively. The proposition, "God knows and cares about you" is cognitive; that is, it is either true or false. The fact that the proposition is always and everywhere true does not make either God or you static beings, nor does it make knowing and caring a static relationship. The content of propositions ought not be confused with the realities designated. The objective validity of propositions about persons does not render personal relationships "static," as often charged, or "lifeless." Precisely the opposite is the case. If it may be equally true that "God does *not* know or care about you," then God may not be living, knowing, and caring and he may indeed be a static principle, impersonal energy, or a dumb idol.

Nevertheless, according to Karl Barth such doctrinal information could not have been revealed by God. "Revelation in fact does not differ from the person of Jesus Christ, and again does not differ from the reconciliation that took place in him. To say revelation is to say, 'The Word became flesh.' "[44] Jesus Christ alone can reveal God to us. Even assertions of prophets and apostles are not God's Word. Barth regards them witnesses and only witnesses who claim no authority at all for themselves. Barth never identifies Paul's words with God's words. "In the one case *Deus dixit,* in the other *Paulus dixit.* These are two different things."[45] No doctrinal propositions, Barth thought, could be revealed, with apparently this one exception: "The Word became flesh." Revelation presents the person of Christ, not information about Christ. But to affirm that, Barth had to allow for at least this one exceptional proposition that holds for both God and man in eternity and time. If the alleged "infinite qualitative distinction" between God's mind and human minds is not so great that one proposition can be true for both, then others may also be affirmed.

Emil Brunner similarly declared that "the Word of God is not doctrine, that God in his Word does not speak 'something true,' but himself."[46] Admittedly, doctrinal assertions are "related instrumentally to the Word of God as token and framework, serving in relation to the reality—actual personal fellowship with God, but they are not the Word of God."[47] "God can, if he so wills, speak his Word to a person even through false doctrine and correspondingly find in a false Credo-credo the right echo of his Word."[48]

The Barth-Brunner concern for personal relationship to God as the end and goal of revelation is commendably scriptural. The God-given means to that end, however, are not erroneous assertions but true assertions. True concepts lead away from idols and to the living God who is there. Conceptual truth can become an idol just as any means can become an end. Nevertheless, viewing revealed assertions as less than true does not remove that danger.

Persons relate well to other persons when there is mutual respect and trust. Personal relationships are not enhanced by untrustworthy sayings. Persons disclose their inner commitments and purposes in nonverbal ways but also with greater explicitness and precision in words.

As Jesus said, "Out of the overflow of the heart the mouth speaks" (Matt. 12:34). The audible words are simply external evidence of the heart's attitude. True statements, therefore, are not a hindrance to knowing the inner person but a help. Even a Freudian slip of the tongue may disclose something about a person.

Removal of the possibility of communication in solitary confinement is a most serious penalty. To remove a personal God from the possibility of communication in assertions conveyed by words does not enhance but hurts the possibility of personal relationships. The gift of speech shows that humanity has been made for fellowship. We cannot live fully as persons apart from our neighbors or apart from God.

Although both Barth and Brunner seek to return to a biblical perspective, their position on revelation is not sufficiently biblical at this point. For example, *Logos* refers to the person of Christ in two passages (John 1:1–14; Rev. 19:13) but to information in scores of other passages. Revelation occurs in linguistic assertions, not in the person of Christ only.

Similarly, Old and New Testament words for *revelation* make it clear that God disclosed himself not only without a verbal message but also, and far more frequently, through messages conveyed by prophets and apostles. Revelation takes place not only in events or happenings but also in interpretations of events, predictions of the significance of coming events, commandments and exhortations, judgments and blessings, promises and covenants. "Revelation" is not confined to the foundational message of Christ but includes also messages of the prophets and apostles.[49]

The terms for "speaking," "saying," and other such words support a doctrine of revelation not only in indescribable experiences that one may have with the person of the living Christ, but also in the words of Christ and God's other spokespeople. The Hebrew noun *dabar* basically means "what God said or says." Of the 242 times the phrase "the word of the Lord" occurs, the expression appears as a technical form for a communicable prophetic revelation 225 times.[50]

Summing up the biblical data, Bernard Ramm found that "revelation is both a meeting and a knowing. Something is said in revelation, and what is said is the root and ground of our knowledge of God." Ramm explained further, "Certainly the word 'revelation' is rich in meaning. God's word to the prophet is revelation; God's act is revelation; the return of Christ is revelation. The concept of revelation in Scripture is too rich to be easily schematized; *it is also rich enough to be applied to the conceptual side of revelation.*"[51]

Responding to Barth and Brunner's view, Ramm asks, "But what does it mean to disclose a person? Certainly two people who are deaf, blind, and mute can hardly have any real encounter with each other apart from touch. Real encounter in life between persons is always within the context of mutual knowledge."[52] Any noncognitive concepts of revelation, like those of the neoorthodox, mystics, and new-consciousness groups fail to fit the biblical evidence. In the next chapter we will consider how divine truth can be expressed in human ways without distortion.

RELEVANCE TO LIFE AND MINISTRY

The Chief End of Special Revelation

The comprehensive purpose of special revelation is the reestablishment of the full communion of sinful people with God. So special revelation is directed to life as a whole—to the intellect and the conscience, the emotions and the will. The divine communication seeks to move the whole person away from enticements to sin and toward spiritual life with God.

Few have expressed the objective of revelation as well as W. H. Griffith Thomas has:

> The essential purpose of revelation is life: the gift of the life of God to the life of man. Its practical character is stamped on every part. The "chief end of revelation" is not philosophy, though it has a philosophy profound and worthy. It is not doctrine, though it has its experiences precious and lasting. It is not even morality, though it has its ethic unique and powerful. Christianity *has* all these, but *is* far more than them all. It is the religion of redemption, including salvation from sin, equipment for holiness, and provision for life to be lived in fellowship with God and for His glory. The "chief end" of revelation is the union [communion] of God and

man, and in that union [communion] the fulfillment of all God's purposes for the world. The elements of sonship, worship, stewardship, fellowship, heirship, practically sum up the purpose of Divine revelation as it concerns man's life—a life in which he receives God's grace, realizes God's will, reproduces God's character, renders God service, and rejoices in God's presence in the Kingdom of grace below and the Kingdom of glory above.[53]

The apostle John wrote his Gospel in order that sinners might obtain spiritual life. His purpose, he said, was "that you may believe [the proposition having been attested by many signs] that Jesus is the Christ, the Son of God, and that by believing [that revealed truth] you may have life in his name" (20:31).

Truth Necessary but Not Sufficient

In bringing the whole person to life, the Holy Spirit has freely chosen to use truth as the necessary instrument. Revealed truths are necessary to direct people away from deceptive idols to the living God. But in and of themselves truths are incapable of doing that. Although necessary, the truths of the gospel are not sufficient because sinners need not only new light but also new sight. No one except the Holy Spirit can grant sight—the ability to receive redemptive doctrines. Hence the necessary condition of spiritual life is revealed truth, but truth can be "received" only by the enablement of the Holy Spirit (1 Cor. 2:14).

Christianity, as J. Gresham Machen said, is "a way of life founded on a message." The gospel "is not a mere expression of Christian experience, but on the contrary it is a setting forth of those facts upon which experience is based."[54]

Bombarded by countless claims from new-consciousness leaders, gurus, and witches of all sorts, people need dependable guidelines to lead them away from idols in their quest for personal transformation through experience of their transcendent Source. People created in God's image are unfulfilled by relativistic agnosticism. Still they want answers. Desiring authority, many have joined one cult after another. But spiritual promiscuity is no more viable than agnosticism. Spiritual fulfillment will never be permanent apart from the changeless Lord of all. The lasting key to spiritual reality is changeless gospel truth from the changeless Lord. "How, then, can they call on the one they have not believed in? And how can they hear without someone preaching to them?" (Rom. 10:14).

A Reliable Guide to Significant Worship

Because Jesus is the second person of the Trinity, he is rightly the object of *worship*. To worship and serve other spiritual masters is sinfully to worship and serve creatures rather than the Creator (Rom. 1:25). Not so when Christians worship the Logos who was with God, was God, and became flesh. The incarnate Word or Son mediates God's blessings to us and exemplifies worship in spirit and in truth.[55]

Revelation provides reliable information as an instrument of the Spirit by which all worship God. The peak worship experience is not a mindless feeling of oneness with the underlying energy of everything in nature. The peak worship experience occurs when we love God with all our minds as well as our hearts (Matt. 22:37).

We recognize the Being of greatest worth—not only with our spirits, but also our minds—by worshiping in spirit and in truth (John 4:24). The ideal is not ecstatic utterance with an unfruitful mind. Rather, Paul said, "I will pray with my spirit, but I will also pray with my mind; I will sing with my spirit, but I will also sing with my mind" (1 Cor. 14:15).

Sound conceptual guidelines in our minds direct our adoration away from the creation and to the Creator-Redeemer-Counselor who hears, speaks, and acts. Worship involves the whole person, including an actively dedicated mind. Studies of the *prayers* of people like Hannah (1 Sam. 2:1–10), David (Psalm 119), Jesus (Matt. 6:9–13; John 17), and Paul (Eph. 1:15–23; 3:14–21) show how their communion with God was shaped by profound knowledge of revealed truths or doctrines.

Many approaches to *meditation* today under the influence of Hindu and Buddhist mysticism ask that a person's mind be rid of all conceptual thought from any source whatever, including propositional revelation. That may be an appropriate way to identify with the impersonal, nonintelligent energy of the cosmos, but it is not an acceptable way to commune with the heavenly Father to whom Jesus asked us to pray without vain repetition.

Authentic spirituality is not a mere social activism (Paul Van Buren), a feeling of dependence on God (Schleiermacher), an ecstatic experience (Tillich), nor even a personal encounter with God. Authentic spirituality involves a personal response to a personal God with assent to the instruction of revelation concerning what is most ultimate and of highest value. Without reliable information one may expend his life for nothing; without faithfulness to the highest values, one may be a hypocrite. Accurate information and fidelity are both crucial for their respective purposes. Neither can substitute for the other.[56] In *A Theology of Christian Devotion* Thor Hall observed, "Spirituality without understanding is not faith; it is superstition. Faith without knowledge is not biblical devotion; it is blind fideism."[57]

A Dependable Source of Comfort and Courage

Belief in the unfailing promises of God may provide *comfort* in sorrow and *courage* in the valley of the shadow of death. At such crucial times, a servant of God who does not think any promise in human concepts and words can be reliable, or isn't sure whether revealed doctrines concerning life after death are "faithful sayings," fails to meet the deepest need of the dying and the sorrowing, who look to a minister at such a time if no other. A psychological survey of terminally ill patients by a University of Denver psychologist showed that most preferred visits by conservative ministers, who read the Bible and prayed, to visits by liberal ministers who did not. Before they officiate at a funeral, ministers need to settle whether they have reason to affirm with conviction, "I am convinced that neither death nor life, neither angels nor demons, neither the present nor the future, nor any powers, neither height nor depth, nor anything else in all creation, will be able to separate us from the love of God that is in Christ Jesus our Lord" (Rom. 8:38–39).

A Solid Base for Unity and Fellowship in the Church

Spiritual life involves reconciliation to God and membership in the church, the body of Christ. A chief end (*telos*) of revelation is spiritual fellowship (*koinonia*) with God and with his people (1 John 1:3–4). A common commitment to a divinely revealed, objectively valid belief system provides a solid base for church *unity*. Those who believed the gospel on the day of Pentecost were baptized and then devoted themselves to the apostle's teaching and to the fellowship, the breaking of bread, and of prayer (Acts 2:41–42). Those who thus preached and received the Word of God began, not another sect of Judaism, but the Christian church. By Spirit-endued belief in Christ-centered revelation they stood against the powerful persecution of the Roman government, they overcame centuries of prejudice against both the Samaritans and the Gentiles to baptize them into the one body of Christ and so into prejudice-shattering fellowship with themselves.

Enduring unity in the church today also needs to be constructed on every member's reflective commitment to the apostles' revealed doctrines. Commitment to truth does not enslave. Propositional truth liberated the early church for service and it can free the church for greater exploits today. In addition to a unity of mighty acts of God (happenings), the first Christians had a unity because of a common assent to revealed gospel beliefs and a common personal trust in the living Christ to whom they referred.

A healthy church needs strong preaching of God's revealed Word. Many ministers do not preach with authority what careful study has shown to be a spiritual reality based on a central doctrine of God's Word, but some "totally other" unknown "X" to which people of God at a certain period endeavor fallibly to point. Christians, knowing that the lordship of Christ comes to expression in Scripture, will attend and support churches that are faithful to the prophetic and apostolic revelations in preaching and practice.

Schools raised up to train people to minister God's revealed truth need to examine themselves to determine whether they are presently serving their educational *raison d'être*. It is not enough to promote the school as a seedbed of revealed thought. Contributors and friends might well ask, "Do all the faculty declare and defend an informational revelation that originated with God and was communicated through the Messiah as well as tested and confirmed prophetic and apostolic spokesmen, whose affirmations are true and not false?" What is the integrating focus of the curriculum, if any? Is every department's teaching faithful to the living God's supernatural revelation in the words of the Jesus of history, the prophets, and the apostles? Believers in propositional revelation from an omniscient God who does not deny himself have the responsibility of developing and defending the coherence of revealed teachings. To affirm that the revelation is noncontradictory and that a systematic theology is possible, is not to hold that anyone can fully comprehend all that was revealed and known. It is only to say that when we claim to know in part, one part of divine revelation will not destroy another. In developing the harmony of the content of universal and particular revelation, attempts to hold a teaching true in theology but false in philosophy or science (double truth) have not long maintained respect.[58]

A Wise Source of Standards for Church Discipline

Churches and schools today could be more glorifying to their Savior and Head if there were more *discipline*. Unfortunately in many organizations an erosion of belief in revealed truths may have made discipline of those who deny the truth nearly impossible. No ethical effort should be spared to correct such situations. Unless normative teachings are implemented by church leaders, the church becomes indistinguishable from the world.

Where discipline is impossible ecclesiastical separation may become necessary. Separation could not be avoided in Luther's day, and many today find themselves in "fellowships" without basic loyalties in common because they are without a shared revelational base.

125

When a well-researched, respectful, loving, and persistent request to return to the purposes of the organization's original documents affirming the normativity of revealed truths shows no prospect of success, the only remaining alternative may be separation with regret.

Jesus Christ holds the church responsible for maintaining doctrinal as well as moral purity (Rev. 2:2, 14, 20). Paul urged the church at Rome to "keep away from" those who caused division by doctrine "contrary to the teaching" they had learned (Rom. 16:17). And Paul left no doubt about the teaching intended, for it is "now revealed and made known through the prophetic writings by the command of the eternal God, so that all nations might believe and obey him" (Rom. 16:26).

An Authentic Exhibit of Justice Tempered With Mercy

By Spirit-endued belief in justice, mercy and love taught by Christ, prophets, and apostles, the early church made a substantial difference in the first-century world. Not only in Israel, but wherever they went, believers in special revelation improved the condition of women, men, children, masters, and slaves. Progressively they realized that every person's dignity as created in the image of God meant having inherent human rights. They called for justice without respect of persons, and honesty rather than false witness against a neighbor. When people realized their inability to live according to such universal norms fully, Christians offered the mercy and love of God for them.

The prophets and apostles warned of judgment and called people to repent of their unfaithfulness to God and others. At the same time they also called people to believe the news of the Messiah's coming atonement and resurrection, and to trust Christ himself. In societies that are far from just—whether communist, socialist, or capitalist—the message of a just amnesty created a forgiving community. Christians are not merely forgiven, they are forgiving. The unjust today cannot succeed in suppressing their guilt nor in denying the reality of their sinfulness. Psychologically and spiritually, spouses, parents, children, employers, and employees need to see the dynamic of Calvary's forgiveness that satisfies justice and graciously provides new life from above.

REVIEW QUESTIONS

To Help Relate and Apply
Each Section in This Chapter

1. *Briefly state the classical problem* this chapter addresses and indicate reasons why genuine inquiry into it is important for your world view and your existence personally and socially.

2. *Objectively summarize the influential answers* given to this problem in history as hypotheses to be tested. Be able to compare and contrast their real similarities and differences (not merely verbal similarities or differences).

3. *Highlight the primary biblical evidence* on which to decide among views—evidence found in the relevant teachings of the major divisions of Scripture—and decide for yourself which historical hypothesis (or synthesis of historical views) provides the most consistent and adequate account of the primary biblical data.

4. *Formulate in your own words your doctrinal conviction* in a logically consistent and adequate way, organizing your conclusions in ways you can explain clearly, support biblically, and communicate effectively to your spouse, children, friends, Bible class, or congregation.

5. *Defend your view* as you would to

adherents of the alternative views, showing that the other views are logically less consistent and factually faced with more difficulties than your view in accounting for the givens, not only of special revelation but also of human experience in general.

6. *Explore the differences the viability of your conviction can make in your life.* Then test your understanding of the viability of your view by asking, "Can I live by it authentically (unhypocritically) in relation to God and to others in my family, church, vocation, neighborhood, city, nation, and world?"

MINISTRY PROJECTS

To Help Communicate This Doctrine in Christian Service

1. *Memorize one major verse or passage* that in its context teaches the heart of this doctrine and may serve as a text from which to preach, teach, or lead small group studies on the topic. The memorized passages from each chapter will build a body of content useful also for meditation and reference in informal discussions.

2. *Formulate the major idea of the doctrine in one sentence* based on the passage memorized. This idea should be useful as the major thesis of either a lesson for a class (junior high to adult) or a message for a church service.

3. *State the specific purpose or goal of your doctrinal lesson or message.* Your purpose should be more than informative. It should answer the question of why Christians need to accept this truth and live by it (unhypocritically). For teaching purposes list indicators that would show to what extent class members have grasped the truth presented.

4. *Outline your message or lesson in complete sentences.* Indicate how you would support the truth of the doctrine's central ideas and its relevance to life and service. Incorporate elements from this chapter's historical, biblical, systematic, apologetic, and relevance sections selected for their direct importance to your purpose for your audience.

5. *List applications of the doctrine* for communicating the difference this conviction makes in life (for sermons, lessons, small-group Bible studies, or family devotional Bible studies). Applications should make clear what the doctrine is, why one needs to know it, and how it will make differences in thinking. Then show how the difference in thought will lead to differences in values, priorities, attitudes, speech, and personal action. Consider also the doctrine's possible significance for family, church, neighborhood, city, regional, and national actions.

6. *Start a file and begin collecting illustrations* of this doctrine's central idea, the points in your outline, and your applications.

7. *Write out your own doctrinal statement on this subject in one paragraph* (in half a page or less). To work toward a comprehensive doctrinal statement, collect your formulations based on a study of each chapter of *Integrative Theology.* As your own statement of Christian doctrine grows, you will find it personally strengthening and useful when you are called on for your beliefs in general and when you apply for service with churches, mission boards, and other Christian organizations. Any who seek ordination to Christian ministry will need a comprehensive doctrinal statement that covers the broad scope of theology.

CHAPTER 4

THE BIBLE AS GIVEN BY INSPIRATION AND RECEIVED BY ILLUMINATION

The Bible
as Given by Inspiration
and Received by Illumination

THE PROBLEM: IN WHAT WAY IS THE BIBLE INSPIRED AND AUTHORITATIVE?

Having shown that God revealed to prophets and apostles not only himself but truths concerning his redemptive purposes, we now face the question of how revelation given in the distant past could be preserved and transmitted to future generations in need of his Word. Judaism and Christianity confess that by Holy Spirit inspiration God ensured the preservation of revelation in a sacred book, the Bible

Since theologians differ widely on the meaning of inspiration, it is necessary to determine what this theological concept entails. Did God inspire the biblical writer or the written document? If inspiration pertains to the prophetic or apostolic record, the question arises how finite, sinful men could state the undistorted truth of God in human language. Did God dictate his Word to the biblical writer, or did the writer, under the general guidance of the Spirit, record in ordinary human fashion the substance of what God had revealed?

It is also a question whether the inerrancy of the Bible can be upheld in the modern world. Must the writing reflect the limitations and frailties of the human author, or did God supernaturally superintend the process so that what the prophet wrote was the Word of God unalloyed by any error? Is it faithful to the teaching of Jesus and the apostles to limit inerrancy to those teachings of the Bible pertinent to salvation? Many today question whether this collection of ancient documents possesses any authority for sophisticated twentieth-century people. Christians need to know on what basis and to what extent the Bible is a binding authority in the modern world.

Many people regard the Bible as a book difficult to understand. Is it reasonable to believe that for the Bible to be properly understood the same God who inspired its contents must also illumine its message to the human mind? Finally, one must confront the issue of the canon of Scripture. How can we today be assured that all the documents God inspired have found their way into the Bible? Can the so-called apocryphal books included in some editions of the Bible be considered inspired? How should the church respond if a copy of a hitherto unknown Davidic Psalm or Pauline letter were to become unearthed?

Since the theology and life of the church is uniquely rooted in the Bible, an authentic understanding of the origin, validity, and relevance of this foundational document is essential.

ALTERNATIVE PROPOSALS IN THE CHURCH

As the issues of biblical inspiration, infallibility, and canon have been addressed in the church, several interpretations have been and continue to be influential.

Roman Catholic Scholasticism

Traditional Roman Catholic theology upheld in principle the divine origin, inspiration, and inerrancy of the Bible. Thomas Aquinas insisted that "the author of Holy Writ is God."[1] Consequently Aquinas refused to concede any errors to the inspired writers: "It is heretical to say that any falsehood whatever is contained either in the Gospels or in any canonical Scripture."[2] The Scriptures represent an incontrovertible authority, whereas the doctors of the church constitute an authority that is merely probable.

In spite of Rome's formal views on inspiration and infallibility, the authority of Scripture in practice was undermined. This was in part because Rome regarded the Bible as obscure and capable of interpretation only by the hierarchy. Thus the church's Magesterium claimed to unfold unerringly the meaning of the Word of God. The authority of the Scripture was also undermined because of the recklessly nonliteral interpretation advanced by many medieval Roman authorities. Wycliffe protested against the debasement and falsification of Scripture by incompetent persons in the Roman church. Luther said that Romanists "treat the Scriptures and make out of them what they like, as if they were a nose of wax, to be pulled about at will."[3] Add to the above the vast complex of papal decretals, conciliar judgments, and canon laws, and it is clear that the Roman church was prior to and above the Scriptures.

The Council of Trent in 1546 affirmed that Scripture and church tradition were given as "dictation by the mouth of Jesus Christ or of the Holy Ghost."[4] Inspired Scripture and inspired tradition are to be venerated "with equal piety and reverence." Trent certified longstanding trends within the Catholic church by declaring the Apocryphal books (except 1 and 2 Esdras and the Prayer of Manasses) to be inspired by God and thus part of the canonical Old Testament. Moreover, it pronounced the Latin Vulgate the authentic version of Scripture and relegated to the Magesterium the prerogative of giving the true interpretation of the Bible.

Protestant Liberalism

Liberal Protestants, for whom supernatural revelation was problematic, minimized or denied altogether the special inspiration of sacred documents. The Deists viewed Scripture as a human book and saw in it many obscurities, contradictions, and immoral prescriptions. They believed that the biblical writers were inspired only to the extent that their literary talents were elevated in moments of special creativity. Many German rationalists rejected divine inspiration altogether. J. S. Semler, for example, traced the idea of verbal inspiration to the legend of the Septuagint, whose translators were said to have been guided in the very words they used. The church appropriated the Jewish doctrine, Semler said, only when it perceived the need to guarantee the contents of the Bible.

Horace Bushnell, the father of American liberalism, likewise rejected verbal inspiration and an infallible Scripture as involving "insuperable difficulties."[5]

Neither, he argued, did God infallibly guide the church in selecting the books that would form the biblical canon. According to Bushnell, God inspired the biblical writers in the same general way that he inspires all persons for the work they perform. Walter Rauschenbusch defined inspiration as "the stirring of the prophetic spirit in living men."[6] Inspiration, so defined, did not cease with the close of the biblical canon, but will continue until the church ushers in the kingdom of God. The Bible, Rauschenbusch says, is a collection of human documents that reflects the frailty and liability to error of its human authors. "Inspiration did not involve infallibility."[7]

James Barr, following Gerhard Von Rad, views the Bible as a collection of the religious traditions of Israel and the church. By inspiration Barr means that God was with his people in the formation of their religious traditions. Since the biblical writers played a pioneering role in the formation of Judeo-Christian traditions, one may call them "inspired" in some special sense. So defined, inspiration has nothing to do with inerrancy and final authority. Indeed, Barr insists that the early church concept of inspired and authoritative Scripture was a gross mistake: it was "the clearest demonstration of the presence of original sin in the early church."[8]

Neoorthodox Theology

Neoorthodoxy views the Bible as a witness to the Word of God, a time-bound, culturally conditioned human word about past revelatory encounters. Barth regards verbal, plenary inspiration as a mechanical process that attributes too much to the Bible and too little to God himself. He judges that the Bible as defined by conservative theology has become a "paper Pope."[9] Barth believes that the biblical writers penned accounts of their revelatory encounters with the transcendent God. The precise *how* of their inscripturation of the Word, however, is an inexplicable mystery. Barth insists that one should not make the mistake of equating Scripture with the Word of God. "It is quite impossible that there should be a direct identity between the human Word of Holy Scripture and the Word of God."[10] Barth avers that to avoid a docetic view of the Bible, one must posit at least a capacity for error, both in the Bible's historical and scientific teaching and in its theological content. "The prophets and apostles . . . were real, historical men as we are, and therefore sinful in their action, and capable and actually guilty of error in their spoken and written word."[11] Nevertheless, as God graciously condescends to speak through a biblical text and the person responds in faith, the human witness acquires the dignity of the Word of God.

Brunner attacked the doctrine of verbal inspiration, calling it a fundamentalist error. "The orthodox doctrine of verbal inspiration has been finally destroyed. It is clear that there is no connection between it and scientific research and honesty; we are forced to make a decision for or against this view."[12] The written word of the Bible is equated with the Word of God only idolatrously, for the former contains "It-Truth," whereas the latter (authentic revelation) contains "Thou-Truth." According to Brunner, Scripture is merely an errant human word about Christ, the divine Word. But in spite of myriads of inconsistencies and contradictions, the Bible becomes the Word of God in that moment of crisis when the individual meets Christ through it. Inspiration connotes the divine illumination of the biblical writers that enabled them to grasp the mystery of Christ and to bear witness to him.

Vatican II Catholicism

The Vatican II Catholic view of the Bible, influenced by Protestant neoorthodoxy, limits the veracity and authority of Scripture to those teachings that pertain to salvation. The original draft of the "Dogmatic Constitution on Divine Revelation" presented to the first session of the Council expressed the traditional Catholic view that Scripture is "absolutely immune from error." This position was challenged and ultimately replaced by a more "modern" stance, the heart of which reads: "The holy books of Scripture must be acknowledged as teaching firmly, faithfully and without error that truth which God wanted to put into the sacred writings for the sake of our salvation" (no. 11). Avant-garde Catholic authorities thus insist that the so-called nonsalvific teachings of the Bible are neither inerrant nor binding on the faithful.

Hans Küng insists that historical-critical studies of the Bible have demolished the classical doctrine of verbal inspiration. The biblical writers were not divinely programmed penmen, but frail human witnesses who testified to their encounter with the divine revelation. The misleading term, inspiration of Scripture, if it be used at all, connotes only that the human witnesses were "*Spirit-pervaded* and *Spirit-filled.*"[13] But inspiration, so defined, applies equally to the totality of the apostolic life and ministry as to the apostles' literary endeavors. Therefore, Küng concludes, the Bible "is unequivocally *man's word*: collected, written down, given varied emphases, sentence by sentence by quite definite individuals and developed in different ways. Hence it is not without shortcomings and mistakes, concealment and confusion, limitations and errors."[14] Indeed, insists Küng, "there is not a single text in Scripture asserting its freedom from error."[15]

"Liberal" Evangelicals

Some Evangelicals (the so-called limited inerrantists) restrict the veracity and authority of the Scriptures to its salvific teachings. C. S. Lewis upheld the theory of degrees of inspiration when he insisted that inspiration is not "always present in the same mode and the same degree" throughout the Bible.[16] Lewis is not disturbed by the presence of errors in the biblical text: "The human qualities of the raw materials show through. Naïvete, error, contradiction, even (as in the cursing Psalms) wickedness is not removed. The total result is not 'the Word of God' in the sense that every passage, in itself gives impeccable science or history."[17] The flawed character of the Bible is seen in the fact that it contains pagan myths (the Genesis account) and nonhistorical narratives (the stories of Jonah, Job, and Esther).

Dewey Beegle speaks of different "kinds" of inspiration. The great "sent ones" of Scripture—Moses, the leading prophets, Jesus, and Paul—were recipients of a special *charismata*, whereas the lesser writers of the Bible wrote on the basis of their natural abilities and status within the covenant community. The former mode of inspiration ceased with the close of the New Testament canon, whereas the latter "process of reinterpretation and application will continue as long as man exists."[18] Two implications of this thesis follow: (1) Contemporary Christian writers are inspired to the same degree as, for example, David, Haggai, or Jude. (2) The Bible amounts to a collection of contradictory traditions, all of which do not fit into a coherent pattern. According to Beegle, the Bible is "inspired from cover to cover, human mistakes and all."[19]

G. C. Berkouwer is said to have moved through three stages in his understanding of Scripture.[20] The first, held in the 1930s before Berkouwer became acquainted with Barth, posited the entire veracity and trustworthiness of the Bible. The second, adopted in the 1940s, stressed Scripture's salvific character. And the third, embraced in the 1960s, focuses on the existential dimension of the Word. Currently Berkouwer is less concerned with such formal issues as inspiration and inerrancy (which he claims border on Docetism) than with the life-transforming message of salvation embedded in the Bible. He is not troubled by the fact that when the Word became Scripture it succumbed to the fate of all writing, that is, to time-bound notions, culturally conditioned expressions, and scientific misconceptions. But none of these imperfections cause the Bible to swerve from its central purpose, which is to uphold the truth of the gospel.

Jack Rogers follows Berkouwer in replacing verbal inspiration and inerrancy with the "organic" concept of inspiration, whereby "the function, the saving purpose, of Scripture [is] the focus of human concern rather than the form of the writing."[21] Rogers draws a distinction between the divine content, or kernel, of the biblical message and the human form, or husk, in which the message is cast. Rogers insists that the Bible is inspired only in terms of the former, i.e., "the central saving message of Scripture," and not in matters of science, history, chronology, or the male-female relation.[22] Infallibility and authority likewise are redefined in terms of the Bible's central purpose. Hence truth (viewed pragmatically, functionally, and existentially) is that which meets people's needs, and error that which willfully deceives. Insofar as the Bible makes people wise for salvation it is infallible, but because by modern standards it contains factual errors, it is not inerrant.

Protestant Fundamentalism

A fundamentalist view of the Bible, such as that advanced by John R. Rice, posits divine dictation to biblical writers who functioned as secretaries of the Holy Spirit. Rice's view of inspiration as dictation implies that God gave the very words that men wrote down in Holy Scripture. "A secretary is not ashamed to take dictation from man. Why would a prophet be ashamed to take dictation from God?"[23] Rice seeks to safeguard the human element in Scripture by maintaining that God prepared the writers in advance so that their style, vocabulary, and personality are included in the writing in accord with God's plan. What he wishes to avoid is that the biblical writers engaged in historical research, utilized oral traditions, or acquired information from eye witnesses. All Scripture came in a straight line from God to the human writers. Rice's theory of dictation borders on the docetic: "The Scriptures are fundamentally the Word of God, not the word of men, except in some incidental and controlled and limited sense."[24]

Most Fathers, Reformers, and Evangelicals

Most orthodox authorities believe that God supernaturally moved the writers of Scripture so that, although they wrote in accord with their own interests, style, and abilities, the resultant documents are his Word, authoritative in matters of faith and practice, and truthful in all they affirm. Many early Fathers stressed the divine side of Scripture by means of vivid analogies. Justin Martyr described inspiration as the process whereby the Holy Spirit worked on the biblical writers much as a musician plays on a harp or a lyre. Athenagoras maintained that the biblical writer was "a stringed instrument

135

which the Holy Ghost put in motion, in order to draw out of it the divine harmonies of life."[25] Tertullian described individual Old Testament texts as "the commandments of God"[26] and the canon as the Scripture of the Holy Ghost.

Irenaeus in the West upheld the verbal inspiration and veracity of the entire Bible: "The Scriptures are indeed perfect, since they were spoken by the Word of God (i.e., Christ) and His Spirit."[27] Gregory of Nazianzus argued that the smallest stroke of Scripture derives from the Holy Spirit, and that even the slightest nuance of the inspired writer is not in vain. Jerome upheld verbal, plenary inspiration, as evidenced by his overstatement that "the individual sayings, syllables, phonetic markings, and punctuations in divine Scripture are filled with meanings."[28]

Irenaeus and Clement of Alexandria accepted as canonical the books of the Apocrypha. On the other hand, Origen, Athanasius, Gregory of Nazianzus, Cyril of Jerusalem, and Jerome (an authority on Hebrew) strongly opposed the extracanonical writings. Against Jerome's will the Apocrypha were included in the Latin Vulgate, yet accorded a secondary status.

Augustine was a staunch defender of the verbal inspiration of canonical Scripture. While asserting that the biblical authors wrote with an active mind, he stressed the divine initiative by stating that the apostles wrote at the command of Christ, the Lord using them "as if they were His own hands."[29] In a letter to Jerome, Augustine said of canonical Scripture, "I believe most firmly that not one of those authors has erred in any respect in writing."[30] The veracity of Scripture extends even to its discussions of natural science and history. By virtue of the divine afflatus, Holy Scripture is endowed with an indisputable authority.[31] Augustine held that the Old Testament contained forty-four books, including six Apocrypha. On certain occasions he differentiated the "canonical" Scriptures received by the Jews from others (the Apocrypha) that were not accepted by the Jews.[32] The uncertainty in Augustine's mind concerning the Apocrypha may be due to his unfamiliarity with Hebrew and his high regard for the LXX translation.

Martin Luther judged that since Scripture is from the Holy Spirit it possesses the authority of God himself. The function of the written Word is to teach Christ, the living Word. So Luther referred to the Bible as the swaddling clothes and manger in which Christ is wrapped and laid.[33] The Reformer repeatedly insisted that in both its salvific and nonsalvific teachings the Scriptures have never erred. "The Holy Spirit is not a fool or a drunkard to express one point, not to say one word, in vain."[34] Luther's German translation of the Bible eliminated the Apocryphal books inserted by Rome. However, he disputed the canonicity of Jude, Hebrews, James, and Revelation, persuaded that none of these books lays the foundations of gospel faith. Using his own criterion of canonicity—namely, that which teaches Christ—Luther assigned these four letters a secondary status in the New Testament. Luther did not hold a low view of the Bible, as critics allege. The fact is that those Scriptures Luther judged canonical he upheld as fully inspired, inerrant, and authoritative. Only his faulty criterion of canonicity caused him to question the integrity of those four books.

Calvin believed that from Genesis to Revelation, "The Bible has come down to us from the mouth of God."[35] God is the author of the words, propositions, and doctrines contained in Holy Scripture. Indeed, Calvin states that the biblical writers were "clerks,"[36] "penmen,"[37] "amanuenses,"[38] and "organs and instruments"[39] of the Holy Spirit.

By these bold metaphors Calvin did not endorse the dictation theory; rather he sought to convey in this way his conviction that God was in sovereign control of the inscripturation of his Word and that he is its ultimate Author. Calvin further believed that, having God as its author, the written Word of God is infallible or inerrant. Thus Scripture "is the certain and unerring Rule,"[40] "sacred and inviolable truth,"[41] the "sure and inviolable record,"[42] "unerring light,"[43] etc. The only errors Calvin admitted were copyists' errors in some manuscripts. Although the Bible is not a textbook of science or history, when it touches on such matters, its judgments are true.[44] Full conviction of the divine authority and veracity of Scripture is imparted by the compelling testimony of the Holy Spirit.[45]

The major branches of Protestantism uphold the high view of Scripture in their confessional statements. So the Lutheran communion in The Formula of Concord (Epitome), the Reformed in The Belgic Confession (Art. III), The Second Helvetic Confession (ch. I), and The Westminster Confession of Faith (ch. I.5, 6, 8), the Anglican tradition in The Thirty-Nine Articles (Art. XX), and the Baptists in The New Hampshire Confession (Art. I).

B. B. Warfield held that the manner of the Word's inscription is best described by the phrases "concursive operation" and "confluent authorship." That is, the human activity involving historical research and logical reasoning was mysteriously cojoined with the divine operation of the Spirit's superintendence, direction, and control. As a divine-human product, Scripture is "God-breathed" (i.e., produced by the creative breath of the Almighty), not in its thought only, but also in its words, and not in part but in full. Thus "the Bible is the Word of God in such a sense that its words, though written by men and bearing indelibly impressed on them the marks of their human origin, were written, nevertheless, under such an influence of the Holy Ghost as to be also the words of God, the adequate expression of His mind and be also the words of God, the adequate expression of His mind and will."[46] As the veritable Word of God, Scripture is inerrant: "No single error has yet been demonstrated to occur in the Scriptures as given by God to His Church."[47]

Carl F. H. Henry defines inspiration as that "supernatural influence upon divinely chosen prophets and apostles whereby the Spirit of God assures the truth and trustworthiness of their oral and written proclamation."[48] Henry stresses that Scripture is inspired in its entirety, that inspiration does not continue, even sporadically, and that the Scriptures written are the very Word of God. Henry refers *inerrancy* to the veracity of the inspired autographs and *infallibility* to the qualified perfection of the manuscript copies and translations. He urges that the term inerrancy not be dropped, but retained and carefully defined. By verbal inerrancy Henry means (1) that the Bible teaches truth in matters of history and science as well as theology and ethics; (2) that God's truth resides in the words, propositions, and sentences of the Bible; and (3) that only the original writings (autographs) are error-free. Inerrancy does not imply modern scientific precision, does not mean verbal exactitude in the apostolic quotation of Old Testament texts, and does not nullify the need for personal faith in Christ, who is the living Word of God.

The Chicago Statement on Biblical Inerrancy, produced by the International Council on Biblical Inerrancy (1978), agrees with the stance of Henry. It affirms that utilizing the distinctive personalities and literary styles of chosen men, the Spirit superintended their writing such that the sum of what was written, to the very words used, constitutes the authoritative Word of God. Since God is the author of Scripture, what is written "is inerrant, being free from all falsehood, fraud, or deceit" (Art. XII). The statement denies that the Bible could be infallible though errant in its assertions. The Statement is sensitive to the cultural contexts in which the biblical documents were written: "Although Scripture is nowhere culture-bound in the sense that its teaching lacks universal validity, it is sometimes culturally conditioned by the customs and conventions of a particular period, so that the application of its principles today calls for a different sort of action."[49]

The Evangelical position on inspired and authoritative Scripture has been further expounded in a number of recent informative studies.[50]

BIBLICAL TEACHING

To determine which historical perspective on Scripture is closest to the Bible's view of itself, we need to survey the relevant biblical materials in the context of progressive revelation.

Pentateuch

At Sinai (Exod. 24:4) Moses wrote down all the case laws and statutes (known as "the Book of the Covenant," 20:22–23:33) that God had given to Israel. Shortly after that God summoned Moses to ascend the mountain to receive the two tablets of stone on which God had written his laws and commands (24:12). The text states that on the tablets the Decalogue was "inscribed by the finger of God" (31:18; Deut. 9:10), where "finger" is a symbol for the creative power of God. Moses explains, "The tablets were the work of God; the writing was the writing of God, engraved on the tablets" (Exod. 32:16). After the tablets had been broken (v. 19), God rewrote the Ten Com-

mandments on new stone tablets that Moses had chiseled out (34:1), and God ordered that they be lodged in the ark of the Testimony (25:16, 21; Deut. 10:5). In one instance, then, a portion of the Word of God (the Decalogue) was put in writing by God himself without any human instrumentality.

Still at Sinai God commanded Moses, "Write down these words, for in accordance with these words I have made a covenant with you and with Israel" (Exod. 34:27). What Moses wrote down by the command of God (dictation?) most likely are Exodus 34:10–26 and "the Book of the Covenant," cited above. The final reference to Moses' literary endeavors, in Deuteronomy 31:24–26, indicates that "Moses finished writing in a book the words of this law from beginning to end." Jewish tradition identifies "this Book of the Law" (v. 26) as the entire Pentateuch, though other scholars limit the writing to Deuteronomy 1–30.[51] Whatever the scope of the writing, Moses ordered the Book of the Law placed with the other sacred writings by the Ark of the Covenant. What Moses wrote were not his own words, but "the commands of the LORD" (Deut. 4:2). By virtue of their divine origin and authority nothing was to be added to or subtracted from these writings accomplished by the hand of Moses (4:2; cf. 12:32).

Historical Books

As God continued to speak to his servants, their writings came to be viewed as divinely authoritative and so were deposited alongside the ark. Thus at the end of his life Joshua recorded the substance of the covenant established at Shechem "in the Book of the Law of God" (Josh. 24:25–26). Similarly Samuel "explained to the people the regulations of the kingship. He wrote them down on a scroll and deposited it before the LORD" (1 Sam. 10:25). During the reign of Josiah in the seventh century Hilkiah the high priest discovered a copy of "the Book of the Law" (2 Kings 22:8) or "the Book of the Covenant" (2 Kings 23:2). This document has been variously identified as the Pentateuch placed beside the ark (Deut. 31:26) or as the books of Exodus and Deuteronomy. The Chronicler's description of the document as "the Book of the Law of the LORD that had been given through Moses" (2 Chron. 34:14) underscores the divine-human character of this Mosaic writing. In the fifth century, following the rebuilding of the walls of Jerusalem, Ezra, Nehemiah, and the Levites interpreted to the people "the Book of the Law of Moses" (Neh. 8:1) or "the Book of the Law of God" (Neh. 8:8). The book, likely the Pentateuch, is described as both the work of Moses and the work of God.

The human side of Scripture is reflected not only in different styles of writing, but in the biblical writers' use of secular archival records, prophetic annals, collections of poetry, and the like. Uninspired sources utilized by the sacred authors in the preparation of canonical Scriptures include the Book of Jashar (2 Sam. 1:18), the book of the annals of Solomon (1 Kings 11:41), the book of the annals of the kings of Judah (1 Kings 14:29), the records of Samuel the seer (1 Chron. 29:29), the records of Nathan the prophet (1 Chron. 29:29), the records of Shemaiah the prophet and of Iddo the seer (2 Chron. 12:15), and the annotations on the book of the kings (2 Chron. 24:27).

Poetry and Wisdom

The unsurpassing excellence of Scripture, befitting its divine origin, is amply attested in the Psalms. Psalm 12:6 declares that "the words of the LORD are flawless, like silver refined in a furnace of clay, purified seven times" (cf. Ps. 18:30; Prov. 30:5). More precious than silver purged of its dross the Word of God is unblemished truth and absolutely trustworthy. The second volume of Psalm 19 upholds the inherent perfections of the Word of the Lord and its spiritual relevance for life. Thus the Law of God, identified by the synonyms "statutes," "precepts," "commands," and "ordinances," is described as "perfect" (v. 7), or without blemish, "trustworthy" (v. 7), or firm or reliable, "right" (v. 8), or the opposite of crooked or perverse, "radiant" (v. 8), or bright as the sun, "sure" (v. 9) or fully dependable, and "altogether righteous" (v. 9), or straight and true. The conclusion of the psalmist's meditation is that the Law of the Lord is more precious than pure gold and sweeter than honey from the comb (v. 10).

Psalm 119 presents an even more extensive portrait of Scripture's impeccable qualities and spiritual benefits, in that order. Without being exhaustive the Law of the Lord is described as "righteous" (vv. 7, 62, et al.), "good" (v. 39), "trustworthy" (vv. 86, 138), "eternal" (vv. 89, 160), awe-inspiring (v. 120), "right" (vv. 128, 137), "wonderful" (v. 129), and "true" (vv. 142, 151). The psalmist explicitly ascribes several of these perfections to the totality of the written Law by means of the qualifier "all" (vv. 86, 151, 160, 172). Scripture's utility relative to the spiritual life is extensive both in its depth and in its breadth: it guards against sin (vv. 9, 11), renews and restores the life (vv. 25, 37, 40, et al.), mediates God's unfailing love (v. 41), offers encouragement in affliction (v. 92), imparts discernment and understanding (vv. 100, 104, 130, et al.), illumines life's pathway (v. 105), and imparts peace to the soul (v. 165).

The humanity of Scripture is reflected in the fact that the Book of Job accurately records the misguided judgments of Eliphaz, Bildad, and Zophar.

Whereas the Scripture affirms that Job was a "blameless and upright" man who "feared God and shunned evil" (Job 1:1), Job's three friends and Elihu erroneously judged that his suffering was a direct consequence of grievous sins he had committed (Job 4:7–9; 36:8–10). Yet at the close of the episode God vindicates Job, rebukes Eliphaz and company for their faithless counsel, and promises that Job will intercede for them! (Job 42:7–8). The point is that inspiration extends to the accurate recording of patently false counsel. A similar accurate recording of obviously uninspired wisdom occurs in the Book of Ecclesiastes. The naturalistic philosophy of the person who lives life without reference to God is faithfully reproduced in Ecclesiastes 1:2; 3:19–21; 9:1, 10.

The human side of the Bible is further seen in the emotional outbursts recorded in the imprecatory Psalms (Pss. 55, 59, 69, 79, 109, 137). The psalmist not only cries out to God, "Let death take my enemies by surprise; let them go down alive to the grave" (Ps. 55:15), but he also utters the harsh wish, "May they be blotted out of the book of life and not be listed with the righteous" (Ps. 69:28). The most violent imprecation of all was uttered against the Babylonian captors who committed atrocities against the inhabitants of Jerusalem: "Happy is he who repays you for what you have done to us—he who seizes your infants and dashes them against the rocks" (Ps. 137:8–9). The preceding statement should be understood as hyperbolic expressions of the distressed spirit who cries out in anguish against the enemies of God and who longs for the vindication of God's honor and justice.

The Book of Proverbs bears within itself clear evidence that it is a compilation (adapted and edited by Solomon) of the nobler aspects of Near Eastern wisdom. Thus in addition to sections written by Solomon himself (Prov. 10:1–22:16; 25:1–29:27), there are collections called "Sayings of the Wise" (22:17–24:22) and "Further Sayings of the Wise" (24:23–34). Proverbs thus likely represents the distillation of the wisdom—writings of many wise men (some of whom received revelation and others who did not) in various places and over a considerable period of time. On this showing, "Proverbs is the scrapbook of common grace."[52]

The Prophets

As for the rest of the Old Testament canon, God dictated a message to Isaiah that the prophet was to record on a scroll (Isa. 8:1). God ordered the writing of another oracle on a scroll that it might serve as a perpetual witness (Isa. 30:8). And the prophet claimed that his prophetic message was preserved in "the scroll of the LORD" (Isa. 34:16). The prophet Jeremiah claimed that his message was given directly by God (Jer. 1:9). Indeed, God commanded Jeremiah to write in a book the very words that the Lord would speak to him (Jer. 30:2). The procedure by which Scripture was produced is delineated in some detail in Jeremiah 36:1–6. The prophet "dictated" to Baruch "all the words the LORD had spoken to him," whereupon the scribe "wrote them on [a] scroll." Jeremiah certifies that a prophetic utterance from Obadiah (Jer. 49:14–19) and from Micah (Jer. 26:18) are the very words of God himself.

Hosea describes God's prophet as an "inspired man" (Hos. 9:7), and Micah claims to be "filled with power" and "with the Spirit of the LORD" (Mic. 3:8). Moreover, God told Habakkuk to inscribe the revelation on tablets so that its message would be plain for all to read (Hab. 2:2). God himself certifies that the written revelation "will not prove false" (Hab. 2:3).

Synoptic Gospels

That inspiration extends to the very form of a word is clear from Matthew 2:15, where God's watchful care over the infant Jesus was viewed as the fulfillment of Hosea 11:1: "When Israel was a child, I loved him, and out of Egypt I called my son" (cf. Exod. 4:22–23). The singular "son" was an unusual designation for the nation Israel (hence the LXX translation, "Out of Egypt I called his children"). Yet only "son" and not "sons" was appropriate to the Holy Spirit's application of the text to Jesus, the Son whom God would bring up out of Egypt.

Jesus unequivocally upheld the authority of the Old Testament as the Word of God in Matthew 5:17–19 (cf. Luke 16:17). In response to the charge that he sought to do away with the Law and the Prophets, Jesus insisted that his mission was to "fulfill" them (v. 17). The verb *plēroō* conveys the idea of "confirm" or "establish." Whereas Matthew emphasizes that Scripture must be filled out, Luke makes the point that Scripture will not be made void: it is impossible "for the least stroke of a pen to drop out [*pesein*] of the Law" (Luke 16:17). Indeed, Jesus insisted that the authority of Scripture extends to its most minute portions. Both the *iota,* possibly a reference to the *yod,* the smallest Hebrew letter, and the *keraia,* the smallest stroke of the pen, would stand until all God's purposes are accomplished.

In dialogue with the Pharisees and the teachers of the Law (Mark 7:5–13; Matt. 15:3–9) Jesus quoted Isaiah 29:13; Exodus 20:12; and Exodus 21:17 and described the words of Moses and Isaiah as "the commands of God." In each case the Old Testament writings as the "Word of God" were clearly differentiated from human "traditions." In Matthew 19:4–5 Jesus cites a word from Moses (Gen. 2:24). Yet instead of introducing the text with "Moses said" or "the Scripture says," Jesus used the formula, "the Creator said." On another occasion Jesus introduced his quotation of Psalm 110:1 with the claim that David spoke these words *"en pneumati"* (Matt. 22:43–44). The indefectibility of our Lord's words in Scripture is asserted in Matthew 24:35: "Heaven and earth will pass away, but my words will never pass away."

The synoptic Gospels assume that the Old Testament is authoritative in its historical teaching. Jesus treated as factual the accounts of Adam and Eve (Matt. 19:4–5), Cain and Abel (Luke 11:51), Noah and the Flood (Matt. 24:37–39; Luke 17:26–27), the destruction of Sodom and Gomorrah (Matt. 10:15; 11:23–24), the experience of Lot (Luke 17:28–32), Moses the lawgiver (Matt. 19:8; Mark 7:10), David eating the shewbread (Matt. 12:3–4; Luke 6:3–4), the splendor of Solomon (Matt. 6:29; Luke 11:31), Elijah and the widow of Zarephath (Luke 4:25–26), Elisha and Namaan the Syrian (Luke 4:27), and Jonah and the fish (Matt. 12:39–41; Luke 11:29–32).

Similarly Jesus and the Evangelists upheld the Old Testament as prophetically authoritative. Typically a contemporary event was noted, an observation was made ("This was to fulfill what was spoken through the prophet"), and the relevant Old Testament prophecy was quoted. The most important acknowledgments of fulfilled prophecy in the synoptic Gospels are: Matthew 1:22–23 (Isa. 7:14); Matthew 2:15 (Hos. 11:1); Matthew 2:17–18 (Jer. 31:15); Matthew 4:13–16 (Isa. 9:1–2); Matthew 11:10 (Mal. 3:1); Matthew 12:17–21 (Isa. 42:1–4); Matthew 13:14–15 (Isa. 6:9–10); Matthew 21:4–5 (Zech. 9:9); Matthew 24:15 (Dan. 9:27); Matthew 26:31 (Zech. 13:7); and Matthew 27:9–10 (Zech. 11:12–13; Jer. 32:6–9). Jesus summed up the authority of prophetic Scripture in this manner: "Everything must be fulfilled that is written about me in the Law of Moses, the Prophets and the Psalms'' (Luke 24:44).

Jesus also regarded the Old Testament as doctrinally authoritative. A dispute over resurrection was settled by appeal to teaching from the Law (Matt. 22:29–32; Exod. 3:6). Similarly the issue of the abomination of desolation in the eschatological future (Matt. 24:15; Mark 13:14) was clarified by appeal to Daniel 9:27; 11:31; and 12:11. That Jesus viewed the Old Testament as being ethically authoritative is clear from the fact that he frequently quoted from it in making statements regarding moral values and conduct (Matt. 4:1–10; 7:12; 22:36–40).

Christ's belief in verbal inspiration and the indefectible authority of Scripture is reflected in the frequently occurring phrases: ''It is written'' (Matt. 4:4, 6, 7, 10; Mark 1:2; 9:13; Luke 19:46), ''Have you never read?'' (Matt. 21:16, 42; Mark 2:25; Luke 6:3), ''This is what is written'' (Luke 24:46), et al. Likewise the singular term ''Scripture'' (*graphē,* Mark 12:10; 15:28; Luke 4:21) and the plural ''the Scriptures'' (*hai graphai,* Matt. 21:42; Mark 12:24; Luke 24:27, et al.) depict the Old Testament uniformly as a book of divine oracles, every portion of which is clothed with irrefragable authority.

Whereas the foregoing data from the Gospels confirms the divinity of the entire Old Testament, the prologue to Luke's Gospel (Luke 1:1–4) sheds light on the human side as it is related to his Gospel. (1) Luke sets forth his human qualifications for writing (v. 2): although a second generation Christian, he has access to oral and written accounts by eyewitnesses. (2) Luke affirms that he has carefully researched the history to ascertain the facts (v. 3a). (3) The historian states the method he has followed in writing (v. 3b): he organizes his material in a connected whole with a set principle or arrangement. And (4) Luke relates his humanly formed purpose (v. 4): ''so that you may know the certainty of the things you have been taught.'' Thus it is evident that Luke ''presents his Gospel as a very human composition.''[53] Nevertheless it constitutes ''the word'' (v. 2) and hence is marked by truth and ''certainty'' (v. 4).

Primitive Christianity/Acts

Peter and John certify that the sovereign God in Psalm 2:1–2 ''spoke by the Holy Spirit through the mouth of . . . our father David'' (Acts 4:25–26). Later Paul said to leaders of the Jews (Acts 28:25), ''The Holy Spirit spoke the truth to your forefathers when he said through Isaiah the prophet: 'Go to this people and say . . .''' (Isa. 6:9–10). Not only did the apostles attribute the Old Testament writings to the Holy Spirit, but they also regarded them as ''truth'' (Acts 28:25), unalloyed by any falsehood. Paul believed the Old Testament to be plenarily inspired, for he declared to Felix, ''I believe everything that agrees with the Law and that is written in the Prophets'' (Acts 24:14).

In the course of defending their ministry the apostles certified the reliability of the Old Testament history. Stephen surveyed the leading events of Old Testament history from Abraham to Solomon (Acts 7:2–47). Before the synagogue rulers at Pisidian Antioch Paul rehearsed the history of the Exodus (Acts 13:17), the wilderness wanderings (v. 18), the destruction of the Canaanite nations (v. 19), the judges (v. 20), and the kings Saul and David (vv. 20–22).

Moreover, the apostles established their preaching and teaching on the authority of Old Testament prophecy. Repeatedly they insisted that the events that had come to pass occurred in direct fulfillment of an Old Testament prediction (Acts 1:16–17; 2:16–21; 3:21–23, et al.). Likewise their ministry was guided by the authority of Old Testament theology. Thus appeal was made to Amos 9:11–12 to settle doctrinal differences at the Jerusalem Council (Acts 15:15–18). The Bereans diligently searched the Scriptures to determine the validity of Paul's gospel (Acts 17:11).

The Pauline Corpus

As shown in the previous chapter, Paul in 1 Corinthians 2:12 acknowledged that the apostles were recipients of special revelation. The following verse indicates that the very words (*logoi*) in which the Gospels were clothed were provided by the Holy Spirit: "we impart this in words not taught by human wisdom but taught by the Spirit" (1 Cor. 2:13 RSV). Verbal inspiration is also attested in Galatians 3:16, where Paul's argument rests on the singular form of "seed" (*zera'*) in the Old Testament. Thus "the promises were spoken to Abraham and to his seed. The Scripture does not say 'and to seeds,' meaning many people, but 'and to your seed,' meaning one person, who is Christ." The Holy Spirit directed Moses to use the collective "seed" in Genesis 12:7; 13:15, et al. rather than the customary plural, since the ultimate fulfillment of the promise centered on Christ.

The *locus classicus* of the doctrine of inspiration is 2 Timothy 3:16: "All Scripture is God-breathed. . . ." "All Scripture" (*pas* with the singular noun without the article) is rightly understood as each individual Scripture within the totality of Holy Writ. The metaphor "God-breathed" (*theopneustos*, from *theos* and *pneō*, to breathe) connotes origination by divine power (cf. Ps. 33:6; Isa. 40:7, 24). What is divinely spirated or breathed out, according to Paul, is not the human writer, but the written Scripture (*graphē*) itself. Some

authorities, such as the RSV margin reading, regard *theopneustos* as a qualifying adjective and translate the verse, "Every Scripture inspired by God is also profitable . . . ," the outcome being to suggest that only certain parts of Scripture are inspired and hence of spiritual profit. It is preferable, however, to take *theopneustos* as a predicate that is coordinated by the conjunction *kai* ("and") with "useful" or "profitable." This construction, commended by the AV, NIV. and others, upholds the parallelism of the two adjectives "God-breathed" and "useful."[54] Paul in these few words has propounded the doctrine of plenary inspiration: every portion of Scripture has its origin with God. And precisely because Scripture is divinely inspired it possesses spiritual utility. Hence Scripture is "useful for teaching, rebuking, correcting and training in righteousness, so that the man of God may be thoroughly equipped for every good work." Unlike some critics, the inspired apostle was not guilty of placing the functional cart (Scripture's utility) before the ontological horse (its plenary inspiration)!

The divine side of Scripture is affirmed in Romans 3:2, where the apostle maintains that the chief advantage of the Jews is that "they have been entrusted with the very words (*ta logia*) of God." *Logia*, translated "oracles" in the AV and RSV. denotes utterances from the very mouth of God.[55] Hence Paul insists that Scripture, as a book of divine oracles, is the pure and absolute Word of God.

Paul also acknowledges the unity of the Word of God inscripturated by means of the expressions "It is written" (Rom. 1:17; 4:17; 11:26; 1 Cor. 1:19; 2:9; Gal. 3:10, 13, et al.), "Scripture" (Rom. 4:3; 10:11; Gal. 3:16; 1 Tim. 5:18), and "the Holy Scriptures" (Rom. 1:2). On other occasions an Old Testament text is quoted, introduced by the word *legei* (Rom. 15:10; 2 Cor. 6:2; Eph. 4:8; 5:14), *eipē* (1 Cor. 15:27), or *phēsin* (1 Cor. 6:16)—all of which are generally translated by the impersonal "It says." However, B. B. Warfield has convincingly shown that in such texts "It says" = "the Scripture says" = "God says."[56] Once again a number of Old Testament texts are apostolically certified as direct utterances of God himself.

The Pauline corpus also attests the divine origin and authority of the then-emergent New Testament writings. Paul not only asserts that Christ was speaking through him (2 Cor. 13:3), but he describes what he *wrote* to the Corinthians as "the Lord's command" (1 Cor. 14:37) and hence endowed with "the authority of the Lord Jesus " (1 Thess. 4:2). Paul also commanded the brethren to lay hold of the traditions (*paradoseis*) taught by the apostles "whether by word of mouth or by letter" (2 Thess. 2:15). Indeed, Paul solemnly charged as with an oath (*enorkizō*) the church at Thessalonica to read his first letter to the gathered body (1 Thess. 5:27). And he urged that his letter to the Colossians be read to the church there and to the Laodiceans (Col. 4:16). Whoever failed to obey the written apostolic teaching would incur severe punishment (2 Thess. 3:14). The inspiration of a specific New Testament text was acknowledged by the apostle when he placed a saying of Jesus (Luke 10:7) on a par with a command of Yahweh through Moses (Deut. 25:4) and referred to both as "Scripture" (1 Tim. 5:18).

The writings of Paul, although replete with evidences of the divinity of Scripture, also attest its human authorship. The apostle said that beyond the household of Stephanas he did not recall if he baptized any others (1 Cor. 1:16). In the area of marital relationships on which Paul had no directive from the Lord, he gave his own opinion (1 Cor.

7:12). In other situations the apostle rendered a personal judgment (1 Cor. 7:40) and gave his own counsel (2 Cor. 8:8–10). Yet his acknowledgment, "I too have the Spirit of God" (1 Cor. 7:40) reminds us that behind his human judgments was the guidance of the Holy Spirit.

Finally, Paul added that for a person to know God as Savior the Holy Spirit must illumine the truths of Scripture and apply them to the heart. The non-Christian has little understanding of God's redemptive purposes (1 Cor. 2:8–9), for a veil covers the sinner's heart (2 Cor. 3:15). However, when the unbeliever turns to Christ, the Holy Spirit removes the veil (2 Cor. 3:16) and unfolds the things of God to the trusting soul (1 Cor. 2:10–11). Whereas spiritual truths appear foolish to the unbeliever, the Spirit imparts to the believer spiritual insight so that the verities of God's Word are understood and appropriated (1 Cor. 2:14–15). Indeed, through the teaching ministry of the Spirit believers possess "the mind of Christ" and thus evaluate life from his point of view (1 Cor. 2:16). Unlike inspiration, illumination does admit of degrees, the extent of the operation being dependent on the faith and obedience of the individual.

The Johannine Literature

According to the fourth Gospel, Jesus commissioned the apostles to be his witnesses (John 1:37–50; 21:16–17). The Lord trained them to be teachers of the New Covenant, using methods similar to those used by the rabbis to train their disciples (John 4:31–38; 6:5–12; 13:1–17, et al.). He also equipped them with the special endowment of the Holy Spirit (John 14:12; 20:21–23). Jesus gave them the words (*hrēmata*) the Father had given him (John 17:8). Moreover, after his death and exaltation Christ would send the Holy Spirit both to remind them of past teaching and to impart new revelations (John 14:26; cf. 16:13–15). Thereafter the apostolic testimony would be guided and preserved by special inspiration of the Spirit (John 15:26–27; cf. Acts 5:32). The Gospel that John wrote, as indeed the entire New Testament does, represents the fulfillment of these promises.

Several Johannine texts teach the divine inspiration and authority of Scripture. The written record of Moses (John 5:45–47) is equated with "the Scriptures" (v. 39) and designated the Father's "word" (v. 38). In John 10:34–36 the "law" of the Jews—i.e., the Old Testament—is expressly denoted "the Word of God." Moreover, Jesus' argument vis-à-vis the Jews turned on a single word in the Old Testament text. If God in Psalm 82:6 called the prophets "gods" (*'elōhîm, theoi*), why should his Jewish opponents level accusations of blasphemy when Jesus claimed to be the Son of God (*huios tou theou*)? In addition, Jesus in this text made the unqualified assertion, "the Scripture cannot be broken." The aorist infinitive passive of *luō* means "to be destroyed," i.e., to be set aside or invalidated.[57] Jesus asserts that since Scripture is the very Word of God, it cannot be deprived of its binding authority. In John 17:17 Jesus intercedes for his disciples with these words: "Sanctify them by the truth; your word is truth" (cf. 8:31–32). Truth (*alētheia*) here means judgments about an object of knowledge that conform perfectly to reality and provide the basis for facticity. As Westcott noted, "The Word of God is not only 'true' but 'truth' and had a transforming virtue."[58] Similarly in John 21:24 John claims "truth" or inerrancy for his written Gospel.

The Book of Revelation unmistakenly claims its own divine inspiration. John, in a condition of openness to the Spirit, was commanded by God to record the content of his vision in the form of letters to seven churches in Asia Minor (Rev. 1:10–11; chs. 2–3).[59] The entire Apocalypse is in view when the heavenly voice commanded John, "Write . . . what you have seen, what is now and what will take place later" (Rev. 1:19). At the close of the book (Rev. 22:18–19) John invokes a curse on anyone who in any way tampers with the text of his prophecy.

The human side of Scripture is reflected in the conclusion to John's Gospel and in the prologue to his first Letter. Concerning the Gospel, we observe (1) John's humanly former purpose, namely that his readers may know that Jesus is the Messiah, and (2) his humanly determined principle of selection, that those signs are narrated that may elicit saving faith (John 20:30–31). In the prologue of his first letter (1 John 1:1–4), against the background of an incipient Docetism, we may discover (1) John's competence for writing, namely, he was an eyewitness of Christ (so he had "heard," "seen," and "touched" him, vv. 1–2); (2) his aim vis-à-vis those tempted by false teaching: that they might have fellowship with the apostles (v. 3); and (3) the personal benefit John expected to derive from writing: "to make our joy complete" (v. 4).

Other New Testament Writings

In the first chapter of Hebrews seven Old Testament texts are quoted by means of the formulae *legei, eipen,* and *eirēken* and are identified as the sayings of God (Heb. 1:5–8, 10, 13). Later words of Moses (Heb. 4:4) and David (4:7; 7:21) are cited as spoken by God himself. On three occasions texts from the Psalms and Jeremiah are quoted and attributed to the mouth of the Holy Spirit (Heb. 3:7–11; 10:15–16; 10:17). And contemplating the Old Testament the author of Hebrews wrote, "You

145

need someone to teach you the elementary truths of God's word all over again" (5:12). Hence not only is the Old Testament regarded as a collection of divine utterances, but it is also shown to possess a relevance and an authority for believers in the present age.

First Peter 1:10–12 affirms that the Old Testament prophets testified of Christ's sufferings and glorification through "the Spirit of Christ in them." Likewise the New Testament apostles were moved by the influence of the same Holy Spirit when they communicated the gospel. Because of the inspiration of both bodies of writings, Old and New Testaments enjoy the same canonical status (cf. 2 Peter 3:2). Second Peter 3:15–16 indicates that Paul wrote "with the wisdom that God gave him." Peter then juxtaposed all Paul's "letters" with "the other Scriptures," thus indicating that the Pauline Epistles were regarded as equally authoritative with the canon of the Old Testament.

The most important Petrine text relative to the inspiration of Scripture is 2 Peter 1:19–21. The phrase "prophecy of Scripture" refers to the entire Old Testament, whose content is broadly prophetic (Acts 3:21–25; Rom. 16:26). Peter teaches that prophetic Scripture did not originate "by the prophet's own interpretation" (the latter word *epilysis,* meaning the unraveling of a problem). Or as Warfield put it, the Scripture "is not the result of human investigation into the nature of things."[60] Unlike the false prophets the Old Testament prophetic writers did not invent the substance of their writing. Rather, "men spoke from God as they were carried along by the Holy Spirit." The term *pheromenoi* (present passive participle of *pherō*) means to be borne or carried along. It is used in Acts 27:15, 17 of a sailing ship being borne along by the wind. "The prophets raised their sails, so to speak (they were obedient and receptive), and the Holy Spirit filled

them and carried their craft along in the direction He wished."[61] The text makes clear that the impulse and the enablement to write was of God the Spirit. Yet the conscious instrumentality of holy writers is fully preserved.

These and other texts that speak to the issue of the Bible's divine inspiration, authority, and illumination bring to mind Warfield's "avalanche of texts" analogy.[62] Warfield observed that an adroit walker might be able to sidestep a limited number of stones that rolled down upon him from above. But one could hardly escape the force of an avalanche of boulders. Analogously, Warfield argued, the number of texts in support of biblical inspiration are so numerous that the Bible reader cannot possibly avoid the sheer force of their demonstration.

SYSTEMATIC FORMULATION

Before determining which of the historical views most coherently and viably accounts for the extensive biblical data, it will help to organize the biblical givens topically on some of the most controversial issues.

Jesus, the supreme revelation of God in history, has ascended to heaven. About four centuries earlier the line of Jewish prophets had ceased. No apostles (as eyewitnesses of Christ) survived the first century. Granted that prophets and apostles articulated divinely revealed truths to the people of their times, how can they help us centuries later? Their revealed teachings have been preserved for successive generations in writing. Given their ability to express truths from God in audible symbols, there can be no a priori objection to the expression of God's words in visible symbols.

The Inscripturation of Revelation by Inspired Prophets

Although Jesus himself did not leave us any writings, the information he constantly derived from the *Old Testament* remains available to us as it was to him. God instructed prophets not only to speak, but also to write. The writing of the Old Testament was *commissioned by God.* Among those commissioned to write were: Moses (Exod. 17:14; 34:27), Joshua (Josh. 24:25–26), Samuel (1 Sam. 10:25), Isaiah (Isa. 30:8), Jeremiah (Jer. 30:2; 36:2, 17, 28–29), Ezekiel (Ezek. 43:11), and Habakkuk (Hab. 2:2). The writings of prophets with credentials were preserved alongside the ark of the covenant in which Moses placed the Ten Commandments (1 Kings 8:9; Deut. 31:24–26; Josh. 24:25–26; 1 Sam. 10:25; Isa. 8:20; 29:18; 34:16).

The prophets' written words served, not as a fallible human witness to their ineffable experiences of the transcendent, but as a nonnegotiable *divine witness against Israel* (Deut. 31:26). In the realistic world view of the Bible, God and the prophets knew that even the people of God tended to rebel against the Lord (vv. 26–27), become unfaithful to God's guidance (Josh. 24:25–27), and instead follow mediums and spiritists (Isa. 8:19).

Given the well-verified fact of human depravity, what Israel needed was not a collection of errant human pointers, but supernaturally inspired standards for reference. "They . . . would not listen to the law or to the words that the LORD Almighty had sent by his Spirit through the earlier prophets" (Zech. 7:12). The inference drawn from human depravity does *not* imply, as many contemporary theologians do, that divinely inspired prophets distort revealed truth by writing it. Rather, the tendency to unfaithfulness underscores the need for the prophets' undistorted truth from God in a public, written form. When people refused to repent and become faithful, God's Spirit-inspired Scripture provided a just basis for their accountability before God and their peers.

Jesus Christ recognized the final authority of the Spirit-inspired prophetic writings. He resisted satanic temptations by quoting the Old Testament, introducing the quotations with "It is written" (Matt. 4:1–10). He said that the Law and the Prophets could not be abolished. All must be fulfilled (Matt. 5:17–18) and ought to be believed (Luke 24:25). All, according to Paul, originated with God (2 Tim. 3:16) and not, according to Peter, with the writers (2 Peter 1:20–21).

The Canon of Prophetic Writings

By what *criteria* were such unimpeachable writings distinguished from others? The primary factor in recognizing the divine authority of these books was *authorship by a tested and verified prophet.* Merely human writings were not invested with divine authority by decision of a council, but books originating with God were recognized as of final authority immediately, upon knowing their authors' authenticity as prophetic spokesmen.

Jesus Christ recognized the entire *Jewish canon* as from God. The Lord referred to each of its three divisions: the Law of Moses, the Prophets, and the Writings (Luke 24:44; the Psalms is the largest book of the Writings). Sometimes he referred to the entire canon as "the Law and the Prophets" (Matt. 5:17), or to the entire Old Testament as "the Law" (as when quoting a Psalm, John 10:34). The Jewish canon at the time of Christ was the same as our Protestant canon; it did not include the apocryphal additions.[63]

Augustine approved the apocryphal books for edifying reading, but not for establishing authoritative doctrine. Jerome, in Augustine's time, about A.D. 400, Gregory the Great, Bishop of Rome (Pope), 590–604, and Cardinal Cajetan (1517–34) at the time of the Reformation, opposed the inclusion of those books in the canon, "the rule for confirming those things which are of faith." The authors of the apocryphal additions to the Old Testament were not recognized prophets inspired of God. Nevertheless, following the Protestant Reformation in 1546 the Roman Catholic Council of Trent declared that anyone who did not receive as canonical these books entire, with all their parts, was anathema![64]

THE TEXT OF THE PROPHET'S INSPIRED WRITINGS

Granting that the thirty-nine books of the Old Testament were supernaturally inspired and authoritative when written, can we know that we have reliable manuscripts of the Old Testament books Jesus approved? A painstaking examination of extant manuscripts, including the Dead Sea Scrolls and the Cairo Geniza, lead to the conclusion that "the material for the establishment of the OT text is many times as great as that for establishing the text for any other ancient document, except the NT. The agreement in the consonantal text of the various MSS is most remarkable, and the great bulk of the very extensive material that has now been found from before the time of Christ agrees very closely with the consonantal text of the MT [Masoretic Text]."[65]

The manuscripts our translators use are generally so accurate that we can say that what those manuscripts teach, God teaches. But because our surviving Hebrew texts have some variations in wordings, careful students of the Old Testament need to compare Scripture with Scripture and not base a doctrine on one verse. Although a given verse may contain a copyist's mistake, the probability that two or more verses on a subject in different contexts each conceal the same error is so small as to be negligible.[66]

In claiming any teaching to be re-

vealed truth, students of theology who are not equipped to evaluate the different manuscripts will avoid some of the dangers of quoting a poorly supported reading by documenting their claim from more than one biblical assertion. No doctrine important for Christian faith or life is drawn from a single passage. When a doctrinal proposition is well-founded in several Old Testament passages, responsibly translated from the Hebrew and Aramaic, and interpreted according to sound principles of hermeneutics, the probability of abusing the revealed message is reduced.

Summing up, the data show that the Old Testament is more than a human witness to revelation—it is (written) revelation. It is a supernaturally inspired inscripturation of information ultimately given by God in various ways to verified prophetic spokesmen divinely commissioned to write its thirty-nine books as a divine witness by which God would evaluate their lives. The teachings of these faithfully copied books were endorsed by the Lord Jesus Christ as conveying objectively valid (inerrant) truth factually and ethically, and so authoritative and necessary to healthy Christian beliefs and experience in the world.

The Inscripturation of Revelation by Apostles

Jesus Christ not only placed his imprimatur on the Old Testament, he also prepared the way for a similar preservation of his teaching to the apostles in the New Testament. Jesus, having all authority in heaven and on earth, *delegated authority* for ministry in history *to his apostles*. The head of the church commissioned and authorized them in his place to prescribe belief and action to the church. No longer mere learners, but apostles, they substituted for their King; witnessed to his life, death, and resurrection; served his purposes; and spoke for him with final authority. As Jesus Christ gave the apostles the right, the Holy Spirit (beginning at Pentecost) gave them the power, the boldness, and the freedom to command, rule, and expect obedience from all who call Jesus Lord and Savior.[67]

Jesus also gave the apostles reason to anticipate further revelation. The Lord said, "I have much more to say to you, more than you can now bear" (John 16:12). The promised Spirit would not only remind them of everything Jesus taught (John 14:26), but also guide the apostles into all truth (John 16:13), tell them what was yet to come, and take from Christ (as he had from the Father) and make it known to them (John 16:13–15).

The apostles, authorized by their Lord, ministered, not only in teaching and preaching, but also in *writing*. Paul's letters were to be read publicly in the churches (1 Thess. 5:25). Paul admonished the Thessalonians saved "through belief in the truth," to "stand firm and hold to the teachings we passed on to you, whether by word of mouth or by letter" (2 Thess. 2:13, 15). The apostle's authority was such that he could add, "If anyone does not obey our instruction in this letter, take special note of him. Do not associate with him, in order that he may feel ashamed. Yet do not regard him as an enemy, but warn him as a brother" (3:14–15). Disobedience to Paul's letters reflected disobedience to God's Word and required disciplinary action.

In an epistle in which Paul had to deal with issues on which he could not quote Jesus Christ, he had to give his own judgment (1 Cor. 7:12, 25). However, he maintained that his judgment was "trustworthy" (7:25). Adequate grounds are not given in 1 Corinthians 7 for arguing that Paul disclaims authority for his writings. In the same epistle he insists, "If anybody thinks he is a prophet or spiritually gifted, let him acknowledge that what I am writing to you is the Lord's command" (1 Cor. 14:37).

The view that the apostles were simply missionaries and not apostles with divine authority does not fit the facts. Paul said he was not ashamed of "the authority the Lord gave" the apostles for building up the body of Christ (2 Cor. 10:8). He warned the church at Corinth in writing so that when present he would not have to be harsh in the use of his God-given authority (2 Cor. 13:10). Anyone who preached a "gospel" contradicting that of Paul could be anathematized, because, as he said, "The gospel I preached is not something that man made up. I did not receive it from any man, nor was I taught it; rather, I received it by revelation from Jesus Christ" (Gal. 1:11–12).

The evidence indicates that Paul's written contributions in the New Testament originated with God, and although expressed in human categories of thought and the common Greek language, conveyed objectively valid and normatively authoritative truth by the inspiration of the Holy Spirit, whom Jesus Christ had promised to send for this purpose.

Peter put Paul's letters on a par with the Old Testament Scriptures (2 Peter 3:15–16). Although Luke was not an apostle, he was a close associate of Paul, traveling with him on his second missionary journey. Luke's Gospel reflects Paul's apostolic authority, and Luke 10:7 was quoted as Scripture alongside a passage from the Old Testament (1 Tim. 5:18). The introduction to the Gospel of Luke shows not only how the writers, supervised by the Holy Spirit, were active in research, but also that Luke consulted all available apostles (eyewitnesses) as he "carefully investigated everything from the beginning" (Luke 1:2–3). Luke's association with Paul also lends Paul's apostolic authority to the Book of Acts.

Peter also identifies himself as an apostle of Jesus Christ (1 Peter 1:1; 2 Peter 1:1). Although Mark was not a disciple, as a close associate of Peter, his gospel presents its material with Peter's authority through his associate. New Testament books not written by apostles were written by apostolic associates and carry apostolic endorsement.

Truth and Error in Apostolic Writings

The apostles commend their writings to us, not only on the basis of the Lord's delegated authority, but also on their *veracious authority*, the authority of truth. True ideas from Jesus Christ conform to the mind of God and to reality, and ought therefore to be believed in order to guide conduct to desirable ends. By what criteria do we know when our affirmations conform to God's thinking and to existence as it is? Three signs of true affirmations are characteristic of apostolic teaching. True statements convey propositions that are (1) empirically reliable, (2) existentially viable, and (3) logically noncontradictory. It follows, then, that *error* is failure to meet these three standards. Because scholars holding a merely dynamic or functional view of inspiration deny that these criteria are biblical it is necessary to document their use in the New Testament especially.

1. The teaching of John's epistles is presented as *empirically reliable*. "That which was from the beginning, which we have heard, which we have seen with our eyes, which we have looked at and our hands have touched—this we proclaim concerning the Word of life" (1 John 1:1). John also stressed empirical verification in his Gospel by recording many visible "signs" indicating that Jesus was the Christ, and especially the

visible, audible, and tangible signs of the Lord's risen body. Christ's appearances convinced skeptical Thomas and the fishermen who, upon arriving at shore, ate a breakfast the risen Lord had prepared for them (John 20–21). The gospel Paul preached had not only been given to him by revelation from Jesus Christ, but also had been verified by many witnesses on many different occasions, including over five hundred at once, who were still living when he wrote (1 Cor. 15:1–11). The hypothesis that factual assertions in Scripture may not be reliable does not fit the factual emphasis of passages like these, and undercuts the gospel itself.

2. John also commends his written message as *existentially viable*. John writes his second Epistle with the authority of an "elder" who experientially knows and loves the truth that lives in us and will be with us forever (2 John 1:1–2). Knowing personally the joy of living the truth, John urges people to walk in the truth (v. 4) and continue in the teaching of Christ, without which they do not have God (vv. 9, 11). In his third Epistle, John appeals to those he loves in the truth, to walk in the truth, and work together for the truth (3 John 1, 3, 4, 8). Clearly in the New Testament truth can be lived, and was personally experienced.

3. The apostles commend New Testament teaching as true, furthermore, because its sayings are faithful, or *logically noncontradictory*. In teaching about faithfulness to oaths made to the Lord, the Master had asked that his followers not swear by heaven, earth, Jerusalem, or their own heads. "Simply let your 'Yes' be 'Yes,' and your 'No,' 'No'; anything beyond this comes from the evil one" (Matt. 5:33–37). James, concerned about a responsible use of the tongue, echoed the Lord's words, saying, "Let your 'Yes' be yes, and your 'No,' no, or you will be condemned" (James 5:12). This teaching of

Christ and James provides background for Paul's second Letter to the Corinthians.

To the Corinthians Paul wrote that his plans were not made "in a worldly manner" so that in the same breath he would say "Yes, yes" and "No, no" (2 Cor. 1:17). Then, of his letter, Paul said, "But as surely as God is faithful, our message to you is not 'Yes' and 'No.' For the Son of God, Jesus Christ, who was preached among you by me and Silas and Timothy, was not 'Yes' and 'No,' but in him it has always been 'Yes.' For no matter how many promises God has made, they are 'Yes' in Christ" (2 Cor. 1:18–20).

Paul warned Timothy about "false doctrines," myths, endless genealogies, meaningless talk and "whatever else is contrary to the sound doctrine that conforms to the glorious gospel of the blessed God, which he entrusted to me" (1 Tim.1:3–11). No contradiction of the revealed message, not even in the name of "profound" or "existentially relevant" theology, could be given assent. So Paul warned Timothy to "guard" the sound doctrine that had been entrusted to his care, avoiding "opposing" ("antithetical" rsv) ideas of what is falsely called knowledge (1 Tim. 6:20).

In view of these New Testament criteria of truth, its words are *faithful,* not only existentially but also factually and logically. The emphasis on not contradicting faithful sayings was not so much based on Aristotle's formulation of the law of noncontradiction as rooted in God's faithful nature: "He who promised is faithful" (Heb. 10:23; cf. Rev. 19:2, 9, 11; 21:5; 22:6). Thus the logical integrity of the inscripturated Word is not imported from Greek philosophy but inherent in the meaning of "faithfulness" on the part of the God who speaks through prophets and apostles. No infinite qualitative distinction between the divine and human minds makes necessary dialectical reasoning in which theologians must say "Yes" and "No" to every relationship between God and humanity. What the Father gave Jesus, he taught, and what Jesus gave the apostles the Holy Spirit inspired them to write. Hence we can confidently rely on their teaching without either intellectual denial or personal disillusionment (Rom. 10:11). People who announce their belief in biblical inerrancy and hold that a biblical affirmation may be contradicted elsewhere in Scripture, miss the mark of a biblical view of personal faithfulness expressed in logical consistency. They also render their belief in inerrancy meaningless. If the contradictory of a biblical affirmation may be true, then no Scripture is dependable.

The Supernaturalness of Apostolic Inspiration

How could finite, forgetful, often uneducated people with sinful biases faithfully teach the truth without error? On their own, these truly human and fallen writers could not. By the Spirit's ordinary illumination, they could not. The issue is not so much the humanness of the writers. Their varied styles, vocabularies, cultural conditionedness, historical standpoints, finite limitations, and sinful tendencies have been thoroughly emphasized from all sides. The additional issue is whether the Spirit's work with them was the ordinary work of illumining all God's people or an extraordinary work for divine spokesmen, a supernatural inspiration.

Does a providential or a miraculous inspiration account most coherently for the relevant data? The New Testament authors were enabled to convey Christ's teachings with fidelity and add their wisdom from above where he had not spoken, by the *supernatural inspiration* of the Holy Spirit. The Spirit overshadowed in both the content taught and the wording conveying it. Christ had endorsed the Spirit-directed writings of the prophets and promised the Spirit to the apostles. Although those promises may have broader applications to all believers, they most certainly apply in a special way to those apostolic men to whom he addressed them and who wrote New Testament books. The New Testament insight into the mystery of Christ was not made known to men in other generations as "it has now been revealed by the Spirit to God's holy apostles and prophets" (Eph. 3:4–5).

The doctrine of the unity of the Gentiles with the Jews in the church was communicated by apostles who were "holy" in that the Holy Spirit "set them apart" from the rest of humanity to contribute these New Testament writings (Eph. 3:3). So they may be classed along with the writers of the Old Testament as prophets. Peter thus associated the apostles with the prophets when he wrote, "I want you to recall the words spoken in the past by the holy prophets and the command given by our Lord and Savior through your apostles" (2 Peter 3:2). Such nonnegotiable authority for human words is more probably than not a supernatural work of God's Spirit.

Since Peter mentioned Paul's Epistles as Scripture (2 Peter 3:16), his teaching about the origin of Scripture holds for New Testament books as well as Old: "Above all, you must understand that no prophecy of Scripture came about by the prophet's own interpretation. For prophecy never had its origin in the will of man, but men spoke from God as they were carried along by the Holy Spirit" (2 Peter 1:20–21). Since the prophetic writings had a superhuman reliability and authority, they must have been supernaturally kept from error, and so must the New Testament books be classified along with the Old.

Paul's awareness of Luke's writings, and surely of other New Testament books toward the end of his life, means that his teaching applies not only to the Old Testament writings, but also the New, when he said that the Scriptures are able to make one wise for salvation through faith in Christ Jesus. But inspiration is not limited to the teachings on salvation. "All Scripture is God-breathed and is useful for teaching, rebuking, correcting and training in righteousness, so that the man of God may be thoroughly equipped for every good work" (2 Tim. 3:16–17).

Given not only the humanness, but also the fallenness of the writers, the point at issue is whether the Holy Spirit worked with them in an extraordinary manner to produce a result with more than fallible human authority. In view of the recognition that the New Testament books were revelation (not merely a human witness to revelation), and were in the part and the whole, of divine, nonnegotiable authority in the churches, we conclude that their inspiration must have been qualitatively different from the Spirit's illumination of other Christian literature. It produced a cognitive miracle. Without a supernatural inspiration, no portion of even the gospel could have been preserved from errancy and fallibility.

The Canon of Apostolic Writings

Granting that apostolic people wrote inspired Scripture in the first century, do we now have the proper books in the New Testament canon? The most influential factor in the recognition of a book's inspired authority was its apostolic origin.[68]

Some twenty of the twenty-seven New Testament books were immediately known to be from Authentic divine spokesmen and for these no difference of opinion occurred in the early church. On such works as Hebrews,

James, 2 Peter, 2 and 3 John, Jude, and Revelation, some question remained into the second and third centuries. For example, although Hebrews was read in many churches, second-century Western writers questioned whether Paul wrote the anonymous book. Eastern writers maintained that he did. This and other controversies "show that second-century Christians were neither credulous nor superficial in their approach to the holy books."[69] Summing up the issue of the New Testament canon, Geisler and Nix write:

> The vast majority of the New Testament books were never disputed from the beginning. Of the books originally recognized as inspired, but later questioned, all of them came to full and final acceptance by the universal church. Some other books which enjoyed wide usage and were included in local lists for a time were valuable for devotional and homiletical use but never gained canonical recognition by the church. Only the twenty-seven books of the New Testament are known to be genuinely apostolic. Only these twenty-seven have found a permanent place in the New Testament Canon.[70]

THE TEXT OF APOSTOLIC WRITINGS

Have we today the same wording in the original texts of the Greek manuscripts that the apostles wrote? The suggestion that the original apostolic writings are unreal or unimportant because they are not extant today reflects a disregard for the authority of the Savior delegated to these authors. Because every scribe, secretary, and typesetter did not have the special inspiration of the Spirit the apostles had does not diminish the evidence for their original authority for doctrine and practice.

What difference does it make if the original was inerrant since we do not have inerrant copies? Although we have not seen the autographs, others did. Tertullian, about A.D. 200, said that the originals of the New Testament could still be inspected. Have we very good copies of merely human books or of divine-human books? The nature of the Scriptures as originally given is at stake in the assertions about the Gospels and Epistles as they came from apostolic men inspired of God. The doctrine of inspiration has to do with the Bible's origin, not its transmission. To claim that one's view of the Bible's origin is unimportant (so long as it "works"), seems theologically irresponsible.

Given the original nature of the inscripturated revelation, however, its transmission to our day also has great importance. The manuscript evidence is even more abundant for the text of the New Testament than of the Old Testament. Although the different families of manuscript copies are in basic agreement, there are differences that occurred through centuries of copying. Why did the Lord permit this? Perhaps it is because the lack of the originals prevents any museum or church from treating them superstitiously as relics. The written form of God's Word was not given for purposes of bibliolatry. Christians do not worship a book, but the God who has not only acted, but also spoken, in the foundational writings of the prophets and apostles.

Variations in the extant manuscripts are generally of very small, scattered details, except for the end of the Lord's Prayer (Matt. 6:13), the conclusion of the Gospel of Mark, the story of the adulteress (John 8:1–11), Romans 16:15–17, and 1 John 5:7. However, these together amount to about one page of the entire Greek New Testament, and though all of them were found insufficiently supported by the better manuscripts, no doctrine of Scripture is affected. And most of the variations, when studied by knowledgeable scholars can be resolved. Thus the text of the originals can be established beyond reasonable doubt in the bulk of the material.

As George Ladd has said,

It is a seldom disputed fact that critical science has to all intents and purposes recovered the original text of the New Testament. There remain indeed numerous debatable and debated readings; but if one compares our four contemporary critical texts of the New Testament, edited by E. Nestle (1963), G. D. Kilpatrick (1958), R. V. G. Tasker and Kurt Aland — M. Black — B. M. Metzger — A. Wikgren (1966), he will find them to be in substantial agreement.[71]

"From a practical view, however," said J. H. Greenlee, "the difference involved in most variants is so slight that little or no difference of meaning is involved." He agreed with Kenyon, "we have in our hands, in substantial integrity, the veritable word of God."[72]

Summing up the data on the New Testament, the Lord Jesus Christ, the supreme revelation of God, prepared the disciples for additional revelation after his departure and delegated authority to his authentic apostles to write, as well as speak, revealed truth foundational for the building of the church in every century and culture. The twenty-seven books of the New Testament, well preserved through the centuries, are not a mere human witness to a noncognitive revelation, but convey teachings ultimately from God and communicated through verified apostolic spokesmen by the supernatural inspiration of the Holy Spirit. What the New Testament teaches, God teaches. What it affirms is objectively valid truth: logically, factually, and ethically (inerrant), and so it is authoritative for Christians in the development of healthy, coherent convictions by which to live in the church and the world (infallible). In a world of relativism and

rationalization, whether accepted or not, it stands written as of self-evaluation, church discipline, and divine judgment. This view of the New Testament is not a late invention of Princeton theologians like B. B. Warfield, or Scottish realists, but the most coherent account of the primary data from the apostles and the Lord himself.

APOLOGETIC INTERACTION

Can the view of the Bible's inerrancy in all that it affirms stand examination and meet challenges? We seek here to indicate, not an answer to every question that can be raised about the Bible's teachings, but the structure of argument by which to address questions with intellectual integrity.

Some have attempted a purely *inductive* approach to the authority of scriptural claims and phenomena. Important as it is to check assumptions by the given data, a purely inductive method of reasoning is unrealistic. No one has a completely objective mind; all people from all sides have preunderstandings. As assumptions are verified or disproved people change their personal and passionate commitments to world views.

Recognizing the inescapability of assumptions, others have tried a purely *deductive* approach from their presupposition of plenary inerrancy. But this approach assumes the point to be established, committing the fallacy of circular reasoning. It is also special pleading, for the revelation claims of any other religion or cult would not be considered justifiable on this method of reasoning.

But there is a third approach, the *verificational* method, which begins with hypotheses and tests them by logical, empirical, and existential criteria. Utilizing this approach, we compare three logically distinct hypotheses that are held in the church today and determine which of them provides the most coherent and probable account of the internal and external biblical phenomena with the fewest difficulties.

Three Hypotheses to Test

The first proposal to be tested is that *the Bible is totally errant.* A number of Protestant and Roman Catholic scholars regard God's mind so totally different from spatially and temporally limited and morally depraved human minds that none of the assertions of the Bible can be cognitively true in and of themselves. The Bible's teachings may be accepted only when confirmed by other disciplines such as archaeology or the psychology of religious experience. At no point do holders of this view identify the assertions of Scripture with divinely revealed, reliable information. So secular humanists holding this view summarily dismiss the Bible as self-contradictory, unreliable, and irrelevant.

The dismissal of cognitive truth in religious language in general, and the Bible in particular, does not keep others from using the Bible for religious experiences of different kinds. Religious secularists and mystics continue to use if for its relevant emotive and experiential values. The allegedly errant scriptural witness is "inspired" when inspiring (to liberals), calling existentialists to become authentic individuals, or becoming the occasion for encounters with God (for the neoorthodox and relational theologians), or when it occasions an immediate, nonpersonal, mystical absorption into God (for mystics).

On any of these "dynamic" perspectives what the Bible affirms is not to be confused with true (objectively, or logically valid) information revealed from God himself. Although G. C. Berkouwer, for example, thinks that Scripture is composed of the relative conceptions of time-bound humans, he thinks that its words "mysteriously" introduce people to the eternal Christ. The function of biblical language is not so much to inform, Berkouwer says, as to point or witness to something beyond itself.[73] It is indeed "mysterious" how the Holy Spirit witnesses to the truth of falsehoods and through them leads people to the real Christ. Faith, then, is not an act of the mind assenting to all scriptural teachings, he claims, but exclusively a matter of choice and trust.[74]

A second hypothesis proposes that some of the Bible's affirmations are errant and some are inerrant; that is, there is *a partial biblical errancy and a partial biblical inerrancy.* Partial inerrancy theories distinguish what is cognitively true from what is not, generally less by subjective experiences and more by rational or doctrinal considerations. G. C. Berkouwer makes an exception to the alleged time-boundedness of all biblical statements about Christ's resurrection. For biblical teaching on the resurrection he declares objective validity by some exceptional "mystery."[75] Some will say that the Bible makes no false or misleading statements on matters of *faith and practice,* redemptive matters, or "saving truth."[76] However, on other subjects (assuming the Bible teaches things that are not important for faith and practice in some direct or indirect way) the Bible may assert falsehoods and mislead.[77] Faith, then, involves sifting the true from the false in Scripture, and God's Spirit illumines both truth and falsehood to direct us away from idols and lead believers to himself. Belief involves assent only to those matters one finds to be essential to "faith and practice," which may vary considerably from person to person.

A third hypothesis proposes a *plenary inerrancy.* This stance asserts the truth, the objective validity, or the inerrancy of all that the biblical autographs affirm on any subject. All Scripture originated with God, and the Holy Spirit uses only truth to lead people away from idols to himself. Faith, then, need not critically distinguish true from false affirmations in Scripture. The critical function is crucial for interpretive purposes, for determining the precise content asserted by the biblical sentences. An inquiry into the meaning of the authors' manuscripts also follows a verification procedure. Acknowledging subjectivity in preunderstandings, we seek as much objectivity as possible. Some interpretations are better informed than others. We survey the interpretive hypotheses, and assent to the best informed interpretation according to standard criteria of truth and to sound principles of hermeneutics.[78]

Comparisons

Similarities may be seen in that all three views affirm in one way or another that Scripture can be and has been a *dynamic* instrument of the Spirit to renew lives. In our terms, all hold that the Bible is "infallible" in that the Holy Spirit witnesses to it to accomplish the purposes for which God sent it (Isa. 55:11). In Christian theology Spirit-illumined biblical teaching serves as the primary means by which people come into fellowship with the living God, who not only created, but also redeems. People who stress the dynamic power of Spirit-illumined Scripture often portray the plenary view as if it displaced the Spirit's power with a "static" body of truths. What is affirmed is that the Spirit's ability to change lives and societies through scriptural teaching depends on its Spirit-inspired truthfulness.

The three views are also similar in that none of the hypotheses has been *completely demonstrated*. There are several reasons for this. Biblical teaching about invisible realities and the meanings of events are by nature unobservable. Even many of the observable events are no longer verifiable because some left no remains at all, and the

visible remains left from others through the centuries has been destroyed. So none of the three hypotheses has been, or can be, completely confirmed or invalidated.

No plenary errantist has verified that *every* biblical statement about the infinite and holy God is false. Dogmatists (sic!) against the truth of religious language and biblical statements in particular support their views by tautologous or stipulative definitions of an alleged "infinite qualitative distinction" between "God's infinite mind" and "human finite minds," and reductively functional or existentialist perspectives of "religious truths," "revelation," and "faith."

Partial inerrantists have not confirmed all of those biblical statements that they hold to be true nor disconfirmed all that they hold to be false. Neither have they succeeded in defining or clarifying a criterion by which adequately to distinguish the one from the other. Agreement has not been reached in distinguishing those statements essential to salvation or "faith and practice" from those with no relation to these purposes. Which are "saving truths" and which are not?

Plenary inerrantists have not verified, nor can they verify, that *every* biblical assertion is true. A doctrine of plenary inerrancy is based on evidence of the view of Jesus Christ as Lord of all, and on the authority of prophets and apostles who had the credentials of supernaturally called spokesmen for God, inspired to write, not merely a human testimony to God, but a divine testimony to man. These lines of evidence are also supported by the classical view in the church and by standard Christian evidences.

A Matter of Probabilities

None of the three views of Scripture has been, or can be "proven" in a complete intellectual sense. The issue becomes, where different, Which of the three hypotheses provides the *most probable* (coherent and viable) account of the relevant lines of evidence with the fewest difficulties? The issue at this point is *not* psychological certitude. Some theological decisions in this complex world are like some political decisions in which we must opt for the proposal with the less severe problems. This being the case, a single historical or scientific difficulty, as is often alleged, does not in itself destroy the plenary inerrancy position. The question for systematic and integrative purposes calls for a judgment only after the court has heard the many relevant lines of evidence—both pro and con. Only then can the jury assess which proposal carries the highest probability with the fewest difficulties. We cannot go into extensive detail again, but seek only to outline a verificational approach to a concept of the Bible's inspiration.

Major Lines of Relevant Evidence

What are the major lines of given *data* that any view must explain? (1) Jesus Christ's view of Scripture; (2) the claims of the prophets; (3) the claims of the apostles (assuming on nos. 1–3 only that the record is of general historical reliability, not of inspired authority for this purpose); (4) the dominant view of the Scriptures throughout the varied history of the church; (5) the humanness (both finiteness and fallenness) of the writers; (6) problem phenomena: difficulties of apparent historical, chronological, and scientific discrepancies; and (7) the positive phenomena: such as the standard "Christian evidences" of fulfilled prophecy and miracles confirming the office and messages of divine spokesmen.

Some errantists tend to sidestep distinctively Christian evidences. However, the fulfillment of specific predictions made scores or hundreds of years in advance still displays a transcendent, divine knowledge. And the "signs and wonders" still exhibit a transcendent, divine power. Scholarly objectivity calls for consideration of such positive indications as well as the negative phenomena.

Evaluation

How well, then, do the three hypotheses account for all seven lines of evidence?

Briefly, although a noncognitive, total errancy hypothesis does seem to fit the finiteness and fallenness of the writers and their passages presenting problem phenomena, it does not provide an adequate account of the other five lines of data presented by Christ, prophets, apostles, Christian evidences, or the history of the doctrine in the church.

Similarly, a partial-inerrancy hypothesis has little problem with the humanness of the writers and their apparent discrepancies, but it fails to provide an adequate account of the view held by Christ, the prophets, and the apostles, as confirmed by signs and wonders and attested by most authorities throughout church history.

A plenary-inerrancy hypothesis has a coherent and adequate explanation of the final authority of Scripture held by Jesus Christ, the prophets, and the apostles and of their confirmation by supernatural signs and wonders and their attestation throughout the history of the church, but it does not have a full explanation of every historical, scientific, or literary difficulty that can be raised.

If the pattern of reasoning, or paradigm, is now clear, we must look more closely at the consistency, adequacy, and viability of each view.

A belief that the Bible is wholly

subject to errancy resolves all tensions between biblical and other sources of knowledge, but it does so at too great a cost. To relinquish the authority of the Bible merely for the sake of harmony with the prevailing voices in the academic community is too great a price to pay. The view loses the relevance of biblical teaching to anything but a non-cognitive relationship to what is felt to be God.

This belief supplies no cognitive criteria by which to distinguish the true God from idols or the personal God of Christian theism from the impersonal God of pantheistic monism. If scriptural doctrine cannot convey truth about the transcendent realm, mystics, occultists, and others have no way to test the spirits to see whether they are of Christ or Antichrist, of God or Satan.

It makes God's thoughts so "totally other" than human thoughts that God himself cannot communicate with the creature he created in his image for the purpose of communicating and working together. In this, it fails to fit the revealed facts concerning the image of God in humanity, including the human mind (Col. 3:10).

In its desire to free the faith from intellectual difficulties with reversible models of scientific knowledge, it commits intellectual suicide. It reduces intellectual content of Scripture to a merely human emotional, functional, relational, and mystical witness. Having done so, its adherents must not be surprised if people who desire to distinguish God from idols and worship God with their minds as well as their hearts, find the view intellectually uncritical, naïve, and dangerous. Inscripturated revelation has to do essentially with the created cosmos and historical events.

The God of the hypothesis that the Bible is wholly subject to errancy is too small to overcome the limitations of human finiteness and fallenness. James Barr, for example, does not identify the Bible with revelation but calls it an errant human witness to revelation (Jesus Christ). "The entire Bible is a human word, subject to the strains, weaknesses and errors of any other book and deserves, indeed requires, to be studied with just the same methods as any other."[79] Ignoring Jesus' teaching about his own teaching as well as that of the prophets, Barr says that "the Spirit's work with the prophets and apostles was not essentially different in kind from the mode in which he is with his people today."[80] Barr's hypothesis may seem to cohere with the problem phenomena and the humanness of the writers, but it fails to account for the overwhelming data from Christ, the prophets, the apostles, the church and the "signs and wonders" in their support.

According to the view of limited inerrancy, "salvific" teaching in Scripture is to be relied on, while other teaching is not. For such a view to be valid, "saving" must be given clear content. If the charge of insufficient definition applies to total inerrantists with respect to "inerrancy," the charge holds with greater force against the lack of definition of what is "soteriological" in the limited-inerrancy view. If it so prescribes the referents of reliable biblical teaching to "faith and practice" that it never can be in opposition to the facts of contemporary historical and scientific interpretations, it faces all the major problems of the belief that the Bible is wholly subject to errancy. The benefit of freedom from conflicts with science and history is won at great cost—the loss of theism and Christianity at its heart and essence.

If the definition of redemptive truth becomes broad enough to include the historical events that founded the Christian faith, then observable matters of fact are reliably true (inerrant) as well as subjective, experiential matters. The nature of Christianity's redemptive message involves truth about the created and fallen world and historical provisions for its redemption. Mystics may divorce Christian faith from science and history, but evangelical Christians will not do so. The mighty acts of God in the world are no mere myths or symbols, but observable events that have made a difference in time, space, and human lives. To suggest that assertions about redemption are inerrant but that matters of history are not shows a dreadful lack of understanding concerning distinctively Christian faith. Christianity is a matter of facts as well as of relations and experiences.

Inadequate guidelines are given for what is essential to believe and practice or what is soteriological. Hence the concept may be too broad and assert the inerrancy of everything taught in Scripture, or it may be too narrow and fail to include all that has been supernaturally inspired for various purposes of church administration, church discipline, etc.

Divine revelation has more than one single "saving" purpose. The Lord of redemption is the Lord of all. Granted that the highest purpose for us is salvation, a personal, moral, and spiritual communion with God is not the sole end for which each paragraph of Scripture was written. Some units of thought tell us about ultimate origins, the Fall, society's need for government, the judgment that falls on evildoers, and the coming divine wrath to overtake the ungodly. If the Bible is partially errant and if all of this is for salvation (faith and practice), then all that the Bible teaches is subject to errancy and the definition of partial inerrancy is inadequate.

The same arguments by which partial inerrantists regard some scriptural teaching errant (the human authors' finiteness and fallenness) apply to all scriptural affirmations. All teachings, including those on faith and practice, are written by finite, fallen persons in human categories of thought expressed in human languages of a given period and culture. Unless a clearly supernatural inspiration of the inerrant portions is affirmed, it is simply a matter of time until the arguments for partial errancy will be extended to the gospel.

Partial inerrancy fights a losing battle because the rules of the contest are set up by the prevailing standards of modernity (in the fields of history, science, etc.) rather than by revealed truths of general or special revelation. A biblical authority dependent on the gaps in present secular knowledge, may gradually evaporate. It is far from the inherent, unshakable revealed authority of which Jesus Christ, the prophets, and the apostles taught.

The appeal of the errantist positions should not be overlooked, however. Whether one believes that the Bible is wholly subject to errancy or that it is only partially so, he seeks to remove even apparent conflict between Christian faith and contemporary knowledge, fluctuating as that is. Because the Bible's authority does not hold except where they define it to hold, however, their view can never be disconfirmed. It is true by their stipulated authority in matters of faith and practice. So the ultimate authority becomes the standard of the historian or scientist rather than the Scripture. However, in the final analysis Scripture must judge science and history, not vice versa.

Improbable indeed is the hypothesis that the Holy Spirit uses erroneous human teachings more dynamically than supernaturally revealed true teachings expressed in faithful words. Untrue teachings lead to idols and dream castles of unreality. The Spirit of truth has chosen to use true concepts to lead people away from idols and illusions to the living God who hears, speaks, and acts. Of course the sovereign Lord has the power to overrule human errors in preaching, but no evidence indicates that the sovereign God chooses to reveal himself and his purposes by originating ("breathing out") errors.

Although restricting the view of the Bible's authority, the partial inerrancy view fails sufficiently to restrict the theologians' authority. "Once historical criticism was seriously applied to the Bible," wrote A. T. and R. P. C. Hanson, "the old doctrines of inspiration and inerrancy were no longer tenable. They vanished like shadows in the light of the day."[81] The Hanson brothers admit that their view is not that of the historic church: "We must candidly reject the ancient oracular view of the Bible and substitute for it the concept of the Bible as witness or testimony."[82] Nevertheless they believe that the biblical compilation of literature gives sufficient evidence for people "to understand and embrace the Way of Life."[83]

With all the frailties of the Hansons' Bible, it functions inexplicably as a norm of doctrine in Christian churches! But they use "norm" and "rule" in a very "restricted" sense. "What the Bible supplies us with is the raw material for doctrine, not the finished product itself."[84] Unfortunately, the Hansons' "finished product" may become more authoritative in practice than the Scriptures themselves. Although their hypotheses may account for some critical problems and the writers' humanness, it faces far more severe problems with the repeated teaching of Christ, the prophets, the apostles, and the church as supported by Christian evidences.

The *plenary inerrancy* view, although not straining to account for most of the major lines of evidence, has been charged by some with (1) unsatisfactory definition of its terms, (2) an insufficient account of the biblical writers' humanness, and (3) an inadequate explanation of the problem phenomena. In intellectual honesty it cannot ignore the difficulties. Plenary inerrantists who overlook these difficulties reflect more about their own intentions (not to admit any difficulties), as a kind of procedural rule, than they inform about the Scriptures themselves. But those who understand the verificational methodology used here cannot justifiably charge that it dismisses logical or factual considerations a priori. How it can meet some major charges against it is outlined in the next three sections.

Inerrancy: Not Defined?
or Defined Away?

Opponents of plenary biblical inerrancy often insist either that no one ever defined inerrancy (truth) to their satisfaction or that the definitions proposed were so complex as to die the death of a thousand qualifications. As the following definitions are proposed for consideration and acceptance, the reader may assess the validity of such objections.

By "inerrancy" we mean that as a product of supernatural inspiration the information affirmed by the sentences of the original autographs of the sixty-six canonical books of the Bible is true.[85]

By "true" content we mean propositions that correspond to the thought of God and created reality because they are logically noncontradictory, factually reliable, and experientially viable. Therefore, as given, the Bible provides a reliable guide for healthfully experiencing the physical, mental, moral, and spiritual realities that people face in time and eternity.

To grasp the truth that was *given*, as fully as possible, a passage of Scripture must be *taken* (interpreted) by a believer in accord with its author's purpose; degrees of precision appropriate to that purpose at that time; and its grammatical, historical, cultural, and theological contexts (all under the illumination of the Holy Spirit who inspired it).

"Infallible" sentences are units of thought faithfully copied from the canonical autographs that convey the content God intended to communicate through his spokesmen and accomplish their divinely intended purpose.[86]

By "plenary" inspiration we mean that as a result of the Holy Spirit's supernatural supervision, all of the parts of the canon equally are God's Word, infallible in wording and inerrant in teaching. Belief in plenary inspiration does not mean that all passages are equally important for answering any given question (How do you receive eternal life? How do you discipline a wayward church member?). It does mean that all that the Scriptures teach is important for some purpose and contributes in some way to the process of becoming thoroughly furnished to every good work (2 Tim. 3:16–17) in God's universal kingdom with its cultural mandate as well as in the redemptive kingdom with its Great Commission.

By the "perspicuity of the Scriptures" we affirm that they were written with sufficient clarity that readers or hearers are accountable for their response to the content conveyed. People without special training may respect the provisional authority of Christians who have given their lives to a study of the Word, but not grant them ultimate allegiance. Even the most gifted teachers are errant and fallible. But whatever the errors of ill-trained or presumptuous interpreters, the Bible's visual symbols in print adequately convey the truth God intended to reveal. And all who can read or hear the Bible are responsible to read it, assent to its teaching, and live by it.

What are thought to be difficulties concerning biblical inerrancy may be difficulties of the Bible's interpreters. Qualifications put on interpreters of Scripture (as taken) are not to be thought to be on the inerrancy of the Bible (as given). If it is thought objectionable that inerrantists qualify interpretation in terms of the writer's purpose, standards of accuracy appropriate to that purpose at that time, and a responsible use of principles of hermeneutics, then the objection may remain. If it be considered strained harmonization to carefully apply criteria of truth and logical principles utilized in the New Testament (differentiating contradictions from subcontraries and merely verbal differences), then objections there must be. Would errantists, however, commend interpretations of their own writings that failed to take account of their purpose, their intended level of technicality, or their context? Is it irresponsible interpretation, not inerrancy as here defined, that has died the death of a thousand qualifications?

Much fuzzy thinking has suggested that biblical inerrancy is meaningless because it is "tied up" with hermeneutics. Inerrancy and hermeneutics are related, but they are as distinct as the important difference between *what is given* by inspiration and *what is taken* by illumination. It is the difference between the content the inspired biblical writers conveyed and the extent to which their readers for two thousand years have grasped it with the help of sound principles of hermeneutics and growing skills in applying them.

No amount of interpretive abuse can change the nature of the biblical message as it was originally given. But "ignorant and unstable people" may distort it "to their own destruction" (2 Peter 3:16). There are crucial questions of interpretation; there are also crucial questions about the nature of the book to be interpreted. The meaning of the Bible's inspiration and inerrancy cannot be reductively treated as one of a hermeneutical wax nose, to be twisted at will. The one type of question does not rule out the other. There is the question of the Bible as given and the question of the Bible as taken. We can confidently assert that the Bible was entirely inerrant when it was written, without claiming that any individual defender of plenary inerrancy holds all aspects of that truth in his own mind and teaching today. "We know in part" (1 Cor. 13:9).

Plenary Inerrancy and the Writers' Humanness

Many contemporary theologians stress the biblical authors' humanness to the point of errancy. They argue that scriptural authors were time-bound and their writings, though not necessarily true, are of functional value. Some of these are Reformed writers such as G. C. Berkouwer and Harry Boer, evangelical writers like Jack Rogers and Charles Kraft, and Roman Catholic writers like Charles Davis, Hans Küng, and Leslie Dewart.[87]

But just as Jesus Christ was truly divine and truly human without sin, so the Scriptures are truly divine and truly human without error. The inerrancy of finite, fallen human authors makes sense within the cultural context in which Scripture was given, the context of a theistic world view that includes orthodox doctrines of God, creation, providence, and miracles. In such a setting it is clear that human writers would not be abstracted from their relationship of dependence on God and treated autonomously. They lived and moved and had their being in the all-wise Lord of all. Created by God in his image, they had a capacity of self-transcendence enabling them to receive changeless truths by general and special revelation. Although physically time-bound, as image-bearers of the divine, they were created with the capacity to receive truths from beyond time by revelation.

Providentially prepared by God in their unique personalities, they also had, of course, characteristics common to all other human persons in all times and cultures. Categories of thought concerning essential human existence, as well as divinely revealed ideas transcending historical flux could be immutable. Beyond that, truth about a unique, once-for-all event in history remains true always. Their teaching, whether common or uniquely theirs, originated not with their own wills, but God's and came to them through a variety of means: audible voice, inner insights, visions, reading, and research. The use of other human sources is not excluded in universal divine providence. What is excluded is the single-cause fallacy operative in much higher-critical thought—that if an author researched and used other sources, his message was not ultimately from God. God in his sovereignty chose to work through means, not only providentially in everything that comes to pass, but also miraculously in overseeing the production of, say, Luke's Gospel (1:1–4) and in the use of other canonical and noncanonical sources.

In all their research, writers were supervised by the Holy Spirit. Just as Jesus was kept from human depravity by a moral miracle at his virgin conception, so the writers of Scripture were kept from human error by an epistemological miracle at their teaching's conception and birth in written form. The Spirit's work with the writers is not appropriately thought analogous to impersonal, mechanical relationships, but rather like worthy personal relationships. They were moved by the Spirit as one wise, loving person influences another alert, teachable, person in innumerable conscious and unconscious ways.

What stands written in human languages, therefore, is not merely human, but also divine. What the sentences convey, God and his spokesmen wanted to convey. What the content teaches, God and his spokesmen teach. The affirmations conform to the mind of God and to the reality God created. In that sense the content is true or inerrant. And in conveying that content the wording is effectual or infallible. The Bible's teachings are objectively normative for all people of all times and cultures whether these teachings are received or not.

Why does the Bible function effectively to bring sinners to Christ and thoroughly equip them for every good work? Because it is God-breathed (divinely originated) and trustworthy in all that it teaches (2 Tim. 3:15-17).[88]

Plenary Inerrancy and Problem Phenomena

Before accepting a challenge to the truth of a scriptural assertion from any field, it is wise to determine what *canons of scientific evaluation* or *criteria of truth* are used. The reign of the strict logical positivist's verificational principle has been brought down. Historical claims cannot be dismissed as meaningless a priori because they are not repeatable or verifiable by the scientific method at present. The highest values of life (such as justice and love) are unverifiable in that narrow sense and many of the most significant events in the world are not repeatable under controlled conditions (e.g., the death of Abraham Lincoln).

Because there are so many conflicting presuppositions from which to understand the past and even to define "history" and other sciences, we need to develop a healthy skepticism regarding claims that "all critics agree. . . ." Universal agreement in our pluralistic world, even among professionals in the same field, seems highly unlikely. Often this claim covers up a hidden premise: "All who agree with me are critical

scholars, all who differ with me are obscurantists."

Because of an insufficiently critical skepticism among Christian people in the nineteenth and twentieth centuries, a movement of critical thinkers starting with naturalistic, evolutionary assumptions developed an imposing consensus in prominent Christian institutions. Nevertheless, there has continued a historic train of "classical criticism" with different presuppositions that faced the same problems with quite different results.

As early as St. Augustine, problems of the similarities and differences in the synoptic Gospels, for example, were faced and found not irreconcilable with the Bible's view of its own origin and nature. Given the distinction between the content asserted and the linguistic vehicle conveying those affirmations, the wording in the three Gospels need not be identical, only the meanings must be noncontradictory. Different sentences can convey the same content from the different perspectives of different witnesses of such events as the resurrection and the healing of a blind person.[89]

A comparison of the evangelical and nonevangelical presuppositions influential in scientific, historical, anthropological, and biblical interpretations has seemed to confine people to reasoning in "hermeneutical circles." However, we need not orbit forever in one or the other set of presuppositions. Difficult as it may be to break out of longstanding assumptions, the following steps applying our verificational methodology make genuine knowledge and exegesis (rather than eisegesis) possible. (1) Increase the consciousness of one's influential presuppositions and hypotheses. (2) Delimit the issue by focusing initially on the meaning of the scriptural teaching as given. (3) Acknowledge that presuppositions are not beyond examination, but are truth-claims or hypotheses to be reexamined. (4) Build on common ground available as human beings in a threatened world avoiding violence and mind-control. (5) Utilize sound criteria of truth in assessing all of the relevant hermeneutical data. (6) Make a fresh, objective examination of the relevant data with a willingness to accept the set of assumptions that without contradiction accounts for the many diverse lines of relevant grammatical, historical, cultural, theological, and experiential data with the fewest difficulties.[90]

With The International Council on Biblical Inerrancy in its Chicago Statement on Biblical Hermeneutics, "WE AFFIRM that any preunderstandings which the interpreter brings to Scripture should be in harmony with scriptural teaching and subject to correction by it. WE DENY that Scripture should be required to fit alien preunderstandings inconsistent with itself, such as naturalism, evolutionism, scientism, secular humanism and relativism."[91]

People concerned about the problem phenomena of the Bible need to be aware that the preponderance of discovery has tended to support the historical specifics asserted in Scripture, turning some who started with errantist perspectives toward more conservative views of Scripture (Sir William Ramsay and William Foxwell Albright). Rather than tending to shatter confidence in the wording of biblical manuscripts, textual criticism has built confidence in it. Higher criticism—concerned with matters of sources, date, and authorship—has had to revise late dates for biblical books in view of recent discoveries. Although many difficult questions have been raised, the Bible's credibility has been enhanced. "After more than two centuries of facing the heaviest guns that could be brought to bear, the Bible has survived, and is perhaps better for the siege. Even on the critics' own terms—historical fact—the Scriptures

seem more acceptable now than they did when the rationalists began the attack."[92]

Just as in issues regarding science and the Bible a moderate concordism is well supported, so in matters of history, and cultural anthropology, the basic characteristics are in harmony with Scripture, and the remaining difficulties may or may not be cleared up by further study, in our lifetimes. Being finite, we must accept the most probable hypothesis with the fewest difficulties. Many difficulties have been helpfully addressed by the better commentators. Also Gleason Archer, in his *Encyclopedia of Bible Difficulties*, proposes resolutions of numerous difficulties.[93]

Attempts to hold to the truth of the Bible in matters of spiritual life, but not in matters of fact are unsuccessful. The Bible itself is in major segments a set of assertions about historical facts. God created and sustains and governs history. The Exodus occurred in history. Jesus became flesh, lived and taught, died and rose again in history. He builds a church that continues to make world history. He understood the Old Testament to teach literal history. Without history Christianity is not Christianity, but some otherworldly mysticism. Theologians who regard the incarnation as mere mythology have missed the central, unique message of the faith.

Granting that some true biblical history is necessary to faith, where is the criterion by which we can decide which biblical history is necessary and true and which historical passages in Scripture are not necessary and may not be true? From Feuerbach, Harnack, and Schleiermacher on, attempts to define the essence of the Christian faith have had far from universal agreement. If a criterion by which to distinguish among true and false historical records in Scripture were proposed, would it not then be a more ultimate authority than the Scriptures themselves? Everyone believes some things in Scripture, like the Golden Rule. Some also believe biblical history that has been confirmed by extrabiblical historical evidence. Others accept biblical references to nature confirmed by science. They do not believe the Bible as such. They accept only those judgments with which they agree on some other ground.

The Bible's purpose is primarily redemptive, but the same bases for our faith in the central redemptive message (which itself involves historical facts—for example, Jesus is the Christ, he died for our sins, he was buried, he rose again), indicate that all that it teaches on other subjects as well is true.

Whether all or part of the biblical history is in view, Colin Brown effectively argued, "If the truth claims of a purported revelation can be shown to be false on a factual level, we can hardly claim it to represent the truth about God and man on any other level."[94]

RELEVANCE TO LIFE AND MINISTRY

The Book With Life-Transforming Power

A French naturalist, Emile Cailliet, had time to think while recovering from wounds of war, but could find "no light beyond the curtain" of his meaningless life. His favorite literary and philosophical works could not speak to the condition that asked, "Who was I anyway? Nay, what was I?" Upon reading the Bible for the first time in his life, he suddenly realized, "This was the Book that would understand me!" He found its pages "animated by the Presence of the Living God and the power of his mighty acts." As Cailliet prayed and read the opening chapters of the Gospel of John, he responded to the person of the gospel and life became meaningful. It was no longer a miserable sequence

of broken vows and vain resolutions. It is a life of love, and power because it is a redeemed and fully surrendered life, a life in line with the will of God. A man of power does not give the impression of strain and effort, but what he does God does in him. God's presence issues in Christlikeness and worship. Worship because the power of the Presence is not a mere duty; rather it is "a delectation wherein a Christian's destiny finds its fulfillment."[95]

The Only Inerrant Guide for Decision Making

What are the most valuable sources of guidance for people in a pluralistic world? They are not horoscopes, Ouija boards, good feelings, inner experiences, or altered states of consciousness. Mindless attempts to grasp ultimate reality sooner or later need to be conceptually interpreted in relation to all knowledge. Feelings and experiences do not come with tags giving their significance in the long run. Uninterpreted experience does not supply guidance. Knowledge by which to guide life includes the data of experience plus interpretation. Then, of course, the question is whose interpretation is most coherent?

How then shall Christians interpret the varied experiences of life? What goals are worth striving for? How do you know? Whatever experiences and feelings a Christian may have, and whatever may be learned from all other fields of knowledge, the teaching of Scripture provides the primary source of reliable information for guidance in life. It takes priority over counsel from any other field of knowledge and rules out any advice that contradicts it.

Biblical revelation stands out like a "light shining in a dark place" until Christ returns (2 Peter 1:19). Knowing that he will soon leave his body (1:13–14), Peter reminds God's people of the exceptional experience of the apostles who saw Christ transfigured (1:16–18). But he does not ask believers to seek a similar, "mountain top" experience! Even more certain than those eyewitness reports of living apostles, is "the word of the prophets . . . you will do well to pay attention to it. . . . For prophecy never had its origin in the will of man, but men spoke from God as they were carried along by the Holy Spirit" (1:19–21).

Biblical teaching has the divine right decisively to determine beliefs and behaviors. This one Book has this *authority* above all other books, for it is different in kind, not merely in degree. No other writing deserves the reading, the meditation, the study that this volume does. But belief in biblical inerrancy does not make biblical interpretation easy for decision making.

Given plenary inerrancy, a sufficient reason for a belief is that the Bible teaches it normatively for all humanity. However, not everything the Bible records is directly exemplary or normative today. Scripture presents not only general principles, but also narrative about particular people and events in particular cultural circumstances. General revelation presented basic truths about the changeless character of God and his moral demands for all people everywhere. And universal moral law is amplified in some biblical passages. But other passages present laws distinctively for the Jewish commonwealth not directly applicable in the same way to all other nations or to churches. In addition the lies of Satan, the grumbling of the people in the wilderness, the sins of many otherwise great leaders, must be distinguished in context for what they are (according to the most coherent account of all the relevant grammatical, historical, cultural, theological data).[96]

By what criteria can we distinguish universal from particular teachings in applying the biblical teaching to our daily lives? Teachings that are true can generally be recognized if they are given in a context that indicates their (1) universality; (2) necessity or unqualified "oughtness" or normativity for all people, for all people of God, for all in national Israel, or for all in Christian churches; and (3) changelessness. Nine commandments, at least, illustrate such absolute truths (the nine of the ten commandments repeated in the New Testament and written on all people's hearts) for all human beings of all time.

Indicative sentences about particular, irrepeatable events are also permanently true. The fact that events rapidly change does not mean that the truth about a given event itself changes. Truths about particular persons or events are not relative nor less true as time passes or as they are communicated around the world.

In one of these ways or another, through scriptural instruction, the Lord Jesus Christ instructs his discerning church. Apart from adherence to the Bible's guidance, talk about Christ as the head of the church can be manipulated in any direction. A Christian church in which the ultimate operative authority is not God's living Word through the written Word is like a body without a head.

Ned Stonehouse said, "Apart from clarity and unity in understanding the Lordship of Jesus Christ as coming to expression in the Holy Scripture, there can be no theological wholeness and no lasting assurance of advancement in theological education."[97]

The Dependable Means to Fellowship With the Living Word

Through the written Word we learn of the living Word: his eternal existence with the Father, his unique incarnation, his matchless life, his inerrant teaching (which renews, liberates, and sanctifies), his mighty miracles, his atoning death, his triumphant resurrection, his ascension, his intercession on our behalf and his coming again in glory and power. If we turn from the Christ of the written Word, to whom shall we go? To Marx? To Lenin? To Mao? To gurus from the Eastern religions? To gurus of the Western new-consciousness techniques? The Christ of the written Word remains incomparable! Are you bowing to the scriptural Christ as Master of your knowing, loving, and serving (epistemologically, affectively, and ethically)?

"The Christian who wants to encounter God without listening to what he has to say," Richard Lovelace writes, "may remain in the condition of a smilingly subliterate and disobedient two-year old. Sanctification of the mind is of pivotal importance in sanctification of the whole life, and sanctification of the mind involves an increasing ability to think biblically under the empowering of the Spirit."[98]

The key to authentic spiritual experience is assent to God's Word as true, that is, as informative concerning what is in reality, and what ought to be. With that guidance, life can be faithfully devoted to the really real and the most significant. "Without reliable information one may expend his life for nothing: without faithfulness to the highest values, one may be a hypocrite. On the one hand, a merely doctrinaire view of truth may lead to an empty idealism or an arrogant legalism. On the other hand, an undirected commitment may lead to a blind emotionalism, a frustrated activism, or a tragic discontinuity with what is and ought to be."[99]

The Truth to Which
the Holy Spirit Witnesses

Because the Bible is God's Word it ought to command belief and action; because readers of it are finite and sinful, they need the aid of the Holy Spirit to relate productively to its ultimate Author and his dynamic purposes in the world. Although doctrine is a reliable indicator of the kind of spiritual life or motivating force within a person or movement, Richard Lovelace has emphasized, it does not necessarily guarantee spiritual life or force within a person or movement (2 Tim. 3:5; 1 Cor. 13:1; Rev. 2:2–4).[100]

If a sound interpretation of Scripture is necessary, but not sufficient to give spiritual vitality, what is? The Scripture properly interpreted by a believer with the *illumination of the Holy Spirit* who inspired it is able to give spiritual vitality. The mind of sinners, according to some, is blind, and divine illumination provides new sight. The will of sinners, according to others, is rebellious and would not accept the biblical verdict of guilt nor the gospel of grace if it could "see" it. A third view suggests that both are correct and the whole person—the thinking, feeling, and willing self—though active in relation to himself and the world, is unresponsive to the truths of special revelation. The Holy Spirit's illumining activity frees a person's capacities in relation to spiritual things. Renewing the capacities to know, love, and obey God, illumination enables sinners to understand that the gospel is objectively true, to assent to its truth for themselves personally, and to commit themselves to the Savior.

The Spirit's activity of illumination for all believers does not reveal new information to be added to the canon of Scripture, nor does it make any believer, however sincere, inerrant or infallible. Neither does it by internal persuasion apart from examination of the evidence settle questions of which books belong in the canon or which reading of a text has the best manuscript support. The witness of the Spirit does not settle controversies about the meaning of a controversial passage apart from study of the text with sound hermeneutics. Nor does illumination displace the need for objective evidences and sound apologetic arguments based on them in preevangelism.

The witness of the Spirit attests the objective truth and meaning of special revelation, beginning at its heart, the gospel. The Spirit inspired the content of the gospel in the Scriptures, and now the Spirit persuades sinners of its truth objectively for all and internally for themselves. In this persuasion the Spirit may use different amounts of the relevant exegetical, historical, literary, and cultural data discovered by long hours of hard study by the inquirer or the ones ministering the Word to him. Hence the gospel appears no longer as foolishness or a stumbling block. The mind, desires, and will are opened to Christ and then one makes the commitment to him as Savior and Lord (1 Cor. 2:14; 12:3).

As a result of the Spirit's witness, believers develop assurance of their identity as children in God's spiritual family and joint heirs with Christ of all his resources for an abundant life (Rom. 8:15–16; Gal. 4:6). Enabled by the Spirit, believers trust and experience God's purposes of redemptive grace (1 Cor. 2:12). They are no longer in bondage to the values of the natural man (v. 14) and grow in evaluating things according to the revealed mind of Christ (vv. 15–16; 1 John 2:20–22, 27).[101]

People do not have to receive the Bible for it to become the Word of God. It *is* the Word of God objectively whether received as such or not. To reject its teaching is to be judged by its teaching. Christians who enjoy the Bible's benefits, receive it and act on it as the oracles of God. God's Spirit abides with believers, enabling them to receive the things that come from him (1 Cor. 2:14). That applies particularly to the Spirit-revealed and Spirit-inspired Scriptures. Receivers enabled by the Spirit delight, not merely in the Bible's verbal sentences, indispensable vehicles that they are, but especially in the great truths they teach and the awesome realities and events to which they refer.

It is the Spirit through the Word who enables receivers to walk faithfully with the Lord they love. When people are unreceptive, the Spirit's presence convicts them of yielding to fleshly desires, however delightful the temporary pleasures of sin may seem. Although some nonredemptive truths are revealed in nature, the necessary instrument of redemptive truth—since the completion of the canon until Christ himself returns—is scriptural teaching received as God's living voice.

Spiritual disciplines helpful in receiving the prophetic-apostolic message include reading it, studying it, memorizing it, and meditating on its application to life. "Be diligent in these matters; give yourself wholly to them so that everyone may see your progress. Watch your life and doctrine closely. Persevere in them, because if you do, you will save both yourself and your hearers" (1 Tim. 4:15).

An Unfailing Stimulus to Faith

Although suffering as a prisoner for proclaiming the gospel, Paul was not disillusioned or in despair. Why? Because of his faith. As he testifies to his faith, its essential elements become clear. "And of this gospel I was appointed a herald and an apostle and a teacher. That is why I am suffering as I am. Yet I am not ashamed, because I *know* whom I have believed, and am *convinced* that he is able to guard what I have *entrusted* to him for that day" (2 Tim. 1:11–12). Truth about God can be known. Zeal for God without knowledge (of the Redeemer) did not suffice for monotheistic and moral Jews (Rom.

10:1–2). Neither did worship of an "unknown God" atone for the cultured Athenians (Acts 17:23–31). In contrast, Abraham was "fully persuaded that God had power to do what he had promised" (Rom. 4:21).

The faith that saves is directed away from human educational, cultural, and religious achievements to the Creator, whose redemptive plan has been preserved and publicized in Scripture. Faith comes by *hearing* the message of special revelation now affirmed by the written Word of God, the hearer *being convinced* that "Jesus is Lord" and *trusting* in him (Rom. 10:4, 8–11, 14). Faith involves knowledge (*notitia*), persuasion (*assensus*), and commitment (*fiducia*). These three elements of faith are operative, not only when one first believes the gospel and trusts the Savior, but also in a growing faith throughout the Christian life.

An Indestructible Weapon for Victory in Spiritual Warfare

How did Christ, who was tempted in every way as we are (Heb. 4:15), avoid yielding to temptation? By quoting Scripture! Starved after forty days of fasting, Jesus was challenged by the Devil to change stones to bread. Jesus answered, "It is written: 'Man does not live on bread alone, but on every word that comes from the mouth of God'" (Matt. 4:4; Deut. 8:3). Jesus also countered the next two temptations with "It is written . . ." and then the Devil left him (Matt. 4:7, 10–11). Satan flees from nothing else like the Word of the Most High. Those who reduce any part of God's inscripturated Word to a mere human witness subject themselves and those they teach to spiritual warfare without some of their most effective weapons.

Although Christ won the decisive victory against Satan, the great dragon continues to tempt, primarily through our own fleshly desires and those of the unregenerate world, to lie, murder, and not hold to the truth (John 8:44). How can we counteract the works of the flesh such as sexual immorality, idolatry, witchcraft, hatred, jealousy, rage, selfish ambition, envy, drunkenness, and orgies (Gal. 5:19–21)? The scriptural instructions concerning these and an unforgiving spirit were given "in order that Satan might not outwit us. For we are not unaware of his schemes" (2 Cor. 2:5–11).

Christians who would take their stand against the Devil's schemes put on the full armor of God (Eph. 6:11). "For our struggle is not against flesh and blood, but against the rulers, against the authorities, against the powers of this dark world and against the spiritual forces of evil in the heavenly realms" (v. 12). In addition to the defensive armor, the one offensive weapon for this spiritual conflict is "the sword of the Spirit, which is the word of God" (6:17). The Word, as always, is accompanied by praying in the Spirit (6:18).

Whether the attraction to displease God is indirect or more directly present, "basic to all victory of the believer over Satan," said a Baptist pastor experienced in a deliverance ministry, "is the absolute truth of Bible doctrine. . . . Satan backs off from nothing but the absolute truth and fact of God's Word. . . . Seeing this truth is perhaps the single greatest key (to victory) in warfare against Satan."[102]

REVIEW QUESTIONS

To Help Relate and Apply Each Section in This Chapter

1. *Briefly state the classical problem* this chapter addresses and indicate reasons why genuine inquiry into it is important for your world view and your existence personally and socially.

2. *Objectively summarize the influ-*

ential answers given to this problem in history as hypotheses to be tested. Be able to compare and contrast their real similarities and differences (not merely verbal similarities or differences).

3. *Highlight the primary biblical evidence* on which to decide among views—evidence found in the relevant teachings of the major divisions of Scripture—and decide for yourself which historical hypothesis (or synthesis of historical views) provides the most consistent and adequate account of the primary biblical data.

4. *Formulate in your own words your doctrinal conviction* in a logically consistent and adequate way, organizing your conclusions in ways you can explain clearly, support biblically, and communicate effectively to your spouse, children, friends, Bible class, or congregation.

5. *Defend your view* as you would to adherents of the alternative views, showing that the other views are logically less consistent and factually faced with more difficulties than your view in accounting for the givens, not only of special revelation but also of human experience in general.

6. *Explore the differences the viability of your conviction can make in your life.* Then test your understanding of the viability of your view by asking, "Can I live by it authentically (unhypocritically) in relation to God and to others in my family, church, vocation, neighborhood, city, nation, and world?"

MINISTRY PROJECTS

To Help Communicate This Doctrine in Christian Service

1. *Memorize one major verse or passage* that in its context teaches the heart of this doctrine and may serve as a text from which to preach, teach, or lead small group studies on the topic. The memorized passages from each chapter will build a body of content useful also for meditation and reference in informal discussions.

2. *Formulate the major idea of the doctrine in one sentence* based on the passage memorized. This idea should be useful as the major thesis of either a lesson for a class (junior high to adult) or a message for a church service.

3. *State the specific purpose or goal of your doctrinal lesson or message.* Your purpose should be more than informative. It should show why Christians need to accept this truth and live by it (unhypocritically). For teaching purposes, list indicators that would show to what extent class members have grasped the truth presented.

4. *Outline your message or lesson in complete sentences.* Indicate how you would support the truth of the doctrine's central ideas and its relevance to life and service. Incorporate elements from this chapter's historical, biblical, systematic, apologetic, and practical sections selected according to the value they have for your audience.

5. *List applications of the doctrine* for communicating the difference this conviction makes in life (for sermons, lessons, small-group Bible studies, or family devotional Bible studies). Applications should make clear what the doctrine is, why one needs to know it, and how it will make differences in thinking. Then show how the difference in thought will lead to differences in values, priorities, attitudes, speech, and personal action. Consider also the doctrine's possible significance for family, church, neighborhood, city, regional, and national actions.

6. *Start a file and begin collecting illustrations* of this doctrine's central idea, the points in your outline, and your applications.

7. *Write out your own doctrinal statement on this subject in one paragraph* (in half a page or less). To work toward a comprehensive doctrinal statement,

collect your formulations based on a study of each chapter of *Integrative Theology*. As your own statement of Christian doctrine grows, you will find it personally strengthening and useful when you are called on for your beliefs in general and when you apply for service with churches, mission boards, and other Christian organizations. Any who seek ordination to Christian ministry will need a comprehensive doctrinal statement that covers the broad scope of theology.

PART TWO

THE LIVING GOD

GOD: AN ACTIVE, PERSONAL SPIRIT

God: An Active, Personal Spirit

THE PROBLEM: HOW SHALL WE VIEW THE REALITY OF GOD ONTOLOGICALLY?

Having shown that God has revealed himself to all persons via general revelation and to specific persons via special revelation preserved in inspired Scripture, we explore in this chapter what God has disclosed about his own person and character. Kant's critical philosophy maintained that the being of God, as a suprasensible reality is beyond the reach of theoretical knowledge. Having forfeited intellectual knowledge of God, Kant claimed that God, or the purposive Mind, is a postulate of the moral life. Beyond this, the moral Ruler and Lawgiver is inscrutable to persons bound to the phenomenal world. Living in the shadow of Kant, can we claim to know anything about God as he is in himself? Furthermore, given the modern aversion to metaphysics, can we represent God as a being (i.e., "One who is" as opposed to becoming or change) who dwells beyond the world? Does Scripture speak of God in essentialist categories, and if so, how valid are such representations? Can the Greek conception of God as the absolute, timeless being be reconciled with the popular Christian notion of God as Savior, Father, and Friend? Moreover, in an age when ultimate reality is viewed in terms of impersonal principles or pulses of energy, can Christians continue to maintain that God is properly a personal being? If such is the case, as evangelical Christians claim, how do the special qualities of maleness and femaleness apply to God?

Given the biblical claim of the unity and indivisibility of God, how shall we understand the relationship between God's being and his attributes? In this regard the proposals of realists, nominalists, and others will be examined. The present chapter searches for a meaningful and fresh way of arranging the perfections of God as presented in Scripture. In addition, we will inquire into the meaning and relevance of the statement that metaphysically God is self-existent, eternal, unchanging, and omniscient.

When considering the being and character of God, certain crucial problems need to be addressed. Is God an impassible being, as some classical authorities maintained, or does God possess authentic emotions in relation to the creature? Does God feel with persons when they grieve, sorrow, or hurt?

177

Moreover, how can God's immutability be reconciled with events in Scripture in which God appears to alter his dealings with persons, as for example, when he replaces blessing with cursing and vice versa?

ALTERNATIVE PROPOSALS IN THE CHURCH

The following represent the principal interpretations advanced by Christendom concerning the being of God and his metaphysical perfections.

Scholastic Thomism

Aquinas and later Thomists, having wedded Aristotelian philosophy to Christian truth, defined God as first unmoved mover, first efficient cause, and absolutely necessary being. By definition altogether immutable and thus lacking beginning and end, God is an eternal being in the sense that his reality is the permanent now. As both eternal and necessary being, God is "pure act (*actus purus*) without any potentiality."[1] It follows that as absolute being God is simple and not composite: "God is His essence, quiddity, or nature."[2] Thomas insists that nothing can be added to God's essence in an accidental way. And because he is simple being, he has both intelligence and a will. Hence God is a living person who contains within himself all the perfections of being. Furthermore, Thomas's immutable God never experiences passions of sorrow, pain, or fear, for God as an incorporeal being has no sensitive appetites. Nevertheless, Thomas's God knows the joy and delight that is rooted in His own nature. Yahweh ("he who is"), the special name of God, "denominates the infinite ocean of substance"[3] and represents God in his divine immutability and eternity. As the soul indwells every part of the body, so God is everywhere in the threefold sense of his presence, his power, and his substance. God's ubiquity as Spirit does not exclude the copresence of other entities.

Hegelian Idealism

Hegel viewed God, the Absolute Spirit, as that immanent reality in the world process that continually unfolds itself through opposing forces in history. The German idealist brought together epistemology and ontology to arrive at a "developmental pantheism." For Hegel, truth (i.e., the Absolute) is the whole, which essentially reaches its completeness through the process of its own development, called Spirit (*Geist*). God, then, is Absolute Spirit, which, like the bud→blossom→fruit sequence, is a living process of negation and mediation. The Absolute is neither above nor with the universe; it is the eternal totality. Ultimate reality is becoming (Being→Nothing→Becoming), hence the Absolute Spirit unfolds itself developmentally through the process of conflicting and contradictory forces in history. God is neither independent nor self-existent, but a total process of self-expression in and through the finite. Although God is "living," he is not personal, for this would limit the Absolute to a particular mode of being. In short, God is impersonal historical oneness, of which the whole process of reality is a teleological movement toward the realization of Absolute Spirit.

Influenced by Hegel, Schleiermacher developed a pantheistic idealism that envisages God as the personification of the "Spirit of the universe." The Absolute, who is never an object of rational thought, nevertheless is a postulate of the creature's sense of dependence. The divine attributes, which place objective reality in God, give expression to the various dimensions of the Christian self-consciousness or feeling of absolute dependence. Following Hegel, Schleiermacher denied immutability in favor of a God who is eternally becoming.

Protestant Liberalism

The older liberalism rejected traditional metaphysical theology as an alien Greek construct and denied that God is a remote, self-sufficient, and unfeeling being. Walter Rauschenbusch affirmed that there are only two concepts of God: the despotic and the democratic. The former view, espoused by classical and Reformation theology, was stimulated by the totalitarian state. It holds that God is sufficient unto himself, remote, and insulated from human suffering. Rauschenbusch insisted that modern theology must democratize its concept of God by viewing him as a Father who feels and suffers with humankind. Given Rauschenbusch's concept of God as the infinite spirit that undergirds the movement for social progress (cf. Hegel), some authorities accuse him of pantheism.

W. A. Brown, who taught at Union Theological Seminary in New York, likewise rejected the classical approach which he perceived begins with abstract notions of God's absoluteness from which are derived such metaphysical qualities as aseity, eternity, and immutability. The liberal theologian began rather with the personality and character of God as loving Father displayed humanwise in Jesus. The attributes are descriptive of God not as he is in himself, but of the Father's relationship with his people. They are a peculiar construct of the Christian thought of God in the mind. God's absoluteness, for example, signifies that "the holy and loving personality whom Christ has revealed is really master of the universe."[4] His omnipresence means that one cannot drift away from God's love and care.

Barthian Neoorthodoxy

Karl Barth followed Kierkegaard in stressing the infinite qualitative difference between God and human beings. The eternal, ineffable "Wholly Other" reveals himself through the Word as a living, personal God who loves in freedom.

Contrary to the immanent God of liberal theology, Barth emphasized the irrevocable otherness of the God of the Bible. Since God and humans are metaphysical opposites, the invisible and ineffable God is known only by his gracious self-revelation in Christ. Barth's conviction that the sovereign God is known only on the basis of his free decision to engage man is reflected in such statements as, "God's being is absolutely His act"[5] and "the operation of God is the essence of God."[6] Revelation indicates that the living, personal, spiritual God is the eternal being who loves in freedom. Barth divides the divine attributes (God *is* his perfections) into two categories: (1) perfections of the divine loving, and (2) perfections of the divine freedom. In the latter category Barth places God's ubiquity, constancy, and eternity. The first of these signifies not God's inactive extension through the universe, but his sovereign dominion over all space. He is everywhere present as Lord, i.e, generally in creation, especially in revelation and reconciliation, and preeminently in Jesus Christ. Constancy signifies not that God is immobile, but that he is true to himself or self-consistent. God is not moved by impulses external to himself; rather his affections of sympathy, compassion, and anger are self-generated from within his innermost being. Finally, eternity connotes that God is "the One who is and rules before time, in time, and again after time, the One who is not conditioned by time, but conditions it absolutely in His freedom."[7]

Protestant and Roman Catholic
Neoliberalism

Recent Protestant and Roman Catholic liberals redefine theism along existentialist lines. God is not a supreme being who dwells in some heavenly realm independent of the world. Above the limiting categories of being and personality, God is said to be the ground and power of being or the infinite horizon of human existence. The relation between God and the world is viewed in terms of the panentheistic model: the reality of God includes within itself the world, but is not exhausted by it.

From an idealistic and anthropological perspective, Tillich transforms the idea of God by upholding "the God above the God of theism."[8] God is not a being alongside of or above other beings, for as such he would be a creature of time and space. Rather God is being-itself (*ipsum esse*) or the creative ground and power of being. More simply put, God represents the depths of one's life or one's ultimate concern—what one takes seriously without any reservation.[9] Thus, according to Tillich, "God does not exist. He is being-itself beyond essence and existence."[10] Indeed, "It is as atheistic to affirm the existence of God as it is to deny it."[11] Tillich claims that the Ultimate or the Unconditioned is not *a person*, but *personal*, where the latter is defined as "the concreteness of man's ultimate concern."[12] To the foregoing *absolute* characteristics are added several *symbolic* descriptions of the Mystery of being: God is living in that he is the ground of life, eternal in that he conquers the nonbeing of temporality, and omnipresent in that by creative participation in the existence of his creatures insecurity and anxiety are overcome.

John Macquarrie likewise opposes the classical theistic model in favor of an existentialist approach along the lines proposed by Heidegger. Thus God, the most ultimate reality, is not a being (*ens*) beyond the world, but the dynamic "act of being (*esse*)."[13] Thus "Being always includes becoming, and . . . the essence of Being is the dynamic act of letting-be."[14] Macquarrie's "organic" model by his own admission is panentheistic: God is related to the world as form is to matter. Macquarrie's God is hardly self-sufficient, for the organic model involves a reciprocity in which God and the world are dependent upon each other. With his emphasis on becoming, Macquarrie joins other authorities in rejecting the divine impassibility. Rather than being immutable, God is said to be "consistent," or preferably, "faithful."

Much of recent Roman Catholic thought, persuaded that classical theology adopted an alien hellenistic cultural form, likewise doubts that God is properly a supreme being. If God is not a *res* (thing), if God has no essence (a scholastic category), then it can be argued that God does not exist. Are Christians then atheists? No, some avant-garde Catholics respond, for Christians do experience the presence of a reality *beyond* being. Given this development, doubts are raised about God's personality, as customarily defined. Thus Hellwig acknowledges that not a few recent Catholic writers view God as "beyond personality."[15] Moreover, with the traditional distinction between the natural and the supernatural being seriously questioned, Catholic "progressives" tend to view the relation between God and the world in terms of the panentheistic model.

Retreating from the idea of a supreme being or transcendent Deity who exists independently of the world, Hans Küng adopts the panentheistic perspective of "God in this world and this world in God."[16] Thus God "is certainly not an infinite, still less a finite, *alongside* or *above* finite things. He is the infinite *in* all that is finite, being itself in all that is."[17] Küng wants to retain the values of a personal God and so asserts that "he is a God with a human face."[18] Yet Küng insists that the primal reason, support, and meaning of all reality is not a discrete person alongside other persons. Since God is not a being, "It is better . . . to describe him not as personal or impersonal, but as transpersonal, superpersonal."[19] The attributes of God, moreover, describe God not intrinsically or independently, but in terms of his relationship to persons and the world.

Leslie Dewart, in *The Future of Belief*, which bears the subtitle *Theism in a World Come of Age*, insists that traditional notions of God's personality, eternity, immutability, and impassibility entered Christian theology by a process of hellenization. If theism is to prove relevant to the modern world, a dehellenization of the doctrine of God must occur. Dewart believes that personality no longer should be predicted of God. "God is, rather than a center of being to which we are drawn, an expansive *force* [italics added] which impels persons to go out from and beyond themselves."[20] In fact, Dewart completely radicalizes the doctrine of God by suggesting that the supernatural is not essential to Christian faith.

I suggest that in the future we may not feel the need to conceive God as a supernatural being. If we discard the hellenic view of nature, the Christian God no longer must, in order to remain free, be graciously and freely self-giving, perform supernatural feats, undertake supernatural functions and roles, or enjoy supernatural status.[21]

Process Theology

The process theism of Whitehead, Hartshorne, and their followers firmly rejects the God of classical theism, which it describes as an Oriental despot, a static sovereign, and an unrelational idol. The proponents of neoclassical theism view the essence of reality as becoming, not being, i.e., as a series of nonsensory experiences or energy events. Hence all reality (including God) is processive, relational, and pragmatic. Thus God cannot be objectified as an existent or a substantial self. Rather, God is a moving pattern of events, or as Cobb puts it, "an occurrence of thinking, willing, feeling, and loving."[22] More specifically, process theology confounds the divine simplicity by positioning a metaphysical dualism wherein God is said to be bipolar. God's abstract or potential nature—eternal, absolute, unconscious, and unchanging—is said to provide the initial aim or intentional purpose for every actual occasion. On the other hand, God's concrete or actual nature—temporal, dependent, relative, and constantly changing—is the composite nature that prehends all actual occasions and assimilates them into its own reality. But since process thinkers plead that to be real is to be actual ("process is reality"), the primordial pole of God is a pure abstraction, a philosophical construct that possesses no reality whatever. With the collapse of the abstract pole God is shorn of most of the perfections traditionally ascribed to God. Thus the Deity is not a person, for personality is said to limit God.[23] Neither is God self-sufficient, for his consequent nature is dependent on the world for its actuality. And God is certainly not changeless, for Yahweh ("I will be what I will be") continually surpasses himself through the myriad experiences of creative becoming. God is omnipresent in the radical sense that all things are taken into or occur within the divine reality. Process theology, in short, postulates an impersonal "God" who is the creative movement in nature.

Protestant Orthodoxy

Most Fathers, Reformers, and Evangelicals view God as an uncreated, noncontingent, living, and active spirit who, on the basis of propositional revelation, can be partially yet truthfully represented in analogical language. This God is invisible, timeless, everywhere present, and impassible in the sense that he is not moved by external forces contrary to his will.

In the midst of pagan polytheism, the early Fathers depicted God as the one uncreated, invisible, immortal, imperishable, and immutable Being. In spite of the Hellenistic language of many early church authorities (e.g., God as unbegotten, absolute Being—*ho ōn*), they consistently viewed God as related to his creation. So Theophilus describes God as constantly "running, moving, active, nourishing, governing, and making things alive."[24]

Clement of Alexandria, influenced by the Platonic idea of the Absolute, affirms that Deity is incomprehensible to the human mind: "God is invisible and beyond expression by words."[25] Unable to say what God *is*, the creature can only assert what God *is not*: i.e., he is unbegotten, invisible, immutable, and imperishable. God even transcends the abstract conceptions the mind frames of him: the One, Good, Mind, Absolute Being, Lord. Although Clement's God is ontologically remote, he nevertheless is relationally near in his power, providence, and love.

Ontological considerations took on fresh importance during the period of the christological and trinitarian controversies. From the revealed name Yahweh (Exod. 3:14), Athanasius conceived of God as the One, the incomprehensible being (*akatalēptos ousia*) or essence. "When it is said, 'I am that I am,' . . . , we understand nothing else than the very simple, and blessed, and incomprehensible essence itself of Him that is."[26] The famous formula of Athanasius—three persons (*hypostaseis*) in one essence (*ousia*)—communicates in Greek philosophical language the conviction that in his most intrinsic being God "is a concrete reality, not a fiction or abstraction."[27]

Augustine insisted that the inexhaustible and ineffable God cannot be fully grasped by human thought and language. The name Yahweh offers the most fundamental representation of what God is in himself—the only real being or substance. Borrowing elements from Neoplatonism, Augustine claimed that God is simple and therefore cannot be differentiated from his attributes. Hence, "in God to be is the same as to be strong, or to be just, or to be wise, or whatever is said of that simple multiplicity or multifold simplicity."[28] Whereas other entities admit of accidents and therefore are subject to change, Yahweh—"I am he who never changes"—is the only immutable essence. Not only God's nature but also his knowing, willing, and decreeing undergo no mutability. Moreover, according to Augustine, in God there can be no suffering. "Be it far from us to surmise that the impassible nature of God is liable to any molestation."[29]

As the real and unchanging being, God is also eternal. Augustine conceives of eternity not so much as endless time (time being a created entity), but as that higher level of existence free of change where there exists no sequence of yesterday, today, and tomorrow. While denying that God is diffused through space as air or light, Augustine affirms that God is wholly everywhere and is contained in no place. "He is not distributed through space by size so that half of Him should be in half of the world and half in the other half of it. He is wholly present in all of it in such wise as to be wholly in heaven alone and wholly in earth alone, and wholly in heaven and earth together; not confined in any place, but wholly in Himself everywhere."[30] Although he used Greek categories of thought, from start to finish Augustine regarded God not as the abstract Absolute, but as a living and active divine person. Thus God is "always working, . . . sustaining, pervading, and protecting; creating, nourishing, and developing; seeking and yet possessing all things."[31]

Melanchthon, the first systematic theologian of the Reformation, viewed God as a unified, uncreated spiritual being who is eternal, incorruptible, and independent. Being (Germ. *Wesen*, Gk. *ousia*) for Melanchthon "means something that definitely exists in and of itself, and is not dependent on some other foundation, as a contingent thing is."[32] Moreover, God's attributes of power, wisdom, righteousness, etc., are one with his essence. "Divine being is divine power, wisdom and righteousness, and these virtues are not to be separated from the Being."[33]

John Calvin was acutely conscious of the glory and majesty of God: "God is incomprehensible, a Spirit above all spirit, light above all light."[34] The name Yahweh denotes the "incomprehensible essence"[35] of the God who is invisible both to the naked eye and to the human mind. On the basis of revelation God is spoken humanwise as a living and active Spirit. Far from the first cause or unmoved mover of scholastic theology, Calvin upheld a God of "a watchful, effective, active sort, engaged in ceaseless activity."[36] The self-existent God is eternal, and because eternal he is unchanging both in his essence and in his purposes. Scriptures that speak of God as repenting or changing his mind pertain not to God as he is in himself, but to our finite understanding of him. God "cannot be touched with repentance, and his heart cannot undergo change. To imagine such a thing would be impiety."[37] A familiar refrain

in Calvin is that the eternal God remains ever like himself.

The Reformed confessions articulate a full-orbed vision of God. The Second Helvetic Confession (1566) declares: "God is one in essence or nature, subsisting by Himself, all-sufficient in Himself, invisible, without a body, infinite, eternal" (ch. III). The Westminster Shorter Catechism (1647) contemplates God as "infinite, eternal, and unchangeable" in his being and perfections. According to the Westminster Confession of Faith (1647), "There is but one only living and true God, who is infinite in being and perfection, a most pure spirit, without body, parts, or passions, immutable, immense, eternal, incomprehensible. . ." (ch. II.1).

Stephen Charnock in his classic book, *The Existence and Attributes of God*, regards God, the first and independent being, as "a pure act, nothing but vigor and act."[38] The proper name Yahweh signifies both his eternity ("I am") and his unchangeableness ("that I am"). The former denotes the duration of the divine essence without beginning, without end, and without succession. The latter signifies that God's essence, perfections, purposes, and promises endure eternally without any variation. The biblical assertions of repentance and passion involve no changes in God himself. Repentance connotes a change in God's external relations, whereas passions of anger, grief, and joy are anthropopathisms adapted to human minds.

W. G. T. Shedd affirms that the fundamental aspects of God are substantiality (essence or substance) and personality (self-conscious being). Because God is both substance and a person, he can possess and exert attributes. Like Hodge, Shedd insists that the attributes are objectively real qualities in God. God is not essence and attributes, but essence in attributes. "The whole essence is in each attribute, and the attribute in the essence."[39] Shedd insists that God is "without passions" in the sense that he is not passively wrought upon by finite entities external to himself. Although independent of the creation and thus impassive, God nevertheless has feelings and emotions. Literally attributes to the Divine are love (*agapē*) and wrath (*orge*). And as the soul is present in every part of the body, so the whole essence of God is present at every point of space as a simple and undivided unity.

Other evangelical discussion of the being of God and the metaphysical attributes include Ronald Nash,[40] Millard J. Erickson,[41] and Carl F. H. Henry.[42]

Protestant Liberalism

BIBLICAL TEACHING

In order to determine which hypothesis is preferred we now turn to the teachings of Scripture, which constitute our primary authority.

Pentateuch

In the opening chapters of the Old Testament, God made himself known through word and deed as a living and active personal Spirit. With the concreteness that characterizes the Hebrew mind the Pentateuch depicts God as the sovereign personal agent who creates man from the dust of the earth and breathes into his nostrils the breath of life (Gen. 1:27; 2:7). Subsequently God planted a garden in Eden, placed Adam and Eve in it to work it, and entered into personal relations with the first couple. The same God disclosed himself to Noah and caused a flood to cover the earth, thereby destroying those who had violated his holy laws. No passive unrelated being, God entered into personal covenant relations with Abraham, Isaac, and Jacob.

When Israel languished in Egypt, God came to Moses at the burning bush (Exod. 3:1–6). The flame of fire in which the angel of the Lord appeared symbolizes the glory and majesty of the invisible God, whereas the fact that the bush was not consumed suggests that God is self-sustaining or life itself. When God disclosed his plan to bring Israel out of Egypt, Moses asked the name of the One who was behind so bold a venture. God's response to Moses was the profound statement "I AM WHO I AM" (*'ehyeh 'ᵃšer 'ehyeh*, Exod. 3:14). Moreover, Moses was to tell the people, "I AM [*'ehyeh*] has sent me to you." The imperfect tense of the verb "to be" or "to exist" denotes that he ever continues to be Yahweh. The Hebrew expression provides no basis for a projection into the future in the sense of "I shall be what I shall be." The self-designation connotes that the God of Israel is the living, awe-inspiring one who is always active in every experience of his people. "I AM" or Yahweh (LXX, *ho ōn*) thus implies (1) that the faithful God is self-existent, in the sense that he possesses his very nature; (2) that he is eternal ("This is my name for ever," 3:15); and (3) that he is unchanging in his person and purposes.[43]

That God is a living and active Deity is seen in the series of nine plagues that released Israel from Egyptian bondage (Exod. 7–10) and in the miraculous passage through the Sea of Reeds (Exod. 14). On the latter occasion Moses told Israel, "The LORD will fight for you" (Exod. 14:14). God's approach to Moses in a dense cloud (Exod. 19:9) at Sinai symbolizes his invisibility and glory. The accompanying fire and smoke (Exod. 19:18) signifies his spirituality; and the thunder, lightning, and earthquake (19:16, 18) signifies his awesome majesty and power (cf. Exod.

24:15–17; Deut. 5:24). The second commandment, which prohibits the making of corporeal representations of God (Exod. 20:4; cf. 34:17), attests the fact that God is an invisible spirit being. Moses later reminded the people, "You saw no form [*tᵉmûnāh*] of any kind the day the LORD spoke to you at Horeb out of the fire" (Deut. 4:15). God's "Presence" (e.g., his glorious person, *pānîm*) would accompany Israel (Exod. 33:14–16); but as God said to Moses, "You cannot see my face (*pānîm*), for no one may see me and live" (Exod. 33:20).

The Pentateuchal theophanies—e.g., the angel who dialogued with Hagar (Gen. 16:7–13) and the three men who conversed with Abraham (18:1–5)—were shown in chapter 3 to be visible representations of God. These temporary manifestations of Deity in forms accessible to the senses no more vitiate the spirit-nature of God than did the later incarnation of Christ. Anthropomorphisms, which figuratively ascribe to God human features such as a face, hands, back (Exod. 33:23), arm (6:6), and finger (Deut. 9:10); humanlike sentiments of grief (Gen. 6:6), anger (Exod. 15:7), hatred (Deut. 12:31), jealousy (Exod. 20:5), and vengeance (Deut. 32:35); and humanlike actions such as knowing (Gen. 18:21), purposing (50:20), choosing (Deut. 7:6–7), performing (Gen. 21:1), and disciplining (Deut. 8:5) confirm that God is not an impersonal force but a personal being endowed with intellect, emotions, and the power of self-determination. Moses justifiably represented God as "the living One" (*hay*, Gen. 16:14) and the living God (*'ᵉlōhîm ḥayyîm*, Deut. 5:26)—a judgment that God himself confirmed (Num. 14:21, 28).

In Oriental cultures a person's name is richly descriptive of his character and significance. Hence, the biblical names of God, no less than the acts of God, are revelatory instruments that disclose who God is. To know God's name is to know God himself (Exod. 3:13–15; cf. Isa. 52:6). The most common name of God, *'ᵉlōhîm*, occurs more than two thousand times in the Hebrew Bible. A designation for the gods of the Semitic peoples, *'ᵉlōhîm* likely was derived from the root meaning "to reverence," or "to fear." Thus, in meaning and context *'ᵉlōhîm* connotes "the Mighty One or "he that is to be feared." Since *'ᵉlōhîm* overwhelmingly governs pronouns and verbs in the singular, its plural form should be viewed as a plural of intensity or majesty.[44]

Yahweh, the self-existent, eternal, and unchanging "I AM," is the God of grace who enters into covenant relations with his chosen people (Deut. 5:2). The glorious incommunicable name that the Jews superstitiously refused to pronounce (cf. Lev. 24:16) is descriptive of none but the God of Israel. Since the name Yahweh occurs some 150 times in Genesis, one meets with initial surprise Yahweh's saying to Moses (Exod. 6:3): "I appeared to Abraham, to Isaac and to Jacob as God Almighty [*'ēl šadday*], but by my name the LORD (Yahweh) I did not make myself known to them." No contradiction in the pentateuchal traditions need be posited. Rather Exodus 6:3 affirms that whereas God formerly had been addressed as Yahweh, only at Sinai was the full import of that "glorious name" (Deut. 28:58) made known.

In addition to his names, God's character is known by the ascription to him of specific attributes. The opening statement of the Bible, "In the beginning God . . ." (Gen. 1:1), suggests an existence that is absolute and not contingent on any other being or power. God's self-existence or aseity is also affirmed in the revelation of the divine name at Sinai (Exod. 3:14). Yahweh thus is upheld as the One who has life in himself, the One who most fundamentally *is*.

The eternity of God is amply affirmed in the five books of the Law. Abraham "called upon the name of the LORD, the Eternal God" (Gen. 21:33). Moreover, implicit in the "I AM" of Exodus 3:14 is the postulate of the divine eternity. In addition, both Moses and Yahweh testify that the Lord will live and reign forever (Exod. 15:18; Deut. 32:40), a fact that is a source of hope and comfort for the godly (Deut. 33:27). The divine eternality suggests (1) that God's existence had no beginning and will have no end, (2) that God transcends the limitations of time ("I AM"), and (3) that God is the cause and ground of time (cf. John 1:3).

A consequent of the divine aseity and eternity is God's immutability. "I AM WHO I AM" (Exod. 3:14) dwells above the flux of the contingent universe. Similarly the oracle of Balaam reads: "God is not a man, that he should lie, nor a son of man, that he should change his mind [*nāham*]. Does he speak and then not act? Does he promise [*dābar*] and not fulfill?" (Num. 23:19). Moreover, the God who is unchanging in his being, character, and counsel is given the title of "Rock" (Deut. 32:4, 15, 18, et al.). As the solid material of which mountains are formed, Rock (*ṣûr*) points up the stability, unchangeableness, and reliability of Israel's God. The fact that in Noah's day God was grieved (Niphal of *nāham*, "be sorry," "mourn over") and purposed to destroy sinners from the face of the earth (Gen. 6:6), does not invalidate the divine immutability. Neither did his decision to stay his hand of judgment following the golden-calf incident (Exod. 32:12–14) and to withhold his judgment of fire against the murmuring Israelites (Num. 11:1, 10) effect any change in God's being, character, or strategic purpose. Rather, God consistently dealt with people on the basis of his changeless character and their moral responses, and these dealings he had

omnisciently included in his overall plan. That God experienced authentic emotions of regret (Gen. 6:6), anger (Num. 11:10), hatred (Deut. 12:31), jealousy (Exod. 20:4–5), and vengeance (Deut. 32:35) demonstrates that the personal God enjoys a healthy and controlled emotional life. Not moved by forces external to himself, God remains himself in the fullness of his own nature.

Historical Books

God is depicted in the documents chronicling Israel's history as a living, active, and personal God. So Joshua describes the One who led Israel to the Promised Land as "the living God [*'ēl hay*] among you" (Josh. 3:10; cf. 1 Sam. 17:26, 36). The historical books depict a God of consummate intelligence and purpose who performs mighty works on behalf of his people. Thus Yahweh's parting of the waters of the Jordan (Josh. 3:14–17) and his toppling of the walls of Jericho (Josh. 6:1–27) further establish him as a living and active God. Similarly Elijah's triumph by the power of the Lord over the 450 prophets of Baal on Mount Carmel evoked this response from the assembled throng: "The LORD—he is God! The LORD—he is God!" (1 Kings 18:39). Numerous other works were wrought in Israel's history by the personal, living God, such as Elijah's rapture in a whirlwind and the rout of the Syrian army that had besieged Samaria. The fall and resettlement of Jerusalem illustrates the working of the living God. The Lord sent numerous messengers to warn his people of their wicked ways. But when the inhabitants of Jerusalem scoffed at the warnings, the Lord "brought up against them the king of the Babylonians . . . and handed all of them over to Nebuchadnezzar" (2 Chron. 36:17). After the people had been held captive for seventy years, "the LORD moved the heart of Cyrus king of Persia" to free the Jewish exiles and permit them to rebuild the temple in Jerusalem (Ezra 1:1-4).

The historical literature also affirms the immutability of Israel's God: "He who is the Glory of Israel does not lie or change his mind; for he is not a man, that he should change his mind" (1 Sam. 15:29). Also the unique title for God, "the Glory of Israel" (*nēṣaḥ yiśrā'ēl*, where *nēṣaḥ* connotes endurance or constancy), admirably attests that God's character and will are unalterable. Nevertheless, in the face of Saul's deliberate disobedience, not only was God grieved (the Niphal of *nāham*) that he had made Saul king (vv. 11, 35), but he also rejected Saul as king of Israel (v. 23). Far from altering his eternal counsel, God in wisdom adapted his immediate response to the then-existing situation. Changes in God's emotional attitudes and tactical responses, consistent with his overall immutability, are also evident in Judges 2:18-23; 2 Samuel 24:16; 2 Chronicles 12:12; 30:8-10.

The first explicit mention of omnipresence—that the totality of God is present everywhere in the universe—occurs in 1 Kings 8:27 (cf. 2 Chron. 2:6), where Solomon acknowledged in prayer, "The heavens, even the highest heaven, cannot contain you. How much less this temple I have built!" The infinite God cannot be confined to an earthly building, for his Spirit-being pervades, indeed transcends, the entire created order.

Poetry and Wisdom

Job contemplates God as an incorporeal spirit being: "When he passes me, I cannot see him; when he goes by, I cannot perceive him" (Job 9:11). Since God is invisible, Job adds, "If I go to the east, he is not there; if I go to the west, I do not find him" (23:8). The invisible God, however, is no mere cosmic force or energy, but a conscious personal agent. The Hebrew plural noun *pānîm* (rendered in the AV by "face," "presence," and "countenance") is symbolic of the person and his attitudes, sentiments, moods, and actions.[45] Accordingly, God causes his face to shine on the saints (Pss. 4:6; 31:16), and sets his face against evildoers (34:16). Believers seek his face (27:8; 105:4) and will dwell in his presence (140:13), whereas God-haters flee from his face (68:2).

That God is properly personal is seen in the fact that he possesses intelligence, emotions, and a will. Job (12:13) teaches that God possesses wisdom (*ḥokmāh*), counsel (*'ēṣāh*), and understanding (*tᵉbûnāh*). God's counsel is formulated, not arbitrarily, but according to a consistent, intelligent plan (Job 38:2). God also possesses the full range of emotions attributed to personality: compassion (Pss. 103:13; 111:4), jealousy (Ps. 78:58), anger (Job 9:13; 19:11), and wrath (Job 21:20). Finally, God possesses a will, or the power of personal choice. He devised an eternal counsel (Ps. 33:11) that cannot be thwarted (Job 42:1) and chose a people for himself (Ps. 135:4).

That God is the "living God" (*'ēl ḥay*, Ps. 84:2) actively engaged in the affairs of his people is plainly seen in several psalms that survey the history of Israel (Pss. 78, 105, 106, 136). Together these psalms form a mosaic of the mighty deeds of the living God on behalf of his people, including the creation, the making of covenants with the patriarchs, the plagues in Egypt, deliverance through the Sea of Reeds, divine guidance in the wilderness and the conquest of Canaan.

Several names of God are found in the poetic and wisdom literature. Apparently derived from a root meaning to be strong, *'ēl* connotes the God of power, greatness, and awe. Uncompounded in Job (5:8; 8:3; 9:2, et al.), *'ēl* is frequently linked with other epithets in the Psalms: "God of glory" (Ps. 29:3), "God of truth" (31:5), "the God of heaven" (136:26), et al. The name *'ēlôah*, which occurs forty-one times in Job (3:4; 4:9; 5:17, et al.), denotes the God of power and comfort. Derived from the verb *'ālāh* ("to go up"), *'elyôn* depicts God as majestic, exalted, and all-powerful. The name also appears in the compounds "God Most High" (*'ēl 'elyôn*, Ps. 78:35; *'elōhîm 'elyôn*, Pss. 57:2; 78:56), and "LORD Most High" (*Yahweh 'elyôn*, Ps. 47:2). The title (*'ēl šadday*) occurs forty-eight times in the Old Testament. God revealed himself to the patriarchs by this compound name (cf. Exod. 6:3), but as *šadday* alone he is known thirty-one times in Job (5:17; 6:4, 14, et al.). The name probably comes from the Akkadian word for mountain, and thus connotes the omnipotent, invincible God, who is the source of all comfort. A shortened form of Yahweh, namely, *yāh*, occurs most frequently (thirty-nine times) in the Psalms (77:11; 89:8; 94:7, et al.).

Although the hymnbook of Israel is chiefly practical, Psalm 36:9 asserts the self-existence of the Lord: "With you is the fountain of life (*mᵉqôr hayyîm*)." Like a spring that brings forth a constant supply of water, God is the unfailing source of life. "All life flows forth from Him, who is the absolutely existing and happy One."[46] Moreover, eternity, in the sense of infinite continuation of existence, is affirmed of God in Job 36:26 ("The number of his years is past finding out") and in Psalm 90:2 ("From everlasting to everlasting you are God"). Psalm 139:7–12 uses dramatic imagery to affirm the divine ubiquity. If one should ascend to the highest heaven, descend to the lowest depths, or fly from East to West with the speed of light, escape from God's personal presence and care is impossible, for he is everywhere.

Prophetic Literature

When Isaiah repaired to the temple to ponder the fate of Judah he experienced a life-transforming vision of the glory of God (Isa. 6:1–5). Isaiah saw with spiritual eyes the Lord seated on a throne, high and exalted, the train of his robe filling the temple. Accompanying phenomena such as the foundations that shook and the smoke that filled the temple (v. 4) recall the revelation of the majestic God at Sinai. Likewise Ezekiel's call to ministry was preceded by an equally magnificent vision of the glory of God (Ezek. 1:1–28). In the midst of a violent thunderstorm the prophet beheld a fiery chariot formed by four living creatures, and above the chariot he saw a throne of sapphire occupied by the figure of a man glowing with fire and surrounded by brilliant light. Prostrated by the awesomeness of the vision, Ezekiel concluded, "This was the appearance of the likeness of the glory of the LORD" (1:28). That God is a personal spirit is seen in Isaiah's ascription to him (Isa. 11:2) of intelligence, specifically "wisdom" (*hokmāh*, discernment), "understanding" (*bînāh*, intelligence), "counsel" (*'ēṣāh*, the ability to plot a strategy), and "knowledge" (*da'at*, insight). So also Isaiah 40:14, 28 and Jeremiah 51:15. In the prophetic literature, God possesses a full range of emotions, including pity (Jer. 16:5; Ezek. 5:11), grief (Isa. 63:10; Jer. 42:10), jealousy (Nah. 1:2; Zech. 1:14), and anger (Isa. 5:25; Jer. 7:20). Isaiah 54:7–8 brings together the profound emotions of burning "anger" (*qeṣep*), "deep compassion" (*rahᵃmîm*), and "kindness" (*hesed*). That God possesses conscious purpose or a will is seen in the fact that he formulates rational intentions (*mahᵃšābôt*, Isa. 55:8—"My thoughts are not your thoughts"), and purposes (*'ēṣôt*, Isa. 46:10—"My purpose will stand, and I will do all that I please."

A common title for God in the prophets is "LORD," which signifies God's sovereign authority, dominion, and rule over persons and nations. The singular noun with the article, *hā-'ādôn*, is applied to God in such texts as Isaiah 1:24; 3:1; Micah 4:13; Malachi 3:1. The plural form (a plural of majesty similar to *'ĕlōhîm*) with the first person singular suffix, *'ădōnāy*, occurs more than three hundred times in the Old Testament and always with respect to God. It is most frequent in the prophetic writings (e.g., Isa. 3:17; Jer. 50:31; Amos 1:8). Very common is the combined name *'ădōnāy-Yahweh*, rendered "LORD God" (AV) or "Sovereign LORD" (NIV), e.g., in Isaiah 7:7; Ezekiel 2:4; 4:14; Amos 1:8. The title *Yahweh ṣĕbā'ôt*, rendered "LORD of Hosts" (AV) or "LORD Almighty" (NIV), occurs nearly three hundred times in the Old Testament, frequently in the prophets (e.g., Isa. 1:9; Jer. 6:6; Mic. 4:4; Zech. 1:3). The title "the Holy One of Israel" (*qĕdôš yiśrā'ēl*) signifies God's absolute moral perfection and separation from evil. It is most common in the prophets, especially in Isaiah (1:4; 5:19; 17:7, et al.). The title "Father" (*'āb*) is used sparingly in the Old Testament. It denotes God as creator (Mal. 2:10), founder of the nation Israel (Isa. 63:16; 64:8), and the One who entered into a saving, covenantal relationship with his people (Jer. 3:19; 31:9).

Although God appears to change his tactical responses to specific situations (Jer. 18:8, 10; 26:3, 13, 19; Jonah 3:9–10), he remains steadfastly immutable in his purposes (Isa. 14:24; 46:10), word (Isa. 31:2), character (Isa. 54:10), and very being (Mal. 3:6—"I the LORD do not change"). Amos affirms that sinful Israel cannot escape God's judgment, for there is no place where he is not (Amos 9:1–4). Whether his people climb to the heavens or seek refuge in a deep pit, hide in Carmel's caves or sink to the bottom of the sea, God is wholly present to execute punishment (cf. Jer. 23:23–24).

Synoptic Gospels

The synoptic Gospels, like the rest of the New Testament, depict God as a God of exceeding glory. The Greek word *doxa*, analogous to the Hebrew *kābôd*, connotes the plenitude of God's perfections or the luminous manifestation of his person. It signifies those fundamental qualities of majesty, splendor, and grandeur that radiate from the sovereign universe.[47] The glory of God is most dramatically portrayed in the Transfiguration event (Matt. 17:1–8). On the mountain Jesus displayed his glorified state as the God-man. Thus Jesus' "face shone like the sun" (Matt. 17:2), where the verb *lampō* signifies to gleam or shine as a bright light. Moreover, according to Mark (9:3), "his clothes became dazzling white" (*stilbonta leuka lian*); the verb *stilbō*, "to gleam," or "glitter," often was used of polished metal surfaces.[48] Or as Luke puts it (9:29), "His clothes became as bright as a flash of lightning" (*leukos exastraptōn*). The narrative closes with the observation that the disciples were enveloped by "a bright cloud" (*nephelē phōteinē*), which is further manifestation of the brilliance or radiance of the glory of God (Matt. 17:5). Whereas the shining of Moses' countenance at Horeb (Exod. 34:29, 35) was a reflected glory, the dazzling whiteness of Jesus' transfiguration represented an effulgence from the source itself, which is none other than the God of glory (cf. 2 Cor. 3:12–18; 2 Peter 1:16–18).

That the God of the synoptic Gospels is a personal, living, and active God is beyond dispute. Luke attests that God hears prayer (1:13), gives gifts to those who ask (11:11–13), supplies the necessities of life (12:14–28), and works justice on behalf of the oppressed (18:7–8). Mary, in her song of praise, gratefully acknowledges God's operations on behalf of his people: "He has performed mighty deeds with his arm" (Luke 1:51); "He has brought down rulers from their thrones" (v. 52); "He has filled the hungry with good things" (v. 53); and "He has helped his servant Israel" (v. 54).

In addition to the common names for God, *theos* and *kyrios*, the synoptic Gospels attest several less common titles of Deity. "The Most High" (*hypsistos*), the correlate of *'elyôn,* affirms the supreme dignity of the God of the Bible over all other gods. Alone (Luke 1:32, 35, 76) or in combination with *theos* (Mark 5:7; Luke 8:28), *hypsistos* was the customary Gentile title for the God of the Jews (cf. Acts 7:48; 16:17). God was addressed in prayer as "Sovereign Lord" (*despotēs*), a title that designates God as owner and ruler of all (Luke 2:29; cf. Acts 4:24; Rev. 6:10). A title that affirms the transcendent power of God is "the Mighty One" (*ho dynatos*), which occurs only in Luke's Gospel (1:49; cf. 22:69).

Primitive Christianity/Acts

Luke the historian and theologian, although primarily concerned with the work of the Holy Spirit, did not neglect the doctrine of God. The active nature of God is attested by his manifold works. God created the world and everything in it (Acts 14:15), sends rain to water the crops (14:17), and supplies food to sustain life (14:17). God made covenants with (3:25) and gave promises to (2:30) the Fathers of old. He raised Jesus from the grave (2:24), poured out the Holy Spirit (2:17), sovereignly calls people to missionary work (16:10), forgives sins (3:19), works miracles through his servants (19:11), and rescues those who serve him (12:11).

God afflicted his adversaries with deadly diseases (12:23), punishes nations (7:11), and one day will bring about the eschatological restoration (3:21). Appropriately, therefore, he is called "the living God" (Acts 14:15).

In the context of the expansion of the apostolic church, Acts focuses on the purposive will of the personal God. Thus Luke writes of "God's set purpose and foreknowledge" (Acts 2:23), "the whole will of God" (20:27), and of David who "served God's purpose in his own generation" (13:36). The Greek word *boulē,* translated ̈purpose" or "will" in the preceding verses, signifies a counsel that originates from God's deliberate predetermination. Moreover, Paul's companions said in regard to Paul: "The Lord's will be done" (21:14), and Ananias declared, "The God of our fathers has chosen you [Paul] to know his will" (22:14). *Thelēma,* "will," in these verses connotes the plan or design of the all-wise Deity (cf. Eph. 3:1–13).

Preaching to Gentiles at Athens, Paul affirmed God's self-existence or aseity. Since God is a noncontingent, perfect being, he needs no provision the creature may bring to him (Acts 17:25). Moreover, Paul's recitation of a piece of Stoic wisdom—"In him we live and move and have our being" (Acts 17:28)—suggests that whereas humans possess a life that is derived from God, the Lord has life absolutely in himself. He is the source and fount of life itself. When Paul adds that God "is not far from each one of us" (Acts 17:27), he asserts God's presence everywhere in the world (ubiquity), while rejecting the Stoic view that regarded God as identical with the world's order (a kind of pantheism).

Pauline Literature

Paul knew nothing of a static sovereign or a deistical deity; rather, the apostle's God is vitally living and dynamically active (2 Cor. 6:16; 1 Tim. 4:10). God's activity of creation, providence, and redemption is summed up in Paul's observation (1 Thess. 1:9) that the Thessalonians turned from idols to serve "the living and the true God" (*theos zōn kai alēthinos*). The absence of the article before "God" stresses God's nature rather than his person. So understood, his "nature is to be God living and true"[49]—living instead of inert, and true instead of unreal. The apostle reminds us that "in all things God works for the good [*synergei*] of those who love him" (Rom. 8:28). Indeed, "there are different kinds of working (*energēmatōn*), but the same God works all of them in all men" (1 Cor. 12:6).

Significantly, Paul levied no ontological embargo in his speech about God. He affirmed not only God's existential relevance but also his ontological reality. Thus in Romans 1:20 the apostle maintains that general revelation mediates to man a rudimentary knowledge of "God's invisible qualities—his eternal power and divine nature [*theiotēs*]." Moreover, according to Colossians 2:9, "in Christ all the fullness of the Deity [*theotēs*] lives in bodily form." The latter term, *theotēs*, focuses on the perfections or attributes that inhere in the divine being.[50] In Philippians 2:6, Paul does not hesitate to speak of the "very nature [of] God," where *morphē theou* denotes the spiritual and incorporeal form or essence that manifests itself outwardly in the divine glory. The "equality with God" [*isa theō*] that Paul attributes to Christ connotes equality of being or "parity in possession of this form of God."[51]

The most common New Testament title for God is *theos*, which in the Septuagint translates the Hebrew *ʾlōhîm* and, to a lesser extent, Yahweh. Thus *theos* designates the all-powerful, eternal, and self-originated Deity, who alone is to be feared. The name *kyrios*—which occurs in every New Testament book except Titus and the letters of John, but most frequently in Paul—translates the Hebrew Yahweh (Rom. 4:8; 10:16), *ʾādôn* (Matt. 22:44), and *ʾdônāy* (Matt. 1:22). *Kyrios* denotes God as the Ruler and Sovereign who exercises legal authority over all things.[52] A title that occurs most commonly in the Pastorals (six times) is *sōtēr* (1 Tim. 1:1; 2:3; 4:10, et al.), which depicts God as the redeemer and deliverer from sin. Twice in the Pauline corpus (1 Tim. 1:17; 6:15) God is addressed as *basileus*, or "king," although the reality of God's kingdom (*basileia*) is more frequently upheld (Rom. 14:17; 1 Cor. 6:10; Col. 4:11). Implicit in the title is the affirmation of God's sovereign rule, royal power, and dominion.

Paul views God's eternity not in the sense of timelessness, but in the sense that his person endures through an endless series of ages. This is expressed by the phrase "forever" (lit. "unto the ages," Rom. 11:36), by "for ever and ever" (lit. "unto the ages of the ages," 1 Tim. 1:17), and by the remarkable compound phrase that literally reads, "to the generations of the ages of the ages" (Eph. 3:21). In 1 Timothy 6:16 Paul speaks of God's immortality (*athanasia*) and in Romans 1:20 of God's "eternal power," where *aidios* connotes steadiness or unalterability through all times. God's unchangeableness follows logically from his eternity. According to 2 Timothy 2:13, God "cannot disown himself," i.e., act in a way contrary to his nature. And Paul's teaching in Romans 11:29 that "God's gifts and his call are irrevocable" (note the emphatic position of *ametamelēta*) is a claim for the unchangeableness of the divine purpose. Yet the immutability of God's person and purpose in no wise means that he fails to experience a healthy and controlled emotional life (e.g., Jer. 9:24).

The Johannine Literature

No New Testament writer tells us more about the nature of God than does John. In brief, God is light (1 John 1:5), God is spirit (John 4:24), and God is love (1 John 4:8). Light (*phōs*, thirty-three times) is one of the great themes of the Johannine literature. Applied to God, the metaphor of light "suggests ubiquity, brightness, happiness, intelligence, truth, purity, holiness. It suggests excellence without limit and without taint."[53] The notion of glory (*doxa*, thirty-five times in the Johannine writings) is closely related to that of light. *Doxa* signifies the manifestation of God's incomparable brightness and splendor. It is the luminous display of God's very being and attributes. Jesus in John 17:5, 22, 24 spoke of the supra-temporal glory that was his by virtue of his eternal relation with the Father. Later, in his apocalyptic visions, John saw the heavenly temple "filled with smoke from the glory of God and from his power" (Rev. 15:8). The new Jerusalem that came down from heaven "shone with the glory of God, and its brilliance was like that of a very precious jewel, like a jasper, clear as crystal" (Rev. 21:11). The city has no need of sun or moon, "for the glory of God gives it light" (Rev. 21:23).

In the second place, Jesus asserts that "God is spirit" (John 4:24). The absence of the article before *pneuma* affirms that God is spirit in his intrinsic nature, and the fact that the word occupies first place in the sentence suggests that he is so absolutely. Because there is no materiality in God, carnal worship is forbidden. It follows that God the Spirit is wholly invisible (John 6:46; 1 John 4:12). Thus it is recorded that Jesus replied to the Jews,

"You have never . . . seen his form" (*eidos*, John 5:37).[54]

Third, by affirming that "God is love" (1 John 4:8, 16), the apostle attests not only that God's essential nature is *agapē*, but also that he is a vital personal agent endowed with volition. So God loves the Son (John 3:35; 5:20), the disciples (John 14:23; 1 John 3:1), and the entire sinful world (John 3:16). That God executes his "will" (*thelēma*, John 6:38–40; Rev. 4:11) and his "purpose" (*gnōmē*, i.e., decision, Rev. 17:17) provides further proof that God is a rational personal agent rather than a blind, impersonal force.

In the fourth place, John declares that God is "the living Father" (John 6:57), and "eternal life" (1 John 5:20). The apostle's assertion that "the Father has life in himself" (John 5:26), conveys the truth that God is the absolutely living One, the spring and source of the vital force called *zōē*. Life is inextricably linked with vitality, and so Jesus makes the claim, "My Father is always at his work to this very day" (John 5:17). The verb *ergazomai* ("to work, perform") suggests that from creation to the present God has been ceaselessly operative in preservation and redemption.

A concomitant of all the above is that God is eternal and unchangeable. John represents the God of the Apocalypse as "the Alpha and the Omega" (Rev. 1:8; 21:6; 22:13), "the First and the Last" (Rev. 1:17; 2:8), the One "who is, and who was, and who is to come" (Rev. 1:4, 8; 4:8). The ascription, "who is" recalls the "I AM" of Exodus 3:14—the self-existent, eternal, unchanging God who is absolute beginning and end. The God of majesty and judgment who occupies the throne "lives for ever and ever" (Rev. 4:9–10; 10:6).

John uses several distinctive titles of God. "The Alpha and the Omega," as mentioned above, denotes the sovereign and immutable Lord of all ages.

"Lord [God] Almighty," *kyrios (ho theos) ho pantokrator* (Rev. 4:8; 11:17; 15:3, et al.), is the Greek equivalent of *Yahweh ṣᵉbā'ôt* and depicts God as the unrivaled and all-powerful ruler of the cosmos. The title "Father," sparingly used of God in the Old Testament, assumes greater importance in the New Testament revelation. Whereas outside the Johannine corpus Father (*patēr*) is used of God as creator and originator (Matt. 6:25–27, 32; 1 Cor. 8:6; Heb. 12:9), John some eighty times refers to God as the Father of Jesus Christ (e.g., John 5:19–22; 11:41; 17:1). Jesus' relation to God the Father was unoriginated and essential. Furthermore, by regeneration and adoption God has become the Father of believers in Christ. The term *patēr* thus signifies the new relation of life and love that Christians enjoy with God (John 4:23; 20:17; 1 John 2:13; 3:1). The Aramaic term *abba*, "dear Father" (Rom. 8:15; Gal. 4:6), is a title of special intimacy found on the lips of a young child.

Other New Testament Books

In the context of his argument for the superiority of Christ and the new covenant the writer of Hebrews extols the glory and majesty of God. Thus he asserts that Christ is "the radiance of God's glory" (*apaugasma tēs doxēs*, Heb. 1:3), where glory is viewed as the brilliant effulgence from a luminous body (cf. Heb. 9:5). The Epistle of Jude concludes (v. 25) with a doxological ascription to "the only God our Savior be glory [*doxa*], majesty [*megalosunē*], power [*kratos*] and authority [*exousia*]." Moreover, the noun *megalosunē*, that speaks of God's majesty, greatness, and dignity, appears in Hebrews as a title of God—namely, "the Majesty in heaven" (Heb. 1:3; 8:1). Consistent with the spirit of the Old Testament on which Hebrews builds, the God of glory and majesty is

upheld as invisible (Heb. 11:27), living (Heb. 10:31), and dynamically active (Heb. 10:30–31). The General Epistles also stress the divine volition in the sense of God's permission (Heb. 6:3), his intention (2 Peter 3:9), and his deliberate design (James 1:18; 1 Peter 4:2).

That an ontological theology constitutes the warp and woof of biblical revelation is seen in Hebrews' assertion that Christ is "the exact representation of his [God's] being" (Heb. 1:3). *Hypostasis*, from *hyphistēmi* (reflexive), "to stand under," signifies that which is the basis of something, as, for example, the foundation of a building or the bottom of the sea. Applied to God, *hypostasis* connotes his substantial nature, essence, or actual being. It is that foundational spirit reality in which the divine attributes inhere.[55] On the other hand, Peter's reference to the believer's participation in "the divine nature" (*theias physeōs*, 2 Peter 1:4) should be viewed as a periphrasis for entrance into the blessings of salvation in Christ (cf. John 1:12; 1 Peter 5:1).

Finally, Hebrews affirms God's unoriginated self-existence (Heb. 2:10), his eternality (Heb. 1:8, 12; 9:14), and the immutability of both his person (Heb. 1:11–12; 6:18) and his purpose (Heb. 6:17). James attests the divine constancy with the claim that the Father "does not change like shifting shadows" (James 1:17): "God never changes (*parallagē*) nor is changed (darkened by a shadow from change)."[56]

SYSTEMATIC FORMULATION

Although finite, fallen people on earth are incapable of inventing the truth about the inner nature of the highest Being, God has chosen to make known some truths about his being and purposes. Biblically revealed information teaches that God is an invisible, personal, and living Spirit, distinguished from all other spirits not only because he is personal, but also because he is self-existent, eternal, and unchanging. Hence God's being is not continuous with the being of any one or thing in creation. Metaphysically, God transcends all people, animals, events, processes, and principles in the cosmos.

Speaking About the Most High

Is it possible to systematize one's thought about the supreme Being "on the other side" of the divide between the eternal and the temporal? Scientists are still working on a unified field theory of physics, and psychologists have yet to complete a systematic view of human consciousness. Can theologians presume to propose a coherent account of the divine Being?

Mystics consider it impious or unspiritual to fine-tune vague notions about higher powers beyond our control, or the highest Power of all. It is more pious, mystics say, to experience God, than to define God. Impressive as that sounds in devotional literature, the inspired Scriptures wisely advise people to know whom they experience beyond themselves because evil as well as good spirits may be encountered. Mystics generally assume that all is one, all is God, and God is good. Hence there are no demonic beings to encounter. Anything or anyone pantheists meet they presuppose to be inwardly divine.

Not all that transcends observable phenomena is of God. Before dismissing conceptual knowledge for religious purposes, pietists should determine (conceptually!) whether ultimate reality is pantheistic or theistic. If in fact not all is God and we are faced with a present dualism (though not an eternal dualism) between God and Satan, good and evil, right and wrong, then we do

well to determine whether the spirits' doctrines are of God or not.

How ludicrous it is to choose for either experience or conceptual truth about God! Distinctively human experience is not irrational or unknowing. And knowing takes place in conjunction with experience. Knowledge and experience, therefore, are inseparable, and each is crucial to meaningful life. On the conceptual level nothing is more important than knowing with what or with whom we have ultimately to do, the cosmos—humanity, the demonic or God. On the experiential level nothing is more important than being properly related to the cosmos and to the living God "on the other side" of the cosmos. Existential experience is no substitute for conceptual knowing, and conceptual knowing cannot displace the need for relating experientially.

Some refrain from giving a clear definition of God for fear of confining God to human concepts. That reasoning, however, confuses words and meanings with their referents in experience. Clarity in thought about God no more restricts the Almighty than defining water as H_2O diminishes the power of Niagara Falls. Since the word "God" has been used in so many diverse ways, it is imperative that a speaker or writer indicate which of those uses he has in mind. We need not fear that our definitions will put God in a straight jacket![57]

Of which God do we here speak? To define anything is to state the essential qualities that make it what it is, as distinct from other, similar things. The essence of anything, as "essence" is defined here, equals its being (substance) plus its attributes, not merely the sum of the attributes. Following Kant's skepticism concerning knowing anything in itself (its essence), many philosophers and theologians have limited their categories or general ways of speaking about God to describing the phenomena of Jewish or Christian religious experience. Abandoning categories of essence, substance, and attribute, they speak exclusively in terms of Person-to-person encounters, mighty acts of God (happenings, or events), divine functions, or divine processes in history. Indeed, God is active in all of these ways, but is not a speechless mime. Inscripturated revelation discloses some truth not only about God's acts but also about his spiritual being and his attributes. We should not be too quick to give up categories of substance and attributes. Revealed truth discloses not only what God does, but also who God is.

God's Being: An Invisible, Personal, Living Spirit

Jesus explained to the Samaritan woman at the well why she should worship God, not at this mountain or that, but in spirit and in truth. "God," Christ said, "is spirit" (John 4:24). Although some interpreters take "spirit" as an attribute, the term "spirit" in Jesus' statement is not an adjective, but a substantive. The noun "spirit" occurs first in the sentence for emphasis. And a substantive interpretation fits best with the cultural context. In the pre-Kantian, first-century world of the biblical authors, spirits were not dismissed with an a priori agnosticism or skepticism. Jesus taught that God is a real nonphysical entity, substance, or being. Skepticisms come and go, but Jesus' teaching that God is spirit will not pass away. Undoubtedly the majority of the world's population, including animists and others, believe in the reality of spirits. Often that belief includes a conception of one supreme Spirit.

As a spiritual entity, God is *invisible*. No one has ever seen God or ever will (1 Tim. 6:16). People in Old Testament history from time to time saw visions of God, temporary physical manifestations

of God, theophanies, and mighty acts of God, but they did not literally see God. The resurrected Jesus explained to the startled disciples that a spirit or a ghost "does not have flesh and bones," as they saw he had (Luke 24:39). Worshipers of the invisible God, therefore, ought not "think that the divine being is like gold or silver or stone—an image made by man's design and skill" (Acts 17:29; cf. Exod. 20:3–4; Rom. 1:23–25). The tendency of many, not just Latter-Day Saints, to think of a flesh-and-bones God (an old man with a long white beard, a glorified police officer, a rock star, or olympic hero) contradicts revealed truth of God's transcendence and invisibility and leads away from the God who is there and leads rather to idolatry. Idolatry, in turn, leads to disillusionment, and despair.

As spirit, furthermore, God is *personal*. Although thinkers in the neo-Platonic and Hegelian traditions use "spirit" to designate an impersonal Absolute, in the biblical context the divine Spirit exhibits personal capacities of self-consciousness, and self-determination. These capacities are inferred from the abundance of Scripture concerning the Spirit's knowing, feeling, and acting, as seen in the preceding discussion. In thinking about God as personal, it is important to deny any moral or spiritual misuse of these capacities. In addition, we have already emphasized the necessity of divesting our understanding of a personal God from any finite, physical limitations.

Distinct from the physical aspects of human personhood, God transcends the physical aspects of both maleness and femaleness. However, since God created both male and female in his image, we may think of both as like God in their distinctively nonphysical, personal male and female qualities. Both male and female are personal in the likeness of God who is personal. From this perspective, scriptural uses of masculine personal pronouns for God (and other male designations such as "Father") primarily convey the connotation of God's personal qualities. Secondarily, the masculine pronouns and titles in some contexts may indicate whatever distinctive functional roles and responsibilities males have in social relationships.

In the Lord's Prayer and elsewhere Jesus' unique emphasis on God as Father becomes meaningless if God is not indeed personal. Similarly, the great doctrines of mercy, grace, forgiveness, imputation, justification, and intercession can be meaningful only if God is genuinely personal. God can hear the sinner's cry for mercy, be moved by it, decide to act, and save the lost. Because God is essentially personal, furthermore, he may be even superpersonal or tripersonal—Father, Son, and Holy Spirit. Whether we are referring to God's oneness or to his threeness, we may think of him as personal. Add to the biblical evidence of God's personhood the astounding fact of persons in the world, and it is most unlikely that hypotheses of God as impersonal can account for the evidence as adequately as the view that God is personal.

The oneness of the divine Being or personal Spirit means that he is *indivisible* or simple. This characteristic is inferred from the first-century cultural understanding of spirit in the context of the biblical teaching about God's oneness. Neither the real personal distinctions of trinitarianism nor the multiple attributes divide the essential unity of the divine Being. The ontological oneness as essential is not torn apart even by the Incarnation, nor even by the death of Jesus. Relationally, or functionally, the incarnate Jesus on the Cross was separated from the Father, who imputed to him the guilt and punishment of human sin. The incarnate, suffering Christ gave up the glory of his

heavenly status to provide a just salvation for sinful humans but did not empty himself of his essential divine nature. As God, he could not deny himself. How the divine attributes relate to the divine being without shattering God's unity is explored in the next section.[58]

As spirit, furthermore, God is *living and active*. In contrast to the passive ultimates of Greek philosophies, "we have put our hope in the living God" (1 Tim. 4:10). The God of Abraham, Elijah, David, Christ, and Paul, actively creates, sustains, covenants with his people, preserves the Messiah's line of descent in Israel, commissions prophet after prophet, sends his Son into the world, provides the atoning sacrifice to satisfy his own righteousness, raises Christ from the dead, builds the church, and judges all justly. Far from being a passive entity like a building, the God of the Bible is an active architect, builder, freedom fighter, advocate of the poor and oppressed, an empathetic counselor, a suffering servant, and a triumphant deliverer.

A living God is no mere passive object of human investigation. Writers like Pascal, Kierkegaard, Barth, and Brunner have helpfully reminded Christians that knowing God is not like knowing soils. However, these writers go too far in claiming that God is merely a revealing subject. To emphasize personal relationships with God they unjustifiably deny the reliability of scriptural information about God. Members of a creative artist's family may know the artist not only with passionate, personal subjectivity, but also with some objective validity through an examination of the artist's portfolio and résumé. Similarly, God is known, not only in passionate commitment, but also by careful study of his creative works (general revelation), written communiques (in Scripture), and, in a lesser way, through theological "résumés" of divine words and works.

In summary, "God is spirit" means that God is one invisible, personal, living, and active being. There are, however, many spirits. To distinguish God more fully from other spirits, attention must be given to distinctively divine attributes.

Relating God's Attributes to God's Being

Before considering the meaning of each attribute, it helps to consider the relationship of God's essential characteristics to God's being. Attributes are not accidentals but essential characteristics. According to Scripture, God's attributes are not outside of God but are predicated of him. God *is* holy, God *is* love. These qualities do not simply describe what God does or how God functions. They define who it is who speaks and acts. The nature of the tree, Jesus emphasized, determines the fruit it bears. What God is determines what God says and does. Scripturally, essence is prior to existential activity. The phenomena of divine relationships are ultimately what they are because they issue from God's "heart," or innermost essence.

Does the fact that there are different attributes shatter God's indivisibility? The essential characteristics are not mere names for human use with no referent in the divine Spirit (nominalism). Nor are the attributes separate from each other within the divine being so that they could conflict with each other (realism). The attributes all equally qualify the entirety of the divine being and each other (modified realism). God is love, and God is holy. Preserving the simplicity of God's being, then, God's love is always holy love, and God's holiness is always loving holiness. It follows that arguments for the superiority of one attribute over another are futile. Every attribute is equally essential in the divine Being.

One characteristic may be more important for our specific purposes at a particular time, but cannot be more essential than another in an uncompounded, unextended, simple, being.

Inseparable from the divine being, then, the attributes govern every divine activity. Because God is wise, he cannot speak or act arbitrarily or foolishly. Since God is faithful and true, he cannot lie. Inasmuch as God is just, he cannot treat people unfairly. Given the fact that God is holy, he cannot be pleased with moral evil. Because God is love, he cannot act toward people apart from their best interests. Since God is eternal, he cannot die. Again, since God is self-existent, it follows that God cannot become dependent on any person, denomination, or nation. Given that God is immutable, he cannot deny himself. By way of contrast, if, for example, the Muslim God can act arbitrarily (condemning the just and rewarding the evil), the Christian God cannot. The sovereignty and freedom of the God of the Bible involves free self-determination according to his nature, but not self-destruction.

Interpreting and Classifying the Divine Attributes

How should people in space and time interpret the divine attributes? Some thinkers who deny a cognitive revelation believe that God is so totally other than humanity that all alleged knowledge of God must be interpreted *equivocally.* Human thought about attributes of God so distorts the way they are that talk about them may amount to nothing more than talk about characteristics of mankind. To imagine that we can span the heavens is to equivocate. As Pope said, "The proper study of mankind is man." Interpretations reducing biblical teaching about God to equivocal teaching about man destroys the nature of a cognitive revelation by an interpretive principle inconsistent with the avalanche of data on revelation and inspiration, and on the cognitive image of God in mankind by creation and regeneration.

Other theologians, often following Thomas Aquinas, hold that our understanding of God's characteristics is to be taken *analogically* or figuratively. God's love or holiness is not exactly like ours at any point because God is so much greater than we are. Much of our knowledge is analogical or figurative where the Bible uses figures of speech. Even then, however, the point illustrated can be stated in nonfigurative language. A univocal point of understanding, the same for God and man, is necessary to determine which figures are appropriately used of God and which are not. Similarly, the ability to determine in what respect an illustration applies to God, and in what respects it does not, presupposes some nonfigurative knowledge of God's nature in itself.

In seeking to define the divine attributes, then, we seek to discover the element of truth that God intended to disclose and that illumined and informed people can understand *univocally,* that is, with one voice, or one nonfigurative, cognitive meaning. Some points of univocal understanding of divine attributes, such as holiness and love, do not imply full comprehension of them, for now we know only in part. But insofar as our assertions about God's holiness and love faithfully represent conceptually revealed meanings, they are true of God and conform in part to God's understanding. Otherwise, God in the unknown "parts" of himself may be unholy and unloving, and revelation becomes irresponsible deception (a hypothesis that does not fit the relevant data).

Our partial knowledge of the incomprehensible God is not like knowledge of an apple, of which one bite may be good and the next have a worm in it. Rather, our limited knowledge of God is better illustrated in a young child's initial knowledge of a triangle in contrast to a geometry professor's knowledge of the triangle. The child learns that a triangle is a three-sided, plane figure. That simple definition applies to the entire triangle and holds good for the professor's lifetime of teaching geometry. The professor may know many more things about sides, planes, figures, and angles, and how to infer from the degrees of two angles what the third is, etc. However advanced in geometry the professor becomes, he never denies that a triangle is a three-sided, plane figure. Our knowledge of God's revealed attributes may be like that of the child. But as univocal, it was, is, and always will be true of God's entire nature as God is and knows himself to be. However advanced knowledge may become in this life or the next, we will not learn that God is not holy or loving.

Theologians have organized their discussions of God's attributes in different ways to help in relating and remembering them. Classifications of divine attributes have been quite diverse, and each has its strengths and weaknesses. We may distinguish those attributes that are absolute and immanent (A. H. Strong); incommunicable and communicable (Louis Berkhof); metaphysical and moral (John Gill); absolute, relative, and moral (H. Orton Wiley); or personal and constitutional (L. S. Chafer). Advantages and disadvantages of these may be seen in their respective theologies.[59] We find it more meaningful to classify God's characteristics in the following important ways: metaphysically, intellectually, ethically, emotionally, volitionally, and relationally.

Metaphysically, God Is Self-existent, Eternal, and Unchanging

Other spirits also are invisible, personal, living, and active. How does the divine Spirit differ from them? Of the significant differences in several respects, we look first at the distinctive metaphysical attributes.

God is uniquely self-existent. All other spirits are created, and so there was a time when they did not exist. They owe their existence to another. God does not depend on the world or anyone in it for his existence. The cosmos depends on God for its existence.

Contrary to the view that we can know nothing in itself (metaphysically), Jesus disclosed the fact that God "has life in himself" (John 5:26). The ground of God's being is not in others; nothing is more ultimate. God is uncaused by anything other than himself. God is the one who always is (Exod. 3:14). To ask, "Who caused God?" is to ask a self-contradictory question, or to fail to understand who Yahweh is. When we say that every effect must have a cause (other than itself), we mean that every finite, limited effect must have its cause in something else. But God is unlimited or infinite and "laws" describing regular relations of finite things do not necessarily apply to him.

To express this truth, the church fathers, writing in Latin, said God's existence was *a se*, from himself. The English term derived from the Latin is "aseity." An understanding of God's self-existence helps one appreciate why God is not dependent on anything. God is unlimited, free, and self-determined both because he is prior to creation and because he is not contingent on any creature unless he has decreed such contingency (as in being moved by our prayers). Anyone who grasps the fact that God has life in himself (whether his understanding is on a popular or on a more technical, philosophical level), has already broken through the antimetaphysical prejudice of much contemporary philosophy and theology, such as the tendency of process theol-ogy to regard God dependent upon natural and historical processes.

God is also eternal and omnipresent. The essential difference between eternity and time, Augustine held, is the difference between the changeless and the changing. With all the flux of history, God in nature, knowledge, and purpose is the same. Transcendent to temporal change, God as eternal is immutable.

Transcendent to temporal change, God is also quantitatively changeless, or everlasting. God has no beginning, growth, old age, or death. The Lord is enthroned as King forever (Ps. 29:10). And "this God is our God for ever and ever" (Ps. 48:14).

Transcendent to temporal change, the eternal God is unlimited by time in his knowledge. God does not learn line upon line, or observation after observation, or conclusion after premise. God is simultaneously conscious of past and future as well as the present. Since God is not limited by the succession of events in time, his knowledge is not contingent on history. Although God is not limited by changes in time, he created time and sustains the succession of events.

Exalted above all limitations of time and change, God has eternal purposes for time and is vitally active to fulfill them in time. According to his changeless purposes, he created changing creatures and time—past, present, and future. Future aeons are not viewed, as in Barth, totally other than the present age, and in them God may be said to have endless time, or unlimited time. But Oscar Cullmann's attempt to reduce eternity to infinitely extended time bounded by creation and eschatological events fails to fit revelation on God's transcendence.

The changing world, although not as important as God, has permanent significance in God's grand design. Because contingent and changing, it is not to be considered unreal, or, as in some Hinduism, maya. No person, family, subculture, tribe, city, or nation is valueless to the omnipresent Lord of all. History is the product of God's eternally wise planning, creative purposes, providential preservation, and common grace. God fills space and time with his presence, sustains history, and gives the temporal realm lasting value. The transcendent One is Lord of history. God does not negate time, but sustains, guides, and brings it to meaningful fulfillment of wise, gracious and just purposes. To fulfill his redemptive purposes God brought the Messiah into the world "when the time had fully come" (Gal. 4:4).

In sum, God is eternal, or everlasting, in his transcendent being and changeless in his universal purposes and knowledge of past, present and future.

Metaphysically, then, God is not only self-existent, and eternal, but also unchanging or immutable. To affirm that God is changeless is not to contradict the truth that the divine Spirit is living and active. It is to say that all the uses of divine vitality and power are consistent with his attributes and purposes. Although some uses may be for reasons wholly within himself, rather than for revealed considerations, God's acts are never arbitrary, fickle, or capricious. Underlying each judgment of the wicked and each pardon of the repentant is his changeless purpose concerning sin and conversion.

The changelessness of God's purposes does not exclude human instrumentality. Sovereignly, God chooses to accomplish some things independently of any human agency and to accomplish other things through the use of human means. These will be not be achieved without the participation of human instruments. As God purposely achieves some things through human instrumentality, the immutability of God's purposes does not imply the insignificance of personal involvement, but just the opposite. Human agency in many respects finds an important place in God's changeless plans for history.

Unlike the Stoic concept of divine immutability, God is not indifferent to human activity and need. Rather, we can always count on God's concern for human righteousness and well-being. God changelessly answers prayer in accord with his desires and purposes of holy love. From the standpoint of human experience it appears (in the phenomenological language of Scripture) that God repents, but in reality it is the ungodly who have changed their minds in respect to sin. When the people of Nineveh repented, God "relented" and in compassion did not bring on them the destruction he had "threatened" (Jonah 3:9–10). God's basic purposes toward the unrepentant and the repentant in Nineveh remained unchanged; only God's activity changed in accord with changes in the spiritual attitudes of the Ninevites.

Even though everything in creation becomes old like a garment, God is the same (Ps. 102:25–27). Because Jesus Christ was no mere part of creation, the passage from Psalm 102 was quoted also of him. The Son of God remains the same (Heb. 1:10–12). "Jesus Christ is the same yesterday and today and forever" (Heb. 13:8).

The meaning of immutability is vividly illustrated throughout Christ's past active ministry on earth. While moving from weddings to funerals, from greedy tax collectors to the poor and powerless, from harlots to self-righteous Pharisees, from the ill to the demonized, he changelessly remained just, loving, and wise. Deeply moved by experiences of caring, temptations, and tragedies, Christ never lost his integrity. Amid the pressures of an active life in history, he exhibited the dependability of the Father, whose immutability deserves our praise, faith, and trust (Heb. 6:17–18).

APOLOGETIC INTERACTION

The Idol of "Mother Nature"

A high school French teacher asked her young nephew, "Is not God merely mother nature?" Unfortunately, the high school student was not well prepared to answer that rather common question. Had he been more conversant with God's distinctive metaphysical characteristics, he could have pointed out how unattributable they are to "mother nature." The world is not self-existent; God has life in himself. The cosmos had a beginning in the finite past and will eventually come to an end; God is eternal. The useful energy of nature is being depleted; God is tireless, he never slumbers nor sleeps (Ps. 121:4). The world constantly changes; God is immutable.

Contradictory characteristics cannot belong to the same reality. The same entity cannot be self-existent and not self-existent, eternal and not eternal, immutable and not immutable. Hence God cannot be equated with "mother nature," atomic energy, natural laws, human beings, or the sum total of the dependent, temporal, changing universe.

In Athens, the university center of the ancient world, Paul exemplified a Christian approach to Gentiles with unsound views of God. The nontheistic Epicureans considered atoms and space the ultimate reality. The pantheistic Stoics regarded the usual order of natural law (an immanent, impersonal Logos) the highest metaphysical reality with which people have to do. Then, of course, there were the agnostics who worshiped and served an "unknown God."[60]

The confusion of the Creator with the creatures continues to be one of the most prominent problems in contemporary Gentile and Jewish thinking. Many speak out in behalf of atheistic humanism, pantheistic mysticism, and religious agnosticism. If a personal God is distinct from the world and is worthy of worship, then people in pluralistic societies need to speak out on behalf of Christian theism. At any level in public educational systems proud of their "academic freedom" little may be said to represent the classical theism of the Judeo-Christian tradition fairly. Like Paul at Athens, theists today need to (1) earn the right to be heard, (2) address the board of education with respect, (3) appeal to any common ground that can be found, (4) proclaim the truth about the living God, and (5) call people to repent of their idolatrous secular humanism, pantheistic mysticism, or religious agnosticism.[61]

The Idol of Energy (Atoms in Space and Time)

With the mushroom cloud has come not only a concern about the future of humanity, but also a preoccupation with energy. People in a desperate quest for lasting meaning think that their ultimate concern has to do with the finite energy of the universe. Then, with energy as their ultimate object of trust, they attribute divine qualities to it.

The energy of the cosmos, rather than God, has come to be regarded as self-existent. From early ideas that energy was "a force," scientists began to think of it rather as "capability to do work." Then science discovered the interconvertibility of energy with matter $(E = MC^2)$ and the conservation of the sum total. From this, the philosopher of science M. Jammer leaps to belief in "the emancipation of energy as an autonomous existent." In place of an autonomous God, Jammer worships and serves "autonomous energy." Following Ostwald, not only has energy become the universal currency of physics, but "all the phenomena of nature were merely manifestations of energy and its manifold transformations." Energy, Jammer maintains, is substance, and "the only substance."[62]

This "dissolution of matter" into energy was welcomed by monistic thinkers because it suggested a unified conception of the universe with energy as the ubiquitous god. New Consciousness and New Age thinkers with Paul Davies in *God and the New Physics* claim that the end result of the new physics is "more like mysticism than materialism."[63] Davies remarks about the "strong holistic flavour to the quantum aspects of the nature of matter" with "everything somehow made up of everything else and yet displaying a hierarchy of structure."[64]

"The Force" is not just for children at the movies. Forms of monism, pantheism, or panentheism underlie many new religious trends in human potential, new consciousness, altered states of consciousness, and the occult. If the inner energy of all humans is divine, then all have infinite potential and anyone may evolve to the next stage in cultural or religious evolution (often imagined to be like an avatar or god). All people are thought to be "spiritually" connected by this energy. Illness is considered an imbalance of energy, a by-product of an unenlightened consciousness. If you will only "eat" of this theory, as the Deceiver said to Eve and Adam, "you will be like God" (Gen. 3:4).

Valuable as modern physical discoveries have been, the energy of the universe is not the unlimited, personal God of the Bible: (1) Energy loses its usefulness, God does not. (2) The energy of the universe had a beginning and will have an end; God does not. (3) The energy of the universe is impersonal; God is personal. (4) The energy of the universe is amoral; God is moral. (5) The energy of the universe can be manipulated by human engineering; God will not be manipulated by physicists or mediums.

God alone sovereignly rules over all the finite energy in the cosmos. The cosmos is not "all that ever was or ever will be." Sagan exclaims, "Passage from the Chaos of the Big Bang to the Cosmos that we are beginning to know is the most awesome transformation of matter and energy that we have been privileged to glimpse."[65] But that awesome transformation of energy cannot compare with power of the Word of the living Lord who spoke energy-matter into existence and sustains it! How like the wisdom of this fallen world, however, to value mother's cooking more than mother, and created energy more than its Creator!

The Idol of "Being Itself"

To think of God as personal, according to Paul Tillich, is idolatrous, because it makes God a limited, finite being. Tillich thought he avoided idolatry by taking the symbol "God" to stand for "being itself" beyond essence and existence. So he could not speak of the existence of God or the essence of the God who is. He thought it idolatrous even to appeal to evidence for the existence of a personal God. The night before he died, Tillich was pleased to learn that he had "fathered" T. J. Altizer's death-of-God theology.

Although rejecting the God of biblical theism, Tillich said he was not an atheist. His god was the power of being (like energy) enabling all things that are to exist. And he insisted that he was not a pantheist. His god was not the universal essence of all forms. Tillich thought that the ground of all that is transcended the essence of existing things in every respect. This, he says, is what the philosophers teach literally and what the biblical writers also teach if interpreted symbolically. Tillich took only one statement about God to be literally true: "God is being itself, not a being."[66] God is beyond all other cognitive, literal assertions. Religious language generally is more like poetry evoking ecstatic religious experience than like scientific or philosophical language. Faith involved no belief of propositions (other than the one) but was an existential leap into the dark to overcome the anxieties resulting from the apparent meaninglessness of life, guilt, and despair in the face of death.

As devout and strategic as Tillich's view may appear, it fails to do justice to the scriptural revelation concerning God. Even when figurative or symbolic language is used of God, the figure illustrates a point that can be expressed in nonfigurative language. Scripturally more than one proposition can be cognitively asserted of God. God is a living, spiritual being who thinks, feels, wills, and is self-existent, eternal, and unchanging. One can have a personal relationship with the God of the Bible, but not with being itself.

Does a personal concept of God, as Tillich thought, make God finite? Specifically we have established that the Creator is not contingent on, or limited by, space, time, or change. God is personal in a far greater way than humans are. As an infinite, or unlimited, personal being, God far supersedes Tillich's unknown, impersonal being itself. Although Tillich claims that "being itself" transcends personhood, he can literally know nothing about the characteristics of being itself. Therefore Tillich cannot know that "greater than personal" (whatever that is) is a more appropriate symbol for his Unknown of ultimate concern than "personal infinite" or "unlimited personal being."[67]

To the extent that Tillich views the orthodox doctrine of God, a finite God,

he is not addressing the view actually held. On the classical understanding, God is unlimited by time, space, and anything else in all creation, except as in his sovereignty he chose to limit himself. Tillich's abstract being itself cannot respond to intercession or act supernaturally on the world. The abstract Ground of Being could not raise Christ from the dead, answer prayer, or, as Billy Graham used to say, "bless you real good."

The question children ask continues to disturb mature clergymen, "Where is God?" As far as possible replies do well to avoid spatial language ("up there," "out there," or "in us" after J. A. T. Robinson's *Honest to God*), for God is spirit. But answers incorporate a nonphysical element of truth that may have been intended in all these perspectives. Aided by biblical revelation, rather than to assert that God is "up there," we may affirm that God is Lord of all (distinct from all and over all). God is not physically "out there," but active in everything that is and happens, in accord with his providential purposes in space and time. And God is not the inner energy of people but is active with his believing people in accord with his redemptive purposes for the present age.

John Gill helpfully distinguished God's glorious presence in heaven (1 Kings 8:27; Ps. 103:19; Isa. 57:15; Heb. 9:24), his providential presence throughout the universe (Ps. 103:19; Jer. 23:22, 24), and his redemptive presence in the bodies of believers now the dwelling place of God (2 Cor. 6:16; 1 Cor. 6:19, 20).[68] Biblical analyses never blur the distinction between Creator and creature. God is not nature nor people, not even redeemed people or their leaders. The God who transcends people continuously acts by his Holy Spirit to conform believers from the inside out to become more like the Lord Jesus Christ in heaven.

The Idol of Evolution

Another influential confusion of the creation with the transcendent Creator absolutizes evolution. Pierre Teilhard de Chardin (1881–1955) sought to synthesize love for God and love for the world, the internal and the external, theology and science. His organizing key was not merely biological evolution, but an expanded, cosmic evolution of the universe. The matter-energy reality, he suggested, had a psychic aspect. So the geosphere evolved into living organisms, the biosphere. After several hundred thousand years, mind appeared developing the neosphere. Later life was hominized with the appearance of humanity.

As life becomes increasingly complex, de Chardin's humanity evolves on a planetary scale of increasing socialization. That would provide personality the power to develop to its fullest and best. This end is not guaranteed, since humanity is free, and so we must work with faith in man and the world toward our ultimate destination or omega point.

An impersonal omega point as a condition or state will not provide sufficient motivation to overcome every obstacle to evolutionary progress. Christianity provides the personalized, motivating omega point in the return of Christ at the end of the age. We may prepare for Christ's return by unifying all people around Christ and loving our neighbors. When humanity is unified, we will have passed from the neosphere to the Christosphere. With Henri Bergson, de Chardin thinks that the universe is "a machine for making gods." It is not surprising, then, that the new consciousness movements frequently quote Teilhard de Chardin's spiritualized version of evolutionary development.

Teilhard's evolutionary scheme has extrapolated from any limited, actual data of development (within the biblical "kinds") to a total philosophy of evolution, which is far from scientific. He assumes a now-controversial Lamarkian development by acquired characteristics from the simple to the complex. (Further evaluation of evolution may be found in the chapter on creation.)

The supreme consciousness at the end of de Chardin's development is far from the transcendent personal God of Christ and Scripture. Like Brahman in Hinduism, Teilhard's evolutionary God seems to depersonalize human beings. At the end they all appear to be absorbed in the divine consciousness.

Teilhard's religious evolution occurs for many or most without benefit of a reception of Christ's once-for-all redemptive provisions by the regeneration of the Holy Spirit. In gaining the cosmic Christ Teilhard has returned to the nature religions and lost the supernatural Savior of the Scriptures. However dedicated, worship and service of evolution rather than the transcendent Lord of all, is idolatrous.[69]

The Idol of Process

Process theology takes dynamic processes in time in much the same way that Teilhard de Chardin took evolution. Philosopher Alfred North Whitehead combined the growing belief in evolution with the newly conceived concept of relativity in his *Process and Reality* (1929). A dynamic world, said Whitehead, could not have a static creator. God, like all other beings, is in some respects incomplete and a companion of man in the creative advance toward perfection.

God, according to Norman Pittenger, is the inescapable energy that moves through all things. That creative energy

is nothing other than love, pure, unbounded love, sharing, participating, giving and receiving. That is the very heart of deity. Cosmic love is present in all creaturely occasions, enfolding them in its concern and working to bring them to actualization. God is the tender lover, the fellow sufferer who understands, the participant in all human experience whether joyful or painful. There is that in every person which will not let go. And that is what we mean by God. It faithfully acts by lure, persuasion, solicitation and attraction to secure the free consent of people to this purpose of good.[70]

Process thought misrepresents a biblical view of God. The God of the Bible has been found to be far from immobile, static, or unconcerned in relation to nature and human history. The Greek philosopher Parmenides may have held such a view of Being, but not biblically informed Christian theologians. We need not reject God's changelessness in essence and purpose in order to emphasize God's dynamic activity in human history. "The biblical God is not static but inexhaustibly dynamic on his own terms, not ours."[71]

Process thought loses any persevering identity of God. The same living God, however, related dynamically to Abraham, David, Christ, Paul, Augustine, Luther, and Billy Graham. Although changeless in essence and purpose, the divine Spirit is changing in specific activities and relationships with changing persons.

Process thinkers miss the mark of the personal God of Scripture who transcends temporal processes as self-existent and eternal. The Lord of all freedom is free from dependence on the temporal, changing world. A God in process does not know the future and is not sovereign. Limited by time, God is not sovereignly in charge, but indebted to all. Human experience is a mode of God's becoming. Again humans are in danger of confusing themselves with deity. Divine grace is replaced by an inherent optimism born of an unfounded faith in cosmic evolution.

The changing process is unworthy of our worship, as Emil Brunner argued. "Were God one who is 'becoming,'

then everything would founder on the morass of relativism. We can measure nothing by changing standards; changeable norms are no norms at all; a God who is constantly changing is not a God whom we can worship. He is a mythological being for whom we can only feel sorry."[72]

Process thinking about God provides some helpful insights into the activities and relationships of God in history but fails to fit the biblical data of God's changeless being. There is no question that the biblical God is engaged in history, but, as Royce Gruenler, a former process theologian, has concluded, "The limitation of God to time and space has to be considered a modern idolatry."[73]

The Idol of Humanism

Humanists regard the highest manifestation of energy, evolution or process to be found in mankind. The ultimate goal according to Humanist Manifesto II (1973) is "the fulfillment of the potential for growth in each human personality." Among the greatest obstacles to achieving this goal are the promises of immortal salvation in the traditional religions. Ethics needs no theological or ideological sanction because it is considered "autonomous" and "situational." Yet Corliss Lamont seems to present an objectively valid propositional truth when he writes in *The Philosophy of Humanism*: "The chief end of thought and action is to further this-earthly human interests on behalf of the greater glory of man"[74]

Not only is the highest goal autonomous human happiness, but also the highest knowledge and power are human. Humanism aims to realize "as close an approach as possible to human omniscience and omnipotence."[75] Human nature is thought to be neither essentially bad nor good, but essentially flexible and educable.[76] But one who is too autonomous is subject to another of the great aims of humanism, "the transformation and socialization of human motives."[77] Why should this be necessary? Each individual has an "unending debt to the collective culture of mankind and his corresponding obligation to serve the common good."[78] Whence arise these universal and necessary obligations when all is relative?

It becomes clear that humanists, who do not worship and serve the God of the Bible, do not stop worshiping and serving. Instead they are "saved" by, and for, the good of universal humanity, however that may be defined by the humanists in power.

That abstract god, even when associated with nature and given the attributes that belong to God alone, lacks the example, the teaching, and the atonement that Christ provides. It also ignores the human disposition to selfishness and the power of the Holy Spirit, the only One who can transform sinful human nature. Abandoning the illusory hope that education and science will solve the world's problems, many naturalistic and secular humanists today realize the need for a transcendent power to deliver human beings individually and collectively.[79]

Making Idols of Biblical Words

Can biblical theologians wisely limit themselves to terms used in Scripture when other words such as *substance, essence, attributes, personhood, transcendence,* and *relationships* are so essential to adequately represent biblical teaching in view of the antimetaphysical temper of the age?

Without question the initial work of exegesis in the Old or New Testament must start with studies of the inspired words. But the concepts conveyed by those words two millennia or more ago may not be conveyed in the same way today. In the light of today's controversies the point of biblical figures of speech may need to be stated nonfiguratively, and communication of the coherent teaching of all the Scriptures about God may call for more technical terms.

For example, George Ladd's chapter "The God of the Kingdom" in *The Theology of the New Testament*, fails to provide an adequate basis for determining whether God is an invisible Spirit, Energy manifest as matter, Being itself, Evolution, Process, or Humanity. Ladd's four headings are "The Seeking God," "The Inviting God," "The Fatherly God," and "The Judging God." But unless Ladd defines God, he may as well speak of the seeking, inviting, fatherly, judging unknown x. Are these four Gods or one? If one, one what? Who or what is engaged in these activities? Are they personifications referring to aspects of mother nature's activities? Or, is God one transcendent personal Spirit who seeks, invites, cares, and judges? A biblical theologian today cannot escape the responsibility of clarifying the agency or agencies responsible for the selected activities regarded divine. In the confusion of a pluralistic society, nothing can be taken for granted. Ladd's descriptive purpose may excuse him from giving the point of biblical figures in nonfigurative language and from defining terms. But his work, as far as it goes, points up the need for an integrative theology.[80]

John Bright's ultimate concern seemed to focus on Israel's faith, rather than the nature of the God in whom they believed. His undefined x, or Yahweh, elected a special people, and exercised sovereign lordship over them through covenants and promises.[81] Again we are told of activities, but not who, or what, acts in these ways. Is the agent beyond nature or is it nature itself? Is the agent personal or merely a literary personification? If biblical theology cannot answer questions like these, for fear of philosophy (the love of wisdom), it lacks the courage of the writers of the biblical revelation. If there is a danger that much theology today may become unscriptural by using extrabiblical words, the same danger haunts biblical theologians who stress biblical verbs and overlook the nouns revealing God's substantive nature.[82]

RELEVANCE FOR LIFE AND MINISTRY

The renewal of Christian witness and mission requires constant examination of the assumptions shaping the church's life. Today, an apparent loss of a sense of the transcendent is undermining the church's ability to address with clarity and courage the urgent tasks to which God calls it in the world.

Eighteen Protestant, Catholic, and Orthodox theologians meeting at Hartford Seminary in 1975 said that the lack of theological affirmation has serious secular and naturalistic implications. The sole purpose of worship becomes the promotion of self-realization and human community. Emphasis on God's transcendence is considered at least a hindrance to, and perhaps incompatible with, Christian social concern and action.[83] In contrast, J. I. Packer considers knowing the transcendent God to provide at once "a foundation, shape and goal for our lives, plus a principle of priorities and a scale of values."[84]

Against Relativizing the Absolute

Those who worship the God of the Bible in spirit and in truth need to be careful not to reduce the Most High to nature, being, evolution, process, humanity, or even religious experiences. The radical biblical distinction between the transcendent Creator and the creature does not permit a monism, even for devotional purposes. Theists may be attracted by the simplicity and neatness of monism but ought not yield to the temptation to blur the distinction between the Creator and the creature. Their worship and service take place in the context of a dualistic world view. The truth of God's transcendence leads their meditation beyond the physical, visible, audible, changing, temporal idols to the God who is, acts, and speaks. Before Jesus ministered to people's needs, he withdrew from them and communicated with his Father in heaven. Failure to understand God's transcendent being can turn one's worship and service into idolatry. "The essence of idolatry," A. W. Tozer said, "is the entertainment of thoughts about God that are unworthy of Him."[85] No church can long serve the God of truth with an untrue and diminished view of who he is. "The first step down for any church," Tozer observed, "is taken when it surrenders its high opinion of God."[86]

Against Absolutizing the Relative

Because God is uniquely one, he cannot be compared to anything else. People either bow to God as Lord of all or devalue him. No one, Jesus taught, can serve two spiritual masters or ultimates. To have divided loyalties at the highest level, is to distort our entire scale of values and our consequent living. The Christian theists' ultimate concern and commitment is to none other than the living God. "A right conception of God is basic not only to systematic theology but to practical Christian living as well. It is to worship what the foundation is to the temple; where it is inadequate or out of plumb the whole structure must sooner or later collapse."[87]

Meditation on nature is radically different for theists than for pantheists. On the one hand, theists look at the beauty and vastness of the Rocky Mountains and appreciate more fully God's transcendent creative wisdom and power. Theists worship the God whose being is distinct from the being of nature. On the other hand, pantheists and panentheists look at the same mountain range and regard it as a partial expression of God's being.

Unfortunately Richard Foster encourages meditation on nature with Evelyn Underhill's statement, "To elude nature, to refuse her friendship, and attempt to leap the river of life in the hope of finding God on the other side, is the common error of a perverted mysticality." Only on a pantheistic or panentheistic hypothesis is worship of God on the other side of nature a "perversion." The transcendent Creator of the cosmos is not to be confused with it. Foster, quoting Underhill, continues, "So you are to begin with that first form of contemplation which the old mystics sometimes called the 'discovery of God in His creatures.' "[88] Theists may also begin meditation on nature, but in doing so they move from its changing being subject to entropy to the unchanging being of God, who neither slumbers nor sleeps (Ps. 121:4).

What, then, is the top priority on the agenda of the church today? According to A. W. Tozer, it is neither in science nor in the arts.

> The heaviest obligation lying upon the Christian Church today is to purify and elevate her concept of God until it is once more worthy of Him—and of her. In all her prayers and labors this should have first place. We do the greatest service to the next generation of Christians by passing on to them undimmed and undiminished the noble concept of God which we received from our Hebrew and Christian fathers of generations past. This will prove of greater value to them than anything that are of science can devise.[89]

Against Visualizing God

Because God as spirit is invisible, no images drawn from visible things will enrich our worship of him. No one ever has seen God nor can see him (1 Tim. 6:16). Physical images are forbidden in worship by the second commandment: "You shall not make for yourself an idol in the form of anything in heaven above or the earth beneath or in the waters below" (Exod. 20:4). Material images, however skillfully done (even on the Sistine Chapel ceiling), fail to convey the truth about God's spiritual being and may lead attention away from the God who is worthy of worship and service. J. I. Packer argues that images dishonor God, for they obscure his glory and mislead people.[90] With the Reformers we suggest the use of imaginative pictures in teaching to illustrate some facets of truth but decry their use in worship. Fantasies may helpfully entertain and illustrate well-founded cognitive truths. But they do not lead to deeper relationships with the God who, as spirit, transcends mountain ranges, oceans, bulls, snakes, elephants, Venus, Hercules, and any saints who are pictured in the classic art of the Christian church.

Since Jesus became incarnate and visible to the senses, it cannot be wrong for teaching purposes to picture Jesus Christ's humanity and his activities in the Gospels on behalf of sinners. Unwisely Richard Foster's *Celebration of Discipline* is criticized for use of the imagination (in a nonmanipulative sense) in meditating on the incarnate Christ. Can we be obedient to the Scriptures, however, and accept Foster's suggestions to use visualization in achieving the objective of "deep inner communion with the Father" when "you look at Him and He looks at you."[91] However well intended, does not worship or meditation that pictures the Father's face violate the second commandment? Has Foster's teaching, beneficial though it is in may respects, lived up to his desire to make Scripture "the central reference point by which all other meditations are kept in proper perspective"?[92]

Pro-Communion, Not Ontological Union, With God

Because God is personal and transcendent to humans on earth and in heaven, the objective in all forms of worship is not absorption into God, nor any form of ontological union of the finite and fallen with the infinite and holy One. According to Scripture, for mere humans, however "enlightened," to consider themselves continuous with Deity is blasphemy.

Only in pantheism are all persons ontologically one. In theism persons are distinct beings created as unique individuals for fellowship with a personal God. The loyalty of persons to one another in families, churches, and nations can reflect a significant solidarity of values, commitments, and relationships, but not a sameness of being.

Although made like God in some respects, humans are not God. God's distinctive ontological attributes are not communicable to human beings. We are not eternal or immutable, and we are not to seek continuity with the incomparable One who is. We become "partakers of the divine nature" (2 Peter 1:4), not ontologically, but in participating in such communicable characteristics as justice and loving personal relationships in God's kingdom. The goal of worship, then, needs to be clarified frequently in societies that do not teach theism in the public schools and are post-theistic as well as post-Christian. The goal in every worship service is not noncognitive mystical union, but communion. "Our fellowship is with the Father and with his Son, Jesus Christ" (1 John 1:3). The teaching and preaching of divine revelation is intended to lead people away from fellowship with darkness (2 Cor. 6:14) and into the fellowship of light (1 John 1:7).

Pro-Change Consistent With God's Revealed Plans

Given the fact that God is living and active, he is not food in the cupboard, passively there until you go for it. We ought not be surprised if God takes the initiative like a woman who has lost a coin or a shepherd who has lost a sheep, or a father whose son is prodigal. Those who imagine that God transcends the personal in such a way that their deity is more like a vapor or a gas diffused throughout the universe may seem philosophically profound, but unfortunately, are profoundly wrong. God is more like a faithful lifeguard or an all-wise personnel manager than an impersonal "Force." A purely contemplative life, inactive in meeting the needs of the spiritually lost and physically deprived, is not godly.

Although Jesus Christ is the same yesterday, today, and forever (in character and purpose), he may use different strategies or methods.

As relational theologian Bruce Larson observed, God "is always changing in his strategy. God is a God of change in both the Old and New Testament." The prophets challenged those who lived in the past. "Forget the former things; do not dwell on the past. See I am doing a new thing!" (Isa. 43:18–19).

"If God is in the business of perfecting his people," Bruce Larson argued, "then change must be in order." Since hope, with faith and love, is one of the three great verities in life, "we must deal with the fact that hope is an attitude about a future state which can only be ushered in by change." Difficult as it is for conservative mentalities to live with changes in strategy and method emotionally, "Christians need to be excited by change, expectant about it. Indeed, Christians should feel at home in change, for God is the initiator of much change."[93] The changes God initiates, and Christians eagerly anticipate, do not contradict his nature and purposes. God's actions are never out of character.

As self-existent, God does not depend on persons or processes in time and space, but uniquely deserves their worship. God does not need our works for his own well-being. He does not lack anything that we can give. God created people in order to give the undeserved benefits of his common and special grace to them, not to fill up some lack in himself. None can compare to the God who has life in himself. So none deserve the same honor, tribute, and praise as the Lord of Life.

As eternal, God is always there desiring personal relationships with his people, sustaining and governing the world, supporting all that is real, good, beautiful, and true. Beyond the limits of time, the fellowship believers have with God continues beyond the grave and beyond history itself. As eternal, God graciously gives sinners the gift of eternal life, life from his transcendent self, from above all temporal sources and resources. The transformations achieved by other agencies or new consciousness powers within ourselves can never have the permanence of the eternal life from above. In the midst of new-age thinking, which declares that people have infinite potential within themselves, ministers of the gospel need to make clear that the source of authentically eternal life transcends all temporal techniques for changing consciousness.

What difference does it make if in nature and purposes God is eternally immutable? However tragic the developments in history may seem, never will God be unfaithful to his plan of redemption. His wisdom, holiness, and love are not affected by entropy or fatigue. None of God's purposes of grace can flicker and fail. The objective validity of God's truth will hold good though heaven and earth pass away.

God will never break faith with those who trust him.

Pro—Freedom Under God

Whether or not we bow to an unpredictably active Lord of all who is distinct from the world is as much a matter of our wills as our intellects. Are we willing to find our freedom under the Almighty? Or do we imagine that to be free we must deny the existence of a living God distinct from the world?

Consider the insightful analysis of one who was for ten years a process theologian and has now returned to faith in the sovereign God of biblical theism. Along with many penetrating criticisms of process thought, Royce Gordon Gruenler says:

> At the heart, I am convinced, the system sets out not so much to defend God against the problem of evil . . . but is designed to assure that we are free from the despotic control of a sovereign God, such as confronts us in the Judeo-Christian Scriptures. . . . In order to be completely free to choose without external compulsion from a sovereign God, other persons . . . must be completely alone on the very edge of creativity . . . like one of Gottfried Wilhelm Leibniz's windowless monads.[94]

The god of process theologians cannot even know the future. To preserve their self-defined freedom, reality itself and God's experience of it must remain open. Starting with human-centered freedom, an evangelical Arminian attracted to process thought argued, "Either the future is open for God, or I am not really free."[95] But the highest freedom delivers us from ultimate loyalty to finite creatures who wish to be gods, including ourselves. Rebels against the omniscient God, as Jesus said, find themselves idolatrously enslaved to sin (John 8:34).

Pro–Transcendent Authority

Paul Tillich's views also seem to reflect rebellion against objective truths delivered from a transcendent God outside of himself. Tillich's world view is motivated by his opposition to "heteronomy," the rule of a law from another than himself. He also rejects "autonomy"—that is, living by the rational structure of one's own mind. Instead, Tillich favored "theonomy," the law of "Being itself" within one's self. Committed to the inner principles of the universe, Tillich did not deny the self nor distinguish the sacred from the secular. His experience of being itself contributed to his sense of wholeness. In the name of ecstatic union with the depth of his own (and others') being, Tillich revolted against the transcendent Lord of all. He, being a man, blasphemously called his own perspective "theonomy." A more descriptive term for anyone whose "ultimate concern" is within himself, however "inexhaustible" the ground of his being, might be "being-onomy." Medically speaking, we might consider it the disease of "being-itus."[96]

A sign in a physician's office reads, "Whether you get well or not may depend upon which of us is the doctor." Whether we find and minister moral and spiritual health or not, may depend on whether we esteem as divine the depth of our inner selves or the transcendent God (uniquely disclosed in Christ and Scripture).

Reason for a Resistance Movement

Eventually a king will come who "will do as he pleases. He will exalt and magnify himself above every god and will say unheard-of things against the God of gods" (Dan. 11:36). Having desecrated the temple and abolished the sacrifices, he will set up the abomination that causes desolation (v. 31).

"With flattery he will corrupt those who have violated the covenant, but the people who know their God will firmly resist him" (v. 32).

Before Daniel's predicted abomination comes to pass, shortly before the Lord Jesus Christ returns to judge the world (Matt. 24:15), Christian theists ought to stand against the burgeoning consensus of movements committed to worship and service of the creation rather than the Creator. Preaching and teaching must prepare people to defend theism and live and work for the glory of God. Throughout the different areas of society, theists need to speak out, in psychology, education, medicine, and politics. As the source of all truth about reality, the transcendent God cannot wisely be dismissed in any area of life.

REVIEW QUESTIONS

To Help Relate and Apply
Each Section in This Chapter

1. *Briefly state the classical problem* this chapter addresses and indicate reasons why genuine inquiry into it is important for your world view and your existence personally and socially.

2. *Objectively summarize the influential answers* given to this problem in history as hypotheses to be tested. Be able to compare and contrast their real similarities and differences (not merely verbal similarities or differences).

3. *Highlight the primary biblical evidence* on which to decide among views—evidence found in the relevant teachings of the major divisions of Scripture—and decide for yourself which historical hypothesis (or synthesis of historical views) provides the most consistent and adequate account of the primary biblical data.

4. *Formulate in your own words your doctrinal conviction* in a logically consistent and adequate way, organizing your conclusions in ways you can ex-

plain clearly, support biblically, and communicate effectively to your spouse, children, friends, Bible class, or congregation.

5. *Defend your view* as you would to adherents of the alternative views, showing that the other views are logically less consistent and factually faced with more difficulties than your view in accounting for the givens, not only of special revelation but also of human experience in general.

6. *Explore the differences the viability of your conviction can make in your life.* Then test your understanding of the viability of your view by asking, "Can I live by it authentically (unhypocritically) in relation to God and to others in my family, church, vocation, neighborhood, city, nation, and world?"

MINISTRY PROJECTS

To Help Communicate This Doctrine in Christian Service

1. *Memorize one major verse or passage* that in its context teaches the heart of this doctrine and may serve as a text from which to preach, teach, or lead small group studies on the topic. The memorized passages from each chapter will build a body of content useful also for meditation and reference in informal discussions.

2. *Formulate the major idea of the doctrine in one sentence* based on the passage memorized. This idea should be useful as the major thesis of either a lesson for a class (junior high to adult) or a message for a church service.

3. *State the specific purpose or goal of your doctrinal lesson or message.* Your purpose should be more than informative. It should show why Christians need to accept this truth and live by it (unhypocritically). For teaching purposes, list indicators that would show to what extent class members have grasped the truth presented.

4. *Outline your message or lesson in complete sentences.* Indicate how you would support the truth of the doctrine's central ideas and its relevance to life and service. Incorporate elements from this chapter's historical, biblical, systematic, apologetic, and practical sections selected according to the value they have for your audience.

5. *List applications of the doctrine* for communicating the difference this conviction makes in life (for sermons, lessons, small-group Bible studies, or family devotional Bible studies). Applications should make clear what the doctrine is, why one needs to know it, and how it will make differences in thinking. Then show how the difference in thought will lead to differences in values, priorities, attitudes, speech, and personal action. Consider also the doctrine's possible significance for family, church, neighborhood, city, regional, and national actions.

6. *Start a file and begin collecting illustrations* of this doctrine's central idea, the points in your outline, and your applications.

7. *Write out your own doctrinal statement on this subject in one paragraph* (in half a page or less). To work toward a comprehensive doctrinal statement, collect your formulations based on a study of each chapter of *Integrative Theology.* As your own statement of Christian doctrine grows, you will find it personally strengthening and useful when you are called on for your beliefs in general and when you apply for service with churches, mission boards, and other Christian organizations. Any who seek ordination to Christian ministry will need a comprehensive doctrinal statement that covers the broad scope of theology.

CHAPTER 6

GOD'S MANY-SPLENDORED CHARACTER

God's Many-Splendored Character

THE PROBLEM: HOW SHALL WE VIEW THE CHARACTER OF GOD INTELLECTUALLY, ETHICALLY, EMOTIONALLY, VOLITIONALLY, AND RELATIONALLY?

In chapter 5 we emphasized the kind of being God is ontologically—a living, active, personal Spirit, who is self-sufficient, eternal, unchanging, and omnipresent. In this chapter we inquire primarily about the capacities and characteristics of the divine being intellectually, ethically, emotionally, volitionally, and relationally. A number of questions and issues are faced in this chapter. For instance: What is included in the claim that God is all-knowing? Does God's knowledge include both his own purposes and the future free acts of persons? How does God's wisdom differ from his omniscience? Does the fact that God shows mercy on some persons but punishes others eternally invalidate the assertion that he is just? How shall we understand the relation between God's justice and his mercy? Moreover, what is involved in the rich claim that "God is love [agapē]"? The reality of God's love (as well as human love) will be shown to be more volitional than emotional.

In the modern world can God's anger and wrath toward persons made in his image be reconciled with his love? Does the claim that God is a jealous and angry God cast any shadow over his holy character? In the day of judgment will God's compassion and mercy prevail over his hatred of evil? Furthermore, what light might contemporary interest in personal authenticity shed on the character of God? Does the perfection of omnipotence mean that God can make a square circle, tell a lie, or destroy himself? How can the belief that God is transcendent be reconciled with the notion that he is immanent in the world in terms of his presence and operations? Does the claim of transcendence cast God in the role of a ruthless despot, as liberals claim? Or is such a notion entirely consistent with an understanding of the supreme Being?

ALTERNATIVE INTERPRETATIONS IN THE CHURCH

The character or perfections of God have been variously interpreted within the Christian tradition, broadly conceived. The following represents a summary of the principal ways in which God's attributes have been understood.

Marcion and the Gnostics

Marcionite and Gnostic dualism drew a radical distinction between the inferior god of the Old Testament (the demiurge or creator) and the greater God revealed in the New Testament (the Redeemer). The former, who created the material world, was a god of anger, mighty in war; he was one who took vengeance on his enemies. Since the creator permitted the Fall, Marcion reasoned, he could not be good, all-knowing, and all-powerful. Several early Fathers, including Tertullian, responded that Marcion's creator god was the Devil of hell. The Redeemer, Marcion continued, was a God of pure love and mercy who revealed himself in Christ. This Most High God never became angry and never inflicted punishment. According to Marcion, the God of grace fought against and vanquished the god of law and justice and so opened the way to salvation for all who trust him. Clearly, Marcion ruptured the unity of God by assuming that the good God could not be just and the merciful God could not be angry.

Scholastic Thomism

The Thomistic school arrived at a fairly traditional understanding of the divine attributes by the special method of rational deduction from the notion of God as first unmoved mover, first efficient cause, and absolutely necessary being. Aquinas reasoned a priori that such a being contains within himself all the excellencies of perfection. Since infinite perfection includes intelligence, there must exist in God the most perfect knowledge. God perfectly knows himself ("necessary knowledge") and all things outside of himself ("knowledge of vision"). Indeed, God knows all things—past, present, and future contingent—not in a temporal succession but simultaneously in the

vision of his eternal now. From the attribute of will (also necessary to perfection) Thomas argued that God is perfect love. Human love is motivated by perceived goodness in its object. God's love, on the contrary, freely creates goodness in all finite things. Since there are not passions in an absolutely perfect being, Thomas understood the emotional attributes of anger, compassion, and jealousy in a metaphorical sense. He argued that what God actually does (creation, preservation, etc.) he accomplishes by his "ordinary power." God's omnipotence—his "absolute power"—exceeds his actual operations in our particular order. Thus, "God's power is not limited to some particular effect, but He is able to do absolutely all things; in other words, He is omnipotent."[1] On closer inspection, it appears that, following Pseudo-Dionysius and others, Thomas arranged the attributes in two categories: those by way of negation (eliminating characteristics that do not apply to the perfect first cause—e.g., *im*material, *in*visible, *in*finite) and those by way of eminence (infinitely elevating perfections found in finite creatures—e.g., *omni*scient, *omni*potent, *all*-loving).

Deism and Socinianism

Deists, who succumbed to the rationalism of the seventeenth and eighteenth centuries, posited a transcendent God who is the first cause of the created order and governs the universe from a distance, much like an indifferent clock-maker who made a clock and then let it run on its own. With their emphasis on the divine transcendence, Deists effectively denied that God is immanent in providential and in redemptive activity. Thus the Deists allowed no special revelation, no fulfilled prophecy, no miracles, and no active providence. They conceded that God is infinitely wise and good and that he righteously rewards good and punishes evil. But, given their denial of God's continued involvement in the universe, they seriously compromised God's love and mercy. Concluding that belief in an all-knowing and all-powerful God would be inconsistent with evil in the world, they also limited his attributes of omniscience and omnipotence.

The rationalistic Socinians (F. Socinus, J. Crell) emasculated the divine omniscience by insisting that God has an imperfect knowledge of future conditional events. Since free human acts are uncertain as to their actualization, it is impossible that God should infallibly foreknow them. The Socinians also assailed the notion of God's retributive justice. "There is no such justice in God that requires absolutely and inexorably that sin be punished."[2] The divine justice was viewed as general moral excellence, on the basis of which God frees sinners from punishment.

Schleiermacher and Ritschl

Schleiermacher prepared the way for the liberal interpretation by viewing God's attributes as explications of the human religious consciousness. This Romantic theologian divided the divine perfections into three categories: (1) the absolute attributes that arise from one's sense of dependence (eternity, omnipresence, omnipotence, and omniscience), (2) the moral attributes, which arise from consciousness of sin (holiness, justice, and mercy), and (3) those attributes that arise from the person's experience of grace (love and wisdom). Schleiermacher insisted that God's knowledge and power are limited to what actually transpires in the world. Since the real world is the complete expression of the divine will and power, nature reflects all there is of God. Schleiermacher regarded justice the causal link by which sin results in

suffering; little place was found in his system for God's wrath.

Schleiermacher's reduction of the divine attributes was carried to more radical ends by Ritschl, an antisupernaturalist theologian who regarded God's moral attributes as fundamental and insisted that the only adequate view of God is love. "There is no other conception of equal worth beside this which need to be taken into account."[3] He maintained that holiness, justice, and wrath are alien to the divine being. The notion of God's distributive justice and anger against sin were particularly opposed. In Ritschl, retribution and punishment were swallowed up by the divine goodness and grace.

Modern Protestant Liberalism

Twentieth-century Protestant liberalism, in its quest to make God relevant to modern minds, so stressed the divine immanence as to equate God with the world order. In general, God's attributes were identified by magnifying the noble qualities of persons. For example, Walter Rauschenbusch claimed that the classical doctrine of transcendence and power represents a totalitarian concept of God, whereas the model of immanence upholds the democratic view. Jesus, he argued, fought against the totalitarian view, by which God was imagined to be remote from humanity, interfering in human affairs only when necessary, and exacting punishment according to a capricious will. By democratizing the God-concept, Jesus upheld God as the Father of all spirits, infinitely loving, and close to all persons. Rauschenbusch was willing to think of God as less than omnipotent and omniscient if such a model would further the kingdom.

A. C. Knudson polemicized against the idea of retributive justice, where the divine righteousness rewards or punishes in accord with one's deeds.

The old view of God as an "unfeeling judge" must be replaced by the modern conception of God as "forgiving love." Claims Knudson, "There would seem to be no principle in the divine nature that requires that rewards and punishments be meted out to men in strict accordance with their deserts. . . . No atonement in the ordinary sense of the term is necessary before the forgiving love of God can become operative."[4]

W. A. Brown claims that all the emotions attributed to God in the Bible are manifestations of love. This is true not only of God's mercy and long-suffering but also of his jealousy and anger. Both sets of attributes reflect God's "desire to win men for himself, and his opposition to any obstacle which stands in the way of his realizing his loving end."[5] Wrath is merely a form of redeeming love. Some scholars also deny anger and wrath in God. Walter Eichrodt, an Old Testament specialist, insists that "wrath never forms one of the permanent attributes of the God of Israel; it can only be understood . . . as a footnote to the will to fellowship of the covenant God."[6] On the New Testament side, C. H. Dodd viewed wrath not as a divine attribute but as the impersonal process of retribution. "We cannot think with full consistency of God in terms of the highest human ideals of personality and yet attribute to him the irrational passion of anger."[7]

Barthian Neoorthodoxy

Against the radical immanentalism of liberal theology, neoorthodoxy stresses the radical otherness of God and the vast gulf that allegedly exists between Creator and creature. Karl Barth, operating from the premise that the attributes of God describe, not his essence but his acts, represents God as "the One who loves in freedom."[8] That is, love constitutes the foreground and

freedom the background of all God's operations. Love is that perfection in God that seeks the creation of fellowship without any regard to worth in the object loved. Freedom means that God is determined and moved by himself and not by anything from without. Viewed as ontic independence, it means that the sovereign God is free to speak or to keep silent, free to adopt or to reject, free to illumine or to blind.

Barth enumerates the perfections of the divine *loving* as grace counterbalanced by holiness, as mercy counterbalanced by righteousness, and as patience counterbalanced by wisdom. The divine righteousness means that violations of God's holiness will incur terrible wrath and punishment. The divine patience means that God does not immediately destroy, but he gives people opportunity to repent. The perfections of the divine *freedom* Barth enumerates as unity and omnipresence, constancy and omnipotence, and eternity and glory. With respect to omnipotence, God's power is not a neutral or a purely physical power; rather, it is a supremely moral power—"the power both to do the sum of whatever is possible for him and therefore genuinely possible, and also not to do what is impossible for him and therefore completely impossible."[9] Omnipotence includes both omniscience and omnivolence. Barth means by the latter that God's will embraces and controls all other wills. Nothing can hinder the will of the God who is capable of willing everything but the absurd. Finally, Barth upholds the unconditioned transcendence of the "wholly Other"; an absolute gulf exists between God and all created beings. Immanence, to Barth, means relatedness to the world through the incarnate Word, Jesus Christ.

Protestant and Roman Catholic Neoliberalism

Recent expressions of Protestant and Roman Catholic liberalism tend to view

God as the creative power immanent in human life and history (panentheism). Traditional notions of omnipresence, omniscience, retributive justice, and wrath are denied as unworthy of the real God. John A. T. Robinson, following Paul Tillich, attacks the classical notion of transcendence that views God as a discrete personal being wholly other to man. To affirm the transcendence of God is to acknowledge "the transcendent, unconditional element in all our relationships, and supremely in our relationships with other people."[10] For John Macquarrie, a Christian existentialist, omnipotence means that "Being itself" is the source and horizon of all possibilities. God's wrath is viewed as positive rather than punitive; it connotes "a transforming of evil into good, a healing of injuries, a restoring of what has been destroyed or blighted."[11]

Process theology affirms that as to his primordial nature, God is supremely absolute and transcendent—the source of all ideals and possibilities—but according to his consequent nature, God is supremely relative and immanent—a participant in the world's evolutionary advance. This increasingly popular form of neoclassical theism insists that God is supremely "creative-responsive Love."[12] The creative side of love (a function of the primordial nature) produces positive transformation in creatures, whereas the responsive side (a function of the consequent nature) ensures that God is changed and enriched through interaction with the world. Process theology wages war against the notion of divine omnipotence, claiming that God works by the solicitation of love rather than by the coercion of power. In addition, followers of Whitehead insist that God does not know future contingent events. Rather, God knows "the purpose He entertains, the potentialities of the created order, and his own ability to overrule for good."[13] Finally, process theology pays little

attention to God's moral attributes (e.g., holiness, justice, truth), choosing rather to stress his feeling qualities (e.g., empathy, patience, tenderness) and aesthetic (e.g., imagination, creativity, refreshment). As Whitehead, the father of process thought, put it, the love of God "is a little oblivious to morals."[14]

On the Roman Catholic side, consistent with the claim that the entire world has been forgiven, Karl Rahner says little about God's justice, anger, and judgment. Thus, "we have more reason to praise his mercy than to fear his justice, because He has allowed his grace to overflow and not his anger."[15] Hans Küng likewise stresses God's benevolence at the expense of his justice and wrath: "He does not demand but gives, does not oppress but raises up, does not wound but heals. . . . He forgives instead of condemning, liberates instead of punishing, permits the unrestricted rule of grace instead of law."[16] In reaction to the distant and unrelated God of the Greeks, Küng stresses the immanence and radical haveability of the ultimate Reality who indwells persons and history. Leslie Dewart avers that the divine omnipotence must be abandoned as a threat to creaturely freedom. God deals with persons, not by "acting upon" them with limitless power, but in terms of "being with" them in reciprocal relations. People today "find themselves compelled by their Christian faith to *disbelieve* in a supreme Being, in a God behind whose kindness and generosity to man stands a supreme, omnipotent and eternal will."[17]

Protestant Orthodoxy

The Fathers, the Reformers, Protestant orthodox theologians, and Evangelicals posit a God who is all-knowing, holy, and loving, who justly rewards good and punishes evil, who detests sin and yet is long-suffering and compassionate with sinners, who is free, authentic, and all-powerful, and who is transcendent in being (as the exalted One) and yet immanent (as the related One) in providential and redemptive activity.

The apologist Theophilus represented God's character by saying what it is not: "In glory he is incomparable, in wisdom unrivalled, in goodness inimitable, in kindness unutterable."[18] To the question "Is God angry?" Theophilus responds, "Yes, He is angry with those who act wickedly, but He is good and kind and merciful to those who love and fear him. For He is a chastener of the godly . . . but He is a judge and punisher of the impious."[19] In the East, Clement upheld God's omniscience by affirming that God comprehends all things past, present, and future in a single glance. Against Marcion he insisted that the good God is both righteous and just. "Being a lover of men, He is a hater of the wicked, entertaining a perfect aversion to all villany."[20] Clement pointed out that the God who is ontologically transcendent, being beyond space and time, is dynamically near through the immanent operations of the Logos. In the West, Tertullian argued that God would not be wholly good unless he were an enemy of evil. The righteous God "knows how to *heal*, but also how to *strike*."[21] Gregory of Nazianzus argued that mercy is God's natural work, whereas anger is his unnatural work. God is naturally inclined to the former but compelled by sin to the latter. Gregory adds that it is impossible for God to be evil or to cause two plus two to equal ten, "for this would be indicative of weakness in God rather than of strength."[22]

Augustine claims that the omniscient God comprehends all things past, present, and future in his single timeless contemplation.[23] The divine foreknowledge connotes not merely prescience but the ordination that ensures things will eventuate in accord with the will of God. One of Augustine's favorite designations for God is that of "truth." God is true (1) in the metaphysical sense that he is the genuine essence; (2) in the ethical sense of a perfect correspondence between his being, deeds, and words; and (3) in the logical sense that he knows things as they really are. The bishop found no inconsistency between the divine justice and mercy. In justice, God rewards good for good and evil for evil; in mercy, he, through justifying grace, rewards good for evil. Emotionally, God "is jealous without any darkening of spirit, wrathful without any perturbation, pitiful without any pain, and patient without any passion."[24] God's anger is not a disturbing emotion; it is his just retribution against sin. Volitionally, Augustine stresses that God is free to do whatever he pleases in heaven or on earth. Apart from any external compulsion, God is free to create, to confer mercy, and to punish. God is omnipotent, not that he can do anything at all (he cannot die, sin, deny himself, etc.), but that he is able to do whatever he wills—God's will and power being inseparable from his essence. Finally, Augustine insists that God is both transcendent and immanent—transcendent above space as the exalted One, immanent in space as the Actuality that fills everything with his being and power.[25]

With Luther, several attributes of God came in for special attention. In his innermost heart, God is "nothing but burning love and a glowing oven full of love."[26] According to Luther, God's love is neither kindled by any worth, nor quenched by any unworthiness, in its object. Further, if love is God's "proper work," being identical with his nature, wrath is that "alien work," contrary to his nature, that is provoked by wickedness. Noteworthy in Luther is the contrast between transcendence and immanence—i.e., between God in himself and God manifested in Christ, between God hidden (*Deus abscondi-tus*) and God revealed (*Deus revelatus*), between the naked God (*Deus nudus*) and God clothed in his promises.[27] To view God as majesty and law breeds despair; to view him as revealed in Christ opens the door to justification.

Calvin argues that the attributes of God that are most important for us to know are his lovingkindness, righteousness, and judgment.[28] God's fundamental disposition toward the elect is gratuitous love. In spite of our corrupt natures and depraved conduct, "He still finds something in us which in lovingkindness He can love."[29] Righteousness connotes that God's will is the supreme standard of justice and equity. "He must naturally love justice and abhor injustice."[30] As for judgment, the wicked are the special objects of God's severity and wrath. "As God is the fountain of all righteousness, He must necessarily be the enemy and judge of man so long as he is a sinner."[31] Whereas Luther stressed the divine condescension, Calvin emphasized God's transcendence, majesty, and freedom. Although God is infinite in majesty, nevertheless he is immanent in his providential and redemptive operations.

The Protestant confessions clearly articulate the divine perfections. The Belgic Confession (1619) affirms that God is "incomprehensible, invisible, immutable, infinite, almighty, perfectly wise, just, good, and the overflowing fountain of all good" (art. 1). According to the Westminster Confession of Faith (1647), God is "almighty, most wise, most holy, most free, most absolute, . . . most loving, gracious, merciful, long-suffering, abundant in goodness and truth, forgiving iniquity, transgression and sin; the rewarder of them that diligently seek him; and withal

most just and terrible in his judgments" (ch. 2).

Charles Hodge and William G. T. Shedd rehearse the consensus of Evangelical opinion on the divine perfections. God's holiness connotes absolute moral perfection—entire freedom from moral evil. His justice is both rectoral and distributive. The former connotes that God has laid down laws that are holy, just, and good. The latter implies that God rewards everyone according to his works. Distributive justice is remunerative in that it rewards virtue; it is retributive in that it punishes evil. "In every instance of transgression, the penalty of law must be inflicted, either personally or vicariously; either upon the transgressor or upon his substitute."[32] Yet the God of the Bible is equally a God of grace and mercy. Grace is God's benevolent compassion toward the person as a guilty sinner, and mercy is his compassion toward the one in misery and wretchedness.

Recent monographs by J. I. Packer,[33] Ronald Nash,[34] and Stephen Davis[35] helpfully discuss the character of God from an Evangelical perspective.

THE BIBLICAL TEACHING

In order to determine which interpretation of the character of God is to be admitted, we turn now to the primary scriptural data.

Pentateuch

God's perfect, all-inclusive knowledge of everything in the universe is attested by Hagar's name for Deity—"the God who sees me" (*ēl rā'î*, Gen. 16:13), and by the fact that Israel's suffering in Egypt was completely transparent to him (Exod. 3:7). God has unerring knowledge of the future, a knowledge that embraces his own actions (Exod. 9:18–20) and the free choices of human agents. Concerning

221

the latter, God knew in advance that Pharaoh would decide to release Israel from Egypt (Exod. 6:1; 11:1) and that once they were in the land Israel would profane the covenant and worship idols (Deut. 31:20–21). There is no suggestion in these texts that God's foreknowledge is the efficient cause of the object of knowledge.

In the patriarchal history, Abraham's servant (Gen. 24:27) and Jacob (Gen. 32:10) praised God for his faithfulness ('ᵉmet) to them. At Sinai Yahweh revealed himself to Moses as "abounding in . . . faithfulnesss" (Exod. 34:6). Moses in turn represented God as wholly dependable or reliable: "He is the Rock [ṣûr] . . . a faithful ['ᵉmûnāh] God who does no wrong" (Deut. 32:4). A prominent theme of the Pentateuch is Yahweh's unswerving faithfulness to his covenant with Israel. Hence Moses' reminder: "He is the faithful [Niphal participle of 'āman, to be firm] God, keeping his covenant of love to a thousand generations of those who love him and keep his commands" (Deut. 7:9; cf. Gen. 9:16; Exod. 2:24; Deut. 4:31).

When Moses testified of Yahweh, "All his ways are just (mišpāt). . . . Upright and just (ṣaddîq) is he" (Deut. 32:4), he affirmed that God consistently acts in accord with his righteous character. God shows no partiality or unfairness in his dealings; he gives to each what is his due. Thus, in the record of the Fall, God inflicted just penalties on the serpent, on Eve, and on Adam (Gen. 3:14–24). He justly punished Cain for his murder of Abel (Gen. 4:10–13) and executed justice by the destruction of the Flood (Gen. 6:5–7). When God unleashed the plagues on Egypt, Pharaoh confessed, "The LORD is in the right" (ṣaddîq, Exod. 9:27). God acted justly in sentencing faithless Israel to forty years of wilderness wandering and in permitting only Caleb and Joshua of that generation to enter the promised land (Num. 14:26–35).

Mercy in Scripture connotes God's goodness to those in distress or deserving judgment. At Sinai, God revealed himself as "a God merciful [raḥûm] and gracious" (Exod. 34:6, RSV), who freely exercises mercy (rāḥam) on whom he will (Exod. 33:19). Later Moses warned Israel that after committing idolatry in Canaan their unity would be dissolved. Yet if they repented, the merciful God would renew the covenant and relieve their misery (Deut. 4:27–31). God's standing promise was that whenever Israel returned from her idolatrous liaisons, he would turn from his anger and "show mercy" (Deut. 13:17).

Prominent in the Pentateuch is the unfailing love (ḥesed, 245 times in the OT) of the Lord who is loyal to his covenant. Thus, Yahweh disclosed himself to Israel as a loving God: "showing love to a thousand generations of those who love me and keep my commandments" (Exod. 20:6; cf. 34:6–7; Num. 14:18–19). God chose Israel and delivered them from the power of Pharaoh simply by virtue of his love ('ahᵃbāh) for them (Deut. 7:7–8; cf. 4:37). If Israel would be faithful to his covenant of love (habᵉrît wᵉhaḥesed, Deut. 7:9), God would love ('āhēb) and bless them (Deut. 7:13).

The word "holiness" (qōdeš) likely derives from the root meaning "to cut" or "to separate."[36] Thus God is holy in the twofold sense that he is separate (1) from all that is finite and earthly and (2) from all that is unclean and defiled. The first dimension of the divine holiness connotes God's transcendence over the creation, the second the ethical perfection of his character. Holiness in the sense of greatness and sovereignty is affirmed in Exodus 15:11: "Who is like you—majestic in holiness, awesome in glory, working wonders?" The word "holy" (qādōš) and cognates occur more than 150 times in Leviticus,[37] chiefly in the sense of ethical purity. Thus, the offerings an Israelite must bring if he would approach God (Lev. 1–7), the special priesthood to mediate access to God (8–10), and the laws concerning purity (11–15) all attest the absolute moral perfection of God's character. The leitmotif of the Book of Leviticus is the divine command "Be holy because I, the LORD your God, am holy" (19:2; cf. 11:44–45).

The history of Israel illustrates God's intense hatred of evil. God's anger was unleashed against Israel for worshiping the golden calf at Sinai (Exod. 32:10–12; cf. Deut. 9:7–8; 19–20), for their discontent with the provision of manna and quail (Num. 11:33), and for their veneration of the fertility god Baal (25:3–9). That God's wrath was kindled by the idolatry of his covenant people is a frequent theme of Deuteronomy (4:25–26; 6:14–15; 29:22–28, et al.). Yet God's anger was tempered by a patience that grants the sinner opportunity to repent—so the Lord is described as being "slow to anger" (*'erek 'appayîm*, Exod. 34:6; Num. 14:18). God repeatedly promised Israel that if they would turn from foreign gods, he would "have compassion" (*rāḥam, nāḥam*) on them (Deut. 13:17; 30:3). To the oppressed, God promises, "I will hear, for I am compassionate" (Exod. 22:27). God's compassion thus represents his love and pity for the weak and unfortunate. Emotionally God is also depicted as jealous or endowed with a righteous possessiveness. Since God reserves for himself the worship of his people (19:5–6), his jealousy is aroused when the redeemed forsake the covenant and cleave to foreign gods (20:5; Deut. 4:24; 32:16). Yahweh himself said, "Do not worship any other god, for the LORD, whose name is Jealous [*qannā'*], is a jealous God" (Exod. 34:14).

Freedom, a quality close to sovereignty, means that God has power to determine his own self according to his nature and purposes. Thus, God is depicted as a sovereign agent who freely creates (Gen. 1:1), freely grants finite people a measure of freedom (2:16–17), freely plans redemption (3:15), freely chooses a special people (12:1–3), freely reveals himself (Exod. 3:2–15) and his moral law (20:2–17), and freely redeems (14:21–30). God is capable of performing these works, since he is "God Almighty" (Gen. 17:1; Exod. 6:3) and "the Mighty One of Jacob" (Gen. 49:24). In the exercise of his omnipotence, God sometimes works directly, without secondary causes, as in the judgment at Babel (Gen. 11:5–9) and the birth of Isaac (Gen. 21:1–2; cf. 17:17). More frequently, God exercises his power through secondary causes, such as may be the case in the destruction of Sodom and Gomorrah (Gen. 19), several of the plagues against Pharaoh (Exod. 7:11), and Israel's passage through the Sea of Reeds (Exod. 14). In the words of Moses, God is "majestic in power . . . , awesome in glory, working wonders" (Exod. 15:6, 11). Nothing is too hard for the Lord (Gen. 18:14).

The God of the patriarchs is transcendent in being, and this means that he is distinct from all that he has created. The divine transcendence is commonly expressed in spatial terms; e.g., he is "the Most High" (Num. 24:16; Deut. 32:8) and "God Most High" (Gen. 14:18–20). The terrifying phenomena of thunder, lightning, fire, and smoke were visible when God descended to the top of Mount Sinai (Exod. 19:18, 20). The biblical view unites the transcendence and immanence of the divine Being, as in Deuteronomy 4:39: "The LORD is God in heaven above and on the earth below." God is also immanent in providential activity, in the sense that he unceasingly directs the affairs of people and nations to their appointed ends (Gen. 39:2–3; 45:7–8; 50:20; Deut. 2:7). The God of Israel likewise is immanent in redemptive activity, manifesting himself with Israel to redeem and comfort (Exod. 3:8; 15:13; Num. 9:15–23).

Historical Books

The accounts of Israel's history attest that God instantly and all-inclusively knows people's thoughts (1 Chron. 28:9), deeds (1 Sam. 2:3), and comings and goings (2 Kings 19:27). God inerrantly knows not only all actualities (2 Chron. 16:9) but also all future contingencies—i.e., yet unrealized events whose occurrence depends on the free choices of human agents. Thus, God knew in advance that David would vanquish the Philistine forces at Keilah (1 Sam. 23:4–5) and that he would be betrayed to Saul if he remained in the area (vv. 10–13). God is also presented as absolutely faithful to his promises (Josh. 23:14) and to his covenant of love established with Israel (1 Kings 8:23; Neh. 1:5). When Israel was oppressed by pagan neighbors, God in fidelity to his covenant preserved his chosen people (2 Kings 13:23). The name Rock (sûr), commonly ascribed to God (1 Sam. 2:2; 2 Sam. 22:32, 47), connotes both the strength and faithfulnesss of Israel's God.

That God is "righteous" (ṣaddîq) connotes his right behavior or holiness in action (Ezra 9:15; Neh. 9:8). God is just (same word, ṣaddîq) in that with absolute equity he apportions to each what is his due (2 Chron. 12:6; Neh. 9:33). Hence David's song celebrating God's deliverance: "To the faithful you show yourself faithful, to the blameless you show yourself blameless, to the pure you show yourself pure, but to the crooked you show yourself shrewd" (2 Sam. 22:26–27). "With the LORD our God there is no injustice or partiality" (2 Chron. 19:7). In some cases a slight offense against his holiness incurs swift punishment (1 Sam. 6:19–20). Yet even when God punishes, he does not utterly abandon his people, for the Lord is "a

gracious and merciful God" (Neh. 9:31). The Lord steadfastly maintains his covenant of love (ḥesed, 1 Kings 8:23; 2 Chron. 6:14).

The history of Israel is replete with God's hatred of evil. Thus, "the LORD's anger burned" against Israel on account of Achan's sin (Josh. 7:1) and against Uzzah for his careless handling of the ark (2 Sam. 6:6–7). God's anger also burned against Israel for serving false gods (1 Kings 14:9, 15; 16:26), for acts of divination and sorcery (2 Kings 17:17), for consulting mediums and spiritists (2 Kings 21:6)—in short, for disobeying the law of God (2 Kings 22:13). Israel's sins stirred up God's righteous possessiveness or jealousy (Josh. 24:19). Thus his response to spiritual infidelity was "jealous anger" (1 Kings 14:22). Nevertheless, God did not impulsively punish, for he also is "slow to anger" ('erek 'appayîm, Neh. 9:17). Indeed, in fidelity to the covenant, God dealt with his wayward people with grace and compassion (2 Kings 13:23).

The plenitude of God's power is seen in the mighty works he performed in Israel. The staying of the waters of the Jordan (Josh. 3), the toppling of the walls of Jericho (Josh. 6), Elijah's victorious contest with the 450 prophets of Baal (1 Kings 18), and the killing of 185,000 Assyrian warriors by the angel of the Lord (2 Kings 19) demonstrate that the Yahweh of Israel is "the great, mighty and awesome God" (Neh. 9:32; cf. 1 Chron. 29:11–12). No person, no force can withstand his power (2 Chron. 20:6).

Poetry and Wisdom

In Israel's devotional literature, God knows people's thoughts and motives (Prov. 24:12), their "secret sins" (Ps. 90:8), their hurts and anxieties (Ps. 56:8), and their every action (Job 31:4; Prov. 5:21).[38] Job describes God as "perfect in knowledge" (dē'āh, Job

36:4; 37:16). Psalm 139 affirms that God knows every aspect of the psalmist's being: his actions (vv. 2a, 3), his mind (v. 2b), and his unformed words (v. 4). David concludes, "Such knowledge [da'at, God's intimate knowledge of him] is too wonderful for me, too lofty for me to attain" (v. 6). Divine wisdom (ḥokmāh, tᵉbûnāh)—the application of knowledge to the realization of moral ends—is a common theme (Job 9:4; 12:13), particularly in connection with the creation and preservation of the universe (Ps. 104:24; Prov. 3:19–20). In Proverbs 8:22–31, God's attribute of wisdom is personified and set forth in highly descriptive language.[39] God's faithfulnesss, a common theme in the Psalter, is limitless (Pss. 36:5; 57:10), inviolable (Ps. 89:33–34), and eternal (Pss. 117:2; 146:6).

Equally common are assertions of God's righteousness and justice. As elsewhere in the Old Testament, justice connotes the principles of retribution whereby God rewards the faithful and punishes the wicked (Ps. 11:5–7; Prov. 24:12). In the Psalms, righteousness frequently signifies God's deliverance of oppressed saints in fulfillment of his covenantal faithfulnesss (Pss. 5:8; 51:14; 71:15–16, et al.). In this latter sense, ṣedāqāh is equivalent to the salvation of the Lord (Ps. 69:27). God's mercy—the concrete manifestation of pity to the weak and afflicted (Ps. 69:14–17)—results in deliverance from trouble (Ps. 40:11) and forgiveness of sins (Pss. 51:1; 79:8). In the Psalms God's covenant love (ḥesed) is richly represented as infinite (Ps. 57:10), "unfailing" (Ps. 107:8), everlasting (Ps. 136), and the saint's chief delight (Ps. 63:3). In the Song of Songs, the love ('aḥᵃbāh) of God is irresistible in attractive power (8:6) and absolutely indestructible (v. 7).

God, moreover, is endowed with the titles "the Holy One" (Job 6:10; Ps. 22:3; Prov. 9:10) and "the Holy One of Israel" (Pss. 78:41; 89:18). Indeed, the attribute of holiness develops into a synonym for Deity, so that God swearing by his holiness is equivalent to God swearing by himself (Ps. 89:35). Psalm 99, where holiness is thrice ascribed to God (vv. 3, 5, 9), affirms the two aspects of his holiness—i.e., transcendent majesty (vv. 1–3) and absolute moral perfection (vv. 4–5).

The literature also upholds God's severe hatred of wickedness (Ps. 45:7) and of the sinner himself. Concerning the latter, God is said to "hate" (śānē') the evildoer (Ps. 5:4–6).[40] Proverbs 6:16–19 enumerates seven abominations (tô'ēbāh), i.e., the attitudes, thoughts, speech, and actions that the Lord hates. Furthermore, "the sacrifice of the wicked" (Prov. 15:8), "the way of the wicked" (Prov. 15:9), "the thoughts of the wicked" (15:26), and the "prayers" of the wicked (28:9) are abominations to the Lord. God responds to evil by unleashing his "burning anger" (ḥᵃrôn 'ap, Job 20:23), furious wrath (Job 40:11), and angry rage (za'am, Ps. 69:24). Psalm 78, a rehearsal of Israel's history from Egypt to the Davidic kingdom, attests God's indignation against his people's stubbornness and disobedience (vv. 21, 31, 49, 58, 59, 62). No less real, however, is the fact that the compassionate God (Pss. 51:1; 86:15) is slow to anger ('erek 'appayîm, Pss. 86:15; 145:8)—i.e., God takes a long deep breath before venting his wrath.

Volitionally, God is free to execute his purposes in nature and history (Job 12:13–25). "Our God is in heaven; he does whatever pleases him" (Ps. 115:3). He is authentic or true in the sense that his words are in harmony with his being and actions ("the God of truth," Ps. 31:5). So his word likewise is veracious and sure ('ᵉmet, Ps. 119:142, 151, 160). Job was captivated by the power of God, i.e., that he is able to do all that he wills to do (Job 9:4, 19; 36:5, 22). Hence his acknowledgment, "I know that you can do all things; no plan of yours can be thwarted" (Job 42:2). The psalmist confesses that God's power has no equal in the entire universe (Pss. 65:6; 66:3). God's will is his power; all that he wills to do, he performs (Ps. 115:3).

God's transcendence, i.e., his otherness vis-à-vis the finite world, is evidenced by the titles "God Most High" (Pss. 57:2; 78:35) and "the LORD Most High" (Ps. 47:2). The God of Israel is "the Most High over all the earth" (Pss. 83:18; 97:9). In a vivid use of spatial language the psalmist states that God is "enthroned so high, he needs to stoop to see the sky and earth" (Ps. 113:4–5, JB). The Psalms correspondingly acknowledge God's immanence in providential activity (Pss. 36:6; 65:9–13) and his immanence in redemptive activity (Pss. 23:4, 6; 78:52–55).

Prophetic Literature

The divine omniscience is the presupposition of all trustworthy prophecy. Because God's knowledge is complete and perfect, through prophets he declares future occurrences (Isa. 42:9; 48:3, 5). So perfect is God's knowledge (da'at) and understanding (t\u1ebbûnāh) that he has complete cognizance of all future contingent events (Jer. 38:17–18), particularly the course of world history (Dan. 2, esp. v. 28). The prophets also testify that God is absolutely faithful to the covenant and the promises made with Israel (Jer. 32:37–40; Ezek. 16:60; Dan. 9:4). Habakkuk 2:4 states that "the righteous will live by his faithfulness" ('\u1ebbmûnāh, i.e., God's moral steadfastness or fidelity to his holy character).[41] In spite of God's stern judgment, Jeremiah could say, "Great is your faithfulness" (Lam. 3:23).

The prophets dwell much on God's righteousness and justice. God is righteous (ṣaddîq) in that he consistently acts in accord with his holy will and character (Jer. 12:1; Dan. 9:7, 14). God is just in the sense that he apportions to each what is his due, i.e., blessings for obedience and punishment for disobedience (Mic. 7:9; Nah. 1:3). Isaiah 53:4–6 teaches that the punishment justice demands would be vicariously inflicted on the Messiah. The frequent combination "justice and righteousness" (mišpāt and ṣedeq/ṣ\u1ebbdāqāh, Isa. 33:5; Jer. 9:24; Hos. 2:19) indicates that God's dealings with people are always characterized by "high principles" and "irreproachable conduct."[42] Such righteous demands are explicable for the reason than that God is the "Holy One" (Isa. 10:17; 40:25; Hos. 11:9, 12), the "Holy One of Jacob" (Isa. 29:23), and the "Holy One of Israel" (thirty times in Isa.; Jer. 51:5; Ezek. 39:7). God's holiness is most clearly displayed in Isaiah's temple vision (Isa. 6:1–5). The winged seraphim in worship, the shaking of the foundations, the darkness, the smoke, the prophet's cry of unworthiness, and the threefold ascription to God ("Holy, holy, holy is Yahweh, ṣ\u1ebbbā'ôt") affirm the majesty, transcendence, and absolute moral perfection of Israel's God. God's holiness in action is evidenced by his judging sin (Ezek. 28:22), by bringing Israel back from captivity (thus preserving the honor of his name, Ezek. 36:20–23; 39:27), and by punishing Israel's oppressors (Hab. 1:12–13).

God's character as love is affirmed with particular force by the prophets, especially Hosea. God's covenant love (hesed) for his people is more unshakable than the mountains—the emblem of stability. They will be moved, but his love shall stand forever (Isa. 54:10). Hosea views God's love (hesed) in terms of a faithful husband's love for his faithless wife (Hos. 3:1). When Israel persisted in apostasy and rebellion, God poured out on them a love that was free, unmerited, and overflowing (Hos. 14:4). Even though Israel spurned him, God refused to give them up (Hos. 11:7–9). The prophet promises that God will renew Israel with his love (Zeph. 3:17).

"The wrath of God is described in the Old Testament with terrible severity, especially by the prophets."[43] Since sin and its perpetrator are inextricably linked, God is said to hate (i.e., despise or detest) the sinner (Hos. 9:15; Mal. 1:3). God's emotional response to violations of his holy law is described in the strongest possible terms: "fiery anger" (Ezek. 21:31), "burning anger" (Isa. 13:13), "fierce anger" (Jer. 4:8, 26), and "indignation" (Nah. 1:6). God's fury against sin is expressed in the most dramatic imagery. As a farmer thrashes his field, so the Lord slashes his sickle across the nations (Hab. 3:12). In anger God gathers sinful humanity into a fiery furnace, much as a smelter melts unrefined metals in a crucible (Ezek. 22:17–22). And God's judgment of sinners is like the ferocity of an angry lion who tears its prey to pieces and carries them off (Hos. 5:14). Nevertheless, the execution of wrath and punishment is God's "strange work," and "his alien task" (Isa. 28:21), in the sense that God takes delight in healing rather than in destroying (Ezek. 18:32). The prophets depict God as jealous (*qānā'*) for the holiness of his name profaned by Israel's defeat (Ezek. 39:25), for his chosen people (Zech. 1:14), and for the holy land (Joel 2:18). Notwithstanding God's hatred and jealousy provoked by sin, God is "slow to anger" (Joel 2:13; Jonah 4:2), in that he sent messengers with repeated warnings (Jer. 7:13, 25) and postponed his judgments (Isa. 48:9). The prophets depict a deeply compassionate God (Hos. 11:8), whose tenderness for his people is more profound than a mother's love for her child (Isa. 49:15). God's compassion—love modified by the wretchedness of people—moved

him to restore captive Israel to the land (Isa. 54:7–8; Jer. 30:18).

God's freedom to actualize his own will is affirmed in Isaiah 46:10: "My purpose will stand, and I will do all that I please." God freely chose Cyrus of Persia to bring Israel back from captivity (Isa. 44:28). When challenged as to his choice of this pagan ruler, God responded with the parable of the potter who freely shapes the clay as he sees fit (Isa. 45:9–13). His is the sovereignty, the freedom, and the power (cf. Dan. 4:35). By his limitless power, God fashioned the heavens and earth (Jer. 10:12; Amos 4:13). The myriad of stars testify to "his great power and mighty strength" (Isa. 40:26). Truly there is nothing that the Lord is incapable of performing (Jer. 32:17, 27), except that which is contrary to his character and will—e.g., condone evil or tolerate wrong (Hab. 1:13).

Synoptic Gospels

Jesus taught that God knows the acts (e.g., giving, praying, and fasting, Matt. 6:4, 6, 18) that people perform in secret. He knows people's needs (Matt. 6:8, 32), their hearts (Luke 16:15), and the minutest details of their lives (Matt. 10:29–30). God has knowledge of future contingencies, for he knew that Tyre and Sidon (Matt. 11:21) and even Sodom (v. 23) would have repented if certain miracles had been performed in their midst. God knows in advance the exact time of Christ's return to earth (Matt. 24:36). In sum, God knows all that possibly can be known.

Jesus also upheld God's justice, or the righteous impartiality of all his ways. In the parable of the persistent widow (Luke 18:1-8), he reasoned that if a corrupt judge works justice, would not God execute justice for his chosen ones? Most assuredly God "will see that they get justice [*ekdikēsis*, just recompense], and quickly" (v. 8).

God's distributive justice is taught in the parable of the talents (Matt. 25:14–29). The first two servants who executed their duties obediently were amply rewarded, whereas the third servant who proved faithless was severely punished. Even a criminal on the cross acknowledged that God administers punishment in accord with his righteous character (Luke 23:41).

Jesus' story of the fig tree (Luke 13:6–9) teaches that God is long-suffering. The vineyard pictures Israel, the cutting of the tree represents God's judgment against sin (Luke 3:9), and the caretaker's plea for an additional year in which to wait for fruit indicates God's patience, which holds his anger in abeyance. God's compassion was amply demonstrated in the ministry of Jesus. The Lord was filled with compassion at the sight of the leper (Mark 1:41), the aimless crowds in Galilee (Matt. 9:36), the widow of Nain whose only son had died (Luke 7:13), and the hungry five thousand (Matt. 14:14). The parable of the wayward son (Luke 15:11–32) teaches that God's love for the lost in Israel is like the father's concern for the prodigal.[44] In each of the above, the verb *splanchnizomai* signifies the messianic compassion of Jesus, whereby his heart was filled with loving tenderness toward those in dire need.[45]

Following the angel's announcement that she would conceive supernaturally, Mary confessed the divine omnipotence with the words "Nothing is impossible with God" (Luke 1:37). Mary's name for God is *ho dynatos*, "the Mighty One" (Luke 1:49). Jesus likewise acknowledged that God's power knows no limits, save his character and will (Matt. 19:26; Mark 14:36). Jesus' healings (Mark 1:23–26; 2:1–12; 3:1–5, et al.), resuscitations (Luke 7:11–16; 8:49–56), exorcisms (Matt. 9:32–33; Luke 8:26–39), and nature miracles (Mark 4:35–41; 6:45–52) were wrought by a mighty power from God.

The Acts of the Apostles

God's immediate knowledge of all things past, present, and future is reflected in the prophetic predictions of Christ's crucifixion and resurrection (Acts 2:23–28; cf. 3:18).[46] James testified that from eternity God knew that the house of David would be restored and the knowledge and worship of God would be opened up to the Gentiles (15:15–18). Peter, on the same occasion, claimed that God knows the secrets of people's hearts (15:8; cf. 1:24).

In his address to the Athenians, Paul declared that God will judge the world through Christ on the basis of the absolute moral equity that is his nature (Acts 17:31). Even pagan Greeks, when they witnessed the principle of retribution at work, were quick to attribute it to "justice" (*hē dikē*, 28:4). The ground of God's justice—the perfect rectitude of his nature—in Acts is seen most clearly in the person of Jesus Christ, "the Holy and Righteous One" (3:14; cf. 4:27, 30). Still, Acts affirms that God is patient in that he grants sinners time in which to repent. With an eye to the Athenians' idolatry, Paul insists that "in the past God overlooked such ignorance" (17:30)—where the verb *hyperoraō* is used in the LXX of God's postponing severe judgment. Formerly God overlooked the spiritual darkness of the pagan world, but he will do so no longer. With the threat of severe judgment, God now calls the pagan world to repent (17:31; cf. 3:19).

God's mighty power is seen in the healing of the crippled beggar (Acts 3:1–8, 12), of Aeneas the paralytic (9:33–34), and of the crippled man at Lystra (14:8–11); in the raising of Dorcas (9:36–41) and of Eutychus from the dead (20:7–10), and in the miraculous deliverance of Peter (12:6–11) and of

Paul and Silas (16:25-26) from prison. Gamaliel reminded the Sanhedrin of the futility of humans contending against the power of God (5:38-39)—the power that created the heavens, the earth, and everything therein (4:24). The main emphasis in Acts is on God's immanence in providential activity (13:17; 17:26-27) and in redemptive activity (2:1-4; 9:5, 17). Nevertheless, Luke also upholds God's ontological transcendence over the world (7:48-50; 16:17).

Pauline Epistles

Although the word "foreknowledge" primarily indicates "foreordaining mercy"[47] or "electing grace"[48] (Rom. 8:29; 11:2; cf. 1 Cor. 8:3; Gal. 4:9; 2 Tim. 2:19), it also *a major ad minor,* connotes God's unerring knowledge of all things in advance, for God knows what he plans. God also possesses a plenitude of wisdom (*sophia*), in the sense of his ability to arrange and adapt all things to the fulfillment of his holy purposes (Rom. 11:33; 16:27; Eph. 1:7-8). The zenith of God's wisdom emerges in his ingenious plan of salvation (1 Cor. 2:7; Eph. 3:10), more particularly as the chief actor in that drama—the crucified Christ (1 Cor. 1:24, 30). Paul repeatedly affirms that God is faithful (*pistos*, reliable or dependable), in that he fulfills all his promises (2 Cor. 1:20), provides escape from trials (1 Cor. 10:13), protects believers from the evil one (2 Thess. 3:3), and preserves the redeemed to the end (1 Cor. 1:8-9; 1 Thess. 5:23-24).

Paul describes the second person of the Godhead as the "righteous Judge" (2 Tim. 4:8) in that he embodies the perfect standard of right (i.e., "right behavior or right disposition").[49] In his dealings with people, God shows no favoritism or partiality (Rom. 2:11; Eph. 6:9). No charge of injustice can be levied against him (Rom. 3:5-6; 9:14),

for he gives to each his desert. More specifically, God's justice is remunerative (Eph. 6:8) and punitive (Rom. 1:32; 6:23; 12:19). In Paul's statement, "the wages of sin is death" (Rom. 6:23), the word *opsōnion* (e.g., wages or recompense) "strictly denotes payment in kind."[50]

The apostle's teaching about God's love is pervasively soteriological. The divine *agapē* is the *raison d'être* for Christ's incarnation and cross (Eph. 5:2)—indeed, for his entire redemptive mission (2 Thess. 2:16; Titus 3:4). God's active, outgoing love is also the basis of the believer's eternal election and adoption (Eph. 1:4-5; cf. Rom. 9:13), in fact, of the entire salvation experience (Eph. 2:4-7). So intense and so powerful is God's love that no person or power in the universe can sever the believer from it (Rom. 8:35-39). The chief demonstration of divine love occurred when Christ voluntarily laid down his life for his enemies (Rom. 5:6-8). Paul stands in no less awe of God's mercy (*eleos*)—"the emotion aroused by someone in need and the attempt to relieve the person and remove his trouble."[51] Eternal election (Rom. 9:16, 18, 23), salvation from sin (Eph. 2:4-5; Titus 3:5), and summons to service (1 Tim. 1:13, 16) are all rooted in God's free mercy and pity.

Paul was acutely conscious of God's severe displeasure toward sin, expressed as the emotional responses of anger (*thymos*) and wrath (*orgē*). The holy God responds with indignation against every violation of his righteous standards (Rom. 1:18; Eph. 5:6). Eschatologically, Paul viewed the day of the Lord as a treasure of accumulated wrath that God would execute justly (Rom. 2:5, 8; 5:9; 1 Thess. 1:10). Paul, however, uses three nouns to indicate that God delays his judgment so as to provide opportunity for repentance: *paresis*, "overlooking" (Rom. 3:25), implies that for a time God ignores and thus passes over sins; *anochē*, "forebearance" (2:4; 3:25), points to God's tolerance of Israel's blindness; and *makrothymia*, "patience" (2:4; 9:22), focuses on delay of the final judgment.

God is authentic in that in his unlimited self-consciousness he knows who he is, his significance, and his distinctive purpose (1 Cor. 2:11). The apostle gives manifold testimony to the omnipotence of God. In Romans 1:20, Paul identifies God's "eternal power" (*aidios dynamis*) as one of his prominent properties. God's power is seen in his role as Creator, Governor, and Consummator of all things (Rom. 11:36; 1 Cor. 8:6), in his work of spiritual "re-creation" (2 Cor. 5:17), and in his raising of Christ from the dead (1 Cor. 6:14; 2 Cor. 13:4). To describe the power of God operative in believers, Paul brings together four descriptive nouns (Eph. 1:19; cf. 3:20): *dynamis* (power), *energeia* (powerful working), *kratos* (effective might), and *ischus* (latent strength). The only qualifier to the divine omnipotence is that God cannot act contrary to his character (2 Tim. 2:13)—in particular, he cannot lie (Titus 1:2).

Johannine Literature

John upholds the divine omniscience when he affirms that God knows all things (*oida*, John 21:17), including every person's heart (*ginōskō*, 1 John 3:20). Jesus Christ, God manifest in the flesh, knew perfectly all that could be known (John 6:15, 64; 18:4; 19:28). Wisdom, moreover, is ascribed both to God the Father (Rev. 7:12) and to the Lamb (5:12).

John's declaration "God is light; in him there is no darkness at all" (1 John 1:5) affirms that God is absolute moral purity, the antithesis of evil (cf. Rev. 15:4), and absolute truth, the antithesis of falsehood (cf. John 14:6). Isaiah's threefold ascription of holiness is directed to God by the four living creatures in Revelation 4:8. Jesus, moreover, ascribes to God righteousness, or holiness in action, by the phrase "righteous Father" (John 17:25). God is absolutely just (*dikaios*) and dependable (*alēthinos*) in all his judgments (Rev. 16:7; 19:2), indeed, in all his ways (15:3). John's trenchant statement "God is love" (*ho theos agapē estin*, 1 John 4:8, 16) affirms that in his very character and activity God is infinite, self-giving affection. The greatest love one can show is to lay down one's life for a friend (John 15:13). God has done this and more, for the Father sent his own Son to die for friend and enemy alike (1 John 4:9). It is with a sacrificial love that God loves his Son (John 3:35; 5:20), Christian believers (John 16:27; 1 John 3:1), and the entire human race (John 3:16).[52]

A leading feature of John's theology is God's hatred of evil and consequent wrath against evildoers. God is said to hate (*miseō*) the idolatry and fornication of the Nicolaitans (Rev. 2:6) and to pour out his wrath (*orgē*) on all who reject the Son (John 3:36). The predominent motif in John, however, is the awesome eschatological wrath God will mete out on the Christ-rejecting world. Thus Revelation expresses God's terrible judgment under various descriptive images, viz., the wine of God's "fury" (*thymōs*) or "wrath" (*orgē*) that sinners must drink (Rev. 14:10; 16:19), as bowls filled with God's "wrath" that must be poured out (15:7; 16:1), as the reaping of a ripe harvest with a sharp sickle (14:17–19), and finally as the winepress of the fury of wrath that God must tread (14:19; 19:15). The first of John's words for anger, *orgē* (seven times), connotes the righteous wrath that arises from deliberate reflection. The more frequent word *thymōs* (ten times) denotes an emotional rage that boils, or a "burning, blistering anger."[53] John reasons that the believer's eternal salvation (John 10:29), all God's eschatological judgments (Rev. 19:1–2; 20:11–15), and his eternal reign of justice and peace (11:17) are grounded in his "great power" (11:17) or omnipotence. A common title for God in the Apocalypse is "Lord God Almighty" (4:8; 11:17; 19:6).

Other New Testament Books

The omniscience of God is asserted by the claim that "everything is uncovered and laid bare before the eyes of him to whom we must give account" (Heb. 4:13). God's trustworthiness is seen in the fact that he is faithful (*pistos*) to his Word and promises (10:23; 11:11). God is absolutely just, for as Peter testifies, he "judges each man's work impartially" (1 Peter 1:17). With respect to the law, God determined that "every violation and disobedience received its just punishment" (*misthapodosia*, recompense or retribution, Heb. 2:2). God could not do otherwise, for he is a God of consummate holiness (Heb. 12:10; 1 Peter 1:15–16).

Yet God takes greater delight in mercy than in punishment: "Mercy triumphs over judgment!" (James 2:13). God's heart overflows with mercy (*eleos*, Heb. 4:16; 1 Peter 1:3), compassion (*oiktirmos*, James 5:11), and love (*agapē*, Heb. 12:6; Jude 1, 21). But should the recipients of his grace prove disobedient, God brings forth anger and wrath as an inexorable law of retribution (Heb. 3:7–11). Still, God is patient, or long-suffering (*makrothymia*, 1 Peter 3:20; cf. 2 Peter 3:9), to the end that sinners might be saved (2 Peter 3:15). His omnipotence in this section is seen chiefly in terms of his ability to equip believers with every resource for holy living (2 Peter 1:3) and to bring saints to their heavenly destination (Jude 24). Since God's power is conditioned by his

holiness, he cannot be tempted by evil (James 1:13) or lie (Heb. 6:18).

SYSTEMATIC FORMULATION

The logical organization of the historically and biblically derived thought about God's many-splendored character began in chapter 5 and continues here. For a comprehensive concept of God, both chapters must be considered together.[54] With these must be integrated chapter 7 on the Trinity.

Intellectually, God Is Omniscient, Faithful, and Wise

God differs from other spirits, not only in being, but also in knowledge. Transcendent to all else, God's intellectual capacities are unlimited by space, time, energy, laws, things, or persons. Hence, God's knowledge is *omniscient*. Immediately, consciously, and comprehensively God is aware of all eternal, changeless reality (himself, his attributes, and his purposes, as well as the decisions and acts executing them) and all of the temporal reality that ever was, is, or will be.

God knows all of nature's energy-matter, laws, animals, and finite spirits. God also knows living people. He knows not only their physical characteristics, but also their inner thoughts, struggles, motives, volitional decisions, and expressions of those determinations in words, acts, events, and happenings. God knows all things (Ps. 139:2–10; John 21:17; 1 John 3:20).

God knows the free wills he purposed to create, sustain, and utilize preceptively or permissively. He knows all the logical, mathematical, moral, spiritual, and empirical possibilities humans face. God also knows the alternative(s) people choose from among these possibilities and the extent to which they can, since the Fall, achieve their chosen goals. God also knows the future of human beings in a way that does not destroy their freedom or responsibility. From different theological perspectives (Arminian and process) it is argued that if God knows the future there can be no human freedom. However, for God to know what a person will choose to do, and the extent to which since the Fall he will be able to achieve it, is not for God to do it in the person's place. God knows what he himself is going to choose and do independently of human agency and what he will accomplish through human self-determination. God's precognition of evil choices by his creatures is not equivalent to God's predetermination of evil.

How can God know the future and not render our involvement in day-to-day experience pointless? An illustration adapted from Augustine may help. Suppose you have memorized the Shepherd Psalm and are going to listen to a member of your Bible study quote it. You know the entirety of Psalm 23 from the beginning to end. But that prior knowledge does not render meaningless the experiential knowledge of quoting it audibly for your family devotions. When you or a student in your class has quoted the first half of the Shepherd Psalm, you can distinguish what part of it is past and what remains to be quoted.[55] In a far greater way the God who is unlimited by time knows the future in its entirety, as we know the whole Psalm simultaneously. The Creator and Sustainer of time also knows what part of history is past and what is future in any time zone on earth at any given date and time.

When we are confronted with the fulfillments of detailed predictions far in advance consistent with God's purposes, we confront signs of the transcendent knowledge of divine omniscience. The prophet Isaiah dramatically pointed up a decisive difference between the God of the Bible and idols: the Lord's ability to predict the future (Isa. 44:7–8, 25–28). Although the idols could not hear or speak anything, God's prophetic spokesman predicted specific details involving many human decisions far in advance concerning Jerusalem, Judah, Cyrus, and the temple.

God is not only all-knowing; he is also intellectually *faithful and true*. Throughout Scripture, knowledge and faithfulness are inseparable. Unless knowledge learned from others comes from people with intellectual honesty, we may be deceived or mistaken in what we think we know. Because God is faithful and true (Rev. 19:11), his judgments (Rev. 19:2) and his words in human language are faithful and true (Rev. 21:5; 22:6). In God's person there is no lack of fidelity, thought, or promise. God is not hypocritical or inconsistent. Descartes's hypothesis that God may be a great deceiver does not fit the biblical facts.[56]

We may hold unswervingly to our hope because he who promised is faithful (Heb. 10:23). He is faithful to forgive our sins (1 John 1:9), sanctify believers until the return of Christ (1 Thess. 5:23–24), strengthen and protect from the evil one (2 Thess. 3:3), and not let us be tempted beyond what we can bear (1 Cor. 10:13). Even if we are faithless, he remains faithful, for he cannot disown himself (2 Tim. 2:13).

Long before God's promises were inscripturated, not one word of any of the good promises he gave through Moses failed (1 Kings 8:56). Isaiah praised the name of God, for in perfect faithfulness God did marvelous things planned long ago (Isa. 25:1). Passages like these convey a basic divine integrity not only in character, but also in thought. No hypocritical contrast can be drawn between what God is in himself and what God has revealed of himself in relation to those who trust his spoken or written Word. God does not contradict his promises in his personal relationships, works, or communications.

Teachings from this God are faithful or consistent, not irresolvably dialectical or paradoxical. The wisdom that comes from the God who is faithful takes everything into account coherently and is not limited to a paradoxical tension or mere complementarity. The interpretations taken from the faithful words of revelation may be contradictory, dialectical, paradoxical, or merely complementary in the minds of theologians. But our psychological tensions ought not be ascribed to God or his revelation as given.

Intellectually, furthermore, God is *wise*. A wise person is more than a walking encyclopedia of facts; a wise person knows how to use knowledge for worthy ends and purposes. Wisdom includes knowledge (*scientia*), but features ability to use eternal truths in abundant living and effective serving (*sapientia*). Knowledge is indispensable to wisdom, and research is indispensable to insight and intuition. Knowing all the relevant data on any subject and all the possible courses of action, God discerningly selects ends—as well as strategies and methods for achieving them—that are consistent with his purposes of holy love. Prudently God not only chooses the right ends, but also does so for the right reasons—his glory in the good of his creatures.

None of God's counsels, decrees, or predeterminations are arbitrary. In wisdom, God thinks, decides, speaks, relates, and acts in ways supportive, rather than counterproductive of his changeless character. God's activities in space, time, and human history are not unprincipled, chaotic, or helter-skelter. In the cosmos, God's program for the world is wisely devised and administered both creatively and redemptively.

Because God does not act arbitrarily, we can put our trust in his justice and love in all of his purposes, strategies, and methods. Although we may not at any given time in our lives be able to see how God is wisely working things together for good (Rom. 8:28), we have sufficient reason to trust in the depth of the wisdom of the only God (Rom. 11:33; 16:27).

Ethically, God Is Holy, Just, Merciful, and Loving

God transcends his creatures, not only metaphysically and epistemologically, but also morally. The Most High is morally spotless in character and action. In essence God is upright, pure and untainted with evil desires, motives, thoughts, words, or acts. God is eternally and unchangeably *holy*. God is holy in a preethical sense, in himself the exalted source and support who is distinct from or transcendent to all that is. Consciousness of the Most High ideally results in a sense of ultimate dependence on him and obligation to him, an awesome worship of him as the Almighty, and praise to him as the Creator.

However, consciousness of God's ontological greatness quickly leads into consciousness of God's absolute moral uprightness. Free from all evil, God loves only the good and right. He values inner authenticity and takes no pleasure in hypocrisy—religious or nonreligious. God takes no pleasure in evil (Ps. 5:4) and cannot tolerate evil (Hab. 1:13). He cannot even encourage sin in any way (James 1:13–14). Desiring transparent authenticity, God hates hypocrisy. Who, then, can stand in judgment before the Holy One who knows everything?

While standing in awe of such metaphysical and moral holiness, Christians are not in awe of "The Holy" as a totally other abstraction, but of "the Holy One" who speaks to the prophets (Isa. 40:25). The Holy One is not merely an object of emotional fascination but also of intellectual understanding (in part) and volitional obedience.

With mind, will, and emotions enhanced by the Holy Spirit, people who are conscious of the presence of God may experience variously an awe, dread, fear, utter unworthiness, and unacceptability. Isaiah heard the angels crying, "Holy, holy, holy is the LORD Almighty; the whole earth is full of his glory," and he saw a vision of the Lord exalted in the temple. "Woe to me!" cried Isaiah. "I am ruined! For I am a man of unclean lips, and I live among a people of unclean lips, and my eyes have seen the King, the LORD Almighty" (Isa. 6:1–5). Nothing contradictory to holiness can be acceptable to the One of nonnegotiable moral standards.

Not solely a product of God's will, holiness is a changeless characteristic of his eternal nature. In this light, Plato's famous question needs to be reworded. Assuming a world of absolute ideas or principles independent of God, Socrates asked, Is the good good because God wills it? Or does God will it because it is good?[57]

In the context of biblical revelation, we must add a third question: "Is the good good because the very essence of God is good?" The good is not a product of an arbitrary decision of a mere will sporting about in a vacuum. Neither is it good because God's will happens to yield to an alleged higher set of (Platonic) principles to which the Creator of all is subservient. Rather, the good is good because it is consistent with God's very nature. God's self-determinations always express who he is. He cannot deny himself. God wills the good and holiness because he is good and holy. God is always displeased with evil and unholiness because in his very essence he is awesomely separate from all the evil and unholy.

In addition to being morally holy, God is morally *just* and *righteous*. Jesus addressed God as "Righteous Father" (John 17:25). So when Jesus suffered, he made no threats. "Instead, he entrusted himself to him who judges justly" (1 Peter 2:23; cf. Rev. 16:5–7). God's upright character is expressed in his moral law and in judgment according to it without respect of persons. For Christians, righteous conduct is in accord not simply with the standards of a community but, beyond that, with the standards of God. Conformity to a standard implies more than a social obligation; it involves conformity to divine authority expressed in Scripture.[58]

Divine judgment is never arbitrary or capricious, but principled and fair. As absolutely honest and just, God declares people to be what they are, sinners. Justice, in matters of merit, judges that morally responsible people should receive exactly what they deserve. Biblical writers frequently protest the injustice experienced by the poor, widows, orphans, strangers, and the godly. Although people often blame God for these circumstances, God pities the poor (Ps. 72:12, 14), and he answers, revives, and acquits them and grants them justice. In righteousness God delivers the needy from persecution and will create a new heaven and earth in which righteousness will dwell (Isa. 65:17).

Since fallen people suppress God's revealed truth and hold it down in unrighteousness, on standards of sheer merit they deserve God's wrath (Rom. 1:18–32). But a perfect righteousness from God has been revealed in the gospel, a righteousness "by faith from first to last" (Rom. 1:17; 3:21). Those who, like Abraham, are fully persuaded that God can do what he has promised (Rom. 4:21), find their faith credited to them for righteousness on the ground of Christ's atonement (Rom. 4:3, 24). The righteous One satisfies justice through mercy, grace, and love.

As *merciful*, God withholds deserved judgment. The "LORD your God is a merciful God" (Deut. 4:31). Daniel exclaims, "The Lord our God is merciful and forgiving, even though we have rebelled against him" (Dan. 9:9). Paul praises the Father of compassion (mercies) and the God of all comfort (2 Cor. 1:3). As *gracious*, God freely gives undeserved benefits to those he chooses. God is "a gracious and merciful God" (Neh. 9:31). "The LORD your God is gracious and compassionate. He will not turn his face from you if you return to him" (2 Chron. 30:9).

God is not only merciful and gracious but also *loving*, with *agapē* love. Frequently people ask, "What was lacking in God's being that made it necessary for him to create?" God "is not served by human hands, as if he needed anything, because he himself gives all men life and breath and everything else" (Acts 17:25). God created, not out of self-seeking love (*eros*), but out of self-giving love (*agapē*). He desired to give of himself for the well-being of those loved, however unlovely and undeserving they might become. God cares and loves because God *is* love (1 John 4:8).

God's great love is likened to that of a father for a son and a mother toward an unweaned baby (Isa. 49:15; 66:13). Out of love God chose Israel (Deut. 7:7) and all the elect (Eph. 1:4). And out of love for the lost world, God gave his only Son (John 3:16). In love God cares for the aged, the oppressed, the poor, orphans, widows, and the ill. God is not unmoved by people in need; he is not impassible. The God of Abraham, Ruth, Job, Jesus, Peter, and Paul suffered!

In empathy God enters into the feelings of his creatures. Beyond that, through participation God incarnate entered into our temptations and sufferings. H. Wheeler Robinson has said, "The only way in which moral evil can enter into the consciousness of the morally good [*sic*] is as suffering."[59] In all Israel's afflictions, God was afflicted (Isa. 63:9). What meaning can there be, Robinson asks, in a love that is not costly to the lover?[60] The God of the Bible is far from apathetic in regard to the vast suffering of people in the world. In love God sent his Son to die so that ultimately suffering may be done away with and righteousness may cover the earth as the waters cover the seas.

Although love involves emotions, it is not here classed primarily as an emotional characteristic of God, because it involves commitment of the whole person, initiated in the will. Love is a settled purpose of will involving the whole person in seeking the well-being of others. As the greatest commandment indicates, love is an ethical obligation (cf. Matt. 22:37). Love will normally involve the intellect and the emotions to different degrees, but love is more than emotional feeling. Since God's love does involve emotions, it is appropriate to consider divine emotions more explicitly.

Emotionally, God Detests Evil, and Is Long-suffering and Compassionate

Passibility, Thomists argued, involves potentiality, and potentiality involves change. Unrealized potential and change in the Deity seemed to contradict their understanding of God's immutability, transcendence, self-existence, and perfection. Suffering, furthermore, seemed incompatible with perfect divine blessedness. Thus, the Thirty-nine Articles of the Church of England affirm that "God is without body, parts or passions."[61] However, that view seemed to others to convey the idea that God was devoid of an affectional nature essential to personality and *agapē* love. As early as the Bishops Conference of 1786, the word "passions" was omitted. Hence Doctrines and Disciplines of the Methodist Church (1960) stops with saying God is "without body or parts" (art. i).[62]

Which of the two hypotheses, that God is impassible and that he is passible, coherently fits the data of Scripture? Unquestionably the Scripture speaks of God as passionately involved with sinners and repentant sinners. Even though its language be taken figuratively, it illustrates a nonfigurative point. God really suffers when people sinfully destroy his creation, and God literally rejoices when one sinner repents.

Indeed, God is devoid of caprice and of passions out of control. God has no selfish anger. But this is not to say that God has no passions and no righteous anger or wrath. As a person God has emotions as well as intelligence and volition, and as an ethical personal being God experiences displeasure with unrighteousness, and he is pleased with righteousness. Concerned for the well-being of his creatures, God can only be repulsed by the injustice, unrighteousness, and corruption that destroys their health physically, emotionally, mentally, and spiritually. The Bible frequently speaks of God's righteous anger with the evil that would destroy his people and their work in the world. Righteous indignation is anger aroused, not by being overcome by emotions irrationally or selfishly, but by an altruistic concern for people who are suffering from injustice, selfishness, greed, lust, envy, jealousy, and lack of self-control in any respect. In a way such as this *God detests evil.*

Jesus, and the Scriptures in general, speak often of God's wrath at injustices such as persistent mistreatment of the poor and needy. Although the Lord is slow to anger, he will in no way leave the guilty unpunished but will pour out just judgment on them (Nah. 1:3). None can withstand his indignation when it is poured out like fire and when it shatters rocks (v. 6). Apart from understanding God's wrath against evil, it is impossible to understand the extent of divine love in the Incarnation, the extent of Jesus' suffering on the cross, the propitiatory nature of his sacrifice, or the prophetic Scriptures speaking of a future day of divine wrath, the great tribulation on the ungodly in the Book of Revelation.

Fortunately, the living God is also patient and remarkably *long-suffering.* Properly jealous for the well-being of the objects of his love, God is angry with injustice done to them, but suffers without losing heart. Being long-suffering with evildoers without condoning their sin, God graciously provides them with undeserved temporal and spiritual benefits. For example, God promised the land to Abraham, but the iniquity of the Amorites was not yet full (Gen. 15:16). Only after some four hundred years of long-suffering and restraint did God allow the Israelite armies to bring just judgment on multiplying Amorite unrighteousness. When Israel worshiped the golden calf and deserved the judgment that was meted out to other idolaters, God revealed himself at the second giving of the Law as "The LORD, the LORD, a God merciful and gracious, slow to anger, and abounding in steadfast love and faithfulness" (Exod. 34:6 RSV). The psalmist could write, "But thou, O Lord, art a God merciful and gracious, slow to anger and abounding in steadfast love and faithfulness" (Ps. 86:15 RSV). However, even the day of God's grace has an end. Eventually, without respect of persons, God's just judgment fell on Israel for its persistent evils. God's long-suffering is a remarkable virtue, but it does not exclude or contradict God's justice.

Although historically many theologians have taught the impassibility of God, the Scriptures do not hesitate to call God *compassionate.* The compassionate feel so strongly for another's sorrow or hardship that they desire to help them. Because of God's great love his people are not consumed, for his compassions for them never fail (Lam. 3:22). Even after Israel's deserved captivity, God again had compassion on them (Mic. 7:19). The God of the Bible is not an apathetic God but One who deeply cares when the sparrow falls. Jesus beautifully displayed this divine-human feeling for the hungry (Matt. 15:32), the blind (Matt. 20:34), and the sorrowing (Luke 7:13). And Jesus taught the importance of divine and human compassion in the accounts of the Good Samaritan (Luke 10:33) and the father's concern for his lost son (Luke 15:20). The divine blessedness is not unrealistic concerning the evils of the world. Deeply moved by all of the depraved conduct of humanity, the omniscient God nevertheless rejoices over many like the prodigal who return to the way of faith, life, and peace.

As incarnate, Christ felt what humans feel in all respects but did not yield to the temptations involved. As God in literal human experience, Jesus wept with those who wept. He also rejoiced with those who rejoiced. The divine-human author of our salvation, however, was made perfect or complete through suffering in this life (Heb. 2:10). Because he himself suffered, he can help those who suffer and are tempted (v. 18). The God revealed in Jesus Christ is no mere apathetic, uninvolved, impersonal principle.

As Christ's holy nature and loving purposes were unchanged by his suffering, so the living God prior to the Incarnation could experience changing emotions without affecting the immutability of his nature and purposes. God's emotions are always consistent with his holiness and love. His emotions are never out of control. Acknowledging healthy emotions in God, we are as concerned to stress that the God of the Bible experiences no unworthy emo-

tions as are those who deny them. God is changelessly just and righteous and will never go back on his word to us. The most important concerns of defenders of divine impassibility may be maintained without denying the point of a multitude of scriptural assertions to the effect that habitual sin receives divine wrath and that repentance causes rejoicing in heaven—and not only among the angels! Whether expressed in figurative language or not, the teaching of Scripture supports these principles.[63]

Volitionally, God Is Free, Authentic, and Omnipotent

Recent existentialist concerns for freedom, authenticity, and personal fulfillment should not be limited to mankind. Biblical writers seem even more concerned that God be understood to be free, authentic, and fulfilled by being able to do all that he chooses in the way he plans to do it.

God is *free*. From all eternity God is not affected by anything contrary to his purposes. Good things, as we have seen, are purposed with divine pleasure and enduement. Evil things are permitted with divine displeasure. But either way, God is self-determined. The essence of freedom is the power to determine one's self apart from external compulsion according to one's own nature and purposes. In God, freedom need not always involve a choice between contrary options. God cannot deny himself. God chooses according to his nature and has the power to pursue what he has chosen.

Given God's changeless nature and purposes, there are many things God cannot do. Although free to be himself, he cannot deny himself. Being self-existent, eternal, and unchanging, God cannot die. Being personal, God cannot be a mere projection, ideal, or impersonal principle. Being holy, God cannot take pleasure in sin. Being loving, God cannot be impatient, unkind, self-seeking, or easily angered (1 Cor. 13:4–5). Because God is love, he never fails (1 Cor. 13:8). Always God's free will exercises itself in a manner consistent with his personal, eternal, living, intellectual, ethical, emotional, volitional self. Divine freedom does not require the power of choice in these matters. Self-determination is the divine kind of freedom, the highest kind of freedom possible.

God is also *authentic*, authentically himself. The God revealed in the Christ who so unalterably opposed hypocrisy is himself no hypocrite. Earlier we emphasized God's intellectual integrity or faithfulness. Here we emphasize his integrity ethically, emotionally, and volitionally. In contrast to persons who struggle to find out who they are, God in his unlimited self-consciousness knows who he is (1 Cor. 2:11). He has a keen sense not only of his own identity but also of his unique significance and distinctive purpose. God's authenticity is displayed in the fact that his words are in harmony with his being and action. No discrepancy can be found between what God says and what he does.

If it is important for each person created by God to achieve fulfillment as a unique person and not be lost in the crowd or become depersonalized, how much more important it is that God knows himself and realizes fully his own uniqueness. As the ultimate being, God is honestly self-assertive. In reality, no one can compare with him. In calling on people to turn from idols, therefore, God in no way is asking of us anything inappropriate or out of accord with reality. In steadfastly opposing idolatry, he seeks to protect people from ultimate concerns that inevitably disillusion and disappoint. God desires our worship for our sakes, so that we will not eventually succumb to despair

as one after another of our finite gods lets us down. In asking for our exclusive ultimate allegiance, God is simply being transparently honest and authentic.

The living God is also *omnipotent*. When Mary wondered how she, a virgin, could give birth to a son, and Elizabeth wondered how she could have a child (John the Baptist) in her old age, the angel declared, "Nothing is impossible with God" (Luke 1:37). God's omnipotence means that God is able to accomplish whatever he wills (e.g., the incarnation of the Son) in the way in which he wills it (the Virgin Birth).

But as we have seen, God does not will to do anything contradictory to his nature and purposes. Deeply distressed and troubled in Gethsemane, Jesus prayed that if possible the hour of death might pass from him (Mark 14:33–35). Was it possible? " '*Abba,* Father,' he said, 'everything is possible for you.' " Jesus knew that the Father was omnipotent. But in addition, he knew that the Father would not act contrary to the redemptive purpose at the Cross. So Jesus added, "Take this cup from me. Yet not what I will, but what you will" (Mark 14:36). Omnipotence does not mean that God does everything by his own immediate power without the use of angelic or human agencies. God does not will to accomplish everything by the same strategy. Some things come to pass without the use of any other agents in creation—i.e., unconditionally (Isa. 14:24–27). But most events occur through the obedience or disobedience of people to divine precepts (2 Chron. 7:14; Luke 7:30; Rom. 1:24). In either case, God's eternal purposes for history are achieved, whether preceptively, with divine pleasure, or permissively, with divine displeasure.

Some have tried to challenge the omnipotence of God by suggesting that God could not create a boulder so heavy that he could not lift it. Or God cannot create two mountains without a valley between them. The problems here do not illustrate a lack of divine power but the contradictory character of the question. God cannot create square circles because, by definition, there can be no square circles. God can do all things, but not nothings. The difficulty with the proposed illustrations is certainly not with God but with the questions.

God has not only the power to effect all his purposes in the way he purposes them but also the authority in the entire realm of his kingdom to do as he wills. God has the right to rule all his creation. God is not a subject of another dominion; he is King, or Lord of all. And by virtue of all his other attributes, God is fit for ruling well all that he created and sustains. God is a wise, holy, and gracious sovereign. Because he is just, God does not punish any sinner more than he deserves. Because he is full of grace, God freely bestows undeserved benefits and gifts as he pleases (Ps. 135:6).

Having permitted sin, God is great enough to limit its extent and to overrule it for good. God permitted evil's most hideous outbreaking in history at Calvary and transformed it into the way of salvation (Acts 4:24–28). Though all the nations and demonic hosts should rage against him, God cannot fail to achieve his purposes in history. For any of the ungodly to go their own ways independently of God's sustaining power and rightful authority is folly. Only a fool, speaking and living by God's sustaining providence, can claim that there is no God. As Cornelius Van Til put it, atheists could not slap God in the face if he did not hold them on his lap. Whether recognized or not by his dependent creatures, God remains omnipotent.

Relationally, the Transcendent Divine Being Is Immanent Universally in Providential Activity and Immanent With His People in Redemptive Activity

God, as we have indicated, is distinct from the world metaphysically, intellectually, ethically, emotionally, and existentially. Biblical theism cannot compromise the biblically founded belief in God's transcendence in pantheistic, panentheistic, or process world views. No more can they accommodate to deism, for God is continuously active throughout the world providentially. God is not so exalted that since creation he cannot know and relate to natural law in the world of everyday experience. The study of scriptural teaching on divine providence has shown that God sustains, guides, and governs all creation. The nature Psalms reflect on God's activity in relation to every aspect of the earth, the atmosphere, vegetation, and animal life (see Ps. 104). God also preserves and governs persons in human history, he judges corrupt societies and blesses the just and the unjust with temporal benefits like the sunshine, rain, nourishment, and drink. Through God's universal providential activity the cosmos holds together and his wise purposes of common grace are achieved.

But just as persons may be present to one another in varying degrees or ways, God may be present in one way to the unjust and in a richer way to the just. You may be superficially present to a stranger on a bus, revealing little about yourself. However, you may be more significantly present with your godly mother who has prayed daily for you all your life, even though she is miles away. God is graciously present in forgiving love with the converted who by faith have been forgiven, reconciled, and redeemed by Christ's precious blood. They become God's people, and

239

he becomes their moral and spiritual Father. "For this is what the high and lofty One says—he who lives forever, whose name is holy: I live in a high and holy place, but also with him who is contrite and lowly in spirit, to revive the spirit of the lowly and to revive the heart of the contrite" (Isa. 57:15). God, who is ontologically transcendent to the world, is immanently present throughout it and related to it by his providential and redemptive activities.

APOLOGETIC INTERACTION

In the previous chapter, I defended belief in divine transcendence against idolatrous tendencies to reduce God so that he is no more than the world. In this chapter, I will defend divine immanence against unbiblical tendencies to think that God is no longer with us in significant activity here and now.

God's Transcendent Omniscience Immanently Revealed in History

Belief in transcendent divine omniscience and wisdom is of little value to mankind at present if no divine truth can be shared with human minds. Some think that God's thought is so transcendent as to be totally removed from human thought. It has become commonplace to say that God can reveal to finite and fallen human minds only himself, but not true information about himself.

Karl Barth and Rudolph Bultmann presupposed Søren Kierkegaard's teaching of infinite qualitative distinction between God and man. The claim provided an effective corrective in the minds of Barth and Bultmann against the continuity that modernism had alleged between the highest human thought and God's thought. But the view that God is totally other precluded the communication of any sound information in Scripture or elsewhere about God as he is in himself or about God's plan of redemption.

The claim that God's mind is totally removed from human minds receives additional support from Eastern mystics who deny any objective validity to conceptual thinking in reference to the eternal. Relativists from many fields also deny that any human assertions, including the Bible's, are capable of expressing the truth concerning God. Then there are the multitudes of Christian devotional writers who imagine that there is "deeper" spirituality in worshiping a God beyond doctrinal or propositional information. In these movements discursive thought (including careful exegesis and doctrinal formulation) tends to become the archenemy of mystical or spiritual experience of God.

From these perspectives people claim that human knowledge is discursive, line upon line, but God's knowledge is immediate and instantaneous without painstaking research or moving from one logical step to another. Our thought distinguishes subject from predicate in propositions (S is P), but God's mind immediately knows S and P simultaneously as SP without separating them with the verb "to be." Our theological knowledge is propositional, God's is said to be nonpropositional.

One wonders, of course, how a person can know so much about the operations of God's mind if it is totally other than ours. Leaving that consideration aside and admitting that God knows all things at once, we may be certain that his knowledge includes the step-by-step reasoning of people limited by time, their need for gathering data for research, and their use of propositions to communicate. Divine knowledge can distinguish conceptually and linguistically a subject from a predicate nominative and an intransitive verb. Even though God is not limited to temporal steps and propositional distinctions, they are not meaningless to him. He is no stranger to the human mind in time. He created and sustains it in order to communicate truth to people.

To communicate with people in time, God can ascribe appropriate qualities to a thing using one word after another without distorting the truth he knows. Whether we think of the whole of Psalm 23 simultaneously or recite it line after line does not affect the the truth in either case. Similarly, simultaneous knowledge in God's mind need be no hindrance to communication of truth to people who think concept after concept and line upon line. Simultaneous knowledge differs from propositional and discursive reasoning, but not infinitely in every respect. It is knowledge. Truth is truth for God and man, whether known immediately or arrived at discursively.

The view that God's knowledge is infinitely other than ours implies a kind of twofold truth: what is true for discursive human reasoning may be false for God, and what is false for human propositional truth may be true for God's immediate, nonconceptual knowledge. Hence, on that assumption any assertion about God in the form "God is X" is false. Then it may even be false to say that God's knowledge is immediate and simultaneous. If God's mind is "infinitely different" in every quality, those words may mean their opposite. Then God's knowledge is not immediate and simultaneous. But, in fact, truth is truth for God and man, whether arrived at immediately or discursively, whether known apart from concepts and propositions or expressed through concepts and propositions.

Truth from immediate experience of God does not contradict truth mediated by scriptural revelation. Assertions about God alleged from interpretations of mystical intuitions of God do not have a higher authority than assertions about God derived from sound interpretations of Scripture. The doctrine of double truth held that an assertion could be true in philosophy but false in theology, or true in theology and false in philosophy (which covered all other fields at that time). Such double truth was condemned in 1277 by Bishop Stephen Tempier of Paris as a denial of the law of noncontradiction for the purpose of asserting heresy.[64] Truth does not contradict truth, in philosophy (or science) and theology. No more does truth from divine revelation contradict truth from religious or mystical experience. Neither need truth in human theology, well-based in inscripturated revelation, contradict truth in the mind of God.

God's truth, in part, can be communicated without distortion to people because God created humans in his image so that he could communicate with them. Although the human mind cannot invent eternal truth, it can receive general and special revelation from the Eternal. Although the Fall has affected the human mind, it has not eradicated it. Common grace enables people to receive revelation in nature, history, and the human heart. The new birth renews the person in knowledge after the image of the Creator (Col. 3:10). This knowledge is not only of temporal things, but also of the present position and nature of the exalted Christ (1:15–20) and knowledge of God's will (1:9). With knowledge like this Christians are able to avoid the deception in merely fine-sounding arguments (2:4) and strengthen the faith they were taught in concepts and words (2:7). Thus the content of the Word of the risen and exalted Christ can inform their teaching and worship (3:16).

In these and other ways the Scriptures presuppose an informative revelation from God, verbally inspired and Spirit-illumined to minds created and renewed in the divine image for the reception of divine truth. Insofar as we have grasped the contextual meaning given by the original writers of Scripture, our biblically based assertions that God is spirit, God is holy, and God is love are true. They are true for the faith and life of Christians and churches because they are true for God as he is in himself.

Since God's omniscience is formed by all the relevant data and principles of reasoning he established in his universe, God's mind is not totally other than human minds. And our judgments are true insofar as they conform to God's by being faithful to, or coherent with, all the obtainable relevant evidence. Even though God's being is transcendent, his revealed truths are with us here and now by his activities of revelation, inspiration, and illumination. Every one of us will be judged by God's all-knowing mind for our response to his truth in our lives and ministries. God may be intellectually transcendent, but he has revealed truths that all of us are accountable to know, believe, love, and obey here and now in history.

God's Transcendent Righteousness Normative in Historical Justice

God and gurus, Hinduism tells us, are not only beyond propositional truths, but also beyond good and evil. No principles of right and wrong hold for God. All duality, including the difference between right and wrong is illusory. Hindus are taught that in reality all is one, beyond all conceptual distinctions. For the "enlightened" all opposites are either nonexistent or identical. If the Absolute is beyond good and evil and is indifferent to what people do on earth, then literally, all things are lawful. This can lead not only to "a holy indifference" to evil, as the Bhagavad-Gita may have intended, but also to a diabolical insensitivity to evil, as in the Charles Manson group. Influenced not only by drugs but also by Eastern

mysticism's monistic disparagement of propositional truth in morality, Manson could not have made a real difference between killing and the loving activities of Mother Theresa![65]

In Zen Buddhism, Alan Watts explained, "there is no good to gain and no evil to be avoided, no thoughts to be eradicated and no mind to be purified, no body to perish and no soul to be saved."[66] The view that in reality there is no distinct good and evil, that moral judgments between right and wrong are illusory, is a form of relativism.[67] Relativism pervades morality it seems, except when the qualifications of our political leaders are being examined. Reflecting the spirit of moral relativism, an advertisement for a New Age organization paradoxically declared, "It is a sin to call a person a sinner!"

In the context of relativism from the East and West, it is more important than ever to be aware of, and defend, not only God's transcendent holiness, righteousness, and justice, but also God's moral norms in all human hearts (Rom. 2:14–15) and in scriptural teaching. Good and evil are not one. They are not to be confused. "Woe to those who call evil good and good evil" (Isa. 5:20). "Let those who love the LORD hate evil" (Ps. 97:10). "Love must be sincere. Hate what is evil; cling to what is good" (Rom. 12:9). The hope of humanity rests on returning to the belief that we do know the difference between right and wrong, that it is a real difference, a difference revealed by God, a difference by which every human being will be judged. No hypothesis is more thoroughly verified by empirical experience documented in the daily news than the hypothesis that in the world there is real evil, real goodness, and a real difference between them. That difference derives from the will of the holy, righteous, and just God. The Holy One is the source and support of abiding moral values in the flux of history. And all rebellion against moral laws is ultimately against the Most High from whose nature they eternally derive.

God's Transcendent Love Immanently Active to Meet Human Need

If God is thought to be totally transcendent intellectually and morally, one wonders how he can be immanently available for personal encounters even in some nonintellectual and nonmoral sense. The exalted Lord of all is omnipresent holistically: intellectually, morally, emotionally, volitionally, existentially, and relationally. In intelligent and just love, God providentially sustains the world and redemptively atones for sin. Providentially, God in his goodness prevents evil, permits it within certain limits, accomplishes things in a fallen world otherwise impossible, and overrules it for good. Mercifully, he has not destroyed the wicked of the world. In long-suffering love, he bears with the just in spite of many failures, while they mature. While we were yet sinners, God in *agapē* love determined to send his Son to provide for our just redemption.

Often it appears that science has all the answers, that events like the Holocaust show how history has got out of hand, and that believers in God are no more involved in meeting human need than are nonbelievers. For reasons like these, William Hamilton argued in an all-night seminar on God in 1970 at the University of Colorado that God is not with us here and now. Belief in a living Lord of history has become meaningless logically and existentially. A sovereign, wise, and loving Lord of history, Hamilton concluded, "died in his times." Instead of personally experiencing in his life immanently the God of holy love, he experienced, he said, the death of such a God. We respect the honesty of a professional theologian who admits that he has not experienced God with him in wisdom, mercy, grace, and transforming power. We can sympathize with him in his concern for intellectual honesty, moral integrity, and the social relevance of the church. But his interpretation of his experience and of the church does not coherently account for all the facts.

Had Altizer and Hamilton lived at the time of the Flood, they might have concluded that God had died in their time. But God was there in righteous judgment on the incorrigibly wicked and in matchless grace for Noah and his family. Had they been pursued by King Saul as was David, the Lord's anointed, they might well have concluded that God was dead. But God was there, and in the appointed time David became king. If any of us had been present when Israel and then Judah were taken into captivity, we might have concluded that God was dead. But God was there in just judgment on evil without respect of persons and he was there in grace, sending prophet after prophet to call his people back to significant fellowship and service.

Finally, in spite of the people's rejecting prophet after prophet, God said, "I will send my Son; surely they will hear him." And Jesus Christ "came to that which was his own, but his own did not receive him" (John 1:11). After multiple rejections, false accusations, and betrayal, Jesus suffered on the Cross. If ever it seemed that God were dead, it was at Calvary. Jesus himself cried out, "My God, my God, why have you forsaken me?" (Matt. 27:46). But the Father was there in righteous wrath judging the sins of mankind and in marvelous grace transforming history's greatest miscarriage of justice into the basis for the world's salvation. In three days Christ rose from the dead in a verifiable triumph over sin, Satan, and the grave.

After the tragedies through which any of us lives personally, nationally, and internationally, it is easy to say that it no longer makes sense to believe that the Lord of all is in control. But the truth is that the eternal, self-existent, divine Being is still with us in holy love, wisdom, and power, here and now. He acts immanently in history in varied and incomprehensible ways to accomplish authentically and sovereignly his absolutely just and gracious purposes.

As we think of his presence, we cannot abstract his love from justice, or wisdom from power, or holiness from mercy. The scriptural data assure us again and again that in all of his perfections the living God is with us here and now and will be through the end of history and eternally. God did not create the world and leave it to carry on as best it could by itself (as deists say). Any philosophy or religious teaching that denies the continuous, immanent presence and activity of the transcendent Lord of all in history does not fit the facts of biblical revelation.

RELEVANCE FOR LIFE
AND MINISTRY

Because God, with all of his attributes, is present and active immanently in history, we have every reason to develop our consciousness of his presence and activity in relation to our own experience. We stand in awe of God's transcendence far beyond us; it is also significant to contemplate in awe the fact that we live and move and have our being (Acts 17:28) because of his immanent preserving and guiding activities. We are ultimately dependent on him. "He himself gives all men life and breath and everything else" (Acts 17:25). Daily, then, we do well to "practice" contemplating "the presence of God" in our own lives and responding appropriately to his immanent presence in activities all around and within us.

Contemplating God as an invisible

spiritual being, we will not expect literally to see or hear him with our physical senses. But since God is personal, we may cultivate a relationship more like our relationship to human persons than to impersonal principles or things. We are open to communication from God as mediated through the Scriptures and immediately attested in our hearts by the Holy Spirit. We enjoy fellowship or communion with God in that we who have always been part of his ontological family are now by grace through faith part of the same moral and spiritual family. We jointly participate not only in the fellowship of the redeemed family of God but also in God's purposes for the world in general and the people of God in particular. A growing appreciation of God's purposes for all humanity and for the members of the church enables us to appreciate the immanent activity of God in our lives. Although the distinct attributes be isolated from one another, it is of value to sketch briefly the import of each as we contemplate God's immanent presence and activities in our world.

The Highest Human Knowledge

Great as it is to know the universe and persons in it in many different ways, it is greater still to know the transcendent Source and Sustainer. Just as we have an exciting affinity with the minds of some people more than with the minds of others, we may develop an increasingly exciting affinity with the mind of God as disclosed in nature and in the inscripturated Word.

Knowing on biblical authority that God is *omniscient*, we may anticipate each day with the confidence that God knows the challenges we face (physically, mentally, and spiritually). Each evening we are conscious that God knows what we have done that we ought not to have done, stimulating confession and repentance. What has been done for his glory that may or may not have received human recognition God also knows. With a growing awareness that God is consistently *faithful*, whatever crises we face, we can daily and nightly confidently rely on his promises and programs. Believing that God is *wise*, however opaque the circumstances at any given time in our lives, we will not despair but trust that what God permits and appoints has a wise purpose consistent with his holy love.

How can we turn our knowledge *about* God into knowledge *of* God? "The rule for doing this is demanding but simple," said J. I. Packer. "It is that we turn each truth that we learn *about* God into matter for meditation before God, leading to prayer and praise *to* God."[68]

Life's *Summum Bonum*

Increasingly conscious of God's ethical nature, we will grow in moral discernment, love all that is good, and expend our energies for ends that please God. Aware that God is absolutely *just*, without respect of persons, we will know that we ought not even try to rationalize even momentary indulgence of fleshly desires, thoughts, words, and behavior. Daily in the presence of the uncompromising Judge we confess and forsake our sins. Increasingly conscious of God's absolute holiness and his call for us to be holy as he is holy, our ultimate concern to please him cannot be shared with another, for none is like him. When our scale of values is scrambled in the pressures of family, business, social movements, and friends, we are daily reminded that no one else, much less our fallen selves, can function as the Most High for our ultimate concern.

In a growing sense of God's *mercy* and *love* to repentant sinners, we are inwardly renewed. Because God first loved us, we respond by loving God with more of our heart, soul, strength, and mind. The chief end of forgiven and regenerated people is not only to glorify God but also to enjoy him forever. People were created not only to serve God but also for loving communion with him. We are here not only to be of influence in the world but also to love, worship, contemplate, and meditate upon God.

What God desires from us more than anything else is our love (Matt. 22:37–38). To enjoy a loving communion with God is the supreme good of every person in time and eternity. Our hearts indeed are restless until they find their fulfillment in God. The unsatisfied, homesick heart will not be satisfied without giving priority to loving God. As John Burnaby summarized this perceptive thought of Saint Augustine: "To be joined to God is the supreme good for man, because there is no human goodness that is not fruit of the marriage between the human spirit and the divine. And Charity, the love of God, is the power that cements and consummates the union."[69]

No competition need be imagined between fulfilling the first and the second greatest commandments, between loving contemplation of God and loving service to needy neighbors. Carrying through the analogy of the highest human love to love of God (common to the Song of Solomon and Christian mystics), Bernard combined the contemplative life with energetic practical activities. The voice of the Beloved says, "Arise and hasten . . . "—that is, to work for the good of others. "It is the sign of contemplation's truth and purity that the spirit which has been enkindled by the divine flame be filled ever and again with zeal to win for God others to love him in like manner."[70]

The Peak Affective Experience

Moved by daily meditation upon God's emotional characteristics, we increasingly seek by the enablement of the Holy Spirit to control our own emotional patterns so that they become more like his. Like the God in whose presence we feel, as well as think and act, we will not cultivate Stoic apathy or Buddhist indifference to reality. Having acknowledged the appropriately intense emotions of God, we should not be shocked when Christians are deeply moved in face of gross sin and repentance from it. C. S. Lewis declared that he gave up atheism because it was too boring!

Those who would be like God increasingly *detest evil*. In the face of social injustice to the poor and powerless, the godly hate oppression, discrimination, selfishness, greed, covetousness, and all the contributing evils. For those who are living consciously in the presence of the Holy One, the sin that is a stench in his nostrils should become as repulsive in their own.

Although hating sin, the devout, like God, will develop an attitude that is *long-suffering* with the sinner. We must be long-suffering with people (relatives, neighbors, fellow students, and co-workers) who are unjust, unkind, unloving, and undeserving because we want them to be long-suffering with us. But far beyond that, God is long-suffering with them and us! With a growing consciousness of God's omnipresence, we develop not only similar intellectual and ethical responses, but also similar emotional responses to God's.

Maturing Christians in a fallen world become more *compassionate*. In the presence of God and the afflicted, they, like their God, are afflicted (see Isa. 63:9). Christians living in the presence of God not only rejoice with those who rejoice but also weep with those who weep. With empathy they enter into others' sufferings and sorrows, bearing others' burdens.

The Ultimate Commitment

Existentially, as they continuously contemplate God's freedom, maturing Christians grow in a responsible and rewarding sense of being *free* by God's grace. They celebrate their liberation from all lesser creatures who may become tyrants by demanding the ultimate allegiance deserved only by God. Delivered by a higher loyalty from the loyalties that enslave, they are free to determine themselves without compulsion or duress. Under the work of God's Spirit they are enabled to accomplish what of their fleshly selves they could not do. Daily commitment to the God of grace frees us to develop the capacity for self-determination according to our new spiritual natures, not ultimately for the sake of pride or privilege but for the glory of God. Not making our own happiness our ultimate concern, we find joy as a by-product.

The freedom of determining one's self need not be sheer rebellion against conformity to the world's mold. It can, with consciousness of never being ultimately alone in the universe, become affirmatively authentic. The Christian, consciously in step with the Holy Spirit, can increasingly avoid hypocrisy and be authentically himself or herself as created, regenerated, and sanctified. The new person, though far from perfect, can become increasingly candid and transparent in relation to God, herself, relatives, neighbors, and church members. People who might otherwise be intimidating do not threaten us when we come from conscious awareness of a higher presence.

Contemplating God's omnipotence takes a huge load off our shoulders, delivering us from unrealistic notions of what we ourselves are responsible for and so freeing us to fulfill more realistic expectations. Living in the presence of the Almighty helps us not to waste energy, and so there will be more power to use for wise purposes. The universe and the church belong to God, not to us. It is God, not any one person on earth at any given time, who bears the ultimate responsibility for God's work in the world and in the church. Young people who have dedicated themselves to the Lord to change not only the church but also the world need high, but not unrealistically high ideals. Each one is but an instrument—one of many persons God has chosen to use in reaching the world and reviving the church. The recognition that it is God, not ourselves, who is omnipotent frees us from the despair of failing to attain unattainable objectives. Freed from these unnecessary frustrations about the future of humanity and of the church, God's servants do not waste energy on futile anxieties. They then discover greater strength in the use of their gifts for the fulfillment of their distinctive purposes in the world and the church.

The Greatest Relationship You Can Enjoy

Relationally, as we meditate on the presence of the transcendent God with all people in providential ways and with the church in redemptive ways, we know that no greater relationship can be enjoyed than with our awesome Creator and Redeemer.

As human beings made in God's image, we have a capacity for consciously transcending ourselves and relating meaningfully to our neighbors (everyone we come in responsible contact with). We have special relationships with colleagues or fellow workers. We may enjoy even deeper relationships with friends. Then there are those intimate family relationships of children, parents, husbands, and wives. As fellow servants of the Lord in a church, we share still deeper spiritual commitments than with unsaved members of our families. But beyond all these is the greatest human relationship of all—an abiding, loving communion with the Lord himself. We can, by grace, transcend our selfish interests and desires and develop a more settled determination to love above all the One who will never leave nor forsake us. And by grace most of us can begin a more vital, personal relationship with God than we have previously cultivated, right where we are, right at this moment.

What, or who, is your ultimate concern? On what or on whom do you place the highest value of all? What is the dominant love, the supreme love of your life?

REVIEW QUESTIONS

To Help Relate and Apply Each Section in This Chapter

1. *Briefly state the classical problem* this chapter addresses and indicate reasons why genuine inquiry into it is important for your world view and your existence personally and socially.

2. *Objectively summarize the influential answers* given to this problem in history as hypotheses to be tested. Be able to compare and contrast their real similarities and differences (not merely verbal similarities or differences).

3. *Highlight the primary biblical evidence* on which to decide among views—evidence found in the relevant teachings of the major divisions of Scripture—and decide for yourself which historical hypothesis (or synthesis of historical views) provides the most consistent and adequate account of the primary biblical data.

4. *Formulate in your own words your doctrinal conviction* in a logically consistent and adequate way, organizing

your conclusions in ways you can explain clearly, support biblically, and communicate effectively to your spouse, children, friends, Bible class, or congregation.

5. *Defend your view* as you would to adherents of the alternative views, showing that the other views are logically less consistent and factually faced with more difficulties than your view in accounting for the givens, not only of special revelation but also of human experience in general.

6. *Explore the differences the viability of your conviction can make in your life.* Then test your understanding of the viability of your view by asking, "Can I live by it authentically (unhypocritically) in relation to God and to others in my family, church, vocation, neighborhood, city, nation, and world?"

MINISTRY PROJECTS

To Help Communicate This Doctrine in Christian Service

1. *Memorize one major verse or passage* that in its context teaches the heart of this doctrine and may serve as a text from which to preach, teach, or lead small group studies on the topic. The memorized passages from each chapter will build a body of content useful also for meditation and reference in informal discussions.

2. *Formulate the major idea of the doctrine in one sentence* based on the passage memorized. This idea should be useful as the major thesis of either a lesson for a class (junior high to adult) or a message for a church service.

3. *State the specific purpose or goal of your doctrinal lesson or message.* Your purpose should be more than informative. It should show why Christians need to accept this truth and live by it (unhypocritically). For teaching

purposes, list indicators that would show to what extent class members have grasped the truth presented.

4. *Outline your message or lesson in complete sentences.* Indicate how you would support the truth of the doctrine's central ideas and its relevance to life and service. Incorporate elements from this chapter's historical, biblical, systematic, apologetic, and practical sections selected according to the value they have for your audience.

5. *List applications of the doctrine* for communicating the difference this conviction makes in life (for sermons, lessons, small-group Bible studies, or family devotional Bible studies). Applications should make clear what the doctrine is, why one needs to know it, and how it will make differences in thinking. Then show how the difference in thought will lead to differences in values, priorities, attitudes, speech, and personal action. Consider also the doctrine's possible significance for family, church, neighborhood, city, regional, and national actions.

6. *Start a file and begin collecting illustrations* of this doctrine's central idea, the points in your outline, and your applications.

7. *Write out your own doctrinal statement on this subject in one paragraph* (in half a page or less). To work toward a comprehensive doctrinal statement, collect your formulations based on a study of each chapter of *Integrative Theology.* As your own statement of Christian doctrine grows, you will find it personally strengthening and useful when you are called on for your beliefs in general and when you apply for service with churches, mission boards, and other Christian organizations. Any who seek ordination to Christian ministry will need a comprehensive doctrinal statement that covers the broad scope of theology.

CHAPTER 7

GOD'S UNITY
INCLUDES
THREE PERSONS

God's Unity Includes Three Persons

THE PROBLEM: HOW OUGHT WE UNDERSTAND THE PLURALITY OF GOD (AS FATHER, SON, AND SPIRIT), GIVEN THE FACT THAT GOD IS ONE?

Israel was repeatedly taught, against the pervasive polytheism of her pagan neighbors, that the Lord is one. Yet in her life before God Israel became aware of one called Seed, Branch, Wisdom, Prophet, and King and of another called Spirit of God and Holy Spirit. Centuries later the church became convinced that Jesus, more than a man, was a divine person come from God, and likewise that the Holy Spirit, more than an impersonal power, was himself a divine personal agent. The problem within the community of faith is how to retain belief in the unity and uniqueness of Yahweh while doing justice to the divinity of Jesus Christ and the Holy Spirit. Both of these realities appear to be established by propositional revelation and personal experience.

The doctrine of the Trinity represents the heart of both Christian theology and the Christian life. Historically, followers of Christ have affirmed that the nature of God is such that the Atonement was made by the second person of the Trinity and salvation applied by the third person. The Trinity thus is profoundly bound up with what it means to be a Christian. Yet many influential thinkers of today question the assertion that God is multiplicity in unity. Is it true that the Trinitarian confession is a contradiction or, to put it more benignly, a paradox? In what sense is oneness ascribed to God? In what sense threeness? Can we talk about an ontological equality among members of the Trinity? What about an ordering relation? How shall we understand the longstanding conviction in the church that the Son is begotten from the Father and the Spirit proceeds from the Father (and the Son)? Moreover, how weighty are the critics' claims that the doctrine of the Trinity represents a cultural Hellenism, i.e., a metaphysical construct alien and unserviceable to the modern mind? These and other important issues will occupy our attention in the discussion to follow.

ALTERNATIVE INTERPRETATIONS IN THE CHURCH

For an issue so central and crucial to the Christian faith, the Trinity has been subjected to numerous explications.

The following views represent the main interpretations of the Trinity as it has been articulated by Christendom throughout its history.

Monarchian Formulations

Various forms of Monarchianism viewed God as an indivisible monad (i.e., Monarch) without any personal distinctions. Adoptionism or dynamic monarchism, as championed by Theodotus of Byzantium and Paul of Samosata, regarded the Logos as an impersonal power operative in the man Jesus by virtue of which he was adopted as God's Son, and it viewed the Holy Spirit equally impersonally as the grace of God in the church. Modalist Monarchianism, which claimed that the three "persons" are merely names for the several manifestations of the one God, assumed two forms. Patripassianism in the West held that the Father descended into the Virgin, was born of her, and himself suffered on the Cross. Sabellianism claimed that Father, Son, and Holy Spirit are simply designations for three different phases under which the one undivided essence operationally manifests itself. Thus it was claimed that God revealed himself as the Father in creation and the giving of the Law, as the Son in the Incarnation, and as the Holy Spirit in regeneration and sanctification. Sabellius emphatically denied that the Son and the Holy Spirit are distinct persons.

Arianism, Socinianism, and Deism

Arians in the patristic era, Socinians at the time of the Reformation, and Deists and rationalists in the seventeenth and eighteenth centuries denied multiplicity within the Godhead, while generally holding that Jesus was a man adopted by God and that the Holy Spirit was an impersonal power or influence from God. Arius, a deacon in the church at Alexandria, argued that because God is eternal, immutable, and indivisible, his essence cannot be communicated to another. Thus whatever else exists must have come into being by God's creative act. So Arius insisted that God created the Son ("Son" being merely a figure of speech) from nothing by an act of his will to be the instrument for the creation of all things. Christ, the highest mediator, neither is consubstantial nor coeternal with the Father. "The Son, begotten by the Father, created and founded before the ages, was not before he was begotten."[1] Insofar as the Holy Spirit was viewed as a quality or as an attribute of God, a strict monotheism was preserved but triunity was denied.

The conviction of the Socinians that no satisfaction is needed for the human spiritual condition prompted them to deny the Trinity and to insist that God is one both in essence and in person. "The divine essence is single only in number, and therefore there cannot be several persons in it. For a person is nothing else than intelligent, indivisible essence."[2] Failing to distinguish between "essence" and "person," the Socinians argued that if the Godhead consists of three persons, there would have to be three essences. They viewed Jesus as a man supernaturally conceived and adopted by God to serve as a moral teacher. At the completion of his mission, Jesus was elevated to heavenly power and immortality. The Spirit, likewise, was not a divine person, but only a power or influence from God. The Socinian form of Arianism thus denied the deity of the Son and the personality of the Holy Spirit.

The English deists rejected the Trinity for the reason that its mystery was said to violate the religion of nature agreeable to reason. Thomas Chubb insisted that Christ was a mere man, the Holy Spirit an enigma, and the Trinity a doctrine of a "triangular" God. German rationalists such as H. Reimarus, G. E. Lessing, and K. G. Bretschneider rejected the Trinity and the two natures of Christ. They viewed God as a loving Father, Jesus as an inspired ethical teacher, and the Spirit as the power at work in persons to effect moral development.

Hegelian Idealism

Hegel regarded the Trinity as a pictorial representation of a philosophical dialectic of process involving thesis, antithesis, and synthesis. According to Hegel, ontologically God is Spirit (*Geist*). God is also unity, i.e., the All-Containing, the Absolute, the Universal in-and-for-itself. Relationally, God is a unity-in-difference, the mediation of the moments of its own self-determination, the eternal synthesis of itself. The Trinity is the God who differentiates himself within himself, but in the process remains identical with himself. Thus God or Spirit is viewed in three forms: *Universality* (eternal being-in-and-with-itself), *Particularization* (being-for another), and *Individuality* (a return from appearance into Self)—i.e., Father, Son, and Holy Spirit, respectively. The relation between Father, Son, and Holy Spirit is merely a figurative expression. The term "Father" is referred to God as he is in himself; the One apart from creation. But just as the universal gives rise to the particular, so in theological terms the Father "begets" the Son, the Other. This is the moment of particularization, differentiation, and determination. The term "Holy Spirit" denotes the relation of the Father and the Son for which the word "love" is the fitting synonym.

Thus Hegel's Trinity is a dialectic movement wherein the thesis (Father) and the antithesis (Son) are united into the higher unity of the Spirit or Absolute Love. Hegel formulated a modern modalism—an economic, not an essential, Trinitarianism. His God is an impersonal and immanental process of Self-Realization. As such the differentiation within the Godhead only represents simultaneous moments in its continuing being, of which the Son is mere finite existence and the Spirit a mere category of expression.

Neoorthodox Theology

The neoorthodox tradition ascribes personality to the unitary essence of God and regards Father, Son, and Holy Spirit as three different modes of operation of the divine being.

For Karl Barth the central thesis of Christianity is that "God reveals himself as the Lord."[3] Moreover, the God who makes himself known through Jesus Christ is seen to be Revealer, Revelation, and Revealedness, which corresponds to Father, Son, and Holy Spirit of Scripture. Such a phenomenon, Barth argues, includes both unity and variety. The unity consists in the "numerical unity of the essence of the three 'Persons.'"[4] The variety that contributes to the "Three-in-oneness" involves, not three personalities, but three modes of being. So as to avoid the error of what he regards as tritheism, Barth ascribes personality to the undivided essence rather than to the threefold differentiation. For Barth, then, Father, Son, and Holy Spirit are "three modes of being of the *one* God subsisting in their relationships with one another."[5] Beyond that, the Trinity is an inscrutable mystery. Barth's replacement of the classical formula with "one divine subject in three different modes of being" leads us to conclude that his position is a form of idealistic modalism.[6]

Emil Brunner rejects the classical Trinitarian formula as "an aberration of theological thought."[7] Consistent with his interest in function rather than ontology, Brunner focuses on the historical revelation of the Trinity, i.e., on the one God who reveals himself to persons in the form of three operations or names—Father, Son, and Spirit. "If the name 'Father' designates the origin and content of the revelation, the Name of the 'Son' designates the historical Mediator, and the 'Holy Spirit' the present reality of this revelation."[8] Modalism enters when the Son and Spirit are viewed as mere aspects of God—the former being God's self-communication and the latter God's indwelling presence. And subordination occurs when "the three Names do not stand alongside of one another but after one another."[9] Brunner believes with Barth that a triad of three equal divine persons necessarily involves tritheism.

Roman Catholic Neoliberalism

Contemporary Roman Catholic neologists repudiate the classical ontological model as embracing an alien Greek metaphysic and follow Barth in upholding an economic Trinity. The unity of God is consistently emphasized, with plurality viewed as aspects of God's self-communication. The belief that God *is* Trinity is thus replaced by the notion that God *reveals* himself as Trinity. This restatement of the Trinity requires a new definition of the meaning of person. According to Dewart, "the different persons are different modes . . . of his self-communication."[10] Contemporary Catholic liberals seek to maintain a link with Christian tradition by formulating an economic view of the Trinity.

Karl Rahner argues that the formula "three persons in one substance" upholds a "vulgar tritheism" more dangerous than Sabellian modalism. Since, according to Rahner, there cannot be three distinct consciousnesses or centers of activity in God, one must adopt an economic approach to the Trinity. The unity of God resides in the one essence, the one cognition, the one consciousness. But since the immanent Trinity *is* the economic Trinity and vice versa, God's unity can be viewed as his one self-communication to the world. This self-communication, however, occurs in three modes. Thus Father, Son, and Spirit are said to be three self-communications of the one God vis-à-vis the world. "The Father is the incomprehensible origin and the original unity, the 'Word' his utterance into history, and the 'Spirit' the opening up of history into the immediacy of its fatherly origin and end."[11] Rahner not only avoids calling Father, Son, and Spirit "persons," but he replaces "tri-une" or "three-in-one" (*Dreieinigkeit*) with "the threefold God" (*Dreifaltigkeit*). Thus Rahner's modalism is openly manifest.

Hans Küng follows Rahner in renouncing the ontological Trinity (a Hellenistic distortion unintelligible to modern people) in favor of an economic Trinity. "The triadic formulas of the New Testament are meant to express not an 'immanent' but an 'economic' theology of the Trinity, not an inner-divine (immanent) essential Trinity in itself but a salvation-historical (economic) unity of the Father, Son, and Spirit in their encounter with us."[12] The unity Küng posits resides in the revelation event, and the diversity in the "roles" that Father, Son, and Spirit perform. What God is in himself is wholly inexplicable.

Protestant Neoliberalism

Contemporary Protestant liberals have generally abandoned the ontological Trinity, believing that there are no personal distinctions within the reality or being of God. The most that can be affirmed is that the Trinity sums up the threefold way in which God is known in personal experience. Suspicious of the traditional metaphysical postulates about God's inner being and relations, W. A. Brown affirms of the Trinity: "It is not a doctrine about God as He is in Himself, but concerning God as revealed. It is a summary of the different ways in which one may know God in experience."[13] Thus God discloses himself in "three aspects"—namely, as the Absolute or ultimate source of life; as the self-revealing one disclosed in nature, history, and Christ; and as the self-imparting one or indwelling Presence. Brown readily admits that his is a "Trinity of consciousness."[14] In a similar vein, Fosdick contemplated only a Trinity of experience, the substance of which is "the grace of the Lord Jesus Christ, the love of God, and the fellowship of the Holy Spirit."[15]

Process theology likewise derives its "Trinity" from the threefold experience persons have of the living God. First there is the experience of God as Creative Source, which provides each entity with its initial aim or intentional purpose. This is said to be God the Father. Second, there is the experience of God as Self-Expressive Act, which provides a person with the pattern by which to realize one's initial aim. This is God the Son. According to Pittenger, Jesus is the "visible human expression of the divine intention. He is the self-expression of the divine purpose for the human race."[16] And third, there is the experience of God as Responsive Movement, which is the power of love eliciting the response of obedience and worship. This is said to be the Holy Spirit.[17] The "Trinity" of process theology thus involves not three persons but one threefold activity. "Process theology is not interested in formulating distinctions within God for the sake of conforming with traditional Trinitarian notions."[18]

Orthodox and Evangelical Theology

The historic Christian church from earliest times—including most Fathers, medieval theologians, Reformers, and Evangelicals—maintains that God is a unitary essence consisting of three co-equal persons—Father, Son, and Holy Spirit. Although ontologically equal, the three persons evince a subordination in economy or modes of operation. Moreover, the Father is unbegotten, the Son was begotten from the eternal essence of the Father, and the Spirit proceeds from the Father and the Son (West) or the Father alone (East).

Early in the second century the *Letter of Barnabas* affirmed a Trinity comprised of God the Father, Christ the preexistent Lord and Judge, and the Holy Spirit who prepares hearts for salvation.[19] The Trinitarian formula preserved in *The Didache* 7.1 indicates that belief in the triune God was assumed by much of the second-century Christian community. Theophilus first used the term "Trinity" (*trias*) to connote within the Godhead the reality of "Father," "Logos," and "Wisdom" (i.e., the Spirit) without fully explicating the relation between the persons.[20] Irenaeus, against the Gnostics, argued that the one Creator and Redeemer God subsists as Father, Son, and Spirit. More clearly than any previous authority, Irenaeus affirmed the eternal preexistence and divinity of the Word[21] (who was eternally generated from the Father) and the Spirit.[22] Irenaeus spoke plainly of the essential Trinity and the functions each person performs in the administration of salvation.[23]

Tertullian, in his complete discussion of the Trinity, claimed that although God is one by unity of substance (*substantia*), the Father, Son, and Spirit are distinct divine persons (*personae*).[24] The first church father to employ the Latin word *trinitas*, Tertullian explained the differences between the persons in terms of their functions in the out-working of salvation.

The church at Nicea (325) and Constantinople (381) countered the Arian

255

theology by upholding the Son's proper coeternity and consubstantiality with the Father. Christ was not created but was begotten by a timeless generation from the substance of the Father. The Council completed its Trinitarian confession by acknowledging the analogous reality of the Holy Spirit. The heart of the Nicene Creed of 381 reads:

> We believe in one God, the Father almighty . . . ; and in one Lord Jesus Christ, the only-begotten Son of God, begotten from the Father before all ages, light from light, true God from true God, begotten not made, of one substance [*homoousios*] with the Father. . . . And in the Holy Spirit, the Lord and life-giver, who proceeds from the Father. Together with the Father and the Son he is worshipped and glorified.

Athanasius insisted that only the triune God is capable of saving from the consequences of sin. Thus, as a matter of salvation, he upheld one divine being who is at once Father, Son, and Holy Spirit. Against Arius he affirmed the strict consubstantiality of the Father and the Son: "He and the Father are one . . . in the identity of the one Godhead."[25] By an inscrutable process the Word was generated eternally from the essence of God. Athanasius went beyond Nicea's simple statement of faith in the Holy Spirit to affirm that the Holy Spirit is fully eternal and in essence divine: he "is one with the Son as the Son is one with the Father."[26] Whereas the Word is begotten, the Spirit proceeds from the Father through the Son.

Basil, Gregory of Nazianzus, and Gregory of Nyssa made lasting contributions to Trinitarian theology. The Cappadocian theologians, perhaps concerned that the three *hypostaseis* might dissolve into the Platonically defined *ousia,* followed Origen in emphasizing the three distinct persons within the Godhead and the primacy of the Father.

Their Trinitarian formula was: "one divine *ousia* in three distinct *hypostaseis*." By *ousia* they meant one invisible, divine nature, and by *hypostasis* they meant mode of being or personal center with independent existence and unique characteristics. The Cappadocians distinguished the three persons (1) by their mutual relations—the Father is unbegotten, the Son begotten, and the Spirit spirated—and (2) by their activities—the Father is the source, the Son the agent, and the Spirit the consummation of all things. Gregory of Nyssa in his essay *On Not Three Gods* refuted the charge that if Peter, James, and John are one human nature but three men, then the Father, Son, and Spirit as one divine nature must be three Gods.

Augustine, in his essay *The Trinity,* began with the single divine essence and thereafter sought to comprehend how the three persons share in the one nature without dividing it. The Trinity consists of the one essence (*essentia*) that includes three distinct subsistences or persons (*personae*).[27] In fact, given his commitment to the Neo-Platonic doctrine of God's simplicity (where the One lacks all distinctions), Augustine seems to hold not merely that the divine essence includes three persons, but also that each of these persons is actually identical to the divine essence. Thus the distinction between persons is not substantial, but only relational; i.e., paternity (the Father begets), filiation (the Son is begotten), and gift (the Spirit proceeds). For Augustine, oneness of essence implies equality of perfections, unity of will, and oneness of operations. The three persons "are infinite in themselves. And so each is in each, all are in each, each is in all, all are in all, and all are one."[28] The Son is eternally begotten from the substance of the Father, whereas the Spirit proceeds eternally from the Father and the Son (*filioque*), although principally from the Father.[29]

Augustine suggested that the Spirit's procession differs from the Son's begetting: the Spirit "came forth, not as one born, but as one given."[30]

Greek theology viewed the Trinity from the standpoint of the Father as the beginning and source of the Godhead. Thus the Son was begotten and the Spirit proceeds from the person of the Father. This was the position of Athanasius, the Cappadocians, the Niceno-Constantinopolitan Creed, and John of Damascus. In the West, on the other hand, where persons were viewed as relations, the Trinity was derived from the being of the Godhead. Hence the Spirit was said to proceed from both the Father and the Son (*filioque*). The *filioque* was expressly affirmed by Hilary, Augustine, and the Athanasian Creed, and it became a major factor in the eleventh-century schism between East and West.

Calvin welcomed the early-church doctrine of the Trinity; namely, that within the unity of the unbegotten essence there exist three distinct persons or hypostases. Each of these subsistences, while related to the others by a common essence, is distinguished by its own peculiar properties, as follows: "To the Father is attributed the beginning of activity, and the fountain and wellspring of all things; to the Son, wisdom, counsel, and the ordered disposition of all things; but to the Spirit is assigned the power and efficacy of that activity."[31] Such differentiation of persons involves an economic ordering that is properly eternal: "The Father is thought of as first, then from him the Son, and finally from both the Spirit."[32] Calvin further elaborates the relation between the one God and the three persons as follows:

Under the name of God is understood a single, simple essence, in which we comprehend three persons, or hypostases. Therefore, whenever the name of God is mentioned without particularization, there are designated no less the Son and the Spirit than the Father; but where the Son is joined to the Father, then the relation of the two enters in; and so we distinguish among the persons. But because the peculiar qualities in the persons carry an order within them, e.g., in the Father is the beginning and the source, so often as mention is made of the Father and the Son together, or the Spirit, the name of *God* is peculiarly applied to the Father.[33]

The Protestant Confessions articulate the consensus of the church concerning God's Trinitarian being. The reader is directed to Art. 1 of the Lutheran Augsburg Confession (1530), Art. XII of The Epitome of the Formula of Concord (1577), Art. I of The Anglican Thirty-Nine Articles (1563), Art. III of the Reformed Second Helvetic Confession (1566), and chapter 2 of The Westminster Confession (1646). The heart of the latter statement reads: "In the unity of the Godhead there are three persons, of one substance, power, and eternity: God the Father, God the Son, and God the Holy Ghost. The Father is of none, neither begotten nor proceeding; the Son is eternally begotten of the Father; the Holy Ghost eternally proceeding from the Father and the Son."

Recent evangelical theology reflects the received doctrine of the Trinity in its Western form. So L. Berkhof,[34] Henry C. Thiessen,[35] and Millard J. Erickson.[36]

THE BIBLICAL TEACHING

To determine which historical interpretation is preferred, we now turn to the primary data of Scripture.

Pentateuch

The fundamental datum of Old Testament theology is the uniqueness and unity of Israel's God. Contrary to the polytheism of Israel's neighbors, Yahweh alone is the true and living God. Thus in the *Shema* Moses declared, "Hear, O Israel: The Lord our God, the LORD is one" (*'eḥād,* Deut. 6:4). If this text focuses primarily on the uniqueness of Yahweh and the obligation to worship him alone, the unity of God follows from that (cf. Exod. 26:6, 11; 36:13, where *'eḥād,* is rendered "a unit"). So Vriezen argues, "The unity and the uniqueness are . . . quite clearly related. The unity indicates that God is not divided. His uniqueness means that Yahweh alone is God."[37] Vriezen correctly urges that God's unity not be sacrificed to his uniqueness. Whereas texts such as Deuteronomy 4:35, 39; 32:39 emphasize God's uniqueness, Numbers 6:27 stresses God's unity, for his "name" (which connotes his person) is single in number.

On the other hand, the Old Testament emphasis on the unity of God's being is supplemented by a certain multiplicity suggesting distinct centers of consciousness. Thus (1) plural pronouns are used to describe the actions of the Godhead (Gen. 1:26; 3:22; 11:7). It is unlikely that the "us" in Genesis 1:26 refers to God and angels, since man alone was created in God's image (Gen. 1:27). The fact that plural pronouns were not used elsewhere in reference to God may suggest that God is calling the reader's attention to something unusual. Moreover, given the fact that the rest of Scripture depicts three persons working together in the *opera ad extra* (Ps. 33:6; John 1:3; 5:17, 19; Col. 1:16), this phenomenon of plural pronouns points to a plurality of persons in the Godhead. "It would seem most acceptable to hold to the interpretation advanced by the ancient church Fathers and universally accepted by scholars of the past, that this is a reference to the Triune God. . . . What is clearly indicated here is that God, in His unity, has a certain plurality."[38]

(2) When God is the subject, the Old Testament occasionally uses plural verbs (e.g., Gen. 35:7) where a single form of the verb would be expected. In a monotheistic context Elohim ordinarily governs verbs, adjectives, and pronouns in the singular. (3) Many early Christian authorities saw in the threefold blessing and threefold repetition of the divine Name (Num. 6:24–26) an adumbration of the Trinity that later would stimulate the explicitly triune apostolic blessing of 2 Corinthians 13:14. (4) Some authorities see in the divine name Elohim a hint of the Trinity. Thus Elohim is "a term conveying both the unity of the one God and yet allowing for a plurality of persons."[39] On balance, however, it is preferable to view this plural name for God in the sense of a plural of excellence or of majesty.[40]

Multiplicity within the divine unity is further suggested by personal entities endowed with divine qualities. (1) Genesis 3:15 refers to the "offspring," or "seed" (*zᵉra'*) of Eve, who is wounded by Satan but who ultimately destroys the evil one. Whereas the seed could be viewed as the people of God collectively (Rom. 16:20), its ultimate reference is to Eve's conquering Seed, the Lord Jesus Christ (Heb. 2:14). The message of victory, moreover, represents the first announcement of the Good News (the *Protoevangelium*). (2) Deuteronomy 18:15 refers to a "prophet" (*nābî'*) like Moses whom God would raise up from the Jews to proclaim his word. The prophet to come refers in the first instance to the succession of prophets who would continue the work of Moses,[41] but ultimately to the prophetic Messiah himself, as the New Testament clearly attests (John 1:21; Acts 3:22; 7:37). (3) Jacob's blessing ("The scepter will not depart from Judah, nor a ruler's staff from between his feet, until he comes to whom it belongs and the obedience of the nations is his," Gen. 49:10) describes the messianic descendant of Judah who would rule the nations with unrivaled authority. Numbers 24:17 similarly depicts the star of Jacob, the kingly Messiah. (4) One of the most enigmatic figures in the Old Testament is the "angel of the LORD" (mal'ak Yahweh). In the Hagar account (Gen. 16:7–14) the angel of the Lord is identified as "the LORD" (v. 13) and yet is different from the Lord God (v. 11b). Abraham's three visitors (Gen. 18:1–33) are described as "three men" (v. 2; cf. vv. 16, 22), of whom the first is said to be "the LORD" (vv. 1, 10, 13, et al.) and the remaining two "angels" (Gen. 19:1). Calvin, like many other authorities, judges that "the chief of the embassy" was Christ.[42] In the account of Abraham's call to sacrifice Isaac (Gen. 22:11–18), the angel of the Lord is a messenger different from the Lord whom Abraham obeyed. According to Exodus 23:20–21, God's "Name" (i.e., the Lord in his self-manifestation) was in the angel who directed Israel's wilderness journey. The angel is endowed with authority and the power to forgive sins. In God's promise to Moses (Exod. 32:34–33:16), the angel of the Lord bears within himself God's "Presence" (33:14). On balance, it seems preferable to view the mal'ak Yahweh as a self-manifestation of the triune God in a visible form.[43] In the light of our discussion about the "seed," "prophet," and "ruler," Jesus' saying to the Jews, "Moses . . . wrote about me" (John 5:46) gains greater clarity.

In the context of a strict monotheism, Genesis 1:2 attests the creative agency of the rûah 'elohîm ("the Spirit of God was hovering over the waters"). Since rûah 'elohîm in the Old Testament consistently indicates the Spirit of God, we do well to understand it in the same sense here. Concerning this active power who prepares the cosmos for God's further creative work, Aalders writes, "There is no doubt that here, in the first verses of the Bible, there is a reference to the Holy Spirit."[44] According to Genesis 6:3, the Spirit of Yahweh is a divine personal agent distinct from the Lord: "The LORD said, 'My Spirit will not contend with man forever, for he is mortal.'" In the Pentateuch, God's Holy Spirit temporarily empowered leaders for the performance of specific tasks (Exod. 31:3; 35:31; Num. 24:2; Deut. 34:9).

Historical Books

Some suggest that a plurality of persons in the Godhead is attested by the humanlike figure who stood before Joshua and identified himself as "the commander of the LORD's army" (Josh. 5:15). The leader of God's angel host is represented not only as holy (v. 15) but as "the LORD" himself (6:2). Some authorities identify this remarkable figure as an appearance of the preexistent Son of God.[45] It seems better to conclude that the prince of the Lord's host was an angel of the Lord (see the discussion on Gen. 16:7–14 and 18:1–33, above).[46] Nathan's prophecy (2 Sam. 7:13–16) directed attention to David's greater Son who was at the same time the Son of the Father. David's dynasty would endure forever in the form of the kingdom reign of the Messiah (2 Sam. 7:16). Hebrews 1:5 attests that Nathan spoke of the second person of the Godhead.

The period of the Judges records many instances in which "the Spirit of the Lord" temporarily came upon people to inspire and empower them for special tasks (Judg. 3:10; 6:34; 11:29, et al.). The same Spirit-anointment occurred during the monarchy (1 Sam. 10:6, 10; 16:13–14; 1 Chron. 12:18). The Spirit also is seen as a divine person active in the composition of the songs of David (2 Sam. 23:2). "At most points . . . context approves and the analogy of the New Testament strongly suggests that the *rûaḥ YHWH* is the Holy Spirit in the fullest Christian sense."[47]

Poetry and Wisdom

Psalm 33:6 may well be a divinely designated intimation of the triune God: "By the word of the LORD were the heavens made, their starry host by the breath of his mouth." Given the fact that the background of verses 6–9 is the Genesis 1 creation account where the work of the Spirit of God is cited, and given the fact that throughout Scripture Christ is depicted as the unique agent of creation, the Christian understands Psalm 33:6 with many early Fathers in terms of the personal Word and Spirit.[48] If this is the case, an economic ordering of persons in the work of creation may be indicated.

The Psalms direct attention to a divine Messiah or "Anointed One" (*māšîaḥ*) who is clearly distinct from Yahweh. Psalm 2 provides a good example. Whereas Psalm 2:1–3 in its historical context describes ungodly rebellion against the Lord and the Davidic king, Acts 4:25–27 interprets these verses in terms of God's "holy servant Jesus." Moreover, whereas Psalm 2:7–9 depicts the installation and rule of the Davidic king, the verses prophetically anticipate the eschatological enthronement and sovereign rule of the messianic King. The saying in Psalm 2:7, "You are my Son; today I have become your Father," is applied by several New Testament writers to major moments in the experience of Jesus Christ: (1) his incarnation (Heb. 1:5), (2) his baptism (Matt. 3:17), (3) his transfiguration (Matt. 17:5; 2 Peter 1:17), (4) his resurrection from the dead (Acts 13:33), and (4) his ascension and session to the right hand of God (Heb. 1:5). The New Testament writers cited Psalm 2:7 to prove that God's promises

made to David (2 Sam. 7:11–16) were being brought to fruition through Jesus Christ, the divine Messiah.

Calvin observes that the statement "Your throne, O God, will last for ever and ever" (Ps. 45:6) "is sufficient of itself to establish the eternal divinity of Christ."[49] The following verse teaches that the One above him is equally "God." In Hebrews 1:8–9 it is unequivocally clear that the first person addressed as "God" is Christ, God's very Son. Psalm 72 highlights the righteousness and universality of David's kingdom. Yet the achievements of the king and his endless reign so far exceed the capability of a human ruler that the Psalm "suggests for its fulfillment no less a person than the Messiah."[50] Beyond the immediate historical situation, the words "The LORD says to my Lord: 'Sit at my right hand until I make your enemies a footstool for your feet'" (Ps. 110:1), should be viewed as an emphatic reference to the future reign of Christ, as Peter made clear in Acts 2:34–35. When Jesus inquired (Matt. 22:44–46) how Christ could be both David's son and David's Lord, he clearly identified himself with the "my Lord" (*'adônî*) of Psalm 110:1. C. S. Lewis agrees that in addition to the primary historical meaning these Psalms "contain a second or hidden meaning . . . concerned with the Incarnation, the Passion, the Resurrection, the Ascension, and with the Redemption of man."[51] The reality of the Messiah as a person coequal but distinct from Yahweh thus is embedded in many of the Psalms.

Proverbs offers a highly suggestive portrayal of wisdom. *Ḥokmāh* reproves and rebukes (1:23, 30), laughs at the calamity of his rejecters (1:30), answers prayer (1:28), exercises love (8:17), and is the source of life and favor (8:35). As indicated in the previous chapter, wisdom in Proverbs is a divine attribute personified in highly descriptive language. Later, the Holy Spirit led the apostle Paul to explicate the wisdom motif christologically (1 Cor. 1:24, 30; Col. 2:3). It is not likely that the writer himself understood *ḥokmāh* as a divine being.[52]

One catches glimpses of the Spirit in the poetic books as a divine person distinct from and sent by Yahweh. Thus, David prays that God's "Holy Spirit" (*rûaḥ qōdeš*), who is "good" (Ps. 143:10), "holy" (Ps. 51:11), and ubiquitous (Ps. 139:7), performs works appropriate to a divine person—i.e., he creates (Job 33:4; cf. Ps. 33:6), renews the earth (Ps. 104:30), guides believers (Ps. 143:10), imparts understanding (Job 32:8), and may be grievously sinned against (Ps. 106:33).

Prophetic Literature

Israel's prophets upheld the same explicit monotheism affirmed by the Pentateuch. God said through Isaiah: "I am the LORD, and there is no other; apart from me there is no God" (Isa. 45:5; cf. 44:6; 46:9). Inherent in God's uniqueness is the idea of unity of his being.

A plurality of persons within the unity of the Godhead may be intimated by the juxtaposition of singular and plural pronouns in Isaiah 6:8: "Whom shall I send? And who will go for us?" A clearer indication of the multiplicity within the Godhead is found in Isaiah 11:1-2. The text reads that "the Spirit of the LORD will rest" on One called "a Branch," thereby equipping him for messianic ministry. In a related passage the Servant-King testifies: "The Spirit [*rûaḥ*] of the Sovereign LORD [*'adōnāy Yahweh*] is on me, because the LORD has anointed me to preach good news to the poor" (Isa. 61:1). Christian faith recognizes that the Son is sent by the Father and anointed for messianic service by the Spirit. Jesus applied this text from Isaiah to his own life and ministry

(Luke 4:18-19). Also, Isaiah 42:5 contains the triad "God the LORD" (*'el Yahweh*), his elect "servant" (*'ebed*), and his anointing "Spirit" (*rûaḥ*). Isaiah 32, descriptive of the righteous kingdom of the Messiah, refers to "the LORD" (v. 6), the "king" who will reign (v. 1), and to "the Spirit" poured out from on high (v. 15).

The Servant declares in Isaiah 48:16: "And now the Sovereign LORD has sent me with his Spirit." Here *'adōnāy Yahweh* sends both his Son and his Spirit in what one authority describes as "a remarkable glimpse, from afar, of the Trinity."[53] Recounting God's faithfulness to his covenant people, Isaiah speaks of "the LORD" (Isa. 63:7), "the angel of his presence" (*mal'ak pānāyw*, v. 9), and "his Holy Spirit" (vv. 10-11).

The prophets unmistakably depict the Messiah-Son as a divine preexistent person. So Isaiah 7:14 speaks of him as "Immanuel" (i.e., "God with us"), which the New Testament pointedly applies to Jesus Christ (Matt. 1:23). The Son whom God would give (Isa. 9:6) is described in terms that imply divinity: "Wonderful Counselor," "Mighty God," and "Everlasting Father [lit., father or possessor of the ages]." The "righteous Branch," the messianic Ruler whom God would raise up from the fallen house of David (cf. Isa. 4:2; 11:1), in Jeremiah 23:6 (cf. 33:15-16) is given the divine title "The LORD Our Righteousness" (*Yahweh ṣidqēnû*). Judaism understood this as a name for the Messiah.[54] Daniel in a vision saw "one like a son of man" led into the presence of "the Ancient of Days." The former was given "authority, glory and sovereign power; all peoples, nations and men of every language worshiped him. His dominion is an everlasting dominion that will not pass away . . ." (Dan. 7:13-14). Jesus understood this passage in terms of his own person (Matt.

26:64), and "son of man" became his favorite self-designation.

Malachi 3:1 states that God will send his "messenger" to prepare the way for "the messenger of the covenant"— figures we understand from Mark 1:1–2 to be, respectively, John the Baptist and Jesus. Yet Malachi expressly identifies the messenger of the covenant to come as "the Lord" (*hā 'ādôn*)—a divine person distinct from "the LORD Almighty" (*Yahweh ṣᵉbāôt*).

We find in the prophets intimations that the Spirit of the Lord is a personal being (Zech. 7:12; Mic. 2:7), one with the Lord (Isa. 30:1; Hag. 2:5), yet distinctly separate from Yahweh (Isa. 48:16; Ezek. 43:5) and endowed with divine perfections (Isa. 11:2; Mic. 3:8). The prophetic promises that God will pour out his Spirit in the new age (Ezek. 36:25–27; Joel 2:28–32) suggest that the Holy Spirit is a divine person sent from the Father (Acts 2:17–18, 33).

Given Israel's inveterate tendency toward polytheism, the primary purpose of the Old Testament was to impress on the chosen people God's uniqueness and unity. Nevertheless a number of texts suggest that the one God of Israel was perceived to be complex in being, even though fuller explication of the Trinity would await New Testament development. Jesus' rebuke of his disciples for their failure to understand what the prophets had written concerning himself (Luke 24:25) and his explication of the Old Testament Scriptures that testify to him (v. 27) suggest that Christ was portrayed in the Bible of the Jews with some clarity.

Synoptic Gospels

Jesus upheld the Old Testament teaching on the uniqueness and unity of God. The Lord reiterated the *Shema* of Israel (Mark 12:29) and accepted the commendation of a Jewish teacher of the Law: "You are right in saying that God is one and there is no other but him" (Mark 12:32; cf. Deut. 4:35). With the advent of Christ, however, the plurality of persons within the Godhead became more evident. Thus, the angel Gabriel's announcement to Mary (Luke 1:30–35) identified three distinct persons: "the Lord God" (v. 32), "the Son of the Most High" (v. 32) or "the Son of God" (v. 35), and "the Holy Spirit" (v. 35), each of whom from the language and context is by nature divine. Yet it is also evident that the three persons are one, for so Jesus and the Holy Spirit are designated, respectively, the "Son" and "the power of the Most High" God (vv. 32, 35). The disclosure of the angel to Joseph (Matt. 1:18–23) reveals a similar triadic pattern.

Jesus' baptism by John (Matt. 3:16–17) attests the reality of the Trinity. (1) Three distinct persons are identified—"God"; "Jesus," or God's "Son"; and "the Spirit of God." (2) Three unique signs are reported— the Father's audible voice, the Son's real flesh, and the Spirit's mystical presence. (3) Three separate actions are cited—the Father's speaking from heaven, the Son's baptism in the Jordan River, and the Spirit's descent like that of a dove. These data indicate that Father, Son, and Spirit are not merely different names for one God, but are three uniquely distinct personal agents. The unity of persons is highlighted by God's identification of Jesus as "my Son, whom I love" (v. 17). Jesus did not become the Son of God at his baptism. Rather, the Spirit came upon the Son to equip him for the messianic work he was about to begin. John's reluctance to baptize Jesus (v. 14) and his admission that *he* ought to be baptized by Jesus suggests that he knew Jesus to be the Messiah. The third person in the scenario is identified as "the Spirit of God" who descended from heaven (v. 16). Fairly has it been said, "Go to the Jordan and you will see the Trinity."[55]

The narrative of the threefold temptation of Jesus by the Devil (Matt. 4:1–10)—which identifies as separate persons "the Lord . . . God" (vv. 7, 10), "Jesus" or "the Son of God" (an assumption, not an issue of doubt, vv. 3, 6), and "the Spirit" (v. 1)—provides an unmistakable allusion to the Trinity. The fact that Satan attempted to kill Jesus as an infant (Matt. 2:13) suggests that the Devil here did not assume Jesus' deity merely for the sake of argument. Jesus' words in Matthew 12:28 reflect a similar Trinitarian pattern: "If I drive out demons by the Spirit of God, then the kingdom of God has come upon you" (cf. vv. 31–32). Our Lord's Great Commission (Matt. 28:19), however, presents a deliberately conceived Trinitarian formula: ". . . baptizing them in the name of the Father, and of the Son and of the Holy Spirit." Unity of being is suggested by the one "name" (*to onoma*) into which converts were to be baptized, and plurality of persons by the three distinct subjects—"the Father," "the Son," and "the Holy Spirit." The deliberate repetition of the article in the phrase *tou patros kai tou kuriou kai tou hagiou pneumatos* is a most concise and unambiguous representation of the coequality of the three distinct persons in being, authority, and honor. It is fitting that Jesus' earthly ministry concludes with so concise a summary of the one God who subsists in three persons.

The Gospels also unfold the unique filial relation that exists between the first two persons of the Godhead. Matthew 11:25–27 makes this point in two ways: (1) Jesus testifies, "All things [i.e., viceregency over the world; cf. Matt. 28:18] have been committed to me by my Father,"[56] and (2) the Son perfectly knows (*epiginōskō*, v. 27) the latter by virtue of an intimate relationship that was experienced both before and after his incarnation. "The saying grounds Jesus' right to be the mediator of knowledge of God to men in the exclusive relationship which a son has with his father, and thus implicitly he claims a unique filial status."[57] At the Transfiguration (Matt. 17:1–8) the Father declared of Jesus: "This is my Son, whom I love; with him I am well pleased" (v. 5). The radiant transformation of Jesus into the appearance of a supernatural figure (v. 2) attests that the Son is no less divine than the Father. Whereas the radiance of Moses (Exod. 34:29, 35) was a reflected glory, Jesus' represents an effulgence from the source—i.e., from his divine person. In Matthew 22:41–45, Jesus claimed that the designation "son of David" fell far short of explicating Christ's true reality. Since "David, speaking by the Spirit, calls him 'Lord'" (v. 43, quoting Ps. 110:1), Christ must be the very Son of God. Matthew 3:3 establishes that Jesus is identical with the Yahweh of Isaiah 40:3. Finally, when asked by the high priest whether he was "the Christ, the Son of God," Jesus responded, "Yes, it is as you say" (Matt. 26:63–64; cf. the more pointed reply in Mark 14:62, "I am").[58] In other texts, Jesus Christ is denoted the unique and beloved Son of the Father (e.g., Matt. 10:32; 16:16–20; 27:40, 43). The Gospels also indicate a functional ordering between the Father, the One who sends, and Jesus, the Son who is sent (Matt. 10:40; Mark 9:37).

Primitive Christianity/Acts

The preaching of the early Christian missionaries includes the basic elements of the Trinity. In the first sermon after Pentecost (Acts 2:14–40) Peter testified that God raised Jesus from the dead and elevated him to his own right hand, thereby attesting that the Nazarene was indeed the "Holy One" (v. 27) and the "Lord and Christ"

(v. 36). "It is especially in the title 'Lord' that the primitive *kerygma* verges toward Trinitarianism."[59] Moreover, Peter's saying that the risen Christ "has received from the Father the promised Holy Spirit and has poured out what you now see and hear" (v. 33) implies not only the unity of Father, Son, and Spirit, but also an ordering principle in their operations. Stephen's speech (Acts 7:48–52) juxtaposes "the Most High" (v. 48), "the Righteous One" (v. 52) who is "the Son of Man standing at the right hand of God" (v. 56), and "the Holy Spirit" (v. 51) whose promptings the Jews have sinfully resisted. Peter's message to Cornelius speaks of "God" (Acts 10:34, 36, 38, et al.), "Jesus Christ"—the "Lord of all" (v. 36) whom God raised from the grave and appointed as judge of humankind—and "the Holy Spirit" (vv. 38, 44). Paul also acknowledged a Trinitarian faith when he said to the Ephesian elders: "I have declared to both Jews and Greeks that they must turn to God in repentance and have faith in our Lord Jesus. And now, compelled by the Spirit, I am going to Jerusalem" (Acts 20:21–22).

The purpose of the early Christian preaching was to convince Jews and Gentiles that Jesus was the promised Messiah and personal viceregent of God. Accordingly, Jesus was designated "the Lord" (Acts 18:9; 23:11), "Lord and Christ" (2:36), "Lord of all" (10:36), "the Holy and Righteous One" (3:14), "the author of life" (3:15), and "Prince and Savior" (5:31). Moreover, the risen Jesus has taken his seat at God's right hand (connoting a dignity equal to that of the Father), sends the Holy Spirit, forgives sins, and executes judgment on all. The only conclusion warranted is that Acts "assigns to Jesus a function and status equal to those of God the Father himself."[60]

Sometimes called "the Acts of the Holy Spirit," Luke's history of the early church focuses attention on the activity of the Holy Spirit, who continues the ministry of the glorified Jesus.[61] That the Spirit is a personal agent is proven by the juxtaposition of the Holy Spirit with the apostles in Acts 15:28 ("It seemed good to the Holy Spirit and to us . . ."). Moreover, the personality and divinity of the Spirit are implied in his manifold operations— i.e., the Spirit baptized the Galilean disciples so they spoke in vernacular languages (1:5, 8), imparted spiritual power for mission (4:8–13, 31; 9:31), directed Philip to Ethiopia and after that snatched Philip away to another place (8:29, 39), gave Agabus the ability to foretell the future (11:28), directed the Antiochene church to select missionaries (13:2, 4), restrained Paul and his companions from preaching in Asia (16:6–7), and appointed overseers for the churches (20:28). The deity of the Holy Spirit is explicitly affirmed in Acts 5:3–4, where lying to the Spirit is equivalent to lying to God: "Ananias, . . . you have not lied to men but to God." We have noted that an economic ordering is implied in Acts 2:33, where the Spirit of the Father was sent, or "poured out," by the Son. In addition, the third person of the Trinity is denoted "the Spirit of the Lord" (8:39) and "the Spirit of Jesus" (16:7).

Pauline Letters

One discovers in the writings of Paul, who had avidly studied the Jewish Scriptures, a firm insistence on the unity and uniqueness of God. The apostle undoubtedly had in mind the Hebrew *Shema* (Deut. 6:4) when he insisted, "There is no God but one" (1 Cor. 8:4) and "There is but one God, the Father" (v. 6).[62] Paul's emphasis on the oneness of God is also reflected in 1 Timothy 1:17 and 2:5.

The juxtaposition of three persons, with equal prominence given to each, provides the second element of the Trinity. In Romans 1:1–4, Paul testifies to "God" the Father, "his Son. . . Jesus Christ our Lord," and "the Spirit of holiness" (a Hebraism for the Holy Spirit). A deliberate Trinitarianism (that may allude to the triple name used in baptism) is found in 1 Corinthians 6:11: ". . . in the name of the Lord Jesus Christ and by the Spirit of our God." Paul's benediction in 2 Corinthians 13:14 reflects the same close association of three coequal persons: "The grace of the Lord Jesus Christ, and the love of God, and the fellowship of the Holy Spirit be with you all."[63] The Trinity is succinctly set forth in Ephesians 4:4–6: "one Spirit . . . one Lord . . . one God and Father of all, who is over all and through all and in all." This remarkable association of persons is seen also in 1 Corinthians 12:4–6: "the same Spirit . . . the same Lord . . . the same God." Titus 3:4–6 presents a triadic pattern that includes "God our Savior," "the Holy Spirit," and "Jesus Christ our Savior." Bernard comments concerning this text: "The co-operation of all three Persons of the blessed Trinity in the work of grace is tersely and pregnantly expressed."[64] The association of three distinct persons in ways consistent with their deity occurs also in Romans 8:1–4; Ephesians 1:3–14; 5:18–20; and 2 Thessalonians 2:13–14. The fact that within the Godhead the three designations occur in various orders implies their ontological equality: God—Son—Spirit (Rom. 1:1–4; Eph. 1:3–14); God—Spirit—Christ (Titus 3:4–6); Christ—God—Spirit (2 Cor. 13:14); Christ—Spirit—God (Rom. 8:1–4; 1 Cor. 6:11); and Spirit—Christ—God (1 Cor. 12:4–6; Eph. 4:4–6; 5:18–20).

Paul specifies that each of the three persons is fully God. The first person of the Trinity, when viewed in relation to Christ, is known by the name "Father" (Rom. 1:7; Eph. 1:17, et al.) Scripture repeatedly attests that, as to his intrinsic being, the Father is "God" (*theos*): so the first person is denoted "God the Father" (Gal. 1:1; Eph. 6:23; Phil. 2:11, et al.) and "the God and Father of our Lord Jesus Christ" (2 Cor. 1:3; Eph. 1:3; cf. 2 Cor. 11:31).

The apostle likewise believed that Jesus Christ is equally God. Many Fathers, Reformers, and modern authorities, together with the AV, RV, NASB, and NIV, take the phrase "who is God over all, forever praised!" (*ho ōn epi pantōn theos eulogētos eis tous aiōnas*, Rom. 9:5) to be in apposition to and, thus, in explication of the preceding "Christ" (*ho christos*). In that case, Paul argues that the Messiah, as to his human descent, came through the line of the patriarchs, but, as to his eternal being, he is sovereignly divine.[65] Philippians 2:6, which depicts Christ as "being in very nature God" (*en morphē theou hyparchōn*), clearly certifies the Lord's deity. The participle *hyparchōn*, ("stronger than . . . the usual verb 'to be,' . . . speaks of what was and is unchangeably His")[66] is concessive in force. As such, it indicates that although possessing the divine nature, Christ nevertheless became a man and assumed a temporary subordination to the Father. The parallel between *morphē theou* and *morphē doulou* (v. 7) implies that if Jesus Christ were truly a servant, then he was truly God. The following expression, "equality with God," refers to the glory and dignity Christ possessed as one coeternal with the Father. In verse 7 the act of emptying (*ekenōsen*) is defined by the following participial construction (*morphēn doulou labōn*). The verb *labōn* is a participle of means, indicating that Christ "emptied" himself *by* clothing his deity with humanity. The allusion to Isaiah 45:23 in verses 10–11, as well as the inverted subject-predicate nominative construction in verse 11 (suggesting that *kyrios* is definite—i.e., "the LORD" = Yahweh) also argue for the claim that Jesus Christ is true God.

The expression "the glorious appearing of our great God and Savior, Jesus Christ" (Titus 2:13) indicates in three ways that Christ is God: (1) The presence of one article before the two nonproper and singular nouns "great God" and "Savior" refers both nouns to the same person; (2) the New Testament speaks of the "appearing" of Christ but never of the Father; and (3) the adjective *megas* in "great God" makes better sense applied to Christ, since the greatness of God was assumed by all. Finally, Colossians 1:19 and 2:9 teach, against the Gnostic division of Deity among the aeons, that the totality of the divine essence (*theotēs*) resides in Christ. Even Thayer, an Arian, maintains that *theotēs* in Colossians 2:9 upholds Christ's deity.[67]

Texts such as Romans 8:3 and Galatians 4:4, which depict the preincarnate Christ as the Son of God (a term descriptive not of function but of nature), suggest the eternal relation the second person of the Trinity has with the Father. This consideration, plus the descriptions of Christ as "the image of God" (*eikōn*, 2 Cor. 4:4; Col. 1:15), "the radiance of God's glory" (*apaugasma*, Heb. 1:3), "the exact representation of [God's] being" (*charaktēr*, 1:3), and "the Word" through whom God reveals himself (*logos*; cf. John 1:1, 14; 1 John 1:1; Rev. 19:13) have prompted many Christian authorities to postulate the eternal generation of the Son from the essence of the Father.

Paul upholds the deity of the Holy Spirit when he states, "The Lord is the Spirit" (2 Cor. 3:17; cf. v. 18). Although some identify *kyrios* as the God of the Old Testament, it seems preferable, given the immediate context (v. 14), to hold that the apostle identifies Christ and the Spirit. That being so, "The Lord and the Spirit are 'one' in the same sense that Jesus said that He and the Father were one (John 10:30)."[68] The deity and personality of the Holy Spirit, however, are demonstrated more through his manifold activities than through specific statements about his person. Thus, the Holy Spirit mediates revelation from God (1 Cor. 2:10a; Eph. 3:5), raised Christ from the dead (Rom. 8:11), searches out the deep things of God (1 Cor. 2:10b–11) so as to interpret spiritual truths to persons (1 Cor. 2:12, 14), fills the Christian with God's love (Rom. 5:5), imparts spiritual gifts to the church (Rom. 12:6–8; 1 Cor. 12:4–11; Eph. 4:11–12), encourages believers in the struggle with the lower nature (Rom. 8:4, 9), promotes hope for the future (Gal. 5:5), and intercedes for the saints before the Father (Rom. 8:26–27).

In sum, "the New Testament thinks of the Spirit as a person, not simply a power; as 'He' not 'It'."[69] Pauline expressions such as "the Spirit who is from God" (1 Cor. 2:12), "the Spirit of God" (1 Cor. 2:14; Rom. 8:9), and "God's Spirit" (1 Cor. 3:16), appear to imply that the Holy Spirit (his person, not his essence) derives from God the Father. According to Charles Hodge, 1 Corinthians 2:10–14 teaches "the Holy Spirit as proceeding from him [i.e., God the Father] and sent by him as the instructor of men."[70] Similarly, when the apostle refers to "the Spirit of Christ" (Rom. 8:9), "the Spirit of the Lord" (2 Cor. 3:17), and "the Spirit of his Son" (Gal. 4:6), he suggests that the Holy Spirit comes forth from the Son.

Alongside the essential equality of persons there exists an economic ordering or functional subordination. Paul implies that, within the administration of the Godhead, the Father has the primacy over the Son (Rom. 8:3; 1 Cor. 15:24, 28; Phil. 2:7–8) and over the Spirit (1 Cor. 6:19; Gal. 4:6), and the Son has priority over the Spirit (Gal. 4:6). With regard to the operations of the Godhead, Father, Son, and Holy

Spirit are source, channel, and agent respectively: all things are of (*ek*) the Father who originates (1 Cor. 8:6; Eph. 2:8; 3:15), through (*dia*) the Son who mediates (Rom. 1:5; Eph. 2:13, 18), and by (*en*) the Spirit who completes the work (1 Cor. 6:11; Eph. 2:18, 22; 3:5). Texts such as 1 Corinthians 15:24, 28 (which states that, after completion of his work, Christ subjects himself to the Father that the latter "may be all in all") prove that the ordering relation is eternal and not limited to Christ's state of humiliation.

In the Pauline writings, each person of the Godhead has a dominant function attributed to him (the principle of appropriation). Thus, chiefly the Father creates (1 Cor. 8:6; 2 Cor. 4:6), the Son redeems (Eph. 1:7; Titus 3:6), and the Spirit sanctifies (Rom. 15:16; 2 Cor. 3:18; 2 Thess. 2:13). Yet by virtue of the common essence, what one divine person performs each may be said to perform (the principle of *perichorēsis*). Accordingly, the Son creates (1 Cor. 8:6; Col. 1:16) and the Spirit creates (cf. Job 33:4; Ps. 33:6); the Father redeems (2 Cor. 5:18–19; Eph. 2:4–5, 8) and the Spirit redeems (Rom. 8:4; Titus 3:5); and the Father sanctifies (Eph. 1:3–4; 1 Thess. 5:23) and the Son sanctifies (Eph. 4:15–16; 5:25–27).

Johannine Literature

The AV reading of 1 John 5:7 provides an explicit declaration of the Trinity: "There are three that bear record in heaven, the Father, the Word, and the Holy Ghost: and these three are one." However, the manuscript evidence for this reading is sufficiently weak that modern translations rightly omit it from the text of 1 John. A copyist, prompted by the triad of earthly witnesses in verse 8 (Spirit, water, blood), was no doubt reminded of the heavenly Trinity and so made the gloss in a Latin version of 1 John about the fifth century.[71]

The distinction between the three persons—the Father, Jesus, and the Spirit—is dramatically set forth in the Johannine corpus. In John 14:16–17, Jesus differentiates between himself, "the Father," and "the Spirit" (who is identified as "another Counselor" [*allos paraklētos*]). The three persons likewise are distinguished in John 14:26 and 15:26. The Holy Spirit is clearly a person, for he is named "Counsellor" or "Comforter" (AV) and he teaches the disciples and testifies to Christ. Moreover, in such texts as John 5:17–23; 6:37–40; 12:49–50 the Father and the Son are represented as distinct persons, as are Jesus and the Spirit in John 5:32 (*allos* connotes "another" rather than "an other"; that is, he is another of the same kind).

Equally clear in John is the fact that the Father, Son, and Spirit are one in being or essence. Thus, the Spirit's presence with the disciples implies the simultaneous presence of the Father and the Son (John 14:16–24). The mutual participation (*communio*) of the Father and the Son and of the Son and the Spirit within the unity of the Godhead is evident in John 16:13–15. The ontological oneness of the Father and the Son is repeatedly asserted by John. So Jesus called God his Father in a manner that implied full equality with God (John 5:18). He claimed to be "in" the Father, even as the Father was "in" him (John 10:38; 14:10–11, 20; 17:21–23). The unity of Father and Son in essence and attributes is evident in John 10:28–30. In verses 28–29 Jesus claims equal power with the Father ("my hand"—"my Father's hand"). His statement "I and the Father are one" (v. 30) was a claim to deity, for the Jews sought to stone him for what they perceived to be blasphemy.[72] The unity of being that there is between the Father and Jesus is seen also in John 14:9; 17:10; 1 John 2:23–24.

John also upholds the full deity of

each of the three persons. The statement "The Father has life in himself" (John 5:26) is an implicit claim to deity. More explicitly, the Father is called "God" in John 6:27; 17:3; 20:17; Revelation 1:6. Moreover, the Son is plainly represented as God. John 1:1 makes a threefold claim for the Word (*logos*): (1) his eternal subsistence: the Word was "in the beginning" (*en archē*); (2) his eternal intercommunion with God: "the Word was with God" (*pros ton theon*); and (3) his eternal identity with God: "the Word was God" (*theos ēn ho logos*). The fact that *theos* (God) occupies first place in the previous clause indicates that it receives the emphasis. And that *theos* lacks the article denotes that the term refers to Christ's nature—i.e., "What God was, the Word was" (NEB). The Greek text gives no support for the rendering of the *New World Translation* (of Jehovah's Witnesses): "and the Word was a god." The preferred reading of John 1:18 describes Jesus Christ as *monogenēs theos*—"only begotten God" or "the only begotten (himself) God"[73]—an uncommon expression that likely was later changed to the simpler *ho monogenēs huios*. Thomas, after observing Jesus' wounded body, cried out, "My Lord and my God!" (*ho kyrios mou kai ho theos mou*, John 20:28). Identically structured phrases separated by *kai* indicate that "Lord" and "God" both describe the risen Jesus. What John says in 1 John 5:20 ("We are in him who is true—even in his Son Jesus Christ. He is the true God [*ho alēthinos theos*] and eternal life") is fully agreeable with other Johannine ascriptions of deity to Jesus the Son (cf. John 10:33, 36; 20:31). Jesus' response to the Jews in John 8:58: "Before Abraham was born, I am" (*egō eimi*) clearly testifies to his deity. The Jews understood that Jesus claimed to be the "I AM" of Exodus 3:14, the eternally existing Yahweh, as their attempt to stone him indicates.

Commonplace in John is the claim that God the Father is the Father of Jesus Christ (e.g., John 3:35; 14:12–13; 16:25–28; 20:17). Since to the Hebrew mind, sonship involves derivation of nature, filial love, and heirship, the Father-Son conceptuality suggests the eternal generation of the Son. When John depicts Christ as "the one who was born of God" (*ho gennētheis*, 1 John 5:18), he may have contemplated the timeless relation of Christ's begetting and sonship. When applied to Christ, *mongenēs* (John 1:14, 18; 3:16; 1 John 4:9) connotes the Son's uniqueness and incomparability; Christ is in a class by himself.

In the Gospel of John, the Spirit, though not explicitly called God, is invisible (John 14:17), eternal (v. 16), omniscient (v. 26), and true (v. 17; 15:26; 16:13). Attributed to him are numerous divine works; e.g., he convicts of sin (John 16:8–11), regenerates (John 3:5–8), guides believers into the truth of God (16:13–15), and gives power for ministry (20:22–23). In sum, "this Spirit is not an agency, but an agent, who teaches and selects; who can be sinned against and grieved; and who in the New Testament, is unmistakably revealed as a distinct person."[74] John 15:26 ("When the Counselor comes, whom I will send to you from the Father, the Spirit of truth who goes out from the Father, . . .") has traditionally been interpreted in the sense of the eternal procession of the Spirit (Olshausen, Lange, Godet, Pieper, et al.). But behind the primary reference to the mission of the Spirit (*para tou patros ekporeutai*) may lie the primary relation of the Spirit to the Father and the Son. Thus Westcott notes, "The revelation of the mission of the Spirit to men (*which proceedeth, I will send*) corresponds with the revelation of the eternal relations of the Spirit (*from the Father, through the Son*)."[75]

Entirely consistent with the ontological equality of persons, John, like Paul, recognizes an ordering relation within the Godhead. Thus, in a functional sense, both in time and eternity, the Father enjoys priority vis-à-vis the Son. This voluntary subordination of the Son to the Father is evidenced in the Father's act of sending the Son into the world (John 3:34; 5:23, 37; 17:3, 18, 25; 1 John 4:9). That Jesus' will and power were always dependent on the Father (John 5:19, 30, 36; 6:38) is reflected by the fact that the Son speaks the Father's message (John 12:49; cf. 3:34), obeys his commands (John 14:31; 15:10), and accepts his purpose of suffering (John 18:11). In sum, with regard to the Son's role as the agent of creation and preservation and with regard to his voluntary humiliation in the incarnate state, Jesus declared, "The Father is greater than I" (John 14:28).

John also states that in terms of the economy of the Godhead the Father has priority vis-à-vis the Spirit, for the Father has sent the Counselor to indwell believers, thereby continuing the work of the glorified Jesus Christ (John 14:16, 26). In like manner, the Son is functionally greater than the Spirit, in that following his ascension the Son sent the Counselor to bless the church (John 16:7; 20:22). In the work of the Godhead, the Spirit faithfully testifies to Christ (John 14:26; 15:26). Finally, in one text (John 15:26) John affirms that both the Father and the Son send the Holy Spirit on his mission.

Other New Testament Literature

Given the Jewish background of the Epistle of James, one is not surprised to find the unity and uniqueness of God upheld: "You believe that God is one; you do well" (James 2:19, RV, RSV). Yet, notwithstanding his own Hebrew background, Peter acknowledged by an early formula the Trinitarian character of God: ". . . chosen according to the foreknowledge of God the Father, by the sanctifying work of the Spirit, for obedience to Jesus Christ" (1 Peter 1:2). Likewise, Jude juxtaposes the three persons as equal in dignity and divinity: "Pray in the Holy Spirit. Keep yourselves in God's love as you wait for the mercy of our Lord Jesus Christ to bring you to eternal life" (Jude 20–21). The absence of a fixed order of persons in the above texts suggests the essential coequality of Father, Son, and Spirit.

Hebrews 1:8–9, quoting Psalm 45:6–7, explicitly states that the Son of the Father is "God." Similarly, Hebrews 1:3 describes the Son as "the radiance of God's glory" (*apaugasma tēs doxēs*) and "the exact representation of his being" (*charaktēr tēs hypostaseōs autou*). The first expression indicates that the effulgence of the eternal Godhead shines forth through the historical existence of the Son, the second that the essence of the Godhead finds perfect expression in the Son, and the present participle (*ōn*, "being') introducing the sentence invests the Father-Son relation with a certain permanence. Peter specifically identifies the second person of the Trinity as God: ". . . through the righteousness of our God and Savior Jesus Christ" (2 Peter 1:1). According to the Granville Sharp rule, the presence of the definite article before "our God" and the absence of the article before "Savior" refers the phrase "God and Savior" to Jesus Christ.[76] Elsewhere the Son is given titles that indicate unqualified deity; e.g., "God" (*theos*, Heb. 1:8), "sovereign Lord" (*despotēs*, 2 Peter 2:1), and "only Sovereign and Lord" (*ton monon despotēn kai kyrion hēmōn*, Jude 4). The last text, Jude 4, satisfies the criteria of the Granville Sharp rule.

The deity of the Holy Spirit is indirectly acknowledged, in the sense that words spoken by him are attributed to God (Heb. 3:7–11; 10:15–17). Moreover, the Spirit performs works that are appropriate only to Deity; e.g., he energized the prophets (1 Peter 1:11), inspired the Old Testament (2 Peter 1:21; cf. Heb. 3:7; 10:15), empowered Christ for his ministry of suffering (Heb. 9: 14), quickened Christ's crucified body (1 Peter 3:18), and sanctifies believers so as to render them fit for heaven (1 Peter 1:2).

SYSTEMATIC FORMULATION

Organizing our thinking about this vast amount of biblical and historical data, we consider several basic topics in a logical order. Most basic in the context of contemporary concerns is the meaning of the biblical teaching that God is one.

The Oneness of God's Being

The Old Testament clearly and repeatedly teaches that "the LORD is one" (Deut. 6:4), denying the reality of other gods and the value of polytheistic worship. When God judges a polytheistic people, the gods in which they took refuge do not help them. "See now that I myself am He! There is no god besides me" (Deut. 32:36–39). In ultimate reality there are not many, separate divine beings. Metaphysically, we have to do with only one divine being.

Debate becomes serious, however, about whether the repeated biblical teachings on God's oneness rule out, not only polytheism, but also Trinitarianism. A priori assumptions will not resolve this issue. Only an examination of the evidence can determine whether "one" is a technical term excluding diversity in unity, as in a mathematical point, or an ordinary multiplicity in unity, as in a body.

According to the *Old Testament*, when a couple marries, the two become

"one flesh" (Gen. 2:24), *one family*. That actual oneness does not exclude but requires two distinct persons. The experienced oneness of marriage does not exclude multiplicity but requires it—and that multiplicity is a multiplicity of persons.

The Old Testament also uses the same word in reference to *one people or nation*. When Moses told the people of Israel the Lord's words and laws, "they responded with one voice" (Exod. 24:3). By that "one voice" a great multiplicity of Israelites unanimously entered into covenant with the Lord. Even though Israel and Judah would later separate and go into different captivities, Ezekiel symbolized their future reunion by joining two sticks together into one stick. So in the hand of God the two would again become one nation (Ezek. 37:19).

Israel's *one tabernacle* was made up of ten curtains (Exod. 26:1) fastened together with fifty loops and gold clasps on each end (26:5–6) so that the tabernacle was a unit (26:6, 11). Indeed, the one tabernacle was composed of many parts. Its oneness did not exclude, but required, multiplicity.

In the Old Testament usage, "oneness" is drawn from the daily experience with the unity of such things as a family, a nation, and a tabernacle. From these and many similar uses, it follows that "when the Jewish writers of the Old Testament taught that God is 'one,' they stressed God's unity while recognizing diversity within that oneness." The Old Testament as well as the New is "strictly monotheistic while at the same time teaching diversity within the unity."[77]

The *New Testament* similarly speaks of the unity of a *family,* as the passage on "one flesh" (Gen. 2:24) is quoted several times (Matt. 19:5, 6; 1 Cor. 6:16; Eph. 5:31). The complexity of one *human body* is also prominent. The "body is a unit, though it is made up of many parts" (1 Cor. 12:12). Analogously, the body portrays the multiplicity in the unity of the *church*. Hence, "in Christ we who are many form one body" (Rom. 12:5). The unity of the body of Christ, the church, includes a relational unity "in heart and mind" (Acts 4:32) and more. For amidst the disturbing differences at Corinth, the members remained in the spirtually organic unity of the body of Christ (cf. 1 Cor. 1:2 with 12:12–13).

Clearly, New Testament assertions that anything is "one," like those of the Old Testament, do not exclude a multiplicity in unity. To attribute a technical, undiversified sameness to the word "one" in the Bible shows a lack of appreciation for its meaning in its own nontechnical frame of reference.

In *everyday experience* we regularly confront diversity in a thing, an animal, or a movement. Although physical analogies fail to portray all the aspects of Trinitarianism, they effectively illustrate the commonness of multiplicity in unity and our ability to speak about it without contradiction. One electrical appliance or watch may be very complex. Essential to one atom are quite different kinds of energy such as electrons, protons, and neutrons. Water, essentially H_2O, may exist not only as a liquid but also as steam or ice. Essential to one triangle are three sides and three angles. Space has three dimensions: length, breadth, and height. Time has reference to past, present, and future. Light rays from the sun heat, illuminate, and cause chemical photosynthesis in plants. If daily we experience plurality in unity, should be be surprised to find it in God?

Although we lack full comprehension of an atom, water, space, time, light, the human body, a church, or a nation, what we do know we can communicate coherently. By distinguishing the respect in which each of these items is one and the respect(s) in which it has

elements that can be differentiated, we remove confusion. Although we lack full comprehension of the Trinity, when we choose to speak with others about the Trinity and expect them to follow us, we must communicate without self-contradiction. If the Christian doctrine of God were contradictory, it would affirm and deny one divine being, or affirm and deny three divine persons. It does not. The Christian doctrine affirms oneness in respect to essence and threeness in respect to centers of consciousness capable of fellowship, communication, and intercession with one another. Keeping the categories of being and persons distinct, we need suffer no tensions about the classical doctrine of the Trinity being contradictory. Any initial appearance of contradiction (paradox) should be handled like the measles: isolate it until the difficulty is resolved.[78]

Granting a multiplicity in divine unity, in what way is God's oneness to be interpreted? Not as a continuity in space, for God is spirit. God is one *substantially* (one spiritual being) and one *essentially* (one spiritual being with all the attributes belonging to him). (Essence = substance + attributes). The unity is not merely of genus, for there are not three gods of the same kind (genus). Only a substantial and essential oneness fits the scriptural data denying polytheism and affirming monotheism. The divine unity revealed in Scripture is not like a mystical Neo-Platonic "One" beyond all categories of human thought. The biblical oneness does not rule out distinguishable attributes and persons.

Church tradition sometimes made matters more difficult than necessary by claiming that, as simple, God can really include no distinctions at all—not between essence and existence, act and potential, person and essence, or anything else. This last requirement of the classic simplicity theory (that persons and essence in God must be identical) traditionally made the doctrine of the Trinity look incoherent. For on the one hand the doctrine of the Trinity claimed that Father, Son, and Spirit are distinct persons (a claim derived especially from the Gospel of John). On the other hand, the same doctrine seemed to imply that all three persons were actually just the same thing as the divine essence. Both the concept of simplicity above presented and the law of noncontradiction allow for differences of respect (one in essence and three in personhood) without inconsistency.

Although God may be experienced as one, the assertion of God's oneness is *not a doctrine describing phenomena* of religious experiences, or human events or relationships. It is a doctrine about ultimate reality, about God as God *is* metaphysically. Those who believe the teaching of biblical revelation cannot join the antimetaphysical temper of the times without devastating results, not only to Trinitarianism, but also to the doctrine of God's oneness. Those who deny any propositional information about God either inconsistently claim to hold that God is ontologically one or, more consistently, find themselves tending toward the new polytheism (discussed below).

Three Personal Consciousnesses in the Divine Being

If in respect to spiritual being God is one, in what respects is God diverse or multiple? We have already seen diversity of attributes, emotions, purposes, and actions. Is there sufficient evidence to add diversity in another respect, that of persons? Could the one underlying common psyche (the unconscious) have three distinguishable centers of consciousness? Like an ocean (of one substance) with three waves (modes of its existence), does the one personal, spiritual Being subsist in three personal modes?

Inscripturated revelation speaks of the one God as Father, Son, and Holy Spirit. The Bible does not use the terms "essence" and "being" but teaches the concept in other words. Similarly, it does not explicitly refer to three "persons" but its statements about God are most coherently explained by the doctrine of three persons in the one divine essence and being. Alternative views throughout the history of doctrine have failed to fit all the biblical data on God's oneness and threeness as adequately. What are some of the more prominent indications of threeness in the oneness of the divine being?

Three are addressed as essentially God and worshiped as persons. First, the Father's deity is recognized in Daniel's prayer: "O Lord, the great and awesome God, who keeps his covenant of love with all who love him and obey his commands" (Dan. 9:4). Jesus' teaching on prayer begins, "Our Father in heaven, hallowed be your name" (Matt. 6:9). Second, Jesus was called "Immanuel—which means, 'God with us'" (Matt. 1:23). Thomas could no longer doubt Jesus' deity when the risen Lord invited him to touch his wounded hands and side. In worship and dedication the doubter exclaimed, "My Lord and my God!" (John 20:28). Third, when the Israelites in the wilderness tempted the Lord (Exod. 17:2–7), they provoked the Holy Spirit (Heb. 3:7–9). And for Ananias and Sapphira to lie to the Holy Spirit (Acts 5:3) is to lie to God (v. 4). To be born of the Spirit (John 3:6, 8) is to be born of God (1 John 5:18). To pray to Father, Son, and Spirit, if they were not essentially God, would be idolatrous. The Bible consistently repudiates the worship of idols, and therefore, in encouraging worship of the Father, Son, and Spirit, it implies their deity

The name of God as used in benediction at the end of worship in the New Testament era is the threefold name of the Father, the Son, and the Holy Spirit. In the earlier Old Testament benedictions priests put the name of the Lord (singular) on the people (Num. 6:27), emphasizing God's unity. As revelation progressed, making more explicit God's triune existence, Paul's benediction placed the name of God on the people by saying, "May the grace of the Lord Jesus Christ, and the love of God, and the fellowship of the Holy Spirit be with you all" (2 Cor. 13:14). And when people confessed faith in Christ publicly by baptism, the name of God was placed on them by "baptizing them in the name [sing.] of the Father and of the Son and of the Holy Spirit" (Matt. 28:19). If the Son and Spirit were not equally God, the benedictory and baptismal formulas would have been unthinkable. The benediction and the baptismal formulas indicate that first-century believers implicitly recognized the essential deity of the Father, but also of the Son and Spirit.

Father, Son, and Spirit *possess the divine attributes*. The Father is eternal (Gen. 21:33; 1 Tim. 1:17), the Son is eternal (John 1:1; 8:58; 17:5, 24; Heb. 7:3; Rev. 22:13), and the Spirit is eternal (Heb. 9:14). The Father is omnipresent (Jer. 23:24; Acts 17:27), the Son is omnipresent (Matt. 28:20), and the Spirit is omnipresent (Ps. 139:7–10). The Father is holy (Lev. 11:45; John 17:11), the Son is holy (John 6:69; Acts 4:27), and the Spirit is holy (Rom. 1:4; Eph. 4:30). The Father is love (Ps. 136:1–26; Jer. 31:3; John 3:16; 1 John 4:8,16), the Son is love (John 15:9, 13; 1 John 3:16), the Spirit is love (Rom. 5:5; Gal. 5:22; Col. 1:8). The Father is omnipotent (Mark 14:36; Luke 1:37), the Son is omnipotent (Matt. 9:6; Luke 8:25; John 10:18), and the Spirit is omnipotent (Luke 1:35; Acts 1:8; 2:2–4, 17–21; 4:31–33).

While sharing the same divine essence, the Father, Son, and Holy Spirit have *personal characteristics*. The three are not just three different roles or "hats" worn by the one God of Judaism and Islam. Nor are they merely three modes of revelation to people in history as in Sabellian modalism. They are three modes of existence within the deity, with distinctive modes of relating to mankind. They are more like multiple personalities (*The Three Faces of Eve*), but all at once, not serially, and all equally righteous, wise, etc.

The Father, Son, and Spirit distinctively have *personal capacities of intellect, emotion, and will*. God the Father is a personal being with intelligent self-consciousness, emotional self-control, and volitional purposes. The Father consciously "knows" (Matt. 6:8, 32), determines himself or wills (Matt. 6:10; 12:50; 18:14), chooses (1 Peter 1:2), and feels without being out of control (Ps. 86:15; Isa. 63:9; Rom. 1:18).

God the Son also knows (John 2:24; 16:30), feels (Matt. 9:36; John 11:35), and wills (Luke 22:42; John 5:30; 6:38). An entire book has been written on the messianic consciousness of Jesus.[79] Readers of the Gospels can hardly fail to see that although Jesus had an affective nature, he was uniquely self-controlled. Furthermore, he was not "under the circumstances" or, like the Pharisees, compelled by what others thought. Rather, Jesus Christ uniquely determined his thought, words, and actions in a manner consistent with his conscious messianic purpose.

Similarly, the Holy Spirit displays intellectual capacities (John 14:26; 15:26; 16:7, 13; 1 Cor. 2:10); affective capacities (Isa. 63:10; Eph. 4:30), producing fruit involving human emotions (Gal. 5:22–23); and will (Gen. 6:3; Isa. 63:10; 1 Cor. 12:11). So each has personal capacities of intellect, emotion, and will, essential characteristics of persons. In other words, each exhibits self-consciousness, self-control, and self-determination. And, as we will see, the three interrelate as persons in "I-Thou" fellowship and intercession.

People who accept the personhood of the Father and the Son may ask, "Is the Holy Spirit personal?" This is understandable since the Old Testament word "spirit" frequently means air in motion, wind, or breath. However, "spirit" in other contexts means disposition of mind, the entire immaterial consciousness of man, a supernatural angelic being, the active power of God, and, finally, the Holy Spirit in a Trinitarian sense (cf. Isa. 48:16).[80] A similar progression of meanings may be seen in New Testament uses of the term "spirit" (*pneuma*). "Jesus understood the Holy Spirit as a personality . . . 'Paraclete,' i.e., the Comforter (Counselor, Advocate)." (John 14:16, 26; 15:26; 16:5)[81]

The Holy Spirit, as "Counselor," is referred to by personal pronouns (John 14:17), and this is not mere literary personification, since he performs personal services like "witnessing" concerning Christ (John 14:26), teaching (John 16:13), revealing (1 Cor. 2:10), and convicting (John 16:8–11). He witnesses with believers' spirits that they are children of God (Rom. 8:16). As an advocate, the Holy Spirit can intercede for believers with the Father (Rom. 8:26). An impersonal power or influence from the Father could not take the initiative and become an advocate of our cause with the Father. The most unmistakable single indication of the Spirit's personal distinctiveness from the Father is his ability to intercede on behalf of Christians with the Father.

To say that we cannot fully comprehend the meaning of "persons" in ourselves, let alone the divine being, is not to say that we do not understand anything about them. We do know that *persons* are intelligent, self-conscious, self-determined, responsible agents capable of appreciating values, choosing

purposes, and sharing them with others in fellowship and action. As active subjects, not mere objects, the divine persons are not to be identified with physical bodies, finite limitations like mutual exclusiveness, or evil. The divine persons are far greater than finite persons and cannot be fully comprehended. George Smeaton argues, "Only remove from the use of the term every notion involving imperfection . . . and it must be admitted that in human language no term can be found better fitted to express the Church's meaning than the term person."[82]

The doctrine of the Trinity affirms that three such personal consciousnesses or agencies compose the oneness of the the divine being. Norman C. Bartlett pictured a "more or less subconscious nature possessed in common" and controlling three free self-consciousnesses.[83] John B. Champion stresses that as persons the Father, Son, and Spirit do not possess an exclusive self-consciousness but an "inter-consciousness" and "other-conscious."[84] John Lawson emphasizes that the most developed, loving human personalities are "not the most fiercely autonomous, but those who are most completely united in mutual accord and sympathy with other persons around them."[85] To help avoid a tritheism with a merely relational unity it is important to contemplate not only the loving interconsciousness of the three, but also something like a common subconscious or metaphysical essence in common. When Scripture speaks of God as one or as spirit, it speaks of God as personal, and this makes possible the tripersonal distinctions.

The view that God does not just function in relation to the world in three different ways but exists as three persons in one spiritual-psychical essence accounts for the varied lines of evidence with the fewest difficulties. The hypothesis of three modes of revelation accounts for evidence of functional distinctions, but such Sabellianism does not account for the scriptural data that make clear that behind the three modes of revelation to mankind in history are three transcendent, ontological modes of being, subsistences, or persons. Our critical method does not just present an unresolved oneness and threeness but decides for the hypothesis with the greatest explanatory power and the fewest difficulties.

Interpersonal Fellowship of Father, Son, and Holy Spirit

Distinguishable as each of the persons in the Trinity is, each functions harmoniously in an unbroken fellowship of love with the others. People sometimes ask, "What was God doing before he created the world?" In prayer Jesus said, "Father, glorify me in your presence with the glory I had with you before the world began" (John 17:5). Again, "Father, . . . you loved me before the creation of the world" (17:24). Before the world was, Father, Son, and Spirit enjoyed the highest of values—unbroken loving relationships.

The unbrokenness of their fellowship is rooted in the fact that each of the three persons functions in accord with the same essential attributes or perfections. Each consciously embraces wisdom, holiness, love, etc. Father, Son, and Holy Spirit will not and cannot act contrary to the common, unchanging divine nature.

The harmony of fellowship is also rooted in the holistic commitment of each of the three persons to function harmoniously with the eternal purposes for history determined from eternity, whether universal in nature and history or redemptive among the people of God. No act contradictory to these purposes can be soundly ascribed to Father, Son, or Holy Spirit.

Administrative Order Among the Three Persons

Although all three distinct persons are equal essentially and enjoy a perfect fellowship, their interrelationships may reflect a distinctive ordering of activities. In the economic ordering of things, in contrast to the essential equality, the Father is mentioned first, the Son is *of* the Father (never vice versa), and the Spirit is *of* the Father and *of* the Son (never vice versa). Why? What is the significance of their respective names "Father," "Son," and "Holy Spirit"? Do the biblical names and illustrations for the three indicate their relationships functionally?

Some people have rejected Trinitarianism on the ground that a person must have a body and three persons cannot occupy the same space at the same time. Such reasoning fails to understand that God is a spirit and transcends limitations of physics. God does not have a flesh-and-bones body. The premise of God's spiritual nature is basic to understanding not only the essential unity of the three persons and their relational communion, but also their administrative order.

In the biblical context the term "Father" is a figure of speech for the creative source of ideas, the fountainhead of planning goals, and the initiator of the mutual relationships and activities. The first person is to the second as the sun is to its brightness (Heb.1:3), an original to its exact copy (Heb.1:3), a speaker to his word (John 1:1) and a father to his unique and only son (John 3:16). The first person emanates the light, determines the nature of the copy, expresses his word, and begets his Son. In less figurative language, the first person creatively designs and initiates relationships and activities. The point illustrated is not a time of origin, but a distinctness of activity with sameness

275

of nature. The first person initiates and purposes.

The second person's relation to the first is scripturally illustrated by the same four interesting figures. What is the point of each in nonfigurative language? First, "the Son is the *radiance* of God's glory" (Heb. 1:3). Jesus Christ is to the Father as the brightness of a ray of light emanating from the sun is to the sun. As light from the sun, Christ sustains all things (v. 3) and exhibits God's transcendent glory.[86] What is the point of the illustration? Although fire and its brightness are of the same nature, they are distinguishable and in an administrative order for operational activities (the brightness comes from and discloses the sun, not the sun the brightness).

Second, Christ is "the *exact representation* of his being" (Heb. 1:3). Again, Christ is "the image of God" (2 Cor. 4:4) and "the image of the invisible God" (Col. 1:15). This figure, like the first, indicates that although the second person is of the same nature as the first, he is distinguishable from the first, and they follow a functional order. Jesus is an exact representation of the invisible being of God. At best these temporal illustrations of the sameness of nature provide only "some slight and small resemblance" of the relationship in eternal reality.[87]

Third, the second person is to the first as a *word* is to its speaker. "In the beginning was the Word, and the word was with God, and the Word was God. He was with God in the beginning" (John 1:1–2). How does a word relate to its speaker? Jesus explained in another context that a person can be judged by his words because "out of the overflow of the heart the mouth speaks" (Matt. 12:34). Analogously, the second person as the Word audibly expresses the overflow of the Father's heart in creating and sustaining the world. He also achieves his loving

purposes of redemption. By becoming flesh (John 1:14), Christ "has made him known" (1:18). Was he the Word of the Father only since his incarnation? Not according to the context. Before creation the Word was with God and was God (1:1).

The most well-known analogy pictures the relationship of the second person to the first as that of a son to his father. "For God so loved the world that he gave his one and only Son" (John 3:16). Not just the first or the highest created being (as Jehovah's Witnesses claim), Jesus is the only Son "who came from the Father" (1:14), the only Son, "who is at the Father's side" (1:18), "his one and only Son" (3:16, 18).

For purposes of systematics it is not enough simply to report that the above passages in the NIV teach the uniqueness of the second person of the Trinity. Building on biblical theology here, we must ask what the concept of uniqueness ("one and only")[88] implies and relate it to a coherent view of the interpersonal activities. We are not turning an action (begetting) into a state of being. We are asking about the point concerning the activities of the first and second persons illustrated by "Father" and "unique Son."

Interestingly, the NIV translators, while preferring to translate *monogenēs* "one and only," include "begetting" in the margin (John 1:14; 3:16, 18). Although both terms were not used in the translation (only begotten), the concepts of uniqueness and begottenness are not logically exclusive. Interpreters need not choose for one against the other. An only son is also begotten! If "begotten" is not explicitly taught in the term *monogenēs*, is it not implied in the Father-Son relationship?

Consider the points illustrated by the figure "unique son." First, the Father/unique-Son terminology illustrates a relationship that is eternal. It did not begin at Bethlehem. John does not say, "God so loved the world that he gave his one and only Son" (John 3:16; cf. 1:18; 1 John 4:9). As B. B. Warfield pointed out, the passage implies that the Son had been in a loving fellowship with the father from eternity.[89] The value of the Father's gift depended on Jesus' unique relationship to the Father prior to his physical conception. If the Word was in the beginning with God and was God (John 1:1), then the Son was in the beginning with God and was God (eternally).

Second, the Father/unique-Son terminology illustrates a relationship that is personal. The second person of the Trinity is a distinguishable person with the same essence. He was not, like the creation, merely created *by* God. Nor was he, like human persons, merely created *by* God *in* God's image. Jesus Christ alone is *of* the same divine nature as the Father's. What figure could better express this Father-Son relationship than that of one person being begotten of the other person? The Son is not merely an impersonal "radiance," "representation," and "Word." The "Son" exhibits the Father's nature as only a person born of another person could do. He is personally unique, as the early church said, because he was "begotten, not made." The point is not that the Son is physically conceived (as if the Father were flesh and bones); God is spirit. And it is not that he had a beginning in time (or had a birthday); the Son of God is eternal. We must dismiss all physical and temporal images of propagation from the figures of "Father" and "Son" (and "begotten," whether implied or read in the margin). The point is that Christ, who is of the same nature as the Father, is a distinguishable person.

Third, the Father/unique-Son relationship well illustrates the point that functionally the begotten One, without ontological inferiority has a derivative role. With respect to active roles, the begetter initiates and commissions, while the begotten lovingly carries out and provides. Eternally, as well as temporally the Father has a priority as the One who commissions and sends. The unique Son in loving fellowship responds as a faithful missionary sent by the Father to serve.

The derivative administrative role of the second person (without resultant ontological inferiority) is better illustrated by "uniquely begotten" than by "unique" or "one and only" alone. Contrary to charges, the Athanasian concept of eternal generation is far from meaningless. Where is a more significant account of the inter-Trinitarian relationship between the Father and the Son than in eternal generation?

> "Generation" makes it plain that there is a divine sonship prior to the incarnation (cf. John 1:18; 1 John 4:9), that there is thus a distinction of persons within the one Godhead (John 5:26), and that between these persons there is priority and subordination of order (cf. John 5:19; 8:28). "Eternal" reinforces the fact that the generation is not merely economic (i.e., for the purpose of human salvation as in the incarnation, cf. Luke 1:35), but essential, and that as such it cannot be construed in the categories of natural or human generation. In virtue of eternal generation, and not in spite of it, the Father and the Son are one (John 10:30).[90]

The concept of eternal generation, furthermore, accounts most coherently for Christ's frequent statements regarding his equality with the Father and his dependence on the Father. This relationship applies to our Savior's temporary condition of humiliation but also reaches far beyond the thirty-three years of his incarnation.

Note that the case for returning to the concept of the "uniquely begotten Son" is not based on nonbiblical, pagan philosophical considerations, but on interpretation of the points illustrated by the Bible's figurative expressions (such as *radiance, image, word,* and *son*) in their immediate and broader contexts. Those biblically revealed points were recognized in the historic creeds ("begotten of the Father before all worlds" [Nicene] and "begotten before the worlds" [Athanasian]). These points cannot be erased by multiplying exegetical "authorities" whose atomistic word studies and biblical positivism may even unconsciously be rooted in an antimetaphysical bias that does not permit them to interpret in nonfigurative language the truth illustrated in figures of speech about God.

Some avoid the point of the figurative language by using synonyms. Calling the Father's relation to the Son that of "paternity" only repeats the figure, however, and does not explain its point. A similar redundancy occurs when the Son's relation to the Father is called filial. Illustrations figuratively communicate a nonfigurative point that a reader must interpret for theological purposes.

Calvin rejected "eternal generation" as a continuous activity in favor of a once-for-all generation in eternity to avoid speculation about continuous generation.[91] Thus Calvin changes the speculation to how a once-for-all act meaningfully happens in an eternal relationship. To say as Calvin did that the Son "derives" from the Father seems hardly less figurative than affirming that the Son "is begotten by" the Father. But in the time of Athanasius and in any period it is crucial to the deity of Christ that he be eternally of the Father.

For summary purposes we now integrate the four biblical analogies considered above as portraying the relationship of the first two persons of the Trinity in their activities. The second person of the Trinity in eternity as well as in time radiates, models, expresses, and exhibits the Father's plans and purposes. Eternally and temporally he radiates the Father's purposes with the brilliance of the sunlight, models them with the accuracy of an exact copy, expresses them with the meaningfulness of a word, and exhibits them with the personableness of a unique Son.

Scripture does not speak as frequently regarding *the Holy Spirit's relation* to Father and Son, but it gives parallels to its teaching about the Son-Word-Image-Radiance. Why do we speak of the third person as "Spirit" rather than another Son? Relationally, the Spirit also is of (*ek*, "out from") God (1 Cor. 2:12), breathed out or spirated from him. What is the point of this illustration? It may be made in others words when Christ says that the Spirit of truth "goes out from the Father" (John 15:26). Other translations have "proceeds from" (AV), "issues from" (Moffatt), and "goes forth from" (Norlie).[92] In a continuous (present tense) "exhalation" of the third person from the first, the Spirit (the breath of God) implements his purposes. As the Word continuously expresses the "heart" of the Father in the ordering of the world, the Spirit continuously emanates from the "lungs" of the Father to bring his purposes to fulfillment.

Never is the first person *of* the third, but the other way around: "the Spirit of God" (Gen. 1:2; Matt. 3:16), "the Spirit of our God" (1 Cor. 6:11), "Spirit of the living God" (2 Cor. 3:3), "the Spirit of the LORD" (Judg. 3:10), and "the Spirit of the Sovereign LORD" (Isa. 61:1).

Does the Spirit proceed, not only from the Father, but also from the Son? The Eastern church has denied that the Spirit proceeds from the Father *and the Son* (*filioque*).[93] However, the Scriptures also refer to "the Spirit of Jesus Christ" (Phil. 1:19), "the Spirit of Jesus" (Acts 16:7), "the Spirit of

Christ" as parallel to "the Spirit of God" (Rom. 8:9), "the Spirit of his Son" (Gal. 4:6), and "the Spirit of the Lord" (Acts 5:9; 8:39). In anticipating the coming of the Spirit at Pentecost, Jesus said that the Spirit would be sent by the Father in Jesus' name (John 14:26), but also that he would send the Spirit from the Father (15:26). The Pentecostal sending of the Spirit by the Father and the Son may not be totally unique but an instance of many such operational orders. Hence scriptural precedent suggests affirming that the Holy Spirit proceeds not only from the Father but also from the Son. Although all three are spirit, the third person is distinctively the One who powerfully brings to fulfillment in our lives the redemptive transformation envisioned by the Father and provided for by the Son.

Since holiness is an attribute of all three persons, why is the third particularly called the *Holy* Spirit? Holiness is not only an attribute but also a distinctive feature of the Spirit's ministry. The third person convicts of sin, regenerates, and sanctifies. Insofar as converted sinners progressively become holy, their virtue can be traced to the Spirit's teaching, illumination, leading, abiding, and cultivating of Christlike holiness. Furthermore, it is important in cultures like those of Bible times, where people are constantly aware of the presence of evil spirits, to regularly distinguish the Holy Spirit from evil spirits.

Summing up revealed truths concerning the interpersonal relations in the Trinity, there is an unbroken fellowship of love among the Father, the Son, and the Holy Spirit. Their equality of essence and fellowship is not affected by the administrative ordering of relationships among themselves in creative (John 1:1–3) and redemptive activity. In that functional order the first person creatively initiates, the second brightly exhibits, and the third effectually brings to fulfillment.

Distinctive, but Harmonious Ministries in History

Systematic thinking requires keeping the essential and functional categories distinct. Whether we read about God in Scripture or speak about him, we must ask whether the referent is (1) God's underlying essence and being, (2) the three divine persons in their distinctive interpersonal relationships, or (3) their distinctive but harmonious ministries to people in space-time history. For example, operationally in space and time, the incarnate Jesus Christ could say, "The Father is greater than I" (John 14:28). Jehovah's Witnesses think this statement contradicts Trinitarianism, but a reference to Jesus' functional self-denial does not alter his continuous essential deity.

Although all three persons are omnipresent and consciously interrelated in all their activities, each has some distinctive historical activities. In regard to *creation*, the Father calls forth energy-matter, the Logos informs it and orders its laws of change, and the Holy Spirit leads it to develop according to its nature and achieve its destiny.[94] The work of the Spirit is to realize the glory of the Father in the life of every creature, Kuyper finds, by "impregnating" (developing) inanimate matter, animating the rational soul, and taking up his abode in the children of God.[95]

In implementing the redemptive program, all three divine persons manifested their presence in distinctive ways at the *baptism* of Jesus marking the beginning of his ministry. However, only Jesus was immersed by John. Only the Father said, "You are my Son, whom I love; with you I am well pleased." And only the Holy Spirit descended on Jesus "in bodily form like a dove" (Luke 3:22).

During the *temptations of Jesus*, our Lord effectively resisted Satan's temptations by conscious prayer to the Father while quoting inspired Scripture in the presence and power of the Holy Spirit.

Recall the interconnections and distinctive roles of the three divine persons in *revelation*: the Father had the creative idea for it, the Son actively expressed and exhibited it, and the Spirit inspired and illumined it.

Most succinctly, in regard to the distinctive roles of each of the three persons in the work of *salvation*, God the Father *planned* it, God the Son *provided* it, and God the Holy Spirit *applies* it.

Such harmonious functional activities of Father, Son, and Spirit reflect a deeper personal unity of conscious thinking, feeling, and willing. And that unity of mind and purpose reveals an even deeper essential oneness of being.

APOLOGETIC INTERACTION

The Many Gods of the New Polytheism

Polytheism has returned as the logical conclusion of relativistic theology done with an antimetaphysical bias. Unable to know anything about God in himself, those who deny propositional revelation limit all theology to information from changing phenomena of religious experience, events, and relationships. People consigned to the resulting total relativism have not only different perspectives of God. They have no way of knowing that they worship the same God, ultimately. In *The New Polytheism: Rebirth of the Gods and Goddesses*, acknowledging the death of a transcendent, omnipotent God and having lost the one *Logos* by whom all things were created and are sustained, David L. Miller can find no single center harnessing all our pluralistic meanings and values. Miller concludes, "Everywhere one stands is a center, . . . when the center is everywhere it is in fact multiple."[96]

God's ontological unity was argued from the universe by the best Greek philosophers (Plato and Aristotle) and from the writings of inspired Hebrew prophets and apostles by Christian theologians. Hebrew and Greek mentalities have some differences, but also some common concerns. Both traditions had good reasons to regard polytheism a hypothesis that did not cohere with the unity evident in the universe or both the universe and the teaching of the Scriptures. Although omnipresent, God cannot be divided into multiple beings. God transcends and rules the diversity of powers in the world. The hypothesis of many gods does not fit the facts of general and special revelation (above) as coherently as the hypothesis of God's oneness in essence.

The Many Spirits of Animism

The polytheist's gods and goddesses are reminiscent of the many "spirits" of animistic cultures and traditional religions.

Again, the hypothesis of many forces beyond our individual and social control simply fails to account for the data of both general and special revelation (above) concerning the *one* Lord of all. Could an animistic or polytheistic commitment also indicate willful disobedience to the one ultimate source of the countless biblical condemnations of polytheism?

The Three Gods of Tritheism

The early church found it important to make clear that in reality there were not three gods in a kind of tritheistic committee, but only one. To preserve the truth of God's ontological unity, church fathers affirmed that Christ was of the same being or substance (*homoousia*) not just of like substance (*homoiousia*) with the Father. With G. L. Prestige in his extensive study *God in Patristic Thought*, "We may therefore conclude that, down to the Council of Nicea, *homoousios* meant 'of one stuff' or 'substance'; and that when it was applied to the Divine Persons, it conveyed a metaphor drawn from material objects . . . with, however, a safeguard to the unity of God."[97] The biblical evidence on the unity of the Son with the Father is not sufficiently accounted for by affirming a relational or functional harmony, true and important as this evidence is. Only *one* transcendent God is present to the world. Only *one* Trinitarian Lord of all knows the future, speaks, and acts, as documented above.

Metaphysical Skepticism and Orthodox Confessions

Since Immanuel Kant's (1724–1804) denials of objective knowledge of anything in itself, especially God, much contemporary thought has limited religious language to the existential, pragmatic, and relational phenomena. Having dismissed all sources of changeless truth about ultimate reality, it became impossible to know even that ultimate reality is one, let alone triune. Neither Leonard Hodgson's inductions from revelatory historical acts, nor Karl Barth's analysis of revelatory activity adequately represent the biblically revealed trinity.[98]

The Episcopal bishop James A. Pike observed that the people of God had experienced God in three ways and said that "three persons in one God" was probably the best statement that the philosophers of the early church could devise, but he wanted to believe in a *big* God, one who could not be enclosed in a philosophical concept. He imagined that if he described God, he would "cabin in" God. The Apostles Creed,

Pike explained, contained several phrases he could not affirm as literal prose sentences, "but I can certainly sing them, . . . because [the creed] affirms the things basically important and true, in poetic terms."[99]

As a member of the World Council of Churches, apparently he subscribed to its basic statement of faith: "The World Council of Churches is a fellowship of churches which confess the Lord Jesus Christ as *God* and Savior according to the Scriptures and therefore seek to fulfill their common calling to the glory of the *one* God—Father, Son, and Holy Spirit."

To become a participant in the World Council and many other such organizations, is it enough to sing about the Trinity while denying the cognitive statements that God is one being existing in three persons? Will today's young seminary graduates, who have reductively empirical or existential assumptions, find it impossible to assert (however well they may sing!) the *ontological oneness* of Father, Son, and Spirit? If so, will they be accepted in churches and schools with orthodox statements of Trinitarianism?

The Anti-Trinitarianism of Jehovah's Witnesses, LDS (and Others)

Jehovah's Witnesses and Latter-Day Saints are among the most aggressive opponents of Trinitarianism whom Christians frequently meet at their door. Their challenges to Trinitarians reflect arguments common to many other groups. Ministers who fail to prepare their people to meet these challenges may expect to lose members to many such groups. After quoting the Athanasian Creed, James E. Talmadge, a leading Mormon theologian comments, "It would be difficult to conceive of a greater number of inconsistencies and contradictions expressed in words so few."[100]

281

Those who oppose the teaching regarding the Trinity usually have not taken sufficient time to examine what they oppose or to define the charge of contradiction, which they make against the doctrine. Trinitarians do not assert one God and three Gods, or only one person and three persons. Such assertions affirm and deny the same thing at the same time and in the same respect. But the historic doctrine affirming oneness in respect to being and threeness in respect to persons, although not fully comprehensible, is not contradictory. Attacks of Jehovah's Witnesses (and others) also confuse the basic categories of thought: ontological (what one is) and functional (what one does). Claiming that the Bible nowhere teaches the equality of the Son with the Father, Jehovah's Witness writers allege that it teaches the very opposite, that the Son is in subjection to the Father and hence inferior to him.[101] When he was preparing his disciples for his imminent death, Jesus said, "The Father is greater than I" (John 14:28). However, this statement does not contradict his other assertions of oneness with the Father in power to keep his followers from perishing (10:27–30). The Jews understood his claim to be God (v. 33) and sought to stone him for blasphemy. During the Incarnation, Jesus humbled himself as a human servant in order to provide for our salvation. While he was on earth Jesus gave up his heavenly glory and, unlike the Father, limited the use of his divine powers, for he came to suffer hunger, fatigue, and death. It is important in relation to the Trinity not to confuse what the second person is with what he does. Jesus *is* one in essence with the Father, but *functionally* he limited himself as a human to provide for mankind's salvation.

Jehovah's Witnesses (among others) also make the mistake of claiming that the doctrine of the Trinity is unbiblical because it was not fully formulated in Scripture until 350 years after the death of Jesus Christ.[102] But its elements are progressively revealed as extensively documented above. "The formulation of the doctrine," Warfield concluded, "although not made in Scripture, is not opposed to Scripture. When we assemble the *disjecta membra* into their organic unity, we are not passing from Scripture, but entering more thoroughly into the meaning of Scripture."[103]

Jehovah's Witnesses (and others, like Victor Paul Wierwille, leading writer of The Way, in *Jesus Was Not God*) also allege that Trinitarianism originated long after biblical times from pagan sources introduced into the apostate church.[104] The Christian church as a whole hardly became apostate before the apostles died! History can find no such departure from the faith when the Nicean and Athanasian statements were formulated. Rather, the early creeds express in a coherent way the complex teachings of Scripture regarding the one God—the Father, the Son, and the Holy Spirit. Doctrinal apostasy becomes apparent by departure of people and movements from the biblically derived creedal statements.[105]

Pantheistic "Trinities" in the West and in the East

Mary Baker Eddy, founder of Christian Science, considered belief in Trinitarianism a belief in polytheism rather than in one ever-present *I AM*.[106] In accord with her impersonal pantheistic assumptions, she proposed an alternative interpretation: "Life, Truth, and Love constitute the triune Person called God—that is, the triply divine Principle, Love. They represent a trinity in unity, three in one, the same in essence, though multiform in office." Mrs. Eddy explained further, "God the Father-mother; Christ the spiritual idea of sonship; divine Science the threefold, essential nature of the infinite."[107]

The Hindu *trimurti* or threefold manifestation of the Absolute—Brahman, or the universe—in its triple role as emanator, destroyer, and preserver has sometimes been thought analogous to the Christian Trinity. Note the pantheistic rather than theistic presupposition, the lack of three persons, and sheer functional modalism. The Divine Light Mission's Guru Maharaj Ji's acrostic for God: Generator, Operator, and Destroyer, even on a functional level is far from similar to a biblically rooted Trinitarianism.

The situation is similar in regard to the Buddhist *trikaya*. The three bodies emanating from the Buddha are: the primordial and ultimate body of Essence, Bliss, and Appearance, which alone is present in earthly existence.[108] Anything experienced in reality may have threeness in unity. To have a significant comparison with Trinitarianism in other religions, one would need to find a concept of a transcendent, personal God as in Judaism with three personal distinctions able to commune and intercede with one another.

Process Theology and Trinitarianism

In the antimetaphysical mood of the times, process Trinitarianism, a Western variety of thought parallel to Buddhism, rejects substantialist, essentialist, and even personalist categories of thought. With Buddhism, John B. Cobb in *Christ in a Pluralistic Age* seeks to rid his readers of attachment to personal existence as a final good.[109] Cobb's God is no longer a personal, triune, transcendent, absolute being. Father, Son, and Spirit are not eternal persons, but changing functions of the whole process in its relations and activities. In place of the historic Christian doctrine of God, Cobb puts an immanent process of eternal and relativistic becoming. "In a system of naturalistic pantheism God has been reduced to the factor of order and value within the evolutionary process."[110] In view of all the evidence above for God's one-in-essence, three-in-persons transcendence, Cobb's hypothesis has little probability.

Muslim Anti-Trinitarianism

From a Muslim point of view belief in the Trinity is not only illogical; it is the major sin one can commit. It is a sign of infidelity! "Infidels now are they who say, 'God is the messiah, Son of Mary'." Although God is merciful with adulterers and liars, Trinitarians deserve hell. "Whoever shall join other gods with God, God shall forbid him the Garden, and his abode shall be the Fire." Why so strong? The creed, repeated many times a day, affirms, "There is no God but one God [Allah]." And the Koran continues, "The Messiah, Son of Mary, is but an apostle."[111] Christians in Muslim countries or witnessing to Muslim exchange students might suggest a study of oneness in the Old and New Testaments, human experience, and the Koran to determine whether it so summarily dismisses any complexity in the divine being. Then the Muslims may consider the extensive evidence above for the three persons in the Trinity.

A lifelong, active member of a large fundamentalist church said she had never heard an entire sermon or Sunday school class on the Trinity. It is little wonder that a veteran Jehovah's Witness, after a lengthy discussion with one who believed in the Trinity said, "I never before met a Trinitarian who actually seemed to believe the doctrine!" Christian movements will continue to lose members to anti-Trinitarian groups unless they teach their people how to handle the Scriptures that teach God's oneness and threeness.

Until a view is proposed that more coherently fits the biblical passages on both the unity and the diversity of the Godhead, we do well not only to believe and to sing about the Trinity, but also to defend Trinitarianism.

Sooner or later every world view not blind to observed diversity and unity in the world must account for both the one and the many in its ultimate reality. No one escapes this problem by abandoning the Scriptures or Christianity. Some philosophers, such as Parmenides, stress the reality of the one to the denial of the reality of the many. Others, like Heraclitus, affirm the reality of the many changing things in everyday experience and deny the reality of an unchanging unity. If the ultimate reality in a world view is one without diversity, it becomes difficult to account for the many. If the ultimate reality in the world view is many, it becomes impossible to account for the unity of the world. In the ultimate reality, the Trinity, Christianity has a coherent account of diversity in the unity in the world and so does not find it unthinkable that the universe (micro and macro) exhibits both multiplicity and unity.

RELEVANCE FOR LIFE AND MINISTRY

A. W. Tozer held that "a right conception of God is basic not only to systematic theology, but to practical Christian living as well."[112] This Christian pietist reasoned, "The essence of idolatry is the entertainment of thoughts about God that are unworthy of Him."[113] It follows that "the heaviest obligation lying upon the Christian Church today is to purify and elevate her concept of God until it is once more worthy of Him—and of her. In all her prayers and labors this should have first place."[114]

Relating to the Trinity Personally

Being made in God's image, we have the capacity to know the triune God, but because of our sins we lack the power to know him as we ought. The renewal of our minds and hearts in the new birth begins the great adventure. An esteemed former colleague a few days before his death spoke of anticipating "the great adventure." We need not wait for it until the next life. For "now begins the glorious pursuit, the heart's happy exploration of the infinite riches of the Godhead."[115]

Relationships with the three persons of the Trinity can be cultivated as with other personal beings. And the divine Father, Son, and Spirit intensely desire a growing relationship with us. God the Father desired our love from eternity; God the Son provided justly for it on the cross; and God the Holy Spirit makes available the resources for a growing personal communion. No one who calls upon the Father, the Son, or the Spirit in repentant faith is ever turned away.

So a conscious, personal awareness of the triune God's omnipresence and redemptive presence may be experienced here and now! (see 1 Cor. 2:9–10a). The awareness may differ in intensity at different times. It varies like one's awareness of a distant loved one over many busy days, months, and years, but is heightened at times by letters, phone calls, and special visits. The variation is in our conscious attention, however, not of divine presence. The triune God is omnipresent, but we may be brought into a more explicit awareness in the body of believers and at the Lord's Table. The relationship is personal or individual as well as communal. As Tozer says, "It does not come through the body of believers, as such, but is known to the individual, and to the body through the individuals who compose it."[116]

Our consciousness may emphasize, as do the Scriptures on different occasions, the divine oneness, or threeness. Initially, from our experience of nature, we may think of the ultimate source of the world and ourselves. Through the Old Testament we may emphasize the Father's personal, covenant-making grace and steadfast love. Through the Gospels we may zoom in on the incarnate Son's self-giving ministry and his death for our sins. And in the study of Acts we focus on the Holy Spirit proceeding from the Father and the Son to form the Christian church and send believers to disciple others throughout the world. The "Great Commission" and the epistles help us put the three persons together as subsistences within the oneness of the divine Being. Many Christians, as they grow in the grace and in the knowledge of the triune God, follow this historical and literary order of learning.

Putting all the teaching on the doctrine of the Trinity together, Herman Bavinck observed,

> is of the utmost importance for practical religion. . . . Religion cannot afford to be satisfied with anything less than God. In Christ God himself comes to us, and in the Holy Spirit he imparts himself to us. . . . Of God, and through God, and in God are all things. . . . We know ourselves as children of the Father, redeemed by the Son, and having communion with both through the Holy Spirit.[117]

So the Trinitarian understanding of God enriches our limited grasp of the one God *above* us, *for* us, and *in* us.

Some people in these existentialist and pragmatic times may be tempted to seek the practical values of Trinitarian worship and service without knowing the true God and his Son Jesus Christ and the Holy Spirit. A writer very sympathetic to existentialism warns:

> One may carry the contrast between the subjective and objective to such a point

that value or science or logic (or doctrine) is unwisely deprecated. In theology, the contrast can be drawn so sharply that faith and reason are driven unwholesomely asunder. Let us be clear that wherever existentialism undercuts the elements of rational structure which are indispensable to both metaphysics and Christian theology, it must be rejected. Properly employed, however, this mode of thinking rightly opens the way to a reformulation of philosophy and Christian doctrine which can render them vital and dramatic instead of rigid and sterile.[118]

Practicing the Presence of the Trinity

It is not uncommon for untrained Trinitarians to worship as "practical unitarians," claiming to believe in the Trinity but praying like Unitarians. Unitarians, Walter Marshall Horton showed, have emphasized at different times ideas representing all three persons. Influenced by the eighteenth-century Enlightenment, Unitarians thought of God as the ungenerated source of all things. Then, under the impact of New England Transcendentalism, stress fell on God as immanent Spirit, close at hand, dwelling in human beings. Although many turned to pure humanism, some consider God to be the Son who comes forth from himself to reveal his nature in creative and redemptive action.[119]

Practical Trinitarians in their devotional outlook ought to appreciate all three emphases at once. In thinking of the presence of God, they think of the creatively purposive Father; the incarnate, active Son; and the abiding, enabling Spirit. Christians discipline their thinking to avoid "Father Only," "Jesus Only," or "Spirit Only" reductionist tendencies. In practicing the presence of the triune God, Trinitarians consciously meditate on the distinctives of the Planner, Provider, and Enabler while aware of their functional harmony and ontological oneness. "May the

285

grace of the Lord Jesus Christ, and the love of God, and the fellowship of the Holy Spirit be with you all" (2 Cor. 13:14).

Praying to the Triune God

Instead of addressing prayer simply to God; Allah; Jehovah; or the God of Abraham, Isaac, and Jacob, Christians may pray to any of the three persons of the Trinity. It not only follows that persons can have personal relationships, but the Scriptures exhort us to pray to the Father (Matt. 6:6) in the name of the Son (John 16:24) through or in the Holy Spirit (Jude 20). Nowhere does the Bible suggest that prayer must always end with a phrase like "in the name of Christ." Many have found it salutary to begin, "Through Jesus Christ our Lord. . . ." A variety in the order and in the use of divine names helps avoid vain repetition.

Prayer addressed to the Son is not merely a matter of inference from Trinitarianism but is also supported by biblical exhortation and example. Jesus invited prayer to himself (Matt. 11:28; John 4:10). Stephen addressed his dying requests to the "Lord Jesus" (Acts 7:59–60). All Christians call upon Christ (Acts 22:16; 1 Cor. 1:2; 1 Thess. 3:11; 2 Tim. 2:22). Throughout eternity, praise will be offered to Christ (Rev. 1:5–6).

Although prayer addressed to the Holy Spirit is not explicitly exemplified in Scripture, it may be inferred. Prayer to "the Lord of the harvest" to send out workers into the harvest field (Matt. 9:38) is most probably to the Holy Spirit, because it is the Holy Spirit who sends out missionaries (Acts 13:2–4), appoints overseers (Acts 20:28), gives gifts, leads, and empowers for harvest ministries. Since the person of the Holy Spirit dwells in believers' bodies and among believers in the church, it is most appropriate to offer "the Lord of

the harvest" thanksgiving, adoration, praise, and petitions.[120]

Relating to Others in Love Like That of the Trinity

"When we confess the faith of the Church in the Holy Trinity," C. W. Lowry perceives, "we affirm our belief that God is Himself the archetype of all community, all fellowship, all love."[121] The unity of the Godhead, because essential, is also relational. Christians are never of the same essence with one another as are Father, Son, and Spirit, but Jesus prayed that believers would have a relational unity similar to that of the Godhead: "that they may be one as we are one" (John 17:21–22).

The ultimate foundation for all community is found, not in the creatures, but in the ultimate nature of things, in the triune Creator. The final reason for families staying together is not legal agreement enforced by state or church, but demonstration of Trinitarian love and grace. And schism in the church is scripturally sinful (1 Cor. 12:25), not only because of the hurt to many members, but also because it violates their unity in Christ's body and its unity in him with the Father and the Spirit.[122]

Tracing Implications of the Simple Gospel

Although the doctrine of the Trinity is not explicitly stated to pre-Christians in the apostles' *kerygma*, it is implied (in part at least) in the acceptance of Jesus Christ as from the Father above in a unique way and as both Lord and Christ. Young children who accept Christ may not be expected to state the doctrine of the Trinity in the technical terms of one essence and three persons; however, children (of all ages!) understand that Jesus is not simply another human, but in a special way the unique Son from God. That understanding, however childlike, implies some grasp of Jesus' Trinitarian relationship to the heavenly Father. All who believe the gospel and are saved know that, in committing their lives to the Lord Jesus Christ, they are worshiping the Creator, not idolatrously worshiping another creature. Surely any brief tract presenting the plan of salvation for children or adults ought to clarify the deity of Jesus and of the Holy Spirit and relate these in some introductory way.

Testing the Doctrinal Orientation of Institutions

Any doctrinal statement for a Christian church or Christian parachurch society should include in some terms belief in the basic truth of Trinitarianism as a requirement of membership, teaching, and leadership. Unfortunately, too many are satisfied with a statement mentioning a unity, and the names of the Father, Son, and Spirit, without specifying the respects in which they are one and three. Hence a relational unity of mind and purpose may be thought sufficient. Others imagine that they hold a biblical view that the three are not coexistent persons, but merely three different modes of revelation by a unitarian deity. Binitarians affirm only two persons, thinking that the Holy Spirit is just an impersonal influence. If our Christian institutions are to remain true to all the strands of biblical teaching about God, then they must require allegiance to an *essential* unity of the three *persons*—Father, Son, and Holy Spirit.

Teaching the Fundamentals of the Faith

Trinitarian doctrine, like any other, needs only to remain untaught for one generation to be lost. Oddly enough, one of the modern movements most neglectful of the doctrine of the Trinity

is modern Fundamentalism. The Fundamentalists did not include the doctrine of the Trinity in their list of the five fundamentals of the faith, nor did they explicitly formulate it in *The Fundamentals* (1912). It is assumed in B. B. Warfield's article "The Deity of Christ," G. Campbell Morgan's work on "The Purpose of the Incarnation," Robert E. Speer's essay on "God in Christ, the only Revelation of the Fatherhood of God," and R. A. Torrey's defense of "The Personality and Deity of the Holy Spirit." The ingredients are there, but not put together to form a coherent teaching about God.[123]

In a pluralistic world constantly face to face with many concepts of God, parents, Sunday school teachers, ministers, and leaders of parachurch organizations who desire the next generation to be Trinitarian, do well to exhibit the loving personal relationships that follow from it and teach Trinitarian truths on which they remain firm even though heaven and earth should pass away.

The Deepest Roots of a Missionary Theology

The very idea of missions, that of sending, is at the heart of Trinitarianism. In love the Father sent the Son. After his death and resurrection the Son says, " 'As the Father has sent me, I am sending you.' And with that he breathed on them and said, 'Receive the Holy Spirit' " (John 20:21–22). The Lord of the harvest, having come at Pentecost and having added many to the church, sent the first missionaries, Paul and Barnabas, from Antioch. Christianity begins with the heavenly mission: the Father sends the Son, and the Father and Son send the Spirit. Christianity continues as the Spirit sends the forgiven people of God to reach the unreached people in their cities and regions and in the uttermost parts of the world with the message of forgiving, sending, ministering love.[124] Gerald H. Anderson writes:

A major cause for confusion in missions today comes from the inadequacy of the various attempts to formulate the theology of mission in recent years . . . from the culture-centered, man-centered, revelation-centered, eschatology-centered, kingdom-centered, Bible-centered, church-centered, and Christ-centered points of view.[125]

Although each of these aspects is essential, none is adequate as the central point or focus of a theology of missions. So Anderson continues, "It remains now for a major attempt to be made at formulating the theology of mission from the view of *radical trinitarian theocentrism*. When it comes, this approach may plant the seed—but only God gives the growth—for a new flowering of missionary endeavor in our time."[126]

Observing that missionary theology is not an appendix to a biblically based theology, George W. Peters takes up the challenge to produce a Trinitarian-based missions theology. His primary chapter concludes:

The triune God in his very being as Spirit, light and love is an outgoing God, a missionary God, ever sending Himself in benevolent relations to mankind, ever searching in love to bestow Himself in blessings upon mankind, and ever spending Himself in great sacrifice to make man's salvation possible. Father, Son, and Holy Spirit are cooperating and coordinating to bring sinners back from their sinful wandering and blundering and restore them to their pristine state, purpose, destiny and glory.[127]

In another attempt to develop a Trinitarian theology of missions, Lesslie Newbigin, in his book *The Open Secret*, neatly organizes his fresh discussion of the mission of the triune God in three chapters: first, "Proclaiming the Kingdom of the Father: Mission as Faith in Action"; second, "Sharing the Life of the Son: Mission as Love in Action"; and third, "Bearing the Witness of the Spirit: Mission as Hope in Action."[128] After a thoughtful chapter on each of these, Newbigin indicates, "This three-fold way of understanding the church's mission is rooted in the triune being of God himself. If any one of these is taken in isolation as the clue to the understanding of mission, distortion follows."[129]

Missionary work could be further strengthened by an even more thorough response to Anderson's call for a radical Trinitarian theocentric missionary theology. The present work should contribute to that as it considers the significance for life and ministry of the Father's grand design for human history, the Son's atoning provision for it, and its implementation at present by the Holy Spirit.

REVIEW QUESTIONS

To Help Relate and Apply Each Section in This Chapter

1. *Briefly state the classical problem* this chapter addresses and indicate reasons why genuine inquiry into it is important for your world view and your existence personally and socially.

2. *Objectively summarize the influential answers* given to this problem in history as hypotheses to be tested. Be able to compare and contrast their real similarities and differences (not merely verbal similarities or differences).

3. *Highlight the primary biblical evidence* on which to decide among views—evidence found in the relevant teachings of the major divisions of Scripture—and decide for yourself which historical hypothesis (or synthesis of historical views) provides the most consistent and adequate account of the primary biblical data.

4. *Formulate in your own words your*

doctrinal conviction in a logically consistent and adequate way, organizing your conclusions in ways you can explain clearly, support biblically, and communicate effectively to your spouse, children, friends, Bible class, or congregation.

5. *Defend your view* as you would to adherents of the alternative views, showing that the other views are logically less consistent and factually faced with more difficulties than your view in accounting for the givens, not only of special revelation but also of human experience in general.

6. *Explore the differences the viability of your conviction can make in your life.* Then test your understanding of the viability of your view by asking, "Can I live by it authentically (unhypocritically) in relation to God and to others in my family, church, vocation, neighborhood, city, nation, and world?"

MINISTRY PROJECTS

To Help Communicate This Doctrine in Christian Service

1. *Memorize one major verse or passage* that in its context teaches the heart of this doctrine and may serve as a text from which to preach, teach, or lead small group studies on the topic. The memorized passages from each chapter will build a body of content useful also for meditation and reference in informal discussions.

2. *Formulate the major idea of the doctrine in one sentence* based on the passage memorized. This idea should be useful as the major thesis of either a lesson for a class (junior high to adult) or a message for a church service.

3. *State the specific purpose or goal of your doctrinal lesson or message.* Your purpose should be more than informative. It should show why Christians need to accept this truth and live

by it (unhypocritically). For teaching purposes, list indicators that would show to what extent class members have grasped the truth presented.

4. *Outline your message or lesson in complete sentences.* Indicate how you would support the truth of the doctrine's central ideas and its relevance to life and service. Incorporate elements from this chapter's historical, biblical, systematic, apologetic, and practical sections selected according to the value they have for your audience.

5. *List applications of the doctrine* for communicating the difference this conviction makes in life (for sermons, lessons, small-group Bible studies, or family devotional Bible studies). Applications should make clear what the doctrine is, why one needs to know it, and how it will make differences in thinking. Then show how the difference in thought will lead to differences in values, priorities, attitudes, speech, and personal action. Consider also the doctrine's possible significance for family, church, neighborhood, city, regional, and national actions.

6. *Start a file and begin collecting illustrations* of this doctrine's central idea, the points in your outline, and your applications.

7. *Write out your own doctrinal statement on this subject in one paragraph* (in half a page or less). To work toward a comprehensive doctrinal statement, collect your formulations based on a study of each chapter of *Integrative Theology.* As your own statement of Christian doctrine grows, you will find it personally strengthening and useful when you are called on for your beliefs in general and when you apply for service with churches, mission boards, and other Christian organizations. Any who seek ordination to Christian ministry will need a comprehensive doctrinal statement that covers the broad scope of theology.

CHAPTER 8

GOD'S GRAND DESIGN FOR HUMAN HISTORY

God's Grand Design for Human History

This chapter considers the question of whether the events of nature and history are related to a transcendent plan or purpose. Previous chapters have shown that God is no impersonal principle or mindless energy, but a thinking and feeling Being who, while sovereign over the cosmos, is actively involved in human life and history. Given God's ultimacy over the universe, the question arises as to how occurrences in the world, in fact, are related to ends God chose before creation. If God has an overall plan, does he determine to accomplish all of his purposes in the same way or does he determine to accomplish some of them supernaturally apart from any normal use of means and others instrumentally through "natural" forces or human agents? When working with persons made in his image, has God resolved to permit actions that displease him? Can all things, including the spread of sin and the destruction of the wicked, be said to be part of God's all-wise and loving plan in the same way? Some Christians have tried to solve such problems by distinguishing between God's decretive will and his permissive will, whereas others deny that God's relation to evil can be reduced to mere permission.

If God's will is the ultimate cause of all occurrences in nature and history, does it follow that creaturely freedom and responsibility are thereby eliminated? If God's will prevails in the world, how could a person justly be judged for his actions? Furthermore, how, if at all, do the actions of thinking and willing persons impinge on God's sovereign purpose? Can God's plan be altered by human choices? How does finite human decision making relate to God's sovereign and eternal plan? The proposals of Calvinists, Arminians, and theologians of other traditions in regard to such questions will be fairly examined. The present chapter interacts with what most Christians perceive to be true: persons are not pawns in the grip of a blind, immoral power, and ultimately life and history are not meaningless but are invested with purpose and direction by virtue of the eternal plan of a wise and loving God.

ALTERNATIVE CHURCH INTERPRETATIONS

The issue of God's eternal purpose, considered in relation to such matters as human freedom and responsibility, the existence of evil, and the perdition of the unsaved, has occasioned much controversy throughout the history of Christianity. Consequently we must carefully examine the leading interpretations of this complex problem within the church.

Pelagian and Liberal Traditions

Pelagianism and modern liberalism have severely weakened the doctrine of effectual decrees out of concern for creaturely autonomy and freedom. Pelagius and certain of his followers, such as Celestius and Julian of Eclanum, believed that the human person is the master of his own destiny and that God did not subject the creature to an inviolable will. Pelagianism thus virtually denied the notion of a supernatural decree, declaring it to be inconsistent with human autonomy and moral responsibility.

In the nineteenth century Albrecht Ritschl claimed that the quest to probe an alleged supramundane will of a hidden God follows the illegitimate method of speculative theology. His position was that the mind of God was disclosed in the history of Jesus of Nazareth. Through Jesus God is known as "loving will" who guides the world toward the realization of the kingdom.[1] The divine purpose reflected in Jesus excludes the exercise of a punitive will.

Twentieth-century liberal theology has similarly depreciated the sovereign purposes of God in its appeal to human freedom and autonomy. W. N. Clarke affirms that divine foreordination would impugn creaturely freedom, the absence of which would render meaningless human responsibility. Thus "nei-

ther foreordination nor fate has slain freedom, but freedom lives."[2] Clarke's bottom line is that the church need not be bound by the picture of a God of immutable and irresistible decrees.

Other liberals argue that Graeco-Roman philosophy bequeathed to the church the idea of God as capricious and having an arbitrary will. According to Rauschenbusch, the doctrine of divine decrees represents the transference of the idea of the coercive and predatory state to the realm of religion. The "despotic" conception of God as arbitrary tyrant must be replaced by the "democratic" idea of God as benign and loving Father.[3] W. A. Brown similarly held that abstract and individualistic notions such as "secret counsel" and "arbitrary will" (as illegitimate Hellenizations) must give way to concrete and social conceptions of God's gracious kingdom purposes disclosed by Jesus of Nazareth.[4]

Process theology rejects the idea of God as the Controlling Power who determines every detail, present and future, of the world's order. Its God foreknows the future only in terms of the future's potentialities. Process theologians argue that the God of classical theism is an obstacle to the freedom, creativity, and growth of persons. Accordingly, the followers of Whitehead insist that God does not coerce or command; rather, he lovingly lures and tries to persuade entities to new opportunities and satisfactions. Indeed, God provides each actuality with a dynamic impulse called the "initial aim," which each person may choose to accept or reject. "Persuasion and not control is the divine way of doing things."[5]

Semi-Pelagian and Arminian Perspectives

Semi-Pelagians and Arminians argue that in relation to persons an effectual decree would vitiate freedom and responsibility and thereby dehumanize the individual. All God's purposes in relation to human destiny are conditional and are based on God's foresight of human decisions. Semi-Pelagians in the fourth and fifth centuries, in the medieval era, and in much of modern Catholic theology maintain that the Augustinian doctrine of decrees represents a crude fatalism. In matters of salvation Semi-Pelagians uphold the priority of the human will over the divine will and so restrict God's decree to foreknowledge of free human choices. Predestination thus is based on foreseen faith and obedience.

James Arminius, emphasizing human freedom and spontaneity, denied that God efficiently wills the actions of free agents. Thus he viewed the decree of predestination passively as a statement of how God works, namely, saving those he foresaw would believe and of judging those he foresaw would not believe.[6] Against Reformed supralapsarianism, Arminius argued that if God actively decreed the Fall, he would be the author of sin. Hence God "neither perpetrated this crime through men, nor employed against man any action either internal or external, by which He might incite him to sin."[7] Reformed theologians charged Arminius with teaching that God's will is ineffectual and mutable and that his purposes may be frustrated.

John Wesley likewise emphasized less the sovereign purpose of God than the free moral response of the human agent. The Calvinist postulate of an unchanging sovereign decree that determines a person's actions and fate would leave one as free as a stone projected from a sling or a toy in the hands of a tyrant. Thus, although Wesley upheld God's unconditional will to service, he affirmed a conditional will to salvation or perdition. God's sovereign will is not the determiner of a person's destiny. The high Calvinist decree of reprobation violates God's goodness, love, and justice. Wesley argued that it depicts God as "more carnal, false, and unjust that the Devil."[8] Richard Watson, who wrote the first Methodist theology, concurred with Wesley. There are, he argued, two classes of divine decrees: "what He has Himself *determined to do*, and what He has *determined to permit* to be done by free and accountable creatures."[9] Contrary to the Reformed belief in the immutability of God's purpose, Watson insists that God's plan may be changed and even revoked: "The Scriptural doctrine . . . consists in His never changing the *principles* of His administration."[10]

Supralapsarian Hypotheses

Some medieval authorities, Reformers, and orthodox theologians uphold a supralapsarian view of the decrees, whereby all things eventuate according to the logically prior, effectual will of God. They reject the thesis of a permissive will as mere permission would undermine certainty of occurrence. The early Middle Ages witnessed the rise of extreme forms of Augustinianism. Gottschalk, the first significant proponent of double predestination, held that God foreordained to life and to death those whom he sovereignly willed. Gottschalk's supralapsarianism, by which God decreed the eternal damnation of souls prior to his decision to create the world and persons, allowed little room for creaturely freedom. For his views Gottschalk was flogged and confined for life. Similar was the position of Ratramnus: "Nothing that happens to men in this world takes place apart from the secret counsel of the Almighty. For God, foreknowing all things that are to follow, decreed before the ages how they are to be arranged through the ages."[11]

Analogous to his dualism between the "hidden God" and the "revealed

God,'' Luther postulated a twofold will in God, namely, his hidden and his revealed will. The former, the inscrutable purpose into which persons dare not pry, includes God's unconditional predestination of some to be saved and his reprobation of the rest to perdition. Appealing to God's hatred for Esau (Rom. 9:13) and his hardening of Pharaoh (Rom. 9:17–18), Luther affirmed that "the will of the Divine majesty purposely abandons and reprobates some to perish."[12] This will to perdition is not unjust, for the will of God is the highest authority; he is obliged to justify his ways to no one. Mortals, however, must turn from the fearsome, hidden will to God's revealed will made known through Christ and the Scriptures. Luther clearly perceives the workings of God's hidden will as supralapsarian. In addition, little room appears to have been left for a person's freedom of choice vis-à-vis God's will. "Just as we do not come into being by our own will, but by necessity, so we do not do anything by right of free choice, but as God has foreknown and as He leads us to act by His infallible and immutable counsel and power."[13] That God is not the author of sin, and that persons bear responsibility for the choices they make is a mystery embedded in the hidden will of God that only eternity will bring to light.

John Calvin likewise stressed God's comprehensive sovereign will, which allows no room for permission: "All the deeds of men are governed not by His bare permission but by His consent and secret counsel."[14] Thus creation, the fall of Adam, the coming of the Mediator, and Christ's death on the cross were all effected by the active will of the sovereign God. Calvin clearly taught double predestination. "Not all men have been created under the same conditions: some are predestined to eternal life, others to eternal damnation. And inasmuch as a man is created

to reach the one goal or the other, we say that he is predestined to life or to death."[15] Concerning the reprobation of the unrighteous, Calvin soberly remarks: "The decree is dreadful indeed, I confess."[16] Calvin, however, proceeds to distinguish between ultimate and proximate causes. Whereas God's sovereign will is the remote cause of the Fall, Adam's unbelief and rebellion is the immediate cause.[17] By appeal to proximate causes Calvin upholds the responsibility of the human agent. "Men act from their own wickedness, so that the whole fault rests on them."[18] Although Calvin's interest in the decrees was more practical than speculative, what statements he made on their logical order point in the direction of supralapsarianism.[19]

Beza's treatment of the decrees was more speculative: "Nothing in the entire world comes to pass without God's will or knowledge. Everything happens in the manner in which God ordained it from eternity. He disposed the intermediate causes in such a powerful and effective fashion that they were necessarily brought to the appointed end to which He ordained them."[20] Within the framework of double predestination, Beza insisted that the will of God is the first and efficient cause of Adam's fall. But Beza distinguished between God's *decree* of election and reprobation and the *execution* of that decree. Although God willed salvation and damnation, his decree was executed by the secondary means of faith and unbelief. By so reasoning, Beza, the supralapsarian, sought to uphold human responsibility while denying that God is the author of sin. Beza referred the above antinomies to the mysterious will of the sovereign God.

In similar manner John Owen extolled the sovereign God who effectively causes all that eventuates. Reluctant to posit mere permission, Owen argued that "God disposes the hearts of men, rules their wills, inclines their affections, and determines them freely to choose and do what He in His good pleasure has decreed shall be performed."[21] God's sovereign plan includes the coordinate poles of election to eternal life and reprobation to eternal death.

Modern Dutch Reformed theology is predominantly supralapsarian on the decrees. Bavinck, however, maintains that "the history of the universe can never be made to fit into a little scheme of logic."[22] Bavinck does insist that nothing comes to pass without first being established in the divine mind. Hence all things—Adam's fall, the rejection of Esau, the perdition of Judas—have been eternally fixed in the counsel of God and so rendered certain. If the language of permission be used at all, permission must be understood as being "positive" and "efficacious."[23] It follows that for Bavinck the decree of predestination includes both election and reprobation; each has its origin in God's sovereign good pleasure.

Barthian Neoorthodoxy

As understood by Karl Barth, God's decree focuses concretely on Jesus Christ, the beginning and sum of the divine purposes. We will see that Barth proposed a novel scheme of double predestination: God chose Christ for rejection ("No") and elected Christ for salvation ("Yes").

Barth insisted that Scripture does not direct attention to the general doctrine of decrees, with election a subfunction thereof; rather election constitutes the *sum* of the gospel, under which is subsumed all other facets of God's purposes for the world. Against liberalism Barth therefore maintained that God's elective decree is sovereign, omnipotent, and effectual.[24] Against orthodoxy he insisted that the static, abstract decree of Augustine and Calvin must be replaced by a dynamic, concrete decree that has its reality in Jesus Christ. Thus Barth claims that Jesus Christ "is God's Word, God's decree and God's beginning. He is so all-inclusively, comprehending absolutely within Himself all things and everything, enclosing within Himself the autonomy of all other words, decrees and beginnings."[25] Jesus Christ is both the beginning and the sum of the purposes of God. Barth then proceeds to affirm a doctrine of double predestination, albeit not a scheme in which election and reprobation are symmetrical decrees, as in Calvin and Beza. Negatively, in Jesus Christ God eternally elected himself for rejection, suffering, and death. In the first instance, then, "predestination is the non-rejection of man. It is so because it is the rejection of the Son of God."[26] And positively, in Jesus Christ God eternally elected sinful persons to salvation and blessedness.[27] Since God has irrevocably said no to himself and yes to humanity, Barth's logic leads to the vestibule of universalism. Hence the church witnesses to this reality: "that this choice of the godless man is void; that he belongs eternally to Jesus Christ and therefore is not rejected, but elected by God in Jesus Christ."[28] Since God's elective decree in Christ preceded all other determinations, Barth identifies his scheme as a "purified Supralapsarianism."[29]

The Infralapsarianism of Some Fathers, Medieval Authorities, Reformers, and Many Evangelicals

Although many early church fathers stressed human freedom vis-à-vis pagan fatalism, other fathers (e.g., Augustine) and medieval authorities (e.g., Anselm, Aquinas), some Reformers (the later Melanchthon), most confessional standards (e.g., Concord, Belgic, Westminster), and many orthodox and Evangelicals (e.g., Hodge, Packer, Henry)

297

affirm that God has decreed certain things unconditionally (creation, the Incarnation, the salvation of believers) and other things conditionally (the rise of evil, the perdition of unbelievers).

Confronted with pagan astrology and the Stoic doctrine of fate (whereby a person's actions were said to be necessitated by forces beyond his control), the apologists circumstantially emphasized human freedom and responsibility rather than inevitability. Tatian insisted that sin is not due to any divine determination, but to the misuse of human free will. "We were not created to die, but we die by our own fault. Our free-will has destroyed us. . . . Nothing evil has been created by God."[30] Irenaeus, in conflict with the Gnostic doctrine of necessity, muted God's effectual will in salvation. Nevertheless, the sovereign will of God in salvation emerges here and there; e.g., "the Son, according to the Father's good pleasure, administers the Spirit charismatically as the Father will, to those whom he will."[31] On the other hand, Irenaeus maintained that God foresaw human rebellion and permitted his free creatures to walk "in the darkness which they have chosen for themselves."[32] Tertullian concluded that God rejects a person according to his desert: "It is not the mark of a good God to condemn beforehand persons who have not yet deserved condemnation.[33] Tertullian acknowledged in God the equivalent of a preceptive and a permissive will. According to the former, God sets before a person precepts to guide his actions.[34] According to the latter, God did not rescind the gift of freedom, for "He did not interfere to prevent the occurrence of what He wished to happen, in order that He might keep from harm what He wished for."[35]

Against the Pelagians Augustine insisted that the effectual and unchangeable will of God is the ground of all occurrences. Election, one component

of God's unconditional will, is that secret, wise, and beneficent purpose whereby God chose out of the mass of fallen humanity a fixed number to be saved.[36] The bishop was careful to differentiate foreordination from fatalism and determinism, in that he upheld the willing agent's psychological freedom and responsibility. Indeed, "our wills are included in that order of causes which is certain to God and is embraced by His foreknowledge."[37] Augustine also postulated in God a conditional or permissive will. God does not will sins; rather, he permits persons to perpetrate wickedness out of respect for creaturely freedom and for the good he will bring about. God "judged it better to bring good out of evil than not to permit evil to exist."[38] The perdition of the ungodly Augustine ascribed not to God's decretive will, but to his foreknowledge and permission. God left the nonelect in the damnation they justly deserve.[39] Augustine occasionally wrote of God's predetermining sinners to damnation.[40] By such language he conceived of the plan of God broadly, as inclusive both of God's order and of his permission: "Nothing comes about unless God wills it so, either by permitting it to happen or himself performing it."[41] Hence for Augustine reprobation is the divine determination that abandoned sinners should pay the penalty for their own sins. Augustine's order of decrees thus was infralapsarian (or sublapsarian): God's decree of election logically follows his decree to create and to permit the Fall.

Thomas Aquinas's treatment of the decrees was Augustinian. He insisted that some events, such as creation and predestination to life, must be attributed to God's unconditional will. Other events, such as the spread of sin and the reprobation of the wicked, are due to God's permissive will.[42] Thomas explained how evil acts form part of God's overall plan. Although the particular cause of an evil deed is the free act of human persons or Satan, God willed to grant the agent freedom to commit the act. "Since the very act of the free will is traced to God as a cause, it necessarily follows that everything happening from the exercise of the free will must be subject to divine providence. For human providence is included under the providence of God, as a particular under a universal cause."[43] Is human effort or prayer incompatible with God's foreordination? No, he answers, since God's eternal purpose, executed with perfect prevision, includes second causes. "Providence [i.e., foreordination] . . . does not do away with secondary causes, but so provides effects that the order of secondary causes falls also under providence."[44]

Most of the post-Reformation Protestant confessions uphold an infralapsarian view of the divine decrees. Thus the Lutheran Formula of Concord commends an effectual divine predestination to eternal life but not to eternal death. The Westminster Confession affirms (without reconciling the paradoxes) that God is the all-determining first Cause; that he willed the means (second causes) as well as the end of all things; that human actions, although self-actualized, fall within the certainty of God's plan; and that God's will is not the effective cause of sin (Art. III.1; V.2). The Reformed Confessions (Second Helvetic, Gallic, Belgic, Dort, and Westminster) uniformly uphold a single predestination to life. Reprobation includes the twofold purpose of preterition and condemnation to a just judgment (e.g., Westminster Confession, Art. III.3,7). Typical is the Synod of Dort: "Not all, but only some, are elected, while others are passed by in the eternal decree; whom God, out of His sovereign, most just, irreprehensible and unchangeable good pleasure, hath decreed to leave in the common misery into which they have willfully plunged themselves" (Art. I.15). Most of the Reformed confessions reflect an infralapsarian outlook, less clearly so in the case of Dort and Westminster.[45]

Charles Hodge, infralapsarian on the decrees, upheld the Reformed emphasis on the God who foreordains whatever comes to pass. God's will is twofold: efficacious (in the sphere of nature and the ethically good) and permissive (in relation to sin). Hodge maintains that "God has a plan or end for which the universe was created, that the execution of that plan is not left contingent, and that whatever is embraced in the decrees of God must certainly come to pass."[46] Against detractors, Hodge insists that God is not the author of sin, that foreordination is consistent with human freedom and responsibility, and that the decrees do not discourage human effort, since God has ordained both the end and the means to it.[47]

Carl F. H. Henry insists that foreknown and permitted human acts inhere in God's eternal plan. His free, unchanging, and effectual decree imposes certainty on events, be they good or wicked. "The fact that God has foreordained human choices and that His decree renders human actions certain does not therefore negate human choice."[48]

Other recent authorities that uphold an infralapsarian or moderately Reformed stance on the decrees include Millard J. Erickson[49] and the revision of Henry C. Thiessen's theology.[50] Louis Berkhof gives more credence to God's permissive decree than do so-called hyper-Calvinists, but in the end he finds elements of truth in both the infralapsarian and the supralapsarian schemes.[51]

BIBLICAL TEACHING

Pentateuch

The opening statements of the Bible indicate that everything has its origin in

God's thought and will. The formula, "And God said, Let there be . . . " (Gen. 1:3, 6, 14; cf. 1:9, 11, 20, 24, 26) connotes creative words spoken with deliberate intention. The burden of Genesis 1 is that the existence of the universe is grounded in God's intelligent and wise purpose. The observation following each creative episode—"God saw that it was good (*tôb*)" (Gen. 1:10, 12, 18, 21, 25; cf. 1:31)—indicates that God's creative purpose had been realized. The adjective *tôb* connotes less an aesthetic judgment than the fact that "the results of His creative work fully conform to His plan and purpose."[52]

In the Garden of Eden the divine prohibition against eating from the tree of the knowledge of good and evil (Gen. 2:17) indicates that God is a God of specific intention. While the tree contained no magical powers, it served as a symbol of God's conditional purpose vis-à-vis the first pair. The threat of punishment for eating the forbidden fruit (Gen. 2:17; 3:3) implies that sin was permitted by God but not necessitated. Genesis 3 depicts God's allowing with displeasure Adam and Eve's exercise of their free agency in disobedience. The narrative suggests that God's will to permit sin renders Adam and Eve's act empirically certain by virtue of his foreknowledge, but not logically certain.[53] God's will is not the immediate cause of the disobedience of the first pair.

God's promise to give Abraham a land, a posterity, and a mission of blessing (Gen. 12:1–3), a promise later repeated to the patriarchs, is an instance of God's efficient will executed with pleasure. However, the decretive will eliminated neither Abraham's active response (Gen. 12:4; 15:6) nor his moral responsibility (Gen. 17:1; 18:19). Several examples in Genesis of apparent rejection warrant comment. God rejected Cain's offering (Gen. 4:3–5) since, unlike that of Abel, it was not

brought in faith (cf. Heb. 11:4). Similarly, Ishmael was rejected both on account of his scornful attitude (Gen. 21:9) and for the reason that not he but Isaac was chosen for blessing (Gen. 21:10). Finally, God sovereignly chose to install Jacob in the privileged line of Abraham and Isaac (Gen. 25:23; cf. Rom. 9:10–13) while bypassing Esau (but note the latter's preoccupation with merely temporal concerns, Gen. 25:30–34).

The history of Joseph sheds light on the secret workings of God's will. Having learned that God would give Joseph dominion over his brothers, the latter deliberately sold Joseph to Midianite merchants, who in turn sold him to an official in Pharaoh's administration (Gen. 37:28, 36). Yet three times the text declares that *God* sent Joseph to Egypt (45:5, 7–8), which suggests that the brothers' evil designs, permitted by God, were incorporated into his larger plan for the Hebrew people. The severe famine that followed (41:32) and Joseph's rise to authority in Egypt (45:9) were brought about by God. Thus at the end of the episode, Joseph declared that although the intentions of his brothers were evil, God had so overruled and ordered circumstances that his sovereign plan for Israel was actualized (50:20).

The ten or so references to God's hardening Pharaoh's heart (Exod. 4:21; 7:3; 9:12, et al.) offer no proof that God efficiently caused the Egyptian's stubbornness, nor on balance do they support the notion of divine reprobation. Prior to mention of the divine hardening, Scripture implies that Pharaoh freely determined to oppose God's purposes (Exod. 1:9–10, 16). In fact, the text plainly states that Pharaoh volitionally hardened his own heart (Exod. 8:15, 19, 32; 9:7, 34, 35, et al.; cf. 13:15; 1 Sam. 6:6). The most coherent and consistent explanation of the hardening is that God, by withdrawing his sustaining Spirit and by giving Pharaoh up to his own impulses, permitted Pharaoh to actualize his hostile designs (cf. Rom. 1:24, 26, 28).[54] A similar situation occurred in the case of Sihon, king of the Amorites, who refused to permit Israel to pass through his territory. Yet the Hebrews so attributed ultimate causality to God that Moses could say, "God had made his spirit stubborn and his heart obstinate" (Deut. 2:30; cf. Num. 21:23), even though God's involvement was limited to permission of the incident.[55]

God's preceptive will—those moral precepts or commandments that God sets before people for their obedience— is given in the Pentateuch in four major codes. (1) The Decalogue (Exod. 20:1–17) expounds God's purpose for his people in terms of their duty to him and their neighbor. The will of God imbedded in the Ten Commandments is frequently broken even by the devout believer. (2) The Book of the Testament (Exod. 20:22–23:33) provides detailed explication of the principles contained in the Decalogue. The conditional nature of the prescriptions is plainly evident throughout the code (Exod. 21:14, 20, 22; 22:1–2, 16, 23, et al.). (3) The priestly codes (large portions of Leviticus and Numbers) proposed God's wise design for the ministrations of the Aaronic priests. That the laws and decrees in these codes are preceptive and conditional is reflected in the repeated pattern "If you . . . , then I will . . . " (e.g., Lev. 26:3–45). God both permits the violation of his preceptive will and unconditionally ordains punishment for lawbreakers. (4) The Deuteronomic codes (Deut. 1–30; Num. 28–30) contain a restatement of earlier law portions. The preceptive nature of God's will emerges through the common theme of the two books, namely, that if Israel would obey God's voice, he would give them the land and expand their influence. Subsequent his-

tory shows that Israel chose to disobey God's preceptive will, that he permitted them to do so, and that God exacted punishment for their disobedience. God's threatened punishment for disobedience and anger toward sin (Num. 15:30–31; Deut. 28:15–29) suggest that he permitted sin but did not effectively cause it.

God's decretive will is illustrated by his election of Israel for special privileges and service. His choice of Israel was rooted, not in any numerical strength or intrinsic worth, but solely in his own sovereign purpose (Deut. 7:6–8; 10:15, et al.). That God's choice of Israel was made in respect of a fallen universe (Deut. 7:6) seems to point in the direction of an infralapsarian understanding of the logical order of the decrees. In Deuteronomy 29:29 Moses states, "The secret things [hannistārōt] belong to the LORD our God." By these words Moses refers to events yet future that are known only to God—specifically to the judgment that would fall if Israel persisted in their radical disobedience (see vv. 21–28). The following words, "the things revealed [hanniglōt] belong to us and to our children forever, that we may follow all the words of this law," refer to God's preceptive will, which if obeyed, will result in God's blessing.

Historical Books

God's decretive will is evident in the promulgation of his covenant with David (2 Sam. 7:12–16). Here God declares his intention to establish through David an eternal house (vv. 11–12), an eternal throne (v. 13), and an eternal kingdom (v. 16). Even though the Davidic kings would prove faithless and incur punishment, God's redemptive purpose would not fail (vv. 14–16). God's will is likewise seen in his purpose to punish idolatrous Israel. Whereas God justly willed that sin must be punished, the moral evil associated with Nebuchadnezzar's ravaging of Judah (2 Kings 19:25) is part of God's permissive will. The same applies to the punishment inflicted on Jerusalem and Judah by the coalition of pagan nations (2 Kings 24:2–3, 20).

The Lord likewise willed the punishment of Eli's sons by death, but it cannot be said that God was responsible for their sins. Referring to Eli's offspring, 1 Samuel 2:25 reads: "His sons, however, did not listen to their father's rebuke, for it was the LORD's will to put them to death." Two points need be made here. First, the Hebrew conjunction *kî*, translated "for," may also mean "so that," indicating the outcome or result of a situation. In addition, the verb *ḥāpēṣ* has an affective rather than volitional focus and fundamentally means "to experience emotional delight."[56] Thus whereas the Lord took great delight in Samuel, his anger toward the sons of Eli was aroused by virtue of their stubborn persistence in sin.

With regard to Eli's sons, "their failure to listen to their father or obey him functions like the hardening of Pharaoh's heart: it justifies Yahweh's death threat against them. Since they would not hear, he took pleasure in killing them."[57] When the Scripture says that an evil spirit from the Lord "tormented" Saul (1 Sam. 16:14) following the departure of the Holy Spirit from his life, we understand that God permitted the affliction as punishment for Saul's callous disobedience. Moreover, 2 Samuel 24:1 states that God "incited" (lit. "moved," *sût*) David to number the troops of Israel and Judah. Yet David acknowledged that he was morally responsible for his act (v. 10), which reflects a sinful trust in numbers. This admission by David agrees with the chronicler's testimony that "Satan . . . incited David to take a census of Israel" (1 Chron. 21:1). Satan, not

God, prompted David to sin. God's involvement in the matter was one of permission, though to the Hebrew mind God is the ultimate (i.e., final) cause of all occurrences.[58] Likewise Rehoboam's rejection of the advice of the wise elders and the defection of the ten tribes was a matter of divine permission, not causality. The outcome, however, was included in God's sovereign plan (1 Kings 12:15; cf. v. 24). We similarly understand the lying spirit that lured Ahab into attacking Ramoth Gilead (1 Kings 22:20–23). "The sending of the evil spirit is to be regarded as done by the permissive will of God instead of by His direct will. Let it be remembered that Ahab had had ample chance to know truth through Elijah, but had stubbornly resisted it."[59] The incident of God's hardening (Piel of *ḥāzaq*, "to make strong") the hearts of the Canaanite city dwellers (Josh. 11:18–20) should be understood in the sense of Pharaoh's hardening in Exodus. The Hebrew mind, which saw God as the ultimate cause of all that is, frequently spoke of God as causing what he merely permits—though self-hardening is acknowledged, as in 1 Samuel 6:6; 2 Chronicles 36:13; cf. Nehemiah 9:16–17, 29. The Hebrews thus shared little of the pagan belief that events happen by "chance" (*miqreh*, 1 Sam. 6:9). Texts that speak of God rejecting (*mā'as*) persons refer not to eternal reprobation, but to God's temporal penal judgments. God rejects those who have first rejected him (1 Sam. 15:23, 26).

Poetry and Wisdom

Job's trials taught him that God is a God of intelligent purpose (*'ēṣāh*, Job 12:13). All his dealings with nature (v. 15), persons (vv. 17–21), and nations (vv. 23–25) were carefully conceived, though not fully understood by humans (Job 42:3). The decree of God is wholly sovereign and free (Job 23:13–14). The Hebrew of Psalm 135:6 literally reads: "Everything that Yahweh willed to do [*hāpēṣ*] he did ['*āśāh*]." The "plan" ('*ēṣāh*) or "purpose" (*maḥ*ᵃ*šābôt*) of the Lord is eternal and unchangeable (Ps. 33:11). Given his wisdom and power, God need not have any contingency plans. Moreover, God's will is effectual (Prov. 19:21), and his "plan" (*mᵉzimmāh*, Job 42:2) is absolutely invincible. God's purpose embraces all things; even the evil deeds of the wicked fit into his overarching plan (Prov. 16:4).

The poetical books acknowledge God's unconditional will. Thus the election, anointing, enthronement, and rule of David, and ultimately of Christ (Ps. 2:7–8), were effected by God's inviolable "decree" (*ḥōq*). Moreover, God willed the punishment of those who refused his grace and rebelled against him. The language of rejection, common in the Psalms and indicated by the verbs *zānaḥ* (Pss. 43:2; 44:9, 23; 60:1, et al.) and *mā'as* (Ps. 53:5; 78:59, 67; 89:38), refers to a temporal forfeiture of privileges as a result of deliberate covenant-breaking. God's work among the Egyptians—"whose hearts he turned to hate (*śāmē'*) his people" (Ps. 105:25)—must be understood in the sense of his hardening of Pharaoh's heart (for human self-hardening, see Ps. 95:8; Prov. 28:14). Scripture refuses to ascribe sin to God's efficient will, as indicated by repeated warnings of judgments against evil practices (Ps. 81:13–15; Eccl. 11:9).

God's preceptive will, which embodies his desired intentions and which may be broken, is suggested by such Hebrew words as *mišpāṭ* ("ordinance," "laws," Ps. 119:91, 103, 149), *tŏrāh* ("instruction," "law," or "teaching," Pss. 1:2; 19:7; 119:1), '*ēdāh* ("statute," Pss. 78:56; 93:5; 119:2, 22, 24), *miṣwāh* ("command," "precept," Pss. 19:8; 78:7; 89:31), '*ēṣāh* ("counsel," Job 38:2; Pss. 73:24; 106:13), *derek* ("way," "path," Job 21:14; 23:11; 31:7), and *rāṣôn* ("will," in the sense of delight or good pleasure, Pss. 40:8; 103:21). God desires that people obey him and realize his moral purposes for their lives (Ps. 51:6; Prov. 19:20). Yet it is clear that God's preceptive will of pleasure frequently is broken by disobedience (Ps. 107:11; Prov. 1:25, 29–30).

God's permissive will is seen in his allowing Satan to strike at Job (Job 2:3–6) and his possessions (Job 1:12). Although Satan was the effective agent of affliction (Job 2:7), Job 42:11 speaks of "all the trouble [*rā'āh*, "misfortune," "adversity"] the LORD had brought upon him" (cf. Job 1:21). Clearly here, as elsewhere, God is said to cause what he merely permits to be done. Other instances of God permitting with displeasure what was contrary to his highest purposes appear in Psalms 78:18–31 and 81:11–12. That sin entered the world by divine permission only is clear from Ecclesiastes 7:29: "God made mankind upright, but men have gone in search of many schemes" (cf. Ps. 92:15).

The Prophets

God's plan ('*ēṣāh*) in the prophets is represented as a coherent whole (Isa. 14:26). Aspects thereof, actualized in time and history, are "great" (Jer. 32:19) and inscrutable (Isa. 55:8). God's will, moreover, is sovereign and free (Dan. 4:35). The imagery of the potter and clay (Isa. 45:9–13), adduced in response to the questions, Why did God bring the captivity? and Why did God choose Cyrus to effect restoration? clearly affirms that God wills events on the basis of his sovereign pleasure. The divine purpose, in addition, is effectual and inviolable. "The LORD Almighty has purposed [*yā'aṣ*], and who can thwart him?" (Isa. 14:27; cf. 55:10–11).

God's sovereign will, effected by

human instrumentality, includes his purpose to liberate Israel from captivity by Cyrus, to repopulate Jerusalem, and to rebuild the temple (Isa. 44:28; 46:10–11; Jer. 29:11). God's word in Malachi 1:2, "I have loved Jacob" refers to God's decision to show compassion to or to sovereignly elect the younger brother to salvation. The parallel clause, "Esau I have hated" (śānē'), connotes God's relative lack of preference for, or his passing over, the firstborn, for reasons known only to himself.[60]

A prominent feature of God's will in the prophets is his decision to punish the wicked (Isa. 14:24–25; 26:21; Jer. 50:45). In the execution of the divine judgment, hostile nations freely act according to their own political and military self-interests (Isa. 23:13; Mic. 4:12–13). Habakkuk wrestles with the problem of why the people of God suffer at the hands of ruthless pagan invaders. Although the language speaks of God "raising up the Babylonians" and employing them as agents of judgment (Hab. 1:6, 12), the Hebrew mind once again ascribes to God's initiative what he merely permits to be done.[61]

In Habakkuk 1:17 the anguished prophet appears to ask God how long the Babylonians will be permitted to ravage the nations without being checked. When in the course of judgment God is said to work ra' or rā'āh (Isa. 45:7; Jer. 18:11; Amos 3:6; Zech. 8:14–15), the meaning is not that God is the author of wickedness but that his punishment takes the form of "disaster" or "calamity."

How should we understand the relation between the will of God and the Messiah's death? Isaiah 53:3–5, 7–9 prophetically depicts the deep physical and emotional sufferings of the Christ, which the Gospels indicate were administered by the Jewish religious leaders and Roman authorities. The latter, then, were the efficient agents of the Messiah's suffering and death. The text of Isaiah 53:10 is somewhat corrupt and could be translated, "But Yahweh took pleasure in his humiliated one."[62] But if the common reading be allowed to stand—"Yet it was the LORD's will to crush him and cause him to suffer" (cf. RSV, NASB, JB)—"perhaps no more is intended than the fact that the servant's anguish was in every way the fulfillment of a great divine plan."[63] That is, God's role in the death of the Messiah (Isa. 53:4, 10) was to permit the foreseen passion of the Lord and sovereignly to ordain the *saving ends* that would be achieved by his death—namely, atonement for sins, declaration of righteousness, and spiritual cleansing for all who believe (Isa. 52:15; 53:5, 10–11).

The prophets upheld God's preceptive will that included his desired intentions for his people. Isaiah 48:17 reads, "I am the LORD your God, who teaches you what is best for you, who directs you in the way you should go" (so also Ezek. 18:21; Hos. 6:6). Yet because God's will of pleasure was scorned, disaster fell upon the people of God (Isa. 1:19–20; Ezek. 18:20). The object lesson of the potter (Jer. 18:1–12), wherein the first pot became marred, prompting the potter to fashion a second pot, teaches that God's will of pleasure for his people was violated by disobedience. God does not compel a person against his will to obey his precepts; rather, with displeasure God permits people to choose their own loyalty (Jer. 2:21; 44:4–5; Hos. 6:6–7). The wicked die (Ezek. 18:23) because God has purposed to honor human decisions. What is hebraistically known as God's stupifying activity (Isa. 6:9–10) represents his permission of creaturely rejection of his Word.[64] God's rejection of his people occurred only (logically) after they had deliberately rejected him (Jer. 6:30; Hos. 4:6; 9:17).

The Synoptic Gospels

Jesus was conscious of the unconditional will of his Father. His model prayer contains the petition "Your kingdom come, your will [thelēma] be done on earth as it is in heaven" (Matt. 6:10). The verbs "come" and "be done"—imperatives of request that stand first in each clause in the Greek—indicate that Jesus petitioned for the historical actualization of God's eternal purpose for history—namely, the establishment of the kingdom on earth. According to Luke 12:32, God by a sovereign determination resolved (eudokēsen) to give his little flock the blessings of his reign. Moreover, Luke affirms that Christ's suffering, death, and resurrection—being fixed in the plan of God—were foretold in prophetic Scripture (Luke 24:46). Luke 22:22 is an important Scripture on the subject of the divine decree: "The Son of Man will go as it has been decreed [hōrismenon, perfect passive participle of horizō, "to determine," "appoint"], but woe to that man who betrays him." This text teaches that the Crucifixion was part of God's overarching decree, though the efficient and blameworthy cause of Christ's death clearly was Judas's act of betrayal (cf. Matt. 26:24). The impersonal verb dei ("it is necessary")[65] connotes that Jesus' preaching ministry (Luke 4:43); his suffering, death, and resurrection (Matt. 16:21; Luke 24:7, 26, 44); and the world-wide proclamation of the gospel (Mark 13:10) were aspects of God's purpose: "The necessity of the events results from the sovereign purpose of God and the inviolability of His word through the prophets."[66]

Some interpreters find in certain sayings of Jesus justification for an alleged decree of reprobation. Matthew 11:25, however, teaches that God by his "good pleasure" (eudokia) has chosen to reveal the significance of Christ's words and deeds to receptive hearts and to hide the same from the proud and self-sufficient. The Lord made the same point in Matthew 13:11. Jesus' parable of the sheep and the goats (Matt. 25:31–46) differentiates between the sheep on the right hand ("blessed" by the Father) and the goats on the left ("cursed" [katēromenoi] by him). The text states that the righteous inherit the kingdom prepared specifically for them (v. 34), whereas the accursed depart into the place of torment prepared, not for them, but for Satan and his angels (v. 41). "The distinctive element in the biblical statement is not the 'congruity' but the 'incongruity' of the 'right hand and the left hand.' "[67] The lost are those whom God has sovereignly chosen to "leave" (aphiēmi, Luke 17:34–35) in their self-chosen state of sinful rebellion.

God's preceptive will is set forth in Jesus' Sermon on the Mount (Matt. 5–7). Access to heaven is predicated on obedience to God's preceptive will of pleasure (thelēma, Matt. 7:21; 12:50). Many people, however, respond like the Jewish leaders who "rejected God's purpose for themselves" (Luke 7:30). The words "for themselves" modify the verb "rejected," thus emphasizing that persons may break God's will of pleasure and thereby incur condemnation.[68] Other instances where God's preceptive will was spurned occur in Matthew 23:37 and Luke 12:47. The Lord takes no pleasure in the death of any of his creatures (Matt. 18:14).

Jesus taught that God's permissive will is characterized by empirical certainty. According to Matthew 24:6, wars "must" (dei) occur, and, according to Matthew 18:7, the working of those who obstruct true faith is "inevitable" (anankē). Some things are rendered certain by God's decreeing their happening, others by his foreseeing their permitted occurrence. God's holy and righteous character ensures that he is not the efficient cause of greed and hatred in the world.

Primitive Christianity/Acts

The record of the church's growth in Acts gives pride of place to God's sovereign will. As in the Gospels, so in Acts Christ's rejection, death, and resurrection were grounded in God's overarching plan. So Peter testifies to the Jews: "This man was handed over to you by God's set purpose [*horismonē boulē*] and foreknowledge [*prognōsis*] and you, with the help of wicked men, put him to death by nailing him to the cross" (Acts 2:23). Peter later declared that the authorities "did what [God's] will [*boulē*] had decided beforehand [*proōrisen*] should happen" (Acts 4:28). These texts teach (1) that Christ's death in respect to its saving end or purpose was willed by God and thus certain of occurrence (cf. Acts 3:18; 17:3); (2) that God permitted the freely conceived plots of Jesus' enemies which were incorporated into his redemptive plan.[69]; and (3) that Christ's death, though part of God's plan, did not exclude Jesus' free giving of himself (Eph. 5:2)—i.e., for Jesus God's will was conditionally experienced.

God's decretive will is further illustrated by the fact that God "set [*etheto*] by his own authority" the time for the restoration of the kingdom (Acts 1:7). In addition, God not only ordained (*hōrismenos*) Jesus to be judge of the living and the dead (Acts 10:42), but he also appointed (*estēsen*) a day for the judgment of the world (Acts 17:31). The account of Paul's shipwreck (Acts 27) teaches that God's sovereign will does not discourage genuine human effort. An angel of God informed the apostle that both he and the others on the ship would survive the storm (Acts 27:22–24, 34). Yet God's purposes would be realized only as the mariners stayed with the ship (v. 31), jettisoned cargo (v. 38), and used their nautical skills to run the ship aground (vv. 39–41). Some of God's purposes are achieved by human instrumentality.

Acts recognizes, in addition to God's decretive will done with pleasure, his permissive will accomplished with his displeasure. At Lystra Paul and Barnabas said the following of God's dealings with the Gentile world: "In the past, he let [*eiasen*, "to permit," "allow"] all nations go their own way" (Acts 14:16). God did not compel obedience to his preceptive will (cf. David's obedience to the same, Acts 13:22). Rather, after issuing adequate warnings, he reluctantly allows people to follow their own desires. Paul's statement that "in the past God overlooked [*hyperidōn*] such ignorance" (Acts 17:30) conveys the same meaning.

Pauline Corpus

Paul's letters contain extensive teaching on the divine decrees. Ephesians 1:9–11 outlines the leading characteristics of God's will. (1) God has but a *single* plan. Verse 9 refers to "the mystery of his will [*thelēma*]" and verse 11 "the plan [*prothesis*] of him who works out everything in conformity with the purpose [*boulē*] of his will [*thelēma*]." (Cf. God's "purpose" in Rom. 8:28; Eph. 3:11.) (2) This plan is an *inclusive* plan; it embraces "everything" (Eph. 1:11) or "all things" (Rom. 8:28). "Everything is comprehended in his purpose, and everything is ordered by his efficient control."[70] (3) His is an *eternal* plan, as indicated by the word *protithēmi* ("to purpose," v. 9), *proorizō* ("to predestine," v. 11), and *prothesis* ("purpose," v. 11). Ephesians 3:11 pointedly speaks of God's "eternal purpose" (*prothesis tōn aiōnōn*). (4) God's plan is also a *free* plan, in that God acts not by internal constraint or by external compulsion, but strictly on the basis of "his good pleasure" (*eudokia*, v. 9; cf. v. 5; Phil. 2:13). And (5) God's plan is an *effectual* plan; what the sovereign God wills unconditionally or conditionally comes to pass (v. 10; cf. v. 13). The end of the divine decrees is God's glory (*doxa*, Eph. 1:6), or the manifestation of the sum of his excellencies.

Elsewhere in Paul's writings it is clear that God sovereignly planned from eternity the scheme of saving sinners through Christ (1 Cor. 2:7; cf. 1:21; Eph. 1:9). The components of God's saving "purpose" (Rom. 8:28) are detailed in Romans 8:29–30 by a series of aorist verbs: God "foreknew," "predestined," "called," justified," and "glorified" his people. That the glorification of the saints is put in the aorist tense indicates that the event was rendered so certain in the divine plan that Paul regards it as an accomplished fact.[71] The apostle believed that God from eternity elected individual sinners to be saved (Eph. 1:4–5, 11; 1 Thess. 5:9; 2 Thess. 2:13; 2 Tim. 1:9). Texts such as Romans 9:15; 1 Corinthians 2:7; Ephesians 1:4; and 2 Timothy 1:9 suggest that God's saving purpose was executed with respect to a fallen world order, a view that agrees with the infralapsarian order of the decrees. It is also clear that God's effectual will to save includes genuine human involvement and responsibility (Phil. 2:12–13; 2 Thess. 2:13).

Paul applies his theology of divine decrees to the historical problem of Israel's unbelief and apparent rejection by God. That the Gentiles and not Israel have found favor with God was foreshadowed by God's love for Jacob and his "hatred" of Esau (Rom. 9:13). The statement "Jacob I loved" connotes that God extended compassion toward Jacob or that he elected him in grace. On the other hand, the statement "Esau I hated" signifies that God purposed not to extend compassion toward Esau or that he chose not to elect him in grace. According to Cranfield, "God has chosen Jacob and his descendants to stand in a positive relation to the fulfillment of His gracious purpose: He has left Esau and Edom outside this relationship."[72] The affirmation that God is merciful to whom he wills (vv. 15, 18) signifies election according to his free self-determination. On the other hand, God's hardening of Pharaoh and Israel (v. 18) connotes not reprobation, but his ratification of their own determination to steel their hearts against the divine will of pleasure. With Shedd we could say that God hardens the hearts of the unsaved in two ways: (1) by permitting the person to exercise his sinful will and (2) by withdrawing his grace so that the person's sinful lusts go unchecked.[73] Paul's statement that God "raised up" (*exēgeira*) Pharaoh—the Hebrew of Exodus 9:16 suggests that God merely sustained Pharaoh in life (see RSV)—was intended to point up God's use of hard-hearted Pharaoh in the out-working of his saving plan. God was not, however, the efficient cause of Pharaoh's actions.

The analogy of the potter and the clay (Rom. 9:20–21), whereby the craftsman fashions out of the same lump one vessel "for noble purposes" (*eis timēn*) and another "for common use" (*eis atimian*) registers the point made earlier that God purposes to sanctify one group of people and to leave the other in their sins. "It should be noted that *eis atimian* implies menial use, not reprobation or destruction. The potter does not make ordinary, everyday pots in order to destroy them."[74] Neither do verses 22–23 support a predestination to destruction. The text states that the saved were "prepared in advance for glory" (*proētoimasen*), whereas the lost are "prepared for destruction" (*katērtismena*). The fact that Paul does not here use the verb *prokatartizō* (cf. 2 Cor. 9:5) suggests that it is not God who reprobated in eternity; rather, the sinner prepared himself for destruction by his own refusal to repent. The emphasis in these verses is not God's reprobation, but the postponement of his wrath against people who are ripe for destruction. In sum, "there appears here no support for any dogma of predestination to damnation, while the parallel foreordination to glory is stated with no uncertainty."[75]

The hardening of Israel cited in Romans 11:7, 25 and their subsequent spiritual insensibility (Rom. 11:8, 10) should be understood in the sense of Romans 9:18. With pleasure God willed the salvation of "a remnant" (Rom. 11:5) within the family of Abraham, but with displeasure he permitted the majority of Israelites to reject his offer of grace (v. 12). We agree with Brunner that "there is no doctrine of a double decree in the New Testament, and still less in the Old."[76] As Paul reflects on God's sovereign and inscrutable decrees, he is compelled to worship and praise the God from whom and through whom and to whom are all things (v. 36).

Paul sees God's decretive will as providing the benefits of Christ's death on the Cross (Gal. 1:4) and as the ground of his apostleship (2 Cor. 1:1; Gal. 1:1, 15–16), the gifts granted by the Spirit to the church (1 Cor. 12:11), and the authority of civil rulers (Rom. 13:1–2).

The hortatory sections of Paul's letters admonish believers to actualize God's preceptive will for their lives. These exhortations to do God's *thelēma* (Rom. 12:2; Eph. 5:17; Col. 4:12; 1 Thess. 4:3) focus on the concrete goal of spiritual maturing or perfection in Christ. Paul's statement that God "wants [*thelei*] all [cf. *pantōn (anthrōpōn)*, vv. 1–2, 6] men to be saved and to come to a knowledge of the truth" (1 Tim. 2:4) refers, not to God's decretive will that shall be effected (so Roman Catholic and other universalists),

but to that general desire or wish of God that is constantly assailed by creaturely freedom.[77]

God's permissive will is seen in the threefold "God gave them over" (*paredōken*) cited in Romans 1:24, 26, 28. God reluctantly permitted humankind to substitute idolatry for the knowledge and worship of the living God. The element of displeasure in God's permissive will stands out in 1 Corinthians 10:5, where it is said of the Israelites who practiced idolatry and sexual immorality, "God was not pleased [*ouk eudokēsen*] with most of them." According to 2 Thessalonians 2:10, 12, the workers of iniquity perish because they refuse to embrace the truth of the gospel. The opening phrase of verse 11, *kai dia toutou* ("for this reason"), introduces the result of this self-chosen unbelief: "God sends them a powerful delusion so that they will believe the lie." Thus Peter suggests that God responds to persistent unbelief with judicial hardening. "God sends a 'working of delusion' in the sense that to be misled by falsehood is the divine judgment inevitably incurred in a moral universe by those who close their eyes to the truth."[78]

John's Writing

According to Revelation 4:11, God's will (*thelēma*) is the ground of the creation of the world and the existence of all that is. That same unconditional will planned the values and ends of Christ's death, so that John could speak of "the Lamb that was slain from the creation of the world" (Rev. 13:8). John's claim that the Father gave certain individuals to belong to the Son (John 6:37, 39) connotes God's decretive will to save. Yet it is clear that this decree of election requires the faith response of the individual ("whoever comes to me," v. 37, and "who looks to the Son and believes in him," v. 40).

Jesus' saying that he came into the world "for judgment" (John 9:39) implies no decree of reprobation, still less a supralapsarian order of the decrees. Rather, Jesus intended that his teaching and miracles would bring people to a point of decision. Those who chose to reject him passed judgment on themselves. Similarly, Jesus' description of Judas as "the one doomed to destruction" (John 17:12) focuses on Judas's self-chosen character and his inevitable end. Thus "even the fall of Judas found a place in the whole scheme of divine Providence."[79]

Jesus' burden was to do the will (thelēma) of the Father who sent him (John 4:34; 6:38). The major moments of Jesus' life were included in the plan of God: namely, his arrest (John 7:30; cf. 2:4), his crucifixion (the verb dei, John 3:14; 12:34), and his resurrection (dei, John 20:9). Each of these events was empirically necessary because it was foreseen by God and included in his eternal purpose.

The Book of Revelation uses the verb of necessity, dei, to speak of those events that "must soon take place" (Rev. 1:1; cf. 4:1; 22:6) in the overall purpose of God. The future course of the world's order includes events both planned and permitted by God. Thus God unconditionally planned the second coming of Christ, the overthrow of Satan, the millennial reign of Christ, the resurrection of the just and the unjust, and the new heavens and the new earth. On the other hand, God has permitted with displeasure the spread of apostasy, the rise of totalitarian regimes, the unleashing of Satanic oppression during the Great Tribulation, and the rebellion of Satan after the thousand-year reign. In spite of all the sin in the world, John insists that God is not the author of evil: "God is light; in him there is no darkness at all" (1 John 1:5). As light (phōs), God is the unimpeachable source of holiness, righteousness, and truth.

Other New Testament Literature

Hebrews attests the immutability and trustworthiness of the divine decree with the phrase "the unchanging nature of his purpose" (boulē, Heb. 6:17). James agrees that no variation occurs in God's willing and doing (James 1:17). This is so because the plan of God is eternal, having been formed before the creation of the world (1 Peter 1:20).

In teaching that Christ "was chosen (proegnōsmenou, perfect passive participle of the verb "to foreknow") before the creation of the world" (1 Peter 1:20), Peter implies that God eternally planned the end and the values of Christ's saving mission (cf. Luke 22:22; Acts 2:23). Although the great moments of Christ's ministry were included in the plan of God, Jesus' statement "I have come to do your will [thelēma], O God" (Heb. 10:7; cf. v. 9) indicates that from his earthly standpoint he conditionally experienced the sovereign will. According to 1 Peter 1:2, God's sovereign decree of election involves (1) the use of foreordained means ("through the sanctifying work of the Spirit") and (2) conscious human participation and responsibility ("for obedience to Jesus Christ"). Jude 4 affirms, not a decree of reprobation, but God's purpose to execute judgment (krima) on false teachings. Likewise 1 Peter 2:8 affirms the divinely appointed ruin of those who persistently reject the gospel. The antecedent of the clause "which is also what they were destined for" (etethēsan) is not the verb "they disobey" (so Calvin, Beza), but "they stumble."[80]

Hebrews 13:20–21 teaches that God desires that his preceptive will be fulfilled: "May the God of peace . . . equip you with everything good for doing his will [thelēma], and may he work in us what is pleasing (*euarestos*) to him, through Jesus Christ." Other references to God's will of pleasure are Hebrews 10:36 and 1 Peter 2:15; 4:2, 19. Similar to 1 Timothy 2:4 is the teaching of 2 Peter 3:9: "The Lord . . . is patient with you, not wanting [*boulomai*] anyone to perish, but everyone to come to repentance." The last two texts teach that God takes no pleasure in the death of the wicked but waits for the unsaved to turn and live (cf. Ezek. 18:23).

According to James 1:13–15 God does not tempt (*peirazō*) anyone to sin. Rather, out of respect for creaturely freedom God permits people to follow their own lusts and to sin. Hebrews' mention of Israel's hardness of heart in Egypt focuses on the individual as the cause of the hardening (Heb. 3:8, 13, 15; 4:7). Scripture suggests that continued resistance to God's grace produces a fixed habit of opposition to God that is not easily broken. One authority observes that the aorist passive subjunctive, *sklērunthē* ("that none of you may be hardened," Heb. 3:13) is best "understood as a passive of permission; i.e., 'allow or permit one's self to be hardened.' "[81] Similarly, Esau was rejected by God only after he had rejected the grace of God freely offered (Heb. 12:17).

SYSTEMATIC FORMULATION

Before seeking as far as possible to order the extensive controversial material from the primary scriptural and secondary historical sources logically, we pause to examine our preunderstandings about causal actions.

Assumptions Concerning Personal and Impersonal Causes

To understand anything, said the Greek philosopher, Aristotle, we must know not only (1) the material of which it is made and (2) the agent who made it, but also (3) the end or purpose in mind and (4) the form given it to satisfy this purpose.[82] In short, Aristotle sought four causes of events in human history and of the whole nature: material, efficient, final, and formal antecedents. The New Testament also, allowing for material factors and forms or essences in the Logos, attributes events to personal (efficient) agencies and their purposes. For centuries afterward theologians continued to investigate not only the nonpersonal materials contributing to the nature of things and events, but also personal causes and teleological ends served.

However, since Hume, Kant and many modern scientists abandoned the early theistic assumptions of scientists and philosophers and overlooked the agency of persons as efficient causes with final causes or purposes. Secular humanism's epistemology tends to limit philosophical inquiry to phenomenal description of observable causes and their forms (formulae). The choices of persons are attributed to other impersonal factors. Our actions may be held to be determined by nonintelligent antecedents. If we perform actions that appear to be uncaused, they are attributed to sheer chance. Secular science now simply describes changes in the forms of matter-energy and does not even ask, let alone answer, questions about personal agency and purpose in the cosmos at large. So, if we have been educated within the assumptions of a nontheistic world view, we may describe only event-causation and whatever meaning individual existentialist types may read into their lives at the moment.

To overcome the sense of pointlessness, non-Christians may inconsistently "borrow" or "steal" from a Christian world view a universally good "purpose" that will automatically work itself out through a Marxist economic dialectic, mere chance, or an undirected evolution. These unwarranted hopes within non-Christian world views need to be unmasked. Then Christians need to place greater emphasis on "agent causation: the notion of a person as an ultimate source of action."[83] Christians need not reject the categories of causality, as Barth does, to emphasize personal categories.

Believing with good reason that the ultimate reality is a transcendent, personal, causal Agent who knows, feels, and wills, it makes sense to inquire whether God has an overarching purpose for the world. If our heavenly Father has a goal for history and is personally involved with the world, lasting significance in human existence can make sense. And human determinations and actions may also be regarded as responsible causes. Issues related to ways in which God works out his plans in history must be reserved for the study of divine providence.

The Meaning of Divine Decrees in General

By the divine decrees we mean the eternal Father's self-determined purposes and strategies that guide his Son's and the Spirit's dynamic activities from the world's creation to history's consummation.

To help grasp the significance of this hypothesis we here briefly present some of its important facets for consideration. Some of the more controversial points will be defended at greater length in relation to soteriology.

The decrees refer to purposes our heavenly *Father* has chosen for creation and human history. Although the distinctive ministries of the Son and the Spirit are often highlighted, the Father's distinctive role may not receive equal time. One characteristic emphasis of the Scriptures attributes to the Father the primary responsibility for electing, predestining, and foreknowing (Matt. 6:10; Eph. 1:3–4). So passages in the Old and New Testaments referring the purposes to "God" (without distinguishing the persons of the Trinity) may be interpreted as meaning the Father's purposes when trinitarian distinctions are in view.

The Father's decrees were not automatically necessitated, but were *free decisions* of purposes for the universe. In making them, God was not coerced by anything outside himself, for nothing else existed beyond the triune essence. As a personal agent God has the intellectual capacity to choose among ends and the volitional ability to move toward their achievement by the strategies he chooses. On our concept of freedom these decisions were self-determined in accord with the Father's nature. It may seem tautologous to insist on a freedom with fidelity to the divine character since that should be implied in *self*-determination. But Barth and James Daane seek to divorce God's freedom from his essence. Daane opposes a decretal theology in which God "is a decreeing God in terms of his ontology, and not in terms of his freedom."[84] According to Daane, "The distinctive feature of God's decree is that it expresses the freedom of the divine will."[85] Indeed God's decrees are chosen freely, but God cannot deny himself, lie, or determine to do anything unholy or unjust. God's choice of ends was not arbitrary but in accord with attributes of wisdom, holiness, and love. The freedom of Christ's heavenly Father cannot be abstracted from his whole being. It is not a mere will that decrees, it is the whole being of God the Father who decrees. The agent choosing the divine purposes is God the Father, not just his will abstracted from him. So we insist that God's freedom does not include the power of choice contrary to his attributes, but the power of self-determination according to them. Note, please, that by holding that God is faithful to wise, holy, and loving ends, *we* do not limit God. Rather, we simply recognize that the Almighty makes decisions with integrity and authenticity. God's sovereignty is absolute, but not tyrannical.

The decrees were also *eternal decisions* giving direction to dynamic action in time. Before the creation of the world the Father envisioned creation's goals. His settled determinations secure the direction of his dynamic acts in history. The changelessness of the decrees need not imply a "fixed" and "static" view of history (as Barth charged). Clarity of purpose and strategy should not be confused with lack of activity. God is not less active for knowing where he is going. Quite the contrary, God's purposes call for the dynamic activities of his spiritual people, his Son, and the Spirit in history.

The Father determined *both purposes and strategies* (ends and means). Beginning students in this doctrine often find insuperable difficulties because they are preoccupied with the notion that God is achieving ends entirely apart from means and processes. The goal of winning a football game is one thing, the team's strategy for achieving that win in different plays is another. Both are indispensable. Thought about the ends should not ignore the strategies for attaining them. Neither should means be mistaken for ends or ends for means. The end is what is aimed at (the final cause), means are the ways the end is brought about. Purposes are intended goals; strategies are the tactics designed to achieve them. God included strategies as well as purposes in his plan.

God's purposes and strategies are *comprehensive but radically different* in relation to moral evil and good. The Father permits the work of Satan; he ordains the work of Christ. Moral evil is included in God's plan, as we shall see, not with pleasure but with displeasure.

To affirm with some Reformed theologians that all the decrees are one may raise unnecessary problems. All may be considered one if it means all God's purposes are just and his different strategies are coordinated in God's mind. If, however, the oneness of the decrees means that the Father determines human enslavement to sin unconditionally with the same pleasure as redemption from sin, that is unthinkable. If God cannot even tempt to sin (James 1:13) and takes no pleasure in death (Ezek. 18:20) its merited consequence (Rom. 6:23), theologians ought not to imply that he has purposed it or contributes to it by the same strategies as he contributes to holiness, which he efficiently encourages and which is an unmerited gift of grace.[86]

Does not the Bible itself say that God can create evil (Isa. 45:7)? Isaiah does not teach the blasphemous idea that the Lord creates sin! What the Lord, the Holy One of Israel (v. 11), initiates is punishment for sin! He created "darkness" or "disaster" (v. 7) in judgment on Egypt when it was dark for three days (Exod. 10:21–23). "He sent darkness and made the land dark—for had they not rebelled against his words?" (Ps. 105:28). So Isaiah predicted that a sudden disaster would come upon Babylon (Isa. 47:11). Amos warned Israel that God would punish her for her sins (Amos 3:2). Only in the context of judgment for sin do the prophets write, "When disaster comes to a city, has not the LORD caused it?" (v. 6).

Like a just judge, God decrees punishment for sin but he does not decree acts of sin! That radical distinction must not be forgotten when we read about "the plan of him who works out everything in conformity with the purpose of his will" (Eph. 1:11). From Paul's generalization it does not follow that God intends moral rebellion and eternal punishment with the same pleasure as moral faithfulness and heaven. What follows from Paul's statement is that in one way or another everything is teleologically related to God. Again, the fact that God "works out everything in conformity with the purpose of his will" in its broader biblical context does not imply that God is the causal agent of evil as well as good nor that he is the efficient cause of sin. Rather, God is the final cause of whatever comes to pass because from eternity God purposefully planned for it all either with pleasure or permissively. Some things he permissively allowed with displeasure and judgment, and some things he predestined with pleasure.

The Father's elective purposes are both *individual and collective*. The decrees do not stop with individuals like Adam, Abraham, and Paul, but encompass whole groups of people. God's purpose to create our original parents and permit their fall encompasses every descendant of theirs, the totality of human persons. Similarly, God's redemptive purposes include people of all times who are justified by faith. Within the category of his people are purposes for such subgroups as Israel (Deut. 7:7–8) and, since Pentecost, the church (1 Peter 1:1–2). God purposed to call these people out from fallen humanity in order that they should bless the whole world. So everyone, individually and collectively, repentant or unrepentant, is in one way or another related to God's purposes.

To speak of God's collective concerns as a corporate election is not to exclude individuals. The Father's condemnation of evil involved the condemnation of all people, Jews and Gentiles, including each person (Rom. 3:10–23). So his redemptive purpose was not directed to an empty corporation or logical class, but to the body of Christ with each of its members. Election need not be of either individuals or a class, but of both.

The election of individuals for salvation is clearly taught by our Lord's explanation of why some responded to his message and others did not (John 6:35–36; 60–71). Those given to him by the Father come to him and are received by him (v. 37) and are kept by him (vv. 39–40). "No one can come to me," Jesus explained, "unless the Father who sent me draws him" (v. 44), or enables him (v. 65). People did not believe the miracles of Jesus because they were not his sheep (John 10:26). His sheep listen to his voice and follow him, and he gives them eternal life; they shall never perish and no one can snatch them out of Christ's hand (v. 27). Since they are given to Christ by the Father, neither can anyone snatch them out of the Father's hand (v. 29). They have been chosen not only for salvation but also for service and that is why the world hates them (John 15:16–19). The Father granted the Son authority over all people that he might give eternal life to all those the Father gave to him (John 17:2). To those given to him Jesus reveals the Father, and they obey the Father's Word (v. 6); they know Jesus comes from the Father (v. 7), Jesus prays for them (v. 9), keeps them (vv. 11–12), asks that they have the full measure of his joy (v. 13), protection from the evil one (v. 15), sanctification (vv. 17–19), the fruitfulness of their message to win others to belief (vv. 20–21), and unity with one another (vv. 22–23). Jesus also anticipated seeing them in glory (v. 24). Not all were given to Jesus by the Father, but some persons clearly were.

God's redemptive purposes are intended for both *salvation and service.* In Old Testament times Abraham, Moses, David, and the prophets were justified by faith and intended to take the message of God's righteousness and grace to the world. In New Testament times Saul was called out of the world for salvation from his sin and for service as the apostle to the Gentiles. The other apostles had been called out from among the masses by Jesus for salvation (including both justification and sanctification) and service. All believers are chosen "to be holy" (Eph. 1:4), "to do good works, which God prepared in advance for us to do" (2:10), "for obedience" (1 Peter 1:2), and for the world-wide proclamation of the gospel (Matt. 28:19, 20). All have gifts for ministry to the church (1 Cor. 12:7).

The Father's elective purposes are *Christ-centered but not Christomonistic* (as in Barth's proposal). Unquestionably Christ has preeminence in the Father's plans for creation (John 1:1–3; Col. 1:15–17) and redemption (Col. 1:18–20; 2:9, 10), but he is not the only one chosen in the redemptive plan. In Christ the Father chose believing sinners in the church to be holy (Eph. 1:4), to be his spiritual children (v. 5), to be redeemed (v. 7), and to know his will (v. 9). As we have seen, these passages are both collectively of the church and individually of its members, so that the Father's plan to provide redemption in Christ includes specific persons to benefit by his provisions. "If there is no election of individuals," as Carl Henry argued against Barth's view, "election can hardly be personal good news."[87]

Furthermore, Henry added, "Unless Christian proclamation reaches the sinner as a condemned and doomed person to whom God offers redemption, it is not the good news intended by the New Testament."[88] Barth's hypothesis that all people are already condemned and already justified in Christ and are simply in need of being informed about Christ does not cohere with the Scriptures. We cannot ignore the crucial distinction between Christ's provisions for reconciliation, redemption, and forgiveness and the sinner's Spirit-enabled reception of these benefits by repentant faith. Jesus Christ was not the only

person in view in the decision to permit sin with its consequences.

According to the Bible, condemnation fell first on Adam and his descendants, individually and collectively. It is on sinners—not on the Savior—that judgment first fell. Logically, as well as historically, only after the condemnation of the entire human race can its guilt and penalty meaningfully be imputed to the dying Christ. And only after Christ has paid the penalty for our sin, can we receive his redemption.

Specific Purposes

Thoughtful children (of all ages) sometimes ask, "Why is there anything at all?" To answer simply and directly, "Because before there was anything else the heavenly Father, who always existed, lovingly planned to create all good things and persons. God decided to create, not because he had to fill up any lack in the divine being, for God is perfect (Matt. 5:48). Things exist because freely and lovingly God determined to share his goodness with other existing beings."

What more specific ends for the creation has God revealed to the prophets (Amos 3:10)? For what eternal purposes can we discover adequate evidence in revelation (explicit or implicit)? God's purposes have been amplified here beyond the minimal logical issues to point up their relevance (often thought to be purely theoretical) and to anticipate an outline of a Christian philosophy of history or theodicy.

1. In holy love God wisely planned *to create the cosmos* to function according to regular physical laws. He also planned *to create persons* to love and serve him in harmony with physical and moral laws. All things, we infer from the subsequent deed, were to be created not only by Christ but also for him (Col. 1:16)—i.e., for his glory (Rom. 11:36). That decision to create other personal

beings would mean the existence of other self-determining agents, other efficient causes of actions and events. They would not be equally ultimate with him, but necessarily persons dependent on him for their existence and persons with a beginning in time and history. As finite beings, their use of their capacity of self-determination would not always necessarily be consistent with their natures. They could changeably exercise their self-determination either morally in harmony with their upright natures, or contrary to them. Similarly people in history would be free to determine their moral choices and actions either consistently with God's precepts, or contrary to them. By choosing to create changing people in history God would create people free to choose not only in accord with their moral natures (as created), but also contrary to them.[89]

2. Although God desired people's faithfulness to himself and the order he established for human good, he planned to *permit self-determining persons to become unfaithful* to him. God did not predestine our first parent's disobedience to his moral law, but permitted it in his plan for history. God also planned to permit people who broke his precepts and covenants to suffer the just consequences of their self-determined disbelief and disobedience. As Augustine said, "There are two kinds of evil—sin and the penalty for sin."[90] There may be no explicit biblical statement to the effect that God knew before the foundation of the world that Adam and Eve would sin, but divine omniscience includes everything. If the Father did not know that Adam and Eve would sin, why did he plan in eternity to atone for sin (Acts 2:23)?

3. Before creation God planned *to send his Son* and through his atonement provide justly for *common and saving grace*. Redemption is provided by the precious blood of Christ who was "cho-

sen before the creation of the world" (1 Peter 1:20). The Father's election of Christ was revealed at Jesus' transfiguration: "This is my Son, whom I have chosen; listen to him" (Luke 9:35). Peter could later say, "This man was handed over to you [who cried, "Crucify him!"] by God's set purpose and foreknowledge" (Acts 2:23; cf. 4:27–28; 1 Cor. 2:7–8; Rev. 13:8).

On the ground of Christ's loving provision, temporal effects of sin would be ameliorated for all in common grace. Then as repentant believers would take the gospel to all, many would be born again. At conversion the seeds of the victory over the habitual, moral, relational results of sin would also be planted.

4. From eternity God planned *to send the Holy Spirit to call out his people for eternal life* from among the human rebels. Many persons would thus repent, believe, and grow in faithfulness. God's people individually and collectively not only share his fellowship but also the mission of his kingdom. "For he chose us in him before the creation of the world to be holy and blameless in his sight . . . to be adopted as his sons . . . when the times will have reached their fulfillment—to bring all things in heaven and on earth together under one head, even Christ" (Eph. 1:4–11; cf. 3:10–11).

"This grace was given us in Christ Jesus before the beginning of time" (2 Tim. 1:9). We rest "on the hope of eternal life, which God, who does not lie, promised before the beginning of time" (Titus 1:2). However unfaithful people may have been prior to their conversion, those united to Christ by faith believe that God's Spirit will bring their lives in this world to a just and wise culmination, as the beginning of life eternal.

In this history-spanning rebuilding of God's rule, the Father planned to send the Son and the Spirit to work in, with, and through his people *collectively* through families (Noah's, Abraham's, etc.), the Israelite nation, and Christian churches.

The Father's plan included preserving the human race from extinction and self-destruction through the *family*. To Adam and Eve God said, "Be fruitful and increase in number; fill the earth and subdue it. Rule over the earth" (Gen. 1:28–30). That cultural mandate came first to a specific couple, a family. While judging the persistently evil with the destruction of the Flood, God would establish a covenant with Noah to save him and his family from destruction (Gen. 6:18).

The Father's plan also included descendants of Abraham's family in the Israelite *nation*. God covenanted with Abraham to make of him a great nation, to bless those who bless him and his descendants, and to bless all people of the earth through him (Gen. 12:2–3). God also promised him countless descendants (Gen. 15:4–5) and a land (Gen. 15:7). God planned to bring them out of slavery in Egypt through Moses (Exod. 3:7–10) and into the land through Joshua (Deut. 34:9; Josh. 1:15). Through Isaiah, God pleaded with the rebellious people in the house of Jacob: "Remember the former things, those of long ago [God's purposes fulfilled in the deliverance from Egypt]; I am God, and there is no other . . . I make known the end from the beginning, from ancient times what is still to come. I say: My purpose will stand, and I will do all that I please. From the east I summon a bird of prey; from a far-off land, a man to fulfill my purpose. What I have said, that will I bring about; what I have planned, that will I do." (Isa. 46:9–11). Earlier Isaiah had alluded to the fact that a plan for one nation involves a plan for all. "This is the plan determined for the whole world; this is the hand stretched out over all nations" (Isa. 14:26).

The primary institution God planned to use in bringing blessing to the whole world in the present era is the *church*. On earth, having become incarnate to do the Father's will, Jesus exclaimed, "I will build my church, and the gates of Hades will not overcome it" (Matt. 16:18). That the building of the church unifying Gentiles and Jews (not merely as classes, but as persons also) was in the Father's plan before creation seems even more explicit in Paul's calling (Eph. 2:15). Although God's intent was not revealed for ages before Paul, it was that the church's race-transcending unity would display the manifold wisdom of God to rulers and authorities in heavenly realms, according to his eternal purpose (Eph. 3:10–11).

5. God ultimately purposed *to unite heaven and earth under Christ*. God sovereignly determined to bring linear history to a just culmination in a final judgment of the evil ones and a climax of grace, bringing all things together in heaven and on earth under one head, even Christ (Eph. 1:10). The people of God in Israel and the churches have an underlying spiritual unity in the first to be elected, Christ. But institutionally the nation remains one kind of organization not reducible to an ecclesiastical organization. And the organized church is made up of people. Because the body of Christ is corporate, societal, and communal, it is an empty fiction without its many members. Hence it seems difficult to exclude persons from election. God's election is not solely christological, nor is it either corporate or individual. The Father elected Christ, the individuals who make up his "body," and the corporate whole of his "body," his people—Israel and the church.

Just as by God's word the heavens existed and the earth was formed, so "the present heavens and earth are reserved for fire, being kept for the day of judgment" (2 Peter 3:7). When the appointed time has come, the Lord God Almighty, who is and was, judges the dead and rewards his servants (Rev. 11:17–18). And how can we have any assurance that after all these years this is still God's purpose? "The Lord is not slow in keeping his promise" (2 Peter 3:9). Although the ungodly will be destroyed, "in keeping with his promise we are looking forward to a new heaven and a new earth, the home of righteousness" (v. 13).

Undoubtedly these promises flow from eternal purposes. The decision to create involved an awareness that in the new "home of righteousness" not only would justice be done, but also mercy and grace would be lavishly experienced. Hence history is neither open-ended nor cyclical, but linear and climactic. Evil will finally be destroyed; universal justice, peace, and love will follow.

Varied Strategies

The great designer of the cosmos is the final cause of everything, for there would be nothing at all if it had not been for his plan to create and sustain the world and life. In the final analysis God has a reason for everything, good and evil. Teleologically we incorporate an element of the supralapsarians' concern that God be sovereign over the evil as well as the good. The final cause of everything's existence, however, is not the efficient cause of everything's activities. Certainly the Holy One is not the efficient cause of morally evil acts to destroy his creatures. The Most High is not the blameworthy cause of rebellion against himself.

To illustrate the difference between being the final cause of something and being its efficient cause, think of an airline established for the final purpose of transporting people and goods from one city to another. Because the final cause or *raison d'être* of the airline is transportation, its workers serve as stewards of that goal. If the airline maintains reasonable standards of safety and competence and if a terrorist blows up one of its planes in the air, the airline company cannot be regarded as the efficient cause or the blameworthy cause of that tragedy. The terrorist's purpose of destroying the flight contradicts the purpose of the airline to complete the flight without accident. The flight's passengers would not have lost their lives in that way if it had not been for that airline company's existence, but the company as such is not the culpable cause of the tragedy. No illustration intended to make clear God's relationship to evil can be perfect, but the above illustration helps us to understand how God can be the final cause of life (even that of the terrorist) and not be culpable for destructive actions efficiently caused by sinners.

By what strategies does God attain his life-giving ends? His miraculous and providential strategies vary significantly. Ordinarily God works providentially through impersonal forces of nature and personal agents (as second causes) to achieve his temporal and preceptive ends. In extraordinary instances (usually related to preserving and establishing his creative and redemptive programs) God chooses to achieve his decretive ends directly through miracles. Consider his miraculous strategy first and then his providential strategy.

1. To achieve certain special decretive purposes God's strategy is to act miraculously, either superseding nature's laws and human agencies or using other means in extraordinary ways. For example, creation *ex nihilo* must necessarily have been achieved without the use of secondary causal factors. At the point of initial creation no other beings or things existed to play an intermediate role in that creative act. In God's

miraculous strategy he is both the final cause and the efficient cause.

Since the creation God is not the only agent and God's miraculous strategies are not always so totally removed from other means. But when means are used in miracles, they are used in an extraordinary manner, as in the following examples. Dust does not ordinarily produce human beings, but God used "dust" in the miraculous creation of man (Gen. 2:7). Ordinarily virgins do not conceive, but in an extraordinary way God enabled Mary to bring the Messiah into the world (Luke 1:35; 2:7). Clay on the eyes does not ordinarily heal blindness, but at the request of Christ it enabled the blind man to see (John 9:7). In such extraordinary uses of means, God not only chooses their final purpose, but also acts as efficient cause.

No amount of opposition from human or demonic terrorists can succeed against God's miraculous strategies. God's plans are great! "O great and powerful God, whose name is the LORD Almighty, great are your purposes and mighty are your deeds. . . . You brought your people Israel out of Egypt with signs and wonders" (Jer. 32:18–21). Kings and kingdoms cannot succeed against God's extraordinary acts. The One enthroned in the heavens laughs when the kings of the earth take their stand against him (Ps. 2:1–2). "Surely, as I have planned, so will it be, and as I have purposed, so will it stand. . . . This is the plan determined for the whole world; this is the hand stretched out over all nations" (Isa. 14:24–26). Again, "He does as he pleases with the powers of heaven and the peoples of the earth. No one can hold back his hand" (Dan. 4:35). God's miraculous strategy for achieving his *decretive will* cannot be thwarted.

2. Although we have found that God is the final cause of whatever comes to pass, ordinarily God has chosen to work through nature's impersonal forces and cognitive precepts. In God's *providential strategy* he remains the final cause of everything but makes use of nature's ordinary energies (as "material" causes) and of people as efficient causes to achieve the ends of his preceptive will. Hence in any historical event on planet earth there may be several causal factors.

In analyzing human events we must avoid the single-cause fallacy and look for many contributing factors. Under divine providence there may be multiple natural factors and one or more persons involved. Creation's laws are uniform but people's responses to God's revealed precepts occur in two radically different ways. People may either (1) believe and obey divine exhortations (as in Exod. 20:1–17) or (2) disbelieve and disobey God's precepts.

God is pleased with belief and obedience to his *preceptive will*; he is not pleased with unbelief and disobedience to his preceptive will. God's permission of disbelief and disobedience to his preceptive will may be referred to as his *permissive will*. With either obedience or disobedience, the all-knowing God is not surprised. Both responses to his instrumental strategy have been included in his all-encompassing plan.

In God's preceptive will more than the Ten Commandments are involved. The preceptive strategy includes the use of all of general revelation and special revelation. God uses the inspired Scriptures "for teaching, rebuking, correcting and training in righteousness" (2 Tim. 3:17). Reports of historical blessings and judgments are given to provide hope and warnings to the receptive, but others may ignore them. Doctrinal passages provide the materials for structuring a world view, but they may be side-stepped by unbelieving thinkers. The Bible's gospel invitations are to be received and acted on, but they may be rejected.

Neither the giving of the law nor the presentation of the gospel as such guarantees a positive response from fallen people. God sent John the Baptist to summon people to repent in preparation for the Messiah's ministry. John baptized those who repented, but "the Pharisees and experts in the law *rejected* God's purpose for themselves, because they had not been baptized by John" (Luke 7:30). The unrepentant sinners in their insolence nullified or set aside (*atheteō*) God's preceptive will (*boulē*) in which he takes pleasure. But they are still within his permissive will, receiving the displeasure of God. The Father's preceptive will not only may be opposed, but in fact the dominant tendency of sinners by nature is to thwart it. Even after God delivered his people from Egypt and miraculously fed them in the wilderness, he lamented, "But my people would not listen to me; Israel would not submit to me. So I gave them over to their stubborn hearts to follow their own devices" (Ps. 81:11–12). The fact that some of God's strategies can be resisted should not lead us to think that all of them can be resisted or thwarted. God's miraculous strategies cannot be thwarted, as we found. Two kinds of strategies, then, are required to account for the evidence: one miraculous and unconditionally effective; the other providential and, up against depraved human nature, in itself relatively ineffective.

Two kinds of strategies are required furthermore, because the evidence indicates two results to the different responses to God's providential or conditional strategy. Some people believe and obey God's preceptive will and therefore please God, and other people are permitted to disbelieve and disobey that will and, by doing so, displease God. The Scriptures imply that God permits what displeases him. Clearly he permits the death of the wicked but takes no pleasure in their death (Ezek. 18:23): "I take no pleasure in the death of anyone, declares the Sovereign LORD" (Ezek. 18:32). God permitted hypocrites to live, but said, "I desire mercy, not sacrifice" (Hos. 6:6). An evident difference occurs between what he desires and what he permits. Again, " 'I am not pleased with you,' says the LORD Almighty" (Mal. 1:10). Clearly among the prophets no contradiction was seen in holding to the permissive will of the Sovereign Lord. None of the prophets claimed to fully understand the relation between God's decretive (unconditional) will and his permissive (conditional) will, but they did recognize the two as significant for their respective purposes.

Many tend to assume that God has only one strategy for achieving his purposes—either an unconditional strategy (hyper-Calvinism) or a conditional one (Wesleyanism or Arminianism).[91] Either symmetrical hypothesis, affirming that God plans to accomplish good and evil in the same way, seems too oversimplified to account for the differences in the relevant data. The biblical evidence above (and in the biblical section) is complex, making more probable the hypothesis that the Father (1) conditionally permits sin with displeasure and (2) unconditionally (for sinners unable to meet the condition of faith) gives the gift of Christ's righteousness.

The Logical Order of Decrees

One cannot state all God's specific eternal purposes at once; so in listing them some order, though artificial, is unavoidable. A temporal order is out of the question, since time had not begun before the creation of the world. The issue is which decrees had logical priority over the others in the Father's plan. Three logical possibilities need to be clearly distinguished: Arminian double foreknowledge, supralapsarian double predestination, and an infralapsarian foreknowledge of sin and predestination to salvation.

For Arminianism God's purposes of salvation and of condemnation are both conditional; so God simply foresaw the Fall with its universal implications and he foresaw those sinners who would believe on Christ. We may call this view double foreknowledge. God foresaw who would fail to meet the condition of faith in Christ and who would meet that condition and be saved. From an Arminian perspective the order of decrees is (1) creation, (2) permission of the Fall and the condemnation of all, (3) the universal provision of Christ's atonement and prevenient grace, and (4) the election of all who meet the condition of faith in Christ. This is a type of infralapsarianism, since the election of the saved logically follows the permission of the Fall (lapse).

From a supralapsarian Calvinistic perspective neither purpose is conditional, so God unconditionally predestines some to be saved and some to be lost. This view is commonly called double predestination—of the lost and the saved. It is called supralapsarianism because the Father's election, determining who will be saved and who will be lost is made logically before (supra) the decision concerning the Fall (lapse) into sin. The logical agenda in God's mind was thought to include the following steps: (1) to glorify himself God predestined some people to eternal life and some to eternal death; (2) as a means to that goal, God decided to create human beings; (3) God decreed the Fall to supply some people for eternal punishment; and (4) so that the elect could be justly saved, he decreed the work of Jesus Christ.

By calling the supralapsarian decree concerning the Fall "permissive," Fred H. Klooster makes the decree of the Fall conditional.[92] But a consistent supralapsarian position regards the decrees as unconditional. It it difficult to soften the blows of double predestination without being inconsistent. As a distinct logical alternative it requires that the decrees concerning the lost be unconditional and not permissive.

A clearly distinct infralapsarian Calvinism regards the decree concerning the lost to be conditional and the decree concerning the saved to be unconditional. God foresaw the fall of all mankind into sin but predestines the unmerited salvation of many, since the depraved will be incapable of meeting a spiritual condition. The Father's choice of the elect is not logically prior to his decision to permit the Fall, but after (infra, or sub) the Fall (lapse). Hence in infralapsarianism God's decrees were made along the lines of this agenda: (1) the creation of all mankind; (2) the permission of the Fall and just condemnation of all; (3) since no sinners could meet the condition of salvation, the predestination of "many" to salvation and permission of others to receive the just penalty for their sins; and (4) the provisions for salvation through the work of Christ and the application of salvation's benefits through the work of the Holy Spirit.[93]

Limiting our concern to the lost at this point, the issue is between infralapsarian permission of sin and its consequences and supralapsarian predestination of them. Is a just God glorified by unconditionally predestining some human beings to eternal punishment independent of their foreseen creation and fall? Could a judgment predestining some to be condemned be made without respect of persons? Finding the supralapsarian position unjust and irreconcilable with Scripture, infralapsarian Calvinists join with Arminians in regarding the degree concerning the Fall to be conditioned on foreseen disbelief and disobedience. It is a permissive decree with displeasure. And it is administered, not to some, but universally without respect of persons. The object of the decree is universal, not particular (Rom. 3:19–20), and its basis is foreseen works of disobedience.

Throughout Scripture just judgment is always merited; saving grace is always unmerited. That categorical difference ought to be reflected from the beginning of a theology about God's eternal purposes. Throughout Scripture punishments must fit the crimes actually committed. Jesus endorsed degrees of punishment when he said, "From everyone who has been given much, much will be demanded" (Luke 12:47–48). Jesus also said that it would be more bearable for Tyre, Sidon, and Sodom on the day of judgment than for those who had rejected him (Matt. 11:20–24). Justice is merited; grace is unmerited. Great harm is done when the distinct categories of grace and works are confused at any point in theology. When people complain that an infralapsarian view of election is unjust, they forget that no one is treated unjustly. A customer confused these categories when complaining that a photograph did not do him justice. The photographer replied, "My friend, what you need is not justice, but mercy!" All are treated justly when all are judged sinners and worthy of condemnation.

If God, by electing many to be saved, passes over some, it may be asked, Is not that the same as predestining them to their unenviable destiny? Admittedly, the end result is the same, but the radical difference is whether that punishment was deserved and whether the sentence of condemnation was justly pronounced. If the sentence was not merited by sinful works but was unconditionally decreed, as in supralapsarianism, it would seem to be unfair indeed. But given the universality of sin and the sentence, as in infralapsarianism, it was not assigned to some with partiality.

And given the degrees of punishment, no one is punished more than he or she deserves. No injustice is done to any sinner by this decree. We could wish that God had found it wise and just to give Christ's righteousness to all sinners, but that theory does not fit the biblical facts. One might more justifiably complain on behalf of the nonelect that undeserving as they are, they did get a gift that others received, though gifts are not appropriately demanded. One cannot rightly complain, however, that God has dealt with the nonelect unjustly. That complaint shows a confusion of logical categories of grace and justice or works.

After a helpful historical overview and summary of the biblical data, Paul K. Jewett, in his *Election and Predestination,* fails to find a clearly distinct infralapsarian alternative to supralapsarianism or Arminianism. Admittedly the "great majority, even in the Reformed tradition, have backed away from the supralapsarian position . . ."[94] because the Scriptures teach an unconditional election and a conditional reprobation.[95] But a Calvinist cannot hold that God simply *foresees* that the reprobate will fall, Jewett says, "without borrowing a leaf from the Arminian's book."[96] Why must Jewett as a Calvinist fear borrowing a word from Arminians if their usage is (in part) from the Bible? A study of "foreknowledge" and "foreknowing" indicates in some cases mere prescience (Acts 26:5; 2 Peter 3:17) and in others a stronger determination (Acts 2:23; Rom. 8:29; 11:2; 1 Peter 1:2, 20). The term *foreknowledge,* like most words, has more than one meaning. It can mean mere prescience of evil in some contexts and predetermination of Christ and salvation in others. Apparently unaware of the twofold usage in Scripture, Jewett returns to a supralapsarian symmetry, saying that "the reprobate are what they are [i.e., morally and spiritually blind] by the positive ordination of God."[97] Inconsistent with his own interpretation of the scriptural difference between conditional and unconditional, he claims that "supra- and infralapsarianism are but nuances of one and the same fundamental approach."[98]

Unable to reconcile the issues, Jewett confesses that for him, "when all is said and done, the problem of reprobation remains unresolved."[99] Since he cannot resolve it, he seems to think no one can, for he then adds, "it would appear, unresolvable."[100] Resorting to "the paradox of grace"[101] and "mystery,"[102] Jewett leaves the impression that any attempt to resolve his contradictions amounts to "artificially contrived compromises."[103]

On the basis of the biblical evidence above, it is far from artificial, we submit, to regard the election of the depraved as unconditional and the reprobation of all in Adam as conditional. Such a clearly distinct logical alternative as infralapsarianism provides is by far the more probable hypothesis than a contradictory one. By taking a position on this controversial doctrine, we make no claim to fully comprehend the ways of God with humans. Rather, applying our verificational method, we find a clearly distinct infralapsarian hypothesis (as here defined) to be more likely true because (1) it is not contradictory, (2) it is able to account for the relevant biblical evidence above with fewer difficulties, and (3) it is tenable without pretense or hypocrisy.

APOLOGETIC INTERACTION

Is the Heavenly Father the Author of Evil?

Although the biblical evidence indicates that God did not initiate evil, some will ask, "If God permits evil, is not God responsible for it? Did not God create people with the potential for rebellion against him?" God is responsible for creating personal agents. They turned aside from him. Not even God could create self-determining persons minus the power of determining their own actions (just as he cannot make square circles). God can be the final cause of the existence of everything without being the efficient, blameworthy cause of any evil acts.

By way of illustration, Henry Ford is the final cause of all Ford cars, for there would not be any if he had not invented them to provide transportation. But Henry Ford, who could well have envisioned misuses of his automobiles, apparently felt it wiser, in a kind of benefit-evil analysis, to invent them than not. However, when a drunken driver of a Ford car takes others' lives in a head-on collision, Henry Ford is not the efficient cause of the tragedy. Similarly, although God is the teleological (final) cause of everything that is, he is not the efficient cause of his creatures' evil choices. The Father chose to create self-determining beings and to work with them preceptively and permissively. People are responsible for their bad decisions and actions. We cannot blame our sinful choices on the Devil or on God.

Others will insist that if God knew that people would sin, he would not have escaped responsibility for their evil if he then created them. As omniscient, surely God knew that human beings, though created in his image and carefully advised to avoid evil, would alienate themselves from one another and from the triune God, would come under condemnation, and would become predisposed to selfishness, materialism, pride, and sensuality. Nevertheless God is not the blameworthy, or efficient, cause of rebellion against himself. God could foreknow with certainty that Adam and Eve would yield to temptation and sin, without himself being their tempter or inducing them to yield. But did he not know that the Tempter would enter the Garden of Eden? Yes, he knew. But God did not send Satan there. And apparently before Satan fell from his created state of perfection, there was no other creature to tempt him; the Devil fell of his own volition. No more ultimate source or explanation for sin can be found than the volition of the creature. God foreknows with certainty what his creatures will decide, but God does not make their decisions for them. When he created their natures by which they are self-determined, he made them good. Since by their own choices persons originated moral evil, God is not the author of sin. "God cannot be tempted by evil, nor does he tempt anyone" (James 1:13).

Although God has not told us specifically why he chose to create, we suggest that in infinite wisdom, taking into account all the data of omniscient foreknowledge in a kind of foreseen benefits-evils analysis, he concluded that it was better to create than not to create. Analogously, although some married couples may hesitate to bring children into a fallen world with all the known risks or evils, most do have children. Apparently they conclude that the evils are far outweighed by the inestimable values of enduring loving relationships with children (and possibly grandchildren) throughout their lives.

What are some of the values that the Father may have had in mind in permitting moral evil with its consequent suffering? Some suffering is justly judgmental. *Retributive* suffering vindicates justice or fairness, a fact that is clear to all who have been treated unjustly or unfairly. (Just laws are of little help to a society if they are not enforced.) Through suffering we receive many other benefits. *Empathic* suffering enriches personal relations. In all of Israel's afflictions, God was afflicted (Isa.

63:9). Paul wrote to the Corinthians "out of much affliction and anguish of heart and with many tears" (2 Cor. 2:4 RSV). Christians find deepening relationships in weeping with those who weep and rejoicing with those who rejoice (Rom. 12:15). Empathic suffering may lead to *vicarious* suffering, supremely exemplified by Jesus Christ on the cross. Then *testimonial* suffering may be experienced by those who follow the example of Christ. We may suffer for righteousness' sake (1 Peter 3:14), for the kingdom of God (2 Thess. 1:5), for the gospel (2 Tim. 2:9), or for bearing injustice (1 Peter 2:19). Pain may serve to prevent greater suffering as an early warning sign to avoid a more serious condition. In this way suffering serves a beneficial *educational* purpose. The greatest good of the Christian life is not freedom from pain, but Christlikeness. God planned to work all things together for good, not for our ease, but for our conformity to Christ's characteristics. So he planned to permit discipline ("for our good"), that those who are trained by it might enjoy the "peaceable fruit of righteousness" (Heb. 12:10–11 RSV). Suffering is usually involved in purification, said C. S. Lewis. And looking back over his life, Lewis mused, "Most of the real good that has been done me in this life has involved it."[104]

In sum, God is not the author of sin, for moral evil, as Augustine taught, is not a substance created by God, but a turning of creatures' wills against God.[105] Evil has no independent status; creatures brought evil into the world. Having permitted creaturely self-determination, God manages evil for the greater good through such activities as the experience of fairness, loving empathy, vicarious giving, faithful witness, and disciplined education.[106]

Do the Father's Decrees Undermine Human Responsibility?

God has chosen not to be the sole efficient cause of events, but to work ordinarily through human persons as self-determining agents. Since he plans not to be the sole efficient cause of events, others will have the privilege of a dependent self-determination and the responsibility for their choices. God has planned for our self-determination even at the cost of permitting sin with its horrid consequences.

How, then, can God know with certainty and even predict what people will do without determining what they will do? For one thing, self-determination is according to one's nature, and God knows human nature with its limited knowledge and power at different times. (1) Prefallen persons were able to determine themselves in obedience to God or the contrary, disobedience to God. (2) As enslaved to sin people are able only to sin. (3) As regenerated by the Holy Spirit believers have two natures, an old and a new, so they again have the power of contrary choice, but faithfulness to God dominates. (4) When believers are resurrected, they will have one new nature confirmed in righteousness, and so they will be able only to glorify God. God as omniscient knows each of these states of the moral nature with certainty.

God also knows the hereditary factors contributing to one's personality. God knows ahead of time, not only the givens at one's conception and birth, but also one's grandparents, great grandparents, the entire family tree. In God's plan from before the foundation of the world God chooses from among all the hereditary factors in human life that make up the specific nature of each unique person. If, for example, he wants a prophet with the basic make-up of a Moses or an Elijah, he does not start looking at the available people, but can plan the appropriate genetic factors in the progenitors. As Erickson explains, God, foreknowing the infinite possibilities, chooses to bring into existence the individual who will freely decide to respond to every situation precisely as God intends. By so doing, God renders *certain,* but not *necessary,* the free decisions and actions of the individual."[107]

God's omniscience from eternity also anticipates environmental, cultural, and subcultural influences and pressures. In the midst of these cultural occasions for our self-determination he can anticipate whether we will succumb or resist. As responsible agents we can consent to, or rebel against, our parents' style of life and our schools and their educational philosophies. Well-known counterculture movements support this ability, as do converts from capitalism to communism, and from communism to capitalism, to new religions and cults, and from them. God knows what we will do because he knows all of the factors contributing to our moral natures and cultural influences.

God also knows what we will choose spontaneously. He made us with a power of creativity like his own. And the completeness of his knowledge does not miss the possibilities and actualities of our creative abilities. Clearly these are within the limits of our physical, mental, moral, and spiritual natures, however, and not unlimited, like his. Spontaneous acts are not nonacts, and they too are known by God. But morally accountable behavior is self-determined, whether spontaneous or routine. According to Millard Erickson's concept of freedom, "the answer to the question 'could the individual have chosen differently?' is yes, while the answer to the question, 'But would he have?' is no."[108] Some concepts of freedom would require total spontaneity or random choice. Erickson's concept of freedom (and ours) more realistically accepts the fact that in human decisions and actions nothing is completely spontaneous or random.

God's plan includes all that he foreknows of the nature of human agency and its enslaved use as fallen. He also knows how it will be used when renewed and spiritually liberated. For morally corrective purposes he may choose to do some extraordinary things to regenerate a person's moral nature and so free up the ability to know, love, and serve him. God's initiative will be required when people are enslaved to sin and neither would nor could deliver themselves. However, God's certain knowledge of what we will do, is not confused in his mind with his certain knowledge of what he will do for us. And he knows what we will do when we are left to our sinful selves and what we will do with his gracious illumination and enablement. Either way our self-determination is involved.

What we determine in and of our sinful selves we cannot blame on our parents, our teachers, the other sex, the government, the Devil, or God. Under whatever pressures, persons are responsible for their responses, from conformity to rebellion. By foreknowing which will be the case with certainty, God does not thereby become the efficient cause or render it necessary by some compulsion. God can know with certainty which of the infinite possibilities we choose without compelling our choices. For our choices we remain responsible, and we will give account to him, the righteous Judge. To the extent that any view of the divine decrees takes away one's sense of accountability to God for his own decisions and actions, that understanding is unbiblical.

How could God's prophets predict specific future events produced by the complexities of human determinations far in advance? By foreknowing all the people involved with all their ordinary and spontaneous determinations, God could anticipate an eventuality with certainty without coercion. For example, in a case like the prediction of the Flood, without altering the responsibility of the wicked for their multiplying sins, God could himself determine their just punishment and introduce for the people of faith a way of deliverance. God could foresee the evils of Joseph's brothers and overrule them for Joseph's good. But God's introduction of beneficial results in no way changed the brothers' responsibility for their jealousy and hatred. More on how this works out in history has been examined in the chapter on providence.

Far from subverting responsibility, Christianity contributes to human responsibility precisely because all people will give account to an all-knowing, holy Judge. If the ultimate reality were impersonal, as in secular and pantheistic world views, we would never give account to an all-knowing Judge of our deeds, whether they are good or bad. In those philosophies we must live with the consequences of our choices, but we need not anticipate personal judgment. Christian theism results, not only in a sense of dependence, but also in a sense of obligation to the revealed purposes of the living God before whom we ultimately stand to give account.

Does Predestination Make History Meaningless?

The prior choice of ends and strategies by a coach does not as such make a football game meaningless. The execution of the plays by responsible members of the team is indispensable. Every business has its purposes. Management without goals would not be effective. With predetermined goals and strategies the manager can get things done through people. But the clarity of objectives does not make the employees' work unnecessary or insignificant. Academic courses have objectives that render the day-by-day activity of students more, rather than less, meaningful. Long trips have planned destinations that lend significance to each day's travel. The prior choice of ends for a career in sports or the military does not make the career meaningless.

So too, the ends God wisely chose for persons, families, nations, and churches mean that our efforts are not merely full of sound and fury, signifying nothing. God's eternal purposes give meaning to history. History is not a ceaseless repetition of meaningless cycles. Nor is human history like a telephone book with a great cast of characters, but no plot! God's grand design gives the course of history a wise, just, and gracious significance not only for time, but also for eternity.

Do the divinely chosen strategies render history meaningless? If God had chosen to accomplish everything independently of human agency by supernatural means, the objection might have force. But since God has sovereignly chosen generally to work in, with, and through people, people are far from unimportant in history. That God should at times plan, in view of permitting self-determining people to fall into sin, to use supernatural remedial strategies does not counter his plan to use human agencies normally. At least insofar as God's strategy is instrumental or conditional, the significance of human choices and activities is not erased but enhanced. And even his supernatural strategy is designed to rescue humans from the results of their sin and guarantee a just culmination of history.[109]

The Futility of Fatalism

According to the fatalistic hypothesis, what will happen, will happen, and nothing we do or do not do can make any difference. An impersonal, irrational, purposeless, inescapable force determines all of the apparently free choices of life. Freedom may not be absent, but it is subjected to a meaningless necessity that has no purpose. Since fatalism implies impersonal, un-

wise, unjust, and unloving ends, then Christianity cannot be classified as fatalistic. The heavenly Father wisely chose holy and loving ends.

Since fatalism also means that human agency makes no difference in the achieving of the ends, Christianity is not fatalistic. The Father sovereignly chose to achieve predetermined objectives generally by an instrumental strategy utilizing human volition, not bypassing it. Foreseeing that human wills would become enslaved to sin, God provided for their liberation to fulfill their destiny. A planned providence provides the loving support that makes life bearable; fate, on the other hand, renders all human striving futile. Christian self-determination is not rendered pointless, but meaningful eternally in the grand design of a personal God who creates personal beings for fellowship and shared objectives in work. Under sheer fate we can only face the future with despair. Under wise, loving, and just providence, we can face it with hope.[110] Is not the theistic option more viable (as well as more coherent)?

The Senselessness of Sheer Indeterminacy or Chance

Chance events in life are uncaused by either impersonal or personal forces. If things fall out by chance, our existence is contingent on uncalculated and uncalculable convergences of atoms in space. Life is then made up of unplanned, irrational happenings. The causes of human choices are not only unknown, but they have no rational antecedents, determinations, or occasions. On this hypothesis human behavior is completely uncaused.

Charles Sanders Pierce thought that the hypothesis of chance events accounts for the diversity of the universe. And William James thought that it provided a way out of the conflict between determinism and free will. Faced with a possible conflict between God's omniscience and chance, James concluded that God knows the ends he wishes achieved, but not necessarily the means to these ends. At various points in God's plan ambiguous possibilities exist, human free will comes into play, determining the means to already determined ends.[111]

In contrast, God's acts are determined not by ambiguity or chance, but by his own holy and loving nature. Similarly when God leaves decisions to human instrumentality, he does not leave them to an arbitrary will sporting in a vacuum but to persons who, among other activities, decide among alternatives and move to accomplish their chosen ends. As the evidence above shows, human decisions are not uncaused; they are self-determined. We cannot blame chance; mature people accept responsibility for their own choices.

The Dehumanization of Naturalistic Determinism

Naturalists picture the cosmos as a most unusual machine (without a personal being inventing, manufacturing, maintaining, and running it). It follows that naturalistic determinists try to show that for everything that happens, there are conditions, such that, given them, nothing else could have happened. People's choices are determined allegedly by antecedent physical and psychological causes, including hereditary factors in the person's genetic make-up and physical condition. This theory, however, fails to account for the data of Scripture and of consciousness. It overlooks the reality of personal agency and reduces persons to events. Nontheistic determinism leaves people irresponsible and unaccountable for moral decisions. Furthermore, a secularistic determinism fails to explain adequately the human ability to rebel

against environmental and cultural influences. Environmental givens— economical, psychological, and otherwise—may preset some insuperable limits. Yet in other respects, people may be strongly influenced, but not invariably determined. Many cultural pressures may be major, but they can be rejected or changed. So in matters of moral responsibility it becomes more accurate to speak of cultural occasions of human decisions, rather than of the cultural determination of those decisions.

The hypothesis of determinism fails to account for the givens of spontaneity, deliberation, free choice, creativity, moral responsibility, and the ability to pursue ends. We are people who act, not merely people who are acted upon. We are not free when we are caused to act by an external force or compulsion. But when we are not under external compulsion, we have power over the determinations of our own wills to cause our own actions. Unlike other living things, we are self-moved and engage in creative activities.[112]

Adam and Eve could have resisted temptation; they could have said no. However culturally or satanically tempted by the thirty pieces of silver, Judas himself coveted the money and responsibly determined to betray Christ. Even spouses or mature children who allow themselves to be dominated by another family member for years may have some responsibility for giving in for so long. In God's plan we are not mere victims; we initially give in to our addictions. In his image we are self-determining, responsible agents within the limits of our created, fallen, and regenerated natures. The glorification of Christians, of course, awaits Christ's second coming.

By way of summary and conclusion, we do not claim to fully comprehend all that is involved in God's sovereign plans from eternity and what the relation of those plans are to human freedom in time, especially in regard to the lost. What we have here found is that, of the hypotheses surveyed, an infralapsarian Calvinist (or Arminian) decree of conditional reprobation is (1) without logical contradiction, (2) the most adequate in accounting for the relevant biblical evidence with the fewest difficulties, and (3) tenable without hypocrisy in the face of either the awful results of sin or the awesome trophies of divine grace. In connection with soteriology more will be said about the decrees concerning the saved.

RELEVANCE FOR LIFE AND MINISTRY

Great Joy in Being Chosen

Everyone who believes does so because he or she is chosen by the Father from the foundation of the world, redeemed by the atonement of Jesus Christ, and enabled by the Holy Spirit. Far from producing pride, the truth of the Father's gracious choice of a sinner who deserved only his wrath, leads to humility before him. Those who are justified by grace through faith have nothing of which to boast (Eph. 2:8–9).

For an example of how acceptance of God's elective purpose can bring blessing, consider the perspective of Charles Haddon Spurgeon, who said:

> I believe the doctrine of election, because I am quite sure that if God had not chosen me I should never have chosen Him; and I am sure He chose me before I was born, or else He never would have chosen me afterwards; and He must have elected me for reasons unknown to me, for I never could find any reason in myself why He should have looked upon me with special love. So I am forced to accept that doctrine. I am bound to the doctrine of the depravity of the human heart, because I find myself depraved in heart, and have daily proofs that there dwelleth in my flesh no good thing.[113]

In many Christian minds lurks the fear that their sanctification, if not their justification, depends on their working for Christ from morning until night. James W. Ney confessed, "When I admitted that according to the Scriptures there was no justification apart from God's loving choice, my life began to change."[114] The burden of his own stewardship was lifted. His work for Christ was no longer done out of fear or necessity, but purely out of love for being accepted though unacceptable.

Relief From the Weight of the World on Our Shoulders

Many other questions trouble young Christians, especially about their work for Christ. "What is my responsibility for the spiritual condition of the billions of people in the world? Am I the ultimately responsible person for winning every relative, friend, acquaintance, and contact to Christ? How can I overcome the constant worry and fear that if any souls perish it will be all my fault?"

Study of our heavenly Father's decrees should help us realize that the weight of the whole world is not on our shoulders. Ultimately it is on God's shoulders. And we are assured that his judgments are absolutely just. No sinners will ever be punished more than they deserve. No sinners have any claim on God's grace. He can freely give it to whom he will.

Jesus illustrated these principles in the parable of the workers in the vineyard, some of whom worked from early morning, others from morning break time, others from the beginning of the afternoon, and some only after the afternoon break (Matt. 20:1–16). No injustices were done to any of the people who worked, whether for all day or a small part of it. Those who worked all day received what they deserved; those who worked less time received the same amount—more than they deserved. Those who worked from early morning for the full day complained that they were treated unjustly (v. 12) But the landowner said, "Friend, I am not being unfair to you. Didn't you agree to work for a denarius? Take your pay and go. I want to give the man who was hired last the same as I gave you. Don't I have the right to do what I want with my own money? Or are you envious because I am generous?" (vv. 13–15). In this teaching Jesus kept the categories of justice and grace (generosity) clear. We will avoid unnecessary worry about injustice if we do not charge God with injustice for his generosity to many sinners. While treating all justly, he has a right to give good gifts generously to the elect. The ultimate responsibility for who receives salvation and who does not is not ours, but his.

True, God's strategy is to use human witnesses in presenting the way of salvation. At most, however, our responsibility is intermediate, not ultimate. The ultimate burden of who is saved and who is lost does not rest with an evangelist, a pastor, a Sunday school teacher, a parent, a missionary, a church board, or the board of a mission society (1 Cor. 3:5–6). It is God who gives the increase (though all of those mentioned above have been used in the history of the growth of the Christian church and its outreach in foreign missions). Christians who have done what they can may rest at night knowing that in the final analysis, God's sovereignty guides the mission boards and the missionaries to the people whom he will enable to respond to the gospel. Liberated from the ultimate burden and confident of being called by God, we can serve God and the lost more effectively.[115]

Many think that acceptance of a Calvinistic view of election destroys any evangelistic zeal and missionary outreach. However, for many the assurance that God has elected some to respond encourages them in the tough tasks of preevangelism and evangelism. God has chosen not only the end of salvation, but also the means—human instruments. As it pleases God he will produce the fruit of our labors.

Others imagine that belief in predestination cuts their desire to pray. If God knows who will be saved, why should we pray for the unreached people we seek to reach with the gospel of grace? The heartfelt intercession of Paul, who wrote much about God's election, pleaded that his fellow Israelites might be saved (Rom. 10:1). If God had done in prevenient grace all that he could justly do for Paul's friends (as Arminians think), there would be no point in praying further for them. In praying for the lost, we express our faith that God can without injustice graciously transform contemporary Sauls into Pauls. When all are on their knees, they seem to be Calvinists.

Similarly, college and seminary studies and sermon and Sunday-school lesson preparations may be viewed as elements in God's instrumental strategy, rather than interruptions in God's work. When God becomes the center and circumference of our theology, our lives begin to show our confidence in him. Peace and joy become realities of experience. Fellowship with the heavenly Father becomes a heartwarming reality for his children, not merely a biblical word-study or a name for a group.

A Transcendent, Changeless Source of Meaning in Life

The Scriptures do not present God's eternal purposes for his people as a source of tension or a logical problem but as a great spiritual blessing in Christ (Eph. 1:3). Indeed the Father's grand design gives purpose to Christians in the present and gives them hope for the future (vv. 8–10).

Many non-Christians have no sense of purpose in the whole of history or in their own lives. Although scientists have generally excluded personal agency and final causes from their methodology, there is continuous evidence of responsible human agencies in our daily activities. How strange to imagine that every meaningful thing we do has a purpose but that the totality of our lives has no point! Purpose in every meaningful human act reflects purpose in the universe as a whole.

Persistent attacks on teleological evidence by those who refuse to believe in the intelligent, purposeful heavenly Father, have caused some existentialist Christians to limit confident affirmation of God's revealed purposeful ends to the subjectivity of believers' hearts. However, the Scriptures are emphatic, and we too should be, that according to one strategy or another, everything in nature, history, and our lives has a purpose in God's grand design.[116]

The Only Assurance That Good Will Triumph Over Evil

People who have no transcendent, sovereign source, support, and guarantor of values, have insufficient reason for believing that history will end in a way that they could approve of.

Many alternative proposals are popular, but they all fail to certify a just end to history. "Evolution" cannot assure us of that hope. Evolution has produced no major change in essential humanness in all the years of human existence on earth. There is no evidence that quantum jumps in evolution will occur or, if they should, that they would be for the better rather than for the worse.

Dialectical materialism has failed to produce a classless, peaceful, society without need for massive military and police might to put down the restlessness of the self-determining human hearts. The hypothesis that forceful revolution can produce permanent peace lacks adequate support in the history of humanity in general and in the history of Marxism-Leninism in particular. Marxism's promise of eventual peace is belied by preparation for war.

To project confidence in a pointless world, however heroic it may seem, is not the mark of intelligent commitment. Instead it represents wishful thinking contrary to the evidence of divine revelation.

Or to hold with Sartre that man is "a useless passion" with no lasting meaning does not provide freedom for significant existential involvement in the battles of life. This philosophy involves mankind in nothing more than an endless, losing fight with ultimate absurdity.[117]

In contrast to the world's unfounded hope for a just peace, Christians may confidently trust in God's changeless nature and eternal plan, which includes the triumphant return of Christ to unify the world. That hope is based on the reliable revelation of God's great purpose. "Because God wanted to make the *unchanging nature of his purpose* very clear to the heirs of what was promised, he *confirmed it with an oath.* God did this so that, by two unchangeable things in which it is impossible for God to lie, we who have fled to take hold of the hope offered to us may be greatly encouraged. We have this hope as an anchor for the soul, firm and secure" (Heb. 6:17–19, italics added).

A Paradigm of Goal-Oriented Living and Ministering

The tendency of many teachers and ministers is to be problem-oriented in serving the Lord, rather than goal-oriented. We cannot ignore problems, but they can best be met from the perspective of long-range, affirmative goals. The Father in heaven established a goal-oriented kingdom that at the same time provides for solving humanity's deepest problem—sin. So at least in our problem solving, we do well to follow our Father's example and have some positive goals encompassing our problems and more. Paul did not simply plead with Euodia and Syntyche to agree with each other in the Lord (Phil. 4:2); he first laid the groundwork for the attempt at problem solving by praying that all members of the Philippian church under Christ might share the objective of "having the same love, being one in the spirit and *purpose*" (2:2). Encouraging others to have attitudes like that of Christ, who gave up glory in heaven out of concern for the interests of others, our attempts to solve disputes among church members should be more effective if these attempts are made in the context of a constructive objective of continuous unity for all members "in spirit and purpose."

Aligning Our Purposes With God's Chosen Ends

Pastors and officers of churches, as other institutions, do well to write out the long-range goals of the institution. Those churches that aim at nothing are sure to accomplish their aim. Each church can profit from the discipline of formulating its *raison d'être* for itself in its particular location at its particular time. The stated purpose provides the reference point for periodic evaluations of the leaders in ministry and of all church officers. How well has the church done in the preceding year in accomplishing its chosen ends? In what ways is it succeeding or failing, and why? By what changes of focus or personnel can it do better?

The reasons for a particular church's existence, however detailed and specific, ought to be in harmony with the ultimate ends God has chosen for the church (both universal and local). When that is the case, there will be regard for nature and its laws as God's creation and respect for the value of self-determining people created in God's image. People's most basic problem will be seen to be moral and spiritual rebellion against God, resulting in alienation from God. And the focal point of ministry in seeking to meet that need will be the proclamation of the atoning provision of Jesus Christ. Other ministries, however beneficial in themselves, must not take the place of the divine priority for Christians individually and collectively in churches in the present age.

From God's general, transcultural exhortations, we know of other divine purposes for our lives and ministries. God desires that his people be stewards of and rule over lower forms of life. God plans to use us as witnesses, as salt, light, saints, ambassadors, co-regents in his kingdom, and co-builders in his church. He desires that we be sanctified through the truth of the Word (John 17:17–19), testify to the truth (18:37), honor God with our bodies (1 Cor. 6:20), and do all to the glory of God (10:31). God also wills that we excel in using our gifts to build up the church (14:12) so that all may reach unity in the faith and become mature in the fullness of Christ (Eph. 4:12–13). In brief, "we make it our goal to please him" (2 Cor. 5:9).

Choosing Strategies in Harmony With God's Strategies

A person or church can have the best list of ends in the world, but they are unlikely to be efficiently achieved without similar consideration of the wisest strategies for achieving them. It is also beneficial to spell out the role and responsibility that each officer fulfills in order to achieve those goals. And these ought to be consistent with the Father's strategies for attaining his ends in the world. No strategy will be attempted to accomplish what God has chosen to do miraculously without human instrumentality, though we will want to be available should the Father desire to work through us in extraordinary ways. We cannot manipulate the Almighty. But the church's primary responsibility is to set its goals for the ordinary, day-by-day responsibilities God has delegated to it.

Coercive means of programing and deprograming persons against their wills should not be used. God himself respected his self-determining creatures enough to permit them to make mistakes. People's value as creatures of God will be esteemed. The human rights of persons in God's image ought to be respected. Christian churches will use only ethically persuasive methods such as preaching, teaching, and personal dialogue. People who do not repent of sin, believe the gospel and trust Christ will not be pressured into church membership, whether younger or older, richer or poorer. Our strategies will take into account not only our good purposes but also the person's abilities to respond to them under normal circumstances. And our strategies will not be completed when justification by faith and church membership are achieved, but assistance will continue for all members in their growth toward the goals of spiritual maturity. The development of worthy ends with commendable strategies will be encouraged by the hope of the coming universal unity at the return of Christ. Until the day of Christ's return, we will recommit ourselves to faithful work toward ends consistent with God's ends, and strategies in harmony with God's strategies. We have been brought from spiritual death to life for a grand purpose. Our election is "a call to service, a summons to be a co-laborer with God in the actualization of God's elective purpose and goal."[118]

Has God a Detailed Plan for Our Lives?

In addition to the general moral and spiritual ends for all Christians, has God a detailed plan for each person, family, and church? Beyond general purposes, evidence indicates that the Father planned a number of specific matters. Apparently God chose Adam and Eve to be the first parents of the human race, Abraham to be the father of a great nation, Noah and family to sustain the race through the flood, Saul to be Israel's first king, David to rule as his successor, the prophets and apostles to be his spokesmen, and Paul to be the catalyst for uniting Gentiles with the Jews in the Christian church. To members of Christ's body the Holy Spirit gives gifts, just as he determines (1 Cor. 12:11). From such indications we might consider it probable that God has specific plans for all of his people.

If God has such detailed plans for us in his comprehensive purposes, he has not, like a travel agent, listed the various routes we are to take to the end of our journey. Instead he made us self-determining beings who can be guided by his entire revelation, both general and special. In seeking to make a decision, we do not ask for a revelation of God's will beyond what he chose to reveal, but for his leading in making a decision in harmony with his revealed purposes and strategies. A Christian way of life based on the primary data of the entirety of revelation, general and special, includes not only explicit moral teachings but many ethical inferences for life and ministry (such as we seek to exhibit briefly in each chapter of this volume).[119]

However, making decisions on matters not specifically discussed according to God's moral principles is often more difficult than it appears. Which principles apply in a given case? What is their order of priority? Exactly how do we apply them? To make decisions in accord with the moral will of God, we do well to take more fully into account the moral and ethical implications of the entirety of Scripture in the coherent manner of Christian writers in *ethics*. The study of secondary sources in moral theology ought not be ignored.[120]

Ordinarily God's promised guidance (Ps. 32:8) of repentant believers (vv. 3–5) who pray for leading (vv. 6–7) is not by the force of "bit and bridle" (v. 9). Neither is it by nonrational means like Ouija boards, witches, or cards, but through his "instruction" and "counsel" (v. 8). The Lord's instruction and counsel is found in the option that most coherently accounts for all lines of relevant data such as: (1) all that special revelation now in Scripture teaches relevant to the options (primarily, but not exclusively moral instruction) and (2) all that general revelation indicates in our experience, including (a) our recognition of our spiritual gifts, (b) the counsel of qualified persons, (c) providentially ordered experiential data and (d) our persistent desire for the option in order to glorify God.

Having gathered all these data, we arrive at a decision about the wisest course of action in accord with the *criteria of God's truth* on any other matter. Our option sufficiently corresponds with God's thoughts when (1) without any contradiction (2) it accounts for all the relevant lines of evidence (explicit and implied) and (3) we can live by it without hypocrisy. The Holy Spirit guides us in the process of decision making according to these criteria. He then witnesses with our spirits to the objective validity of the truth discovered and its personal, subjective applicability, and this gives us a sense of peace.

The degree of psychological assurance of having discovered a course of action pleasing to God depends on many intellectual factors contributing to a well-founded conviction. Intellectually the degree of probability depends on (1) the amount of relevant material from general and special revelation perused, (2) the validity of our interpretive principles and our skill in the art of applying them, (3) the soundness of our criteria of truth and skill in applying them to all the relevant areas of instruction and life, and (4) the reliability of our method of reasoning for arriving at well-founded conclusions.[121] With strong probability that a decision based on the convergence of many of these factors is right, there should develop a strong inner assurance that we have a course of action in accord with his plan.

We need all of these checks and balances because we are so easily tempted to take short cuts, prematurely claiming to know God's plans with finality when, much like presumptuous prophets, we think and speak out of our own hearts. Another reason why we need these checks and balances is that on a similar issue equally able and dedicated Christians often come to different and even opposite conclusions. In life's decisions we generally act on conclusions with degrees of intellectual probability depending on the extent of the relevant evidence and our skill in handling it (2 Tim. 2:15). But knowing God's good purposes for us and his promise to lead us in our sincere search, we endeavor to order our lives for his glory. Through this process the Holy Spirit gives the psychological assurance that he has led us with his "eye."

We ought never dictate to God what we have concluded he must will. However, assured of the Lord's leading, we will always proceed on ventures with the proviso of James, "If it is the Lord's will, we will live and do this or

333

that" (James 4:15). That qualification need not reflect a lack of faith on our part that what God promised he will do (Rom. 4:21). Rather, it may indicate awareness that we are not inerrant in even the best judgments of our finite minds concerning the future.

REVIEW QUESTIONS

To Help Relate and Apply Each Section in This Chapter

1. *Briefly state the classical problem* this chapter addresses and indicate reasons why genuine inquiry into it is important for your world view and your existence personally and socially.

2. *Objectively summarize the influential answers* given to this problem in history as hypotheses to be tested. Be able to compare and contrast their real similarities and differences (not merely verbal similarities or differences).

3. *Highlight the primary biblical evidence* on which to decide among views—evidence found in the relevant teachings of the major divisions of Scripture—and decide for yourself which historical hypothesis (or synthesis of historical views) provides the most consistent and adequate account of the primary biblical data.

4. *Formulate in your own words your doctrinal conviction* in a logically consistent and adequate way, organizing your conclusions in ways you can explain clearly, support biblically, and communicate effectively to your spouse, children, friends, Bible class, or congregation.

5. *Defend your view* as you would to adherents of the alternative views, showing that the other views are logically less consistent and factually faced with more difficulties than your view in accounting for the givens, not only of special revelation but also of human experience in general.

6. *Explore the differences the viabil-*

ity of your conviction can make in your life. Then test your understanding of the viability of your view by asking, "Can I live by it authentically (unhypocritically) in relation to God and to others in my family, church, vocation, neighborhood, city, nation, and world?"

MINISTRY PROJECTS

To Help Communicate This Doctrine in Christian Service

1. *Memorize one major verse or passage* that in its context teaches the heart of this doctrine and may serve as a text from which to preach, teach, or lead small group studies on the topic. The memorized passages from each chapter will build a body of content useful also for meditation and reference in informal discussions.

2. *Formulate the major idea of the doctrine in one sentence* based on the passage memorized. This idea should be useful as the major thesis of either a lesson for a class (junior high to adult) or a message for a church service.

3. *State the specific purpose or goal of your doctrinal lesson or message.* Your purpose should be more than informative. It should show why Christians need to accept this truth and live by it (unhypocritically). For teaching purposes, list indicators that would show to what extent class members have grasped the truth presented.

4. *Outline your message or lesson in complete sentences.* Indicate how you would support the truth of the doctrine's central ideas and its relevance to life and service. Incorporate elements from this chapter's historical, biblical, systematic, apologetic, and practical sections selected according to the value they have for your audience.

5. *List applications of the doctrine* for communicating the difference this conviction makes in life (for sermons, lessons, small-group Bible studies, or

family devotional Bible studies). Applications should make clear what the doctrine is, why one needs to know it, and how it will make differences in thinking. Then show how the difference in thought will lead to differences in values, priorities, attitudes, speech, and personal action. Consider also the doctrine's possible significance for family, church, neighborhood, city, regional, and national actions.

6. *Start a file and begin collecting illustrations* of this doctrine's central idea, the points in your outline, and your applications.

7. *Write out your own doctrinal state-* *ment on this subject in one paragraph* (in half a page or less). To work toward a comprehensive doctrinal statement, collect your formulations based on a study of each chapter of *Integrative Theology.* As your own statement of Christian doctrine grows, you will find it personally strengthening and useful when you are called on for your beliefs in general and when you apply for service with churches, mission boards, and other Christian organizations. Any who seek ordination to Christian ministry will need a comprehensive doctrinal statement that covers the broad scope of theology.

Notes

Preface

[1] Bernard Ramm, *After Fundamentalism: The Future of Evangelical Theology* (San Francisco: Harper & Row, 1983), 27.

[2] Ibid.

[3] For additional comparison and contrast of these three methods of decision making, see Gordon R. Lewis, "Schaeffer's Apologetic Method," in Reflections on Francis Schaeffer ed. Ronald W. Reugsegger (Grand Rapids: Zondervan, 1986), 69–104.

Chapter One

[1] Francis Schaeffer, *A Christian Manifesto* (Westchester: Crossway, 1981), 4.

[2] B. A. Demarest, "Systematic Theology," *EDT,* 1064–66; George Ladd, *A Theology of the New Testament* (Grand Rapids: Eerdmans, 1974), 25–26; David Wells, *The Search for Salvation* (Downers Grove: InterVarsity, 1978), 23–28, 36–46; Klaus Bockmuhl, "The Task of Systematic Theology," ed. Kenneth S. Kantzer and Stanley N. Gundry, *Perspectives on Evangelical Theology* (Grand Rapids: Baker, 1979), 3–14.

[3] Cornelius Van Til, *An Introduction to Systematic Theology* (Unpublished syllabus, 1971). Rousas John Rushdoony, *The Necessity for Systematic Theology* (Valliceto, Calif.: Ross House, 1979).

[4] Gordon Clark, *Karl Barth's Theological Method* (Philadelphia: Presbyterian and Reformed, 1963). Carl Henry, *God, Revelation and Authority* (Waco: Word, 1976), vol. 1.

[5] Millard J. Erickson, *Christian Theology,* 3 vols. (Grand Rapids: Baker, 1983–85), 1:21.

[6] John Jefferson Davis, *Foundations of Evangelical Theology* (Grand Rapids: Baker, 1984).

[7] Considering biblical teaching as evidence, compare the steps in a scientific method in Irving M. Copi, *Introduction to Logic,* 6th ed. (New York: Macmillan, 1982), 470–75.

[8] Erickson, *Christian Theology,* 1:78.

[9] For initial ideas in this direction from the Old Testament see Walter Kaiser, *Toward an Exegetical Theology* (Grand Rapids: Baker, 1981), 139. More will be said on this in future volumes, d.v.

[10] For criteria of truth and ways of defending the existence of the God revealed in the Jesus of history and the teaching of Scripture, see Gordon R. Lewis, *Testing Christianity's Truth Claims* (Chicago: Moody, 1976), esp. chapters 7–10, and appendix.

[11] Adapted from Henry A. Virkler, *Hermeneutics: Principles and Processes of Biblical Interpretation* (Grand Rapids: Baker, 1981), 117.

[12] On the missiological issue of contextualizing the message in terms of the hearers' horizons see John Jefferson Davis, "Contextualization and the Nature of Theology" in his *The Necessity of Systematic Theology* (Grand Rapids: Baker, 1978), 169–85.

[13] *Metaphysical Bible Dictionary* (Lee's Summit, Mo.: Unity School of Christianity, 1954); Mary Baker Eddy, *Science and Health with Key to the Scriptures* (Boston: First Church of Christ Scientist, 1932).

[14] For chapters on the doctrinal use of Scripture see Bernard Ramm, *Protestant Biblical Interpretation* (Boston: W. A. Wilde, 1956) and Berkeley Michaelsen, *Interpreting the Bible* (Grand Rapids: Eerdmans, 1963).

[15] See Copi, *Introduction to Logic,* chapter on defining terms, 138–73.

[16] William L. Reese, "Laws of Thought," in *Dictionary of Philosophy and Religion* (Atlantic Highlands, N.J.: Humanities, 1980), 297.

[17] See Copi, *Introduction to Logic,* chapter on immediate references, 177–202.

[18] See John Jefferson Davis, *Foundations of Systematic Theology* (Grand Rapids: Baker, 1984), 136.

[19] Bruce Demarest, "Christendom's Creeds: Their Relevance in the Modern World," *Journal of Evangelical Theological Society,* vol. 21, no. 4 (Dec. 1978): 345–56.

[20] L. Harold DeWolf, *The Case for Theology in a Liberal Perspective* (Philadelphia: Westminster, 1959), 19–41.

[21] Anthony Thiselton, *The Two Horizons* (Grand Rapids: Eerdmans, 1980).

[22] Charles Kraft, *Christianity in Culture* (Maryknoll: Orbis, 1979).

[23] John Jefferson Davis, "Contextualization and the Nature of Theology" in his *The Necessity of Systematic Theology* (Grand Rapids: Baker, 1978), 169–85.

[24] For reading on cultural factors in interpretation see Walter C. Kaiser, "Legitimate Hermeneutics," in *Inerrancy,* ed. Norman L. Geisler (Grand Rapids: Zondervan, 1980), 141–44; Gordon R. Lewis, "The Human Authorship of Inspired Scripture" in *Inerrancy,* 229–51; Alan Johnson, "History and Culture in the New Testament Interpretation," ed. Samuel J. Schultz and Morris Inch, in *Interpreting the Word of God* (Chicago: Moody, 1976), 128–61; R. C. Sproul, *Knowing Scripture* (Downers Grove: InterVarsity, 1977), 101–12; Henry A. Virkler, *Hermeneutics: Principles and Processes of Biblical Interpretation* (Grand Rapids: Baker, 1981), 211–32.

[25] On breaking out of the hermeneutical circles or assumptions, see Gordon R. Lewis, "A Response to Presuppositions of Non-Evangelical Hermeneutics" in *Hermeneutics, Inerrancy and the Bible,* Earl D. Radmacher and Robert D. Preus, eds. (Grand Rapids: Zondervan, 1984), 615–26.

[26] Watchman Nee, *The Spiritual Man* (New York: Christian Fellowship Publications, 1968), 3 vols.

[27] Clark Pinnock, "Prospects for Systematic Theology," ed. David F. Wells, *Toward a Theology for the Future* (Carol Stream: Creation House, 1971), 96.

[28] A. J. Ayer, *Language, Truth and Logic* (New York: Dover, 1946), 114–20.

[29] Alan Watts, *The Way of Zen* (New York: Random House, 1957), 115.

[30] Alan Watts, *Beyond Theology: The Art of Godmanship* (New York: Vintage Books, 1964).

[31] John Bright, *The Authority of the Old Testament* (Grand Rapids: Baker, 1978), 159.

[32] Ibid., 116.

[33] Ibid., 131.

[34] Ibid., 140.

[35] Ibid., 47–48, 115, 125.

[36] Ibid., 130.

[37] John Gill, *Body of Divinity* (Atlanta: Turner Lasseter, 1957), xxiv–xxv.

[38] Andrew Murray, *With Christ in the School of Prayer* (New York: Loizeaux Brothers, n.d.), 171–72.

[39] Ibid.

[40] Francis Brown, S. R. Driver, and C. A. Briggs, *A Hebrew and English Lexicon* (Oxford: Clarendon, 1907), 54; Gerhard Kittel, *TDNT,* 10 vols., 1:232–47.

[41] Gordon R. Lewis, "God's Word: Key to Authentic Spirituality" in *A Call to Christian Character,* ed. Bruce Shelley (Grand Rapids: Zondervan, 1970), 111.

[42] Thor Hall, *A Theology of Christian Devotion* (Nashville: The Upper Room, 1969), 90, 74–75.

[43] W. G. T. Shedd, *Dogmatic Theology,* 3 vols. (Grand Rapids: Zondervan, n.d.), 1:5.

[44] For an exposition and defense of post-Reformation Lutheran orthodoxy see Robert D. Preus, *The Theology of Post-Reformation Lutheranism,* 2 vols. (St. Louis: Concordia, 1970–72); for the views of Reformation and post-Reformation divines, see Heinrich Heppe, *Reformed Dogmatics* (London: Allen and Unwin, 1950).

[45] Cited in Hubert Cunliffe-Jones, *History of Christian Doctrine* (Philadelphia: Fortress, 1980), 431.

[46] Karl Rahner, *TI,* 5:115–34.

[47] Hans Küng, *On Being a Christian* (Garden City, N.Y.: Doubleday, 1976), 21.

[48] Paul Tillich, *The Courage to Be* (New Haven: Yale University Press, 1952), 179.

[49] Ibid., 177–80.

[50] Frank Vanden Berg, *Abraham Kuyper* (Grand Rapids: Eerdmans, 1960), 282.

[51] A. C. Headlam, *Christian Theology* (Oxford: Clarendon, 1934), 3–4.

Chapter Two

[1] A. C. Headlam, *Christian Theology* (Oxford: Clarendon, 1934), 7.

[2] Thomas Aquinas, *ST,* I.12.13.

[3] Henry P. Van Dusen, *The Vindication of Liberal Theology* (New York: Scribner, 1963), 77.

4 L. Harold DeWolf, *A Theology of the Living Church* (New York: Harper, 1953), 24.

5 Ibid., 65.

6 Friedrich Schleiermacher, *The Christian Faith* (Reprint, Philadelphia: Fortress, 1976), 133.

7 Paul Tillich, *Systematic Theology,* 3 vols. (Chicago: University of Chicago Press, 1951–63), 1:110.

8 Ibid., 1:12.

9 Karl Rahner, *TI,* X:36.

10 See ibid., V:115–34 for Rahner's development of this expression.

11 Cited by Henri Bouillard, *The Knowledge of God* (New York: Herder & Herder, 1967), 12–13.

12 Karl Barth, *CD,* vol. 2, pt. 1, 173.

13 Ibid., vol. 1, pt. 1, 192.

14 Ibid., vol. 1, pt. 2, 306.

15 For Barth's development of this idea, see *CD,* vol. 2, pt. 2, 306ff. and vol. 2, pt. 2, 345ff.

16 G. C. Berkouwer, "General and Special Revelation," in *Revelation and the Bible,* ed. C. F. H. Henry (Grand Rapids: Baker, 1976), 15.

17 Van Til maintains not only that the sinner cannot know God's general revelation, but that "the natural man is spiritually blind with respect to everything."*An Introduction to Systematic Theology: In Defense of the Faith* (Nutley, N.J.: Presbyterian and Reformed, 1974), 82.

18 Theophilus, *To Autolychus,* I.5; cf. Tatian, *Address to the Greeks,* IV; XII.

19 Clement of Alexandria, *Miscellanies,* V.13.

20 Tertullian, *The Apology,* XVII.6; *Against Marcion,* I.10.

21 Origen, *On First Principles,* I.1.6; Athanasius, *Against the Heather,* III.35–36; Cyril of Jerusalem, *Catechetical Lectures,* IX.16; XI.2; Gregory of Nyssa, *The Beatitudes,* sermon no. 6.

22 Augustine, *Sermons on the New Testament,* XCI.2.

23 Martin Luther, *LW,* vol. XXVI, 299.

24 John Calvin, *Institutes of the Christian Religion,* I.xvi.1.

25 Charles Hodge, *Systematic Theology* (Reprint, Grand Rapids: Eerdmans, 1973), 21–25.

26 Carl F. H. Henry, *God, Revelation and Authority,* 6 vols. (Waco: Word, 1976–83), 1:399–402; 2:69–76, 83–90.

27 Henry C. Thiessen, *Lectures in Systematic Theology* (Grand Rapids: Eerdmans, 1979), 7–10.

28 Dale Moody, *The Word of Truth* (Grand Rapids: Eerdmans, 1981), 57–77, 276–77.

29 Millard J. Erickson, *Christian Theology,* 3 vols. (Grand Rapids: Baker, 1983–85), 1:154–74.

30 Walter Brueggemann, *Genesis* (Atlanta: John Knox, 1982), 16.

31 In subsequent chapters of Genesis Moses presents a rich description of God's character, his works, and especially the unfolding of his saving purposes vis-à-vis his chosen people Israel.

32 According to Francis I. Anderson, the focus of God's universal revelation in the Job text is twofold: "So far as the world is concerned, God's wisdom is seen in its variegation and its order. So far as man is concerned, God's wisdom is expressed in his moral conduct." *Job* (Downers Grove: InterVarsity, 1976), 262.

33 Bertil Gärtner, *The Areopagus Speech and Natural Revelation* (Lund: Gleerup, 1955), 178.

34 See William Neil, *The Acts of the Apostles. NCBC,* 191.

35 *BAGD,* 291.

36 John Murray, *The Epistle to the Romans,* 2 vols. (Grand Rapids: Eerdmans, 1959), 1:40.

37 So G. C. Berkouwer, *General Revelation* (Grand Rapids: Eerdmans, 1955), 175–87. According to Berkouwer the law of God works on the human heart from without; it is not implanted in the heart as an innate endowment.

38 The NIV margin reading (so also the AV) sets forth the preferred translation. "Everyman . . . coming into the world" is the rabbinic way of saying, "Everyone who is born." See R. V. G. Tasker, *St. John* (London: Inter-Varsity, 1960), 46.

39 Tasker, *St. John,* 42.

40 Alfred Plummer, *The Gospel According to St. John* (Grand Rapids: Baker, 1981), 68.

41 For a thorough study of the biblical content see Bruce Demarest, *General Revelation: Historical Views and Contemporary Issues* (Grand Rapids: Zondervan, 1982), 227–62. For an example of reading more into divine revelation in nature than warranted scripturally or experientially see A. H. Seiss, *The Gospel in the Stars* (Grand Rapids: Kregel, 1972). The stars are "signs" of agricultural, not redemptive significance (Gen. 1:14). In an agricultural context, the stars served as signs of "seasons," "days," and "years" for planting and

harvesting. See Basil F. C. Atkinson, *The Book of Genesis* in *The Pocket Commentary of the Bible* (Chicago: Moody, 1957), 18.

[42] H. P. Owen, "Theism," *EP*, 8:97.

[43] William Reese, *Dictionary of Philosophy and Religion: Eastern and Western* (Atlantic Highlands, N.J.: Humanities, 1980), 462.

[44] Friedrich Schleiermacher, *The Christian Faith*, ed. H. R. Machintosh and J. S. Steward (Philadelphia: Fortress, 1976), 133.

[45] Immanuel Kant, *Critique of Practical Reason*, II, Conclusion, ed. R. M. Hutchins, *Great Books of the Western World* (Chicago: Encyclopedia Britannica, 1952), 42:360.

[46] Reinhold Niebuhr, *The Nature and Destiny of Man* (New York: Scribner, 1943), 135.

[47] Gordon R. Lewis, "Faith and Reason in the Thought of St. Augustine" (Unpublished dissertation, University Microfilm Syracuse University, 1959), 25–54.

[48] Gordon R. Lewis, *Testing Christianity's Truth Claims* (Chicago: Moody, 1976) compares six systems of reasoning to the existence of the God revealed in the Jesus of history and the teachings of Scripture.

[49] Dale Moody, *The Word of Truth* (Grand Rapids: Eerdmans, 1981), 59.

[50] Emil Brunner, *Revelation and Reason*, 76.

[51] J. N. D. Anderson, *Christianity and Comparative Religion* (Downers Grove: InterVarsity, 1970), 102, 105. See also A. H. Strong, *Systematic Theology* (Philadelphia: Judson, n.d.), 843–44; W. G. T. Shedd, *Dogmatic Theology*, 3 vols. (Grand Rapids: Zondervan, n.d.), 2:704–12.

[52] Charles Hodge, *Systematic Theology* (Grand Rapids: Eerdmans, 1946), 2:646–48; Robert E. Speer, *The Finality of Jesus Christ* (Westwood, N.J.: Revell, n.d.); Gordon Lewis, *Judge for Yourself* (Downers Grove: InterVarsity, 1977), 26–35.

[53] Corliss Lamont, *The Philosophy of Humanism* (New York: Frederick Unger, 1982), 197.

[54] Ibid., 286.

[55] S. H. Kellogg, *A Handbook of Comparative Religion* (Grand Rapids: Eerdmans, 1951), 7–9.

[56] Aldous Huxley, Introduction, in *The Song of God: Bhagavad-Gita* (New York: New Americana Library, 1951), 12.

[57] Ibid., 13.

[58] Huston Smith, *Forgotten Truth: The Primordial Tradition* (New York: Harper & Row, 1976), 152.

[59] Ibid., 52–56.

[60] Ibid., 58.

[61] C. S. Lewis, *Miracles* (New York: Macmillan, 1948), 105.

[62] Ibid., 101.

[63] L. Harold DeWolf, *The Case for Theology in a Liberal Perspective* (Philadelphia: Westminster, 1959), 32.

[64] John Hick, *Philosophy of Religion* (Englewood Cliffs: Prentice-Hall, 1963), 76. Compare Barth's denials of propositional truths in revelation.

[65] On Barth's changing views of divine transcendence with his criticisms of his own earlier position, see Karl Barth, *The Humanity of God* (Richmond: John Knox, 1960), 37–65.

[66] Barth, *CD*, vol. 1, pt. 1, 252.

[67] Karl Barth, "No!" in Emil Brunner and Karl Barth, *Natural Theology*, trans. Peter Fruenkel (London: Geoffrey Bles, Centenary Press, 1946), 62.

[68] Barth, *CD*, vol. 1, pt. 1, 10.

[69] Karl Barth, *Epistle to the Romans*, trans. Edwyn C. Hoskyns (London: Oxford, 1963), 47. For a biblically based evaluation of Barth's and others' views see Demarest, *General Revelation*, 1–226.

[70] For a critique of non-Christian values and a defense of Christian values see Edward John Carnell, *A Philosophy of the Christian Religion* (Grand Rapids: Eerdmans, 1952), condensed in Gordon R. Lewis, *Testing Christianity's Truth Claims*, 210–30.

[71] Augustine, *The Happy Life*, trans. by Ludwig Schupp, *Writings of Saint Augustine*, vol. 1, *Fathers of the Church*, 43–84.

[72] Stanley L. Jaki, *The Road of Science and the Ways to God* (Chicago: University of Chicago Press, 1978), 180.

[73] Lausanne Covenant, International Congress on World Evangelization (Wheaton: Lausanne Committee on World Evangelization, 1974), Article 5.

[74] Waldron Scott, *Bring Forth Justice* (Grand Rapids: Eerdmans, 1980). For reformed ways of developing the implications of general revelation for society see H. Henry Meeter, *The Basic Ideas of Calvinism* (Grand Rapids: Kregel, 1967) and Henry R. Van Til, *The Calvinistic Concept of Culture* (Grand Rapids: Baker, 1972).

[75] David Chilton, *Productive Christians in an Age of Guilt Manipulators: A Biblical Response to Ronald Sider* (Tyler, Tex.: Institute for Christian Economics, 1981); cf. Ronald

Sider, *Justice: The Bible Speaks on Hunger and Poverty* (Downers Grove: InterVarsity, 1980).

[76]Waldron Scott, ed., *Serving Our Generation: Evangelical Strategies for the Eighties* (Colorado Springs: World Evangelical Fellowship, 1980).

[77]Brenda Munsey, *Moral Development, Moral Education and Kohlberg* (Birmingham: Religious Education Press, 1980).

[78]For discussions of points of contact with non-Christians in six systems of apologetics see Gordon Lewis, *Testing Christianity's Truth Claims,* and Gordon Lewis, "Van Til and Carnell," ed. E. R. Geehan, *Jerusalem and Athens* (Phillipsburg, N.J.: Presbyterian and Reformed, 1971), 349–68.

[79]C. F. D. Moule, *The Phenomenon of the New Testament* (Naperville, Ill.: Allenson, 1967), 19.

[80]See references in note 51.

[81]See references in note 52.

[82]Lit-sen Chang, *Strategy of Missions in the Orient: Christian Impact on the Pagan World* (Phillipsburg, N.J.: Presbyterian and Reformed, 1970).

[83]B. B. Warfield, *Selected Shorter Writings* (Phillipsburg, N.J.: Presbyterian and Reformed, n.d.), 27, 45.

[84]Ibid., 45.

[85]Lit-sen Chang, *Strategy of Missions in the Orient,* 105.

Chapter Three

[1]"Revelation," *The Encyclopedia of the Lutheran Church,* 2:2052.

[2]Council of Trent, Session IV (April 8, 1546). See Philip Schaff, *Creeds of Christendom,* 3 vols. (Grand Rapids: Baker, 1977), 2:80.

[3]Cited in Edward G. Waring, *Deism and Natural Religion* (New York: F. Unger, 1967), 109.

[4]G. E. Lessing, cited in Peter Gay, *The Enlightenment* (New York: Knopf, 1966), 330.

[5]F. Gerald Downing, *Has Christianity a Revelation?* (Philadelphia: Westminster, 1964), 238.

[6]Karl Barth, *CD,* vol. 1, pt. 2, 237.

[7]Ibid., vol. 1, pt. 1, 136.

[8]Emil Brunner, *Revelation and Reason* (London: SCM, 1947), 8.

[9]H. Richard Niebuhr, *The Meaning of Revelation* (New York: Macmillan, 1941), 16.

[10]Hans Küng, *On Being a Christian* (Garden City, N.Y.: Doubleday, 1976), 467.

[11]Rudolph Bultmann, *Existence and Faith* (London: Collins, 1960), 100.

[12]Athanasius, *The Incarnation of the Word,* XIII.

[13]Ibid., XIV.

[14]Augustine, *Confessions,* VI.5.8.

[15]John Calvin, *Institutes of the Christian Religion,* I.vi.3.

[16]Carl F. H. Henry, *God, Revelation and Authority,* 6 vols. (Waco: Word, 1976–83), 2:7.

[17]Ibid., 12.

[18]B. B. Warfield, "The Biblical Idea of Revelation," in *The Inspiration and Authority of the Bible* (Nutley, N.J.: Presbyterian and Reformed, 1970), 82–96.

[19]Millard J. Erickson, *Christian Theology,* 3 vols. (Grand Rapids: Baker, 1983–85), 1:175–98.

[20]Bernard Ramm, *Special Revelation and the Word of God* (Grand Rapids: Eerdmans, 1961).

[21]Ronald H. Nash, *The Word of God and the Mind of Man* (Grand Rapids: Zondervan, 1982).

[22]Cf. Deut. 34:11: "Moses . . . did all those miraculous signs and wonders the LORD sent him to do in Egypt—to Pharaoh and to all his officials and to his whole land." See also Deut. 7:18–19.

[23]C. Brown, *"chrēmatizō," NIDNTT,* 3:324.

[24]G. D. Lass, *A Theology of the New Testament* (Grand Rapids: Eerdmans, 1974), 392.

[25]B. Gärtner, *"epiphaneia," NIDNTT,* 3:319.

[26]Cf. Bernard Ramm, *Special Revelation and the Word of God,* 110.

[27]Robert E. Webber, *God Still Speaks: A Biblical View of Christian Communication* (Nashville: Thomas Nelson, 1979), 69–72.

[28]Augustine, "Retractions" I.3.2, trans. Robert P. Russell, in *Fathers of the Church: A New Translation,* ed. Ludwig Schopp et al., "Writings of St. Augustine" (New York: CIMA, 1948), 1:332n.

[29]Jean Wahl, *A Short History of Existentialism* (New York: Philosophical Library, 1949), 19; Jean-Paul Sartre, *Existentialism* (New York: Philosophical Library, 1947), 15; Gordon R. Lewis, "Augustine and Existentialism" *Bulletin of the Evangelical Theological Society* vol. 8, no.1 (Winter 1965), 13–22.

[30] Edward John Carnell, *Introduction to Christian Apologetics* (Grand Rapids: Eerdmans, 1948), 60; Bernard Ramm, *Special Revelation and the Word of God* (Grand Rapids: Eerdmans, 1961), 143–54.

[31] See on the Logos: Ronald Nash, *The Word of God and the Word of Man*, 6 vols. (Grand Rapids: Zondervan, 1982), 59–69; Henry, *God, Revelation and Authority* 3:164–247.

[32] Few works on revelation consider Christ's view of his own teaching. Donald Guthrie has a brief section arguing that "of utmost importance for any approach to the authority of the NT is the attitude which Jesus took to his own teaching," but that statement seems difficult to reconcile with his earlier agreement with Cullmann that the concept of prophet and teacher "played no significant part in NT Christology." *New Testament Theology* (Downers Grove: InterVarsity, 1981), 960–61 and 269–70. Barth also had sections studying the verbs for Jesus' evangelizing, preaching, and teaching, but he did not develop Jesus' view of his own teaching. *CD*, vol. 4, pt. 2, 194–209.

[33] Francis Brown, S. R. Driver, and Charles A. Briggs, *A Hebrew and English Lexicon of the Old Testament* (Oxford: Clarendon, 1907); Rudolph Bultmann, *"alethia," TDNT*, 1:241–47; Anthony Thiselton, "Truth," *Dictionary of New Testament Theology*, ed. Colin Brown (Grand Rapids: Zondervan, 1978), 897–901.

[34] Allan A. MacRae, "Prophets and Prophecy," *ZPEB*, 4:880; Bernard Ramm, *Special Revelation and the Word of God*, 59.

[35] Josephus *Apion* I.8.

[36] A. A. MacRae, "Prophets and Prophecy," *ZPEB*, 4:903.

[37] R. E. Higginson, "Apostolic Succession," *EDT*, 73.

[38] Donald Guthrie, *New Testament Theology*, 769.

[39] Evaluated by contemporary Roman Catholic theologian Richard P. O'Brien, *Catholicism* (Minneapolis: Winston, 1980), 240.

[40] Thomas Dehany Bernard, *The Progress of Doctrine in the New Testament* (London: Macmillan, 1879), 1–207.

[41] John Baillie, *The Idea of Revelation in Recent Thought* (New York: Columbia University Press, 1956), 47.

[42] Ibid., 49.

[43] Antony Flew, *A Dictionary of Philosophy* (New York: Martin's Press, 1979), 271.

[44] Barth, *CD*, vol. 1, pt. 1, 134.

[45] Ibid., 125–27.

[46] Emil Brunner, *Truth as Encounter* (Philadelphia: Westminster, 1943), 13l; for an evaluation of Brunner see Paul Jewett, *Emil Brunner's Concept of Revelation* (London: James Clarke, 1954), esp. 139–85.

[47] Emil Brunner, *Truth as Encounter*, 133.

[48] Ibid., 137.

[49] W. Mundle, "Revelation," *NIDNTT*, 3:312–16.

[50] Earl S. Kalland, *"Dābār," TWOT*, 1:180.

[51] Bernard Ramm, *Special Revelation and the Word of God*, 150–51.

[52] Ibid., 159.

[53] W. H. Griffith Thomas, "Revelation," in *Hastings Dictionary of the Bible*, ed. James Hastings (New York: Scribner, 1909, reprint 1951), 797.

[54] J. Gresham Machen, *Christianity and Liberalism* (Grand Rapids: Eerdmans, 1946), 21, 19.

[55] Geoffrey Wainwright, *Doxology: The Praise of God in Worship, Doctrine and Life: A Systematic Theology* (New York: Oxford, 1980), 86.

[56] Gordon R. Lewis, "God's Word: Key to Authentic Spirituality," in *A Call to Christian Character*, ed. Bruce Shelley (Grand Rapids: Zondervan, 1970), 105–20.

[57] Thor Hall, *A Theology of Christian Devotion* (Nashville: The Upper Room, 1969), 4.

[58] See Martin Pine, "Double Truth," in *Dictionary of the History of Ideas*, ed. Philip P. Wiener (New York: Scribner, 1973), 2:31–37.

Chapter Four

[1] Thomas Aquinas, *ST*, I.1, q. 1, art. 10.

[2] Thomas Aquinas, *Job*, XIII.1.

[3] Cited by Philip Watson, *Let God Be God!* (Philadelphia: Fortress, 1947), 12.

[4] Council of Trent, session IV, April 8, 1546.

[5] Horace Bushnell, *Nature and the Supernatural* (New York: Scribner, 1858), 33, 493.

[6] Walter Rauschenbusch, *A Theology for the Social Gospel* (New York: Macmillan, 1917), 192.

[7] Ibid., 191.

[8] James Barr, *The Bible in the Modern World* (London: SCM, 1973), 43. Later in the same book Barr asserts that from the modern point of view, the early church's doctrine of Scripture appears to be the result of "an authority neurosis." Ibid., 113.

[9] Barth, *CD*, vol. 1, pt. 2, 525.

10 Ibid., 499.

11 Ibid., 529. For Barth's ascription of error to the Bible, see also ibid., 507, 530, 533.

12 Emil Brunner, *The Mediator* (Philadelphia: Westminster, 1947), 105.

13 Hans Küng, *On Being a Christian* (Garden City, N.Y.: Doubleday, 1976), 465.

14 Ibid., 463.

15 Ibid., 466-67. Many contemporary Catholic authorities have adopted a lower view of inspiration. So Richard P. McBrien limits inerrancy "to those essential religious affirmations which are made for the sake of our salvation." *Catholicism* (Minneapolis: Winston, 1981), 64. Monika Hellwig asserts that God's revelation about Jesus has been transmitted through various historical channels, "none of which is free from human error and the ambiguities of history." *Understanding Catholicism* (New York: Paulist, 1981), 3. Consequently there are no formal statements that may be taken as the final authority on many matters of faith and life. Anthony Wilhelm, in his classic introduction to Catholicism, insists that "although the Catholic church reverences the Bible, the biblical authors in their writings were, like us, sinful, subject to error." *Christ Among Us: A Modern Presentation of the Catholic Faith* (New York: Paulist, 1981), 159.

16 Cited by Norman L. Geisler, *Decide for Yourself* (Grand Rapids: Zondervan, 1982), 95-96.

17 C. S. Lewis, *Reflections on the Psalms* (New York: Harcourt, Brace, 1958), 111-12.

18 Dewey Beegle, *Scripture, Tradition and Infallibility* (Grand Rapids: Eerdmans, 1973), 76.

19 Ibid., 208.

20 See R. C. Sproul, "The Case for Inerrancy: A Methodological Analysis," in *God's Inerrant Word*, ed. John W. Montgomery, (Minneapolis: Bethany, 1974), 243-44.

21 Jack Rogers and Donald McKim, *The Authority and Interpretation of the Bible* (San Francisco: Harper & Row, 1979), 30.

22 Ibid., 393.

23 John R. Rice, *Our God-Breathed Book— The Bible* (Murfreesboro, Tennessee: Sword of the Lord, 1969), 287.

24 Ibid., 141.

25 Athenagoras, *A Plea for the Christians,* IX.

26 Tertullian, *A Treatise on the Soul,* XXVII.

27 Irenaeus, *Against Heresies,* II.28.2.

28 Jerome, *Patrologia Latina,* ed. J. P. Migne, vol. XXVI, 481; cited by Otto Weber, *Foundations of Dogmatics,* 2 vols. (Grand Rapids: Eerdmans, 1981–83), 1:232.

29 Augustine, *Harmony of the Gospels,* I.35.54.

30 Augustine, "Letter," LXXXII.3.

31 "Faith will totter if the authority of Scripture begins to shake." Augustine, *On Christian Doctrine,* I.37.4.

32 For Augustine's discussion of the value of the Apocrypha, see *On Christian Doctrine,* II.8.12–13 and *City of God,* XVIII.36.

33 Neoorthodox authorities deny that Luther established an identity between the Word of God and the written Scriptures. They maintain that Luther viewed the Scriptures as a vehicle of the Word, i.e., as a witness to Christ. On this showing the Bible is the authoritative Word of God only as it witnesses to Christ and as the Spirit animates the text to the life. "For Luther, Scripture is not the Word, but only witness to the Word, and it is from Him whom it conveys that it derives the authority it enjoys." J. K. S. Reid, *The Authority of Scripture* (New York: Harper, 1957), 72.

34 Martin Luther, *WA,* LIV:39.

35 John Calvin, *Institutes,* I.18.4.

36 John Calvin, *Harmony of the Gospels,* 1:127.

37 John Calvin, *Psalms,* 3:205.

38 Calvin, *Institutes,* IV.8.8–9.

39 John Calvin, *Philippians, Colossians, I & II Thessalonians,* 87; *Minor Prophets,* 3:197; cf. *Pastoral Epistles,* 249.

40 Calvin, *Psalms,* 1:11.

41 Calvin, *Institutes,* III.2.6.

42 John Calvin, *Job,* 744.

43 Calvin, *Psalms,* 4:480.

44 Calvin, *Psalms,* 5:184–85.

45 Calvin, *Institutes,* I.7.5; I.8.13; *John,* 2:101. Neoorthodox authorities such as K. Barth, W. Niesel, and J. K. S. Reid deny that Calvin taught a doctrine of verbal inspiration and verbal infallibility. "Calvin is no verbal inspirationist" (Reid, *Authority of Scripture,* 36; cf. 47). According to the neoorthodox, Calvin taught that the Bible is not the Word of God, but is only a witness to the Word, i.e., to Christ himself. The written record *becomes* the Word of God as the Spirit vivifies it to the hearer or reader. So Reid, ibid., 51.

46 B. B. Warfield, "The Real Problem of Inspiration," in *The Inspiration and Authority*

of the Bible, ed. Samuel G. Craig (Philadelphia: Presbyterian and Reformed, 1970), 173.

47 Ibid., 225.

48 Carl F. H. Henry, *God, Revelation and Authority,* 6 vols. (Waco: Word, 1976–83), 4:129.

49 "Exposition," of the "Articles of Affirmation and Denial," reprinted by Henry, *God, Revelation and Authority,* 4:218. Clark Pinnock, in *The Scripture Principle* (San Francisco: Harper & Row, 1984), attempts to mediate between a conservative evangelical posture on one hand, and a liberal evangelical or neoorthodox stance on the other. Whereas in his earlier work, *Biblical Revelation* (Chicago: Moody, 1971), Pinnock vigorously insisted that the Bible is the Word of God, in *The Scripture Principle* he implies that the Bible plus the Holy Spirit is the Word of God (pp. 57, 198), or that the Bible contains the Word of God (pp. 56, 99). In his earlier work, Pinnock argued that Jesus and the biblical writers taught the full inerrancy of Scripture, and that errors in the Bible would impugn the character of God. In *The Scripture Principle,* however, Pinnock claims that neither Jesus nor the apostles taught inerrancy (p. 57): "The case for inerrancy just isn't there" (p. 58; cf. p. 59). Pinnock now argues that the Bible is infallible in its testimony to Christ, but is flawed in its teachings concerning science and history (pp. 99–100; 104–5). The Genesis record of the Fall is probably "saga" to be interpreted existentially (pp. 67–68, 116), and the Jonah story is "a didactic fiction" (p. 117). Given these admissions, it is difficult to see how Pinnock's position can be accommodated to the historic position of the church.

50 For example, Roger R. Nicole and J. Ramsey Michaels, eds., *Inerrancy and Common Sense* (Grand Rapids: Baker, 1980); D. A. Carson and John D. Woodbridge, eds., *Scripture and Truth* (Grand Rapids: Zondervan, 1983); Ronald Youngblood, ed., *Evangelicals and Inerrancy* (Nashville: Thomas Nelson, 1984); and Gordon R. Lewis and Bruce Demarest, eds., *Challenges to Inerrancy: A Theological Response* (Chicago: Moody, 1984).

51 Joshua refers to this Mosaic writing as "the Book of the Law of Moses" (Josh. 23:6; cf. 1:7–8).

52 Charles G. Martin, "Proverbs," *NLBC,* 703.

53 E. Earle Ellis, *The Gospel of Luke. NCBC,* 64.

54 This construction is preferred by J. N. D. Kelley, *A Commentary on the Pastoral Epistles* (Grand Rapids: Baker, 1981), 203.

55 Cf. B. B. Warfield: The Scripture as *ta logia* are "one continuous oracular deliverance from God's own lips." *Inspiration and Authority,* 404.

56 B. B. Warfield, " 'It Says:' 'Scripture Says:' " *Inspiration and Authority,* 299–348.

57 F. Büchsel, *"luō," TDNT,* 4:336.

58 B. F. Westcott, *St. John* (London: John Murray, 1882), 245. Cf. A. C. Thiselton, "Truth," *NIDNTT,* 3:889–93.

59 H. B. Swete observes that John was so steeped in the Scriptures that 278 of the 404 verses of Revelation contain references to the Old Testament. *Apocalypse of St. John* (London, 1907), cxxxv.

60 B. B. Warfield, *Inspiration and Authority,* 136.

61 Michael Green, *2 Peter and Jude, TNTC* (London: Tyndale, 1968), 91. K. Weiss, *"pherō," TDNT,* 9:58, prefers to translate *pheromenoi* by the weaker term "impelled."

62 Warfield, *Inspiration and Authority,* 119–20. Said Warfield about the biblical texts in support of the orthodox view of the Bible: "There are scores, hundreds of them: and they come bursting upon us in one solid mass. Explain them away? We should have to explain away the whole New Testament."

63 On Jesus' view of the OT see, John W. Wenham, *Christ and the Bible* (Downers Grove: InterVarsity, 1972), 11–81.

64 On the OT canon see R. Laird Harris, "Canon of the Old Testament," *ZPEB,* 1:709–31; R. Laird Harris, *Inspiration and Canonicity of the Bible* (Grand Rapids: Zondervan, 1957), 131–95.

65 "Text and Manuscripts of the Old Testament," *ZPEB,* 5:696.

66 MacRae, ibid.

67 J. Norval Geldenhuys, *Supreme Authority: The Authority of the Lord, His Apostles and the New Testament* (Grand Rapids: Eerdmans, 1953), 16–64.

68 Donald Guthrie, "Canon of the New Testament," *ZPEB,* 1:733.

69 Andrew F. Walls, "The Canon of the New Testament," in *EBC,* 1:638.

70 Norman L. Geisler and William E. Nix, *From God to Us: How We Got Our Bible* (Chicago: Moody, 1974), 125.

71 George Ladd, *The New Testament and Criticism* (Grand Rapids: Eerdmans, 1967), 80–81.

72 J. H. Greenlee, "Text and Manuscripts of the New Testament," *ZPEB,* 5:713.

[73] G. C. Berkouwer, *Holy Scripture* (Grand Rapids: Eerdmans, 1975), 358, 361.

[74] Ibid., 54, 279.

[75] Ibid., 253.

[76] Pinnock, *Scripture Principle*, 128.

[77] Steven T. Davis, *The Debate About the Bible* (Philadelphia: Westminster, 1977), 15. For discussions of limited inerrancy by Richard J. Coleman, J. Barton Payne, and Vern S. Pothyress, see Youngblood, ed., *Evangelicals and Inerrancy*, 161–85.

[78] For one who practices a similar approach, though with less of a structured methodology, see Millard J. Erickson, *Christian Theology*, 3 vols. (Grand Rapids: Baker, 1983–85), 199–240.

[79] James Barr, *The Scope and Authority of the Bible*, 18–20.

[80] Ibid.

[81] A. T. Hanson, and R. P. C. Hanson, *Reasonable Belief: A Survey of the Christian Faith* (New York: Oxford University Press, 1980), 42.

[82] Ibid., 43.

[83] Ibid., 45.

[84] Ibid., 46.

[85] Gordon R. Lewis, "What Does Infallibility Mean?" *Bulletin of the Evangelical Theological Society*, 6 (Winter 1963): 18–27; reprinted in Youngblood, ed., *Evangelicals and Inerrancy*, 35–48. See also Kevin J. VanHoozer's challenge of our view of propositional revelation in "The Semantics of Biblical Literature," in D. A. Carson and John D. Woodbridge, eds., *Hermeneutics, Authority, and Canon* (Grand Rapids: Zondervan, 1986), 53–104. Interacting in some measure with G. R. Lewis, "What Does Infallibility Mean?" VanHoozer seeks to preserve a cognitive communication that allows for greater appreciation of the ordinary language of Scripture and its diverse literary forms. Although he has purposes similar to ours, such as not divorcing propositional and personal revelation, his chapter has several problems: (1) It leaves the misimpression that defenders of propositional revelation regard the entire Bible as informative (p. 59), thus overlooking half of my article devoted to its expressive, directive, interrogative, exclamatory, and pictorial or imaginative uses of language. (2) His chapter fails to emphasize that diverse literary forms in ordinary language such as parables, though not propositional in form, teach a propositional point that Jesus himself on occasion "translated" into formal assertions (Matt. 13:18–23). Such "translation" did not distort the figurative purpose! No "logical gap" need be manufactured either between a parable and its propositional interpretation or between sentences' verbal signs and their meanings (the content signified). (3) In defining language acts as "*something* propounded for consideration" (p. 92), VanHoozer fails to provide a meaningful alternative to propositional content. (4) VanHoozer has not answered "the strongest argument for the existence of propositions" (p. 60), the fact that the same content can be asserted in all the different languages in which the Bible is translated. (5) He manufactures "disparate views" and alleged "confusion" between Henry, Clark, and G. R. Lewis/Obitts when admittedly all three scholars are agreed as to the general thrust of propositional revelation (p. 59). This illustrates the danger of magnifying differences of wording when on this point the thought is essentially the same. (6) VanHoozer seems to belong among those who commit the "heresy of propositional paraphrase" (p. 67), for among his three requisites for a successful speech act is a propositional condition (p. 96). Propositional conditions specify the kinds of *content* that are appropriate for various "illocutionary forces" including states of affairs and future events (p. 96). (7) In his search for a broader criterion of truth, he adopts the narrower one. At best a "correspondence" test can confirm empirical claims (not mere words, symbols), but comes far short of the breadth of a coherence test in relation to the nonempirical teachings of Scripture. (8) He has not indicated how phenomenal human speech acts can refer to the metaphysical reality of who God is. The concern for a propositional revelation was designed to counter not only noncognitive, but also antimetaphysical notions of revelation. (9) His own definition of infallibility, though different in words, is little different from ours in meaning. He writes, "Infallibility means that speech acts are performed successfully" (p. 100). (10) VanHoozer's allegation that our view is similar to Barth's (p. 58) is impossible to follow. How is a doctrine of revelation and inspiration—one that indicates that all the Bible's verbally conveyed teachings *are* divine revelation—similar to one that claims that the Bible's teachings are not revelation and errantly "point" to the living person of Christ only?

[86] Ibid.

[87] For a brief evaluation of these positions see Gordon R. Lewis, "The Human Authorship of Inspired Scripture," ed. Norman Geisler, *Inerrancy* (Grand Rapids: Zondervan, 1979), 229–40.

[88] Ibid., 240–64.

[89]Gordon R. Lewis, "A Comparison of Form Criticism and Classical Criticism of the Gospels," in *More Evidence That Demands a Verdict*, ed. Josh McDowell (Arrowhead Springs: Campus Crusade for Christ, 1975), 335–40.

[90]Gordon R. Lewis, "Non-Evangelical Hermeneutics: Response," in *Hermeneutics, Inerrancy, and the Bible*, ed. Earl D. Radmacher and Robert D. Preus (Grand Rapids: Zondervan, 1984), 613–25.

[91](Article XIX), ibid., 885–86.

[92]"The Bible: The Believers Gain," *Time Magazine* (December 30, 1974), 41.

[93]As an example of the thoroughness with which evangelical scholars have faced the issues and dealt with them, see Gleason L. Archer, *Encyclopedia of Bible Difficulties* (Grand Rapids: Zondervan, 1982).

[94]Colin Brown, "Revelation," *NIDNTT*, 3:334.

[95]Emile Cailliet, *Journey Into Light* (Grand Rapids: Zondervan, 1968), 11–18, 98, 105–6.

[96]See J. Robertson McQuilkin, "Problems of Normativeness in Scripture: Cultural Versus Permanent" and the Papers in Response by George W. Knight and Alan F. Johnson, ed. Earl D. Radmacher and Robert D. Preus, *Hermeneutics, Inerrancy, and the Bible*, 219–82; Alan F. Johnson, "History and Culture in New Testament Interpretation," in *Interpreting the Word of God*, ed. Samuel J. Schultz and Morris A. Inch (Chicago: Moody, 1976), 128–61.

[97]Ned B. Stonehouse, "Review of Theological Education in America" in *Christianity Today* (Feb. 16, 1959), 36.

[98]Richard F. Lovelace, *Dynamics of Spiritual Life* (Downers Grove: InterVarsity, 1980), 282–83.

[99]Gordon R. Lewis, "God's Word: Key to Authentic Spirituality," in *Call to Christian Character*, ed. Bruce Shelley (Grand Rapids: Zondervan, 1970), 111.

[100]Ibid., 283–84.

[101]On illumination see Bernard Ramm, *The Witness of the Spirit* (Grand Rapids: Eerdmans, 1960), 130 pp.

[102]Mark I. Bubeck, *The Adversary* (Chicago: Moody, 1975), 94.

Chapter Five

[1]Thomas Aquinas, *ST*, vol. 1, pt. 1, q. 3, art. 2.

[2]Aquinas, *Summa Contra Gentiles*, I. 21. 1.

[3]Aquinas, *ST*, vol. 1, pt. 1, q. 13, art. 11.

[4]W. A. Brown, *Christian Theology in Outline* (New York: Scribner, 1911), 113.

[5]Karl Barth, *CD*, vol. 2, pt. 1, p. 272.

[6]Ibid., vol. 1, pt. 1, p. 426.

[7]Ibid., vol. 2, pt. 2, p. 619.

[8]Paul Tillich, *The Courage to Be* (New Haven: Yale University Press, 1952), 177–78.

[9]"Whatever concerns a man ultimately becomes God for him." Paul Tillich, *Systematic Theology*, 3 vols. (Chicago: University of Chicago Press, 1951–63), 1:211.

[10]Ibid., 205.

[11]Ibid., 237.

[12]Ibid., 223.

[13]John Macquarrie, *Principles of Christian Theology* (New York: Scribner, 1977), 206.

[14]Ibid., 122. Yahweh, according to Macquarrie, means, "I cause to be," or "I bring to pass." Ibid., 196–97.

[15]Monika Hellwig, *Understanding Catholicism* (Ramsey, N.J.: Paulist, 1981), 191.

[16]Hans Küng, *On Being a Christian* (Garden City, N.Y.: Doubleday, 1976) 82, 295.

[17]Ibid., 303.

[18]Ibid., 308.

[19]Ibid., 303.

[20]Leslie Dewart, *The Future of Belief* (New York: Herder & Herder, 1966), 189.

[21]Ibid., 211.

[22]John B. Cobb, Jr., "The World and God," in Ewert H. Cousins, ed., *Process Theology* (New York: Newman, 1971), 158.

[23]According to H. N. Wieman and W. M. Horton, God "is not a personality, but God is more worthful than any personality could ever be." *The Growth of Religion* (Chicago: Willett, Clark, 1938), 362–63.

[24]Theophilus, *To Autolychus*, I.4.

[25]Clement of Alexandria,, *Miscellanies*, V.11. Cf., "God is one, and beyond the one, and above the Monad itself." *The Instructor*, I.8.

[26]Athanasius, *De Synodis*, III.35. So also Gregory of Nazianzus, *Oration*, XXX.17–18, who links Yahweh with the special, absolute name *ho ōn*.

[27]G. L. Prestige, *God in Patristic Thought* (London: SPCK, 1952). 17.

[28]Augustine, *On the Trinity*, VI.4.6.

[29]Augustine, *On Patience*, I.

30 Augustine, *Letters*, CLXXXVII.14. Cf. *Sermon on the Mount*, II.9.32; *City of God*, *VII.30*.

31 Augustine, *Confessions*, I.4.4.

32 Philip Melanchthon, *Loci Communes*, I; cited by Clyde L. Manschreck, ed., *Melanchthon on Christian Doctrine* (Grand Rapids: Baker, 1982), 8.

33 Ibid.

34 John Calvin, *Calvin: Theological Treatises*, ed. J. Baillie, J. T. McNeill and H. P. Van Dusen, *LCC* (Philadelphia: Westminster, 1954), XXII:302.

35 John Calvin, *Institutes of the Christian Religion*, III.xxx.40.

36 Ibid., I.xvi.3.

37 John Calvin, *Minor Prophets*, 1:402.

38 Stephen Charnock, *The Existence and Attributes of God* (Grand Rapids: Kregel, 1958), 80.

39 W. G. T. Shedd, *Dogmatic Theology*, 3 vols. (Grand Rapids: Zondervan, n.d.), 1:334.

40 Ronald Nash, *The Concept of God* (Grand Rapids: Zondervan, 1983).

41 Millard J. Erickson, *Christian Theology*, 3 vols. (Grand Rapids: Baker, 1983–85), 1:263–81.

42 Carl F. H. Henry, *God, Revelation and Authority*, 6 vols. (Waco: Word, 1976–83), 5:9–306.

43 "*Hayah* means to be, to exist and not: to be here—ready to help. God is not called the 'One who is' because He is faithful, but He is faithful because He is the 'One who is.' " Paul Heinisch, *Theology of the Old Testament* (Collegeville, Minn.: Liturgical Press, 1955), 45.

44 See Jack B. Scott, "'*elohim*," *TWOT*, 1:44–45 for a discussion of the traditional interpretation. Erickson, *Christian Theology*, 1:328–29, explores the possibility that the plural may be a "quantitative plural," which connotes diversity within the Godhead.

45 Victor P. Hamilton, "*pānîm*," *TWOT*, 2:727.

46 Franz Delitzsch, *Biblical Commentary on the Psalms*, 3 vols. (Grand Rapids: Eerdmans, 1952), 2:6.

47 According to Charles Hodge, "The glory of God is the manifested excellence of God." *A Commentary on the Epistle to the Ephesians* (Reprint, Grand Rapids: Baker, 1980), 38.

48 Fritz Rienecker and Cleon L. Rogers, Jr., *A Linguistic Key to the Greek New Testament* (Grand Rapids: Zondervan, 1982), 112.

49 Leon Morris, *The First and Second Epistles to the Thessalonians*. NICNT (Grand Rapids: Eerdmans, 1959), 63.

50 "*Theotes* indicates the divine essence of the Godhead, the personality of God; *theiotes*, the attributes of God, His divine nature and properties." W. E. Vine, *Expository Dictionary of New Testament Words* (Westwood, N.J.: Revell, 1961), 329.

51 John Eadie, *A Commentary on Philippians* (Reprint, Grand Rapids: Baker, 1979), 105.

52 *Kyrios* "expresses particularly his creatorship, his power revealed in history, and his just dominion." H. Bietenhard, "Lord," *NIDNTT*, 2:514.

53 Alfred Plummer, *The Epistles of St. John* (Reprint, Grand Rapids: Baker, 1980), 23.

54 *Eidos*, from *eidō*, "to see," signifies "the expression of the essence in visible form." G. Braumann, *eido*," *NIDNTT*, 1:704.

55 F. F. Bruce paraphrases *charakter tes hypostaseōs autou* as, "the very image of the substance of God—the impress of His being." *The Epistle to the Hebrews* (London: Marshall, Morgan & Scott, 1965), 5. See also J. Hering, *The Epistle to the Hebrews* (London: Epworth, 1970), 5; and B. F. Westcott, *The Epistle to the Hebrews* (London: Macmillan, 1889), 13.

56 Peter Davids, *Commentary on James*. NTGTC (Grand Rapids: Eerdmans, 1982), 88.

57 For a definition of God see G. R. Lewis, "God, Attributes of," *EDT*, 451.

58 On divine simplicity see Henry, *God, Revelation and Authority*, 5:127–40; Ronald Nash, *The Concept of God* (Grand Rapids: Zondervan, 1983), 85–97.

59 A. H. Strong, *Systematic Theology* (Philadelphia: Judson, 1907), 247–49; Louis Berkhof, *Systematic Theology* (Grand Rapids: Eerdmans, 1959), 55–56; John Gill, *Body of Divinity* (Atlanta, Georgia: Turner Lassetter, 1957), 34–35; H. Orton Wiley, *Christian Theology*, 3 vols. (Kansas City, Mo.: Beacon Hill, 1959), 1:325–29; Lewis Sperry Chafer, *Systematic Theology*, 8 vols. (Dallas: Dallas Seminary Press, 1947), 1:189–91, 212.

60 Kenneth F. W. Grove, *The Gospel in a Pagan Society* (Downers Grove: InterVarsity, 1975), 125 pp.

61 Gordon R. Lewis, "The Gospel on Campus" (in four parts) *His* (Oct., Nov., Dec. 1966, and Jan. 1967).

62 M. Jammer, "Energy" *EP*, 2:511–17.

63 Paul Davies, *God and the New Physics* (New York: Simon and Schuster, 1983), vii.

64 Ibid., 163.

[65] Carl Sagan, *Cosmos* (New York: Random, 1980), 4, 21.

[66] Tillich, *Systematic Theology,* 1:268.

[67] For an evangelical evaluation of Tillich see R. Allen Killen, *The Ontological Theology of Paul Tillich* (Kampen: J. H. Kok N. V., 1956), 253–57.

[68] Gill, *Body of Divinity, 43.*

[69] On Teilhard de Chardin see: J. J. Duyvene De Wit, "Pierre Teilhard de Chardin" in *Creative Minds in Contemporary Theology,* ed. Philip Edgcombe Hughes, (Grand Rapids: Eerdmans, 1966), 407–48; N. M. Wildiers, *An Introduction to Teilhard de Chardin,* trans. Hubert Hoskins (New York: Harper and Row, 1968); David Gareth Jones, *Teilhard de Chardin: An Analysis and Assessment* (Grand Rapids: Eerdmans, 1970).

[70] Norman Pittenger, "Process Theology Revisited," *Theology Today,* XXVII, 2 (July 1970): 213.

[71] Royce Gordon Gruenler, *The Inexhaustible God* (Grand Rapids: Baker, 1983), 126.

[72] Emil Brunner, *The Christian Doctrine of God* (Philadelphia: Westminster, 1950), 269.

[73] Gruenler, *The Inexhaustible God,* 105; on process theology see also Norman Geisler, "Process Theology" in *Tensions in Contemporary Theology,* ed. Stanley N. Gundry and Alan F. Johnson (Chicago: Moody, 1976), 237–84; Norman Geisler, "Process Theology and Inerrancy," ed. Gordon Lewis and Bruce Demarest, *Challenges to Inerrancy: A Theological Response* (Chicago: Moody, 1984), 247–84.

[74] Corliss Lamont, *The Philosophy of Humanism* (New York: Frederick Ungar, 1982, 6th ed.), 227.

[75] Ibid., 143.

[76] Ibid., 241.

[77] Ibid., 240.

[78] Ibid., 241.

[79] For evaluations of humanism see Norman L. Geisler, *Is Man the Measure? An Evaluation of Contemporary Humanism* (Grand Rapids: Baker, 1983); James Hitchcock, *What Is Secular Humanism?* (Ann Arbor, Mich.: Servant Books, 1982); Robert E. Webber, *Secular Humanism: Threat and Challenge* (Grand Rapids: Zondervan, 1982).

[80] George E. Ladd, *A Theology of the New Testament* (Grand Rapids: Eerdmans, 1974), 81–90.

[81] John Bright, *The Authority of the Old Testament* (Grand Rapids: Baker, 1975), 130–34.

[82] Gordon R. Lewis, "Categories in Collision?" ed. Kenneth S. Kantzer and Stanley N. Gundry, *Perspectives on Evangelical Theology* (Grand Rapids: Baker, 1979), 259–64.

[83] "The Hartford Appeal for Theological Affirmation," *Christianity and Crisis,* vol. 35, no. 12 (July 12, 1975), 168–69.

[84] J. I. Packer, *Knowing God* (Downers Grove: InterVarsity, 1974), 29.

[85] A. W. Tozer, *The Knowledge of the Holy* (New York: Harper, 1961), 11.

[86] Ibid., 12.

[87] Ibid., 10.

[88] Richard Foster, *The Celebration of Discipline* (New York: Harper, 1978), 25.

[89] Tozer, *Knowledge of the Holy,* 12.

[90] Packer, *Knowing God,* 40–41.

[91] Foster, *Celebration of Discipline,* 27.

[92] Ibid., 26.

[93] Bruce Larson, *The Relational Revolution* (Waco: Word, 1976), 94–95.

[94] Gruenler, *Inexhaustible God,* 18–19.

[95] Ibid., 38–39.

[96] See note 67.

Chapter Six

[1] Thomas Aquinas, *SCG,* II.22.8.

[2] Faustus Socinus, *Prelectiones Theologicae,* ch. 16.

[3] Albrecht Ritschl, *The Christian Doctrine of Justification and Reconciliation* (Clifton, N.J.: Reference Book Publishers, 1966), 273.

[4] Albert C. Knudson, *The Doctrine of God* (Nashville: Abingdon, 1930), 345–46.

[5] W. A. Brown, *Christian Theology in Outline* (New York: Scribner, 1941), 11.

[6] Walter Eichrodt, *Theology of the Old Testament,* 2 vols. (Philadelphia: Westminster, 1961–67), 1:262.

[7] C. H. Dodd, *Romans* (London: Hodder & Stoughton, 1946), 24.

[8] Barth, *CD,* vol. II, pt. I, pp. 257, 322, passim.

[9] Ibid., 533.

[10] J. A. T. Robinson, *Honest to God* (London: SCM, 1963), 52.

[11] John Macquarrie, *Principles of Christian Theology* (New York: Scribner, 1977), 365.

[12] John B. Cobb, Jr., and David R. Griffin, *Process Theology* (Philadelphia: Westminster, 1976), 61.

[13] Ewert H. Cousins, *Process Theology: Basic Writings* (New York: Newman, 1971), 27.

[14] Cited with approval by Norman Pittenger in *God's Way With Men* (London: Hodder & Stoughton, 1969), 22.

[15] Karl Rahner, *TI*, 9:136.

[16] Hans Küng, *On Being a Christian* (Garden City, N.Y.: Doubleday, 1976), 312.

[17] Leslie Dewart, *The Future of Belief* (New York: Herder & Herder, 1966), 204–5.

[18] Theophilus, *To Autolychus*, I.3.

[19] Ibid.

[20] Clement of Alexandria, *Miscellanies*, VII.3.

[21] Tertullian, *On Purity*, 2.

[22] Gregory of Nazianzus, *Fourth Theological Oration*, 11.

[23] Augustine said of all occurrences in the past, the present, and the future: "All of these are by Him comprehended in His stable and eternal presence." *City of God*, IX.21.

[24] Augustine, *On Patience*, 1. That Augustine believed God experiences a healthy and controlled emotional life is clear from Confessions, I.4.4: "Thou knowest, but art not disturbed by passion; Thou art jealous, but free from care; Thou art repentant, but not sorrowful; Thou art angry, but calm."

[25] For Augustine's interpretation of the divine transcendence and immanence, see *Confessions*, I.2–3; *Soliloquies*, I.1.3–4.

[26] Martin Luther, *LW*, LI:95.

[27] Luther, *LW*, I:11–14; III:138, 276; XII:312–13; *LW* Companion Volume, "Luther the Expositor," 56.

[28] John Calvin, *Institutes of the Christian Religion*, I.x.2.

[29] Ibid., II.xvi.3.

[30] Ibid., II.xxiii.4.

[31] Ibid., III.xvii.2.

[32] W. G. T. Shedd, *Dogmatic Theology*, 3 vols. (Reprint, Grand Rapids: Zondervan, n.d.), 1:373.

[33] J. I. Packer, *Knowing God* (Downers Grove: InterVarsity, 1973).

[34] Ronald H. Nash, *The Concept of God* (Grand Rapids: Zondervan, 1983).

[35] Stephen T. Davis, *Logic and the Nature of God* (Grand Rapids: Eerdmans, 1983).

[36] Th. C. Vriezen argues that the root denotes the idea of brilliance, by virtue of which the person cannot behold God. *An Outline of Old Testament Theology* (Wageningen: H. Veenman, 1958), 149.

[37] Gordon J. Wenham, *The Book of Leviticus. NICOT* (Grand Rapids: Eerdmans, 1979), 18. Wenham estimates that Leviticus contains 20 percent of the total occurrences of qādōš and cognates in the Old Testament.

[38] Cf. Ps. 33:13–14: "From heaven the LORD looks down and sees [rā'āh] all mankind; from his dwelling place he watches [šāqah] all who live on earth."

[39] Cf. Louis Goldberg, *"hokmāh," TWOT*, 2:283: "Wisdom should not be regarded as God but it does belong to God; it is one of his attributes."

[40] Gerard Van Groningen, *śānē', TWOT*, 1:880, states that the verb śānē' conveys God's emotional attitude of detesting and despising both evil and the evildoer. "God's hatred for idols and feasts is also directed against people (Mal. 1:3; Pss. 5:5; 11:50). In each case the character and/or activities of the hated ones are expressed; thus God is opposed to, separates himself from, and brings the consequences of his hatred upon people not as mere people, but as sinful people."

[41] R. E. H. Stephens, "Habakkuk," *NBCRev*, 770, comments that the ground or support of the righteous person's faith is God's faithfulness. "The 'faithfulness' of which he [Habakkuk] now speaks is not only moral endurance to the end, but the persistent belief that God will be true to Himself. 'Faith' in this narrower sense is an essential element in the wider fidelity, as Paul and Luther clearly saw."

[42] H. C. Leupold, *Exposition of Isaiah*, 2 vols. (Grand Rapids: Baker, 1968), 1:513.

[43] Vriezen, *Outline of Old Testament Theology*, 157.

[44] E. Earle Ellis, *The Gospel of Luke. NCBC* (Grand Rapids: Baker, 1968), 1:513.

[45] H. Köster, *"splanchnizomai," TDNT*, 7:553–55.

[46] For a discussion of the relationship between the death of Jesus Christ and God's all-encompassing plan for the world, the reader is directed to chapter 8, "God's Grand Design for Human History."

[47] F. F. Bruce, *Romans. TNTC* (London: Tyndale, 1963), 176.

[48] Matthew Black, *Romans. NCBC* (Grand Rapids: Eerdmans, 1981), 125.

49 William Dyrness, *Themes in Old Testament Theology* (Downers Grove: InterVarsity, 1979), 53. Cf. *TDNTAbr*, 170.

50 F. Godet, *Commentary on St. Paul's Epistle to the Romans* (New York: Funk & Wagnalls, 1883), 262. Cf. O. Becker, *"opsonion," NIDNTT*, 3:144–45.

51 Fritz Rienecker and Cleon Rogers, Jr., *A Linguistic Key to the Greek New Testament* (Grand Rapids: Zondervan, 1980), 525.

52 A distinction can be made between two important words for God's love. *Phileō* denotes affection, concern, and fondness resulting from a personal relationship, and in this sense it is used of God's love for the Son (John 5:20) and for Christian believers (John 16:27). *Agapaō/agapē* connotes affection or deep regard resulting from a deliberate choice, and so is used of God's love for Christ (John 3:35; 10:17; 15:9; 17:24, 26), Christian believers (John 17:23; 1 John 3:1; 4:19), and the entire human race (John 3:16). See W. Günther, "love," *NIDNTT*, 2:542, 544, 548.

53 Rienecker and Rogers, *Linguistic Key*, 847. Cf. H. Schönweiss, "anger, wrath," *NIDNTT*, 1, 105–6.

54 For a connected study of this approach to the divine attributes see also G. R. Lewis, "God, Attributes of," *EDT*, 451–59.

55 Augustine, *Confessions*, XI.31.

56 René Descartes, *Meditations*, III, ed. Hutchins, *Great Books of the Western World*, 31:82.

57 *Euthyphro*, ed. Hutchins, *Great Books of the Western World*, 7:196.

58 Colin Brown, "Righteousness," *NIDNTT*, 3:352–73.

59 H. Wheeler Robinson, *Suffering: Human and Divine* (New York: Macmillan, 1939), 178.

60 Ibid., 156.

61 *Book of Common Prayer* (New York: Church Pension Fund, 1945), 603.

62 *Doctrines and Disciplines of the Methodist Church, 1960* (Nashville: Methodist Publishing House, 1960), 30.

63 For further discussion see G. R. Lewis, "Impassibility of God," *EDT*, 553–54.

64 Martin Pine, "Double Truth," in *Dictionary of the History of Ideas*, ed. Philip P. Wiener (New York: Scribner, 1973), 2:31–37.

65 R. C. Zaehner, *Our Savage God: The Perverse Use of Eastern Thought* (New York: Sheed and Ward, 1974), pp. 9–17.

66 Alan Watts, *The Way of Zen* (New York: Random, 1957), 152.

67 Ibid., 40.

68 J. I. Packer, *Knowing God* (Downers Grove: InterVarsity, 1974), 18.

69 John Burnaby, *Amor Dei: A Study of the Religion of St. Augustine* (London: Hodder & Stoughton, 1938), 141.

70 Ibid., 262.

Chapter Seven

1 Arius, *Letter to Alexander of Alexandris*, 4.

2 *Racovian Catechism*, 22.

3 Karl Barth, *CD*, vol. 1, pt. 1, pp. 351, 353, 382.

4 Ibid., 402. Here Barth argues that God's essence is his act of revelation. "God's essence and His operation are not twain but one. . . . The operation of God is the essence of God." Ibid., 426.

5 Ibid., 366. Barth, defining person as a center of conscious individuality, concludes that in God there are not three Thou's—three personal subjects—but only one. His suborthodox understanding of the Trinity follows from this crucial judgment.

6 So argues Sylvester P. Schilling in his book *Contemporary Continental Theologians* (Nashville: Abingdon, 1966), 36: "[Barth] definitely espouses a modalistic trinitarianism." The same conclusion is reached by Jürgen Moltmann in *The Trinity and the Kingdom* (San Francisco: Harper & Row, 1981), 139–44.

7 Emil Brunner, *The Christian Doctrine of God* (Philadelphia: Westminster, 1949), 226. "The idea of *'una substantia'* has had a particularly disastrous influence. . . . Similarly, the idea of Three Persons is more than questionable."

8 Ibid., 206–7.

9 Ibid., 223.

10 Leslie Dewart, *The Future of Belief* (New York: Herder & Herder, 1966), 148.

11 Karl Rahner, *The Trinity* (New York: Seabury, 1974), 47.

12 Hans Küng, *On Being a Christian* (Garden City, N.Y.: Doubleday, 1976), 475.

13 W. A. Brown, *Christian Theology in Outline* (New York: Scribner, 1911), 156.

14 Ibid., 157.

15 Harry Emerson Fosdick, *The Living of These Days: An Autobiography* (New York: Harper, 1956), 64.

16 Norman Pittenger, *The Holy Spirit* (Philadelphia: United Church Press, 1974), 123.

[17] The Spirit "is the 'responding,' the conforming, the returning of the 'amen' of God through the whole creation and in deity itself." Pittenger, *Holy Spirit*, 59.

[18] John B. Cobb, Jr., and David R. Griffin, *Process Theology: An Introductory Exposition* (Philadelphia: Westminster, 1976), 110.

[19] *Letter of Barnabas*, 2:9; 12:8 (Father); 5:5; 7:2 (Son); 6:14; 12:2; 19:7 (Holy Spirit).

[20] Theophilus, *To Autolychus*, 2.15.

[21] Irenaeus, *Against Heresies*, II.30.9; III.6.1–2; III.8.3; IV.6.6; and passim.

[22] Irenaeus, *Proof of the Preaching*, 5; idem., *Against Heresies*, V.12.2.

[23] Irenaeus, *Proof of the Preaching*, 7; idem., *Against Heresies*, V.10; IV.6.7; 20.1,4.

[24] Tertullian, *Against Praxeus*, II, V–VII, XIII; *Apology*, XXI.

[25] Athanasius, *Oration Against the Arians*, III.4; cf. IV.1.

[26] Athanasius, *Letters to Sarapion*, I.20–21; *Oration Against the Arians*, III.25.

[27] Augustine, *The Trinity*, VII.6.11. Or, "one substance or essence" subsisting in "three persons."

[28] Ibid., VI.12.12; cf. idem., *Enchiridion*, 38; *On Christian Doctrine*, I.5; *The Trinity*, V.8.9; XV.5.8.

[29] Augustine, *The Trinity*, XV.20.38; 17.29; 26.47.

[30] Ibid., V.14.15.

[31] John Calvin, *Institutes of the Christian Religion*, I.13.18.

[32] Ibid.

[33] Ibid., I.13.20.

[34] L. Berkhof, *Systematic Theology* (Grand Rapids: Eerdmans, 1941), 82–99.

[35] Henry C. Thiessen, *Lectures in Systematic Theology*, rev. by Vernon D. Doerksen (Grand Rapids: Eerdmans, 1979), 89-99.

[36] Millard J. Erickson, *Christian Theology*, 3 vols. (Grand Rapids: Baker, 1983–85) 1:321–42

[37] Th. C. Vriezen, *An Outline of Old Testament Theology* (Wageningen: Veenman & Zonen, 1958), 175. Peter C. Craigie, *The Book of Deuteronomy*. NICOT (Grand Rapids: Eerdmans, 1976), 169, concurs: "The word ['eḥād] expresses not only uniqueness but also the unity of God." M. Dahood believes that God's uniqueness lies in the foreground, for he translates the verse "Obey, Israel, Yahweh. Yahweh our God is the Unique." Cited by Craigie, *Deuteronomy*, 169.

[38] G. Ch. Aalders, *Genesis*, 2 vols. (Grand Rapids: Zondervan, 1981), 2:70.

[39] Jack B. Scott, "'elōhîm," *TWOT*, 1:470.

[40] So *Gesenius' Hebrew Grammar*, ed. E. Kautzsch (Oxford: Clarendon, 1976), 398–99.

[41] Craigie, *Deuteronomy*, 262, comments: "The singular ('a prophet') is a collective form indicating a succession of prophets."

[42] John Calvin, *Commentary on Genesis*, 1:470.

[43] "The evidence for the view that the angel of the Lord is a preexistent appearance of Christ is basically analogical and falls short of being conclusive. . . . It is best to see the angel as a self-manifestation of Yahweh in a form that would communicate his immanence and direct concern to those to whom he ministered." Thomas E. McComiskey, "Angel of the Lord," *EDT*, 48. For extended exegetical argumentation, see William Graham MacDonald, "Christology and 'The Angel of the Lord,'" in *Current Issues in Biblical and Patristic Interpretation*, ed. Gerald F. Hawthorne (Grand Rapids: Eerdmans, 1975), 324–35. Cf. H. Bietenhard, "angel," *NIDNTT*, 1:101.

[44] Aalders, *Genesis*, 1:55. Henri Blocher claims, "The part played alongside God by His Word, which distinguishes and communicates, and by His Spirit, which is a living presence, suggests that the writer's monotheism is not as simple as might appear." *In the Beginning* (Downers Grove: InterVarsity, 1984), 70.

[45] Hugh J. Blair, "Joshua," *NBCRev*, 239.

[46] See also Martin Woudstra, *The Book of Joshua* (Grand Rapids: Eerdmans, 1981), 105.

[47] J. Barton Payne, "rûah," *TWOT*, 2:837.

[48] H. C. Leupold argues as follows concerning the phrase "the breath of his mouth": "in which, without any doubt, God's Holy Spirit was potently at work" to bring into being all the heavenly bodies. *Exposition of the Psalms*, 2 vols. (Columbus: Wartburn, 1959), 1:272.

[49] John Calvin, *Commentary on the Psalms*, 5 vols. (Grand Rapids: Eerdmans, 1949), 2:183. What likely was opaque to the psalmist was brought to light by the New Testament, following the Incarnation.

[50] Derek Kidner, *Psalms 1–72*. TNTC (London: Inter-Varsity, 1973), 254.

[51] C. S. Lewis, *Reflections on the Psalms* (New York: Harcourt, Brace, 1958), 99. Cf. Derek Kidner, *Psalms 73–150*. TOTC (London: Inter-Varsity, 1975), 393.

[52] Cf. Derek Kidner, *Proverbs*. TOTC (London: Tyndale, 1964), 79: "The personification

of wisdom, far from overshooting the literal truth, was a preparation for its full statement, since the agent of creation was no mere activity of God, but the Son, His eternal Word, Wisdom, and Power."

[53] Derek Kidner, "Isaiah," *NBCRev*, 616.

[54] See Charles L. Feinberg, *Jeremiah: A Commentary* (Grand Rapids: Zondervan, 1982), 163.

[55] Abraham Calov, cited by Robert D. Preuss, *The Theology of Post-Reformation Lutheranism*, 2 vols. (St. Louis: Concordia, 1970–72), 2:129.

[56] Alfred Plummer comments that "the aorist points back to a moment in eternity and implies the preexistence of the Messiah." *An Exegetical Commentary on the Gospel According to Matthew* (Reprint, Grand Rapids: Baker, 1982), 168.

[57] I. Howard Marshall, *"huios tou theou,"* *NIDNTT*, 3:641.

[58] For a complete discussion of Jesus' response to the high priest, see Plummer, *Matthew*, 378–79.

[59] R. S. Franks, *The Doctrine of the Trinity* (London: Duckworth, 1953), 10.

[60] I. Howard Marshall, *The Acts of the Apostles. TNTC* (Grand Rapids: Eerdmans, 1980), 296.

[61] "The dominating theological motif in Acts is the presence and work of the Holy Spirit." F. F. Bruce, "The Acts of the Apostles," *NBCRev*, 972.

[62] The pagan Greeks (v. 5) believed in "many 'gods'" (i.e., idols) and "many 'lords'" (i.e., mythological heroes). In contradistinction, Paul emphasizes the uniqueness of "one God, the Father" and of "one Lord, Jesus Christ" (v. 6). When Christ is separately mentioned in context, Paul denominates God as "the Father" (e.g., Rom. 1:7; 2 Cor. 1:3; Eph. 1:17).

[63] "The distinct personality and the divinity of the Son, the Father, and the Holy Spirit, to each of whom prayer is addressed, is here taken for granted. And therefore this passage is a clear recognition of the doctrine of the Trinity." Charles Hodge, *II Corinthians* (Reprint, Grand Rapids: Baker, 1980), 314.

[64] J. H. Bernard, *The Pastoral Epistles* (Reprint, Grand Rapids; Baker, 1980), 179.

[65] See F. F. Bruce, *Romans. TNTC* (London: Tyndale, 1963), 187. Also John Murray, *Romans. NICNT*, 2 vols. (Grand Rapids: Eerdmans, 1959–65), 2:246: "Grammatically or syntactically there is no reason for taking the clauses in question as other than referring to Christ." Romans 9:5 may be punctuated differently than the above have suggested (see AV, RV, RSV marg., NEB marg.), in which case the text would then make no explicit claim of deity for Christ. The orthodoxy of believing Christians who favor one of the alternative forms of punctuation ought not to be impugned.

[66] F. Foulkes, "Philippians," *NBCRev*, 1132.

[67] Joseph Henry Thayer, *A Greek-English Lexicon of the New Testament* (New York: American, 1889), 288.

[68] R. V. G. Tasker, *2 Corinthians. TNTC* (London: Tyndale, 1958), 66.

[69] Leon Morris, *1 Corinthians. TNTC* (London: Tyndale, 1958), 173.

[70] Charles Hodge, *1 Corinthians* (Reprint, Grand Rapids: Baker, 1980), 40.

[71] For a discussion of the history of the *Comma Johanneum*, see Bruce M. Metzger, *The Text of the New Testament* (New York & Oxford: Oxford University Press, 1968), 101–2.

[72] B. F. Westcott comments: "It seems clear that the unity here spoken of cannot fall short of unity of essence." *The Gospel According to St. John*, 2 vols. in one (Reprint, Grand Rapids: Baker, 1980), 2:68.

[73] F. F. Bruce maintains that these two expressions best represent the meaning of *monogenēs theos* (cf. NASB), *The Gospel of John* (Grand Rapids: Eerdmans, 1983), 44. Modern lexicography judges that *monogenēs* derives from *monos* and *genos* and thus bears the meaning "one of a kind" or "unique." The NIV works a conflation of sorts by translating *monogenēs theos* as "God the only Son." Whichever translation is accepted, however, the deity of Christ is established.

[74] Charles Hodge, *Systematic Theology;* 3 vols. (Reprint, Grand Rapids: Eerdmans, 1973), 1:447.

[75] Westcott, *St. John*, 2:214.

[76] See J. H. Moulton, *A Grammar of the New Testament Greek. Vol. I: Prolegomena* (Edinburgh: T. & T. Clark, 1908), 84.

[77] Herbert Wolf, *"'ehad,"* *TWOT* (Chicago: Moody, 1980), 1:30.

[78] J. Oliver Buswell, Jr., "The Place of Paradox in Our Christian Testimony," *Journal of the American Scientific Affiliation*, vol. 17, no. 1 (March 1965): 96.

[79] Geerhardus Vos, *The Self-Disclosure of Jesus* (Grand Rapids: Eerdmans, 1954).

[80] J. Barton Payne, *"rûah,"* *TWOT*, 2:836–37.

[81] T. S. Caulley, "Holy Spirit," *EDT,* 523.

[82] George Smeaton, *The Doctrine of the Holy Spirit* (Edinburgh: T. & T. Clark, 1882), 100.

[83] Norman C. Bartlett, *The Triune God* (New York: American Tract Society, 1937), 81.

[84] John B. Champion, *Personality and the Trinity* (New York: Revell, 1935), 97.

[85] John Lawson, *Comprehensive Handbook of Christian Doctrine* (Englewood Cliffs, N.J.: Prentice-Hall, 1967), 123.

[86] Augustine, "Sermons on NT Lessons" LXVII, 11.

[87] Ibid.

[88] K. H. Bartells, "One," *NIDNTT,* 2:725.

[89] See B. B. Warfield, *The Lord of Glory* (Reprint, Grand Rapids: Zondervan, n.d.), 198–99; see also Gordon Clark's defense of eternal generation in his work *The Trinity* (Jefferson, Md.: Trinity Foundation, 1985), 109–26.

[90] G. W. Bromiley, "Eternal Generation," *EDT,* 368.

[91] B. B. Warfield, *Calvin and Augustine* (Philadelphia: Presbyterian and Reformed, 1956), 250.

[92] Curtis Vaughn, ed., *The New Testament From 26 Translations* (Grand Rapids: Zondervan, 1967).

[93] For a discussion of the debate see George S. Hendry, *The Holy Spirit in Christian Theology* (Philadelphia: Westminster, 1956), 30–52.

[94] Abraham Kuyper, *The Work of the Holy Spirit* (Grand Rapids: Eerdmans, 1956), 19–21. See also Dorothy Sayers, *The Mind of the Maker* (London: Methuen, 1941).

[95] Ibid., 24.

[96] David L. Miller, *The New Polytheism* (New York: Harper & Row, 1974), 11.

[97] G. L. Prestige, *God in Patristic Thought* (London: SPCK, 1952), 213.

[98] Gordon R. Lewis, "Triune God: Revelational Bases for Trinitarianism," *Christianity Today,* 7 (Jan. 4, 1963): 20–22.

[99] James A. Pike, "Three-Pronged Synthesis," *The Christian Century,* 21 (Dec. 21, 1960): 1497–98.

[100] James E. Talmadge, *Articles of Faith* (Salt Lake City: Church of Jesus Christ of Latter-Day Saints, 1952), 48.

[101] *The Truth That Leads to Eternal Life* (New York: Watchtower Bible and Tract Society, 1968), 22–23.

[102] Ibid.

[103] B. B. Warfield, "Trinity," in *ISBE,* 5:3012.

[104] *Let God Be True,* 2d ed. (New York: Watchtower Bible and Tract Society, 1946), 111.

[105] For more detailed response to the Jehovah's Witnesses see Gordon R. Lewis, *Confronting the Cults* (Phillipsburg, N.J.: Presbyterian and Reformed, 1966), 23–29; Anthony Hoekema, *The Four Major Cults* (Grand Rapids: Eerdmans, 1963), 270–76.

[106] Mary Baker Eddy, *Science and Truth With Key to the Scriptures* (Boston: The Trustees Under the Will of Mary Baker Eddy, 1906), 256.

[107] Ibid.

[108] John A. Hutchison, *Paths of Faith* (New York: McGraw-Hill, 1975), 636.

[109] John B. Cobb, *Christ in a Pluralistic Age* (Philadelphia: Westminster, 1975), 220.

[110] Bruce A. Demarest, "Process Trinitarianism" in *Perspectives on Evangelical Theology,* ed. Kenneth S. Kantzer and Stanley N. Gundry (Grand Rapids: Baker, 1979), 31.

[111] *The Koran,* CXIV, Sura V. 77, trans. M. Rodwell (New York: Dutton, 1953), 494.

[112] A. W. Tozer, *The Knowledge of the Holy* (New York: Harper, 1961), 10.

[113] Ibid., 11.

[114] Ibid., 12.

[115] A. W. Tozer, "The Pursuit of God," in *The Best of A. W. Tozer,* ed. Warren Wiersbe (Grand Rapids: Baker, 1978), 15.

[116] Ibid., 15.

[117] Herman Bavinck, *The Doctrine of God* (Grand Rapids: Eerdmans, 1955), 333.

[118] David E. Roberts, *Existentialism and Religious Belief* (New York: Oxford, 1957), 10.

[119] See Walter Marshall Horton, *Christian Theology: An Ecumenical Approach* (New York: Harper, 1955), 195.

[120] See E. H. Bickersteth, *The Trinity* (Grand Rapids: Kregel, 1959), 134–35n.

[121] C. W. Lowry, *The Trinity and Christian Devotion* (New York: Harper, 1946), 157.

[122] Bernard Piault, *What Is the Trinity?* trans. Rosemary Haughton, *Twentieth Century Encyclopedia of Catholicism* (New York: Hawthorn, 1959), 17:139.

[123] See Claude Welch, *In This Name* (New York: Scribner, 1952), 94.

[124] See Charles W. Lowry, *The Trinity and Christian Devotion,* 157.

[125]Gerald H. Anderson, "The Theology of Mission Among Protestants in the Twentieth Century," in *The Theology of Christian Mission*, ed. Gerald H. Anderson (Nashville: Abingdon, 1961), 15.

[126]Ibid.

[127]George W. Peters, *A Biblical Theology of Missions* (Chicago: Moody, 1972), 81.

[128]Lesslie Newbigin, *The Open Secret* (Grand Rapids: Eerdmans, 1978), esp. 20–72.

[129]Ibid., 72.

Chapter Eight

[1] "God is conceived as loving will, when we regard His will as set upon the bringing forth of His Son and the community of the kingdom of God; and if we abstract from that, what we conceive is not God at all." A. Ritschl, *The Christian Doctrine of Justification and Reconciliation* (Reprint, Clifton, N.J.: Reformed Book Publishers, 1966), 283.

[2] William Newton Clarke, *An Outline of Christian Theology* (Edinburgh: T. & T. Clark, 1909), 146.

[3] Walter Rauschenbusch, *A Theology for the Social Gospel* (New York: Macmillan, 1917), 174–79.

[4] William Adams Brown, *Christian Theology in Outline* (New York: Scribner, 1911), 89–95, 182–83, 190–94.

[5]John B. Cobb, Jr., and David Ray Griffin, *Process Theology: An Introductory Exposition* (Philadelphia: Westminster, 1976), 53.

[6]Arminius "believed that the sublapsarian unconditional predestination view of Augustine . . . is unscriptural." J. K. Grider, "Arminianism," *EDT*, 79.

[7]Jacob Arminius, *The Writings of Arminius* (Reprint, Grand Rapids: Baker, 1977), 4:82.

[8]John Wesley, "Sermon CXXVIII," in *The Works of John Wesley*, 14 vols. (Grand Rapids: Zondervan, n.d.), 7:383.

[9]Richard Watson, *Theological Institutes*, 2 vols. (New York: Lane & Scott, 1851), 2:423.

[10]Ibid., 426.

[11]Ratramnus, *On Predestination*, I.

[12]Martin Luther, *The Bondage of the Will*, *LW*, 33:146

[13]Luther, *Bondage of the Will*, *LW*, 33:191. For Luther's treatment of Judas's betrayal in relation to God's will, see ibid., 185, 193.

[14]John Calvin, "Articles Concerning Predestination," *LCC*, 22:180. Cf. *Institutes of the Christian Religion*, III.23.8.

[15]Calvin, *Institutes*, III.21.5. Cf. "God once established by His eternal and unchangeable plan those He long before determined once for all to receive into salvation, and those whom, on the other hand, he would devote to destruction." Ibid., III.21.7.

[16]Ibid., III.23.7. Although sovereign election to life is more prominent, Calvin regards reprobation to death as the logical consequence of the positive decree. For his treatment of reprobation see further ibid., I.18.2; II.4.1,3–5; III.22.6,11; III.23.1–10; III.24.12–14; "Articles Concerning Predestination," 179–80.

[17] "While . . . God holds the Devil and the godless subject to His will, nevertheless God cannot be called the cause of sin, nor the author of evil, nor subject to any guilt." Calvin, "Articles Concerning Predestination," 179.

[18]Calvin, "Brief Reply in Refutation of the Calumnies of a Certain Worthless Person," *LCC*, 22:342. Cf. *Institutes*, III.21.1,4; III.23.2–5.

[19]See Calvin, *Institutes*, III.23.3,7–8.

[20] Theodore Beza, *Quaestiones et responsiones* (Geneva, 1570), 107; cited by John S. Bray, *Theodore Beza's Doctrine of Predestination* (Nieuwkoop: De Graf, 1975), 88.

[21]John Owen, *The Works of John Owen*, ed. by William Gould; 16 vols. (Edinburgh: Banner of Truth Trust, 1965–68), 10:42.

[22]Herman Bavinck, *The Doctrine of God* (Reprint, Grand Rapids: Baker, 1977), 391.

[23]Ibid., 360, 386. "The final answer to the question why a thing is and why it is as it is must ever remain: 'God willed it,' according to his absolute sovereignty." Ibid., 371.

[24]Barth grants the usual distinctions between God's absolute and conditional will and between his efficient and permissive will. But since the divine decision establishes the conditions by which all things eventuate, the latter terms in each of the above pairs dissolve into his sovereign decree. *CD*, vol. 2, pt. 1, pp. 590–97.

[25]Ibid., vol. 2, pt. 2, p. 95. "Before Him and without Him God does not, then, elect or will anything." Ibid., 94.

[26]Ibid., vol. 2, pt. 2, p. 167.

[27] "God has ascribed to man . . . election, salvation, and life; and to Himself He has ascribed . . . reprobation, perdition, and death." Ibid., vol. 2, pt. 2, p. 117.

[28]Ibid., 306.

[29]Ibid., 142. For Barth's complete discussion of the supra-infra debate, see ibid., 127–145.

30 Tatian, *Address to the Greeks*, XI.

31 Irenaeus, *Proof of the Apostolic Preaching*, 7. Cf. *Against Heresies*, V.2.2.

32 Irenaeus, *Against Heresies*, V.29.2.; cf. IV.39.3–4.

33 Tertullian, *Against Marcion*, II.23. Cf. "What God has justly decreed, having no evil purpose in his decree, He decreed from the principle of justice not malevolence." Ibid., II.24.

34 Ibid., II.6.

35 Ibid., II.16.

36 Augustine, *Concerning the Predestination of the Saints*, 11, 18–19, 32–37; *On the Gift of Perseverance*, 41–42, 47; *On Admonition and Grace*, 13–14, 32.

37 Augustine, *The City of God*, V.9.

38 Augustine, *Enchiridion*, 27.

39 Augustine, *The City of God*, XXI.12; *Enchiridion*, 27; *On the Gift of Perseverance*, 16.

40 Augustine, *The City of God*, XV.1; *Enchiridion*, 26; *On the Gospel of St. John*, 43.14; 48.4,6.

41 Augustine, *Enchiridion*, 95; cf. *On the Trinity*, III.4.

42 "As predestination includes the will to confer grace and glory, so also reprobation includes the will to permit a person to fall into sin and to impose the punishment of damnation on account of that sin." Thomas Aquinas, *ST*, vol. I, pt. 1, q. 23, art. 3.

43 Ibid., q. 22, art. 2.

44 Ibid., q. 23, art. 8. Thomas adds: "Secondary causes cannot escape the order of first universal cause . . . , indeed, they execute that order." Ibid.

45 Richard A. Muller states, "The infralapsarian view is the confessional view of the Reformed churches," in *Dictionary of Latin and Greek Theological Terms* (Grand Rapids: Baker, 1985), s.v., *supra lapsum*, 292.

46 Charles Hodge, *Systematic Theology*, 3 vols. (Reprint, Grand Rapids: Eerdmans, 1973), 1:542. He also writes, "The decrees of God are in no case conditional. The event decreed is suspended on a condition, but the purpose of God is not. It is inconsistent with the nature of God to assume suspense on His part." Ibid., 1:540.

47 Ibid., 1:545–48.

48 Carl F. H. Henry, *God, Revelation and Authority*, 6 vols. (Waco: Word, 1976–83), 6:85.

49 Millard J. Erickson, *Christian Theology*, 3 vols. (Grand Rapids: Baker, 1983–85), 1:345–63.

50 Henry C. Thiessen, *Lectures in Systematic Theology*, rev. by Vernon D. Doerksen (Grand Rapids: Eerdmans, 1979), 100–110.

51 L. Berkhof, *Systematic Theology* (Grand Rapids: Eerdmans, 1941), 100–108, 115–25.

52 G. Ch. Aalders, *Genesis*; 2 vols. (Grand Rapids: Zondervan, 1981), 1:57. Cf. Claus Westermann, *Creation* (Philadelphia: Fortress, 1974), 61; Andrew Bowling, *"tob," TWOT*, 1:345–46.

53 Against the sweeping judgment of L. Berkhof, *Systematic Theology*, 108, and certain other Reformed theologians, to the effect that God's permissive will renders the entrance of sin into the world *logically* certain.

54 See Paul's discussion of the hardening of Pharaoh's heart under the Pauline literature, later in this section, pp. 305–6.

55 According to J. A. Thompson: "The demands of God, once rejected, became a hardening influence on Sihon's heart, so that he was unable to respond favorably to Israel's request." *Deuteronomy. TOTC* (London: Inter-Varsity, 1974), 95.

56 Leon J. Wood, *"ḥāpēṣ," TWOT*, 1:310.

57 Ralph W. Klein, *1 Samuel. WBC* (Waco: Word, 1983), 26.

58 "From the biblical viewpoint, all things have their ultimate source in God. Even the wrath of men and Satan ultimately further the divine purposes." Fred E. Young, *The Wycliffe Bible Commentary*, ed. Charles F. Pfeiffer and Everett F. Harrison (Chicago: Moody, 1962), 304.

59 Ibid., 339.

60 "Loved" thus connotes "preferred," and "hated" metaphorically signifies "not preferred." "The Hebrew word for 'to hate' often means to scorn, or to rank something lower than something else, while 'to love' may mean to choose something and rank it higher than something else." Th. C. Vriezen, *An Outline of Old Testament Theology* (Wageningen: Veenman & Zonen, 1960), 167. For the imagery see Genesis 29:30–31; Deuteronomy 21:15–16; Proverbs 13:24; Matthew 6:24; cf. Matthew 10:37 with Luke 14:26.

61 See Ebenezer Henderson, *The Twelve Minor Prophets* (Reprint, Grand Rapids: Baker, 1980), 298: "God is often said to do what He permits to be done by others."

62 Claus Westermann, *Isaiah 40–66. OTL* (Philadelphia: Westminster, 1969), 266.

[63] H. C. Leupold, *Exposition of Isaiah*, 2 vols. (Grand Rapids: Baker 1968–71), 2:232. Cf. Edward J. Young, *The Book of Isaiah*, 3 vols. *NICOT* (Grand Rapids: Eerdmans, 1965–72), 3:354: "They were only obeying what the Lord permitted them to do." So also Alfred Martin and John Martin, *Isaiah: The Glory of the Messiah* (Chicago: Moody, 1983), 141: "What Christ suffered at the hands of men was tragic. . . . Nevertheless, in and through that tragedy God was working out His sovereign purpose of grace. Isaiah emphasizes that in verse 10."

[64] In Isaiah 6:9–13, God commanded Isaiah to make the people callous through his preaching. God gave his word through the prophet, to which the people chose to respond perversely, thus provoking God's just retribution.

[65] "The *dei*, as often in the Gospels, may mean 'by God's decree' (Matt. 24:6; 26:54), which is true of the good, but not of the evil." Alfred Plummer, *The Gospel According to St. Matthew* (Reprint, Grand Rapids: Baker, 1982), 250.

[66] E. Earle Ellis, *The Gospel of Luke. NCBC* (Grand Rapids: Eerdmans, 1981), 277.

[67] Emil Brunner, *The Christian Doctrine of God: Dogmatics* (Philadelphia: Westminster, 1950), 1:237.

[68] Ellis, *Luke*, 120.

[69] Some authorities such as A. H. McNeile, *The Gospel According to St. Matthew* (Reprint, Grand Rapids: Baker, 1982), 250, and I. Howard Marshall, *The Acts of the Apostles. TNTC* (Grand Rapids: Eerdmans, 1980), 75, view the divine determination and the human betrayal as an insoluble paradox. Marshall comments: "Here we have the paradox of divine predestination and human responsibility in its strongest form." We suggest that the apparent paradox is solved as one divides the problem and distinguishes between (1) God as the final cause who ordains the saving values of Christ's death and (2) the human agent (Judas) as the efficient, blameworthy cause of Christ's sufferings.

[70] Charles Hodge, *Ephesians* (Reprint, Grand Rapids: Baker, 1980), 28.

[71] Niger Turner points out that the verb "glorified" (*edoxasen*) is likely a proleptic aorist: "The timeless [proleptic] aorist is a suitable tense to express this projection of the future into the present as if some event had already occurred." In J. H. Mounton, ed., *A Grammar of New Testament Greek*, s.v. "syntax" (Edinburgh: T. & T. Clark, 1963), 3:74.

[72] C. E. B. Cranfield, *The Epistle to the Romans*, 2 vols. *ICC* (Edinburgh: T. & T. Clark, 1975–79), 2:480. F. F. Bruce observes

that the terse statements about Jacob and Esau describe "God's choice of Jacob and passing over his brother." *Romans. TNTC* (London: Tyndale, 1963), 188. Cf. W. G. T. Shedd, *Commentary on Romans* (Reprint, Grand Rapids: Baker, 1980), 286.

[73] Shedd, *Romans*, 292. We agree with Charles Bigg, *The Epistles of St. Peter and St. Jude. ICC* (New York: Scribner, 1909), 133, that the doctrine of reprobation "is irreconcilable with the idea [or character] of God."

[74] Cranfield, *Romans*, 2:492.

[75] F. Davidson and Ralph P. Martin, "Romans," *NBCRev*, 1035. Other texts adduced by some in support of reprobation, such as 1 Corinthians 9:27; Galatians 4:30; 2 Timothy 2:20; 3:8, are best understood as not positing an unconditional will of perdition in God.

[76] Brunner, *The Christian Doctrine of God*, 331.

[77] J. H. Bernard remarks, "That the divine intention may be thwarted by man's misuse of his free will is part of the great mystery of evil, unexplained and inexplicable." *The Pastoral Epistles* (Reprint, Grand Rapids: Baker, 1980), 41.

[78] F. F. Bruce, *1 & 2 Thessalonians. WBC* (Waco: Word, 1982), 174. Cf. I. Howard Marshall, *1 and 2 Thessalonians. NCBC* (Grand Rapids: Eerdmans, 1983), 204: "Those who refuse to believe and accept the truth find that judgment comes upon them in the form of an inability to accept the truth."

[79] B. F. Westcott, *The Gospel According to St. John*; 2 vols. in 1 (Reprint, Grand Rapids: Baker, 1980), 2:251.

[80] Bigg, *St. Peter and St. Jude*, 103.

[81] Fritz Rienecker and Cleon L. Rogers, Jr., *A Linguistic Key to the Greek New Testament* (Grand Rapids: Zondervan, 1982), 673. Cf. U. Becker, "hard, hardened," *NIDNTT*, 2:156: "In the NT men who do not open themselves to the Gospel are described as hardened."

[82] Aristotle, *Metaphysics* I.3.

[83] Alvin Plantinga, "Advice to Christian Philosophers," *Faith and Philosophy*, 1, 3 (July 1984): 266.

[84] James Daane, *The Freedom of God* (Grand Rapids: Eerdmans, 1973), 60.

[85] Ibid., 170.

[86] For an analysis and refutation of the single decree see ibid., 45–73.

[87] Henry, *God, Revelation and Authority*, 104.

[88]For an evangelical evaluation of Barth's view of election see ibid., 90–107.

[89]The concept of human free agency here presented focuses on human self-determination, not in a vacuum, but dependent on God and in accord with the different moral condition of human nature at different times. Our view differs from that of Norman Geisler and many others who fail to take into account the differing states of human nature affecting the power of self-determination (1) prior to the Fall, (2) after the Fall, (3) after regeneration, and (4) after glorification. In agreement with Geisler's chapter entitled "God Knows All Things," we affirm that before the Fall humans had the power of contrary choice and that God simply knows all things. But differing with Geisler, we state that after the Fall God foreknows that people with depraved natures use their power of self-determination only sinfully. Left to mere divine prescience, none would believe. So that many would believe and benefit by Christ's atonement, the Father chose to grant them (the elect) repentance and a radically new heart. Then with the new nature and the old, believers have the power of contrary choice again. But in heaven, they will no longer be able to sin. Hence our view of human freedom includes the strength of a view like Geisler's in relation to evil and a view like John S. Feinberg's Augustinian soft (persuasive) determinism in relation to the redemption of depraved sinners. Our view differs from Feinberg's chapter "God Ordains All Things" by holding more consistently that God does not ordain evil. For a brief comparison, if we were to write a chapter in their series, it might be entitled "God Knows All Things and Ordains Some (Redemptive) Things." For Feinberg's and Geisler's concepts see their chapter edited by David Basinger and Randall Basinger, in *Predestination and Free Will* (Downers Grove: InterVarsity, 1986), 19–43, 64–84.

[90]Augustine, *Against Fortunatus*, 15.

[91]Unfortunately most of the Arminian debate has been directed against supralapsarian double predestination, and vice versa. Inadequate focus has been given either in exposition or debate to a clear infralapsarian alternative. The infralapsarian view here developed is not answered by the critical evaluations of supralapsarianism, for example, in Clark Pinnock, ed., *Grace Unlimited* (Minneapolis: Bethany Fellowship, 1975) or in Roger Forster and V. Paul Marston, *God's Strategy in Human History* (Wheaton: Tyndale, 1973).

[92]F. H. Klooster, "Supralapsarianism," *EDT*, 1060.

[93]R. V. Schnucker, "Infralapsarianism," *EDT*, 560–61.

[94]Paul K. Jewett, *Election and Predestination* (Grand Rapids: Eerdmans, 1985), 93.

[95]Ibid., 94.

[96]Ibid., 95.

[97]Ibid., 96.

[98]Ibid.

[99]Ibid., 97.

[100]Ibid.

[101]Ibid., 106.

[102]Ibid., 108.

[103]Ibid.

[104]C. S. Lewis, *Letters to Malcolm* (New York: Harcourt, Brace and World, 1963), 109.

[105]Augustine, "The Free Choice of the Will" II, 20. cf. his *Confessions* VII, 16.

[106]For further discussion of the purposes of suffering, see Gordon R. Lewis, "Suffering and Anguish" ed. Merrill C. Tenney, *ZPEB* 5:530–33.

[107]See Erickson, *Christian Theology*, 1:368, especially note 11.

[108]Ibid., 359.

[109]See B. B. Warfield's discussion of God's miraculous strategy in "Christian Supernaturalism" in *Biblical and Theological Studies* (Philadelphia: Presbyterian and Reformed, 1952), 1–21.

[110]See Donald Bloesch, "Fate, fatalism," *EDT*, 407.

[111]See Stephen M. Cahn's discussion of Pierce and James's "Dilemma of Determinism," *EP*, 2:73.

[112]Richard Taylor, "Determinism," *EP*, 2:359–71; Norman L. Geisler, "Freedom, Free Will and Determinism," *EDT*, 428–30.

[113]Charles Haddon Spurgeon, *Lectures to My Students* (Grand Rapids: Zondervan, 1954), 80.

[114]James W. Ney, "Revolution," *His*, 21, 2 (November 1960): 35.

[115]For application of the sense of being called by God in the Christian life see Gordon MacDonald, *Ordering Your Private World* (Nashville: Nelson, 1984), 55–65.

[116]See Emile Cailliet, *The Recovery of Purpose* (New York: Harper, 1959).

[117]Jean-Paul Sartre, *Existentialism and Human Emotions* (New York: Philosophical Library, 1957), 90.

[118]Daane, *Freedom of God*, 150.

[119] Whereas all of the Bible is inspired and profitable in various ways (2 Tim. 3:16–17), Gary Friesen tends to limit the data of the Bible for decision making to "those areas specifically addressed by the Bible, and the revealed commands and principles of God." *Decision Making and the Will of God* (Portland: Multnomah, 1980), 163.

[120] See Carl F. H. Henry, *Christian Personal Ethics* (Grand Rapids: Eerdmans, 1957); idem, *Christian Social Ethics* (Grand Rapids: Eerdmans, 1964).

[121] It might help to review the steps in the method of theological decision making in chapter 1 of this book.

General Index

Scripture Index

Proverbs